수능직방

능
방

실수 없는 수능 듣기 만점 공략!

Listening

수능 듣기 실전 모의고사 **20회**

LEVEL **2**

저자 및 연구진

저자

Jason Lee

연세대학교 영어교육 석사
Jason Lee Academy 대표
www.jasonlee.co.kr
jasonlee@jasonlee.co.kr

연구

Jason Lee Academy 연구원

연구실장: 김희선
Ryan DeLaney 수석연구원: University of Southern Indiana/University of Cambridge(CELTA)
서지연 연구원: 한국외대 영어과(쭈)
박주현 연구원: 고려대 영어교육 석사
박성우 연구원: 연세대 영어영문학 석사
백재민 연구원: 연세대 영어영문학 석사
박동준 연구원: 서울대 경영학과(쭈)
박국일 연구원: Boston University(쭈)
이민령 연구원: 고려대 경영학과
Taylor Lagieski 연구원: University of Montana/ University of Cambridge(CELTA)

감수

양유리 선생님: 연세대 영어교육 석사, 양천고 교사
김세리 선생님: 연세대 영어교육 석사, 화곡중 교사

평가

김동원(성균관대) 김정호(인제의대) 김효중(육군사관학교) 박찬슬(서울대) 이승혁(경희대)
이우진(제주의대) 이종식(서울시립대) 임재훈(연세대) 장정우(美미시간주립대) 조원우(연세대)
최진명(서울대) 탁우령(고려대) 황인찬(서울대)

수능직방 **Listening** LEVEL 2

지은이   Jason Lee
펴낸이   최회영
영문교열   윤은지, Eric Williams
펴낸곳   (주)웅진컴퍼스
등록번호   제22-2943호
등록일자   2006년 6월 16일
주소   서울특별시 서초구 강남대로39길 15-10 한라비발디스튜디오193 3층
전화   (02)3471-0096
홈페이지   http://www.wjcompass.com

ISBN   978-89-6697-889-2

13 12 11 10 9 8
26 25 24

Printed in Korea

이 책을 내며

　　최근 수능 영어는 많은 변화를 겪고 있습니다. 2013학년도까지 15년간 기본 틀을 유지하며 난이도만 조절해 오던 데서 벗어나 2014학년도에 갑자기 수준별 시험(A·B형)으로 출제되더니 2015학년도부터는 A·B형 구분을 없애고 다시 단일형으로 바뀌었습니다. 급기야 2018학년도 수능 시험부터는 절대평가로 바뀌게 되었습니다. **급변하는 대입 영어 정책에 수험생과 학부모의 마음이 무거운 상황에서, 수능 영어 어떻게 준비해야 할까요?**

　　'최적의 수능 대비'와 '실질적인 영어 실력 향상'이 동시에 가능한 교재로서 불철주야 연구와 노력을 다하여 수능직방 Voca 시리즈에 이어 이번에 수능직방 Listening 시리즈를 출간하게 되었습니다. 그 특징은 다음과 같습니다.

　　첫째, 평가원의 최신 수능 개편안 및 출제 방침, 그리고 수능 연계 EBS 교재를 활용한 출제 경향까지 과학적으로 철저히 분석·반영하였습니다. 즉, 코퍼스 언어학에 기반을 둔 Jason Lee Academy는 이번 수능직방 Listening 개발 과정에서도 고유의 특허 기술을 활용하여 수능·평가원 모의고사의 어휘 수준과 문장 수, 선택지 길이와 한 문장에서의 최대 어휘 수까지 분석·반영하였습니다.

　　둘째, EBS 수능 연계 교재 및 최근 7년간의 시·도 교육청 모의고사 듣기 평가에서 정답률이 낮았던 문항들(60% 이하)을 엄선하여 비슷한 난이도로 재구성하였습니다.

　　셋째, 모든 문제와 지문은 수능·평가원 출제 경험이 있는 학교 선생님들의 조언과 감수를 거쳐 최신 수능이 요구하는 기준을 만족시키도록 구성되었고, 앞으로 출제 가능성이 없는 유형은 배제하였습니다.

　　넷째, 학생 개인별 맞춤 학습, 완전학습이 가능하도록 3종의 음원(문제풀이용, 문항별, 실전보다 빠른 듣기용 MP3 음원)과 무료 Mobile App을 제공합니다.

　　다섯째, 실제 원어민의 대화, 담화에 가깝게 구성하여 수능 시험을 준비하면서 살아있는 영어(Real English) 실력까지 갖출 수 있습니다. 국내 유명 어학원과 학교에서 강의 경력이 풍부한 원어민 선생님들이 교재 기획·개발 전 과정에 참여하였기 때문입니다.

　　저희 Jason Lee Academy 연구진과 웅진컴퍼스 모두의 열정과 노력이 여러분의 수능 만점과 영어 실력 향상이라는 결실로 이어지리라 확신합니다

강남 Jason Lee Academy에서

수능 출제 경향 분석 및 대비 전략

🍃 수능 듣기의 역사

수능 영어에서 가장 큰 변화를 겪은 영역은 단언컨대 듣기 영역입니다. 1994학년 1차 수능 8문항을 시작으로 1996학년에 10문항, 1997학년 17문항으로 늘어났고, 1998학년 수능부터 2013학년까지 15년간은 거의 비슷한 유형과 포맷을 유지하였습니다. 하지만 2014학년 6월 평가원 모의고사부터 '외국어 영역'에서 '영어 영역'으로 이름도 바뀌고 A형, B형으로 수준별 시험을 치르게 되면서 수능 영어 시험에 많은 변화가 나타났습니다. 그중 듣기 영역이 문항 수와 구성 면에서 가장 큰 변화가 있었습니다. 17문항에서 22문항으로 증가하여, 듣기 비중이 기존 약 37.78%에서 약 48.89%로 대폭 상승하였습니다. TOEIC과 TEPS 등의 시험과 매우 유사한 '짧은 대화 응답'과 '한 지문 두 문항' 등과 같은 신유형이 나타났습니다. 하지만 야심 차게 시작된 수준별 시험은 난이도 조절 실패 등의 이유로 2014학년 수능이 처음이자 마지막 시험이 되었고 2015학년부터 다시 듣기 문항 수도 기존 17문항으로 돌아가게 되었습니다. 다만, 2014학년의 22문항 체제에서 문제 유형은 그대로 유지하되, 중복 유형을 줄여 17문항으로 만든 점은 주목할 만한 대목입니다.

🍃 NEW 통합형 수능 영어 듣기 출제 경향 분석 및 학습 전략

<u>우리가 준비해야 하는 수능 영어 듣기</u>는 크게 4가지, 세부적으로는 총 15가지 유형으로 구성되어 있습니다.

1. 대의 파악 (2014학년 5문항 → 2015학년 이후 3문항)

대화 · 담화를 듣고 전체적인 내용을 이해하거나 추론하는 능력을 측정합니다.

① 대화 · 담화 목적
② 대화 · 주제/요지
③ 대화 · 담화자 주장/의견
④ 대화자 심정/관계, 대화 장소 → 관계의 비중이
　 압도적으로 높음

학습 전략

◈ 대화 도입부를 들으면서 대화/담화가 일어나는 상황, 장소, 대화자 간의 관계를 유추해 본다.
◈ 대화자가 반복, 강조하는 핵심 단어 · 표현에 집중한다.
◈ 너무 광범위하거나 지엽적인 선택지는 피한다.

2. 세부 사항 (2014학년 9문항 → 2015학년 이후 7문항)

대화 · 담화의 핵심적 내용과 전개 방식에 비추어 제시된 특정 정보를 가급적 정확하고 신속하게 파악할 수 있는 능력을 측정합니다. 직접적으로 제시된 정보를 구체적인 사항에 초점을 맞추어 정확하게 파악하는 연습이 필요합니다.

① 그림 내용 일치/불일치 → 대부분 불일치 문제
② 한 일/할 일/부탁한 일
③ 5W1H 세부사항 → 6하 원칙 중 주로 '이유'를 묻는
　 유형으로 출제
④ 숫자 관련 정보 → 고난도 문항으로 출제
⑤ 대화 언급/불언급
⑥ 담화 내용 일치/불일치 → 주로 불일치로 출제
⑦ 도표 내용 일치/불일치

학습 전략

◈ 평소 들으며 내용을 메모하는 연습을 하자.
◈ 계산 문제는 넓은 공간에 식을 세우고 복잡한 식은 대화가 끝난 후 계산한다.
◈ 내용 일치/불일치 문제는 선택지 순서대로 나오기 때문에, 선택지를 미리 봐놓고 줄을 그어가며 푼다.

3. **간접 말하기 (2014학년 6문항 → 2015학년 이후 5문항)**

실제 일상생활에서 흔히 발생할 수 있는 의사소통 상황과
관련된 듣기 자료를 통해 이해한 바를 가상의 말하기 상황에
적용할 수 있는 능력을 측정합니다.

① 짧은 대화 응답
② 대화 응답
③ 담화 응답

◈ 교과서 주요 의사소통 기능 표현을 미리 익혀두자.
◈ 미리 선택지의 내용을 읽고 무슨 내용인지 파악한다.
  (대화/담화를 듣고 난 후 선택지 내용을 읽으면, 시간에 쫓겨
  다음 문제까지 영향을 받기 때문이다.)
◈ 선택지의 내용을 두 개 이상 모르면, 과감히 그 문제는 건너
  뛰고 다음 문제에 집중하자.

4. **복합 (2014학년 2문항 → 2015학년 이후 2문항)**

하나의 대화·담화문을 통해서 주로 전체적인 흐름 파악과 세부적인 내용 파악 능력을 동시에 측정하고자 출제합니다.

① 하나의 대화·담화문 2문항

◈ 대화/담화가 시작되기 전에, 문제와 선택지를 반드시 미리 읽어놓아야 한다.
◈ 들으면서 본인만 알 수 있도록 최대한 간결하게 메모하는 습관을 평소 들여놔야 한다.
◈ 세부적인 내용은 처음에 놓쳤더라도 두 번째에서 만회할 기회가 있다. 포기하지 말자.
◈ 상위권의 경우, 한 번 들을 때 두 문제를 정확하게 맞힐 수 있도록 집중한다. 그래야 시간을 아껴서 독해에 더 투자할 수 있다.

🍃 수능 영어 듣기 만점 전략

1. **평소 매일 꾸준히 듣는 연습이 필요합니다.**
   노력에 비해 당장 실력이 늘지 않는 듯해도, 영어 실력은 결국 계단식으로 향상된다는 것을 기억하세요.

2. **안 들리는 원인을 파악하여 보완하세요.**
   자신이 자주 틀리는 문제 유형, 모르는 어휘, 취약점을 파악해서 보완하세요. 받아쓰기(Dictation) 및 오답 노트 작성이 도움이
   됩니다.

3. **들으면서 메모하는 연습을 해 보세요.**
   문장 전체를 꼼꼼히 받아 적기는 사실 쉽지 않은 일입니다. 따라서 나만의 전략을 세워 평소 최대한 간결히 메모하는 습관을
   들여야 합니다. 예를 들어, Studying English를 받아 적어야 한다면 다 적는 것이 아니라 Stu~g Eng~ 처럼 본인만이
   알아볼 수 있도록, 기호 또는 축약 등의 방법을 이용하면 유용합니다.

4. **실제 수능보다 빠른 속도로 듣는 연습을 하세요.**
   실제 시험 당일에는 심리적으로 위축되고 긴장한 탓에 자칫 속도가 빠르지 않음에도 불구하고 순간적으로 놓칠 수가 있습니다.
   따라서 평소 실제 수능보다 빠른 속도의 대화/담화문을 긴장감을 유지하며 듣는 연습을 하세요. 실전 감각을 키울 수 있습니다.

❘ BONUS TIP ❘

평가원 공식 발표에 따르면, 2014학년도 수준별 영어 A형을 끝으로 **'지도를 활용한 길 찾기'** 문항은 더는 출제되지 않습니다.
또한, 1997학년도 수능부터 2013학년도 수능까지 13번으로 출제되었던 **'그림 상황에 맞는 대화를 고르기'** 문제도 신수능에서는
더 이상 찾아보기 어렵습니다.

구성과 특징

{ Step 1 }

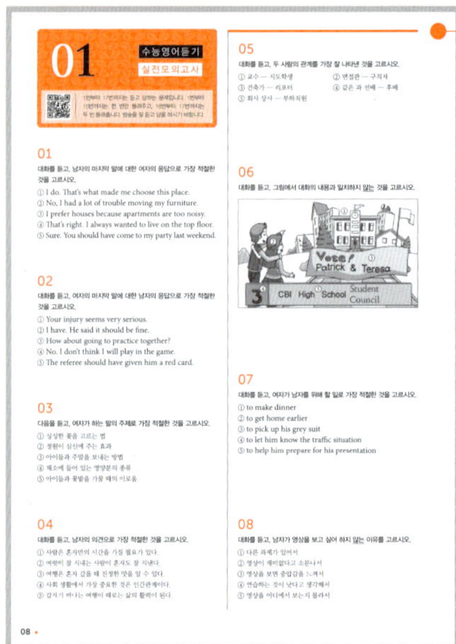

100% 수능 실전 모의고사

▶ **수능 최신 출제 경향 반영**: 평가원에서 제시한 수능 출제 방침과 수능 개편안을 최고의 연구 · 집필진이 철저히 분석, 반영하여 문항유형 및 배치, 어휘의 난이도와 script 길이까지 실전과 100% 동일하게 구성하였습니다.

▶ **바로 듣는 바로 푸는 QR Code 수록**: 언제 어디서나 자투리 시간에도 듣기 학습이 가능합니다.

{ Step 2 }

Dictation (받아쓰기)

▶ **Lexical Chunk(의미 단위)별로 빈칸 구성**: 정답을 찾는 데 꼭 필요한 핵심 어구 및 수능 필수 어휘를 듣고 받아쓰는 연습을 통해, 해당 표현을 완전히 자신의 것으로 소화할 수 있고 수능 출제 포인트가 어디에 있는 지까지 파악하게 되어, 결국 수능 고득점으로 이어집니다.

▶ **문항별 MP3 음원 제공**: 자신이 틀린 문제, 다시 듣고 싶은 표현만 빠르게 찾아 학습할 수 있도록 문항별로 구분해둔 파일도 제공합니다.

{ Step 3 }

친절한 정답 및 해설

▶ **친절하고 상세한 정답 및 해설, 해석과 소재와 핵심 어휘까지 빠짐없이 수록**: 학습자 스스로 꼼꼼히 복습이 가능하도록 구성 하였습니다.

▶ **평가원 지침에 따라 분류한 수능 듣기 문제 유형**도 문항별로 친절히 표기해 놓았습니다. 자신이 자주 틀리는 문제 유형이 무엇인지 파악하고 부족한 점을 보완하는 데에 도움이 될 것입니다.

완전학습을 위한 **무료 제공**

※ 용도별 MP3 음원 3종 (문제풀이용, 빠른 듣기용, 문항별)
www.wjcompass.com/sjlistening

※ 수능직방 Listening 전용 Mobile App 제공
Apple App Store / Google Play Store 접속 후,
'수직리스닝'을 검색하세요.

목차

수능 출제 경향 분석 및 대비 전략 ⸺ 04
구성과 특징 ⸺ 06

01회 실전 모의고사 ⸺ 08

02회 실전 모의고사 ⸺ 14

03회 실전 모의고사 ⸺ 20

04회 실전 모의고사 ⸺ 26

05회 실전 모의고사 ⸺ 32

06회 실전 모의고사 ⸺ 38

07회 실전 모의고사 ⸺ 44

08회 실전 모의고사 ⸺ 50

09회 실전 모의고사 ⸺ 56

10회 실전 모의고사 ⸺ 62

11회 실전 모의고사 ⸺ 68

12회 실전 모의고사 ⸺ 74

13회 실전 모의고사 ⸺ 80

14회 실전 모의고사 ⸺ 86

15회 실전 모의고사 ⸺ 92

16회 실전 모의고사 ⸺ 98

17회 실전 모의고사 ⸺ 104

18회 실전 모의고사 ⸺ 110

19회 실전 모의고사 ⸺ 116

20회 실전 모의고사 ⸺ 122

★ **책 속의 책**: 정답 및 해설
★ **무료 제공**: 수능직방 Listening 전용 Mobile App

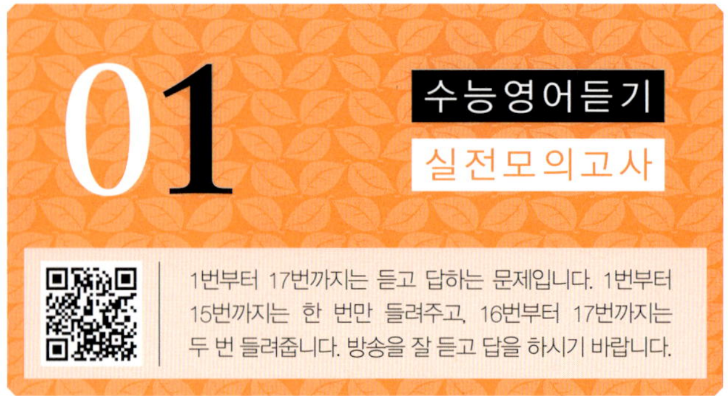

1번부터 17번까지는 듣고 답하는 문제입니다. 1번부터 15번까지는 한 번만 들려주고, 16번부터 17번까지는 두 번 들려줍니다. 방송을 잘 듣고 답을 하시기 바랍니다.

01

대화를 듣고, 남자의 마지막 말에 대한 여자의 응답으로 가장 적절한 것을 고르시오.

① I do. That's what made me choose this place.
② No, I had a lot of trouble moving my furniture.
③ I prefer houses because apartments are too noisy.
④ That's right. I always wanted to live on the top floor.
⑤ Sure. You should have come to my party last weekend.

02

대화를 듣고, 여자의 마지막 말에 대한 남자의 응답으로 가장 적절한 것을 고르시오.

① Your injury seems very serious.
② I have. He said it should be fine.
③ How about going to practice together?
④ No. I don't think I will play in the game.
⑤ The referee should have given him a red card.

03

다음을 듣고, 여자가 하는 말의 주제로 가장 적절한 것을 고르시오.

① 싱싱한 꽃을 고르는 법
② 정원이 심신에 주는 효과
③ 아이들과 주말을 보내는 방법
④ 채소에 들어 있는 영양분의 종류
⑤ 아이들과 꽃밭을 가꿀 때의 이로움

04

대화를 듣고, 남자의 의견으로 가장 적절한 것을 고르시오.

① 사람은 혼자만의 시간을 가질 필요가 있다.
② 여럿이 잘 지내는 사람이 혼자도 잘 지낸다.
③ 여행은 혼자 갔을 때 진정한 맛을 알 수 있다.
④ 사회 생활에서 가장 중요한 것은 인간관계이다.
⑤ 갑자기 떠나는 여행이 때로는 삶의 활력이 된다.

05

대화를 듣고, 두 사람의 관계를 가장 잘 나타낸 것을 고르시오.

① 교수 — 지도학생
② 면접관 — 구직자
③ 건축가 — 리포터
④ 같은 과 선배 — 후배
⑤ 회사 상사 — 부하직원

06

대화를 듣고, 그림에서 대화의 내용과 일치하지 <u>않는</u> 것을 고르시오.

07

대화를 듣고, 여자가 남자를 위해 할 일로 가장 적절한 것을 고르시오.

① to make dinner
② to get home earlier
③ to pick up his grey suit
④ to let him know the traffic situation
⑤ to help him prepare for his presentation

08

대화를 듣고, 남자가 영상을 보고 싶어 하지 <u>않는</u> 이유를 고르시오.

① 다른 과제가 있어서
② 영상이 재미없다고 소문나서
③ 영상을 보면 중압감을 느껴서
④ 연습하는 것이 낫다고 생각해서
⑤ 영상을 어디에서 보는지 몰라서

09

대화를 듣고, 여자가 지불할 금액을 고르시오.

① $20　　② $25　　③ $27　　④ $30　　⑤ $33

10

대화를 듣고, 건물에 관해 두 사람이 언급하지 <u>않은</u> 것을 고르시오.

① 겉모습　　　　② 주소　　　　③ 용도
④ 층수　　　　⑤ 건축 년도

11

Big Bear Resale Services에 관한 다음 내용을 듣고, 일치하지 <u>않는</u> 것을 고르시오.

① 고객들이 원치 않는 물건을 팔아준다.
② 20년 동안 운영해 왔다.
③ 골동품 가게, 폐품 처리장과 일을 한다.
④ 직접 와서 사진을 찍어서 웹사이트에 올려준다.
⑤ 픽업과 배달 서비스는 유료이다.

12

다음 표를 보면서 대화를 듣고, 두 사람이 선택할 동아리를 고르시오.

Jeremy's Academy English Clubs

	Club Name	Meeting Schedule	Activities	Number of Members
①	Great Storytellers	Wed. 5:00 p.m.	Reading & Listening	20
②	Global Leaders	Fri. 5:30 p.m.	Speaking & Writing	20
③	Drama Addicts	Mon. 4:30 p.m.	Reading & Acting	15
④	Better on Paper	Tue. 4:30 p.m.	Reading & Writing	10
⑤	Real Debaters	Fri. 3:00 p.m.	Speaking & Debating	10

13

대화를 듣고, 여자의 마지막 말에 대한 남자의 응답으로 가장 적절한 것을 고르시오.

Man: ________________________

① I should cancel the meeting.
② I think you need to see a doctor.
③ Thank you so much. I owe you one.
④ I already copied all of the information.
⑤ Okay, great. Get some help from Craig.

14

대화를 듣고, 남자의 마지막 말에 대한 여자의 응답으로 가장 적절한 것을 고르시오.

Woman: ________________________

① I'm sorry, but you can't. My phone is broken.
② Sure. Playing computer games helps me relax.
③ No problem. That's what friendship is all about.
④ You're right. Everyone has different preferences.
⑤ You should probably find a different game to play.

15

다음 상황 설명을 듣고, Taylor가 기차역 직원에게 할 말로 가장 적절한 것을 고르시오.

Taylor: ________________________

① I had a great visit with my friend here in New York.
② Can you tell me how to get to my train platform?
③ Is there any other place I can get my ticket?
④ This is the nicest train station I've ever seen.
⑤ I'd like one ticket for Minneapolis, please.

[16-17] 다음을 듣고, 물음에 답하시오.

16

여자가 하는 말의 주제로 가장 적절한 것은?

① Different types of social networking
② Community involvement through the co-op
③ Organizational methods using social networking
④ Attending upcoming social events in the community
⑤ Benefits of joining community involvement programs

17

여자가 언급한 social media의 하나로 언급되지 <u>않은</u> 것은?

① Twitter　　② KakaoTalk　　③ Facebook
④ Instagram　　⑤ YouTube

01 DICTATION

01

M: ___________ ___________ ___________ ___________ ___________ ___________ your new apartment, Wanda?

W: I did. It wasn't too hard because I live on the first floor.

M: That's cool. Do you have a patio at your apartment?

W: (I do. That's what made me choose this place.)

02

W: Oh, you have a cast on your finger. Did you get hurt?

M: Yes. I was slide tackled during practice and I ___________ ___________ ___________ ___________.

W: You should really see a doctor. Have you visited Dr. Kebb?

M: (I have. He said it should be fine.)

03

W: How do you usually spend weekends with your kids? Have you considered planting a flower garden with them? Gardening is a great way to get your kids outdoors, teach them life skills, and ___________ ___________ ___________ ___________ all at the same time. Flower gardens are beautiful, and choosing different flowers and watching them grow is a lot of fun. If ___________ ___________ ___________ your kids not spending enough time outside or worried that they're not learning to be responsible, a flower garden can help with both issues. While you're ___________ ___________ ___________ ___________, your kids will see why it's important to take care of things and always finish what they start. This will allow them to naturally develop personal and social responsibility. This spring, try something new for family time: plant a flower garden, and ___________ ___________ ___________ ___________!

04

W: Hey Jeff, I haven't seen you at work lately. Where have you been?

M: I took a few weeks off to ___________ ___________ in India.

W: You went alone?

M: Yep. I really enjoy traveling alone.

W: Didn't you ___________ ___________?

M: Not really. I think being alone is great for your mental well-being. ___________ ___________ ___________ ___________ ___________-___________, and it's less stressful than traveling with others.

W: So you think it's important to take time to be alone?

M: Absolutely.

W: Well, personally, I get really uneasy and anxious when I'm alone. ___________ ___________ ___________ ___________ ___________ ___________, I guess.

M: I used to be that way, too. But I learned to ___________ ___________ ___________, and it's really helped me in my social life. It's helped me become more comfortable with myself and with others.

W: Aha, I guess I understand what you mean.

05

W: Good morning.

M: Oh, you must be Ms. Jackson. Have a seat.

W: Thank you.

M: I've been ___________ ___________ ___________ ___________ and I see that you graduated as the valedictorian of your university. I'm very impressed.

W: Well, I majored in architecture. I've been interested in it since I started playing with building blocks as a child, so ___________ ___________ ___________ ___________ ___________.

M: Excellent. I also see here that you interned with Carter & Young.

W: That's right. I worked at their office during summer vacation last year.

M: Great. So, how did you hear about this position?

W: I was referred here by my professor.

M: All right. If ___________ ___________ ___________ ___________ ___________, what kind of architecture are you interested in working on?

W: I'm very interested in commercial development.

M: It seems like __________ __________ __________ __________ __________ __________ __________ __________ __________ __________.

W: I appreciate you saying that.

06

W: Hey, Patrick!

M: Hi, Teresa. What are you up to?

W: I've almost finished our campaign poster.

M: Great! Did you find a good picture of the school to use in the background?

W: I did, and I used that picture of us pointing as the foreground.

M: It looks great. I also like the banner you drew next to us.

W: I couldn't __________ __________ __________ __________ __________ campaign slogans, though. Sorry.

M: That's all right. By the way, I don't think that the candidate number looks good on the right side.

W: Now that you mention it, it probably __________ __________ __________ __________ __________. How about our school's name and the position we're running for at the bottom?

M: I think that's fine. You've done a great job, Teresa.

W: Thanks. Remember, we need to start the election campaign by 8:30 tomorrow morning.

M: All right. I'll be there __________ __________ __________ __________ __________ __________. Thanks again.

07

[Cell phone rings.]

W: Hey, honey. Are you __________ __________ __________ __________?

M: Yes, but the road is really crowded. I wonder __________ __________ __________ __________ __________.

W: Has there been an accident or something?

M: I'm not sure what's going on. You can have dinner without me if you're hungry.

W: All right. When do you think you'll be home?

M: I really don't know. But can you __________ __________ __________ __________?

W: Of course. What's up?

M: Can you stop by the dry cleaner's and pick up my grey suit? I want to wear it tomorrow for my big presentation.

W: Sure, I'll go over there and get it now.

M: Thanks so much, sweetie. __________ __________ __________ __________ __________ so you just need to pick it up. I hope I can make it home soon.

W: Okay, honey. See you when you get here.

08

W: Hey, Tommy. Have you watched any videos of __________ __________ __________ __________ __________?

M: Not yet. But I've heard he's amazing.

W: You heard right. Everyone on the Internet __________ __________ __________ __________ __________. Would you like to see some highlights?

M: Hmm. . . I don't think I should.

W: Why not? Wouldn't you like to see why he's so good?

M: I'd rather wait until __________ __________ __________.

W: But wouldn't you be more prepared for the game if you watched some video?

M: I think practice is a better way to prepare.

W: That's what a lot of the other players said. They said __________ __________ __________ __________ __________ __________ __________ __________.

M: They're right. Watching videos is a waste of time. My time would be better spent in the gym than the living room.

09

M: Thanks for calling Brother's Pizza. __________ __________ __________ __________ __________?

W: Yeah, I'd like a large triple-cheese pizza. How much will that be?

M: One large special-topping pizza is normally $25, but today is Customer Appreciation Day, so you can get any large pizza for the price of a __________-__________ __________.

W: Oh, great. __________ __________ __________, I'd like to add an order of chicken wings.

M: Sure. Will that be all for you today?

W: Yeah, that's all.

M: Okay. The pizza is $20 and the chicken wings are $10 so your total today comes to $30.

W: ___________ ___________ ___________ ___________ ___________ ___________ ___________ for this order?

M: Yes, of course. Is it a coupon from our website?

W: Yeah. It's for 10% off.

M: Just give it to the delivery man when he comes.

10

M: Hey, what's that you're looking at on your computer?

W: Just some pictures from my summer vacation to London. Would you like to see them?

M: Sure. *[Pause]* This building is interesting. ___________ ___________ ___________ ___________ ___________.

W: That's right. Londoners have nicknamed it "The Gherkin" because it looks like a gherkin, a small pickle.

M: What's its real name?

W: 30 Saint Mary Axe. ___________ ___________ ___________.

M: What's inside it?

W: Well, it's located in the financial district of London, so ___________ ___________ ___________ ___________ ___________ ___________, along with several restaurants.

M: How tall is it?

W: I think it's around 180 meters tall. ___________ ___________-___________ ___________ ___________.

M: Did you go inside?

W: I did. I have pictures of the interior. Would you like to see them?

11

M: Is your house ___________ ___________ ___________ ___________ ___________ ___________ you don't need? Do you have old TVs, refrigerators, or computers sitting around collecting dust? Well, Big Bear Resale Services is just the place for you. We've been in the business of ___________ ___________ ___________ ___________ for 20 years. We work with the best

antique shops, scrapyards, and private buyers to assure you'll get the most money ___________ ___________ ___________, ___________ ___________. All you have to do is pick up the phone and call us. We'll come to your place, appraise your old goods, photograph them, and post the photos on our website in order to ___________ ___________ ___________ ___________. Then we'll pick your items up and ___________ ___________ ___________ ___________. Call Big Bear Resale Services today!

12

W: Hi, Aaron. I'm thinking about joining an afterschool English club.

M: Mr. Baek ___________ ___________ ___________ ___________ ___________ ___________ ___________, too.

W: Hey, let's join one together then. I'm kind of new to the school and you're pretty much my only friend.

M: That's a great idea. He gave me this schedule. What about this club? I've always wanted to try out acting.

W: I really want to join that one, too, but I have piano lessons after school on Mondays. What about the debate club? I've always been interested in arguing.

M: ___________ ___________ ___________ ___________ ___________ that lets us read a lot. I don't really care much for speaking or debating.

W: Well, I guess ___________ ___________ ___________ ___________ ___________ ___________ ___________ ___________. Which one should we choose?

M: It looks like this one has a lot more members. Let's join that.

W: Yeah, that way I have a better chance of making new friends.

M: Exactly. I'll sign us up.

13

W: ___________ ___________ ___________ ___________ ___________ ___________ ___________ ___________?

M: Have you seen Craig?

W: Craig? He called me earlier today and said he was sick, so he wasn't coming in.

M: Are you serious? He's called in sick three times this month.

W: I guess he's been quite ill for a few weeks now. Is there a problem?

M: He and I are supposed to meet our business partners today, and he's the one __________ __________ __________ __________.

W: Oh, no. Really?

M: __________ __________ __________ __________ __________ sometimes. Anyway, have you seen the handouts he had prepared for the meeting?

W: What did they look like?

M: They had a lot of information and data __________ __________ __________ __________ and sales rankings for the last quarter.

W: __________ __________ __________ __________ __________, and if I find them I'll bring them to you.

M: (Thank you so much. I owe you one.)

14

M: Hey, Carol. I see that you're playing that new *Candy Stomp* game on your phone.

W: Yeah. My friend James recommended that __________ __________ __________ __________.

M: I've really wanted to try it, too. __________ __________ __________ __________ __________ when you're finished?

W: No problem. I'll give it to you in a few minutes.

M: Awesome. Hey, have you ever played *Battle of the Clans*? It's pretty fun.

W: I did once, but I thought it was boring.

M: Really? It's so popular.

W: Well, it was a little __________ __________ __________ __________ __________. I enjoy simple games.

M: I don't think it's complicated at all. Even my little cousin can play it.

W: I couldn't get into it. I guess I'm just not like everyone else.

M: Well, __________ __________ __________ __________ __________ __________, can they?

W: (You're right. Everyone has different preferences.)

15

W: After visiting his friend in New York City, Taylor is on his way to Grand Central Station to take a train back to his hometown, Minneapolis. __________ __________ __________ __________ __________ __________ __________ is much more congested than he thought it would be, and the taxi is driving very slowly. Taylor is afraid that he's going to __________ __________. When he arrives at the station, he sees that he has twenty minutes __________ __________ __________. The ticket line is very long. He sees a station worker and wants to ask him __________ __________ __________ __________ __________ where he can buy his ticket. In this situation, what would Taylor most likely say to the station worker?

Taylor: (Is there any other place I can get my ticket?)

16-17

W: Good afternoon, everyone. I'm sure you all know about the social events our city has to offer, but do you know about the co-op? Our city's co-op is very important to our community. It's open daily so that members can trade fresh produce and recipe ideas as well as __________ __________ __________ __________, such as fund raisers and volunteer projects. This allows members of the community to join together __________ __________ __________ __________. You might wonder how you can join the co-op and participate. Well, __________ __________ __________ __________ __________, such as Twitter and KakaoTalk, to communicate with one another and promote upcoming events. We also have a Facebook page and occasionally run online campaigns to raise money. You can also check our YouTube page to see what kind of projects we've done in the past. __________ __________ __________ __________ __________ __________ your fellow community members by joining the co-op. Thank you for your time.

1번부터 17번까지는 듣고 답하는 문제입니다. 1번부터 15번까지는 한 번만 들려주고, 16번부터 17번까지는 두 번 들려줍니다. 방송을 잘 듣고 답을 하시기 바랍니다.

01

대화를 듣고, 남자의 마지막 말에 대한 여자의 응답으로 가장 적절한 것을 고르시오.

① I'm studying to be a nurse.
② No. I haven't been home yet.
③ You should go to the hospital.
④ Yes. I saw the doctor this morning.
⑤ Sounds good. I hope I get better soon.

02

대화를 듣고, 여자의 마지막 말에 대한 남자의 응답으로 가장 적절한 것을 고르시오.

① I'll keep on watching it, then.
② You should continue watching it.
③ I've never watched that TV show before.
④ I'd like to borrow it when you're finished.
⑤ You can watch it on TV on Saturday nights.

03

다음을 듣고, 남자가 하는 말의 목적으로 가장 적절한 것을 고르시오.

① 공원 내 이용시설을 알려주려고
② 캠핑장 이용 수칙을 안내하려고
③ 환경 보호의 중요성을 강조하려고
④ 위험 야생 동물 신고를 촉구하려고
⑤ 소지 불가한 물품 목록을 공지하려고

04

대화를 듣고, 두 사람이 하는 말의 주제로 가장 적절한 것을 고르시오.

① 명상을 하는 방법
② 명상의 긍정적 효과
③ 기분 전환 방법의 소개
④ 팟캐스트에서 강의 듣는 법
⑤ 운동이 우리 몸에 주는 이점

05

대화를 듣고, 두 사람의 관계를 가장 잘 나타낸 것을 고르시오.

① director — actress
② art director — judge
③ boss — office worker
④ customer — hairdresser
⑤ personal trainer — model

06

대화를 듣고, 그림에서 대화의 내용과 일치하지 <u>않는</u> 것을 고르시오.

07

대화를 듣고, 여자가 남자를 위해 할 일로 가장 적절한 것을 고르시오.

① 아이 돌보기
② 거실 재배치하기
③ 공항으로 마중 가기
④ 시내 관광 계획 짜기
⑤ 고객에게 식사 대접하기

08

대화를 듣고, 남자가 여자를 찾아온 이유를 고르시오.

① 경기 시간 변경을 알리려고
② 상대 팀에 관해 알아보려고
③ 새 유니폼 구매를 요청하려고
④ 주문한 유니폼의 색상을 확인하려고
⑤ 신임 지도 교사에게 인사를 드리려고

09

대화를 듣고, 남자가 지불할 금액을 고르시오.
① $45　② $54　③ $55　④ $60　⑤ $64

10

대화를 듣고, 자원봉사 활동에 관해 언급하지 <u>않은</u> 것을 고르시오.
① 자원봉사 할 사람　② 자원봉사 할 장소
③ 자원봉사 활동 내용　④ 자원봉사 시작 방법
⑤ 자원봉사 하게 될 시간

11

과학 박람회에 관한 다음 내용을 듣고, 일치하지 <u>않는</u> 것을 고르시오.
① 첫 번째 라운드에서 25명이 선발되었다.
② 최종 라운드의 아이디어는 실제 생활과 관련이 있고 유용해야 한다.
③ 최종 라운드는 5월 22일부터 2주 동안 열릴 것이다.
④ 사용한 재료의 수와 종류는 평가에 반영되지 않는다.
⑤ 수상자의 작품은 특허권을 얻을 수 있다.

12

다음 표를 보면서 대화를 듣고, 여자가 선택한 에어컨을 고르시오.

Air Conditioners

	Window Unit	Remote Control	Cooling Power (BTU)	Oscillation	Price
①	X	O	8,000	X	$240
②	O	X	5,000	X	$215
③	X	O	5,000	O	$260
④	X	X	8,000	O	$230
⑤	X	X	8,000	O	$275

13

대화를 듣고, 여자의 마지막 말에 대한 남자의 응답으로 가장 적절한 것을 고르시오.

Man: _______________________________

① Don't worry about it. I can do it alone.
② Congratulations on making it into the show.
③ Cheer up! You'll have another chance next year.
④ No problem. I'll give you a call when I'm finished.
⑤ It's all right. You really don't need to apologize to me.

14

대화를 듣고, 남자의 마지막 말에 대한 여자의 응답으로 가장 적절한 것을 고르시오.

Woman: _______________________________

① Relax. You shouldn't be so hard on yourself.
② It's great that you're following your dreams.
③ You should audition for some movies.
④ We should watch the movie together.
⑤ You should consider a new career.

15

다음 상황 설명을 듣고, Jayden이 Lucy에게 할 말로 가장 적절한 것을 고르시오.

Jayden: Lucy, _______________________________

① make sure to tell me if you need my help.
② I hope that you do really well in the magic club.
③ I need you to handle your responsibilities for this project.
④ you should make an effort to balance school and home life.
⑤ why don't we take a break for a while if it's too much work?

[16-17] 다음을 듣고, 물음에 답하시오.

16

여자가 하는 말의 주제로 가장 적절한 것은?
① Combining professional education with liberal arts
② Employment opportunities for liberal arts majors
③ Reasons for decreasing interest in liberal arts
④ The impact of liberal arts on humanity
⑤ The benefits of studying liberal arts

17

언급된 과목이 <u>아닌</u> 것은?
① philosophy　② education　③ history
④ languages　⑤ mathematics

녹음을 다시 한 번 듣고, 빈칸에 알맞은 말을 쓰시오

01

M: Hello, Lilly. You don't look so well. You look really tired.

W: I'm all right. I've just __________ __________ __________ __________ __________ __________ __________ all day.

M: That sounds awful. __________ __________ __________ __________ __________ __________ __________?

W: (Yes. I saw the doctor this morning.)

02

W: I heard that you're watching one of my favorite TV series.

M: Is it really one of your favorites? I'm only on the second episode. __________ __________ __________ __________.

W: Yeah. __________ __________ __________ __________ __________, but it gets really interesting later.

M: (I'll keep on watching it, then.)

03

M: Hi. Welcome to Walker Mountain State Park Campground. I'm park ranger Frank Reynolds, and I'd like to discuss the rules we expect you to follow here at the state park. Due to pollutants in soap and other cleaning goods, we ask that you only shower and __________ __________ __________ __________ __________ __________. We also ask that you tend to your campfires and extinguish them before midnight. Fireworks are __________ __________ __________ __________. As you can imagine, untended campfires and fireworks can cause forest fires, which will __________ __________ __________ __________ __________ __________. __________ __________ __________ __________ __________ a park ranger if you witness anyone violating these rules. Thank you for listening and we hope that you enjoy your time here at Walker Mountain State Park.

04

W: Hi, Chase. What are you listening to?

M: Hey, Hailey. I'm listening to a __________ __________ __________.

W: Meditation, huh? I've never tried it.

M: I'm learning a lot from the podcast. Did you know that you can benefit from meditation __________ __________ __________ __________ __________? For example, it boosts your energy.

W: That's interesting. So if I get tired in the afternoon, it will help if I meditate.

M: That's right. They're also talking about how meditation can help you sleep at night and relieve stress.

W: Really? That must be why people who meditate are always in such a great mood.

M: Could be. They also said that meditation can improve your health and __________ __________ __________.

W: So __________ __________ __________ __________ __________ __________?

M: Yeah, it's great for your overall health.

W: I guess I should start meditating.

M: I think I'm going to start, too.

05

M: Cindy, how's it going with trying to memorize your lines?

W: Very well, Mr. Reynolds.

M: I hope you can do it quickly. We don't have a lot of time.

W: Well, __________ __________ __________ __________ __________, and I just got the script this morning.

M: I understand. But we only have the space __________ __________ __________ __________, and we need to work on your intonation.

W: All right, let's start now. I think I'm ready.

M: Great. Come in stage left and __________ __________ __________ __________ from there.

W: Okay. *[Pause]* "In delivering my son from me, I bury a second husband." How was that?

M: Good. Now, __________ __________ __________ __________ __________ from stage right.

W: All right. *[Pause]* "In delivering my son from me, I bury a second husband." __________ __________ __________ __________?

M: It did, actually. It seems more natural.

W: Great. I'm so excited for opening night!

M: I'm glad to hear that. I know you'll do a great job.

06

M: This place is pretty amazing, isn't it?

W: Yeah, I'm having a great time. But it's pretty cold, don't you think?

M: Well, __________ __________ __________ __________ __________ __________. Look, back near those icicles. That's a very peculiar ice sculpture back there.

W: You mean the one with the monkey riding the animal?

M: Yeah. What kind of animal do you think it is that he's riding?

W: It looks like a pig. Anyway, I can't believe they __________ __________ __________ __________ __________ __________ __________.

M: Yeah. It looks really neat. Do you want to check out the inside?

W: Well, I'm having a lot of fun on this seesaw right now.

M: I'm not. You're a lot bigger than me, so __________ __________ __________ __________ __________ __________.

W: You're right. __________ __________ __________ __________ __________, it's not a lot of fun to be on the bottom all the time.

M: Yeah. So, how about we go over to the castle?

07

W: Sweetheart, can you help me __________ __________ __________ this Friday?

M: I'm afraid I can't. Can we do it next Friday?

W: Did something come up?

M: Yes. I have an important client coming in from LA, and __________ __________ __________ __________ __________ over the weekend.

W: Will you be busy all weekend?

M: I'm not sure. She's arriving Friday morning, and __________ __________ __________ __________ __________ __________ at the airport.

W: Do you need to __________ __________ __________ __________ with her?

M: She wants to take a tour of the city, so I have to show her around.

W: Well, why don't you invite her to dinner, __________ __________ __________ __________ __________?

M: That sounds great. Can you cook something French for us?

W: Okay. I'll go grocery shopping on Thursday, then.

08

M: Hi there, Mrs. Temmel.

W: Good morning, John. Come in. What can I do for you?

M: I need to talk about the basketball team.

W: What about it?

M: Well, you know we bought new team uniforms last season.

W: I remember. They were really __________ __________ __________ __________ __________ __________.

M: Right, but __________ __________ __________ __________ __________ __________ is using the same colors on their uniforms.

W: You mean Mound High School?

M: Yes. I saw some of their students wearing them the other day.

W: Okay, so are you suggesting we buy new uniforms again?

M: I am. That way, we can use different uniforms for different matches.

W: All right, let me talk with the principal and __________ __________ __________ __________.

M: I'd really appreciate that, Mrs. Temmel. Please let me know what you guys decide.

09

W: Good morning. What can I do for you today?

M: Hi. I'm looking to __________ __________ __________ __________ __________ for the day.

W: Great. Well, we have 50cc scooters and 125cc motorbikes.

M: I see. ___________ ___________ ___________ ___________?

W: The motorbikes are $30 a day. The scooters usually cost you $25, but we're ___________ ___________ ___________-___________ ___________, so you get an additional 10% off.

M: Awesome! I don't think we'll be driving them very far, so we'll just take two scooters, please.

W: Great. Do you need to rent helmets as well?

M: Of course. I'd like to be safe while riding. How much are they?

W: Helmets are $5 a day. They're not included ___________ ___________ ___________.

M: I see. Well, I guess we'll take two scooters and two helmets, then.

W: All right. We'll get them ready for you.

10

W: Good morning, everyone. I'm Terry Loggins, and I'm here to take any questions you might have about volunteering in your community.

M: Hi, Terry. I've been wanting to get my kids ___________ ___________ ___________ for some time now.

W: What type of volunteer work did you have in mind?

M: Well, they're both still in middle school, so they really can't do too much.

W: Oh, there are still positions available. They could help out at soup kitchens or retirement homes, or they could help single moms and senior citizens ___________ ___________ ___________ ___________ ___________ such as mowing the lawn or taking out the trash.

M: Those are some really great recommendations. ___________ ___________ ___________ ___________ ___________?

W: Just stop by your city hall. They should have ___________ ___________ ___________ ___________ ___________ ___________ ___________.

M: That sounds easy enough.

W: It is easy, and it'll mean a lot to those you help!

11

W: We've just finished the first round of the science fair, and there are 25 students who have made it through the preliminaries ___________ ___________ ___________ ___________ ___________ ___________ ___________ ___________ ___________.

All of the students who qualified for the final round submitted ideas that are ___________ ___________ ___________ ___________ in today's world. ___________ ___________ ___________ ___________ ___________ two weeks from today, on May 22nd, in the Student Center's Event Hall. This time, students will make working models of their ideas. They will be judged not only on whether or not they can make their ideas work, but also on ___________ ___________ ___________ ___________ ___________ ___________ ___________ was used to make them. The grand-prize winner will receive $5,000 toward obtaining a patent and producing an actual prototype of the idea.

12

M: Hello. What can I help you with today?

W: Hello. I'm looking for an air conditioner for my new apartment.

M: All right. How about this one? It's a window unit and it has a lower power rating, so ___________ ___________ ___________ ___________ ___________ ___________ ___________.

W: Oh, I'm not looking for a window unit.

M: Okay. Well, these are quite popular these days. ___________ ___________ ___________ ___________ ___________ ___________.

W: I don't think I need a remote. I would like an AC that's more powerful, though.

M: Okay. Do you want one that oscillates, as well?

W: Absolutely.

M: That narrows your choices down to these two. ___________ ___________ ___________ ___________?

W: ___________ ___________ ___________ ___________ ___________ ___________ $250, if possible.

M: Then this one is perfect for you.

W: Great. I'll take it.

13

M: Laura, you don't look so well. Are you all right?

W: I'm fine. __________ __________ __________ __________ __________.

M: Come on. You can tell me anything. What's the matter?

W: Well, you know how I tried out for the school's talent show last week?

M: Yeah, I remember. You spent hours working on your juggling act.

W: Right. So, I checked the bulletin board today, and I didn't make it into the show.

M: Really? How is that even possible? You're great.

W: I thought __________ __________ __________ __________. I didn't make any mistakes at all.

M: I understand your frustration. __________ __________ __________ __________ __________ __________ when I tried out for the drama club.

W: It's just so heartbreaking. __________ __________ __________ __________.

M: (Cheer up! You'll have another chance next year.)

14

M: Hi. I think we've met before. Isn't your name Jamie?

W: Yes, I'm Jamie. You're Ricky, from my high school, right? It's been a long time.

M: It sure has. The last time I saw you was at graduation, I think. That's been almost eight years!

W: Wow! It's hard to believe it's been that long. So, what've you been up to?

M: I've been living in Los Angeles for the past few years. I've been trying to __________ __________ __________ __________ __________ as an actor.

W: Really? __________ __________ __________ __________ __________ __________?

M: Just one as a vampire in a commercial for heartburn medication.

W: Oh, I know that commercial! It's __________ __________ __________ __________. It's so funny.

M: Thanks, but I was really hoping to get into a Hollywood feature. I have some auditions next week.

W: (It's great that you're following your dreams.)

15

M: Lucy and Jayden are students at the local high school. This semester they are taking a science class together. The students in the class were assigned team projects. Lucy and Jayden are working as a team and __________ __________ __________ __________ __________ __________. The problem is that Lucy has joined the magic club and needs to attend practices often. Therefore, she can't __________ __________ __________ __________ __________. In the beginning, Jayden understands Lucy's situation. But he __________ __________ __________ __________ when she continues to put off her responsibilities. Jayden wants to talk to Lucy about this. What should he say to her in this situation?

Jayden: Lucy, (I need you to handle your responsibilities for this project.)

16-17

W: Universities and colleges all around the country have been experiencing __________ __________ __________ __________ __________ __________ __________ __________. Many influential members of our great nation believe that the liberal arts are useless. They encourage students to study other subjects because they might lead to a better job. Let's take a minute to consider whether or not liberal arts are useful. __________ __________ __________ __________ __________ __________ future jobs by providing them with an invaluable set of skills that no other subjects offer. Studying philosophy, history, and languages __________ __________ __________ __________ __________ that are essential for survival in the real world and could not be obtained from subjects like mathematics. These problem-solving skills help create a __________ -__________ __________. I urge you to rethink your position on liberal arts. Consider signing up for classes that will, in many ways, make you a better person.

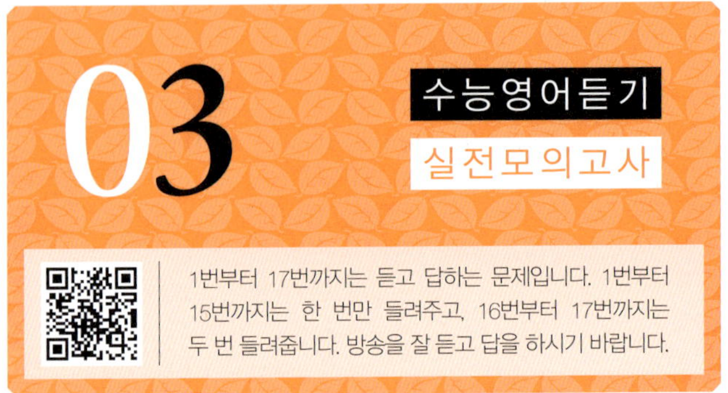

01

대화를 듣고, 여자의 마지막 말에 대한 남자의 응답으로 가장 적절한 것을 고르시오.

① Well, let's look at the weather.
② Yeah, me too. I'm really excited.
③ I'll come by your house in the evening.
④ Oh, that's fine. We can do it another time.
⑤ I think we should study more for our test.

02

대화를 듣고, 남자의 마지막 말에 대한 여자의 응답으로 가장 적절한 것을 고르시오.

① No. I did it on my own.
② Perhaps by next Monday.
③ Sure. Let me do it for you.
④ I like chemistry more than physics.
⑤ Yes. They'll leave in a couple of days.

03

다음을 듣고, 남자가 하는 말의 요지로 가장 적절한 것을 고르시오.

① 스포츠 활동은 학업에 지장을 준다.
② 여자가 남자보다 학업 성적이 우수하다.
③ 지나친 스포츠 활동은 학생들의 건강을 해친다.
④ 학생들의 스포츠 활동은 학업 이상의 것을 줄 수 있다.
⑤ 학교는 학생들을 위한 운동기구와 프로그램을 마련해야 한다.

04

대화를 듣고, 여자의 의견으로 가장 적절한 것을 고르시오.

① 아이들도 간단한 음식은 만들 줄 알아야 한다.
② 음식을 가리지 말고 골고루 먹어야 한다.
③ 자신의 방은 항상 깨끗이 정리해야 한다.
④ 바쁠 때는 패스트푸드를 먹을 수 있다.
⑤ 건강을 위해 정크푸드를 삼가야 한다.

05

대화를 듣고, 두 사람의 관계를 가장 잘 나타낸 것을 고르시오.

① 학부모 — 교사
② 승무원 — 승객
③ 상사 — 부하직원
④ 학생 — 지도교사
⑤ 아동전문가 — 고객

06

대화를 듣고, 그림에서 대화의 내용과 일치하지 <u>않는</u> 것을 고르시오.

07

대화를 듣고, 여자가 남자에게 부탁한 일로 가장 적절한 것을 고르시오.

① to get party decorations
② to help start a book club
③ to reserve enough tables
④ to give a call to close friends
⑤ to give her directions to the party

08

대화를 듣고, 여자가 음반을 사러 갈 수 <u>없는</u> 이유를 고르시오.

① 가족여행 준비를 해야 해서
② 다른 친구와 약속이 있어서
③ 저녁 식사 준비를 도와야 해서
④ 버스 터미널에 마중을 나가야 해서
⑤ 엄마가 청소하는 것을 도와야 해서

09

대화를 듣고, 남자가 지불할 금액을 고르시오.

① $73 　② $80 　③ $87 　④ $89 　⑤ $107

10

대화를 듣고, 음악 캠프에 관해 두 사람이 언급하지 <u>않은</u> 것을 고르시오.

① 캠프 시기 　② 캠프 기간 　③ 캠프 위치
④ 셔틀버스 운행 　⑤ 나이 제한

11

실험에 관한 다음 내용을 듣고, 일치하지 <u>않는</u> 것을 고르시오.

① 8살에서 10살 사이의 영국 학생들이 참가했다.
② 쌍방향 책상은 학생들의 공감능력 향상을 보기 위한 실험이다.
③ DeskTouch는 기술을 통해 학습 효과를 높이도록 고안되었다.
④ 스마트폰이나 iPad처럼 기기를 터치하는 것에 반응한다.
⑤ 모든 책상은 중앙 책상과 쌍방향으로 연결되어 있다.

12

다음 표를 보면서 대화를 듣고, 두 사람이 선택할 게스트 하우스를 고르시오.

	Name	Rate per Night	Location	Hot Tub
①	Bright Chalet	$65	Mountainside	Yes
②	Sky Chalet	$60	Mountainside	No
③	Gold Chalet	$50	Mountainside	Yes
④	Royal Chalet	$70	In Town	Yes
⑤	Star Chalet	$50	In Town	No

13

대화를 듣고, 여자의 마지막 말에 대한 남자의 응답으로 가장 적절한 것을 고르시오.

Man: _______________________________

① It's all right. I bought a new sleeping bag.
② I really appreciate your recommendations.
③ Do you think I can borrow his hiking boots?
④ That would be great. I really need to save money.
⑤ That's awesome. He seemed like he really had fun.

14

대화를 듣고, 남자의 마지막 말에 대한 여자의 응답으로 가장 적절한 것을 고르시오.

Woman: _______________________________

① Yeah, I really enjoy red wine with dinner.
② I think it's your turn to cook dinner for me.
③ Sorry, but we don't have time to drink it now.
④ All right. Just don't drink it in the living room.
⑤ Don't worry. I won't get any wine on your carpet.

15

다음 상황 설명을 듣고, Linda가 Mike에게 할 말로 가장 적절한 것을 고르시오.

Linda: _______________________________

① It could be colder up there than you think.
② Please be safe and camp only in areas where it's permitted.
③ You should wash your jacket before you leave. It's really dirty.
④ You can't leave the house until you've finished washing your clothes.
⑤ Climbing mountains is fun, but it can be dangerous. Please be careful.

[16-17] 다음을 듣고, 물음에 답하시오.

16

남자가 하는 말의 목적으로 가장 적절한 것은?

① to bring people with like minds together
② to show appreciation for the artists' help
③ to provide advice on how to buy artwork
④ to promote innovation in the art industry
⑤ to help creators receive funding for projects

17

프로젝트 분야로 언급되지 <u>않은</u> 것은?

① 영화 　② 패션 　③ 발명품
④ 만화 　⑤ 출판

03 DICTATION

01

W: I'm so happy now that final exams are finished.

M: So am I. Do you want to ___________ ___________ ___________ ___________ with me this weekend?

W: That sounds lovely, but I already have ___________ ___________ ___________ ___________ ___________.

M: (Oh, that's fine. We can do it another time.)

02

M: Clara, don't you think the physics assignment is ___________ ___________ ___________ ___________?

W: It was quite difficult, but I was able to finish it last night.

M: You must be joking! Your parents ___________ ___________ ___________ ___________, right?

W: (No. I did it on my own.)

03

M: You would think that participating in high school athletic programs would ___________ ___________ ___________ ___________ ___________ a student's grades. However, recent research shows that, in general, students who play sports do better in school than those who don't. Exercise has a positive effect on learning, memory, and concentration, which can ___________ ___________ ___________ ___________ ___________ in the classroom. The effects of participating in sports sometimes ___________ ___________ ___________ ___________, as student athletes also learn valuable lessons about other skills that are important in life, such as teamwork and goal-setting. Working with coaches, trainers, and teammates to ___________ ___________ and achieve other goals teaches students skills that are important to success and so can help them throughout their lives.

04

W: Tom, what's going on in here?

M: What are you talking about, Mom?

W: This place is ___________ ___________. Look at all of this garbage!

M: Yeah, you're right. Sorry about that, Mom. I'll ___________ ___________ ___________ now.

W: And look at what caused the mess. There are fast food bags, junk food boxes, soda cans, and candy wrappers all over the place. You didn't eat all of that, did you?

M: I did. I was so hungry.

W: But all of this stuff is really bad for you. None of it is healthy at all.

M: Well, you never ___________ ___________ ___________ ___________ ___________, so every once in a while I eat a lot of it when you're not home.

W: I don't want you to eat that stuff because I ___________ ___________ ___________ ___________.

M: I understand. I'll try not to eat junk food anymore.

W: Just remember how important your health is.

05

M: How about this weather?

W: It's awful, isn't it? The forecast says it's supposed to be rainy all week.

M: Are we still going to work outside today?

W: No. I have some work for you to do in the office.

M: That's great. ___________ ___________ ___________ ___________ if I work outside.

W: There's something I've been meaning to talk to you about, Frank.

M: Sure. What is it?

W: Well, you ___________ ___________ ___________ ___________ ___________ lately. Is everything all right?

M: Honestly, my son has been having a lot of difficulties at school, and ___________ ___________ at home. I'm really worried about him.

W: I can understand. I have two children myself. But, you know, kids will be kids. You just have to let them develop naturally.

M: Thanks for the advice, Mrs. Stark. What is it you need me to do today?

W: I'd like you to ___________ ___________ ___________.

06

M: What's that you're working on, Sandra?

W: It's ___________ ___________ ___________ my new band. We have a show coming up next week.

M: It looks pretty cool. So your band is called Bastion?

W: That's right. I wrote our name ___________ ___________ ___________ ___________ ___________ . I also drew some skulls next to it.

M: I see that. I guess you're a rock 'n' roll band. That's a pretty cool guitar you drew on the left side.

W: Yeah, that's my guitar: a Bender P-159.

M: It looks like you put a picture of yourself on the right. Where's your guitar?

W: Well, I couldn't find a picture of me with my guitar so I chose one where I'm not holding it.

M: Cool. You wrote the date and the venue ___________ ___________ ___________ , huh?

W: That's right. We're playing at the Denton Shelter House at 9 p.m. on the 27th.

M: Awesome. I might ___________ ___________ ___________ ___________ .

07

W: Hi, Oliver! You made it just in time!

M: Really? What's going on?

W: I was just ___________ ___________ ___________ ___________ ___________ Elena's birthday this weekend.

M: Oh, nice. Will it be a surprise party?

W: No. I think we'll just ___________ ___________ ___________ ___________ ___________ ___________ get together at Joe's Crab Shack.

M: Sounds good. I know she's wanted to go there for a while.

W: I was thinking of inviting all of our good friends.

M: I like that idea. What can I do to help?

W: ___________ ___________ ___________ ___________ to the party store and picking up balloons and "Happy Birthday" signs?

M: Of course. I'll head over there ___________ ___________ .

W: Awesome. This is going to be a great party.

M: Yeah, I'm really excited!

08

W: Hey, Julian. What's up?

M: Not too much. I'm just reading this music review in the school newspaper.

W: That's cool. What album is it?

M: Kenny North's new album, *Graduate School*. ___________ ___________ ___________ ___________ ___________ ?

W: Of course. A lot of people are talking about it these days.

M: Yeah, I'm thinking about buying it. Do you want to come over and listen to it with me after school?

W: I'd love to, but I really can't. I ___________ ___________ ___________ ___________ ___________ after school today.

M: Really? Why?

W: My brother's ___________ ___________ ___________ ___________ to visit.

M: So you need to pick him up from the bus station?

W: My dad is going to pick him up. I have to ___________ ___________ ___________ ___________ ___________ .

M: I see. Well, I hope you have a great time catching up with your brother.

09

W: Welcome to Jenna's Butcher Shop. What can I do for you?

M: I'm looking for some steaks.

W: Steaks, huh? What kind of steaks do you want?

M: Well, I'm ___________ ___________ ___________ tomorrow with my parents-in-law, so I'd like something that would impress them.

W: Well, we're having a sale on premium T-bone steaks. ___________ ___________ ___________ $20 a steak.

M: That sounds amazing. I'll take four, please.

W: No problem. ___________ ___________ ___________ ___________ baked potatoes. Would you like a bag?

M: Sure. How much are they?

W: They're usually $9 a bag, but you seem like a loyal customer, so I'll give them to you for $7.

M: That's great. I'll take one bag of potatoes, then.

W: All right. So, we have four premium T-bones and a bag of potatoes. ___________ ___________ ___________ ___________ ?

M: I believe that's it. Here's my card.

10

[Telephone rings.]

W: Hello?

M: Hi, Stacy. This is Dominic. Is Russell around? My son is really wanting to play with him today.

W: Oh, Russell isn't here. He's at music camp today.

M: Music camp, huh?

W: Yeah. The local orchestra holds one every summer. The students get to practice with professional musicians.

M: _________ _________ _________. Where is it?

W: It's at the auditorium, right across from the library.

M: I see. Do they still have any spots available?

W: They do. I just signed Russell up yesterday, and they still had several left. They also have a shuttle bus that picks the students up.

M: That's great. Do they have any _________ _________?

W: It's for kids age ten and up. You can find all the information on the orchestra's website.

M: Nice! I'll check it out. I think my son would love to join.

11

M: Since 2009, eight- to ten-year-old students across Britain have been involved in a very cool experiment: to see if replacing pencils, paper, and even calculators with hi-tech interactive desks would help _________ _________ _________ _________! The project was created by Britain's Dunham University and SinergyCom. The hi-tech desks, called DeskTouch, are just one of several research projects _________ _________ _________ learning through technology. They've been fitted with software that responds to one's touch, much like a smartphone or iPad. All of the desks _________ _________ _________ _________ _________ from which the teacher can create and send math problems to the students and then check them afterwards.

12

W: Hey sweetheart, you know that Billy finishes up school in less than a month, right?

M: Yeah. He's _________ _________ about his summer vacation. I've been thinking that we should do something special this year.

W: What did you have in mind?

M: Well, you know how I've said that I've always wanted to go to The Smoky Mountains?

W: Yeah. We _________ _________ _________ _________ _________ _________.

M: Right. So I've been searching the Internet, and I found this list of chalets in the mountains. Tell me what you think.

W: Well, I don't think we should spend more than $60 a night.

M: Yeah. I'd prefer to stay on the mountain, though. The towns there look so touristy.

W: I agree. I guess that leaves these two, then.

M: Hmm. . . let's go for the one that has a hot tub. _________ _________ _________.

W: Sure. Go ahead and book it.

13

W: Hey, Eddie. You look busy. Should I come back another time?

M: I'm just finishing up here. I'm almost _________ _________ _________ _________ _________ to Nepal.

W: That's exciting. Did you buy everything I recommended?

M: I did. Thanks for the recommendations. I bought a new pair of boots and a tent.

W: That's great. Oh my! Is this your sleeping bag? I think it's too thin. _________ _________ _________ _________.

M: I think you're right, but sleeping bags are expensive. I _________ _________ _________ _________ a new one.

W: Hmm. . . I think I might be able to help.

M: Really? Do you have one I can borrow?

W: Well, my father has one that he never uses. I'll see if he'll _________ _________ _________ _________.

M: (That would be great. I really need to save money.)

14

W: Hey, thanks for coming. Welcome to my new apartment.

M: I'm sorry I'm late. I had to __________ __________ __________ __________.

W: Wine, huh? It isn't red wine, is it?

M: It is. Don't you like red wine?

W: I do. But I just __________ __________ __________ __________ __________ in my living room. I don't want you to spill any on it.

M: Don't worry about it. I'll be extra careful.

W: I'm not sure if I trust you. Remember when we ate spaghetti together and you got sauce all over your white shirt?

M: That was a one-time mistake. You're __________ __________.

W: I'd really feel more comfortable if you didn't drink it. I want to keep this apartment spotless.

M: If that's how you feel, I'll __________ __________ __________ __________ __________.

W: (All right. Just don't drink it in the living room.)

15

W: Mike, a high school student, is planning on spending the weekend with his friends. They've __________ __________ __________ __________ in the mountains. However, Mike's mom, Linda, is worried about her son. She's been camping in the late summer and knows that it can get quite cold in the mountains. She __________ __________ __________ __________ __________ __________, but he refuses. He thinks that wearing a winter jacket in the summer is ridiculous and doesn't want to __________ __________ __________ __________. Linda isn't sure if he'll need the jacket or not, but she wants to try to convince Mike to take it __________ __________ __________. In this situation, what would Linda most likely say to Mike?

Linda: (It could be colder up there than you think.)

16-17

M: Crowd funding has become a great way for people around the world to __________ __________ __________ for their artistic endeavors. Many creative people have ideas that they would love to put into practice, but lack the money necessary to make that happen. That's where our program, Donation Station, comes in. Donation Station connects artists and other creative people to investors who believe in their projects. To get started, all you need to do is __________ __________ __________ on the Donation Station website and describe your project. If investors like it, they can send you the funds you need to __________ __________ __________ __________. Do you have a great idea for a movie, but lack the money to produce it? Donation Station can help. Perhaps you have a new fashion design or a useful invention, or maybe you need help publishing a book. Donation Station realizes that creativity is essential for our society and helps advance the whole world. That's why we try to help make your dreams reality. Sign up right now at our website to __________ __________ __________ __________ __________ __________.

04 수능영어듣기
실전모의고사

01

대화를 듣고, 여자의 마지막 말에 대한 남자의 응답으로 가장 적절한 것을 고르시오.

① Your lessons have really helped me.
② That's okay. You just need to practice.
③ I'll come by your house at around noon.
④ I'm happy to share my music collection with you.
⑤ Hold on! You need to tune the guitar before playing it.

02

대화를 듣고, 남자의 마지막 말에 대한 여자의 응답으로 가장 적절한 것을 고르시오.

① Okay. I guess the tip isn't included in the bill.
② Sounds good to me. How about I cook for you?
③ I didn't really care for the pasta at that restaurant.
④ Sure. That way you won't have to go to the grocery store.
⑤ All right. I heard about a new Mexican restaurant down the street.

03

다음을 듣고, 여자가 하는 말의 목적으로 가장 적절한 것을 고르시오.

① 팬들의 적극적인 응원을 부탁하려고
② 공식 웹사이트의 개설을 안내하려고
③ 팬들의 의견 제안 방식의 변경을 공지하려고
④ 경기장과 시설의 보수 공사 계획을 알려주려고
⑤ 효과적인 팬들의 의견 제안 방법을 추천 받으려고

04

대화를 듣고, 두 사람이 하는 말의 주제로 가장 적절한 것을 고르시오.

① 한국의 다양한 미신
② 돌잔치에서 지켜야 할 예절
③ 한국 돌잔치의 특별한 전통
④ 돌잔치 문화의 지나친 상업화
⑤ 한국 부모들의 자녀에 대한 큰 사랑

05

대화를 듣고, 두 사람의 관계를 가장 잘 나타낸 것을 고르시오.

① 선배 — 후배
② 교사 — 학부모
③ 교수 — 회사 직원
④ 입사 지원자 — 면접관
⑤ 인사팀 담당자 — 학생

06

대화를 듣고, 그림에서 남자가 선택한 차량을 고르시오.

07

대화를 듣고, 여자가 남자를 위해 할 일로 가장 적절한 것을 고르시오.

① 여행 경험 들려주기
② 웹 사이트 읽어주기
③ 일본어 강좌 소개해주기
④ 가볼 만한 곳 추천해주기
⑤ 호텔 예약 방법 알려주기

08

대화를 듣고, 남자가 늦게 귀가하는 이유를 고르시오.

① 오랜만에 만난 친구와 이야기가 길어져서
② 휴대폰이 고장 났는데 수리가 오래 걸려서
③ 스쿨버스가 고장이 나서 대중교통을 이용하느라
④ 사고가 났는데 친구가 다쳐서 같이 병원에 가느라
⑤ 길이 통제되고 주변 교통수단을 이용할 수 없어서

09

대화를 듣고, 여자가 지불할 금액을 고르시오.

① $30 ② $44 ③ $50 ④ $54 ⑤ $60

10

대화를 듣고, 여자가 본 영화에 관해 두 사람이 언급하지 <u>않은</u> 것을 고르시오.

① 영화 제목 ② 영화 주제 ③ 영화 길이
④ 관람 소감 ⑤ 상영관 위치

11

컴퓨터 게임 대회에 관한 다음 내용을 듣고, 일치하지 <u>않는</u> 것을 고르시오.

① 다음 주말에 개최된다.
② 두 가지 전략 게임을 한다.
③ 컴퓨터를 상대로 하는 게임도 있다.
④ 이 대회에 아마추어는 참가가 불가능하다.
⑤ 참가 신청서 제출 마감은 1월 7일까지이다.

12

다음 표를 보면서 대화를 듣고, 두 사람이 선택한 기부 내용을 고르시오.

Make a Difference Charity

	Option	Category	Project	Donation Amount
①	A	Overseas	Disaster Relief	$200
②	B	Overseas	Medical Care	$250
③	C	Overseas	Disaster Relief	$350
④	D	Domestic	Education	$100
⑤	E	Domestic	Medical Care	$200

13

대화를 듣고, 여자의 마지막 말에 대한 남자의 응답으로 가장 적절한 것을 고르시오.

Man: ____________________

① New York is beautiful this time of year.
② I'm sorry to hear you had such bad luck.
③ It's nice that the police were able to find it.
④ You should arrive at the airport an hour early.
⑤ I should be more careful the next time I travel.

14

대화를 듣고, 남자의 마지막 말에 대한 여자의 응답으로 가장 적절한 것을 고르시오.

Woman: ____________________

① Well, I'm thinking of donating money to this website.
② Right. Killing elephants is illegal in many countries.
③ Why don't we check out the elephants at the zoo?
④ No problem. You can borrow this documentary.
⑤ People shouldn't hunt elephants for ivory.

15

다음 상황 설명을 듣고, Jane이 Tim에게 할 말로 가장 적절한 것을 고르시오.

Jane: Tim, ____________________

① your workout and dieting habits are not healthy.
② your diet and exercise routine is working well.
③ you still seem to be out of shape.
④ you need to work out more.
⑤ you have to study harder.

[16–17] 다음을 듣고, 물음에 답하시오.

16

남자가 하는 말의 목적으로 가장 적절한 것은?

① to provide some advice on mountain biking
② to persuade others to take up mountain biking
③ to identify the health benefits of mountain biking
④ to explain reasons why mountain biking is popular
⑤ to warn of potential dangers during mountain biking

17

남자가 언급하지 <u>않은</u> 것은?

① 헬멧 ② 물 ③ 날씨
④ 지도 ⑤ 여벌 옷

녹음을 다시 한 번 듣고, 빈칸에 알맞은 말을 쓰시오

01

W: Daniel, you're becoming a really __________ __________ __________.

M: __________ __________ __________ __________ __________. Have you ever tried playing an instrument?

W: I love music, but I don't have any musical ability.

M: (That's okay. You just need to practice.)

02

M: I'm getting hungry. What would you like to eat?

W: I'm not sure. Do you want to __________ __________ __________ __________ again?

M: We're __________ __________ __________ __________ eating out. Let's eat at home tonight.

W: (Sounds good to me. How about I cook for you?)

03

W: Good morning, fans. I understand some of you have suggestions about the new stadium and its facilities. __________ __________ __________ __________ __________ __________ you've dropped in the box that we put up in the stadium several months ago. However, we've decided to make this process easier by __________ __________ __________ __________ __________ __________. This will allow you to do it from anywhere at any time. It's so simple. Just go to the official website, __________ __________ __________ "__________" __________, type your suggestion into the box provided, and click "Submit." This new system also __________ __________ __________ __________ to your suggestions in a timely manner. Thank you for your time.

04

W: Jimmy, I have a party invitation for you.

M: Wow, your son's first birthday. How exciting!

W: Yeah. Can you make it to the party?

M: In Busan? Of course! And I heard there's a __________ __________ __________ __________ a child's first birthday.

W: Yes, there is. At its first birthday party, a baby chooses from one of several __________ __________ __________.

M: So, does the item the baby chooses predict his or her future?

W: That's right. For instance, if my son chooses a pencil, we believe it means he'll have a __________ __________ __________.

M: I see. What else can the baby choose from?

W: Well, if he chooses money then he'll be wealthy. If he chooses a spool of thread, it means he'll have a long life.

M: That makes sense. I'm really looking forward to your baby's party!

05

[Telephone rings.]

W: Hello?

M: Hi, Aria. This is Walter.

W: Hello, Walter. How is everything?

M: Great, thanks. I just wanted to take some time to thank you for recommending the two interns that are working with us now. We really __________ __________ __________ __________ __________ __________.

W: Great! I'm glad to hear that hiring my students has worked out so well for you.

M: __________ __________ __________ __________ __________ that I'm actually calling to ask if you have any other students you could recommend.

W: Sure. Which department needs interns?

M: We have __________ __________ __________ __________ __________.

W: I see. I think I know the perfect students for those positions. I'll notify them after class next week.

M: Great. Please __________ __________ __________ __________ __________ and have them call me directly.

W: Will do, Walter.

M: Thank you.

06

W: Hi. Welcome to Isaac's Rent-a-Car. What can I do for you today?

M: Hello. I have a reservation to pick up a vehicle this afternoon. My name is Robert Clay.

W: Just a second. Okay, I have your reservation right here, Mr. Clay. ___________ ___________ ___________ ___________ ___________ and tell me which car you'd like.

M: ___________, ___________ ___________ ___________ ___________ ___________ ___________-___________ ___________. I'm traveling alone.

W: I see. How about the convertible, then? It's sporty, so it's fun for people driving alone.

M: Well, the air is quite smoggy today. I don't want to ___________ ___________ ___________ ___________ ___________ ___________.

W: Okay. I guess that narrows it down to these two.

M: Hmm. I don't want a gray car. Gray is a bit of ___________ ___________ ___________ ___________.

W: Uh-huh. Well, I suppose this one is the best fit for you then.

M: Looks good. I'll take it. Here's my credit card.

07

W: Hey, what are you up to?

M: I'm searching the Internet for a hotel room for my vacation.

W: That's cool. ___________ ___________ ___________ ___________?

M: Tokyo. Have you ever been?

W: Tokyo? Yeah, I've been. I stayed at the Tokyo Palace Hotel. It was wonderful.

M: I looked at rooms there, but they're far too expensive for me.

W: I see. Well, you should check out ___________ ___________ ___________ ___________ ___________ ___________. It's called *tokyodeals.com*.

M: Cool. Let me check it out. *[Pause]* Oh, here it is. But I think ___________ ___________ ___________ ___________ ___________ to me.

W: Why's that?

M: The website is in Japanese. I can't read Japanese at all. Can you?

W: Sure. I studied Japanese in college. Want me to help you?

M: That would be awesome! Thanks for your help.

08

[Telephone rings.]

W: Hello?

M: Hey, Mom. It's Tom.

W: Where have you been, Tom? ___________ ___________ ___________ ___________ ___________ ___________ an hour ago. It's seven o'clock.

M: ___________ ___________ ___________ ___________ earlier. I even had to borrow someone's phone to call you now.

W: Okay. So you're not home now, and you're calling me, which means you won't be home soon. What's the matter?

M: Didn't you hear that ___________ ___________ ___________ ___________ ___________ in front of the park?

W: No. Are you all right?

M: Yeah, I'm okay. I was on the other side of the park when it happened.

W: So why haven't you come home yet?

M: Because the police and fire department have blocked the roads around the park. Traffic's really bad, and the subway ___________ ___________ ___________ ___________ ___________ ___________ ___________ ___________.

W: That's awful news. Did you have dinner?

M: I had some fruit and a little salad a while ago. I'm okay.

W: All right. Take care. I'll see you later.

M: Okay, Mom. See you soon.

09

M: Hi. Welcome to Franklin University's Arts Center. What can I do for you today?

W: Hello. I'd like tickets for two adults and two children, please.

M: No problem. *[Keyboard typing sound]* That'll be $44.

W: Do these tickets __________ __________ __________
the Harmony Blues show?

M: I'm sorry, but they don't. Tickets to that performance cost an additional $4 a person.

W: I see. What is the cost per ticket, then, __________
__________ __________?

M: They're $18 for adults and $12 for children.

W: Okay. I'd like to get those tickets for two adults and two children. Oh! I almost forgot about these coupons I have for 10% off. Here they are.

M: *[Pause]* I'm sorry, but __________ __________
__________ __________ __________ the performance tickets.

W: Oh. Well, that's all right. Here's my card.

M: Thank you, ma'am.

10

W: Hey Pablo, have you ever seen the documentary *An Unfortunate Fact*?

M: I haven't. What's it about?

W: It's about climate change. It discusses the dangers that __________ __________ __________.

M: Hmm. . . I think I've heard about it. I really like science documentaries. How was it?

W: It was __________ __________ __________-
__________. It made me think hard about the future of the world.

M: Was it a long documentary?

W: It was about two hours. __________ __________
__________ __________, but if you like science documentaries, I'm sure you'll enjoy it.

M: I'd love to see it, but I don't think I'll have time this weekend. Do you think __________ __________
__________ __________ __________ __________
next weekend?

W: I have no idea. You could check their websites for information.

M: Yeah, all right. I look forward to talking with you more about it once I've seen it.

11

M: Good afternoon, gamers! My name is Nimbus, and
__________ __________ __________ __________
at the PC Playground next weekend. These contests

are for players of real-time strategy games. We'll be playing two different games in our contests: *Suncraft* and *League of Heroes*. In the *Suncraft* contest, you will play side-by-side with professional *Suncraft* players. For the *League of Heroes* contest, players will be grouped into random teams and compete against computer AI __________ __________ __________
__________. For these contests, we will only accept amateurs. __________ __________ __________
__________ __________ __________. To apply, visit our website at *www.PCPlayg.co* and submit your application before January 7th. We wish you all the best of luck and __________ __________ __________
__________ __________ __________.

12

W: Hey sweetheart, I think I've found the charity that I'd like to donate to this year.

M: Great! Is it another children's charity?

W: Not this time. It helps people of all ages. It's called *Make a Difference*, and we can choose to help __________ __________ __________ or here in our own country.

M: Well, didn't we __________ __________ __________
__________ __________ __________ last year? I think this year we should help people overseas.

W: Me, too. I've been watching the news a lot lately, and I think that we should donate money to victims of that terrible tsunami.

M: It does look awful, doesn't it? __________ __________
__________ __________ __________ __________
__________.

W: All right. So, how much do you think we should donate?

M: I don't think that we can afford anything more than $300.

W: Then that leaves us with this option.

M: Good! It feels great to use our money to help others.

13

M: Hey, Samantha. Did you enjoy your trip to New York?

W: I don't think it __________ __________ __________
__________ __________.

M: Really? That's a shame. What went wrong?

W: Pretty much everything. When I got to New York, the airline had lost my baggage. It took three days for them to find it.

M: That's awful, but I know how you feel. __________ __________ __________ __________ __________ __________ when I went to Rome.

W: Oh, that was just the start of it. While I was sitting at a cafe enjoying my coffee, someone stole my briefcase.

M: Really? That's unfortunate.

W: Unfortunate? I was infuriated! And the police couldn't help me. But __________ __________ __________ __________ __________ __________ __________.

M: You __________ __________ __________ __________, right?

W: Nope. My flight back to Seattle __________ __________ __________ __________ __________. Then when I went to claim my luggage, it was missing again.

M: (I'm sorry to hear you had such bad luck.)

14

M: Hey Brittney, what's that you're looking at?

W: Oh, I'm searching online for ways to save the elephants.

M: You want to help elephants, huh?

W: Yeah. __________ __________ __________ __________ with kind hearts. __________ __________ __________ __________ __________ __________.

M: That's interesting. I never knew that.

W: It's the truth. But there are a lot of poachers out there that hunt elephants for their ivory.

M: Still? I thought people __________ __________ __________ __________ __________. How many elephants are killed each year just for their tusks?

W: As many as 40,000 a year, some experts say.

M: That's terrible. What do people want the ivory for?

W: It can be used to make collectible figurines, billiard balls, and traditional medicines

M: That's so sad. What can we do to help?

W: (Well, I'm thinking of donating money to this website.)

15

M: Jane's son, Tim, a middle school student, is really concerned about __________ __________ __________ __________ __________ __________. Jane knows that it's good to be aware of your health, but she thinks Tim takes it too far. She has noticed that he's been going to the gym for hours a day and __________ __________ __________ __________ __________. This concerns her because he seems to be getting too skinny. He looks unhealthy. But Tim thinks that he needs to lose more weight. Jane thinks he's becoming obsessed, and she worries it's going to lead to a serious health problem. She wants to try to __________ __________ __________ __________ __________ __________ __________ __________ __________ __________. What would Jane most likely say to Tim in this situation?

Jane: Tim, (your workout and dieting habits are not healthy.)

16-17

M: Good morning, everyone. Today, we're going to talk about mountain biking. As you know, mountain biking is a great way to exercise. It's also a nice way to __________ __________ __________ __________. But while it may be fun and beneficial to your well-being, it's also very dangerous. Be sure to __ __________ __________ __________ before your next trip. First of all, please __________ __________ __________ __________. Always, and I mean always, wear a helmet. Protecting your head is crucial when mountain biking. Another very important thing to consider is water. Mountain biking is physically exhausting, so __________ __________ __________ __________ __________. You'll also want to check the weather before going out on the mountain. You wouldn't want to get stranded in the rain. And lastly, bring a map and compass. That way, if you get lost, you can find your way back down. Keep these tips in mind on your next mountain biking trip.

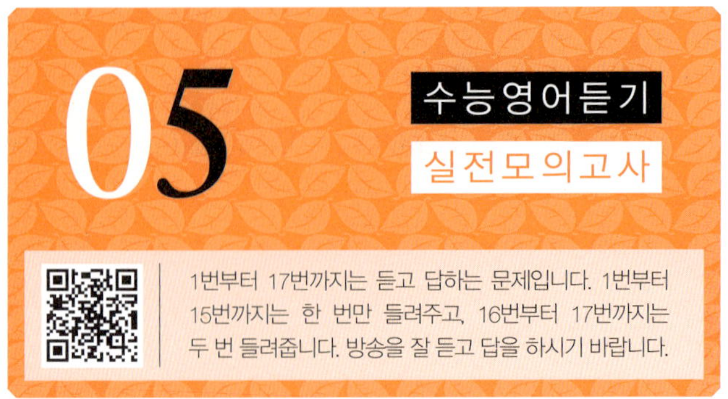

01

대화를 듣고, 여자의 마지막 말에 대한 남자의 응답으로 가장 적절한 것을 고르시오.

① That's fine. I'll pay with my credit card.
② Well, then I need to get my money back.
③ It looks like you were really overcharged.
④ I apologize. There has been a misunderstanding.
⑤ We can give you a 5% discount on your next purchase.

02

대화를 듣고, 남자의 마지막 말에 대한 여자의 응답으로 가장 적절한 것을 고르시오.

① I look forward to interviewing him tonight.
② It's important to be thoroughly prepared.
③ You should bring some flowers.
④ She will graduate next year.
⑤ I think getting a job is.

03

다음을 듣고, 남자가 하는 말의 주제로 가장 적절한 것을 고르시오.

① 컴퓨터 보안 프로그램의 중요성
② 온라인상 개인정보 도용 방지 요령
③ 웹사이트 비밀번호 분실 예방 방법
④ 온라인 개인 정보 유출의 피해 사례
⑤ 전자상거래의 개인 정보 유출 위험성

04

대화를 듣고, 여자의 의견으로 가장 적절한 것을 고르시오.

① 수업 시간에 필기를 빠짐없이 해야 한다.
② 휴대폰으로 인터넷 하는 시간을 줄여야 한다.
③ 성적 향상이 높은 친구의 방법을 따라야 한다.
④ 성적에 대한 지나친 스트레스를 경계해야 한다.
⑤ 방해요소를 제거하여 학습 집중력을 높여야 한다.

05

대화를 듣고, 두 사람의 관계를 가장 잘 나타낸 것을 고르시오.

① 의사 — 환자
② 사장 — 비서
③ 영화배우 — 매니저
④ 투숙객 — 호텔 직원
⑤ 관광 가이드 — 관광객

06

대화를 듣고, 그림에서 대화의 내용과 일치하지 <u>않는</u> 것을 고르시오.

07

대화를 듣고, 남자가 여자를 위해 할 일로 가장 적절한 것을 고르시오.

① 집안을 정리해 주기
② 자전거 주문해 주기
③ 택배 확인해주기
④ 간식 사다 주기
⑤ 설거지 해 주기

08

대화를 듣고, 여자가 공항에 마중 나갈 수 <u>없는</u> 이유를 고르시오.

① 회사에 갑자기 급한 일이 생겨서
② 집에 손님이 오기로 되어 있어서
③ 비행기 도착 시간이 너무 늦어서
④ 기념품 목록을 작성해 줘야 해서
⑤ 딸을 피아노 레슨에 데려가야 해서

09

대화를 듣고, 남자가 지불한 금액을 고르시오.

① $15 ② $20 ③ $27 ④ $36 ⑤ $40

10

대화를 듣고, 수업에 관해 두 사람이 언급하지 <u>않은</u> 것을 고르시오.

① 수업 과목 ② 수업 장소 ③ 수업 횟수
④ 수업 요일 ⑤ 수업료

11

Johnny Bahama's Sea Tours에 관한 다음 내용을 듣고, 일치하지 <u>않는</u> 것을 고르시오.

① 하는 내내 가이드가 있다.
② 하루에 네 번 투어가 있다.
③ 체력적으로 힘든 활동이다.
④ 구명조끼를 착용해야 한다.
⑤ 예약은 전화로도 가능하다.

12

다음 표를 보면서 대화를 듣고, 두 사람이 선택한 프로그램을 고르시오.

Upton Library Summer Program Schedule

	Program	Days	Time	Activities	Fee
①	Reading	Mon. ~ Wed.	16:00 ~ 17:00	Reading	$20
②	Reading	Thu. & Fri.	15:00 ~ 16:30	Active Reading	$30
③	Writing	Wed. & Thu.	16:00 ~ 17:30	Creative Writing	$40
④	Writing	Thu. & Fri.	17:00 ~ 19:00	Nonfiction Writing	$50
⑤	Art	Wed. ~ Fri.	16:00 ~ 17:30	Painting	$60

13

대화를 듣고, 여자의 마지막 말에 대한 남자의 응답으로 가장 적절한 것을 고르시오.

Man: _______________________________________

① I don't want him to join any school clubs.
② I'd like to know how to teach students better.
③ I'll tell him to be at school on time from now on.
④ I feel relieved to hear he behaves so well in school.
⑤ I think I should advise him to be active in your class.

14

대화를 듣고, 남자의 마지막 말에 대한 여자의 응답으로 가장 적절한 것을 고르시오.

Woman: _______________________________________

① I'm not too busy now, so I can come with you to see him.
② That's a shame, but I'm sure he'll understand the situation.
③ I'm sure you can pass the exam, since you've worked so hard.
④ That's right, but he must be too busy to go camping with you.
⑤ The assignments should be submitted by email to the teachers.

15

다음 상황 설명을 듣고, Carl이 정비사에게 할 말로 가장 적절한 것을 고르시오.

Carl: _______________________________________

① I think that I should get a second opinion.
② How much is it going to cost to fix my car?
③ I don't think I have any spark plugs in my car.
④ How long will it take to change the spark plugs?
⑤ That's great! I was worried that it was a serious problem.

[16-17] 다음을 듣고, 물음에 답하시오.

16

남자가 하는 말의 <u>주제</u>로 가장 적절한 것은?

① to inform people of a new herbal supplement
② to provide tips on improving memory and brain function
③ to suggest a supplement proven to help Alzheimer's patients
④ to remind people of the dangers of taking herbal supplements
⑤ to help people recognize the warning signs of Alzheimer's disease

17

Ginkgo biloba에 관한 내용과 일치하지 <u>않는</u> 것은?

① 독일에서 쓰이는 예방법이다.
② 독일 외 다른 나라에선 쓰지 않는다.
③ 뇌활동과 기억력 회복에 도움을 준다.
④ 뇌로 가는 혈액의 순환을 증가시켜준다.
⑤ 복용 20분 내에도 효과가 나타날 수 있다.

01

W: Where did you get the postcards? Were they expensive?

M: I picked them up ___________ ___________ ___________ ___________. I got the whole set for $10.

W: Really? I bought the same cards yesterday for $15 in town.

M: (It looks like you were really overcharged.)

02

M: Next Monday, my daughter is going to ___________ ___________ ___________, but I have a job interview at the same time.

W: But you can't do both.

M: I know. Which do you think is more important?

W: (I think getting a job is.)

03

M: Due to recent technological advances, people are spending more and more time on the Internet. As many of you may know, this has led to the rise of online predators that are looking to steal your personal information. I'm here today to offer some tips on ___________ ___________ ___________ ___________ ___________ ___________. For one thing, it's very important to change the passwords of your online accounts regularly. Furthermore, you should use unique ___________ ___________ ___________ ___________ ___________ ___________. These passwords should contain numbers, letters, and special characters, such as asterisks or punctuation. You should ___________ ___________ ___________ ___________ ___________ ___________. Be careful when inputting your information ___________ ___________ ___________. Finally, when using a public computer, be sure to log out completely. Close the browser when you're finished.

04

M: Tiffany, you're really ___________ ___________ ___________ ___________ ___________. You've also been participating more often.

W: It's funny you've noticed, but yes I have.

M: How are you doing it? You were struggling so much earlier in the semester.

W: I've been trying to read the textbooks before class at home and ___________ ___________ ___________ ___________.

M: How can I improve my concentration and interest when I study, like you have?

W: It's quite simple, actually. Just get rid of all of the things that can be a distraction.

M: You mean I should turn off my TV and stop browsing the Internet?

W: Well, everything is ___________ ___________ ___________. But you should make time to study, and only study during that time.

M: That makes sense. Sometimes I like to study with the TV on, but I find it to be really distracting.

W: I'm sure you can improve in class if you just get rid of the things that are distracting you.

05

W: Good morning, Boris. How are you feeling today?

M: A lot better, thanks. I'm really enjoying my time here at the resort. It's a lot more comfortable than the last place we stayed.

W: I'm glad you like it. The view from ___________ ___________ ___________, right?

M: It's lovely. I really don't want to leave.

W: Well, what would you like for breakfast? I can have room service send up steak and eggs if you'd like.

M: That sounds great. So, ___________ ___________ ___________ ___________ for today? Is that magazine shoot today or tomorrow?

W: That's tomorrow. You have a television interview at the local station today.

M: I see. Thanks, Diane. I really appreciate all of your help. By the way, ___________ ___________ ___________ ___________ ___________?

W: Next Monday. Our set manager __________ __________ __________ __________ to prepare.
M: That sounds great. Thanks again.

06

W: Hello, Jayden. What are you using the computer for?
M: I'm working on a new design for our website. Check it out.
W: It's looking a lot nicer. I really like the __________ __________ __________ __________ __________ __________.
M: Thanks. I wanted to make it more user-friendly.
W: I like the picture of the soccer player on the top, too. Is that a link to the players' biographies underneath it?
M: It sure is. I thought it would be nice for the fans to learn more about the players.
W: What is that picture?
M: It's a picture of the player of the month. He's __________ __________ __________ __________.
W: How about the video under the picture?
M: That's a video of some of the highlights of the year so far.
W: How about __________ __________ __________ __________ __________ __________?
M: There's one at the bottom of the page.

07

[Telephone rings.]
W: Hello?
M: Hi, darling. __________ __________ __________ __________ __________ __________?
W: Not yet. I just finished my work. I'll leave the office in five minutes. Did you have dinner yet?
M: Yeah, Richard and I had hamburgers. Oh, a large box came for you in the mail today. What's in it?
W: That must be Richard's new coat. __________ __________ __________ __________ on the Internet the other day.
M: Ah, I see.
W: So, I've had a really long day. I think I'll be __________ __________ __________ __________ __________ __________ when I get home. Will you take care of them?

M: Sure. I'll do them with Richard.
W: That's great. I'll __________ __________ __________ __________ __________ and pick up some dessert for you guys on the way home.
M: That sounds nice.
W: Is there anything specific you'd like?
M: Some chocolate and maybe some ice cream. I'll see you when you get here.

08

[Cell phone rings.]
M: Hello?
W: Hey, sweetheart. How was your presentation?
M: It went really well. My clients seemed very impressed.
W: That's great. Are you going to make it home today?
M: Yep. I __________ __________ __________ for this afternoon.
W: Awesome. The kids will be so excited to see you. __________ __________ __________ __________ __________.
M: Yeah, I'm really excited to get home so I can be with the family. Do you think you can pick me up at the airport?
W: Maybe. What time does your flight arrive?
M: It lands at 4:45.
W: Oh. Well, I don't think I'll be able to get there until later. I have to __________ __________ __________ __________ __________ __________ at 5.
M: No problem. I'll __________ __________ __________.
W: Sorry, sweetheart. Oh, could you __________ __________ __________ __________ __________ on your way back?
M: Sure. See you tonight.

09

W: Good evening. What can I do for you?
M: Hello. I'd like tickets to the play for my wife and myself, please.
W: Well, sir, __________ __________ __________ __________. The only seats left are in Section C or in Section F on the balcony.
M: I guess one of those will be fine. How much are they?

W: The Section C tickets are $20 and the Section F tickets are $15.

M: Why are the tickets in Section C so much more expensive?

W: ___________ ___________ ___________ ___________ in Section C, sir.

M: I guess I'll take two tickets in Section C, then. Do you offer any discounts?

W: ___________ ___________ ___________ ___________ ___________ ___________ 65 can receive a 10% discount.

M: I'm 67, and my wife turned 65 last month. Here's my credit card and our IDs.

W: Very well, sir. Here are your tickets. You can enter through the door on your right. Enjoy the play.

M: Thank you.

10

W: Hey Felix, I heard that you're trying to ___________ ___________ ___________ ___________ by tutoring.

M: I am. Do you know anyone who's looking for a tutor?

W: Well, my little sister is ___________ ___________ ___________ and could really use some help.

M: What kind of math does your sister need help with?

W: ___________ ___________ ___________ ___________ at the moment.

M: Oh, no problem. How often would she be able to meet?

W: Twice a week. Tuesdays and Thursdays would probably be best.

M: Okay. How long should the lessons be?

W: I think if it's twice a week, an hour-long lesson should be enough.

M: All right. And how much is your mom ___________ ___________ ___________?

W: She said $40 a lesson seems fair, but you might be able to negotiate with her.

M: No, that's great. Why don't you give your mom my phone number and have her call me? That way we can work out the rest of the details.

W: Sure. No problem.

11

W: Have you ever wondered what it would be like to swim with dolphins, fish, and other marine life? Join Johnny Bahama's Sea Tours, where you can experience ___________ ___________ ___________ ___________ ___________. Oh, you've never snorkeled before? That's no problem. We have ___________ ___________ ___________ ___________ ___________ ___________ ___________ ___________ of the way. We offer daily tours at 9 a.m., 1 p.m., and 4 p.m. Due to the physically demanding nature of the activity, only snorkelers age fifteen and older are allowed on these tours. We also ask that all snorkelers ___________ ___________ ___________ ___________ at all times. You can make reservations at your hotel lobby or by calling 110-555-7570 between the hours of 7 a.m. and 6 p.m. Thank you for listening and have a wonderful stay here on our beautiful island.

12

M: Hey sweetheart, the library is offering some summer programs for children. I think ___________ ___________ ___________ ___________ ___________ one of them.

W: That sounds great. Do you have any information on them?

M: Sure. Here's the flyer they gave me.

W: *[Pause]* Leslie has swimming lessons on Mondays, so she ___________ ___________ ___________ ___________ on that day.

M: Yeah. She also has summer camp every day until three o'clock, right?

W: Right. So we need to find a program that starts after 3:30.

M: All right. Well, I ___________ ___________ ___________ ___________ ___________ an artist, so maybe we can put her in one of the other classes.

W: Yeah. That narrows our choices down to these two.

M: All right. I think $50 is a bit much, don't you?

W: I agree. I guess we should enroll her in this program, then.

M: I'll go over to the library tomorrow and ___________ ___________ ___________.

13

M: Hi, Ms. Swanson. I'm Daniel Hoult, Edward's father.

W: Oh, Mr. Hoult. It's a pleasure to meet you. Come in, please.

M: Thank you. How is my son doing in school?

W: Well, Edward __________ __________ __________ __________.

M: Is that so?

W: Yes. He's always smiling, and he tries to actively participate in class.

M: Isn't he a little aggressive, though?

W: No. He sometimes gets overly excited with his friends, but he __________ __________ __________ __________ __________ __________.

M: He gets irritated rather easily at home.

W: Well, students are often very different at home than at school.

M: You mean the other students are the same way?

W: Yes, Mr. Hoult. Edward's just fine here. He __________ __________ __________ __________ __________ everything.

M: (I feel relieved to hear he behaves so well in school.)

14

M: Jenny, how was your hiking trip over the weekend? You went with your family, right?

W: Actually, my father and I were alone this time, and it was __________ __________ __________ __________ __________ __________!

M: Just you and your father?

W: Yes. We talked about a lot of things. I felt grown-up and __________ __________ __________ __________.

M: I bet you did. I miss my father a lot. He's been away for a year.

W: He's in Dubai, right? __________ __________ __________ __________ __________ during winter vacation?

M: He asked me to come, but I don't have time. I have to attend the winter pre-college program.

W: Oh. I heard that the __________-__________ __________ __________ __________ __________.

M: Yes, it is. There are a lot of assignments and reading. I feel bad that I won't be able to visit him, though.

W: (That's a shame, but I'm sure he'll understand the situation.)

15

W: On the way to work, Carl begins to have car trouble. He __________ __________ __________ __________ __________ and explains that his car sometimes stalls when it's idling. The mechanic has a look at his car and discovers that he needs to change the spark plugs. Fortunately for Carl, this is a rather simple and cheap solution, so he instructs the mechanic to go ahead and change the plugs. Carl __________ __________ __________ __________ __________ __________ __________, so he wants to ask the mechanic __________ __________ __________ __________ __________ __________. In this situation, what would Carl most likely say to the mechanic?

Carl: (How long will it take to change the spark plugs?)

16-17

M: Alzheimer's disease is __________ __________ __________ __________ __________ in today's world. It's an awful disease that negatively affects a person's language, comprehension, memory, and thought processes. The disease most often affects the elderly, but Alzheimer's has been known to strike adults as young as 40. Through much research, doctors are now very confident that the disease can be prevented. __________ __________ __________ __________ in Germany is treatment with ginkgo biloba. The popular herbal supplement has been used for years in China and other countries in order to improve the circulatory system as well as increase brain function. Clinical studies have shown its ability to restore memory and __________ __________ __________ to the brain. It's so potent, in fact, that the effects of the supplement can be detected within 20 minutes of use. __________ __________ __________ __________ __________, Alzheimer's patients may see dramatic improvements.

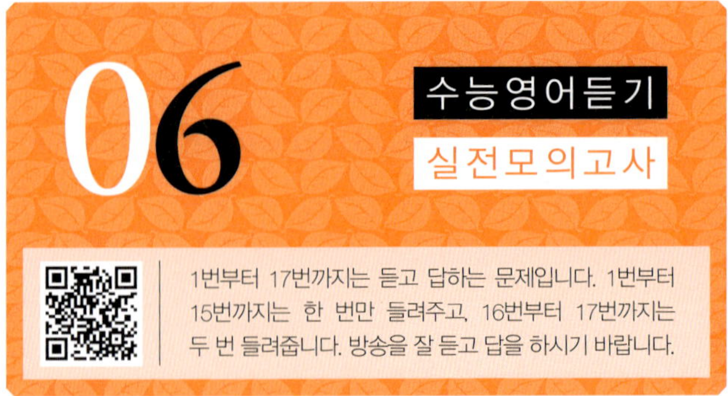

01

대화를 듣고, 남자의 마지막 말에 대한 여자의 응답으로 가장 적절한 것을 고르시오.

① Yeah. What a perfect way to spend a summer evening.
② Are you going to make your famous chicken salad?
③ Why don't you invite everyone to the party?
④ Just bring some snacks. It's not a big deal.
⑤ Do you need any help baking the pie?

02

대화를 듣고, 여자의 마지막 말에 대한 남자의 응답으로 가장 적절한 것을 고르시오.

① A penny for your thoughts.
② It looks like I only have coins.
③ The arcade is only two blocks away.
④ A ten-dollar bill, a five, and the rest in coins.
⑤ Do you know where I can find a change machine?

03

다음을 듣고, 여자가 하는 말의 목적으로 가장 적절한 것을 고르시오.

① 재난대책본부 견학 내용을 안내하려고
② 증가하는 자연 재해의 심각성을 알리려고
③ 교내 토네이도 대비 훈련에 대해 안내하려고
④ 단체 이동시 질서 유지의 중요성을 알리려고
⑤ 재난대처를 위해 지역 사회의 협력을 촉구하려고

04

대화를 듣고, 매출 증가를 위한 남자의 의견으로 가장 적절한 것을 고르시오.

① 주변에 다른 음식점과 협력해야 한다.
② 음식을 만들 재료를 싸게 구입해야 한다.
③ Blackbeans보다 싼 가격에 메뉴를 제공해야 한다.
④ Blackbeans보다 광고를 크고 확실하게 해야 한다.
⑤ Blackbeans에서 제공하지 않는 메뉴를 제공해야 한다.

05

대화를 듣고, 두 사람의 관계를 가장 잘 나타낸 것을 고르시오.

① 작가 — 편집자
② 기자 — 조각가
③ 사진작가 — 모델
④ 꽃가게 주인 — 고객
⑤ 카페 주인 — 배우

06

대화를 듣고, 그림에서 대화의 내용과 일치하지 <u>않는</u> 것을 고르시오.

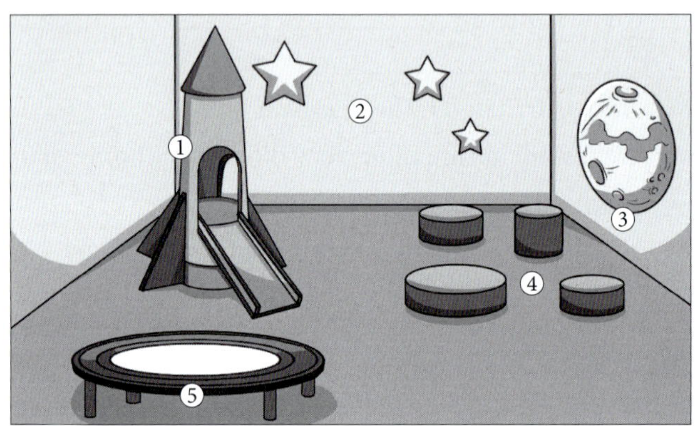

07

대화를 듣고, 여자가 남자를 위해 할 일로 가장 적절한 것을 고르시오.

① 도서 목록 만들어 보내 주기
② 남자가 읽을 책 추천해주기
③ 여름방학 때 함께 책 읽기
④ 학생들에게 책 읽어 주기
⑤ 서재의 책 정리 도와주기

08

대화를 듣고, 남자가 학교에 갈 수 <u>없는</u> 이유를 고르시오.

① 남동생을 돌봐야 해서
② 늦게까지 일해야 해서
③ 출장 준비를 해야 해서
④ 저녁 식사를 준비해야 해서
⑤ 과학 전시회를 준비해야 해서

09

대화를 듣고, 여자가 지불할 총 금액을 고르시오.

① $180　② $200　③ $225　④ $250　⑤ $271

10

대화를 듣고, 겨울철 호주 여행에 관해 두 사람이 언급하지 <u>않은</u> 것을 고르시오.

① 관광객 수　② 물가　③ 교통수단
④ 날씨　⑤ 낮의 길이

11

Sloth에 관한 다음 내용을 듣고, 일치하지 <u>않는</u> 것을 고르시오.

① 하루에 18시간 잠을 잔다.
② 나무 높은 곳에서 쉰다.
③ 땅에서 먹이를 찾는다.
④ 포식자들에게 취약하다.
⑤ 먹이를 많이 먹는다.

12

다음 표를 보면서 대화를 듣고, 여자가 선택한 제품을 고르시오.

2015 Zoo Used Car Sales

	Model	Year	Mileage	Price	Warranty
①	Cheetah	2008	20,200 miles	$10,000	1 Year
②	Cheetah	2011	35,000 miles	$12,000	6 Months
③	Cheetah	2014	26,000 miles	$25,000	1 Year
④	Hawk	2009	70,500 miles	$8,000	6 Months
⑤	Hawk	2013	45,000 miles	$15,000	1 Year

13

대화를 듣고, 남자의 마지막 말에 대한 여자의 응답으로 가장 적절한 것을 고르시오.

Woman: _______________________

① Any time. Remember to do it or you may be in trouble.
② You're right. I shouldn't have used the graph to begin with.
③ Don't worry. The graph gives all the information you'll need.
④ The graph actually came from another person in the office.
⑤ You're welcome. Tomorrow, we can hand in our reports together.

14

대화를 듣고, 여자의 마지막 말에 대한 남자의 응답으로 가장 적절한 것을 고르시오.

Man: _______________________

① Which tablet would you recommend?
② I agree. You really need to buy a new tablet.
③ Which app do you use the most these days?
④ Yeah, it does. I think I need to cut down on my use.
⑤ The tablet was actually too expensive for my budget.

15

다음 상황 설명을 듣고, Dave가 Roy에게 할 말로 가장 적절한 것을 고르시오.

Dave: _______________________

① Could you give me some advice about making friends?
② I really appreciate you helping me make new friends.
③ I don't think I'll be able to make the party today.
④ I'll see you during practice tomorrow, Roy.
⑤ I had a lot of close friends on my old team.

[16-17] 다음을 듣고, 물음에 답하시오.

16

남자가 하는 말의 주제로 가장 적절한 것은?

① Ways to be a clever consumer
② Where to find consumer reviews
③ How to write an effective shopping list
④ Reasons to be a more conscious shopper
⑤ Benefits of using coupons when shopping

17

남자가 언급한 것이 <u>아닌</u> 것은?

① 쇼핑 리스트　② 웹 사이트　③ 중고 거래
④ 영수증　⑤ 스마트폰 앱

01

M: Hi, Amanda. What are you baking?

W: I'm going to __________ __________ __________ __________ tomorrow night's dessert.

M: That sounds great. Tomorrow is the outdoor barbeque dinner, right?

W: (Yeah. What a perfect way to spend a summer evening.)

02

W: It's finally the weekend. Let's go play some games at the arcade.

M: That sounds great, but __________ __________ __________ __________. Do you have change for a twenty-dollar bill?

W: I think so. __________ __________ __________ __________ __________?

M: (A ten-dollar bill, a five, and the rest in coins.)

03

[Chime bell rings.]

W: Good morning, students. This is your vice principal, Mrs. Lee. Tornado season is approaching, so the school is going to have a tornado drill after lunch today. Be sure to __________ __________ __________ __________ when the siren goes off. Please don't rush, and exit the room __________ __________ __________ __________. Your teachers will usher you into the basement, where you will receive instructions on __________ __________ __________ __________ __________ __________ __________ __________. Local firefighters will __________ __________ __________ to help with the procedure. The drill shouldn't take more than thirty minutes to complete. Please pay attention, as this drill is for your own safety. Thank you for your cooperation.

04

W: Justin, we need to sit down and talk about our cafe.

M: Sure. Is something wrong?

W: __________ __________ __________ __________, as you know.

M: Yes, I know. __________ __________ __________ __________ since Blackbeans opened across the street.

W: Well, I was thinking we should __________ __________ __________.

M: Really? I don't think we should do that.

W: But it may be the only way to get our customers back into the cafe.

M: I think we should __________ __________ __________ __________ __________ that Blackbeans doesn't.

W: I really like that idea!

M: We need to remind people that __________ __________ __________ __________ __________. Should we place an ad about it?

W: Absolutely. I'll come up with a draft first thing tomorrow.

M: I think our logo and some pictures of all the items we offer that Blackbeans doesn't would make a perfect ad.

W: Great suggestion.

05

M: Hi, Ms. Sampson!

W: Hello, Steve. I appreciate you coming today.

M: Let's get started. So, this time you're __________ __________ __________ __________.

W: Yes, I am. This is the first time that I've decided to devote all my effort to the human face.

M: Are you enjoying yourself?

W: I really am. Actually, I'm now considering focusing all my work on the human body rather than abstract art.

M: That sounds exciting. I love the expression this model used for this sculpture. Is she someone you know?

W: Yes, she owns a coffee shop in my neighborhood. ____________ ____________ ____________ ____________ ____________ ____________ ____________, and she was more than happy to help out.

M: I see. Would you mind doing me a favor?

W: Of course. What is it?

M: I want to use a photo in our article. ____________ ____________ ____________ ____________ next to your favorite piece?

W: Sure.

06

M: It looks like you're almost ready to open up the daycare, Pam.

W: Yeah, we've ____________ ____________ ____________ ____________ ____________ ____________ ____________ over the last couple of weeks. Check out the playroom.

M: It looks great. The rocket in the corner is awesome!

W: Yeah, I think it will be fun for the children to play on. I painted some stars on the back wall, too.

M: I see that, as well as the moon over on the right.

W: That's right. What do you think about ____________ ____________ ____________ ?

M: It looks great. The cylinder chairs are quite space-like.

W: I thought so, too. And we've tried to make them different sizes.

M: The table ____________ ____________ ____________ ____________ ____________ ____________, though.

W: I agree. A square table in this room ____________ ____________ ____________.

M: I'm sure the children won't care.

07

W: Hey, Mr. Smith. What are you up to?

M: Hello, Serena. I'm just looking up books.

W: What for?

M: I'm trying to find books that the students in my English class will find interesting. I'd like them to choose one to read over the summer.

W: Oh, so you're making a summer reading list. What books have you chosen so far?

M: I only have a couple. I'm going to need a lot more. It's hard to find books that ____________ ____________ ____________ ____________ ____________.

W: I'm sure I can help. I read a lot ____________ ____________ ____________ ____________.

M: Really?

W: Sure. I can make a list of ____________ ____________ ____________ ____________ and email it to you.

M: That would be nice of you. Thanks for your help.

W: It's my pleasure. I hope you have a great summer vacation.

08

[Cell phone rings.]

W: Hello, Dad. What's up?

M: Hey, Elsa. Are you going home anytime soon?

W: I'm still at school. I don't know when I'll finish here.

M: I was wondering if you could pick up a couple of pizzas on your way home. ____________ ____________ ____________ ____________.

W: Well, I still have a bit of work to do here. The science fair starts tomorrow, you know.

M: Right. Now I remember. Are you planning on having dinner near the school?

W: Yeah, I'll ____________ ____________ ____________ ____________ at the diner next door.

M: All right. So, when are you going to head home?

W: Probably not until around eight o'clock. Is there any way you could come and pick me up?

M: I don't think I can. I'm working late tonight. Will you call your brother and tell him that ____________ ____________ ____________ ____________ ____________ ____________ tonight?

W: Sure. I'll give him a call.

09

[Telephone rings.]

M: Thank you for calling Together Chicken. What can I do for you?

W: Hi. I'd like to ____________ ____________ ____________ for tomorrow. We're going to need twenty orders of chicken for our club meeting.

M: No problem. What kind of chicken do you want?

W: Well, I think we're going to go with some garlic chicken and some smoked chicken.

M: All right. How many of each would you like?

W: We'll take ten orders of each. How much will it be?

M: Garlic chicken is $10 an order, and smoked chicken is $15.

W: Well, __________ __________ __________ __________ than I thought it would be.

M: Oh! I almost forgot. We offer a 10% discount on orders of ten or more chickens.

W: Oh, that's good. I'm going to need them delivered to Jason Bourne Academy at noon.

M: No problem. We'll send them over then.

10

M: Hey Maggie, what do you have going on this winter vacation? Any plans?

W: Well, __________ __________ __________ __________ __________, and I'm thinking about taking a trip to Cairns in Australia.

M: Hmm. . . I really don't think that's a very good idea.

W: Why not?

M: Well, first off, it's peak season, so __________ __________ __________ __________ __________.

W: Really?

M: For sure. And it's more expensive there during peak season.

W: I had no idea.

M: It's also really hot at that time of year because Australia is in the southern hemisphere. It'll be summer there.

W: Oh. I thought that it would be quite mild. I really hate the heat. Is there anything good about visiting Australia at that time of year?

M: Well, __________ __________ __________ __________ __________ __________, so you can get in more time at the beach.

W: That's nice, I guess. But maybe I should find somewhere else to go this winter.

11

M: Today, I'd like to talk about the sloth. The sloth is one of the sleepiest animals in the world! It sleeps 18 hours a day. Why would an animal sleep so much? Scientists believe that this is a way for the sloth to protect itself. It rests and sleeps high up in the trees, but the food it eats is located down on the ground below. Since the sloth is a very slow-moving animal, it is very __________ __________ __________ while it's on the ground looking for food. Over time, this sleepy animal has learned to live on very little food, so it only needs to spend a small amount of time hunting. This does not explain why the sloth sleeps so much, though. Possibly, sleeping helps it to __________ __________ __________. Or maybe it's just really lazy!

12

M: Good afternoon, ma'am. What can I do for you today?

W: Hi. I'm looking to buy a used car for my son.

M: __________ __________ __________ __________ __________ __________ __________?

W: Well, he likes fast cars so we've been looking at different sports cars.

M: Okay. I think __________ __________ __________ __________ __________ __________ __________ __________. [Mouse clicking sound] Here's a list of our used sports cars.

W: Hmm. . . I don't think we want a car that's more than five years old.

M: Well, the previous owner of __________ __________ __________ __________ __________ out of these five.

W: I understand that, but I'm looking for a newer car—one that has less than 50,000 miles on it.

M: Okay. How much are you looking to spend?

W: I don't want to spend more than $15,000.

M: Then we've narrowed it down to these two.

W: Great. I don't want to spend the extra money if something goes wrong, so I'll take the one __________ __________ __________ __________.

M: Okay. Let's go and take a look at it.

13

W: What are you working on?

M: I'm trying to finish my economics report. Did you get yours done?

W: I did. I turned it in yesterday.

M: You always finish so quickly. I hope I'll be able to
___________ ___________ ___________ ___________
___________.

W: Don't worry, you'll be fine. There's plenty of time.
[Pause] I really like that graph. It looks great!

M: Thanks. I like it, too. I copied off of a website I found
while doing my research.

W: Really? Did you ___________ ___________ ___________
___________ ___________ ___________?

M: No, I didn't. Should I have?

W: Absolutely! You always need to ___________
___________ when you're using someone else's work.

M: I didn't know it applied to the Internet, too. Thanks
for letting me know.

W: (Any time. Remember to do it or you may be in
trouble.)

14

W: Rudy, is that your new tablet? It looks really cool.

M: Thanks. I bought it last weekend.

W: Where did you buy it from?

M: I went to William's Electronics Mart.

W: ___________ ___________ ___________ ___________
___________ ___________ ___________
___________?

M: Yeah, no problem. Here you go.

W: It's so neat. This must be the latest model. How do I
get to the start menu?

M: Just push the round button ___________ ___________
___________ ___________ ___________ ___________.

W: *[Pause]* Oh, okay. It looks like ___________
___________ ___________ ___________ a lot of cool
apps.

M: Yeah, I've actually been spending a lot of time on it
since I bought it.

W: Do you use it every day?

M: Definitely. I would say I use it about four hours every
day.

W: Really? Four hours? Doesn't that seem like a little
too much?

M: (Yeah, it does. I think I need to cut down on my use.)

15

M: Dave recently transferred to a new baseball team.
He's always had a hard time ___________ ___________
___________ ___________ ___________. After his first
practice, the team manager, Roy, recommends
having a party in the locker room. Roy thinks it'll
be a great opportunity for Dave to get to know
his teammates. Dave is ___________ ___________
___________ ___________ ___________, but, after some
deliberation, he agrees to join the party. Dave develops
a close friendship with some of his teammates during
the party. He would like to let Roy know that he
enjoyed the party and ___________ ___________
___________ ___________ ___________ ___________.

In this situation, what would Dave most likely say
to Roy?

Dave: (I really appreciate you helping me make new
friends.)

16-17

M: Good morning, listeners. I'd like to talk to you today
about how you can be a smarter shopper and spend
your money wisely. Here are some tips you can
use to become a keen consumer. First, consider
the difference ___________ ___________ ___________
___________ ___________ ___________ ___________
___________. ___________ ___________ ___________
___________ ___________, and be sure to place
those that are most important higher up on your
shopping list. Second, do some product ___________
___________ ___________ ___________ ___________.

There are several websites online that provide
reviews and reports on a wide range of products, such
as electronics, vehicles, and household appliances.
Third, be conscious of the prices of what you buy
and be sure to check your receipts to ___________
___________ ___________ ___________ ___________
___________. Finally, be sure to look for coupons
and sales. You can search the Internet for deals.
There are even applications for your smartphone
that can provide coupons to save you money. Keep
these tips in mind the next time you go shopping.
Thank you for listening.

1번부터 17번까지는 듣고 답하는 문제입니다. 1번부터 15번까지는 한 번만 들려주고, 16번부터 17번까지는 두 번 들려줍니다. 방송을 잘 듣고 답을 하시기 바랍니다.

01

대화를 듣고, 남자의 마지막 말에 대한 여자의 응답으로 가장 적절한 것을 고르시오.

① No. I don't like the training facility.
② Thanks. I really needed this job.
③ Yes. They need more trainers.
④ I'm afraid I don't need a job.
⑤ Okay. I'll help you.

02

대화를 듣고, 여자의 마지막 말에 대한 남자의 응답으로 가장 적절한 것을 고르시오.

① He is almost two years old.
② His favorite food is chicken.
③ Children should eat healthy food.
④ Your son may have an allergy to milk.
⑤ I appreciate you taking care of my son.

03

다음을 듣고, 여자가 하는 말의 목적으로 가장 적절한 것을 고르시오.

① 헌혈증 기증을 부탁하려고
② 병문안 가기를 부탁하려고
③ 헌혈의 중요성을 강조하려고
④ 건강 검진 일정을 공지하려고
⑤ 학생의 수술 경과를 알리려고

04

대화를 듣고, 남자의 의견으로 가장 적절한 것을 고르시오.

① 휴대폰의 사용시간을 줄여라.
② 휴대폰의 다양한 기능을 익혀라.
③ 친구의 의견을 잘 듣고 존중하라.
④ 공공장소에서 휴대폰 사용을 자제해라.
⑤ 맹목적으로 최신 유행을 쫓으려고 하지 마라.

05

대화를 듣고, 두 사람이 대화하고 있는 장소로 가장 적절한 곳을 고르시오.

① 스키장　　　　② 눈썰매장　　　　③ 아이스링크
④ 야외 수영장　　⑤ 농구 경기장

06

대화를 듣고, 그림에서 대화의 내용과 일치하지 <u>않는</u> 것을 고르시오.

07

대화를 듣고, 남자가 여자를 위해 한 일로 가장 적절한 것을 고르시오.

① 손상된 파일 복원해 주기
② 보고서 출력물 가져다 주기
③ 보고서 철자 오류 수정해 주기
④ 보고서에 수록할 자료 검색해 주기
⑤ 철자 검사 프로그램 사용법 알려주기

08

대화를 듣고, 여자가 주문을 취소하고자 하는 이유를 고르시오.

① 다른 상품을 잘못 주문해서
② 상품이 제때 도착하지 않아서
③ 오프라인이 훨씬 더 저렴해서
④ 배송지 주소를 잘못 입력해서
⑤ 주문한 것과 다른 상품이 도착해서

09

대화를 듣고, 남자가 지불할 금액을 고르시오.

① $40　　② $45　　③ $50　　④ $55　　⑤ $60

10

대화를 듣고, 보아뱀에 관해 두 사람이 언급하지 <u>않은</u> 것을 고르시오.

① 새끼 낳는 방법　　② 새끼의 먹이
③ 알이 부화하는 장소　　④ 낳는 새끼의 수
⑤ 새끼들의 허물 벗기

11

Eiffel Tower에 관한 다음 내용을 듣고, 일치하지 <u>않는</u> 것을 고르시오.

① 1887년에 건설을 시작해서 2년 후에 완성되었다.
② 관광객들이 접근할 수 있는 층은 총 세 개 층이다.
③ 전세계에서 가장 방문자가 많은 유료 기념물이다.
④ 첫째 층에서 둘째 층까지 계단이 300개가 넘는다.
⑤ 가장 위층까지 관광객들이 걸어서 이용할 수 있다.

12

다음 표를 보면서 대화를 듣고, 남자가 선택한 것을 고르시오.

	Location	Hotel Included	Price per Person
①	Honolulu, USA	X	$1,050
②	Las Vegas, USA	O	$750
③	Rio de Janeiro, Brazil	X	$900
④	Cancun, Mexico	O	$850
⑤	Kingston, Jamaica	O	$700

13

대화를 듣고, 남자의 마지막 말에 대한 여자의 응답으로 가장 적절한 것을 고르시오.

Woman: _______________________________

① Bus rides are great for reflecting on your day.
② I think so, too. He should play with a safer one.
③ That's right. It's bad manners to speak loudly in public.
④ Sounds good. I really like listening to music on the bus.
⑤ I agree. I'll go ask the driver to turn the volume down a bit.

14

대화를 듣고, 여자의 마지막 말에 대한 남자의 응답으로 가장 적절한 것을 고르시오.

Man: _______________________________

① I have never seen the kids have so much fun.
② I'm pretty good at designing haunted houses.
③ That's a great idea. It'll be exciting for the kids.
④ No problem. I'll let the parents know our plan.
⑤ That's a good plan. The kids love costume contests.

15

다음 상황 설명을 듣고, Aiden이 Mr. Lincoln에게 할 말로 가장 적절한 것을 고르시오.

Aiden: _______________________________

① You should reconsider your priorities.
② When is the due date for this assignment?
③ Can we reschedule the meeting for a later date?
④ Is it okay if I keep these books for two more days?
⑤ Could you postpone the due date of my assignment?

[16-17] 다음을 듣고, 물음에 답하시오.

16

여자가 하는 말의 목적으로 가장 적절한 것은?

① to recommend Thai silk clothing
② to introduce Chatuchak Market in Bangkok
③ to describe the variety of souvenirs in Thailand
④ to discuss the importance of markets in Thai culture
⑤ to explain the size and popularity of Chatuchak Market

17

태국 비단에 대한 설명으로 언급하지 <u>않은</u> 것은?

① 값이 싸고 고품질이다.
② 전통 태국 의상에 사용된다.
③ 가장 많이 사는 기념품이다.
④ 여러 종류의 비단 제품이 있다.
⑤ 비단 스카프 가격은 40달러 이하이다.

07 DICTATION

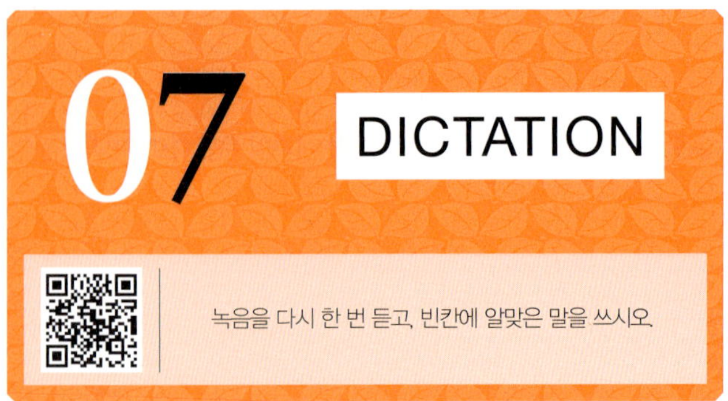

01

M: Is it true that you started working at the __________ __________?

W: It's true. I started at the beginning of the month.

M: __________ __________ __________ __________ __________ __________ __________. Are they hiring anyone else?

W: (Yes. They need more trainers.)

02

W: I'm getting worried about my son. He suddenly turned red after breakfast.

M: I see. Let's __________ __________ __________ __________ __________. [Pause] What have you been feeding him?

W: Well, he had milk and bread this morning.

M: (Your son may have an allergy to milk.)

03

W: Good morning, everyone. This is your vice principal, Rebecca Smith. I think most of you know Helena Simson, one of your classmates. Her mother is in the hospital waiting to __________ __________-__________ __________. I've just heard from Helena's homeroom teacher that her mother is supposed to have the surgery very soon. I've been informed that __________ __________ __________ __________ __________ __________ __________ __________ for the surgery. I strongly believe it lies with us to help each other in times like this. So, if any of you want to donate blood to Helena's mother, please __________ __________ __________ __________ __________ __________ __________ __________. Your blood could save someone's life. Thank you for your heartwarming help on behalf of Helena and her mother.

04

W: Hey Dad, can I ask you a question?

M: Of course. What is it, dear?

W: I'd like to upgrade my cell phone.

M: What's the matter with the one you already have?

W: Nothing really, but I've had it for two years, and I'd like to get a new one.

M: Lizzy, if there's nothing wrong with the phone, why would you replace it?

W: Because it's old. It's not even a smartphone.

M: You know __________ __________ __________ __________ of a cell phone is to make calls. I'm a business man, and I don't even have a smartphone.

W: Please, Dad. You know that a cell phone is much more than a phone these days.

M: Maybe I'm not making myself clear. You shouldn't always feel the need to do something __________ __________ __________ __________ __________.

W: Okay, Dad. I'll give it some more thought.

05

W: It's much more exciting than I expected.

M: Right. I used to go skating every winter when I was a kid.

W: Can we __________ __________ __________ for a minute, though? I'm feeling tired.

M: All right. Let's sit down for a while. Do you want me to get you something to drink?

W: Yes, a soda would be great. But isn't it difficult to buy something while wearing skates?

M: No. You don't need to go to the counter. You can call them and they'll bring your order for you.

W: That sounds good. I really want something to drink.

M: Me too. I didn't think __________ __________ __________ __________ __________. I thought it would be cold the whole time we were on the ice.

W: It's all because you didn't __________ __________ __________ __________ __________. Do you even remember how many laps we went around this ice rink?

M: I'm so sorry. I was so excited that I didn't even think about it.

06

M: Hannah, is this a picture of the play you acted in last semester?

W: It sure is. We worked so hard on that performance.

M: The tiger looks very realistic. Is the rabbit __________ __________ __________ __________ __________ his friend, the deer?

W: That's right. It's the Aesop's Fable about the tiger and the rabbit.

M: The set looks really cool.

W: Thanks. The drama club got together and designed it all. See the rocks in the background? I painted them.

M: Wow! You did a great job. That tree on the right side looks very realistic, too. It really gives the feeling of being in Africa.

W: Yeah, that's what we were going for.

M: Did you also __________ __________ __________?

W: No. We rented them from Fat Panda's Costume Shop.

M: I see. Well, it seems like __________ __________ __________ __________ __________ __________ __________ into this play.

07

M: Sophie, I heard you were writing a report on the Cold War.

W: Yes. You've been too busy to help me with it.

M: I'm sorry. But __________ __________ __________ __________ __________ today because I finished my own report.

W: Well, I've already finished writing it!

M: I know. __________ __________ __________ __________ __________ __________ __________, so I read it while you were at school.

W: Oh. Did you like it?

M: Yes, I did. Your ideas on the environmental problems of the Cold War were very interesting.

W: Thanks. I spent a lot of time researching that part.

M: But there were some spelling errors, so __________ __________ __________ __________ __________ __________.

W: That was nice of you.

M: If you want, I'll teach you how to use the spell checker.

W: That's a good idea.

08

[Telephone rings.]

M: Good morning, this is Genie's Online Store.

W: Hi. I'm calling __________ __________ __________ a couple of books I ordered last week.

M: Sure. What's the problem? Were they damaged?

W: No. They were supposed to be here by Saturday, but it's already Monday and they're not here yet.

M: I see. I'll check your order. Can you please give me your seven-digit order number?

W: __________ __________ __________ __________ __________ __________ at the moment. My name is Ella Hanley. Does that help?

M: Yes. Please hold on for a minute while I check for you.

W: No problem.

M: *[Keyboard typing sound]* I apologize, but it looks like __________ __________ __________ __________ __________. It should be there by Thursday.

W: Thursday, huh? That's unacceptable. __________ __________ __________ __________ __________ __________ on Wednesday.

M: I'm very sorry, ma'am.

W: Will you please cancel my order? I'll get them from the local bookstore.

09

[Telephone rings.]

W: Thank you for calling the Henderson Employment and Training Office. May I help you?

M: Hi. I saw a flyer about a career fair at the end of the month. I was wondering __________ __________ __________ __________ __________ __________.

W: Sure. We still have tickets.

M: Awesome. I need five of them. How much do they cost?

W: If you __________ __________ __________ __________, they cost $10. They're $20 at the door.

M: I see. Do you offer any group discounts?

W: I almost forgot—__________ __________ __________ __________ __________ __________. You can get a 10% discount for groups of 5 to 10, and a 20% discount if you buy more than 10 tickets.

M: That's awesome. So, a 10% discount for me. I'll buy them now, then.

W: No problem. If you have your ___________ ___________ ___________ ___________ ___________, I can take your information now.

10

W: Good morning, Theo. Did you have a good weekend?
M: Yeah, it was all right. I didn't do anything special. I did ___________ ___________ ___________ ___________ ___________ ___________ that I found interesting.
W: Really? What about reptiles?
M: Well, did you know that ___________ ___________ ___________?
W: Of course. I thought that was common knowledge.
M: It is. But some species of snakes, such as the boa constrictor, give live birth.
W: No way. How do they do that?
M: ___________ ___________ ___________ ___________ ___________ ___________ ___________ and once they hatch, they give birth.
W: That's incredible. How many babies can a boa have?
M: Anywhere from six to thirty-nine.
W: That's incredible. I had no idea.
M: It's true. Baby boas also ___________ ___________ ___________ within ten days of being born.
W: Wow. Animals are truly amazing, huh?

11

W: Today, I'm going to talk to you about the Eiffel Tower. It's ___________ ___________ ___________ ___________ ___________ ___________ ___________, but did you know that it was originally built as a watch tower? The tower's construction started in 1887 and was completed two years later. During its construction, the Eiffel Tower surpassed the Washington Monument to assume the title of ___________ ___________-___________ ___________ in the world. The tower has three levels that visitors can access, and it is the most visited monument that requires an entry fee in the world. Visitors can ascend ___________ ___________ ___________ ___________ ___________ to the first and second levels. The walk from ground level to the first level is over 300 steps, as is the walk from the first to the second level. The top level is ___________ ___________ ___________ ___________ ___________ ___________ ___________.

12

W: Welcome to ABC Travel. What can I do for you today?
M: Hi. ___________ ___________ ___________ ___________ ___________ ___________ ___________ for my business partners and me.
W: I'm sure I can help you with that. When are you planning on traveling?
M: We're looking at the last weekend of this month.
W: All right. Would you like to travel abroad or stay in the United States?
M: I'd like to go somewhere exotic, so how about somewhere outside of the United States?
W: Do you want your package to ___________ ___________ ___________ ___________ ___________?
M: Yes, please. I'd like it to be all-inclusive, if possible.
W: Sure. Let's see here. We have a destination that meets your criteria for only $850 per person.
M: ___________ ___________ ___________ ___________ ___________ ___________ ___________ ___________. I'm not looking to spend more than $750 per person.
W: That leaves us with one option.
M: I've always wanted to go there. Reserve four spots, please.

13

W: Hi, Stan!
M: Oh, hey Candace. I didn't know you take the bus home.
W: Well, I usually drive, but my car is in the shop this week. Anyway, ___________ ___________ ___________ ___________?
M: Oh no, this isn't the bus I take home. I'm actually going to the mall.
W: I'm sorry. You're going to fall?
M: No. I said that I'm going to the mall. There's a new toy that I want to pick up for my kid.
W: I see. The mall is really close to my place, so I know it very well.
M: I'm sorry, Candace, but I can't hear you too well. The music on this bus is incredibly loud.

W: Yeah, I hate it __________ __________ __________ __________ __________. When I ride the bus, I just want to __________ __________ __________ __________ __________ __________.

M: And why does he have to play heavy metal music? It's the worst.

W: (I agree. I'll go ask the driver to turn the volume down a bit.)

14

W: Hey Andrew, I need to talk to you about something.

M: Of course, Grace. What's up?

W: It's about the Halloween party. Have you __________ __________ __________ __________ __________?

M: Not yet. We should probably plan it together, don't you think?

W: Yeah, that would be perfect. I have some ideas for a couple of games and events.

M: All right. Well, last year the parents brought candy and we had a costume contest with the kids.

W: Don't you think that's __________ __________ __________ __________? Why don't we do something a little more special, like make a haunted house for them?

M: You mean you want to use the library __________ __________ __________ __________ __________ __________?

W: Exactly! We can call it the "haunted library" tour. Don't you think the kids would love it?

M: (That's a great idea. It'll be exciting for the kids.)

15

M: Aiden is the captain of his high school basketball team, which keeps him busy after school. He also __________ __________ __________ __________ __________ __________ at the school, such as the chess club, the movie club, and student government. When he isn't busy with these activities, he uses what little time he has to do his homework and study for exams. Aiden needs to read for an important assignment in Mr. Lincoln's class and won't be able to finish it __________ __________ __________. He would like to ask the teacher __________ __________ __________ __________ __________ __________ __________ __________ __________. In this situation, what would Aiden most likely say to Mr. Lincoln?

Aiden: (Could you postpone the due date of my assignment?)

16-17

W: Good morning, fellow classmates. I'd like to talk to you today about a very special market in Bangkok, the capital city of Thailand. Chatuchak Market is __________ __________ __________ __________ in the world. The market has more than 8,000 stalls and spans over 27 acres. More than 400,000 people visit the market every weekend. Visitors can enjoy local Thai food, buy souvenirs, shop for vintage sneakers, or even buy an exotic pet, such as a baby squirrel or a monkey. You can also buy something made of the cheap, high-quality silk that Thailand is famous for. This silk __________ __________ __________ __________ __________ __________. You can buy silk scarves, blankets, or neckties. __________ __________ where in the market you buy it, you can spend anywhere from $4 to $40 on a silk scarf. However, __________ __________ __________ __________ __________ __________ at Chatuchak Market. You can also buy purses, Muay Thai boxing shorts, jewelry, and ceramics. Now I'd like to show you some pictures I took of Chatuchak Market when I visited there last spring.

01

대화를 듣고, 남자의 마지막 말에 대한 여자의 응답으로 가장 적절한 것을 고르시오.

① Sorry, but I forgot to write it down.
② I'll send someone right over to help.
③ You can save 10% on your next rental.
④ It shows here that you reserved a sports car.
⑤ I'd like to change my reservation to a minivan.

02

대화를 듣고, 여자의 마지막 말에 대한 남자의 응답으로 가장 적절한 것을 고르시오.

① Why don't we check out the menu before we decide?
② I am not looking forward to meeting this weekend.
③ You go. I really need to complete this before 5 p.m.
④ I thought everything we had last time was great.
⑤ Do you have any advice on good dinner places?

03

다음을 듣고, 남자가 하는 말의 주제로 가장 적절한 것을 고르시오.

① 과다한 염분 섭취가 건강에 미치는 영향
② 피클 속 비타민K와 나트륨에 대한 오해
③ 피클이 함유하고 있는 영양성분
④ 고혈압을 예방하는 음식의 소개
⑤ 피클의 섭취와 건강과의 관계

04

대화를 듣고, 여자의 의견으로 가장 적절한 것을 고르시오.

① 컴퓨터 교체 주기가 점점 길어지고 있다.
② 최신 컴퓨터의 기능들을 많이 활용해야 한다.
③ 컴퓨터를 직접 고침으로써 수리비를 아껴야 한다.
④ 컴퓨터 구입에 있어 디자인 요소를 고려해야 한다.
⑤ 컴퓨터의 일부만 교체하고 가급적 버리지 말아야 한다.

05

대화를 듣고, 두 사람의 관계를 가장 잘 나타낸 것을 고르시오.

① 기자 — 편집장
② 학과장 — 학교직원
③ 신입회원 — 동아리장
④ 학생 — 진로 상담교사
⑤ 라디오 진행자 — 게스트

06

대화를 듣고, 그림에서 대화의 내용과 일치하지 <u>않는</u> 것을 고르시오.

07

대화를 듣고, 남자가 여자를 위해 할 일로 가장 적절한 것을 고르시오.

① 일 도와주기
② 함께 외출하기
③ 점심 주문하기
④ 커피 사다 주기
⑤ 보고서 대신 작성하기

08

대화를 듣고, 여자가 남자의 DVD를 가져오지 <u>않은</u> 이유를 고르시오.

① DVD를 분실해서
② 날짜를 잘못 알아서
③ 다른 장소에 들렀다 오게 돼서
④ 동생의 숙제를 도와주느라 잊어서
⑤ 자신의 발표 내용을 검토하느라 바빠서

09

대화를 듣고, 여자가 지불할 금액을 고르시오.

① $15　　② $17　　③ $45　　④ $47　　⑤ $60

10

대화를 듣고, 두 사람이 훈련 시설에 대해 언급하지 않은 것을 고르시오.

① 설계자　　　　② 건축 기간　　　　③ 완공 시기
④ 건축 비용　　　⑤ 내부 시설

11

EcoBag에 관한 다음 내용을 듣고, 일치하지 않는 것을 고르시오.

① 전 세계 학교에 사회적 인식을 불러일으키기 위해 만들어졌다.
② 지퍼를 제외한 가방 전체가 재활용된 플라스틱으로 만들어졌다.
③ 가방의 끈과 손잡이는 튼튼하면서도 편안하고 가볍다.
④ 키가 자라서 가방이 작아지더라도 다시 재활용될 수 있다.
⑤ 한 개를 구입하면 회사가 다른 학생에게 한 개를 기부한다.

12

다음 표를 보면서 대화를 듣고, 두 사람이 선택할 기부 프로그램을 고르시오.

Guardian's Charity for Animals Donation Plan

	Option	Project	Payment frequency	Amount
①	A	Animal Shelter	One-Time	$75
②	B	Animal Shelter	Monthly	$10
③	C	Wild Sanctuary	Monthly	$5
④	D	Wild Sanctuary	Monthly	$20
⑤	E	Wild Sanctuary	One-Time	$50

13

대화를 듣고, 여자의 마지막 말에 대한 남자의 응답으로 가장 적절한 것을 고르시오.

Man: ________________________________

① Sorry, but only fans can vote.
② These are our mascot choices.
③ No. You can't participate in the event.
④ You have to sign up for the event early.
⑤ You're right. I'm going to buy one right now.

14

대화를 듣고, 남자의 마지막 말에 대한 여자의 응답으로 가장 적절한 것을 고르시오.

Woman: ________________________________

① I'll get you a souvenir from the science museum.
② I've really been looking forward to this field trip.
③ I visited the science museum when it opened.
④ The debate team has to compete on Friday.
⑤ It takes hard work to be part of any team.

15

다음 상황 설명을 듣고, Bill이 Martin에게 할 말로 가장 적절한 것을 고르시오.

Bill: Martin, ________________________________

① you should lead the way and I will follow you.
② I can always tell whether it's going to rain or not.
③ let's go running when we're sure that it won't rain.
④ always dry out your workout gear after you use it.
⑤ always be careful when riding your bike in bad weather.

[16-17] 다음을 듣고, 물음에 답하시오.

16

남자가 하는 말의 목적으로 가장 적절한 것은?

① 재활용 센터에 필요한 폐품을 모으기 위해
② 재활용 제품을 판매하는 회사를 홍보하려고
③ 재활용 제품 사용하기 운동에 참여를 유도하려고
④ 폐품을 재활용한 제품이 품질도 좋음을 알리려고
⑤ 폐품을 재활용한 제품 제작 아이디어를 공모하려고

17

언급된 물건이 아닌 것은?

① frames　　　② furniture　　　③ lamp shades
④ bookshelves　⑤ planters

01

[Telephone rings.]

M: Thank you for calling Bird's Car Rental. May I help you?

W: Yes. I was just calling to ___________ ___________ ___________ I made online.

M: Sure. Do you have your reservation number?

W: (Sorry, but I forgot to write it down.)

02

W: Oh my! Look at the time. We should go eat soon.

M: In a minute. I just want to finish this last piece of work.

W: You can do that after lunch. ___________ ___________ ___________ for some fresh air.

M: (You go. I really need to complete this before 5 p.m.)

03

M: Do you like hamburgers? Do you also like the pickles that are served with those hamburgers? Were you aware that pickles are actually quite healthy? That's right. Pickles not only taste great, but they are low in fat and calories as well. They are also a great source of Vitamin K, which ___________ ___________ ___________ ___________ ___________ ___________ by thickening the blood. Eating just half a pickle provides 17% of your daily requirement of Vitamin K. However, ___________ ___________ ___________ ___________, pickles can also ___________ ___________ ___________ ___________ because they are very high in sodium. You can fulfill over half of your daily sodium recommendation by eating just one whole pickle. Pickles can be enjoyed daily, but be sure not to eat too much.

04

W: Darling, my computer is having some issues. ___________ ___________ ___________ ___________.

M: Hmm. . . I suppose we can go shopping for a new computer this weekend.

W: I don't think we need to get a brand-new one. This one is pretty new.

M: These days technology changes so quickly that many people replace their computers ___________ ___________ ___________ or so.

W: That's true. It just seems like such a waste. We can probably just replace the screen, right?

M: I guess so. But ___________ ___________ ___________ ___________ ___________ ___________ ___________.

W: You're right, but other than the screen, ___________ ___________ ___________ ___________ ___________ ___________. I think I can use it for at least two more years.

M: Okay. If that's what you want.

W: We should try to get it fixed. I'll ___________ ___________ ___________ the repair shop.

05

M: Good afternoon, Mrs. Towns.

W: Hi, Hugh. Have you put any more thought into what we talked about last week?

M: I have, and I think I've ___________ ___________ ___________. I want to be a journalist.

W: A journalist, huh? What made you think of that?

M: Well, I've been watching a lot of video clips from Voice News. The work of the reporter seems so ___________ ___________ ___________.

W: I see. Well, what kind of skills do you need to be a journalist?

M: You need to be naturally curious and ___________ ___________ ___________ ___________ ___________ and investigating.

W: I see. I think that the local college has some great courses that would teach the skills that successful journalists need.

M: Really?

W: Yeah, I've heard great things. Also, you should ___________ ___________ ___________ ___________. I'm sure you can learn a lot about the process there.

M: Great idea. I appreciate all the advice, Mrs. Towns.

W: Anytime, Hugh.

06

M: What's this line all about, Dee?

W: They're waiting to take photos with their companions. Let's get in line.

M: All right. But don't you think this photo zone __________ __________ __________ __________?

W: Yeah, it's kind of silly, isn't it? Are we supposed to sit on the sofa? I'd rather stand.

M: Yeah, and __________ __________-__________ __________ __________ __________ __________. It looks old.

W: Look at the big flower next to the couch.

M: Is that a sunflower? It really doesn't match our prom's theme.

W: There are stars on the wall, too. It's like night and day in the same photo. What were they thinking?

M: I do like the poster on the wall. It kind of __________ __________ __________ __________ in high school.

W: I agree with you there.

M: All right, it's our turn. Be sure to smile!

07

M: Hey, Rachel! Are you __________ __ __ __________ __________ __________?

W: I want to, but I'm really busy today. What about you?

M: Yes. I have a break, so I'm going to get some food. Would you like me to __________ __________ __________ __________ __________?

W: It's really nice of you to ask, but actually working on this report is making me nervous. __________ __________ __________ __________ __________ __________.

M: Really? That's too bad. Well, how about some coffee then? Do you like Starbeans coffee?

W: Yeah, sure I do. I really love their vanilla lattes.

M: Okay, a vanilla latte it is. I'll be back in 30 minutes. Oh, what size would you like?

W: Wow, __________ __________ __________ __________ __________ __________. A tall-sized one is fine. Thank you so much!

M: Don't worry about it. I'll be back soon.

08

M: Hey, Carrie. What's up?

W: I'm just __________ __________ __________ __________ for Mr. DeWitt's class. I'm pretty stressed about it.

M: I can understand. So, did you remember to bring the DVD about Peru that I let you borrow?

W: Woops, I totally forgot. I'm really sorry, Conner. I can bring it to you tomorrow.

M: What? You forgot it again? I told you that I needed it for my presentation this afternoon.

W: I'm sorry. It just __________ __________ __________. I forgot to bring it because I was helping my brother with his math homework this morning.

M: You explanation __________ __________ __________ __________, Carrie.

W: I'm really sorry. I'll go home at lunch and get it for you.

M: All right. I'll meet you here at the end of the lunch period.

W: Okay. Sorry again. See you later.

09

W: Excuse me. I'd like to exchange these baby shoes for a different pair.

M: Why do you want to exchange them?

W: Actually, my friend bought these for my daughter in this shop, but we got the same shoes from another person a month ago.

M: Oh, I see. We have many kinds of shoes here. Do you see any that you like?

W: Let me see. . . Oh, these will __________ __________ __________ __________. The ribbon on the side of the shoes is so cute. How much are these?

M: They're $60.

W: How much more do I have to pay after the exchange, then?

M: The shoes you brought back were $45, so you only have to __________ __ __ __________.

W: Okay. Here's my credit card. Oh, I also need a hairband for my daughter. __________ __________ __________ __________ __________?

M: Yes, of course. __________ __________ __________ __________ __________ __________ __________. It's just $2.

W: Good. I'll take it, too.

10

W: Welcome to our facility, Dr. Fecc.

M: Hi, Ms. Johnson. It's great to finally meet you. This training facility is unbelievable.

W: We're very proud of our team's facility. Would you like a tour before we get to business?

M: I'd love a tour. Thanks. So, I heard that the EPL chose this facility as the best in the league last season.

W: That's true. It was __________ __________ __________-__________ __________ Pete Parker.

M: Yeah, I've heard of him. Did it take a long time to complete?

W: It only took about two years. We were able to start training here last spring.

M: __________ __________ __________ __________ __________ __________ this place?

W: Well, where do I start? It has an Olympic-size swimming pool, a tennis court, a sauna, a steam room, __________ __________ __________ __________ __________ __________ __________.

M: That's amazing. Wait. . . you have a restaurant in here, too. This place is truly incredible.

11

M: This morning, I'd like to talk about a great new invention for the environment. It's called the EcoBag. As you probably assumed, it's an eco-friendly backpack. Amanda Stevens, a professor's daughter, created this great backpack to bring social awareness to schools around the world. EcoBag is __________ __________ __________ __________ __________ __________. Even the zippers are made this way. The straps and handle of the bag are made from a blend of recycled fabric and plastic so they are not only strong, but comfortable and lightweight. __________ __________ __________ __________ __________ __________ __________, it can be recycled. What's more, if you __________ __________ __________, the company will donate another bag to a student in need. So you see, the EcoBag is a great way to do your part by helping the environment and the needy.

12

M: Hey honey, what's that you're looking at?

W: It's a brochure for Guardian's Charity. They accept donations to help animals.

M: Right. That's a great program. Are you thinking about donating?

W: Well, what do you think? You do like helping animals, don't you?

M: Of course I do. Remember, how last year we __________ __________ __________-__________ __________ to the local animal shelter? Let's try a different project this year.

W: All right. I read an article recently about wildlife sanctuaries and how they help __________ __________ __________ __________ return to their natural habitats.

M: That sounds interesting. I think we should make a __________ __________ __________ __________ __________.

W: That's a great idea. It's more affordable and more meaningful if we donate money month-by-month. How much do you think we should donate?

M: I don't think we can afford anything more than $10.

W: Okay. It looks like this option is ideal for us.

13

W: Hey, I have some exciting news! Our team is having an interesting event on their website.

M: Really? What is it?

W: They're calling it the "Choose Your Mascot" event and __________ __________ __________ during the next game.

M: I don't quite understand. Are they letting the fans choose what their mascot is going to be?

W: That's it. __________ __________ __________ __________ __________ __________ what the team mascot is.

M: And it will be any mascot the fans vote for?

W: Yep, __________ __________ __________ __________ __________ __________.

M: That's different. Can anyone participate in the event?

W: No. Only fans __________ __________ __________ __________ __________ can participate.

M: That's interesting. I want to help choose the next mascot.

W: Well, you're going to have to get a ticket for Saturday's game.

M: (You're right. I'm going to buy one right now.)

14

M: Hey, have you heard that plans for our field trip have changed?

W: No. I haven't heard anything about it.

M: Yeah. It's supposed to rain on Friday so we can't __________ __________ __________ __________ __________. We're going to the science museum instead.

W: That's a shame. But you must be happy. You went to the amusement park with your family last week, right?

M: Yeah, and I've really wanted to visit the science museum ever since it opened. __________ __________ __________ __________ __________ __________ __________ members of our science club.

W: Well, I can't go on the field trip this Friday.

M: Really? Why not?

W: __________ __________ __________ __________ to the debate team.

M: Really? I didn't know there was a debate on Friday.

W: There isn't, but we really need to prepare for next week's contest.

M: I see. You're really __________ __________ __________ __________.

W: (It takes hard work to be part of any team.)

15

W: Bill is watching TV in his house when he __________ __________ __________ from his friend, Martin. The two friends are usually quite active but haven't been able to get together in a few weeks because of the bad weather. This evening, Martin __________ __________ __________ __________. Bill really wants to __________ __________ __________ __________ __________ and get some exercise outside, but he's still worried about the weather. Last summer, he was out for a bike ride rather far from the city and __________

__________ __________ __________ __________ __________ __________ __________. Because of that bad memory, he decides to __________ __________ __________. What would Bill likely say to Martin in this situation?

Bill: Martin, (let's go running when we're sure that it won't rain.)

16-17

M: Everyone knows that __________ __________ __________ is great for the environment, but is the quality as good as buying brand-new items? When you buy from Greenbacks, the answer is always "Yes." We collect discarded items and __________ __________ __________ __________ __________ that are both interesting and high in quality. We also offer very reasonable prices. Nothing in our inventory is more expensive than $100. We carry furniture made from discarded commercial wood, lamp shades made from old clothes, and bookshelves made from antique ladders. If you need new planters for spring, __________ __________ __________ __________ Greenbacks. We have repurposed many things, such as crates, boots, and jars, to give your garden a sharp, new look. All of our items are unique, so your purchases will make great conversation pieces. Check out our website at *www.greenbacksrepurpose.com* to join many others in the repurposing movement. __________ __________ __________ __________ with Greenbacks.

수능영어듣기
실전모의고사

09

1번부터 17번까지는 듣고 답하는 문제입니다. 1번부터 15번까지는 한 번만 들려주고, 16번부터 17번까지는 두 번 들려줍니다. 방송을 잘 듣고 답을 하시기 바랍니다.

01

대화를 듣고, 남자의 마지막 말에 대한 여자의 응답으로 가장 적절한 것을 고르시오.

① Sorry, but all sales are final in this store.
② We should be able to repair the screen next week.
③ I'm sorry, but we don't accept returns after 30 days.
④ You're going to need a receipt if you want a refund.
⑤ We have been having a lot of problems with this product.

02

대화를 듣고, 여자의 마지막 말에 대한 남자의 응답으로 가장 적절한 것을 고르시오.

① No problem. We will be departing shortly.
② That's great. This has really been a pleasant flight.
③ Yes. We sincerely apologize for the inconvenience.
④ That's right. We will be arriving to the airport on time.
⑤ Sorry for your troubles. I'll get you some water immediately.

03

다음을 듣고, 여자가 하는 말의 목적으로 가장 적절한 것을 고르시오.

① 보수공사로 인한 이용 통제를 공지하려고
② 안전사고에 대한 예방 교육을 실시하려고
③ 새로 단장한 커뮤니티 센터를 홍보하려고
④ 궂은 날씨로 인한 시설피해를 알려주려고
⑤ 학교행사 변경 내용과 장소를 안내하려고

04

대화를 듣고, 두 사람이 하는 말의 주제로 가장 적절한 것을 고르시오.

① 음악 감상이 운동에 주는 긍정적 효과
② 공원 내 조깅 전용 도로 설치의 필요성
③ 보행자를 위한 운전자의 배려 부족 현상
④ 헤드폰 끼고 음악 들으며 뛰는 것의 위험성
⑤ 공공장소에서 음악 들을 때 지켜야 할 매너

05

대화를 듣고, 두 사람의 관계를 가장 잘 나타낸 것을 고르시오.

① 상담사 — 구매자
② 기자 — 지역주민
③ 방송 작가 — 시청자
④ 영화 감독 — 연기자
⑤ 뉴스 진행자 — 프로듀서

06

대화를 듣고, 그림에서 대화의 내용과 일치하지 <u>않는</u> 것을 고르시오.

07

대화를 듣고, 남자가 여자에게 부탁한 일로 가장 적절한 것을 고르시오.

① to talk to Mr. Stevenson
② to sign up for her course
③ to supervise his new club
④ to participate in his new movie
⑤ to show him how to use a camera

08

대화를 듣고, 남자가 잠자리에 들지 <u>못하는</u> 이유를 고르시오.

① 친구와 전화 통화하느라
② 탄산음료를 너무 많이 마셔서
③ 친구들이 놀렸던 것이 속상해서
④ 내일 할 연설을 연습하고 싶어서
⑤ 내일 있을 시험 준비를 해야 해서

09

대화를 듣고, 여자가 지불할 금액을 고르시오.

① $70 ② $75 ③ $80 ④ $85 ⑤ $95

10

대화를 듣고, 연례 마라톤에 관해 두 사람이 언급하지 <u>않은</u> 것을 고르시오.

① 완주 거리 ② 당일 복장 ③ 현재 등록 인원
④ 수익금 사용처 ⑤ 완주 기념품

11

Miller Brody에 관한 다음 내용을 듣고, 일치하지 <u>않는</u> 것을 고르시오.

① 1920년 Tennessee에서 외아들로 태어났다.
② Minnesota 대학에서 박사 학위를 받았다.
③ 동료 교수들과 충돌 없이 잘 지냈다.
④ 재임기간 동안 많은 책을 출판했다.
⑤ 유럽에서 각국의 사람들을 만났다.

12

다음 표를 보면서 대화를 듣고, 두 사람이 선택할 관광지를 고르시오.

Madison Tourism

	Activity	Duration	Price	Hotel Pickup
①	River Zipline	2 hours	$90	No
②	Canoe Trip	5 hours	$70	Yes
③	Wine Tasting	4 hours	$50	Yes
④	Downtown Walking Tour	2.5 hours	$20	Yes
⑤	Butterfly Garden Tour	1 hour	$10	No

13

대화를 듣고, 여자의 마지막 말에 대한 남자의 응답으로 가장 적절한 것을 고르시오.

Man: ____________________

① I told the usher to make them be quiet.
② I met the actor that played the main role.
③ I asked the usher if I could go to the toilet.
④ I'll never forget that amazing performance.
⑤ After watching the play, I complained to the theater.

14

대화를 듣고, 남자의 마지막 말에 대한 여자의 응답으로 가장 적절한 것을 고르시오.

Woman: ____________________

① Okay, perfect. I'm very happy to help.
② We appreciate your donation. Thanks so much.
③ I'd rather not look at those pictures. They're so sad.
④ Thanks for the advice. I'll be sure to never do it again.
⑤ Just print your name, then sign here. That's all we need.

15

다음 상황 설명을 듣고, Katie가 Kenny에게 할 말로 가장 적절한 것을 고르시오.

Katie: ____________________

① There are other movies we can choose.
② You won't get a reward for volunteering.
③ We already have enough people volunteering.
④ I'd like to help out by working at the orphanage.
⑤ It's very fun and I'm sure the children will love you.

[16-17] 다음을 듣고, 물음에 답하시오.

16

남자가 하는 말의 목적으로 가장 적절한 것은?

① 새로운 레스토랑을 홍보하려고
② 복합 쇼핑몰의 탄생을 알리려고
③ 세계 최대의 호텔을 소개하려고
④ 라스베가스 내의 관광법을 알려주려고
⑤ 세미나와 회의를 위한 장소를 추천하려고

17

매일 공연을 볼 수 있는 장소로 언급된 곳은?

① Area A ② Area B ③ Area C
④ Area D ⑤ Area E

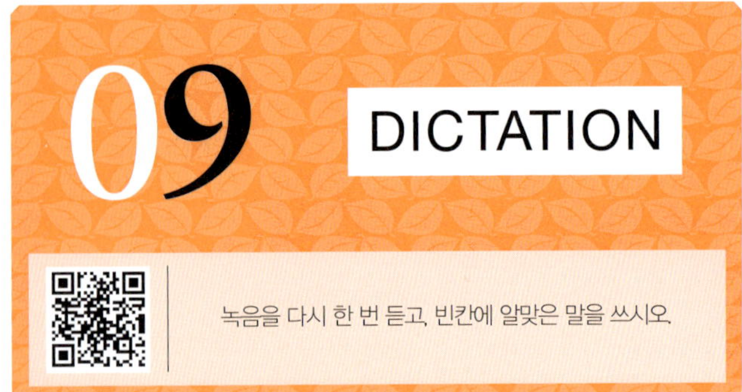

09 DICTATION

01

M: Hi. I'd like to ___________ ___________ ___________.

W: I see. When did you purchase it?

M: Let me check the receipt. *[Pause]* It looks like I picked it up a little over a month ago.

W: (I'm sorry, but we don't accept returns after 30 days.)

02

W: Excuse me, sir. When will we land in Seattle?

M: We should be arriving in Seattle at around 7 p.m.

W: I see. So we're running a little bit ___________ ___________.

M: (Yes. We sincerely apologize for the inconvenience.)

03

[Bell rings.]

W: Good afternoon, everyone. Could I please have your attention? This is your principal, Mrs. Jones. ___________ ___________ ___________ ___________ ___________, the school's gym will be closed for construction for the next three weeks. Students must stay out of the gym ___________ ___________ ___________. We apologize for the problems this closure will cause, but it is for the safety of the students. I assure you that ___________ ___________ ___________ will be safer and much nicer when it reopens on February 22nd. Any activities that were scheduled to take place in the gym will be moved down the street to the community center. You can find ___________ ___________ on our website. Thank you for understanding our situation.

04

W: Hey, darling. I'm going to ___________ ___________ ___________ ___________ downtown.

M: Okay. Oh, I see you're bringing your headphones. Do you plan on listening to music during your run?

W: Of course. I just got the new Maroon 5 album. I'm looking forward to listening to it.

M: I don't think you should listen to music while you run.

W: Why not? Running is boring. Listening to music ___________ ___________ ___________ ___________.

M: If you wear your headphones, you won't be able to hear the passing traffic. It's dangerous.

W: Hmm. . . I never really considered that.

M: Yeah, it's important to ___________ ___________ ___________ ___________ ___________ when you're outside. I wouldn't want you to get hurt.

W: I understand. I guess I'll listen to this album ___________ ___________ ___________ ___________.

M: I just want you to be careful, sweetheart.

05

W: Hey there, Sam. What are you holding?

M: Hi, Erica. Actually, these are ___________ ___________ ___________ ___________ ___________.

W: Really?

M: Yes. Apparently some of our audience doesn't like our news content.

W: Sam, you're the one who wanted to make the local news more light-hearted.

M: I know, but I guess it's not working if we're disappointing our viewers.

W: So should I start reporting on more serious news?

M: Yeah, I guess so. ___________ ___________ ___________ ___________ ___________ so we can all discuss this matter?

W: That's a good idea. What should I do?

M: ___________ ___________ ___________ ___________ all of the staff and have everyone meet in the boardroom after lunch?

W: Okay, got it. But I would like to just say that I really enjoyed the way we were doing the news.

M: I know. Me, too. We'll talk about everything in the meeting.

06

W: Oh, my! What happened to your apartment, Alvin?

M: Wow! It looks like someone broke in and __________ __________ __________.

W: Yeah, whoever was in here broke your mirror.

M: __________ __________ __________ __________, too. This is terrible.

W: There's a bat by the table. That's probably what they used to smash everything.

M: I think you're right. I've never had this happen to me before. Why would someone do this to me?

W: Well, at least the tree hasn't been destroyed.

M: I don't think they took anything. I don't see anything missing. My books are just the way I left them on the floor.

W: I wonder how they got in.

M: Maybe they __________ __________ __________ my open window.

W: Probably. It doesn't look like they used the door.

07

W: Hello, Daryl. What can I do for you?

M: Well, Ms. Peterson, I'd like to ask you about something.

W: Sure, you know you can ask me anything.

M: Some friends and I are really __________ __________ __________ __________ and we want to know if we can start a movie club.

W: Well, first off, I think you should talk to Mr. Stevenson. He's the one __________ __________ __________ __________ __________.

M: Yeah, I talked to him. He said we need a teacher to supervise us.

W: Okay, so who were you thinking of?

M: We know __________ __________ __________ __________ in video production.

W: Oh, you knew that? So you want me to supervise your club?

M: We would really like that. Will you do it?

W: Of course I will. It actually __________ __________ __________ __________ __________ __________.

M: Thanks a lot, Ms. Peterson!

08

M: Hey, Mom. Do we have any coffee left?

W: I think so. Why?

M: I'm in the mood to have a cup.

W: It's far too late to drink coffee. It has a lot of caffeine in it, so it'll __________ __________ __________ __________ __________ __________.

M: Well, I kind of need the energy.

W: Why do you need to __________ __________ __________?

M: I have to __________ __________ __________ in Spanish class tomorrow, and I want to practice it.

W: I've heard you in your room practicing all week.

M: Yeah, I've actually been practicing since last week.

W: So __________ __________ __________ __________ __________ __________.

M: Well, I'm afraid that I'll make a mistake and everyone will laugh at me.

W: I see. Well, I don't think you have anything to worry about. If you make a mistake and everyone laughs, just laugh with them.

M: Okay. Thanks for the advice, Mom.

W: Anytime. Now get ready for bed.

09

M: Welcome to Chester Science Center. How may I help you?

W: Hi. I need tickets for two adults and one child, please.

M: Sure. It's $30 for an adult and $20 for a child.

W: All right. Do these tickets __________ __________ __________ __________ __________?

M: Well, they include all of the shows and main attractions, including the hands-on science show and the aquarium.

W: That's great. What about the planetarium? __________ __________ __________ in the ticket price?

M: It's not. However, you can purchase Science Center Plus tickets that include all of the shows and attractions as well as the planetarium and laser show.

W: All right. How much are those tickets?

M: They're __________ __________ __________ __________ __________ __________.

W: Sounds great. I'll take three of them.

M: Sure. Two adults and one child, right?

W: That's right. Here's my card.

10

M: Cathleen, did you know that they're __________ __________ __________ __________ on the 27th of this month?

W: Yeah, I did know that.

M: Well, do you want to join the race?

W: I'd like to, but it seems like 26 miles will be __________ __________ __________ __________ __________ __________.

M: Yeah, it is pretty far. But you don't have to run the whole thing. You can walk when you need to.

W: Really? That doesn't sound so bad.

M: There are a lot of people running it this year. Almost 2,000 have registered, according to the website.

W: Oh, my! That's a lot of people.

M: It's for a good cause, you know. The __________ __________ is $40, but the proceeds will be used to beautify the riverfront park.

W: I see.

M: You also get a t-shirt and your name on a plaque if you finish the run. We can do it together. I'll help you finish it.

W: All right. __________ __________ __________ __________ to think about it. I'll let you know before next week if I'm going to join or not.

11

W: Good morning, class. Today, I want to talk to you about an American psychologist named Miller Brody. He was born in 1920 in Tennessee, the only son of a hardworking businessman and a house wife. He graduated from the University of Minnesota in 1945 with __________ __________ __________ __________ and started teaching at the University of Montana the following year. He was handsome and fun so his students really loved him, though he was often __________ __________ __________ __________ __________ __________. Throughout his career, he published books that focused on the psychological impact that __________ __________ __________ __________ have on people. He went to Europe after marriage, where he held discussions with many scholars from different countries in hopes of discovering the origins of the social class system in America. Miller Brody __________ __________ from natural causes in 2002.

12

W: Hey, sweetheart. I found this pamphlet down in the lobby. It gives information on Madison's tourist attractions.

M: That's cool. We should find something to do tomorrow.

W: All right. Well, I'd like to __________ __________, but five hours is a little too long, don't you think?

M: Yeah. That's also too expensive. Let's find something that doesn't cost as much.

W: Okay. Well, we could check out the butterfly garden. I heard that it's beautiful this time of year.

M: We could check that out, but they don't __________ __________ __________ from the hotel.

W: Yeah, it would be a real pain to get out there.

M: You're right. Well, that __________ __________ __________ __________ __________. Which do you think will be more fun?

W: I think it'll be __________ __________ __________ __________ __________ __________ __________.

M: I agree. Let's check this one out, then.

13

W: Hey, Tom! Did you enjoy the play last night?

M: Well, the play itself was really good, but I didn't enjoy my time at the theater much.

W: Oh, I thought you were really excited to see that play. What happened?

M: Yeah, I was excited to see it because I love the actor that __________ __________ __________ __________. But I __________ __________ __________ __________ with a couple of people.

W: At the theater? What caused the argument?

M: They were sitting in my seats, and even after I pointed that out to them, they insisted that the seats were theirs.

W: It is __________ __________ when people do that!

M: That's not all. The usher came over to handle the situation and had a look at our tickets. After a closer look, it seems that the clerk had printed the wrong tickets for me, so __________ __________ __________ __________ __________ __________.

W: You must have been furious. What did you do in the end?

M: (After watching the play, I complained to the theater.)

14

W: Hey, Cameron. What does your picket sign say? "Stop animal testing"?

M: Oh, hi Ellie. Yeah, it's __________ __________ __________ __________ __________ __________ __________.

W: A lot of people I know are against that as well, but I'm not sure why.

M: Well, people shouldn't use animals to test products being developed for human use. These pictures show all kinds of terrible things being done to animals in testing labs.

W: Wow, I'm really shocked. I didn't know they treated them like that.

M: They can kill __________ __________ __________ a day just to research the effects of one product!

W: I think it's great that you're __________ __________ __________ __________ __________. Is it possible for me to make a donation?

M: That would be great, Ellie. Go to our website for all the information you need.

W: (Okay, perfect. I'll be happy to help.)

15

M: Kenny asks his friend Katie to go to see a new movie. Katie __________ __________ __________ because she has plans to help at the orphanage this afternoon. Kenny asks Katie why she volunteers and she tells him that helping others, especially children, is very rewarding for her. Kenny has considered volunteering because he also likes helping others. However, he doesn't know if he can __________ __________ __________ __________ because he doesn't think that he is good with children. Katie would really like for Kenny to join her at the orphanage and wants to

__________ __________ __________ __________ __________. In this situation, what would Katie most likely say to Kenny?

Katie: (It's very fun and I'm sure the children will love you.)

16-17

M: The Venetian Hotel in Las Vegas is a unique experience. Since it opened its doors in 1999, The Venetian has been the largest hotel in the world. Complete with more than 7,000 rooms, the hotel is __________ __________ __________ __________ __________. The restaurant complex, which offers a variety of food from around the world, can be found in Area A, which also houses the piano bar. Area B holds the casino, where patrons win big every night. In Area C, you can find a shopping mall featuring stores that carry designer brands such as Coach, Prada, and Louis Vuitton. Area D is home to The Venetian's entertainment district, where __________ __________ __________ __________ __________ __________ perform every day and night. You might see a circus, a magic show, watch Barbara Streisand sing, or see any of several other Vegas-style shows. Finally, there is Area E, the lobby and ballroom area. This area also commonly plays host to conventions and seminars. If you ever find yourself in Las Vegas, __________ __________ __________ __________ __________ __________ __________ in the world, The Venetian Hotel.

1번부터 17번까지는 듣고 답하는 문제입니다. 1번부터 15번까지는 한 번만 들려주고, 16번부터 17번까지는 두 번 들려줍니다. 방송을 잘 듣고 답을 하시기 바랍니다.

01

대화를 듣고, 남자의 마지막 말에 대한 여자의 응답으로 가장 적절한 것을 고르시오.

① Okay, I'll call the service center now.
② I'll make sure to take good care of it.
③ I think we should buy the same model.
④ We should try to save energy if possible.
⑤ Make sure he knows to come as soon as he can.

02

대화를 듣고, 여자의 마지막 말에 대한 남자의 응답으로 가장 적절한 것을 고르시오.

① Actually, I'm not sure if I need a car wash.
② No, not really. They do a great job.
③ I think so. They have no money.
④ I don't wash my car.
⑤ It's not my car.

03

다음을 듣고, 남자가 하는 말의 목적으로 가장 적절한 것을 고르시오.

① 아파트 주변 위험 시설을 안내하려고
② 애완동물 유기에 대한 폐해를 알리려고
③ 애완동물 돌보기 대행서비스를 홍보하려고
④ 아파트 내 치안 강화 활동에 동참하도록 격려하려고
⑤ 애완동물이 이웃에 피해를 끼치지 않도록 요청하려고

04

대화를 듣고, 여자의 의견으로 가장 적절한 것을 고르시오.

① 산에서 자신의 쓰레기를 다시 가지고 와야 한다.
② 산에 오를 때는 장비와 옷을 갖추어야 한다.
③ 산에서도 쓰레기 분리수거를 해야 한다.
④ 다양한 등산 코스 개발이 필요하다.
⑤ 산 위에 쓰레기통을 설치해야 한다.

05

대화를 듣고, 두 사람의 관계를 가장 잘 나타낸 것을 고르시오.

① 의사 — 환자
② 감독 — 배우
③ 농구감독 — 리포터
④ 교장 선생님 — 학생
⑤ 심리치료사 — 의뢰인

06

대화를 듣고, 그림에서 대화의 내용과 일치하지 <u>않는</u> 것을 고르시오.

07

대화를 듣고, 남자가 여자에게 부탁한 일로 가장 적절한 것을 고르시오.

① to give him a ride somewhere
② to lend him money for the bus
③ to check when his bus will arrive
④ to let him know where the bus stop is
⑤ to show him how to find an application

08

대화를 듣고, 남자가 요즘 조깅을 하지 <u>않는</u> 이유를 고르시오.

① 교통사고 부상 때문에
② 다른 운동이 좋아져서
③ 이사를 했기 때문에
④ 드럼 연습을 하느라
⑤ 시험 준비 때문에

09

대화를 듣고, 여자가 지불할 총 금액을 고르시오.

① $18　　② $20　　③ $22　　④ $24　　⑤ $26

10

대화를 듣고, 두 사람이 언급하지 <u>않은</u> 것을 고르시오.

① 여자가 주문했던 책의 권 수
② 여자가 주문했던 책의 종류
③ 잘못 배송된 책의 작가
④ 잘못 배송된 책의 처리 방법
⑤ 운송료 지급

11

학교공개 행사에 관한 다음 내용을 듣고, 일치하지 <u>않는</u> 것을 고르시오.

① 한 학기 동안 학생들이 만든 작품을 보여준다.
② 가족이나 친척을 데려오는 행사이다.
③ 3월 26일 수요일에 열린다.
④ 행사는 네 시간 동안 진행된다.
⑤ 선착순으로 입장한다.

12

다음 표를 보면서 대화를 듣고, 두 사람이 선택할 관광 스케줄을 고르시오.

Boat & Snorkeling Tours

Option	Boat	Lunch	Goggles	Trek Fins
① A	7 hours	Provided	Provided	Not Provided
② B	6 hours	Not Provided	Provided	Provided
③ C	6 hours	Provided	Not Provided	Provided
④ D	5 hours	Not Provided	Not Provided	Provided
⑤ E	5 hours	Provided	Provided	Not Provided

13

대화를 듣고, 남자의 마지막 말에 대한 여자의 응답으로 가장 적절한 것을 <u>고르시오</u>.

Woman: ______________________________

① You need to always be polite while on the phone.
② Okay, good. That way you won't miss my call.
③ I would prefer you took the subway home.
④ Be sure to talk softly on your cell phone.
⑤ You should shut off your phone.

14

대화를 듣고, 여자의 마지막 말에 대한 남자의 응답으로 가장 적절한 것을 고르시오.

Man: ______________________________

① Yeah, there's no way for her to find a decent job.
② Yes, I always wanted her daughter to get a great job.
③ What a surprise! I haven't invited them to the party.
④ No need to worry. Alyssa found out you were concerned.
⑤ Yes. Now I understand that worrying only makes matters worse.

15

다음 상황 설명을 듣고, Rachel이 그녀의 아버지에게 할 말로 가장 적절한 것을 고르시오.

Rachel: ______________________________

① Sorry about all of this, Dad.
② Calm down, Dad. It'll be okay.
③ Really? So shouldn't I ask her?
④ See, I knew she would help us!
⑤ Maybe we should have taken the bus.

[16-17] 다음을 듣고, 물음에 답하시오.

16

남자가 하는 말의 목적으로 가장 적절한 것은?

① to provide surveillance camera installation instructions
② to convince people to purchase surveillance cameras
③ to explain how surveillance cameras can prevent crime
④ to demonstrate the effectiveness of surveillance cameras
⑤ to propose a reduction in the number of surveillance cameras

17

감시 카메라가 설치된 곳으로 남자가 언급하지 <u>않은</u> 것은?

① 학교　　　　② 사무실　　　　③ 엘리베이터
④ 상점　　　　⑤ 자동차

10 DICTATION

01

M: Wow, it's so hot in here. Let's turn on the air conditioner, Amy.

W: It's not working properly. We can't use it until it's fixed.

M: Well, we should ___________ ___________ ___________ as soon as possible then.

W: (Okay, I'll call the service center now.)

02

W: The weather is nice today.

M: Yeah, I'm going to wash my car.

W: How much does it cost to wash your car?

M: I usually ___________ ___________ ___________ ___________.

W: Really? Isn't that too expensive?

M: (No, not really. They do a great job.)

03

M: Over the last few weeks, we've received several complaints about neighborhood dogs barking late into the evening. These dogs have become ___________ ___________ ___________ ___________ ___________ ___________ ___________, especially those who have to work early in the morning. It has ___________ ___________ ___________ ___________ ___________, last night, a resident called the police, who came out to the neighborhood to deal with the problem. ___________ ___________ ___________ ___________ ___________, we have also received several complaints that pet owners are not cleaning up after their pets. We at Greenville Apartments urge our residents to ___________ ___________ ___________ ___________ to keep our neighborhood clean and quiet. We appreciate your efforts.

04

W: Daniel, it's beautiful up here. The mountain air is so clean, and the views are amazing.

M: I agree. It's truly wonderful. But, I think ___________ ___________ ___________.

W: It's hard to leave, but it is getting dark. We should go soon.

M: First, where do you think I can ___________ ___________ ___________ ___________ ___________?

W: There doesn't seem to be any place to put it. Let's just take it with us.

M: Okay, but it would be so much easier if they'd put some trash cans up here.

W: Yeah, but then they'd have to hire someone to come ___________ ___________.

M: Well, without trash cans, people just throw their trash anywhere they want.

W: True, but if there was a trash can, it would fill up and then overflow and trash would ___________ ___________ ___________.

M: I suppose you're right.

W: I really don't think taking our trash with us is a big deal.

M: I guess it's not.

05

W: Excuse me, Mr. Wise, but ___________ ___________ ___________ ___________ ___________?

M: Sure, Shelly. Come on in. What can I do for you?

W: I just wanted to apologize for my performance last night. I really ___________ ___________ ___________ ___________ ___________.

M: Yeah, you weren't as into the performance as you usually are. You made a lot of mistakes.

W: I know. I should have been more focused. I've just been really frustrated lately, and it's been ___________ ___________ ___________ ___________ ___________.

M: Frustrated about what?

W: Well, I'm falling behind in math class. I've been stressed out about that.

M: I see. Would you like me to replace you for a couple of shows so you can __________ __________ __________ __________?

W: No, it's fine. I've spoken to my teacher. She's agreed to let me retake the last exam.

M: All right. Well, forget about last night. Let's just focus on tomorrow's performance.

W: Okay. Thanks, Mr. Wise.

06

W: I love coming to town for the Spring Festival, Carl. It's so much fun!

M: Me, too. There's so much to do.

W: Absolutely. Let's get something to eat first.

M: Sure. But I need to go to the ATM to get some money.

W: That's perfect. __________ __________ __________ __________ __________ __________ __________ the bank.

M: Nice! What do you want to do after we eat?

W: Well, I always like riding the rides, especially that big wheel.

M: I don't think I can ride with you. __________ __________ __________ __________.

W: That's too bad. Well, I guess you can __________ __________ __________ __________ __________ __________. You can also listen to the band like those people over there.

M: There aren't any bands playing right now, unfortunately.

W: I'm sure you can find something to do while you wait.

M: Sure. Anyway, let's get something to eat!

07

W: Hello, Mr. Brown. It's nice to see you here. Are you waiting for a bus?

M: Yeah. Are you going somewhere, Laura?

W: I'm going home. I'm __________ __________ __________, too. Which one are you waiting for?

M: Number 52. I've been waiting for almost 10 minutes. Ah, do you have a smartphone with you?

W: Yes. Why do you ask?

M: I heard there's a __________ __________ __________. Can you let me know what time my bus will arrive?

W: Of course. Actually, I just installed that app on my phone this morning. Just a second. *[Pause]* Let's see. Here it says bus 52 __________ __________ __________ __________ about five minutes.

M: Oh, that's great. Thank you, Laura.

W: No problem. Oh, __________ __________ __________. See you tomorrow, Mr. Brown.

08

W: Pardon me. Don't we know each other?

M: Cynthia! It's me, Mason!

W: Oh, my goodness, __________ __________ __________. How are you?

M: I'm doing really well. I don't think we've talked since you moved away.

W: I think you're right. Are you still playing music? You always loved the drums.

M: I am. I still really love to play.

W: What about jogging? I __________ __________ __________ __________ a lot.

M: I haven't jogged in a long time, actually.

W: Really? Why not?

M: __________ __________ __________ __________ __________ __________ __________ about a year ago. I can't really run at all.

W: That's terrible. I'm so sorry to hear that. I hope they caught the person that did it.

M: Yes, they did. He actually stopped the car and called the police himself. Anyway, I should be going.

W: Yeah, me too. Let's try to __________ __________ __________!

M: Of course.

09

M: Good morning, Ms. Smith.

W: Good morning, Mr. Baron. All your vegetables __________ __________ __________ today.

M: Yes. I'd especially recommend the onions and the carrots. They just arrived.

W: They do look really fresh. __________ __________ __________ __________?

M: The onions are $2 each, and the carrots are sold by the kilogram. One kilogram of carrots is $6.

W: Then, I'd like one kilogram of carrots and two onions, please.

M: Okay. __________ __________?

W: Yes, I need to buy some pumpkins and some potatoes to make soup.

M: Pumpkins are $5 each, and one kilogram of potatoes is $4.

W: I think two pumpkins and one kilogram of potatoes should be enough. Could I __________ __________ __________?

M: Yes, of course. I'll have someone bring them by in about two hours.

W: Great. Here's my credit card.

10

[Telephone rings.]

M: Shine On Top Bookstore. What can I do for you?

W: I __________ __________ __________ __________ and received them this morning, but there's a mistake with one of them.

M: Okay. May I have your name, please?

W: Yes. It's Rebecca Jackson.

M: Let me just pull up your purchase. *[Keyboard typing sound]* You ordered a collection of essays and a science textbook, right?

W: Yes. The problem is that the essay collection I received is __________ __________ __________ __________ __________.

M: Oh, I'm sorry about that. What's the title of the book you received?

W: It's *A Big Dream*. What I ordered was *Just a Dream* by John Thomas.

M: I __________ __________ __________ __________. We'll have the correct book shipped out to you right away.

W: What should I do with the book I have now?

M: Could you please return it to us by mail? We'll __________ __________ __________ __________.

W: Okay. I'll send it tomorrow.

11

W: Good afternoon, everyone. I'm Lilly Stevens, art director here at Maple's Academy. Today I'd like to announce a special open house event at our school. This event allows students to bring their families to the academy to __________ __________ __________ __________ they've created this semester. You can bring not only your parents, but also your __________, __________, __________ __________ __________. We will also host several activities, such as sculpting and tie-dyeing, that you may choose to participate in with your relatives. This open house event __________ __________ __________ __________ __________ in the activities center from 5 to 9 p.m. on Wednesday, March 26th. You will need to __________ __________ as there is only enough space to accommodate 100 guests. Please visit our website for more information.

12

W: Hey, sweetheart. What's that you're looking at?

M: It's a __________ __________ __________ __________ __________ __________ __________. I think we should do some snorkeling before we go home.

W: That's a great idea. Let's __________ __________ __________. I think it'll be a great experience for the kids. How about the seven-hour tour?

M: Seven hours is far too long for the kids to be on a boat. Don't you think __________ __________ __________ __________ __________?

W: You're probably right. Let's go for a shorter one, then.

M: All right. Do you think we should go on one of the tours that provides lunch?

W: I don't really think that's necessary. We bought a lot of food for our trip. I can make some sandwiches.

M: All right. So, we're obviously going to need goggles, unless we want to buy our own. What about trek fins? Do you think we'll need them?

W: Absolutely. Snorkeling is always __________ __________ __________ __________.

M: Okay. Well, I think we've found the perfect tour for us.

13

W: Are you __________ __________ __________ __________ __________ __________ __________ today between the Devils and the Rangers?

M: I sure am! I'm really excited for this game.

W: Did you get tickets yet?

M: Yes, of course.

W: What time will the game finish?

M: They usually end between 9:30 and 10:00 p.m.

W: Oh, really? I didn't know they lasted that long. I'll come __________ __________ __________.

M: That'd be great, Mom. Where should I meet you?

W: __________ __________ __________ __________ __________ when I arrive at the stadium.

M: All right, great. I'll be sure to have my cell phone with me.

W: Are you sure you'll be able to hear it ring? The stadium is so noisy.

M: I'll __________ __________ __________ __________ and put it in my front pocket so that I feel it when you call.

W: (Okay, good. That way you won't miss my call.)

14

W: Hello, dear. How was your time with all of your friends?

M: It was great. We __________ __________ __________ __________ and then went to the park.

W: That sounds like a lot of fun.

M: Yeah, it really was. We were all having such a good time that we wanted to keep it going, so __________ __________ __________ __________ __________ __________.

W: That was a great idea.

M: Oh, Lauren told me that her daughter landed a job in Phoenix.

W: That's nice. __________ __________ __________ __________? You've been so concerned about Alyssa getting a job.

M: Maybe a bit, but I know our Alyssa will find herself one soon.

W: You seem less worried about it than you were before.

M: Well, I just __________ __________ __________ that there's nothing I can do about it.

W: You're right. There is no use worrying. It won't change anything.

M: (Yes. Now I understand that worrying only makes matters worse.)

15

W: Rachel and her father have been driving around the parking lot at the mall for 10 minutes. It's Saturday and the lot is nearly full. Rachel's father __________ __________ __________ __________. Rachel takes out one of her dolls and __________ __________ __________ __________ a parking space for them. Rachel's father asks what she's doing. She tells him that one of the characters in her favorite cartoon always says if you ever need help, you should ask a friend. Her father tries to explain that this is not the kind of help her cartoon was talking about, but Rachel insists. __________ __________ __________ __________, they see a spot open up in front of them. What would Rachel most likely say to her father?

Rachel: (See, I knew she would help us!)

16-17

M: Good evening, everyone. I'd like to take some time tonight to talk about closed-circuit television, or surveillance cameras for short. In this country, there are more than three million surveillance cameras __________ __________ __________ __________ __________. Some people believe that these cameras prevent crimes from being committed, as criminals are cautious around cameras. However, many of us feel that surveillance cameras can __________ __________. These cameras are everywhere: in our schools, offices, shops, and even our cars. While they might record potential criminals, they also record innocent passersby. There are even stories of people installing surveillance cameras to __________ __________ __________ __________ and other people. This conduct is clearly against the law, but is rarely punished. The police also seem to agree that we should reduce the number of surveillance cameras and increase the number of patrol officers. We should work together to __________ __________ __________ __________ __________ in our city in order to __________ __________ __________ __________ __________.

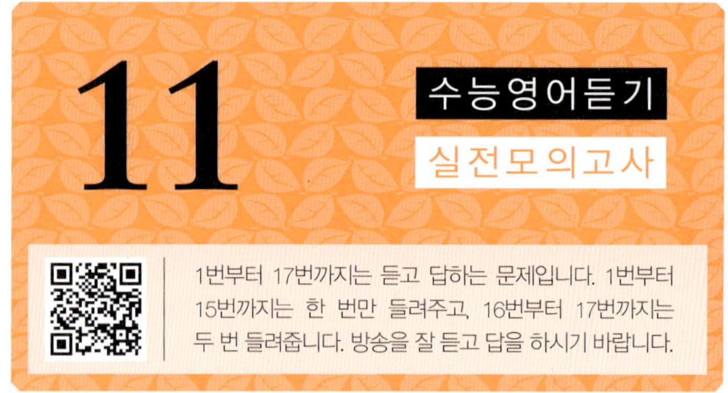

01

대화를 듣고, 남자의 마지막 말에 대한 여자의 응답으로 가장 적절한 것을 고르시오.

① No. This is too big for my house.
② I needed your advice before I bought it.
③ Sure. I'm going to hang the TV on the wall.
④ You have to clean the living room regularly.
⑤ I thought you said it was okay to buy a new TV.

02

대화를 듣고, 여자의 마지막 말에 대한 남자의 응답으로 가장 적절한 것을 고르시오.

① She must be proud of you for winning the prize.
② Yeah, the bakery sells delicious apple pies.
③ I'll make a special cake for your birthday.
④ I don't like alcoholic beverages.
⑤ Great. I'll bring some drinks.

03

다음을 듣고, 여자가 하는 말의 목적으로 가장 적절한 것을 고르시오.

① 연극 동아리의 모임 장소를 공지하려고
② 연극 동아리의 공연을 홍보하려고
③ 연극 동아리의 역사를 소개하려고
④ 연극 동아리 가입을 권유하려고
⑤ 연극 동아리 창단을 제안하려고

04

대화를 듣고, 두 사람이 하는 말의 주제로 가장 적절한 것을 고르시오.

① 다이어트에 효과적인 물
② 수돗물 공급 중단의 원인
③ 탄산수가 건강에 좋은 이유
④ 충분한 수분 섭취의 필요성
⑤ 과도한 탄산수 섭취의 문제점

05

대화를 듣고, 두 사람의 관계를 가장 잘 나타낸 것을 고르시오.

① 고객 — 부동산 중개업자　　② 방문객 — 정원 관리사
③ 세입자 — 집주인　　　　　④ 투자가 — 금융설계사
⑤ 학부모 — 교사

06

대화를 듣고, 그림에서 대화의 내용과 일치하지 <u>않는</u> 것을 고르시오.

07

대화를 듣고, 남자가 여자를 위해 할 일로 가장 적절한 것을 고르시오.

① 밴드 리더의 전화번호 알려주기
② 밴드 공연 관람권 예매해 주기
③ 밴드 합주 연습실 제공해 주기
④ 밴드 오디션 참가 신청해 주기
⑤ 밴드 기타 연주자 구해 주기

08

대화를 듣고, 여자가 청바지를 자선단체에 기부하려는 이유를 고르시오.

① 키가 커지면서 바지가 맞지 않게 되어서
② 너무 많이 입었기 때문에 싫증이 나서
③ 자선단체에 물건을 보내고 싶어서
④ 유행에 뒤떨어지는 디자인이라서
⑤ 새로운 청바지를 선물 받아서

09

대화를 듣고, 남자가 지불할 금액을 고르시오.

① $30　　② $35　　③ $40　　④ $45　　⑤ $50

10

대화를 듣고, 컴퓨터 게임 토너먼트에 관해 두 사람이 언급하지 <u>않은</u> 것을 고르시오.

① 장소　　　　　② 요일　　　　　③ 대상 연령
④ 준비물　　　　⑤ 시작 시간

11

겨울 방학 캠프에 관한 다음 안내 방송을 듣고, 일치하지 <u>않는</u> 것을 고르시오.

① 자원봉사 학생들을 모집하고 있다.
② 캠프는 각각 12월과 1월에 실시된다.
③ 수업마다 다른 장소에서 캠프를 진행한다.
④ 자원봉사 신청서는 8월 31일까지 내야 한다.
⑤ 캠프 상담자들은 일주일에 3일 일해야 한다.

12

다음 표를 보면서 대화를 듣고, 여자가 구입할 CCTV를 고르시오.

CCTV Systems

	Model No.	Video Resolution	Infrared	Memory	Price
①	XT221	1280 x 480	X	32GB	$200
②	XT331	1920 x 1080	X	64GB	$350
③	S401	1280 x 480	O	32GB	$260
④	S501	1920 x 1080	X	32GB	$290
⑤	S502	1920 x 1080	O	64GB	$400

13

대화를 듣고, 남자의 마지막 말에 대한 여자의 응답으로 가장 적절한 것을 고르시오.

Woman: ______________________________

① I'm not surprised. I knew you would like the movie.
② I don't understand why people like dinosaur movies.
③ I guess we should take a break and eat some snacks.
④ You're right, but I didn't know they were so interesting.
⑤ You will be scared if you watch another dinosaur movie.

14

대화를 듣고, 여자의 마지막 말에 대한 남자의 응답으로 가장 적절한 것을 고르시오.

Man: ______________________________

① I think you should follow your dreams.
② I think I ought to major in accounting.
③ Really? I'll go there for help right now.
④ You should choose a major soon.
⑤ There aren't many jobs in art.

15

다음 상황 설명을 듣고, Morty가 카드 판매자에게 할 말로 가장 적절한 것을 고르시오.

Morty: ______________________________

① Have you sent me the refund yet?
② Could I please purchase another set of cards?
③ How large is your collection of baseball cards?
④ I was wondering if you knew any other card dealers.
⑤ I haven't received the cards yet. Have you sent them?

[16-17] 다음을 듣고, 물음에 답하시오.

16

남자가 하는 말의 주제로 가장 적절한 것은?

① Ways to rescue mistreated animals
② Efforts to save endangered animals
③ Ways in which animals help humans
④ The role of animals in entertainment
⑤ Negative effects of using animals for help

17

언급된 동물이 <u>아닌</u> 것은?

① elephant　　② deer　　③ bear
④ dog　　　　⑤ hog

11 DICTATION

01

M: Honey, did you buy this new TV?

W: Yes. Don't you remember? I told you we needed a better one with a clearer picture.

M: Yes, but why did you buy it __________ __________ __________ __________ ?

W: (I thought you said it was okay to buy a new TV.)

02

W: Robert, Helena's seventeenth birthday is __________ __________ __________ __________ .

M: Oh, I nearly forgot. It's March 23rd. How about a surprise party for her?

W: Sounds great. Then I can prepare her favorite dish: apple pie.

M: (Great. I'll bring some drinks.)

03

W: Hello, I'm Grace Stamos, a junior journalism major. As freshmen, you've been here for about three months now. Are you enjoying your time here at the university? Is everything __________ __________ __________ __________ __________ __________ ? If you're looking to do more, you might think about __________ __________ __________ __________ .

The club has been a big part of the university for over 50 years, and many of our incoming freshmen __________ __________ . Making new friends is easy __________ __________ __________ __________ __________ , and you'll get to visit all the cool clubs and theaters in the city when you do your performances. I'm positive you'll find the club very enjoyable. If you would like to meet new people and __________ __________ __________ __________ __________ __________ here, then join the Drama Club today!

04

M: Wow! It's such a hot day. Did you bring anything to drink, Katie?

W: Sure.

M: Thanks. *[Pause]* Wait, why did you bring soda?

W: That's sparkling water.

M: Sparkling water, huh? Why not regular water? This stuff __________ __________ __________ __________ .

W: Well, sparkling water has benefits that you can't get from regular water. It's really __________ __________ __________ __________ __________ .

M: I see. Why is that?

W: It suppresses your appetite, so that makes it great for dieting. Since I started drinking sparkling water, I've lost almost 4 kilograms.

M: That's incredible.

W: It's also a lot healthier than tap water in this area. I saw on the news that __________ __________ __________ __________ __________ for a few months.

M: I see. I guess I should start __________ __________ __________ .

05

[Cell phone rings.]

M: Good morning, Ms. Tanner. This is Joseph Lancaster.

W: Mr. Lancaster, it's so nice to hear from you. Have you decided on a property?

M: Yes. My wife and I have decided to go with the Main Street property.

W: Ah, the two bedroom home with three bathrooms. It really is a wonderful property. It's __________ __________ __________ __________ __________ __________ .

M: Yes, we really love all the open space in the yard.

W: It's a perfect place for raising your kids. They'll have __________ __________ __________ __________ __________ .

M: Yes, I agree. I was wondering if it would be all right to plant a small garden in the yard as well.

W: I'm sure it'll be fine. I've been working with the property owner for years.

M: Great. So when can I __________ __________ __________ __________ __________ __________ ?

W: Can you stop by the office this afternoon? The property owner will be here, too.
M: Sure. I'll come by at around 4 p.m.

06

M: Look, dear. I found this old picture in the attic.
W: Oh, my goodness. I haven't seen this picture in a very long time. That is the playground my father built for me and my brother, Tim, when we were younger.
M: So the little girl is you. You're ___________ ___________ ___________ ___________.
W: That's right. Wasn't I cute?
M: That man holding your hand ___________ ___________ ___________ ___________. He looks so young!
W: Well, he was. We all were!
M: The boy playing in the sand is Tim, right?
W: Yeah, he always liked to get dirty.
M: The slide looks like it was a lot of fun.
W: It was so much fun. All of the neighborhood kids ___________ ___________ ___________ ___________ ___________.
M: So, when was this photo taken?
W: When do you think?
M: Everything looks so green. I'm guessing it was taken in the summer.
W: Yeah, it was. Summers were always the best because we didn't have to go to school.
M: ___________ ___________ ___________ ___________ ___________! It looks like you had an awesome summer.
W: I really did, thanks to my dad.

07

W: Oh, you're looking at an audition notice for a jazz band at a jazz cafe downtown. Are you interested in joining?
M: Not me. My sister is. She plays guitar in a jazz band.
W: Is her band going to ___________ ___________ ___________ ___________?
M: They want to. The problem is that their drummer broke his arm last week.
W: Oh, no! He won't be able to play the drums yet, then.

M: Yeah. So the band leader is trying to get a new drummer ___________ ___________ ___________ ___________.
W: Hmm. . . Do you think I could meet him?
M: Why? Do you play the drums?
W: Yes, I play a little. And I've been wanting to ___________ ___________ ___________ for a long time.
M: Great! I'll ask my sister for his cell phone number and ___________ ___________ ___________ soon.
W: Thanks. I hope I'm good enough to play with them.

08

M: Stacy, your jeans are on the floor. Will you pick them up, please?
W: Can I just leave them there for now, Brian? I'm ___________ ___________ ___________ ___________ later today.
M: Really? But they look new.
W: They are new, basically. I've only worn them a couple times.
M: Why are you giving them up? They seem to be really good quality.
W: I know, and I do like them, but I just can't wear them.
M: ___________ ___________ ___________ ___________? Why not?
W: They're too small for me.
M: Okay, but I thought ___________ ___________ ___________ ___________ ___________. These days I see kids in really tight jeans all the time.
W: Yeah, but they're also too short for me.
M: Aha.
W: I bought those jeans last summer, and since then ___________ ___________ ___________ almost two inches.
M: Well, I suppose we need to buy you some new jeans soon.

09

M: Hi. I'm looking to buy a new pair of headphones.
W: Sure. Do you have a particular brand or style in mind?
M: Well, I want something that's comfortable because I'll be wearing them ___________ ___________ ___________.
W: All right. I think you'll really like this pair.

M: What can you tell me about them?

W: They're incredibly popular these days. They have ___________ ___________ ___________ for comfort and use new technology for optimal sound.

M: That sounds great. How much do they run?

W: They retail for $50, but they're 10% off this week.

M: Awesome! I also found this coupon for $10 off on your website. Can I ___________ ___________ ___________ ___________ ___________ ?

W: Absolutely. We can give you an additional $10 off the discounted price.

M: Nice. I'd like to ___________ ___________ ___________ ___________ ___________ .

W: Sure, no problem.

10

W: Sweetheart, how about taking Albert to the ___________ ___________ ___________ tomorrow?

M: That sounds great! I saw a poster that said ___________ ___________ ___________ at PC Playground Arena.

W: That's the place! They hold tournaments the last Saturday of every month.

M: Are you sure Albert would be interested in it? ___________ ___________ ___________ ___________ ___________ ___________ ___________ first-person shooters.

W: I don't think so. I'm sure he'll enjoy it. It was actually his idea to go.

M: Okay. ___________ ___________ ___________ ___________ ___________ ___________ ___________ ?

W: I'd say we should bring lunch, some snacks and drinks, and maybe our Ryan and Jason t-shirts so we can cheer them on.

M: That's quite a lot for an afternoon event. Do you think we should leave early?

W: I don't think we should leave too early. It starts at noon, so let's leave at around 11.

M: All right. ___________ ___________ ___________ ___________ ___________ 11.

11

W: Attention, everyone. The New Poets Society is accepting applications from new students who are interested in poetry and art. There will be poetry camps during the winter vacation, and we would like to have as many student volunteers to ___________ ___________ ___________ ___________ as possible. Volunteer camp counselors are responsible for monitoring the younger students and modeling appropriate behavior and safety. Winter camps begin December 23rd and January 7th, and ___________ ___________ ___________ ___________ ___________ at the Walker Art Center in Minneapolis. ___________ ___________ ___________ ___________ no later than August 31st. Camp counselors will be required to work at least eight hours a day, three days a week. If you would like any additional information on the winter camps, please visit us on the web at *www.winterpoets.com*.

12

W: Hey, Samuel. Didn't you buy a CCTV system for your house?

M: I did. Why?

W: Well, my husband and I are shopping for one, but I really don't know much about them. Can you help me?

M: Sure. Let me see that brochure. *[Pause]* Okay. You'll probably want to ___________ ___________ ___________ ___________ first.

W: Well, which one do you recommend?

M: I think ___________ ___________ ___________ ___________ , ___________ ___________ .

W: Okay. I'll go with the high resolution.

M: Do you think you'll ___________ ___________ ___________ ___________ ___________ ?

W: The ones with infrared seem much more expensive. I don't really think I'll need it.

M: Okay. The next thing to consider is its storage capacity.

W: Well, I don't really think I'll need too much. What do you think?

M: I don't really use up much space on mine. I think 32GB should be enough space.

W: Great. I guess this is the one for me. Thanks for helping.

13

M: __________ __________ __________ __________
__________ the movie, Debra?

W: I loved it, Dad! Let's watch it again.

M: I knew you'd like it, but let's __________ __________
__________ and then watch something else.

W: I don't want to see anything else. Let's watch *Before Time* again!

M: We just saw that. Let's put in a different movie. Seriously. What about *Teddy Rex*? I heard that's a good one.

W: All right, but it'd better be __________ __________
__________ *Before Time*!

M: It's going to be even better. We'd better get it started soon __________ __________ __________
__________ __________.

W: I won't. Now put on *Teddy Rex*, Dad.

M: I'm quite surprised, Debra. You said that dinosaurs were scary just before we started watching *Before Time*.

W: (You're right, but I didn't know they were so interesting.)

14

M: Hey, Lynn. Do you know what you want to major in yet?

W: I do. I recently decided on online journalism. What about you?

M: I'm still undecided.

W: __________ __________ __________
__________ accounting. You really __________
__________ __________ __________ numbers and managing money.

M: You're right. But I don't know if I want to work with numbers. I'm also interested in art and art history.

W: So you're not sure what to major in?

M: Yeah, I just don't know what to do.

W: Well, __________ __________ __________ __________
visit Ms. Marshall in the counseling center?

M: Why would I visit her? I don't have any behavioral problems.

W: Ms. Marshall can give you an aptitude test to see __________ __________ __________ __________. I think it will help you make a decision.

M: (Really? I'll go there for help right now.)

15

M: Morty likes to collect things. Baseball cards are his favorite thing to collect. A few weeks ago, Morty __________ __________ __________ __________
__________ on the Internet that offered 20 unopened packs of baseball cards for $20. He decided to jump on this deal, and immediately transferred the payment to the card dealer. After one week of waiting and checking the mailbox every day, the cards still hadn't arrived. He decided to __________ __________ __________, but the cards still didn't come. __________ __________
__________, and today he has decided to call the card dealer. After three rings, the dealer answers the phone. In this situation, what would Morty most likely say to the card dealer?

Morty: (I haven't received the cards yet. Have you sent them?)

16-17

M: Good morning, everyone. In our last class, we talked about how animals are often mistreated and used for entertainment and discussed the examples of elephants and bears in circuses. In today's class, I'd like to talk about how people use animals to help them __________ __________ __________
__________ __________ __________. You may have seen our first animal in a shopping mall or walking down the street. This is a seeing-eye dog, and it __________
__________ __________ with their day-to-day lives. Seeing-eye dogs, usually golden retrievers, help their owners cross the street and __________
__________. These dogs also offer companionship and are generally very caring creatures. The next animal we're going to talk about is the truffle hog. People in North America and Europe use hogs to __________ __________ __________
__________ __________ called truffles. Hogs have a great sense of smell and can identify truffles that are __________ __________ __________ __________
__________ __________. Hogs have a natural affinity to search for food underground, so they are perfect for this task.

12

1번부터 17번까지는 듣고 답하는 문제입니다. 1번부터 15번까지는 한 번만 들려주고, 16번부터 17번까지는 두 번 들려줍니다. 방송을 잘 듣고 답을 하시기 바랍니다.

01

대화를 듣고, 여자의 마지막 말에 대한 남자의 응답으로 가장 적절한 것을 고르시오.

① You need to take a medical exam.
② You should fill out an application first.
③ Sure. The interviewer will see you now.
④ We scheduled an appointment for you yesterday.
⑤ We're busy right now, but we'll contact you next week.

02

대화를 듣고, 남자의 마지막 말에 대한 여자의 응답으로 가장 적절한 것을 고르시오.

① I agree with you. It's too expensive.
② I'd like to know what the present is.
③ You're right. Van Gogh is the best artist ever.
④ Do the tickets cost just $10? That's a real bargain.
⑤ I can't believe it! How did you know that I love his work?

03

다음을 듣고, 여자가 하는 말의 목적으로 가장 적절한 것을 고르시오.

① 건강 음료의 중독성을 설명하려고
② 경기력 향상 방법을 안내하려고
③ 건강에 좋은 식단을 권장하려고
④ 체력 유지의 중요성을 알리려고
⑤ 스포츠 음료를 홍보하려고

04

대화를 듣고, 두 사람이 하는 말의 주제로 가장 적절한 것을 고르시오.

① 머리를 맑게 해주는 식이요법
② 긴장감이 학습 효율에 미치는 영향
③ 시험으로 인한 긴장을 완화하는 방법
④ 학업 점수를 올릴 수 있는 공부 방법
⑤ 지나친 운동이 두뇌에 미치는 부정적 영향

05

대화를 듣고, 두 사람의 관계를 가장 잘 나타낸 것을 고르시오.

① 약사 — 환자
② 판매원 — 고객
③ 기자 — 기부자
④ 간호사 — 헌혈자
⑤ 변호사 — 의뢰인

06

대화를 듣고, 그림에서 대화의 내용과 일치하지 <u>않는</u> 것을 고르시오.

07

대화를 듣고, 여자가 할 일로 가장 적절한 것을 고르시오.

① 회의자료 복사하기
② 인력관리부서에 가기
③ 수정 테이프 구입하기
④ 인터넷 카페에 전화하기
⑤ 프린터 수리기사 기다리기

08

대화를 듣고, 여자가 해변에 갈 수 <u>없는</u> 이유를 고르시오.

① 과제를 해야 해서
② 몸이 좋지 않아서
③ 고향으로 가봐야 해서
④ 아르바이트를 해야 해서
⑤ 조별 과제 모임이 있어서

09

대화를 듣고, 새 고속도로 이용 시 단축될 시간과 고속도로 이용 요금을 바르게 짝지은 것을 고르시오.

	단축될 시간	고속도로 이용 요금		단축될 시간	고속도로 이용 요금
① 약 15분	—	$2	② 약 15분	—	$3
③ 약 25분	—	$2	④ 약 25분	—	$3
⑤ 약 40분	—	$5			

10

대화를 듣고, 캠핑에 관해 두 사람이 언급하지 <u>않은</u> 것을 고르시오.

① 캠핑 가는 요일
② 남자가 여자에게 알려줄 일
③ 캠핑 가는 데 걸리는 시간
④ 캠핑에서 먹을 음식
⑤ 짐을 싸야 할 항목

11

Georgetown's Musical Mondays에 관한 다음 내용을 듣고, 일치하지 <u>않는</u> 것을 고르시오.

① 첫 행사는 4월 22일에 시작한다.
② 밴드의 리드보컬이 팬들과 만날 것이다.
③ 밴드의 공연은 6시부터 8시까지 있을 것이다.
④ 초등학생 이상의 어린이부터 입장할 수 있다.
⑤ 수익금은 Georgetown 예술문화협회에 전달될 것이다.

12

다음 표를 보면서 대화를 듣고, 두 사람이 선택한 자전거 강좌를 고르시오.

	Lesson	Instructor	Day	Years of Work Experience
①	A	Sally Fields (female)	Thursday & Friday	8
②	B	Tom Ford (male)	Monday & Wednesday	10
③	C	Wendy Fry (female)	Tuesday & Wednesday	5
④	D	Brenda Benson (female)	Monday & Friday	7
⑤	E	Steve Anderson (male)	Wednesday & Thursday	6

13

대화를 듣고, 남자의 마지막 말에 대한 여자의 응답으로 가장 적절한 것을 고르시오.

Woman : ________________________________

① You've never gotten stage fright before.
② I'm sure. You've been practicing hard.
③ I couldn't have done it without you.
④ No. I'm too nervous to perform.
⑤ Okay. I should give it a try.

14

대화를 듣고, 여자의 마지막 말에 대한 남자의 응답으로 가장 적절한 것을 고르시오.

Man: ________________________________

① Yes. I'll go back when my kids are a bit older.
② Actually, I wish I had never left America as a child.
③ Exactly. It would be hard to communicate overseas.
④ That's correct. Hard work made everything possible.
⑤ I really wanted to study abroad but couldn't afford it.

15

다음 상황 설명을 듣고, Greg이 Henry에게 할 말로 가장 적절한 것을 고르시오.

Greg: ________________________________

① Emails are a great way to show your appreciation.
② It doesn't matter what they donated. It's the thought that counts.
③ I think that we should put together some gift baskets to show thanks.
④ I don't think that we should focus so much time on writing thank-you notes.
⑤ I think that handwritten thank-you notes are the best way to show appreciation.

[16-17] 다음을 듣고, 물음에 답하시오.

16

남자가 하는 말의 주제로 가장 적절한 것은?

① Tips on staying cool in hot weather
② What to do in emergency situations
③ How to save energy for the environment
④ Energy consumption of digital electronics
⑤ Dangers of overloading an electrical outlet

17

열을 발생시키는 전자제품으로 언급되지 <u>않은</u> 것은?

① 냉장고
② 전화기 충전기
③ 전자레인지
④ 커피메이커
⑤ 컴퓨터

녹음을 다시 한 번 듣고, 빈칸에 알맞은 말을 쓰시오

01

W: Hi. I finished ___________ ___________ ___________ ___________. Is there anything else I need to do?

M: No, that's it. You're free to go.

W: I see. When will you call me to set up an interview?

M: (We're busy right now, but we'll contact you next week.)

02

M: Rosa, I've prepared something special for you. Would you like to know what it is?

W: Oh, yes please. Tell me quickly.

M: ___________ ___________ ___________ ___________ ___________ the Van Gogh exhibition!

W: (I can't believe it! How did you know that I love his work?)

03

W: Hello, players. As you all know, sometimes it's hard to keep your energy levels up during a game. Playing sports naturally drains your energy. There is one thing you can do to help ___________ ___________ ___________—drink Rad CraCra. Rad CraCra helps keep you in the game. Its special mix of vitamins and minerals helps you ___________ ___________ ___________ ___________ ___________. It's cheap, too. One can of Rad CraCra only costs about a dollar, but it's all you need to ___________ ___________ ___________ ___________ ___________ ___________. It's a high-quality product that's about half the price of other sports drinks. Its effects even ___________ ___________ than those more expensive products. So, drink Rad CraCra anytime you need an extra boost.

04

W: Hey Joe, what's wrong? ___________ ___________ ___________ ___________.

M: Well, Mom, I'm very nervous about my English exam.

W: Calm down! You've been studying all week, so I'm sure you'll do great.

M: I'm just so worried. I can't ___________ ___________ anything else.

W: Have you tried doing some yoga or having a conversation with your friends?

M: I chatted on the phone with Molly, but it didn't really help. How do you relax when you're stressed?

W: I usually ___________ ___________ ___________ ___________ when I need to relax.

M: Do you think that will help? I think I'll get tired if I jog.

W: Exercising releases endorphins in your brain that help you think more clearly. I'm sure it'll make you feel better.

M: Yeah? Well, I'm going to try to jog ___________ ___________ ___________ ___________. Thanks for your help, Mom.

05

W: Good afternoon. ___________ ___________ ___________ ___________ ___________?

M: I am, but I'm a bit nervous. This is the first time I've done it.

W: That's great! Welcome. ___________ ___________ ___________ ___________ ___________ ___________ is fill out this form.

M: Sure. [Pause] Okay. I'm finished. What's the next step?

W: Now we need to prick your finger to check your blood type.

M: Sure. But I'm a little afraid of needles.

W: It will only hurt a bit. [Pause] All right, that's it. Are you currently on any medication?

M: Well, I ___________ ___________ ___________ ___________ ___________ ___________ a few days ago. Is that okay?

W: That shouldn't be a problem. Have a seat over here and roll up your sleeve, please.

M: I'm running a little late for a meeting. This won't take long, will it?

W: It usually takes about 20 minutes to give blood. We really appreciate your donation.

06

M: Check out this picture from my childhood, honey.

W: You were so cute back then. Look at you in your baseball uniform.

M: Yeah, I used to love baseball. I even wore my uniform in the winter. That's my first mitt.

W: Really? I see that you're holding a snowball in your left hand. __________ __________ __________-__________ when you were young?

M: Yeah, I was ambidextrous when I was a child. I could never decide __________ __________ __________ __________.

W: I like the snowman you built. I guess you gave him your cap.

M: That's right. He's wearing my Ravens baseball cap. I'm wearing my Lions cap.

W: So I guess you were the pitcher and he was the batter, huh? He has your bat.

M: Yeah. I didn't have many friends growing up, so in the winter, I built my own.

W: __________ __________, sweetheart.

07

W: Hey, Bill. Do you have any whiteout?

M: I do. What do you need it for?

W: There's a mistake on this handout for today's partner meeting. I need to correct it.

M: I think you should __________ __________ __________ on your computer and print it again. Partner meetings are important.

W: I know. But __________ __________ __________ __________, and the meeting is in 30 minutes.

M: Yeah, I know. You'll need to go down to the human resources department and use theirs.

W: I need color copies, though. Theirs is only black and white.

M: Well, otherwise you'll have to wait until __________ __________ __________ __________ __________.

W: I can't wait that long. Do you think the Internet cafe down the road has a color printer?

M: I'm not sure, but I can __________ __________ __________ __________ and you can call them.

W: That would be great, Bill. Thanks for helping out.

M: No problem.

08

M: Hey, Sammie. How's everything at your new school?

W: It's all right. I'm starting to __________ __________ __________ __________ __________.

M: That's great. Hey, you remember Jeff, right? Well, we're going to the beach for the weekend.

W: That's cool. So, I guess he got back from his semester in Barcelona.

M: That's right. We're going to the beach to catch up and __________ __________ __________ __________. You should come with us.

W: I'd love to, but I don't think I can. I have a lot of homework to do.

M: School is __________ __________ __________ on the weekends, too?

W: Sometimes. This weekend is especially busy. I have a big chemistry report due on Monday, and an English exam on Tuesday.

M: Sounds like __________ __________ __________ __________.

W: You're right. I've been stressed out all week.

09

W: Honey, how about going to Grove Beach tomorrow?

M: Isn't it too far from here? __________ __________ __________ __________ __________ to get over the mountain on those curvy roads.

W: We don't have to go that way anymore. We can go on the new highway that opened last month.

M: Really? You mean we don't have to drive on __________ __________, __________ __________ __________?

W: Right. It only takes about 15 minutes to get over the mountain using the highway.

M: Wow, that's fantastic.

W: But it's not free. We have to pay for it.

M: How much is it?

W: Well, the government's original plan was to charge $5. But civil organizations requested that they __________ __________ __________.

M: So was it lowered?

W: Yeah, the government __________ __________ __________ $2 less than they originally planned.

M: Oh, great.

10

M: Darling, would you like to come camping with us next Saturday?

W: I don't know. I'm not sure I'll have fun there.

M: Sure you will. The lake is so pretty. I can teach you how to build a fire and set up a tent.

W: All right, I'll come. But you need to __________ __________ __________ __________ __________ __________ so I don't get bored.

M: Sure, sweetheart. The area we're going to __________ __________ __________ __________. You can look it up online if you like.

W: How far away is it from here?

M: It's about three and a half hours by car, but __________ __________ __________ __________ __________ is so beautiful.

W: That sounds nice, actually. So, what do we eat while we're up there?

M: We'll eat the fish that we catch, and of course we'll have other food too, like hot dogs and hamburgers.

W: All right. Do you need any help packing for the trip?

M: Nope! __________ __________ __________ __________ __________ __________. Your only job is to be my company!

11

M: Good morning, everyone. As you know, the weather is warming up, which means it's about time to kick off Georgetown's Musical Mondays by the river. The first event is __________ __________ next Monday, April 22nd at six o'clock. The famous blues band Back Section Action will be coming to perform at Riverside Park. The lead singer of the band will meet with fans after the show. The band will __________ __________ __________ at six o'clock and finish at around eight. As with all of our events, this is __________ __________-__________ __________, so bring your friends and the entire family. There will be a $5 fee __________ __________ __________, and all of the proceeds will go to the Georgetown Arts and Culture Society. Thank you for your time.

12

M: Hey sweetheart, I think that we should start teaching Adam how to ride his bike __________ __________ __________.

W: That's a great idea, but I don't think it's safe to do it around here. The streets are too busy.

M: Well, I found __________ __________ __________ __________ __________ at Freedom Park. These instructors specialize in teaching children to ride for the first time.

W: That's really cool.

M: I thought so, too. So, do you think we should hire a male or female instructor?

W: I think we should go with a woman. He really seems to prefer his female teachers at school.

M: Great. Well, he can't take the class with this one. He has baseball practice on Mondays.

W: Of the two that are left, I think we should go for the one __________ __________ __________.

M: I agree. It looks like we've found our instructor.

13

W: So Larry, __________ __________ __________ __________ __________ __________ __________ this year's talent show?

M: I'm not so sure.

W: Why not? You're great at juggling, and you've been working so hard at it.

M: I'm just worried that I'll make a mistake and everyone will laugh at me.

W: You need to be confident and believe in yourself, Larry. __________ __________ __________ __________ __________ __________ __________ when they perform in front of people.

M: Thanks for trying to help, Mom.

W: Well, are you going to __________ __________ __________ __________?

M: Hmm. . . I still don't know.

W: Come on! Show some confidence! It's not like you to be afraid!

M: After my disaster onstage last year, I'm not sure if I have it in me.

W: Relax. __________ __________ __________ __________ and everyone makes mistakes.

M: So, you think I'll do better this year?

W: (I'm sure. You've been practicing hard.)

14

W: Nicholas, I think I saw you in the city the other day. You were talking to a very attractive woman.

M: Ah, I remember that. I was talking to Clarice Heisenberg. She works for the family business. She handles all of our overseas accounts.

W: __________ __________ __________ __________ eavesdrop, but I couldn't help noticing that you were speaking in a different language.

M: Yes, Clarice is from Germany. She can speak English, but it's easier for her to speak German, and I like practicing.

W: __________ __________ __________ you spoke German.

M: Yes, I actually was born in Germany and lived there for 10 years as a child.

W: Really? I had no idea. Why did you live in Germany?

M: My father's business was based there.

W: That is so interesting. Will you ever __________ __________ __________ __________?

M: (Yes. I'll go back when my kids are a bit older.)

15

M: A severe tornado recently destroyed a neighboring town, so Greg and Henry held a charity event to __________ __________ __________ __________ __________. The event was a success because many caring individuals donated money and basic necessities like canned goods and bottled water. Greg and Henry delivered the goods to the victims, who

__________ __________ __________ __________ the donations. Greg and Henry have decided that they would like to show thanks to those who donated. Henry thinks that __________ __________ __________ __________. Greg agrees that email would be convenient, but he feels that they should send handwritten notes because they are more personal and sincere. In this situation, what would Greg most likely say to Henry?

Greg: (I think that handwritten thank-you notes are the best way to show appreciation.)

16-17

M: This summer has been rather hot, hasn't it? In fact, the entire Earth is getting hotter and hotter because of global warming. If you want to __________ __________ __________ __________ __________ __________, wear proper clothing. Light colors reflect light, and with it heat, but dark colors absorb it. So wearing lighter colors will keep you cooler. You should also __________ __________ __________ __________ __________ when you're not using them. For example, phone chargers don't need to be plugged in if the phone is not charging. Also, to stay cool, __________ __________ __________ __________ __________ with a clock. Microwaves and coffee makers are good examples of electronics with clocks that __________ __________ __________ __________ __________. Computers also generate a lot of heat, so you should shut down your computer if you're not using it. Lastly, stay downstairs if possible. A basement is always cooler than the rest of the house. Normally it's about five to ten degrees cooler than the other floors.

01

대화를 듣고, 여자의 마지막 말에 대한 남자의 응답으로 가장 적절한 것을 고르시오.

① Me, too. I like Chinese food a lot.
② Sounds good. Let's grab some popcorn.
③ I like romance movies more than action.
④ Well, I'd like to eat dinner after the movie.
⑤ Great idea. I know a nice restaurant nearby.

02

대화를 듣고, 남자의 마지막 말에 대한 여자의 응답으로 가장 적절한 것을 고르시오.

① She should be in her office. I'll introduce you two.
② If that's the case, you should find a new office.
③ My office is on the sixth floor of this building.
④ This isn't your office. Your office is over there.
⑤ The new team member seems like a great fit.

03

다음을 듣고, 여자가 하는 말의 목적으로 가장 적절한 것을 고르시오.

① 식습관 변화의 원인을 분석하려고
② 동물 실험 반대 운동을 소개하려고
③ 채식주의자가 되는 이유를 설명하려고
④ 육식 위주 식단의 부작용을 경고하려고
⑤ 종교적 신념과 음식과의 상관관계를 알리려고

04

대화를 듣고, 남자의 의견으로 가장 적절한 것을 고르시오.

① 블루레이 재생기의 사용법을 잘 숙지하고 사용해야 한다.
② TV 자막을 활용하면 효과적으로 외국어를 학습할 수 있다.
③ 미국 드라마 시청은 영어 청취력 향상에 매우 효과적인 방법이다.
④ 너무 빠른 속도의 외국어 TV 프로그램은 외국어 습득에 방해가 된다.
⑤ 청각 장애를 가진 사람들을 위해 자막이 있는 프로그램을 늘려야 한다.

05

대화를 듣고, 두 사람이 대화하고 있는 장소로 가장 적절한 곳을 고르시오.

① 세미나실　　　② 음반 매장　　　③ 악기 판매점
④ 종합 경기장　　⑤ 밴드 대회장

06

대화를 듣고, 그림에서 대화의 내용과 일치하지 <u>않는</u> 것을 고르시오.

07

대화를 듣고, 여자가 남자에게 부탁한 일로 가장 적절한 것을 고르시오.

① to clean out the closets
② to prepare food for dinner
③ to call ahead to the restaurant
④ to feed the dogs before dinner
⑤ to turn off all the lights in the house

08

대화를 듣고, 남자가 내일 오토바이를 타러 갈 수 <u>없는</u> 이유를 고르시오.

① 출장 준비를 해야 해서
② 회사 일이 늦게 끝나서
③ 오토바이를 수리해야 해서
④ 가족 모임에 참석해야 해서
⑤ 여동생 이사를 도와줘야 해서

09

대화를 듣고, 두 사람이 공항을 향해 출발할 시각을 고르시오.

① 6시 ② 5시 ③ 5시 30분
④ 4시 30분 ⑤ 4시

10

대화를 듣고, 중고 판매점에 관해 두 사람이 언급하지 <u>않은</u> 것을 고르시오.

① 매장의 위치 ② 매장의 규모 ③ 폐점 시간
④ 할인 혜택 ⑤ 택배 서비스

11

Melon plant에 관한 다음 내용을 듣고, 일치하지 <u>않는</u> 것을 고르시오.

① 남아메리카의 남쪽 지역이 원산지이다.
② 오렌지색 꽃은 봄에 2주간 볼 수 있다.
③ 야생 꿀벌에 의해 수분이 이루어진다.
④ 열매는 달고 즙이 많아 사람이 먹을 수 있다.
⑤ 씨는 심한 화상 치료를 위한 연고로 만들어진다.

12

다음 표를 보면서 대화를 듣고, 두 사람이 구입할 태블릿 컴퓨터를 고르시오.

Tablet Computers

	Model	Price	Screen Size	Warranty
①	ZX-1	$169	7 inch	2 Years
②	ZX-2	$219	10 inch	2 Years
③	LV-101	$199	8 inch	1 Year
④	LVX-101	$279	10.4 inch	1 Year
⑤	Ai-6	$299	11 inch	1 Year

13

대화를 듣고, 여자의 마지막 말에 대한 남자의 응답으로 가장 적절한 것을 고르시오.

Man: ____

① That's incredible. Isn't technology amazing?
② You should get fitted for C-Braces right away.
③ I appreciate the advice. I'll get a new set of crutches.
④ That's right. I'm going to be able to walk again soon.
⑤ I heard that people with your condition can walk again.

14

대화를 듣고, 남자의 마지막 말에 대한 여자의 응답으로 가장 적절한 것을 고르시오.

Woman: ____

① I'm sure you can find a balanced solution.
② I need some help downloading this new game.
③ It's too expensive for kids to play sports these days.
④ Can you tell me the name of the baseball team he plays on?
⑤ I think you need newer hardware in order to play that game.

15

다음 상황 설명을 듣고, Michael이 아내에게 할 말로 가장 적절한 것을 고르시오.

Michael: ____

① I turned in the report last week.
② Let me know if I can help you with it.
③ The documents are on the kitchen table.
④ Will you bring the documents to my office?
⑤ Could you help me a bit with the report, please?

[16-17] 다음을 듣고, 물음에 답하시오.

16

여자가 하는 말의 목적으로 가장 적절한 것은?

① to explain how to effectively avoid mouth breathing
② to emphasize the delicacy of the respiratory organs
③ to highlight the importance of nose breathing
④ to explain the benefits of breathing filtered air
⑤ to describe several methods of breathing

17

Mouth breathing의 단점으로 언급되지 않은 것은?

① 불면증 유발 ② 폐에 불순물 유입
③ 질병 감염에 대한 취약성 ④ 폐에 찬 공기 유입
⑤ 호흡기 염증 유발

13 DICTATION

01

W: We've got some time before the movie starts. Let's have dinner.

M: Good. _________ _________. What are you in the mood for?

W: I'd like to eat Japanese food. What about you?

M: (Great idea. I know a nice restaurant nearby.)

02

M: So, I just started working here and I have no idea _________ _________ _________ _________.

W: _________ _________ _________ _________ the marketing manager, Sarah, about it.

M: Do you know where she is? I've never met her.

W: (She should be in her office. I'll introduce you two.)

03

W: In our last session, we learned that not eating meat is common in many religions, especially Buddhism and Hinduism. In today's session, I want to look at some other reasons for not eating meat and becoming a vegetarian. Many people choose vegetarianism because they _________ _________ _________ _________ _________ _________ _________ _________. They believe eating less animal meat and more fiber will _________ _________ _________ _________ _________ heart disease, cancer, and diabetes. Vegetarians also have ethical concerns. They don't like that certain animals, like cows and chickens, are fed different chemicals to make them bigger. There are also _________ _________ _________ _________ _________ _________ _________ _________ for any reason at all. Can you think of any other reasons for being a vegetarian? Please share your ideas with us.

04

W: Is that a Blu-ray player? It looks a little different.

M: It actually provides subtitles for people with hearing disabilities.

W: Really? That is a very interesting idea. I didn't know that technology was available.

M: Well, _________ _________ _________ _________ every TV show. But it works with most, and you can order more online.

W: But you don't have a _________ _________. Why do you have this machine?

M: Because we're _________ _________ _________ _________ live with us for a year, and I thought it would help her with her English skills.

W: That's very thoughtful of you, but how do you know she likes to watch TV?

M: We asked her in an email. She said she loves to watch American dramas, but the dialogue is sometimes so fast that she can't understand it.

W: Well, then this thing should really help her.

M: I hope so. It wasn't cheap.

05

W: Wow! This place is _________-_________. It's so loud!

M: Yeah, today is the last day of the competition. The final four bands are going to start playing soon.

W: Right. I didn't know it'd be this noisy and crowded in here.

M: It's a rock 'n' roll competition, Clara. Of course it's going to be noisy.

W: I thought so, but I didn't expect this. This is madness.

M: Yeah. It's incredible, isn't it? The annual Battle of the Bands competition _________ _________ _________ _________ in the past few years.

W: For sure. I guess the bands all saved their best songs for this performance, huh?

M: Yeah, my brother said that his band is going to _________ _________ _________, _________ _________ for the finals.

W: That makes a lot of sense.

M: I'm really looking forward to seeing him play.

W: Me, too.

06

M: Hey, Maro. What are you looking at?

W: It's a picture of my cat, Dubu, and me. Have a look.

M: *[Pause]* You look so young in this picture. __________ __________ __________ __________ ?

W: It must've been soon after I got Dubu. I used to wear glasses, you know.

M: I've never seen you wear them. I like Dubu's color. It's such a nice, solid grey.

W: Yeah. What do you think about the shirt?

M: I think it's kind of cheesy—I don't really like polka dots. Is that a heart pendant __________ __________ __________ __________ __________ ?

W: Yeah, I thought it was cute so I bought it for him. He's also playing with his favorite toy.

M: It's a ball, right?

W: That's right. I buy him new toys all the time, but __________ __________ __________ __________ __________ .

M: That's cool. He seems like a nice cat.

07

W: Finally, we're finished cleaning the house.

M: Yeah, but it wasn't easy. I had no idea it would be such hard work.

W: __________ __________ __________ __________ it's really hot outside today, either.

M: But in the end, we did a great job. Everything looks much nicer.

W: I agree. Oh, look at the time. We __________ __________ __________ . What should we make?

M: I don't want to make anything. Let's get out of the house and go somewhere for dinner. We deserve it.

W: Good idea. I don't want to __________ __________ __________ in the kitchen, since we just cleaned it.

M: That's right. I just want to relax and enjoy the rest of my day.

W: Will you __________ __________ __________ before we go? I want to wash up quickly for dinner.

M: Of course.

W: Thank you, dear.

08

W: Hey, Marcus. Is your motorcycle out of the shop yet?

M: Yeah, I got to ride it to work this morning. __________ __________ __________ __________ __________ __________ . What do you say we go on a ride after work today?

W: I don't think I can. Let's go tomorrow afternoon.

M: Saturday afternoon? Why not tonight?

W: Well, you know how we have that big business trip next week? __________ __________ __________ __________ __________ __________ before I leave work today.

M: Oh. But I don't think I can go for a ride tomorrow.

W: Why not? Do you have something planned for the weekend?

M: Yeah, I have to meet my sister tomorrow morning.

W: What're you going to do?

M: She's moving into a new apartment, and she needs my help.

W: __________ __________ . Anyway, I hope you enjoy spending time with your sister. We'll find some time to go riding soon.

M: Sounds good.

09

M: I can't believe it's already been a year since Marcia left.

W: I know it. I can't wait to catch up with her.

M: When does her flight arrive from Korea?

W: It should be here at 6 p.m.

M: Okay, then we should leave here at around five to make sure we __________ __________ __________ __________ .

W: Yeah, but there's a lot of traffic these days because of road work. I think we need to leave earlier.

M: Okay, how about half an hour earlier?

W: Good idea. I'm going to go to the grocery store now and pick up some things for dinner tonight.

M: __________ __________ __________ __________ __________ __________ to leave?

W: Of course. See you then.

M: Okay, great. Make sure you're not late. Today is really important!

W: I know. __________ __________ __________ __________ .

10

W: Hey Jason, did you buy the computer game for next month's competition?

M: Yeah, I picked it up at Big Panda's Resale Shop. It looks brand new, and I only paid $15 for it.

W: Really? That's _________ _________ _________ _________ _________ _________ _________ a new one. How far away is this shop?

M: It's right down the street, near the old high school.

W: So it's quite close.

M: It is. It's in a _________-_________ _________ that's full of used books, games, and movies.

W: Wow! That's quite big. I think I'll go down there and have a look for some games as well. What time does it close?

M: I think it closes at 10 p.m., but you should probably call first to make sure.

W: That's a good idea.

M: Oh! Also, if you show them your student ID, they'll _________ _________ _________ _________ _________ _________ _________.

W: That's awesome! I appreciate the help.

11

W: This morning, I'd like to talk about the melon plant. _________ _________ _________ southern regions of South America, and its orange blossoms can be seen at midnight every night for two weeks in the spring. _________ _________ _________ wild honey bees that inhabit the area. When pollinated, the blossoms appear to glow at night. The fruit which the plant produces is a special kind of melon found only in this specific area. Its taste is similar to watermelon or cantaloupe, very sweet and juicy. However, the fruit cannot be eaten because the bees that pollinate the melon plant are poisonous and _________ _________ _________ _________ _________ their poison in the plant. Even though the fruits cannot be eaten, their seeds _________ _________ _________ _________ _________ _________ used to treat severe sunburn.

12

M: Hey sweetie, I think it's about time we got a new tablet. The one we have is too old and slow.

W: I've noticed that, too. Have you found any that you like?

M: I have. I've made _________ _________ _________ _________ _________ _________. Take a look.

W: *[Pause]* I think this one looks all right. It's the cheapest, too.

M: Yeah, it's cheap. But it's not very big. It's actually smaller than the one we have.

W: Really? Well, this one has the biggest screen. It's also a really popular brand.

M: I've been thinking about that one. _________ _________ _________ _________ _________ _________ spending more than $250 on a tablet, though. Let's find something a bit cheaper.

W: All right. So that means that we should decide between these two. This one is more expensive, but _________ _________ _________ _________ _________.

M: Yeah, I think the longer warranty is important. If it breaks, we can replace it pretty easily.

W: All right. Let's get this one, then.

13

M: Hey, Lana. Where's your wheelchair?

W: I didn't bring it today.

M: So _________ _________ _________ now, then?

W: Nope. I don't need crutches either.

M: I see. So how are you going to get around? _________ _________ _________ _________ without help.

W: I can walk without a wheelchair or crutches now. I don't ever have to use them again.

M: What? That's impossible! You've been unable to walk your whole life!

W: I just got fitted for C-Braces.

M: What are C-Braces?

W: They're special, computer-controlled braces that I can attach to my legs and walk without any other help. They're a brand-new technology.

M: So you mean you're basically able to walk now?

W: That's right. I can _________ _________ _________ _________ _________ _________.

M: (That's incredible. Isn't technology amazing?)

14

W: What are you up to, George?

M: I'm downloading a new game on my computer.

W: Why are you downloading another new game?

M: Well, Teddy loves these educational games and they're free, so ________ ________ ________ ________ ________.

W: Don't you think he has enough games already?

M: I don't think so. He's at an age where he learns so fast.

W: I see. But if you download too many games, then ________ ________ ________ ________ and not want to go outside and play.

M: I'm not worried about that. We also ________ ________ ________ ________ gymnastics and baseball.

W: I think that's a good idea, but those activities are only twice a week. He can play games every day.

M: Yeah, I see your point. ________ ________ ________ ________ ________ ________ he can spend on the computer.

W: (I'm sure you can find a balanced solution.)

15

W: Michael has ________ ________ ________ ________ ________ ________ at work today. He submitted his last report a couple of days late because ________ ________ ________ ________ ________ ________ ________. His boss wasn't happy with the delay, so he's very motivated to get this one in on time. Once he arrives at work, he ________ ________ ________ to take out the documents and finds that they're not there. He panics at first and doesn't know how to react. He calls his wife at home and she tells him he has left them on the kitchen table. He's glad that he hasn't lost the report, but ________ ________ ________ ________ ________ ________ ________. In this situation, what would Michael most likely say to his wife?

Michael: (Will you bring the documents to my office?)

16-17

W: Good afternoon, everyone. I want to talk to you all today about how breathing properly can really benefit your overall health. First, you should breathe through your nose. Mouth breathing is more common, but using your nose is actually more natural and therefore healthier. ________ ________ ________ ________ ________ ________ against all of the impurities that can be found in the air we breathe. Mouth breathing doesn't purify the air at all, so things like dust and dirt don't get filtered out. This can ________ ________ ________ ________ ________ ________ ________ or some other airborne illness. Breathing with your mouth also allows cold air to enter the lungs, which can ________ ________ ________ ________ ________ ________ ________. Breathing through your nose, however, ________ ________ ________ and gives you more energy. By filtering and keeping the air warm, the nasal passages only allow in air that is fit to enter the lungs. This means that all of the delicate organs that depend on air will work their best.

1번부터 17번까지는 듣고 답하는 문제입니다. 1번부터 15번까지는 한 번만 들려주고, 16번부터 17번까지는 두 번 들려줍니다. 방송을 잘 듣고 답을 하시기 바랍니다.

01

대화를 듣고, 남자의 마지막 말에 대한 여자의 응답으로 가장 적절한 것을 고르시오.

① I'm ready to go to the match.
② We should go see a movie instead.
③ We should leave tomorrow morning.
④ You forgot to turn in your homework.
⑤ It shouldn't take more than 15 minutes.

02

대화를 듣고, 여자의 마지막 말에 대한 남자의 응답으로 가장 적절한 것을 고르시오.

① Thanks for closing the windows.
② The weather is wonderful today.
③ You're right. I've been exercising often.
④ It's really rewarding to help other people.
⑤ I think I caught a cold from my classmate.

03

다음을 듣고, 남자가 하는 말의 목적으로 가장 적절한 것을 고르시오.

① 스포츠 광장에서 개최하는 프로그램을 소개하려고
② 공원 내 스포츠 광장 건립의 필요성을 강조하려고
③ 새로 개장한 스포츠 광장의 이용을 장려하려고
④ 공원 내 스포츠 광장 건립 계획에 반대하려고
⑤ 공원 시설에 대한 개선 및 보수를 촉구하려고

04

대화를 듣고, 두 사람이 하는 말의 주제로 가장 적절한 것을 고르시오.

① 다양한 민간요법의 재료
② 청결한 등산화의 중요성
③ 음식물 쓰레기 처리 방법
④ 바나나 껍질의 다양한 용도
⑤ 바나나를 주재료로 한 요리

05

대화를 듣고, 두 사람의 관계를 가장 잘 나타낸 것을 고르시오.

① 소설가 — 학생
② 평론가 — 기자
③ 영화감독 — 교사
④ 가수 — 공연 기획자
⑤ 영화관 직원 — 배우

06

대화를 듣고, 그림에서 대화의 내용과 일치하지 <u>않는</u> 것을 고르시오.

07

대화를 듣고, 여자가 남자에게 부탁한 일로 가장 적절한 것을 고르시오.

① 애완용 새 사주기
② 새집 만들어 주기
③ 새들한테 모이 주기
④ 새들이 많은 길 산책하기
⑤ 새들을 위해 같이 나무 심기

08

대화를 듣고, 남자가 콘서트에 갈 수 <u>없는</u> 이유를 고르시오.

① 표가 매진돼서
② 콘서트가 취소돼서
③ 어머니가 팔을 다쳐서
④ 상사 대신 출장을 가야 해서
⑤ 남동생의 결혼식에 참석해야 해서

09

대화를 듣고, 여자가 지불할 총 금액을 고르시오.

① $112　　② $116　　③ $120　　④ $132　　⑤ $140

10

대화를 듣고, 여드름 피부 관리 방법에 관해 여자가 언급하지 <u>않은</u> 것을 고르시오.

① 깨끗한 피부를 유지하기　　② 여드름을 자극하지 않기
③ 여드름에 연고 바르기　　④ 여드름을 짜지 말기
⑤ 기름진 음식 피하기

11

Maple syrup에 관한 다음 내용을 듣고, 일치하지 <u>않는</u> 것을 고르시오.

① 식민지화 이전부터 사용되었다.
② 주로 상처 치료에 널리 사용되었다.
③ 캐나다 퀘벡이 세계 최대 생산지이다.
④ 옥수수 시럽보다 영양분이 더 풍부하다.
⑤ 심장병을 예방하고 면역 체계를 강화한다.

12

다음 표를 보면서 대화를 듣고, 남자가 선택한 전자레인지를 고르시오.

Microwave Ovens

	Model	Price	Power (Watts)	Rotate	Size (Cubic feet)
①	A	$90	950	X	0.7
②	B	$130	950	O	0.9
③	C	$190	1200	O	0.9
④	D	$240	1200	X	1.2
⑤	E	$270	1200	O	1.2

13

대화를 듣고, 여자의 마지막 말에 대한 남자의 응답으로 가장 적절한 것을 고르시오.

Man: ________________________________

① French is more difficult than English.
② It seems that we should depend on theories.
③ They say fluency is more important than accuracy.
④ The theories emphasize the use of correct grammar.
⑤ They point out that theory and practice are different.

14

대화를 듣고, 남자의 마지막 말에 대한 여자의 응답으로 가장 적절한 것을 고르시오.

Woman: ________________________________

① I'll be sure that I invite her to the party.
② Sure. I can do that. I'd be happy to help.
③ Great. I'll take some pictures after lunch.
④ I made the collage and it looks really nice.
⑤ Sounds good. I'll be sure to bring some snacks.

15

다음 상황 설명을 듣고, Neil이 아내에게 할 말로 가장 적절한 것을 고르시오.

Neil: ________________________________

① I've always wanted to take a long trip like this.
② Now that I'm retired, I can go fishing whenever I want.
③ I really hope we can find something interesting to do.
④ I think we should go on a backpacking trip together.
⑤ I guess you're right. Traveling that long is too difficult for me.

[16-17] 다음을 듣고, 물음에 답하시오.

16

남자가 하는 말의 목적으로 가장 적절한 것은?

① to provide tricks on keeping fruit fresh
② to warn of the dangers of skipping breakfast
③ to recommend the best time of day to eat apples
④ to offer new and exciting ways to enjoy breakfast
⑤ to suggest eating fruit in the morning to benefit health

17

사과의 건강상 이점으로 언급되지 <u>않은</u> 것은?

① 비타민C의 공급원이다.　　② 소화를 촉진시킨다.
③ 체중 관리에 좋다.　　④ 뼈를 튼튼하게 한다.
⑤ 여러 가지 암을 예방한다.

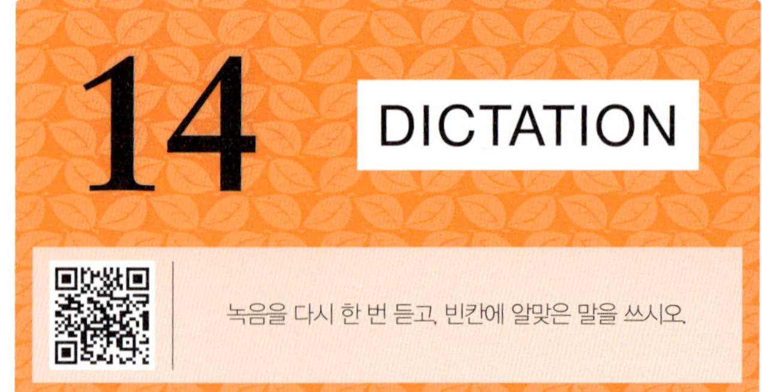

01

M: Hey Mia, are you ready to go to the tennis match yet?

W: Almost. I just need to finish __________ __________ __________ __________ __________ on my math homework.

M: __________ __________ __________ do you think it will be?

W: (It shouldn't take more than 15 minutes.)

02

W: Hey Kevin, it's pretty cold in here. Let's close the windows.

M: I'm __________ __________ __________ __________ today.

W: What's the matter? __________ __________ __________ __________ __________ __________ this morning.

M: (I think I caught a cold from my classmate at school.)

03

M: Good evening, everyone. I'm Scott McGee, and I would like to talk to you all tonight about our city's plan to construct a sports arena at Central Park. I'm sure you can all agree that Central Park provides __________ __________ __________ __________ __________ __________ for everyone. We picnic there in the spring and summer, and we __________ __________ __________ __________ __________ __________ year-round. But if we allow the city to build the arena, we won't have space to do those things anymore. __________ __________ __________ __________ __________ __________ __________ __________ from people going to the arena for sports games and other events. I strongly believe that __________ __________ __________ __________ __________ __________! I would like to think everyone here shares my opinion.

04

W: Don't throw that away, Cody.

M: Why not? It's just a banana peel.

W: There are __________ __________ __________ __________ __________.

M: Yeah, I've seen you make compost out of them for the garden. Is that what you're talking about?

W: Well, yes. But there are also many other uses for banana peels. For example, did you know you could use them to __________ __________ __________ and other itchy rashes?

M: That's interesting. So, you're going to __________ __________ __________ __________ __________ in case you get bitten by a bug?

W: Well, no. I was actually going to use that peel to polish my leather shoes.

M: Oh, maybe I'll use one to polish my shoes. What else are they good for?

W: If we put them outside the window, they'll attract birds and butterflies.

M: That's cool. Now I see why you __________ __________ __________ __________ __________ __________.

05

[Telephone rings.]

W: Hello?

M: Hi, this is Ryan James. I just received your email, and I'd like to __________ __________ __________.

W: Really? That's good news. We really appreciate you taking time out of your busy schedule to visit our school.

M: Not a problem. __________ __________ __________ __________ __________ __________ at the graduation ceremony.

W: Great. __________ __________ __________ __________ __________ __________ to many of the students here at Henderson County High School.

M: Oh, I'm ecstatic to hear that from you.

W: Some of our students would love to speak to you in person. Is there any way you could __________ __________ __________-__________-__________ __________ __________ __________?

M: I don't see why not. I really respect my fans and love to hear from them, especially the young ones.

W: I'm sure they'll be excited to get to __________ __________ __________ __________.

06

M: I like what you did to your dorm room, Clara.

W: Thanks. It was pretty tough moving the desk and the bed.

M: Is that __________ __________ __________ on your bed?

W: Yeah, I've had it since I was young. His name is Geoffrey, and he's a giraffe.

M: Cool. Oh, nice map. Are the pins in it __________ __________ __________ __________ __________ __________?

W: That's right. I put the whiteboard next to it to write my schedule on. I'm really forgetful, you know.

M: I also like that lamp. __________ __________ __________ __________ the room well.

W: That was another gift I got from my grandmother.

M: That's a nice laptop on your desk. Did you bring it from home?

W: Yes, my father gave it to me __________ __________ __________ __________.

M: Well, your room __________ __________ __________ __________ __________ than mine. I like it.

W: Oh? Now I'm curious to see your room.

07

W: I've always liked this trail, Dad.

M: I'm glad to hear that. It's always been one of my favorites, too.

W: I love seeing all of the pretty birds.

M: Yes, there are a lot of them out here.

W: Dad, __________ __________ __________ __________?

M: Birds live in the trees. They build bird homes called nests in the branches way up high.

W: Do birds __________ __________ __________ __________ __________?

M: I'm not sure about that, sweetheart. I think there are birds that don't have houses, though.

W: Really? That's sad. Can we build houses for them?

M: If you __________ __________ __________ __________ __________ __________ __________, then sure we can.

W: I really do, Dad. I want all birds to have nice homes.

M: All right. Then next weekend, we'll build some birdhouses and __________ __________ __________ __________ __________.

W: Great! Thanks, Dad.

08

W: Why are you __________ __________ __________ today, Jim?

M: You know I've been looking forward to Eric Benet's concert. He's my favorite singer.

W: Of course. You've been very excited. What's the matter?

M: __________ __________ __________ __________ I can't go to the concert.

W: Why not? __________ __________ __________ __________?

M: No. I have to go to Shanghai for a meeting.

W: Wasn't __________ __________ __________ __________ __________ that meeting?

M: Yes, he was. But he broke his arm playing tennis last Sunday, so he can't go.

W: That's too bad. What are you going to do with your ticket?

M: I already gave it to my brother.

W: You mean the one who got married last year?

M: Yes. He was so happy about the ticket.

W: Good for him. __________ __________ __________ __________ __________ see Eric Benet someday, Jim.

09

M: Hi. Is there something I can help you with today?

W: I'm looking for some hiking boots. Can I __________ __________ __________ __________ those leather ones?

M: Those are actually men's shoes.

W: I know. I'm shopping for my teenage son. How much are they?

M: They were originally $100, but __________ __________ __________ __________ __________ for 20% off. They were very popular last season. I'm sure he'd like them.

W: I think so, too. I'll take a pair in size 9. Oh! I also need a couple of hiking poles for the two of us.

M: Sure. We have those in pink, purple, green, or blue.

W: I'll take one in purple and one in blue, please. How much are they?

M: They're $20 apiece.

W: Does that 20% discount __________ __________ __________ __________ __________ as well?

M: I'm sorry, but the discount only applies to the shoes.

W: That's all right. Here's my card.

10

M: Oh, no! There are so many pimples on my face.

W: It's just a little acne. It's totally normal to have that __________ __________ __________ __________ __________. By the time you're out of your teens, it will have gone away almost completely.

M: Yeah, I understand all of that. But I still don't like looking at all of these pimples.

W: It's not fun, I know.

M: What should I do about it?

W: Just be sure to keep your skin clean and clear and __________ __________ __________ __________ __________.

M: All right. I can do that.

W: When you see a pimple, you should resist __________ __________ __________ __________ __________.

M: Really? I want to get rid of them right away, though.

W: Most people do, but popping them only makes it worse.

M: Do certain foods cause acne?

W: If __________ __________ __________ __________, you should avoid greasy foods.

11

W: Today I'm going to tell you a little bit about the sweet treat that we call *maple syrup*. __________ __________ __________, the native peoples of North America collected this syrup by tapping into maple trees and collecting the liquid sap that seeped out. They found that maple syrup was a natural sweetener that could be included in many of their recipes. Today, Quebec, a province in Canada, is the world's largest producer of maple syrup. It produces about __________-__________ __________ __________ __________ __________. Compared to other sweeteners, such as cane sugar or corn syrup, maple syrup is __________ __________ __________ of important vitamins and nutrients. Many doctors believe that __________ __________ __________ __________ __________ __________ __________ __________ each day can help prevent heart disease as well as __________ __________ __________ __________.

12

W: Hi. Is there something I can help you find?

M: Yes. I'm looking to buy a new microwave. What do you recommend?

W: Okay, have a look at this one.

M: __________ __________ __________ __________ __________ __________, given that it costs less than $100.

W: You might be right. What about this one? We just got this model in last week. It seems really popular.

M: It's visually appealing, but it has the same amount of power as the cheap one. I'm looking for a more powerful model.

W: Okay. This one is also quite popular, and it's just as new. It also came in last week.

M: What are __________ __________ __________ __________?

W: Well, it rotates, but it's pretty small. Its interior is only 0.9 cubic feet.

M: We heat up some pretty large dishes around my house so I think a larger one would probably be better.

W: Okay. How about this one?

M: It looks great. It rotates, and the interior looks bigger. Oh, the sticker on the panel says it's 1.2 cubic feet. I think I'll take this one.

W: Great. I'll help you load it into the cart, and you can take it to the front to check out.

13

W: Issac, how do you like our French teacher?

M: I think he's all right, but you don't really seem to like him.

W: I just think __________ __________ __________
__________ __________ and not enough basic
grammar.

M: You don't like that?

W: I don't really like it because I think grammar is the
most important part of __________ __________
__________ __________.

M: Are there any recent studies that support your idea?

W: Not really.

M: Well, why do you think so?

W: I mean, if you don't speak using ______________
__________ __________, you'll sound funny.

M: __________ __________ __________ __________
on the basis of many recent theories of language
education.

W: Really? What do those theories say?

M: (They say fluency is more important than accuracy.)

14

M: Hey Stacy, __________ __________ __________
__________ __________ this weekend?

W: I'm not sure yet. Why do you ask?

M: I'm __________ __________ __________ __________
__________ for Bruno. He's turning 30. I think he'd
like it if you came.

W: That sounds great. I was wondering if he was going
to have a party. I'm glad to come.

M: Cool. Well, I want everyone to be at my house by
5 o'clock.

W: That's perfect for me. Do you __________ __________
__________ __________ __________ __________
__________? I can pick up some snacks or something.

M: I think we'll have plenty of snacks. Just bring yourself.

W: Are you sure I can't __________ __________
__________ __________? Bruno is a great friend. I'd
like to show him how much he means to us.

M: Well, in that case, there is something you can do for
the party.

W: What is it?

M: Susie is making a collage with pictures of all of us at
work. It would be great if you could help her choose
some pictures.

W: (Sure. I can do that. I'd be happy to help.)

15

M: Neil, a successful lawyer, was __________ __________
__________ __________ for years. When he finally
retired, he spent a lot of time fishing, drinking
coffee at cafes, or exercising. __________ __________
__________ __________ __________ __________
__________ __________ and has decided that he
should do something more interesting. He wants
to travel through Southeast Asia for a few months.
When Neil discusses his plans with his wife, she
refuses to go with him, saying that __________
__________ __________ __________ for that long.
__________ __________ __________ __________
__________ __________ to let him go alone because
he may never get a chance to travel again. In this
situation, what would Neil most likely say to his
wife?

Neil: (I've always wanted to take a long trip like this.)

16-17

M: How often do you eat breakfast? Do you find yourself
too busy to make time for the most important meal
of the day? Next time you're in a hurry, __________
__________ __________ __________ __________
__________ __________ the door. Fruit is a great
way to give you that much-needed morning boost.
If you have to choose just one fruit, go for an apple.
Apples are the healthiest fruit. You might remember
hearing the old proverb, "__________ __________
__________ __________ __________ __________
__________ __________." Apples are packed with
Vitamin C and __________ __________, __________
__________ __________ __________ __________
manage your weight. They're also great for
__________ __________ __________ and lowering
your cholesterol. Apples prevent heart disease and
lung, breast, colon, and liver cancer. Apples have the
nutritional benefits that'll help you lead a healthy
life. Apples are easy to eat and require very little
preparation time. So next time you're too busy for a
full breakfast, __________ __________ __________.

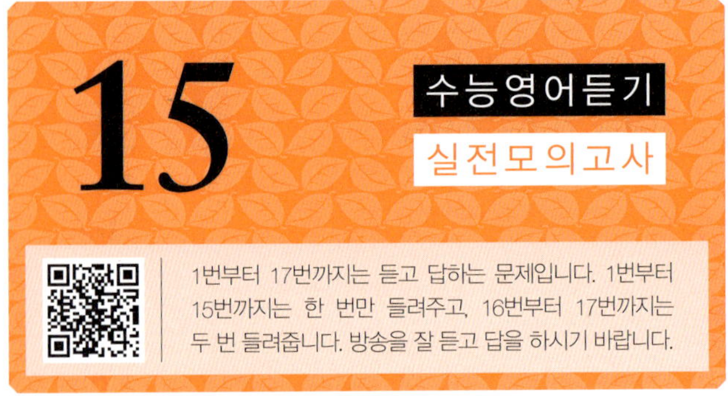

01

대화를 듣고, 여자의 마지막 말에 대한 남자의 응답으로 가장 적절한 것을 고르시오.

① I knew the shop would close eventually.
② I found out the clothes are good quality.
③ Yesterday you asked me what size I wear.
④ I shouldn't have put the box on the table.
⑤ You put the date on your phone to remember it.

02

대화를 듣고, 남자의 마지막 말에 대한 여자의 응답으로 가장 적절한 것을 고르시오.

① Thank you, but I bought a new calculator.
② You don't have to bring your lunch. It's free.
③ Please bring my science report when you come.
④ Let's meet somewhere else. The library is closed now.
⑤ I don't think we're going to use it. Just bring your textbook.

03

다음을 듣고, 남자가 하는 말의 목적으로 가장 적절한 것을 고르시오.

① 새로 개통된 지하철을 홍보하려고
② 지하철 탑승 시의 에티켓을 알려주려고
③ 도시 내 지하철의 필요성을 강조하려고
④ 지하철 공사 기금 마련을 위한 토론을 알리려고
⑤ 지하철 이용 시 불편한 점을 교통부에 항의하려고

04

대화를 듣고, 두 사람이 하는 말의 주제로 가장 적절한 것을 고르시오.

① 국립 공원 운영 자금에 대한 지원을 확대해야 하는 이유
② 국립 공원에서 애완동물에 대한 규정이 엄격한 이유
③ 국립 공원에서 애완동물 입장을 허용하는 이유
④ 국립 공원에서 야생동물에 대한 대처 방법
⑤ 국립 공원에서의 환경친화적인 캠핑 방법

05

대화를 듣고, 두 사람의 관계를 가장 잘 나타낸 것을 고르시오.

① 기자 — 평론가
② 할머니 — 손자
③ 요리사 — 식당 손님
④ 구직자 — 인사담당자
⑤ 심사위원 — 대회참가자

06

대화를 듣고, 그림에서 대화의 내용과 일치하지 <u>않는</u> 것을 고르시오.

07

대화를 듣고, 남자가 여자를 위해 할 일로 가장 적절한 것을 고르시오.

① 선물 사기
② 집안 청소 하기
③ 저녁 식사 준비하기
④ 크리스마스 계획 세우기
⑤ 공항으로 어머님 모시러 가기

08

대화를 듣고, 남자가 점심을 사무실에서 먹어야 하는 이유를 고르시오.

① 회의 시작 시간이 변경되어서
② 프레젠테이션 준비가 덜 되어서
③ 손님들이 일찍 올 것에 대비해서
④ 이메일을 확인할 시간이 필요해서
⑤ 드라이클리닝 맡긴 정장을 찾아야 해서

09

대화를 듣고, 여자가 받을 거스름돈의 액수를 고르시오.
① $15 　② $20 　③ $30 　④ $40 　⑤ $45

10

대화를 듣고, 아파트 임대에 관해 언급되지 <u>않은</u> 것을 고르시오.
① 위치 　② 가격 　③ 편의시설
④ 침실의 개수 　⑤ 선호하는 층

11

Berry Delicious Day에 관한 다음 내용을 듣고, 일치하지 <u>않는</u> 것을 고르시오.
① 행사는 토요일 오전 10시에 시작한다.
② 행사 당일에는 입장료 없이 무료로 입장할 수 있다.
③ 수확한 베리로 만든 파이로 어려운 사람들을 도울 수 있다.
④ 참가자는 활동을 위해 반바지를 입는 것이 좋다.
⑤ 애완동물을 데리고 오지 않는 것이 좋다.

12

다음 표를 보면서 대화를 듣고, 두 사람이 예약할 캠핑카를 고르시오.

RV Rental Options

	Model	Sleeping Capacity	Water Hookup	Stove & Refrigerator	Price per Day
①	Bronze	4	No	No	$140
②	Silver	5	No	Yes	$150
③	Gold	5	Yes	No	$160
④	Platinum	5	Yes	Yes	$180
⑤	Diamond	6	Yes	Yes	$200

13

대화를 듣고, 여자의 마지막 말에 대한 남자의 응답으로 가장 적절한 것을 고르시오.
Man: _______________________________________
① That's a good idea. I'll do that now.
② I gave Mrs. Garcia a key to the house.
③ We should have enough fish food to last.
④ Okay. I'll see if he can bring them to me.
⑤ Yeah. I've already turned on my cell phone.

14

대화를 듣고, 남자의 마지막 말에 대한 여자의 응답으로 가장 적절한 것을 고르시오.
Woman: _______________________________________
① The stadium doesn't open until one o'clock.
② Sure. I'll bring the materials to you as soon as I can.
③ Do you think I'll be able to cancel the presentation?
④ Not bad. When does the presentation need to be ready?
⑤ Okay. I'll give him a call and see if he can bring them to me.

15

다음 상황 설명을 듣고, Jason이 Ryan에게 할 말로 가장 적절한 것을 고르시오.
Jason: _______________________________________
① I really appreciate you being so kind to me.
② Let's get in there and try our best in this match.
③ Congratulations on winning the championship.
④ We couldn't have made it to the finals without you.
⑤ Aren't you happy that they canceled the championship?

[16-17] 다음을 듣고, 물음에 답하시오.

16

남자가 하는 말의 주제로 가장 적절한 것은?
① How people contribute to pollution
② Things to do to improve our air quality
③ The effects of pollution on the environment
④ The benefits of adopting energy-saving habits
⑤ Causes and solutions for environmental pollution

17

남자가 언급하지 <u>않은</u> 것은?
① to pick up garbage
② to recycle
③ to use solar energy
④ to use public transportation
⑤ to conserve energy

녹음을 다시 한 번 듣고, 빈칸에 알맞은 말을 쓰시오.

01

W: I've got a gift for you in this box. You'll never guess what it is!

M: Let me try to guess. Hmm. . . it's some kind of clothes, right?

W: Yes! ___________ ___________ ___________ did you know that?

M: (Yesterday you asked me what size I wear.)

02

M: Helen, could you help me with my science report after school?

W: Of course. ___________ ___________ ___________ ___________ in the library?

M: Sounds good. Do I need to bring a calculator?

W: (I don't think we're going to use it. Just bring your textbook.)

03

M: Hello, everyone. Subways are ___________ ___________ ___________ ___________ ___________-___________ ___________ of transportation for our citizens. That's why we need a subway system that reaches more people and carries them to more destinations around the city. We have contacted the Department of Transportation, but at this time they don't think there is enough money to build a subway system that ___________ ___________ ___________ ___________ ___________. It's our duty, however, to do what is best for our community, so we will be ___________ ___________ ___________ ___________ ways to raise money. This may include other social programs and services. Thanks to everyone here for taking the time to listen to my ideas.

04

M: I think I'll drive out to Yosemite National Park this weekend.

W: Really? That will be a great trip.

M: Do you know what the policies are on bringing pets into the park?

W: Actually, the national parks ___________ ___________ ___________ ___________ about pets.

M: Do they? But pets are supposed to be ___________ ___________ ___________ ___________. Why are the rules so strict?

W: Well, pets can harm smaller animals that inhabit the national parks.

M: Yeah, I guess you're right. I wouldn't want that.

W: The park's rules are also there ___________ ___________ ___________ ___________, you know.

M: How's that?

W: Well, there have been a number of cases where people's pets were attacked and sometimes killed by wild animals.

M: Oh my! Then I'll definitely ___________ ___________ ___________ ___________ ___________ for this trip. Thanks for the information.

05

W: We really enjoyed your dish this evening. You really create some unique flavors.

M: Thanks. I've been experimenting with different combinations.

W: Where did you learn to ___________ ___________ ___________ ___________ ___________? I've never seen anyone use that technique.

M: Well, I was raised by my grandmother, and I used to watch her in the kitchen. I learned everything I know from her.

W: She seems like a wonderful teacher. What were ___________ ___________ ___________ ___________ ___________?

M: I spent two years studying local flavors in southern Mexico. It really changed my perspective on the art.

W: You seem completely ___________ ___________ ___________ ___________. We're glad to have you here.

M: Thank you for giving me a chance.

W: We'd like to invite you to join us in __________ __________ __________ __________ __________ __________.

M: Really? Thank you for the opportunity.

06

W: Hey Spencer, why were you so late to the meeting this morning?

M: It's been a rough day for me. I've had so many problems.

W: Really? What happened?

M: Well, I left home really early so I could make it to the meeting on time, but there was __________ __________ __________ __________ __________.

W: I see. So they closed the road?

M: That's right. I wasn't really __________ __________, and I ran into a barrier that broke my window.

W: That's awful.

M: That's not all. My GPS couldn't __________ __________ __________, so I had to use a regular map.

W: I haven't seen one of those in years.

M: I got lost, so I had to ask a woman with a smartphone to help me.

W: Well, it's great that you can __________ __________ __________ __________ __________.

M: I suppose you're right. I guess it could have been worse.

07

M: Sweetie, I'm home. What's up?

W: I just got a phone call from my mom. She's coming to visit for the holidays!

M: That's great!

W: Yes, I think so too. But __________ __________ __________ __________ __________ __________, and I didn't plan on her coming!

M: Sweetie, it's okay. Don't worry about that.

W: I still need to prepare the house, and I haven't even __________ __________ __________ yet.

M: Let me help you. Should I work on the house or go shopping for a gift?

W: Well, since I know her tastes a little better than you, I think I should buy her gift.

M: Okay, __________ __________ __________. I'll try to get the house cleaned up a bit, then. When do you expect her to arrive?

W: Her flight arrives at 7 p.m., so I'll __________ __________ __________ __________ __________ after work tomorrow.

M: Okay. That sounds good.

08

W: Good morning, Mr. Shepherd.

M: Hello, Paula. Did you get everything prepared for my meeting this evening?

W: I spent all last night working on it, but I finally finished your presentation.

M: That's great. Did you also __________ __________ __________ __________ __________ __________ __________?

W: I did. It's in the closet in your office.

M: I really appreciate all the __________ __________ __________ __________ __________ __________. Now, let me take a look at the presentation.

W: I emailed it to you. Just check your inbox. Oh, by the way, the meeting __________ __________ __________ __________ for one o'clock.

M: What? That's too early. I won't have time to eat before the meeting.

W: Don't worry about it, sir. I've already __________ __________ for you. You can eat it here at the office.

M: Oh, great. Thanks.

09

M: Hi. Are you ready to check out?

W: Sure. I'm sorry about being a couple of minutes late.

M: That's no problem, ma'am.

W: That's good to know. The last place we stayed at __________ __________ __________ __________ __________ __________ __________ for checking out five minutes late.

M: Don't worry about it. It's no inconvenience to us if you're a couple of minutes late. Would you like me to __________ __________ __________ __________ __________?

W: No, thanks. I have the cash right here.

M: All right. It looks like your total comes to $120, and that __________ __________ __________.

W: Wait, what? You said that it was going to be $110 when we checked in yesterday.

M: That's the price of the room, but it shows here that __________ __________ __________ __________ last night.

W: I didn't realize that the movie we ordered was going to be so expensive. Here's $150.

M: All right. *[Pause]* Here's your change.

10

W: Honey, let's look in classified ads for an apartment. We have to decide on which one to rent __________ __________ __________ __________ __________ __________.

M: Right. Which area do you prefer, Demarest or Willington?

W: Actually I prefer Demarest, but the apartments there are generally a lot more expensive.

M: Then let's look at the Willington area. It's also quite __________ __________ __________ __________ __________ __________.

W: Okay. I think $2,000 a month is the most we can afford for rent.

M: I agree. What about the size? Don't you think we need at least three bedrooms?

W: Yes, you're right. The boys will want to have their own rooms.

M: They also want to live in an apartment that's above the 7th floor.

W: Same here. __________ __________ __________ __________ __________, the better the view will be.

M: Well, it won't be easy to find an apartment that __________ __________ __________ __________ __________.

11

M: Good morning, students. My name is Dustin Swift, and I'm speaking to you on behalf of Blue Mystic Berry Farm. I'd like to announce "Berry Delicious Day." Along with strawberries and blueberries, we'll also be allowing you to pick blackberries, raspberries, and boysenberries for you to harvest on Berry Delicious Day, which is this Saturday. The event begins at 10 a.m. and runs until 2 p.m. __________ __________ __________ __________, so tell your parents to bring the whole family. Some of the berries you pick will be used to make pies that will be sold to benefit the Homeless Shelter. Be sure to __________ __________. You should wear long-sleeved shirts and pants to __________ __________ __________ __________ the berry bushes. Some berries are harmful for pets, so we ask that you please __________ __________ __________ __________ __________. We hope to see you on Saturday here at Blue Mystic Berry Farm.

12

M: Hey, I've been looking at RV rentals for our camping trip this summer. I think we should make a reservation really soon.

W: Yeah, we should. We don't want to wait until it's too late.

M: Well, I found this company that __________ __________ __________ __________.

W: Let's have a look. *[Pause]* Since the whole family is going, we're going to need an RV that can sleep at least four people.

M: That's right. But maybe we should get one that's a bit bigger. I'd prefer one that sleeps at least five.

W: All right. Well, do we really need a water hookup?

M: It'll be much nicer if we have one. That way we can __________ __________.

W: All right. What about a stove and a refrigerator? We do most of our cooking outdoors.

M: I say we take that option. It's such a hassle to bring coolers to keep our food cold.

W: All right. That __________ __________ __________ to these two, then.

M: I don't think we need to spend the extra money. Let's go for the cheaper one.

W: Sounds good. Go ahead and make the reservation.

13

W: Hey sweetheart, we're going to be late. __________ __________ __________ __________?

M: I'm trying to hurry, but I think I've lost my cell phone.

W: I think I saw it on the couch earlier.

M: Ah, here it is. Okay, so is there anything else we need to take care of before we go?

W: Oh! Who's going to __________ __________ __________ while we're away?

M: Relax. Mrs. Garcia said that she'll take care of them.

W: Okay. We have to make sure to bring the tickets. __________ __________ __________ __________, right?

M: I didn't, but I have them saved on my cell phone.

W: Saved on your cell phone? Don't we have to print them out anymore?

M: Nope. I have the e-tickets right here. We just have to show them at the kiosk.

W: E-tickets, huh? __________ __________ __________ __________. Nevertheless, I think we should print them out just in case.

M: (That's a good idea. I'll do that now.)

14

[Cell phone rings.]

M: Hello?

W: Hey Charlie, this is Riley.

M: Hey, Riley. What's going on?

W: Well, __________ __________ __________ __________ __________ the EPL headquarters for the conference.

M: Are you ready to give your presentation about our new stadium?

W: I'm ready. But. . .

M: But what? Is there a problem?

W: Well, I seemed to have left all of the presentation materials on my desk in my office. __________ __________ __________ __________ __________ bring them to me?

M: I wish I could help, but there's no way I can bring them. I'm not at the office right now.

W: Well, it's already noon and the meeting starts in an hour. If I went back to pick them up, there's no way I'd __________ __________ __________ __________ __________ for the meeting.

M: That's __________ __________ __________. Give Kyle a call. He should be in the office.

W: (Okay. I'll give him a call and see if he can bring them to me.)

15

M: Ryan and Jason have just lost in the championship round of a tournament for players of the popular first-person shooter, *Counter Strike: GO*. Ryan made a couple of big mistakes early in the match; __________ __________ __________ __________ __________ __________ that they lost. Jason finds Ryan sitting outside on the sidewalk after the match. He notices that Ryan looks upset and __________ __________. Jason is not upset at all. He's actually proud that they made it to the championship. He knows that Ryan __________ __________ __________ and that they were able to make it to the championship __________ __________ __________ __________ __________, and he wants to cheer Ryan up. In this situation, what would Jason most likely say to Ryan?

Jason: (We couldn't have made it to the finals without you.)

16-17

M: These days, humans are beginning to __________ __________ __________ __________ __________ __________. There are many factors that contribute to pollution. Some of them are natural, but most of them are man-made and preventable. To start with the obvious, people often pollute streets and waterways with litter. It's our duty to pick up after ourselves to help preserve and beautify our environment. Recycling is a great way to help the environment because it __________ __________ __________ __________ __________ __________ that goes into landfills. Personal vehicles also contribute significantly to air pollution. Therefore, riding bikes or __________ __________ __________ can help the environment. Power plants also pollute our air. If we cut down on our energy usage at home, we can cut down on emissions from power plants. We should be sure to use energy-efficient bulbs and __________ __________ __________ __________. This will not only cut down on air pollution, but will also save us money.

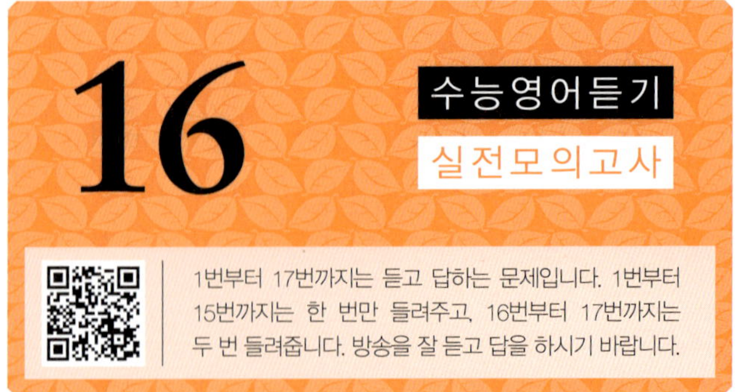

01

대화를 듣고, 남자의 마지막 말에 대한 여자의 응답으로 가장 적절한 것을 고르시오.

① Okay, please follow me there.
② I'm sorry. You'll have to wait in line.
③ *Wrong Number* is no longer showing.
④ Only balcony seating is available for that show.
⑤ No, that's not okay. You should speak to a manager.

02

대화를 듣고, 여자의 마지막 말에 대한 남자의 응답으로 가장 적절한 것을 고르시오.

① I heard the news about the environment this morning.
② I have spare coffee mugs. I can give you one.
③ Using a paper cup is so convenient.
④ You're wrong. I prefer tea to coffee.
⑤ I won't drink coffee from now on.

03

다음을 듣고, 여자가 하는 말의 목적으로 가장 적절한 것을 고르시오.

① 교내 식당의 메뉴 개선을 제안하려고
② 교내 식당의 시설 개선을 요청하려고
③ 학생들의 교내 식당 이용을 촉구하려고
④ 학교 시설에 대한 안전 점검을 요구하려고
⑤ 학생들의 학교 웹사이트 이용을 권장하려고

04

대화를 듣고, 두 사람이 하는 말의 주제로 가장 적절한 것을 고르시오.

① 휴대폰 구입 시 유의할 점
② 운전 중 휴대폰 사용의 위험성
③ 청소년들의 지나친 휴대폰 사용
④ 휴대폰 이용 시 헤드폰 사용방법
⑤ 휴대폰 사용이 건강에 미치는 영향

05

대화를 듣고, 여자의 심정으로 가장 적절한 것을 고르시오.

① embarrassed   ② guilty   ③ happy
④ relaxed   ⑤ stressed

06

대화를 듣고, 그림에서 대화의 내용과 일치하지 <u>않는</u> 것을 고르시오.

07

대화를 듣고, 남자가 여자에게 부탁한 일로 가장 적절한 것을 고르시오.

① to make a reservation
② to purchase vitamins
③ to suggest gift ideas
④ to prepare dinner
⑤ to buy a card

08

대화를 듣고, 여자가 남편에게 화가 난 이유를 고르시오.

① 휴일인데 일하러 나가서
② 집을 너무 어질러 놓고 나가서
③ 행동하기 전에 너무 많은 생각을 해서
④ 가족 사진이 들어있는 USB를 잃어버려서
⑤ 자신의 USB 드라이브를 허락 없이 가져가서

09

대화를 듣고, 여자가 지불할 금액을 고르시오.

① $100   ② $105   ③ $110   ④ $120   ⑤ $125

10

대화를 듣고, The Prized Prince에 관해 두 사람이 언급하지 <u>않은</u> 것을 고르시오.

① 판매 부수   ② 저자   ③ 출판사
④ 장르   ⑤ 영화 제작 계획

11

Science Fair에 관한 다음 내용을 듣고, 일치하지 <u>않는</u> 것을 고르시오.

① 서너 명으로 구성된 팀 단위 프로젝트이다.
② 주제는 제한 없이 자유롭게 선택하면 된다.
③ 작동이 되는 모델은 만들 필요가 없다.
④ 지원서를 5월 5일까지 제출해야 한다.
⑤ 질문이 있으면 과학 선생님께 한다.

12

다음 표를 보면서 대화를 듣고, 남자가 선택할 바퀴를 고르시오.

Mackie Performance Wheels

	Model	Wheel Size (inches)	Color	Price
①	A	22	Mixed	$950
②	B	24	Mixed	$1,100
③	C	22	Black	$900
④	D	24	Black	$1,000
⑤	E	22	Black	$1,200

*wheel: (자동차) 바퀴(휠)

13

대화를 듣고, 여자의 마지막 말에 대한 남자의 응답으로 가장 적절한 것을 고르시오.

Man: ______________________________

① I'd take the military aptitude test if I were you.
② I think you should do what you're passionate about.
③ I haven't decided what kind of career I want to pursue.
④ It's really difficult to be a successful architect these days.
⑤ You'd better collect as many military strategy books as possible.

14

대화를 듣고, 남자의 마지막 말에 대한 여자의 응답으로 가장 적절한 것을 고르시오.

Woman: ______________________________

① Yes. The old phone can't run new apps.
② His phone works well, but it's not very stylish.
③ You're right, but I don't know which one is best.
④ Right. I never owned a smartphone when I was young.
⑤ Yeah, but he's usually complaining about how slow his phone is.

15

다음 상황 설명을 듣고, Nancy가 Maya에게 할 말로 가장 적절한 것을 고르시오.

Nancy: ______________________________

① You should join the weight-loss clinic.
② I know a lot about weight loss and nutrition.
③ Overeating can cause serious health problems.
④ If you're pregnant, then you'll naturally be eating more.
⑤ Have them choose a few items that fit into your nutrition goals.

[16-17] 다음을 듣고, 물음에 답하시오.

16

여자가 하는 말의 목적으로 가장 적절한 것은?

① 먼지가 우리 몸에 주는 악영향을 설명하려고
② 청소 대행 업체인 자신의 회사를 홍보하려고
③ 알레르기 유발 물질에 대해 경고하려고
④ 먼지를 줄이는 청소 요령을 알려주려고
⑤ 새로 나온 청소도구들을 소개하려고

17

여자가 언급하지 <u>않은</u> 것은?

① 진공청소기 사용하기   ② 베개와 쿠션 털기
③ 바닥 닦기   ④ 침구 세탁하기
⑤ 환기시키기

16 DICTATION

01

M: Hi, can I have two tickets for *Wrong Number*?

W: Sure. What time would you like to see the movie?

M: 7 p.m., please. Two adults ___________ ___________ ___________ ___________.

W: (Only balcony seating is available for that show.)

02

W: Oh, I see you're using your own coffee mug.

M: Yes. Using ___________ ___________ ___________ is never good for the environment.

W: ___________ ___________ ___________ ___________. I think I should buy one for myself so that I can join you.

M: (I have spare coffee mugs. I can give you one.)

03

W: Good morning, students. Are you ___________ ___________ ___________ ___________ this afternoon? I would imagine you all say "Yes." Then, how do you feel about the cafeteria here at school? Do you think the facilities are nice? Probably not. There have been quite ___________ ___________ ___________ ___________ ___________ ___________ recently from a number of students. Some of them have even written messages on the school's website. I am one of those students. Unfortunately, I don't think the school is listening. Our cafeteria is giving our school a ___________ ___________. That reputation will continue to get worse if we don't improve the facilities. We need to ___________ ___________ ___________ soon to ensure a better school life for all of us.

04

M: Whoa, my cell phone is really heating up.

W: You really shouldn't use it for so long.

M: What do you think about ___________ ___________ ___________ ___________ ___________?

W: I know a lot of studies have shown that ___________ ___________ ___________-___________ ___________ ___________ ___________ can cause brain tumors.

M: I heard that on the radio the other day.

W: The electromagnetic waves are ___________ ___________ ___________ ___________. It's been shown in many studies.

M: I understand, but the reason I need to use my cell phone so often is for work.

W: Well, there are some ways to use it carefully. For instance, you should use earphones so that ___________ ___________ ___________ ___________ ___________ ___________ ___________ ___________.

M: All right, I'll start wearing my earphones more often.

W: There are other safety precautions you can take, too. You can look them up on the Internet.

05

M: Hey, Monica. How was the game?

W: Well, I can tell you this: I'm not going to watch another one anytime soon.

M: Why? I thought you really enjoyed football. Didn't your team do really well last year?

W: Yeah, they won the Super Bowl. But then the coach retired. They got a new one, and the team has been playing terribly!

M: Sounds like ___________ ___________ ___________ ___________ ___________ this new coach.

W: I think the team is doing worse because of him.

M: Is he really that bad?

W: Well, just look at ___________ ___________ ___________. We haven't won any away games this year.

M: Relax. I'm sure they will do better later in the season.

W: I hope so, but ___________ ___________ ___________ ___________. They lost to a team much weaker than them last week.

M: What about the game today?

W: They played one of the best teams in the league, so of course they lost.

06

W: This here is your office, Mr. Smith.

M: Wow! It's __________ __________ __________ __________ __________. Look out the window. What a wonderful view of the mountains!

W: It's lovely, isn't it? That's why we put the chair __________ __________ __________.

M: That's great. And I guess that's my new laptop on the desk.

W: It sure is. We just bought it last week. It should have everything you need already loaded onto it.

M: __________ __________ __________ __________ __________ __________ about that clock, though.

W: What do you mean?

M: Look at how big it is. And it's so distracting.

W: You're __________ __________ __________ __________ __________ __________, if you'd like.

M: How did you know I love coffee?

W: You look like a coffee drinker, Mr. Smith. I'm just kidding. All of our offices have an electric coffee pot in them. Anyway, welcome to our building.

M: Thank you very much.

07

M: Linda, __________ __________ __________ __________ __________ __________ for Dad's retirement party?

W: Yeah, I have a couple of choices in mind. The first is a new Mexican grill and the other is a Greek restaurant.

M: Well, you know Dad loves Greek food, so why don't we go to the Greek restaurant?

W: __________ __________ __________ __________.

M: Also, have you bought him a gift yet?

W: I haven't. Have you?

M: I haven't, either. We could buy a gift together. Maybe we could __________ __________ __________ __________ __________ he likes.

W: That's a wonderful gift idea.

M: All right, great. I'll pick some up while I'm at work tomorrow. __________ __________ __________ __________ __________?

W: Sure. I know a great place.

08

M: Perfect. I'll see you tomorrow, then.

W: Okay. See you then.

08

W: Thanks for cleaning up the living room, Thomas.

M: No problem, Mom.

W: Hey, __________ __________ __________, have you seen my USB drive?

M: I don't think so. Why?

W: Well, I thought I __________ __________ __________ __________ __________ __________, but I can't seem to find it today.

M: Oh, right. I saw Dad pick it up.

W: Oh? Did he take it into the office?

M: Yes. He said that he needed it to get some files off of his coworker's computer.

W: Really? You're kidding me. He took off with my USB drive without asking first?

M: You mean __________ __________ __________?

W: Absolutely not. He knows that it has some of our family photos on it. It's really important to me.

M: Maybe he just forgot.

W: Sometimes I don't understand your father. __________ __________ __________ __________ __________ __________ __________.

M: Relax, Mom. I'm sure everything will be all right.

09

W: Hi. I'm looking to buy a new sweater for my son.

M: I'd love to help. How old is he?

W: He's 15. He usually wears an adult medium.

M: Great. Well, we have a couple of different materials to choose from. Would you __________ __________ __________ __________ __________ __________?

W: Well, what's the price difference?

M: The cotton sweater is $55, and the wool one __________ __________ __________ __________. The cotton one is really popular these days.

W: That's great. I'll take the cotton sweater, then. I want to buy him a pair of jeans.

M: Okay. These skinny jeans __________ __________ __________ __________ __________ the sweater. Their normal price is $50, but they're on sale for 10% off.

W: Does that discount apply to the sweater, too?

M: I'm sorry, but it only __________ __________ __________ __________.

W: That's fine. I'll take both anyway. Here's my card.

M: Great. Thank you.

10

M: Amy, are you already reading another book?

W: Yeah. I finished up the last one and started on this one this morning. It's called *The Prized Prince*.

M: I think I've heard of it. __________ __________ __________ __________ __________-__________ __________ recently?

W: That's right. It's sold over two million copies.

M: That's a lot. Why is it so popular?

W: Well, first of all, it was written by Steve Queen. He's really famous, you know.

M: Steve Queen, huh? So it must be __________ __________ __________.

W: Nope. He actually wrote a romance novel this time.

M: Oh, __________ __________ __________ __________ __________ __________ __________ romance novels. They're so boring.

W: This is a bit different from your average romance novel. I read online that they're going to make a movie out of it.

M: That's cool. In that case, I might __________ __________ __________ __________.

W: You should. I'll let you borrow it when I'm finished.

11

W: Good morning, everyone. I'd like to talk about this year's Science Fair. This year everyone will be working on a team, and you'll film your projects __________ __________ __________ __________.

Your team will be made up of three or four classmates. Every team will __________ __________ __________ __________ from this year's science catalog. The topics include underwater breathing, race car design, the process of compacting trash, and the behavior of robot maids. Of course your projects do not have to be working models, but only proof of concept. Please __________ __________ __________, along with the names of all your team members and the topic you have chosen, by May 5th at 5 p.m. If you have any questions, please __________ __________ __________ __________. I am looking forward to seeing everyone's work.

12

W: What can we do for you today, sir?

M: I'm looking for some new wheels for my car. I don't like the factory ones that came with it when I bought it.

W: I see. It looks like __________ __________ __________ 22- or 24-inch wheels.

M: I'd like to ride a little low, so I think the 22-inch ones __________ __________ __________ __________.

W: All right. Would you prefer mixed or solid black rims?

M: Mixed is a little too fancy for me. I like black wheels. __________ __________.

W: All right. I think you'll love this model.

M: Those are cool! How much are they?

W: They're on sale this week for $1,200. That's after a 40% discount.

M: That's still a little too expensive for me. I'm looking to __________ __________ __________ __________ __________ __________.

W: All right. I suppose these are what you're looking for, then.

M: They're cheaper, but they look just as good. I'll take them.

13

M: Hey, Chloe. What are you up to?

W: I'm just looking at the results of the military aptitude test I took a couple of weeks ago.

M: Oh. __________ __________ __________ __________ take a look?

W: Of course not.

M: *[Pause]* Wow! You got some impressive results. It says that you are great with __________ __________ __________ __________ __________. You'll be best as an architect or strategist.

W: Yeah, but I don't know if I like the results.

M: Really? Why not?

W: Well, my parents want me to __________ __________
__________, but I've always wanted to be a writer.
I don't think I'm very good at writing now, but I've
been practicing.

M: Well, it's always difficult to decide between what
you want to do and what you're good at.

W: You're right. What would you do __________
__________ __________ __________?

M: (I think you should do what you're passionate
about.)

14

M: Hey Mrs. Lewis, what are you doing on the computer?

W: Oh, hey Chris. I'm just looking for a new smartphone
for my husband.

M: I see. Is his birthday coming up or something?

W: That's right. He __________ __________-__________
next month.

M: He must be really excited to get a new smartphone.

W: He doesn't know yet. But he's always complaining
that __________ __________ __________ __________
__________ __________.

M: How old is it?

W: About four years old.

M: Yeah, __________ __________ __________
__________ nowadays.

W: Right. He's having a lot of trouble __________
__________ __________ with his current phone,
and he can't run some of the newer apps.

M: You should probably buy him one of the newest
models. That way, it's sure to last a long time.

W: (You're right, but I don't know which one is best.)

15

W: Nancy is an employee at a weight-loss clinic. She's not
a personal trainer, but she __________ __________
__________ __________ __________ __________
__________ at the clinic, so she is well versed in
nutrition and how to stay healthy. One afternoon,
she __________ __________ __________ __________
__________ __________, Maya, in the hallway of
her apartment building. Maya is carrying a bag of
groceries. When she sees Nancy, she __________

__________ __________ __________ __________
__________ about the food she's bought. She says
she's trying to buy healthy food, but she needs to
buy for herself, her husband, and her son, and she
__________ __________ __________ __________
__________ __________ __________ __________.

What would Nancy most likely tell Maya in a
situation like this?

Nancy: (Have them choose a few items that fit into
your nutrition goals.)

16-17

W: Good afternoon, everyone. My name is Mary Anne
Philips, and I am the lead nurse at the Big City
Health Department. I'd like to talk to you briefly
about allergens and, in particular, dust. Dust can
have many __________ __________ __________, so
we should strive to make our homes __________
__________ __________ __________. There are
several methods of cleaning that can drastically
reduce the amount of dust in your home. First of
all, how often do you run your vacuum cleaner?
I think you should do it __________ __________
__________ __________ __________. Second,
beating your pillows and couch cushions out once
a week also gets rid of dust. Mopping your floor
often may seem like an inconvenience, but I can
tell you that it's necessary to clean up the dirt and
dust you might have missed while vacuuming.
Finally, you should wash your bedding often,
especially if you or someone you live with has
allergies. __________ __________ __________
__________ __________ __________, and you'll be
able to maintain a clean and healthy home. Thank
you for your time.

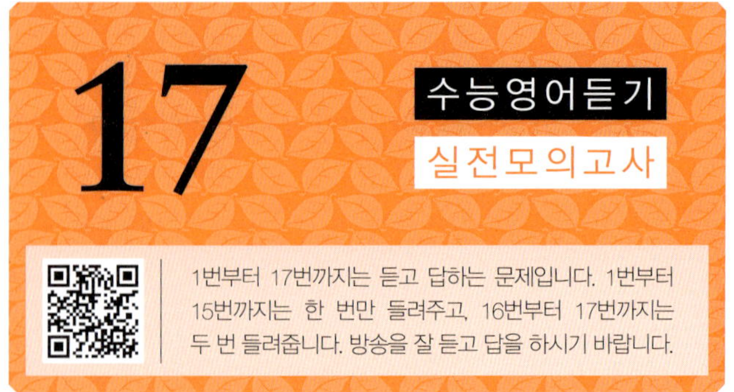

01

대화를 듣고, 여자의 마지막 말에 대한 남자의 응답으로 가장 적절한 것을 고르시오.

① I'm sorry, but we're sold out.
② You can have them tailored here.
③ I don't usually sell designer jeans.
④ Well, I can give you 10% off today.
⑤ Well, I'd like to see some other options.

02

대화를 듣고, 남자의 마지막 말에 대한 여자의 응답으로 가장 적절한 것을 고르시오.

① That's okay. I'll drive my car today.
② Is there a repair shop around here?
③ I guess I'll have to catch a taxi, then.
④ Oh, no! I think your car has a flat tire.
⑤ I need to stop by the grocery store first.

03

다음을 듣고, 여자가 하는 말의 목적으로 가장 적절한 것을 고르시오.

① 정기적인 건강 검진의 중요성을 알리려고
② 성공적인 심장병 치료 사례를 소개하려고
③ 심장병의 원인에 대해 설명하려고
④ 걷기 운동의 중요성을 알려주려고
⑤ 올바른 걷기 자세를 소개하려고

04

대화를 듣고, 남자의 의견으로 가장 적절한 것을 고르시오.

① 공무원들의 방만한 업무 행태를 개선해야 한다.
② 급커브 지역에 경고 표지판이나 전등을 설치해야 한다.
③ 운전자들은 과속하지 않고 신호를 잘 준수해야만 한다.
④ 낡고 훼손된 도로 교통 표지판을 모두 재정비 해야 한다.
⑤ 시에서 교통사고를 줄이기 위한 캠페인을 자주 벌여야 한다.

05

대화를 듣고, 두 사람의 관계를 가장 잘 나타낸 것을 고르시오.

① 집주인 — 수리공
② 건물주인 — 세입자
③ 건설업자 — 의뢰인
④ 건축 설계사 — 인부
⑤ 부동산 중개인 — 고객

06

대화를 듣고, 그림에서 대화의 내용과 일치하지 <u>않는</u> 것을 고르시오.

07

대화를 듣고, 여자가 할 일로 가장 적절한 것을 고르시오.

① 사진 찍기
② 입장권 사기
③ 지도 출력하기
④ 지도 받으러 가기
⑤ 주차 공간 찾아보기

08

대화를 듣고, 남자가 내일 학교에 일찍 오지 <u>못하는</u> 이유를 고르시오.

① 수학 숙제를 아침에 해야 하기 때문에
② 아침에 일찍 일어날 수가 없기 때문에
③ 등교 길에 Cup 카페에 들렀다 가야 하기 때문에
④ 아침에 엄마의 집안일을 도와드려야 하기 때문에
⑤ 걸어서 남동생을 학교에 바래다 줘야 하기 때문에

09

대화를 듣고, 여자가 지불할 금액을 고르시오.

① $60　　② $100　　③ $120　　④ $140　　⑤ $160

10

대화를 듣고, 여자가 학습에 대한 조언으로 언급하지 <u>않은</u> 것을 고르시오.

① 하루에 공부하는 시간　　② 공부하는 장소
③ 수업을 듣는 태도　　④ 사용하는 교재
⑤ 대학 진학 동기

11

The Reptile World Exhibit에 관한 다음 내용을 듣고, 일치하지 <u>않는</u> 것을 고르시오.

① 다양한 파충류들을 볼 수 있는 박람회이다.
② Mega Village 야생동물협회에서 개최한다.
③ 동물들에게 가까이 다가가서는 안 된다.
④ 무료 입장이지만 예약을 해야 한다.
⑤ 더 많은 정보는 홈페이지에 있다.

12

다음 표를 보면서 대화를 듣고, 남자가 빌릴 차를 고르시오.

Leicester Rental Cars

	Model	Type	Rental Price per Day	Capacity (Persons)	Number of Vehicles Available
①	Cube	Economy	50	4	1
②	Compact	Economy	55	4	2
③	Grandio	Family	60	5	2
④	Inistina	Family	65	7	0
⑤	Bentiz	Luxury	75	7	3

13

대화를 듣고, 여자의 마지막 말에 대한 남자의 응답으로 가장 적절한 것을 고르시오.

Man: _______________________________

① I'm sure everything will be fine in your new business.
② It's always nice to see my former employees succeed.
③ Work hard, but don't forget the important things in life.
④ It was great to see you. I'll stop by your office sometime.
④ You shouldn't exercise intensively for more than 3 hours.

14

대화를 듣고, 남자의 마지막 말에 대한 여자의 응답으로 가장 적절한 것을 고르시오.

Woman: _______________________________

① Sounds good. I hope they win!
② I'll cheer for your team with you.
③ Sure. I'll come over around 7 p.m.
④ Great. They may also come to cheer.
⑤ Actually, I'm really busy this weekend.

15

다음 상황 설명을 듣고, Candace가 Larry에게 할 말로 가장 적절한 것을 고르시오.

Candace: _______________________________

① If you have any problems, be sure to let me know.
② You should be more careful when you're running outside.
③ I don't think there's anything you can do to clean those papers.
④ Don't worry about it. There will be another bus in a few minutes.
⑤ I'm also responsible for this. I shouldn't have been using my phone.

[16-17] 다음을 듣고, 물음에 답하시오.

16

남자가 하는 말의 목적으로 가장 적절한 것은?

① 해외 자원봉사 단체를 홍보하려고
② 해외 자원봉사의 이점을 알려주려고
③ 해외 자원봉사의 종류를 소개하려고
④ 해외 자원봉사의 신청 방법을 설명하려고
⑤ 해외 자원봉사에 관한 수기를 공모하려고

17

언급된 해외 봉사 활동이 <u>아닌</u> 것은?

① 물 정화방법 가르치기
② 아기들 밥 먹이기
③ 집 짓기
④ 영어 가르치기
⑤ 아픈 아이들 돌보기

17 DICTATION

01

W: I really like these pants. How much are they?

M: Those are $100. They're designer jeans, __________ __________ __________ __________.

W: Oh, my. That price is a little high for me. __________ __________ __________ __________ __________?

M: (Well, I can give you 10% off today.)

02

M: Get up, Annie! It's after ten! You're going to __________ __________ __________ __________!

W: Relax! It only takes twenty minutes to drive there.

M: Don't you remember? Your car is __________ __________ __________ __________.

W: (I guess I'll have to catch a taxi, then.)

03

W: How do you stay healthy? Do you exercise regularly? Do you go for walks? Were you aware of the __________ __________ __________ __________? In short, your life will be better if you walk more. I'd like to tell you the story of my friend Roger Williams, who __________ __________ __________ __________. He was told by several doctors that his disease could never be completely cured. __________ __________ __________, he no longer suffers from the disease at all. It was walking that helped him. He made walking a big part of his daily routine. Many other people will testify that walking has changed their lives for the better. Walking is __________ __________ __________ __________ __________ __________ __________ __________; it is necessary for everyone.

04

W: Hi, Mr. Anderson.

M: Thanks for meeting me this morning. I wanted to bring this road to your attention.

W: Yes, I can see why. It looks very dangerous.

M: It is dangerous. There aren't enough warning signs or lights __________ __________ __________ __________ __________ __________ __________ __________ __________ __________ __________.

W: Can you see the road from the house?

M: Yeah, I can. I can't tell you how many accidents I've seen.

W: Do you think they're occurring because people are driving too fast?

M: I do think people are driving too fast. I believe more warning signs will significantly __________ __________ __________ __________ __________.

W: Have you __________ __________ __________ __________ __________ __________ in the past?

M: I have, several times. But no one seems to care. They've never gotten back to me with a response.

W: I see. I'm going to __________ __________ __________ __________ __________ __________ as soon as I get to the office.

M: Really? That would be wonderful. Please tell them __________ __________ __________ __________ __________.

05

[Telephone rings.]

W: Hello. This is Brittney Smith.

M: Hi, Ms. Smith. This is Dominic Antonoff. You took me to several buildings yesterday, and I was wondering if I could ask you a few questions.

W: Hello, Mr. Antonoff. __________ __________ __________ __________ __________ __________?

M: That one on Water Street. Does it have a walk-in freezer?

W: Give me one second while I check that. *[Pause]* Yes, it does.

M: That's great. Oh, but does it have central heating and air conditioning?

W: It does. Is that a problem?

M: Hmm. . . __________ __________ __________ __________. What about the building on 6th Street? Is it still available?

W: Yes, __________ __________ __________.

M: Would it be a problem if I remodeled the storefront?

W: I think that would be okay.

M: Great. And did you ask the owner if I could __________ __________ __________ __________ __________ __________ __________?

W: Yes, I asked him. He said that'd be okay.

06

W: Hey, Jay. How was your vacation?

M: It was great. My family really loved __________ __________ __________ __________ __________. Here. I have a photo.

W: *[Pause]* Cool. That's __________ __________ __________ __________ __________ __________?

M: It sure is. We stayed on the Big Island of Hawaii.

W: It looks like you all are really enjoying the view.

M: That's right. My wife and I enjoyed just relaxing at the resort. And those are my favorite sunglasses.

W: Nice. Are those __________ __________ __________ __________ __________ __________?

M: Yes. That's my son and daughter. They really enjoyed the weather there.

W: What kind of drink is that your wife is drinking? It looks fancy.

M: That's a Blue Hawaiian. It's a popular drink in Hawaii.

W: So, who took this picture?

M: My brother did. I wanted to __________ __________ __________ __________ __________, but I lost it that day.

W: Isn't that it on the floor?

M: Oh, it is. __________ __________ __________ __________.

07

W: Sweetie, I can see a sign for Rain Valley Park over there.

M: Look at all of the people! __________ __________ __________ __________ __________ __________.

W: Yeah. Oh, the parking lot is over there!

M: Okay, great. We can park there and __________ __________ __________ __________ __________. Do you think it will take long to get there?

W: I think it will take about 20 minutes. Once we're down there, we can sit by the river.

M: Wow! There are so many cars.

W: Do you think we'll be able to find a parking space?

M: I'll find one. Don't worry about it. You should get out here and __________ __________ __________ __________. I think the line is over there.

W: Okay, that's a good idea. Do you have the map I printed out?

M: I do. __________ __________ __________ __________. I'll be sure to bring it.

W: Great. I'll meet you __________ __________ __________ __________ __________ __________.

08

[Telephone rings.]

M: Hello?

W: Hey Mel, it's Katie.

M: Hey, Katie. What's up?

W: Not too much. So, __________ __________ __________ __________ __________ __________ __________ Mr. Levine assigned today?

M: I just finished before you called.

W: I really don't understand math. __________ __________ __________ __________ __________ __________ with them?

M: Sure, no problem.

W: Great. Do you think you could come to school early tomorrow? We could meet, and you could help me with the questions then.

M: Hmm. . . I don't think I'll be able to come to school early tomorrow. I have to __________ __________ __________ __________ __________.

W: Why doesn't your mother take him?

M: Well, __________ __________ __________ __________ __________ tomorrow morning. I can help you now. How about we meet at Cafe Cup?

W: That sounds great. Thanks a lot.

09

M: Welcome to Seoul Art Center. What can I do for you?

W: I need to buy some tickets for my family for today's exhibition.

M: No problem. __________ __________ __________ __________ __________?

W: Well, I need them for my husband, my daughter, and myself, but my daughter is a high school student. So two adults and one student, I guess.

M: Very well. Adult tickets cost $60 each and a student ticket is $40. Your daughter has her student ID, right?

W: Yes, she does. Here it is.

M: Great. So, two adults and one student, right?

W: That's correct. Oh! I almost forgot that my daughter __________ __________ __________ __________ __________ __________. Can I still use it?

M: Let me check __________ __________ __________ __________.

W: It should be. She just got it last week.

M: *[Pause]* You're right. You can get your daughter's ticket for half price.

W: Excellent. Here's my card.

10

M: Can I speak with you for a minute, Ms. Whitman?

W: Yes, of course you can. What can I help you with?

M: My grades are still quite low, even though I've been studying much more.

W: Well, let's find the problem. __________ __________ __________ __________ __________ __________ __________?

M: I study at home until about midnight on weekdays, so I guess about four hours. But __________ __________ __________ __________ my siblings.

W: It's easy to be distracted when you're studying late at night. Why don't you try studying in the library?

M: You're right. I think I need to __________ __________ __________ __________.

W: Yes. You should also make sure the books you're using are the best.

M: Oh, I see.

W: Do you know why you want to go to university?

M: I guess I haven't thought too much about it.

W: I believe you'll get more from your studying if you have a clear idea of what you want to do.

M: Okay. Thanks a lot for the advice, Ms. Whitman.

11

M: Good afternoon, students. Would you like to come face-to-face with a cobra? Would you like to __________ __________ __________ __________

__________? If so, you should come out to the Reptile World Exhibit at Mega Village Fairgrounds this weekend. The exhibit will __________ __________ __________ __________ __________ __________, from geckos and iguanas to pythons and gators. The exhibit is presented by Mega Village Wildlife Association and __________ __________ __________ __________ __________ and personal with some unique wildlife. It's very informative and educational. __________ __________ __________ __________, but we ask that you reserve your tickets ahead of time. Please visit the Mega Village Wildlife Association's website for more information. Thank you for listening.

12

W: What can I do for you, sir?

M: I'd like to __________ __________ __________ __________ __________ __________ __________. Would you recommend one?

W: All right. We have economy, family-sized, and luxury cars. How many people are there in your family?

M: There are four people, including me.

W: I think a family-sized or luxury one __________ __________ __________ __________ you.

M: What are the differences between those and the economy ones?

W: Besides the differences in rental price and gas mileage, economy cars don't have much space, so the four of you would feel pretty uncomfortable.

M: Well, we'll also need some space for luggage, so __________ __________ __________ __________ __________ __________ __________ __________ __________ __________.

W: Why don't you rent a luxury one, then? It's spacious enough for seven people, so your family will feel quite comfortable.

M: But the rental price is too expensive for me. Oh, here's a family-sized one with the same capacity as the luxury one.

W: Sorry, sir. This model is not available at the moment. They're __________ __________ __________.

M: Then there is no other choice. I'll take that one.

13

W: Hi, Rodrick.

M: Oh, hey Karen. Long time no see.

W: For sure. You know, it's been about a year since I left your company. I really miss working there.

M: We miss you, too. Say, you look a bit different. Did you lose any weight?

W: I did. I've ___________ ___________ ___________, and I've been doing this intense exercise routine.

M: That's great, but don't overdo it. I had a friend who ___________ ___________ ___________ ___________.

W: Don't worry. I'm being quite careful.

M: Okay. So, how's your new business coming along?

W: Well, it's ___________ ___________. I have so much work to do and not enough time to do it.

M: I understand. I also had a tough time when I first started my business.

W: I guess starting a business is always difficult. ___________ ___________ ___________ ___________ ___________ for me?

M: (Work hard, but don't forget the important things in life.)

14

W: Did you get a chance to see the baseball game last night?

M: I did. ___________ ___________ ___________! I was so happy Los Angeles beat Detroit

W: I'm actually a Detroit fan, but the Los Angeles team played so well.

M: The pitcher for LA did an awesome job. ___________ ___________ ___________ ___________.

W: Yeah, he did. It looked like he hurt his arm ___________ ___________ ___________ ___________ ___________ ___________, ___________.

M: I saw that, too. I expected to see a relief pitcher, but no one came out.

W: It was such a long game. Those players must have been so tired.

M: Yeah, it went thirteen innings. That's a long game!

W: It sure is.

M: When does Detroit play again?

W: Thursday night.

M: I'll come over and ___________ ___________ ___________ ___________ ___________.

W: (Sounds good. I hope they win!)

15

M: Candace is a busy career woman. One day, she has an important business meeting, so she's writing an email on her phone while walking to the bus stop. A middle-aged man named Larry is out for his morning jog. ___________ ___________ ___________ and stumbles into Candace, who drops some important papers onto the wet ground. Larry picks them up and tries to dry them off, but ___________ ___________. He is extremely apologetic and ___________ ___________ ___________ ___________ ___________. Candace thinks that this is also her fault because she was distracted at the time of the accident. In this situation, what would Candace most likely say to Larry?

Candace: (I'm also responsible for this. I shouldn't have been using my phone.)

16-17

M: Hello, students. I'd like to talk to you today about our ___________ ___________ ___________ ___________. Volunteering abroad can be a challenging experience. You will undoubtedly face hardships, and you may have a difficult time adjusting. However, the experience is ___________ ___________ and will certainly change your perspective on the world. You'll learn where your priorities lie as you ___________ ___________ ___________ ___________. Your worldview will expand because living in a foreign land will change you. You'll adopt a new set of customs and rules. You'll try food that you've never even dreamed of, and ___________ ___________ ___________ in a foreign language. Most importantly, you'll help those who need help. You may find yourself teaching Africans how to purify water, ___________ ___________ in India, building housing in Myanmar, or taking care of sick children in Indonesia. Volunteering abroad is truly a unique experience, and you'll definitely be a better person because of it.

18

1번부터 17번까지는 듣고 답하는 문제입니다. 1번부터 15번까지는 한 번만 들려주고, 16번부터 17번까지는 두 번 들려줍니다. 방송을 잘 듣고 답을 하시기 바랍니다.

01

대화를 듣고, 남자의 마지막 말에 대한 여자의 응답으로 가장 적절한 것을 고르시오.

① Sure. I like trying foreign foods.
② Yes. It's only a five-minute walk.
③ No. I'm not very good at cooking.
④ I'm not sure. I've never eaten there.
⑤ Yes. It's going to be closed tomorrow.

02

대화를 듣고, 여자의 마지막 말에 대한 남자의 응답으로 가장 적절한 것을 고르시오.

① Thanks. I really need one in this weather.
② Yes, you should check tomorrow's weather.
③ That's all right. You can borrow my umbrella.
④ Usually, but I was in a big hurry this morning.
⑤ I'm glad that the weather will be nice tomorrow.

03

다음을 듣고, 남자가 하는 말의 목적으로 가장 적절한 것을 고르시오.

① 야외 활동 시 뇌우에 대처하는 방법을 알려주려고
② 뇌우로 인한 사고 대책반 신설을 촉구하려고
③ 뇌우 속 야외 활동의 자제를 촉구하려고
④ 재난 시 시설물 이용 방법을 설명하려고
⑤ 기상 변화 예측법에 대해 알려주려고

04

대화를 듣고, 두 사람이 하는 말의 주제로 가장 적절한 것을 고르시오.

① 다른 나라 친구와 불화가 생기는 이유
② 나라마다 다른 개인 위생의 인식 차이
③ 이탈리아 사람들의 인사 방법
④ 외국인 친구와 친해지는 방법
⑤ 정확한 언어 사용의 필요성

05

대화를 듣고, 두 사람의 관계를 가장 잘 나타낸 것을 고르시오.

① 환자 — 응급실 의사
② 관람객 — 박물관 직원
③ 관광객 — 관광 가이드
④ 승객 — 비행기 승무원
⑤ 보행자 — 교통 경찰관

06

대화를 듣고, 그림에서 대화의 내용과 일치하지 <u>않는</u> 것을 고르시오.

07

대화를 듣고, 남자가 여자를 위해 할 일로 가장 적절한 것을 고르시오.

① 공항으로 마중 나가기
② 여행 이야기 들려주기
③ 퀴즈 예상 문항 알려주기
④ 중국에서 만난 친구 소개해주기
⑤ 수업시간에 받은 자료 갖다 주기

08

대화를 듣고, 남자가 테니스 경기를 관람하지 <u>못한</u> 이유를 고르시오.

① 폭우로 경기가 취소돼서
② 경기 일정을 잘못 알아서
③ 테니스 경기를 안 좋아해서
④ 어머니의 가게를 대신 봐야 해서
⑤ 해야 할 공부와 숙제가 너무 많아서

09

대화를 듣고, 여자가 지불할 금액을 고르시오.
① $90　　② $100　　③ $110　　④ $120　　⑤ $130

10

대화를 듣고, 컴퓨터에 관해 두 사람이 언급하지 <u>않은</u> 것을 고르시오.
① 모니터 크기　　② 레이저 프린터　　③ 영상통화
④ 무료 백신　　⑤ 보증기간

11

The Great Tusk Concert에 관한 다음 내용을 듣고, 일치하지 <u>않는</u> 것을 고르시오.
① 세계 최대 동물 복지 단체가 후원한다.
② 유명 가수들과 배우들이 공연한다.
③ 행사 날짜는 6월 15일이다.
④ 수익금은 코끼리들을 위해 사용된다.
⑤ 홈페이지를 통해 표를 구매할 수 있다.

12

다음 표를 보면서 대화를 듣고, 두 사람이 선택한 RV캠프장을 고르시오.

Sunset Lake RV Park

	Campground	Water Hookup	Pets	Electricity	Fee
①	A	O	Allowed	X	$23
②	B	X	Allowed	O	$27
③	C	O	Allowed	O	$32
④	D	X	Prohibited	X	$20
⑤	E	O	Prohibited	O	$27

13

대화를 듣고, 남자의 마지막 말에 대한 여자의 응답으로 가장 적절한 것을 고르시오.

Woman: _______________________________
① I don't think so. He should have called earlier.
② It's always nice to hear from you. Take care.
③ Sorry, but the news is too good to be true.
④ Actually, I don't know who that person is.
⑤ Of course. I'll be looking forward to it.

14

대화를 듣고, 여자의 마지막 말에 대한 남자의 응답으로 가장 적절한 것을 고르시오.

Man: _______________________________
① I'm really glad that I asked you for help.
② I hope you get accepted to that university.
③ You should really ask your parents for advice.
④ If that's the case, that's the one you should go to.
⑤ You really learn a lot about yourself at university.

15

다음 상황 설명을 듣고, Valerie가 동물보호소 직원들에게 할 말로 가장 적절한 것을 고르시오.

Valerie: _______________________________
① Please do not let any visitors into the animal shelter.
② We're struggling to get funding, so we'll have to close.
③ We shouldn't allow visitors to feed the animals human food.
④ We're going to have to buy more fresh food for the animals.
⑤ We need to make sure that the animals are eating the appropriate food.

[16-17] 다음을 듣고, 물음에 답하시오.

16

여자가 하는 말의 주제로 가장 적절한 것은?
① The effects of natural ingredients on skin
② Why we should always use sunscreen
③ The benefits of regular sunbathing
④ Alternatives to after-sun products
⑤ The best after-sun care products

17

여자가 언급하지 <u>않은</u> 것은?
① 찬물　　② 우유　　③ 식초
④ 알로에　　⑤ 오이

18 DICTATION

01

M: Hey Pat, have you been to that Sushi Safari restaurant yet?

W: I have. I went on ____________ ____________ ____________. It's great!

M: I think ____________ ____________ ____________ ____________ ____________ ____________. Is it close to here?

W: (Yes. It's only a five-minute walk.)

02

W: Wade, ____________ ____________. What happened?

M: It's really coming down out there. I didn't think to bring an umbrella with me.

W: Yeah, that's tough. Don't you ____________ ____________ ____________ ____________ every day?

M: (Usually, but I was in a big hurry this morning.)

03

M: Almost everyone ____________ ____________ ____________ ____________ when the weather is nice. It's important to keep in mind that ____________ ____________ ____________ ____________ ____________ rather quickly. You should know what to do in case this ever happens. If you ____________ ____________ ____________ ____________ ____________ ____________, you should seek shelter in a building or in your car. If those options aren't available, then you should find the lowest area around you and avoid open spaces. If you're in an open space and are taller than everything around you, you're at a higher risk of ____________ ____________ ____________ ____________. Always avoid trees and telephone poles. Follow this advice and you'll be prepared next time bad weather hits.

04

M: Are you all right? You seem worried.

W: Do you know Dimitri?

M: Sure. The Italian. He is a very friendly guy.

W: Yes, he is. And I like him. But have you noticed how he always has really bad breath?

M: Actually, I have. Does it upset you?

W: I think he's interesting and ____________ ____________ ____________ ____________ ____________, but his breath is unbearable.

M: Just relax. ____________ ____________ ____________ ____________ ____________ ____________ where he's from.

W: Is it? I've never been, so I have no idea.

M: Well, ideas about personal hygiene differ all over the world.

W: So these differences probably lead to social problems, right?

M: Yes, they do. It's important for everyone to try to understand that people are different.

W: ____________ ____________ ____________ ____________. I think Dimitri and I will get along better now.

M: I'm glad to hear it.

05

W: Excuse me, sir. Do you have a bandage on you?

M: Of course. I ____________ ____________ ____________-____________ ____________ on all the tours I lead. What happened?

W: I tripped and scraped my knee on the museum steps.

M: Then you're going to need a big one. Give me a second. *[Pause]* Here you go.

W: Thanks. Also, I wanted to tell you that my husband and I are ____________ ____________ ____________ ____________ ____________ ____________ ____________.

M: Awesome. ____________ ____________ ____________ ____________ to ensure that you have a great time.

W: So, when are we going to get to the cave?

M: We should be there at around one o'clock.

W: That's pretty soon. That cave has a lot of history, doesn't it?

M: That's right. During the mid-1800s, it was used as a hideout for Jesse James and his bandit gang.

W: That's so interesting. There's a lot of neat history around here, huh?

M: There is. This is a very historical area. It has a lot of natural beauty, too.

06

W: Wow! This band is really good, Joey!

M: Yeah, they're one of my favorite jazz bands. They're called Jazz Hands.

W: Interesting name. I love how they have a female violinist. She's wonderful.

M: __________ __________ __________ __________. The guitarist in the back is one of the best lead guitarists in the city.

W: __________ __________. It's cool that the lead singer plays guitar while he sings.

M: Yeah. I love the sound of his voice. __________ __________ __________ __________.

W: The piano player seems a bit out of place, though. He's sitting down while the rest of the band is standing.

M: Well, he's playing the piano. You can't really stand while you play it. You need to use the pedals.

W: Oh, right. Anyway, I'm really glad you brought me to this jazz club, Joey.

M: I'm really happy that you came with me.

07

[Cell phone rings.]

M: Hello?

W: Hi, Ted. This is Grace. How have you been?

M: Grace! Are you back?

W: Yes. The __________ __________ __________ __________ __________, so I flew back home last night.

M: Did you? Ms. Stone said you'd be back in school on Monday. How was China?

W: It was great. I feel much more confident when I speak to people in Chinese.

M: Great! We're all looking forward to talking with you about your time in China, especially the teachers.

W: I'd like to meet them as soon as possible, but I'm a bit worried since I've missed the first two weeks of class.

M: Right. . . We have two quizzes next week.

W: Really? __________ __________ __________ __________ __________ __________.

M: Well, I've got the handouts from the teachers. I'll bring them to you if you want.

W: Would you? That'd be great!

M: __________ __________ __________ __________?

08

W: Hey Davis, __________ __________ __________ __________?

M: I'm going over to my mom's flower shop. She needs to __________ __________ __________ at the post office, so I'm going to look after the store for her.

W: That's nice of you. Oh, you went to the tennis match last Sunday, right? How was it?

M: It was actually on Saturday, not Sunday.

W: Oh. Anyway, you must've had a great time. You love tennis.

M: I did go to the stadium, but the match was canceled.

W: Really? Why?

M: Thunderstorms. __________ __________ __________ __________ before it even started.

W: Oh, that's right! The weather was nasty on Saturday. That's too bad.

M: Yeah. I was really excited to go. I haven't had time to see a match this season with all the homework and studying I've had to do.

W: Yeah, I know the feeling. Sorry to hear you missed it.

09

W: Oh my! Are these antiques real?

M: They are. A few of the pieces were given to me by my grandmother.

W: Are those lamps over there expensive?

M: The lamp made of brass is $40, and __________ __________ __________ __________ __________ is $60.

W: I think the glass lamp is really nice, but __________ __________ __________ __________ __________ __________ __________.

M: I'll sell it to you for the price of the brass lamp if you really like it.

W: Wow, really? Okay, I'll take it! Also, how much are those lovely plates?

M: The bigger ones are $10 each, and the smaller ones are $5 each.

W: Okay, I'll take these two large plates.

M: Are there any other items __________ __________ __________ __________ __________?

W: I do really like that chair.

M: Yes, it's lovely, isn't it? Actually it's the last one. The others sold for $70, but I'd be happy to give you that one for $50.

W: Okay, wonderful. Thanks so much!

10

M: Hey, sweetheart. Your package arrived today.

W: That's great. __________ __________ __________ __________ __________ setting up this new computer.

M: It seems to be a lot bigger than our old computer.

W: It sure is. It's a lot faster, too. I purchased it as a set that included a 21-inch monitor and a laser printer.

M: It looks quite complicated. I wish I were __________ __________-__________.

W: It's really easy, honey. I can teach you how to use it.

M: That's great. Can this computer run Cacao Chat? All of my coworkers have been talking about it.

W: Of course it can. You can also enjoy video calling for free.

M: That's cool. Did you __________ __________ __________ __________ it?

W: Yeah. If anything happens to it in the next two years, they'll come and fix it.

M: Well, __________ __________ __________ __________ __________ __________ __________ __________ in a safe place so we don't lose them.

W: Great idea.

11

M: Good morning, everyone. This is Ronnie Maroon with GBC News. I'm pleased to announce that __________ __________ __________ __________ __________ __________ in our lovely city. It's called The Great Tusk Concert, and it's sponsored by the Earth Wildlife Federation, the largest animal welfare organization in the world. The Great Tusk Concert will feature performances by __________ __________ __________ __________ __________ __________ music, movies, and television, and they're looking forward to bringing the community together for a spectacular evening. The event will be held on July 15th at the Metropolitan Opera House. The proceeds of this event will benefit elephants around the world that are __________ __________ __________ __________. For more information and to purchase tickets, visit the event's homepage at *www.thegreattuskconcert.com*.

12

W: Hey, sweetheart. __________ __________ __________ __________ __________?

M: I'm just checking our options for our RV trip next month. There are five campgrounds around the lake that we're going to.

W: That's cool. Can I help choose one?

M: Sure. So, what kinds of things do you think we need to consider as we choose?

W: Well, I think having a __________ __________ is pretty important.

M: I agree. Our RV has a shower, so we're going to need a water hookup if we want to use it.

W: Right. So we need to choose one of these three.

M: Okay. I guess we should probably rule out this one, __________ __________ __________ __________ __________.

W: Yeah. I really want to take Baxter with us. I think he'll love the experience.

M: __________ __________ __________ __________ __________ these two.

W: Do you think we can make it for three days without electricity?

M: I think it's possible, but I'd rather have electricity just in case we need it.

W: All right. Well, I guess you should make a reservation for this campground.

13

M: You want to know what happened to me last night, Maria?

W: What happened?

M: Do you know who Dan is?

W: Of course. We played lacrosse together throughout high school, but then he moved to Texas __________ __________ __________ __________.

M: Right. Anyway, he sent me a Face Friend message last night.

W: Really? How's he doing?

M: I guess he's thinking of moving back here for work and was just reaching out to people he __________ __________ __________ __________ __________.

W: It would be great to see him. I wonder if he's changed much.

M: Well, __________ __________ __________ __________ __________. He will be in town in two weeks to look at apartments.

W: Wow! That's great news!

M: Yeah, __________ __________ __________ __________ __________ __________ __________ somewhere downtown. Do you want to join us?

W: (Of course. I'll be looking forward to it.)

14

M: Hey Leah, did you get into the university you wanted?

W: I did, Paul. In fact, __________ __________ __________ __________ __________ __________.

M: Two universities, huh? Well, have you decided which one you're going to yet?

W: They're both great schools. The main difference is that Upstate is a state-run university and Lakeside is private.

M: Yeah, they both have great reputations.

W: Right. I don't know how I'll ever choose between the two.

M: __________ __________ __________ __________. I know how you can decide, though.

W: How? I really need some advice.

M: __________ __________ __________. When it's in the air, you'll notice that there's a particular side you want it to land on.

W: I'll try it out. *[Pause]* You're right. When it was in the air, I was hoping for Upstate University.

M: (If that's the case, that's the one you should go to.)

15

M: Valerie recently started her own animal shelter and is very passionate about her work. She trains her staff so that she's sure __________ __________ __________ __________ __________ __________.

She wants the staff to be especially careful what they feed the animals, as each species has __________ __________ __________. One day, she notices that some of the animals are getting sick. She looks in a cage and sees that a rescued raccoon is eating bird food. She's worried that if animals continue eating the wrong types of food, they could die. She __________ __________ __________ __________ __________ __________ __________ to address this issue. In this situation, what would Valerie most likely say to her staff?

Valerie: (We need to make sure that the animals are eating the appropriate food.)

16-17

W: Good morning, everyone. People have known for a long time about the damage the sun can do to your skin, but certain products, like "after-sun care," lead us to believe that __________ __________ __________ __________ __________.

In fact, a lot of these so-called after-sun products can actually __________ __________ __________ __________ __________ __________ because their oil __________ __________ __________ __________ __________. So what can we do to really protect ourselves? How should we deal with sunburn? Simply keeping the skin cool will do the trick. You can immerse yourself in cool water or use vinegar. If you __________ __________ __________ __________ __________ and place it on your sunburn, the vinegar will __________ __________ __________ __________ __________ __________. It's amazing, but it's also a little smelly. If you don't want to have to smell that smell, a layer of aloe vera or thinly sliced cucumber does the same thing.

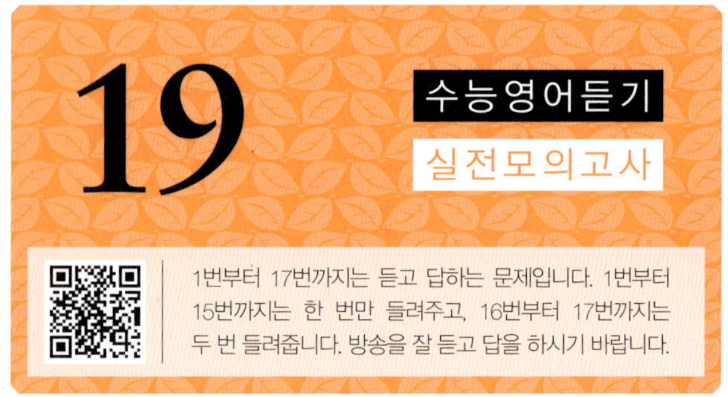

1번부터 17번까지는 듣고 답하는 문제입니다. 1번부터 15번까지는 한 번만 들려주고, 16번부터 17번까지는 두 번 들려줍니다. 방송을 잘 듣고 답을 하시기 바랍니다.

01

대화를 듣고, 여자의 마지막 말에 대한 남자의 응답으로 가장 적절한 것을 고르시오.

① The cafe is about an hour away.
② It should be ready in about 15 minutes.
③ Waffles with apple pie is a popular choice.
④ People say that potatoes are bad for your health.
⑤ I brought some up the other day from the market.

02

대화를 듣고, 남자의 마지막 말에 대한 여자의 응답으로 가장 적절한 것을 고르시오.

① Wow, I love Dragon Heart!
② I'm really busy this Saturday.
③ Sorry, but he said it's sold out.
④ I have two tickets for the concert.
⑤ You should definitely call him and ask.

03

다음을 듣고, 여자가 하는 말의 목적으로 가장 적절한 것을 고르시오.

① 인턴십 채용 절차를 공지하려고
② 로스쿨에 대한 전망을 분석하려고
③ 인턴십에 지원할 수 있는 자격을 알리려고
④ 법률 관련 실무 경험의 중요성을 알리려고
⑤ 로스쿨의 일부 문제점에 대한 개선을 요구하려고

04

대화를 듣고, 두 사람이 하는 말의 주제로 가장 적절한 것을 고르시오.

① 운동과 과학의 관계
② 맨발로 뛰기의 장점
③ 체중 감량을 위한 운동법
④ 달리기가 학습에 미치는 영향
⑤ 달리기 전용 신발 착용의 이점

05

대화를 듣고, 두 사람의 관계를 가장 잘 나타낸 것을 고르시오.

① 경찰관 — 운전자
② 자동차 수리공 — 고객
③ 보험 판매원 — 보험 가입자
④ 공장 관리자 — 기술자
⑤ 중고차 판매원 — 차 소유자

06

대화를 듣고, 그림에서 대화의 내용과 일치하지 <u>않는</u> 것을 고르시오.

07

대화를 듣고, 여자가 남자에게 부탁한 일로 가장 적절한 것을 고르시오.

① to get her cell phone
② to charge her cell phone
③ to keep an eye on her bag
④ to get her a phone charger
⑤ to take her to the bus station

08

대화를 듣고, 남자가 집에서 공부하려는 이유를 고르시오.

① 같이 공부하면 집중이 잘 안돼서
② 집에 있는 책상과 의자가 더 편해서
③ 카페에는 재미있는 할 거리가 많아서
④ 새로 생긴 카페에 사람이 너무 많아서
⑤ 카페 외부 공사로 인한 소음이 시끄러워서

09

대화를 듣고, 여자가 토네이도 발생 지역에 전달할 총 기부금액을 고르시오.

① $20　　② $50　　③ $75　　④ $90　　⑤ $95

10

대화를 듣고, 남자가 브로콜리의 건강상의 이점으로 언급하지 <u>않은</u> 것을 고르시오.

① 콜레스테롤 감소　　② 뼈 건강 증진　　③ 암 예방
④ 체중 감소　　⑤ 식욕 증진

11

Common raven에 관한 다음 내용을 듣고, 일치하지 <u>않는</u> 것을 고르시오.

① 주로 북반구에서 발견된다.
② 인간과 공존한 지는 오래되지 않았다.
③ 생존 성공의 결정적 요인은 식습관에 있다.
④ 여러 음식에서 영양 공급원을 잘 찾아낸다.
⑤ 많은 스포츠팀의 마스코트로 사용되어 왔다.

12

다음 표를 보면서 대화를 듣고, 두 사람이 함께 수강하기로 한 강좌를 고르시오.

Sports Center Summer Program Schedule

	Class	Instructor	Days & Time	Price	Age
①	Swimming (Beginner)	C. Williams	Tue./Thu., 6:00 ~ 7:00	$40	10+
②	Swimming (Advanced)	M. Hines	Mon./Thu., 8:00 ~ 9:00	$46	10+
③	Aerobics	M. Krupa	Wed./Fri., 19:00 ~ 20:00	$22	12+
④	Badminton	C. Paul	Mon./Wed., 16:00 ~ 17:00	$26	10+
⑤	Racquetball	L. James	Tue./Thu., 19:00 ~ 20:00	$26	13+

13

대화를 듣고, 여자의 마지막 말에 대한 남자의 응답으로 가장 적절한 것을 고르시오.

Man: _______________________________________

① Your dog has a very serious injury.
② Where do you think you lost your pet?
③ No, he'll be fine. Good luck in the contest.
④ Can you tell me why you decided to get a pet?
⑤ I'm sorry, but your pet can't join the pet contest.

14

대화를 듣고, 남자의 마지막 말에 대한 여자의 응답으로 가장 적절한 것을 고르시오.

Woman: _______________________________________

① That's a great idea, as long as you can afford it.
② I'm glad that you have a loyal customer base.
③ Do you think I could take out a small loan?
④ I'm sure that promotion helped out a little.
⑤ Advertisements are usually quite effective.

15

다음 상황 설명을 듣고, Casey가 Danny에게 할 말로 가장 적절한 것을 고르시오.

Casey: _______________________________________

① Let's take a helicopter tour of New York.
② That's all right. I'm sure we'll make the next helicopter.
③ That sounds interesting, but I'm not getting in a helicopter.
④ That sounds great. I've always wanted to see the canyon from above.
⑤ Let's check out the Grand Canyon Museum and get more information.

[16-17] 다음을 듣고, 물음에 답하시오.

16

남자가 하는 말의 주제로 가장 적절한 것은?

① The necessity of to-do lists
② How to organize your own desk
③ Tips for becoming more organized
④ Reasons to use calendars and planners
⑤ Advantages of using smartphone applications

17

언급된 항목이 <u>아닌</u> 것은?

① 달력　　② 일정 계획표　　③ 스마트폰
④ 시계　　⑤ 할 일 목록

01

W: I think I'm ready. ____________ ____________ ____________ ____________ ____________?

M: Of course. What would you like this morning?

W: I'll have bacon and eggs with a side dish of baked potatoes. ____________ ____________ ____________ ____________ ____________?

M: (It should be ready in about 15 minutes.)

02

M: I really want to go to the Dragon Heart concert at the Olympic Stadium this Saturday!

W: Yeah, me too. ____________ ____________ ____________ ____________ ____________?

M: I'm not sure, but my friend, Kevin, ____________ ____________ ____________ ____________ ____________.

W: (You should definitely call him and ask.)

03

W: Hello, everyone! I'd like to talk to you all today about an opportunity you won't want to miss. If anyone here is considering going to law school, the internship I want to share with you is a great way ____________ ____________ ____________-____________. However, there are some things you need to be aware of. This particular internship is open to undergraduate and graduate students currently enrolled at our school. But, please ____________ ____________ ____________ ____________ the only undergraduates who ____________ ____________ ____________ ____________ ____________ are those who are currently seniors. Candidates who are law students and have some exposure to the field will be given preference. Finally, applicants must be 28 years old or younger. If you would like to ____________ ____________ ____________, ____________ ____________ ____________ in law, please apply today.

04

W: Hey Cody, what are you up to?

M: I'm reading about ____________ ____________ ____________ ____________.

W: I heard that a lot of people are trying that these days.

M: You're right. Some researchers believe that running barefoot can be great for your health.

W: What are the benefits?

M: Well, it can ____________ ____________ ____________.

W: Really? How so?

M: When you run with shoes on, ____________ ____________ ____________ ____________ ____________ ____________ the shoe. Without shoes, you're able to spread your toes, which can give you more balance.

W: That's cool. Does it help with anything else?

M: It's great for the muscles in your legs. Most running shoes have a raised heel, so your Achilles tendon and calf muscles aren't exercised as much.

W: I see why so many people are starting to run barefoot. I might give it a shot.

M: I'm considering ____________ ____________ ____________ ____________.

05

M: Hi. What can we do for you?

W: Well, I got in an accident recently. Ever since then, the red lights on the dashboard have been flashing.

M: We'll ____________ ____________ ____________ for you. Are you having any other problems?

W: Yeah. When I drive faster than 70 kilometers per hour, my car ____________ ____________ ____________ ____________ ____________.

M: Hmm. . . it sounds like a problem with your tires.

W: My insurance should cover any of the repairs I need, right?

M: I'm afraid I don't know anything about that. You'll have to call them.

W: I'll give them a call after lunch. How long do you think the repairs will take?

M: Well, it depends on __________ __________ __________ __________ __________ __________ __________. I'll be able to tell you more after we have a look at it.

W: I have a couple of other __________ __________ __________ __________ __________ around the area. Is it okay if I come back later?

M: Sure, that's fine. Just leave your phone number. We'll call you once we've got a better idea of what's wrong with it.

W: Sounds good.

06

W: Hi, Peter. I'm sorry for being late. I've been very busy.

M: That's okay. I've got the campsite almost set up. What do you think of what I've done so far?

W: You did a great job. I like that you put the tent by the river.

M: Yeah, that way we can go swimming or fishing easily. It'll also be great to enjoy dinner just next to the water.

W: Ah, so that's why you put the table and chairs between the tent and the river. But where's the icebox? It should be __________ __________ __________.

M: Oh, I forgot about that. It's in the tent. __________ __________ __________ __________ and put it under the tree.

W: But then it'll be next to the fire. It's probably dangerous to have the fire so close to the tree, anyway.

M: __________ __________ __________. Let's put it out later and make a new one closer to the water. By the way, I hung the hammock between the trees. What do you think?

W: That's perfect. Good job!

07

W: Hey, Jeff. I'm really sorry I'm late.

M: I was seriously worried. I didn't think __________ __________ __________ __________ __________. I tried to call, but you didn't answer your phone.

W: Well, I hopped in the taxi and __________ __________ __________ before I realized I'd left my cell phone at home and had to go back. Then there was __________ __________ __________ on the way here.

M: Yeah, it's always bad like that on Friday evenings.

W: I didn't know that. Hey, do you know if there's a convenience store around the bus station?

M: There's one right over there. Why?

W: Well, when I went back home to get my phone, __________ __________ __________ __________ __________ __________. I need to buy another one. Watch my bag, will you?

M: Sure. I'll wait here.

W: Thanks. It should only be a few minutes.

08

M: Hey Kate, __________ __________ __________ __________ __________ __________ tomorrow?

W: I don't think so. It looks like __________ __________ __________ __________ __________. How about you?

M: I've been studying in the cafe in the new Student Center.

W: Oh? How is it?

M: It's pretty cool. They have a few new restaurants, a recreation room with a ping-pong table, and a basketball court.

W: That's awesome. I might go play some ping-pong after the exam.

M: The new pizza shop they have there is really good, too.

W: Nice. What about having lunch there and studying together in the cafe, then?

M: I'd love to get lunch, but I think studying there is a bad idea.

W: Really? Why's that?

M: The terrace of the cafe __________ __________ __________ __________, so it's quite noisy.

W: I see. I guess I'll study at home then, too.

09

M: Good morning, Mrs. DeLaney. Are you busy? I need to talk to you about something.

W: Hey, Taylor. Come on in. What do you need?

M: I'm sure you heard about the tornadoes in Kentucky last week.

W: I did. It sounds awful. Many homes __________ __________ __________.

M: Well, a lot of the students got together to __________ __________ __________ __________ __________. Everyone pitched in $3.

W: That's really nice of you. I'm sure it'll be helpful.

M: I hope so. Everyone seemed happy to help.

W: All twenty-five students donated? That's quite a bit of money.

M: Yeah, and here it is. I was wondering if you could send it to them __________ __________ __________.

W: I'd love to. I'll even donate $20 myself.

M: Thanks, Mrs. DeLaney. I really hope that this money helps.

W: I'm sure it will, Taylor.

10

M: I'm feeling great today. This new diet I just started is amazing. How about you? How're you doing?

W: Not as well as you. I guess I should try out your diet. What kinds of foods are you eating?

M: I'm eating a lot more vegetables. I'd recommend you do that, too. Broccoli is great for you.

W: Really? What are the health benefits of broccoli?

M: Well, first of all, __________ __________ __________ __________ __________ __________, which is great for lowering your cholesterol.

W: Okay. What else?

M: It's full of Vitamin C and Vitamin K, which __________ __________ __________ __________. It's also a great source of antioxidants that can help prevent cancer and keep you healthy.

W: That's great. I'd also like to lose a little bit of weight. Can broccoli help with that?

M: It sure can. Remember how I said broccoli is full of fiber? That means it makes you feel full __________ __________ __________ __________ __________.

W: Wow! I guess broccoli really is a super food!

11

M: The common raven, widely known as the northern raven, is a large black bird __________ __________ __________ __________ __________ __________. It is the most common bird of its kind. In fact, from an evolutionary perspective, the species has been very successful. It __________ __________ __________ __________ for thousands of years, and in some areas has been so numerous that it was considered a pest. One crucial part of the raven's success comes from its diet. These birds are extremely versatile and opportunistic in __________ __________ __________ __________, feeding on rotting flesh, insects, cereal grains, berries, fruit, small animals, and food waste. They have also been considered a __________ __________ and have been used as a mascot for many different sports teams, including the National Football League's Baltimore Ravens.

12

W: Hey Garrett, I found this schedule for this summer's programs at the sports center. It made me think: we should get some exercise this summer. It'd be a shame to just __________ __________ __________ __________ __________ __________.

M: You're right. What classes are you looking at?

W: How about a swimming class? I want to become a better swimmer.

M: Actually, I have a phobia of water.

W: How about the aerobics class, then? I think it'll be fun.

M: That sounds all right, but we have book club meetings on Wednesday nights.

W: That's right. Well, I guess we only have these two choices then.

M: I like that they're pretty cheap. __________ __________ __________ __________ __________ more than $30.

W: So, which one is better for you?

M: Well, we can't take the class on Tuesdays and Thursdays. It's for older kids.

W: That's right. Let's __________ __________ __________ __________ __________, then.

M: Sounds like a plan.

13

M: Have a seat here, please. So, what's the matter with your dog?

W: Well, he can't walk properly.

M: Let me have a look at his feet. *[Pause]* Well, there's the problem. __________ __________ __________ __________ __________ __________ __________. Do you know why?

W: I have no idea.

M: Fortunately, it's not that serious. The swelling should subside in about a week or so.

W: In a week? Actually, __________ __________ __________ __________ __________ __________ the Handsome Dog Contest next week.

M: You mean that contest hosted by The Dog Lovers' Club?

W: That's right. Do you think it's okay for him to __________ __________ __________ __________? I'm worried that he won't be able to.

M: Don't worry about it. Oh, so that's 9 days from now. Yes, he'll be completely fine by then.

W: That's good. I was really worried about him.

M: (No, he'll be fine. Good luck in the contest.)

14

W: Hi, Mr. Goodman. How is business at the store these days?

M: Actually, sales haven't been all that great lately.

W: That's too bad. The economy is in horrible shape nowadays.

M: Yeah. I need to do something about it soon.

W: How are you going to change the economy?

M: I can't change the economy, but I can change __________ __________ __________ __________ in it.

W: So you mean like __________ __________ __________ __________?

M: Well, I was thinking about putting out some coupons in the daily newspaper. I want to give people more for their money.

W: Well, that is very kind of you, but won't you still be losing money?

M: Yes, at first. But I think people will see that I'm trying to accommodate them __________ __________ __________ __________ __________, and that will help me __________ __________ __________ __________ __________.

W: (That's a great idea, as long as you can afford it.)

15

W: Casey lives in New York City, but she has decided to visit her friend Danny in Tucson, Arizona. Casey makes the long journey, and Danny is delighted to see her. He takes her on a tour of his city. __________ __________ __________ __________ __________, Casey tells Danny that she has always wanted to see the Grand Canyon. They set out to go to the Grand Canyon the next day and find a __________ __________ __________ __________ __________ __________. They stay there awhile, and then Danny suggests they take a helicopter ride around the canyon __________ __________ __________ __________ __________ __________ __________. Casey, however, __________ __________ __________ __________ __________ and doesn't want to ride in a helicopter. In this situation, what would Casey most likely say to Danny?

Casey: (That sounds interesting, but I'm not getting in a helicopter.)

16-17

M: Do you frequently find yourself searching frantically for something on your messy desk? Have you missed meetings or appointments because you're just too unorganized? Well, I'm here today to offer some tips on __________ __________ __________ __________ __________ __________. First, organize your desk. Don't be a hoarder. Throw away things that you don't need or that are unimportant. Second, use a calendar, planner, or smartphone to __________ __________ __________ __________ __________. Calendars and planners are a bit outdated, but they can get you organized. Technology is your friend, and there are many apps that can help you organize your schedule. Third, __________ __________ __________ __________ __________. To-do lists are a great way to organize your day, and there are many great smartphone applications that can help. Finally, __________ __________ __________ __________ __________. Stop procrastinating and stick to a schedule. __________ __________ __________ for the items on your to-do list. Combine items to save time. If you follow these tips, I'm sure you'll lead a more organized and productive life.

1번부터 17번까지는 듣고 답하는 문제입니다. 1번부터 15번까지는 한 번만 들려주고, 16번부터 17번까지는 두 번 들려줍니다. 방송을 잘 듣고 답을 하시기 바랍니다.

01

대화를 듣고, 남자의 마지막 말에 대한 여자의 응답으로 가장 적절한 것을 고르시오.

① Thanks for the suggestion.
② Yeah, I'm great at shooting.
③ That's okay. I don't really like basketball.
④ You should go to basketball practice today.
⑤ I thought you were interested in basketball.

02

대화를 듣고, 여자의 마지막 말에 대한 남자의 응답으로 가장 적절한 것을 고르시오.

① Help me become a better player.
② Play the instrument you're best at.
③ You shouldn't play the drum in the tryouts.
④ The marching band contest is this weekend.
⑤ Playing instruments is great for relieving stress.

03

다음을 듣고, 남자가 하는 말의 목적으로 가장 적절한 것을 고르시오.

① 팬 미팅 행사가 취소된 것을 사과하려고
② 유명 작가의 작품 세계를 설명하려고
③ 새로운 독립 영화 감독을 소개하려고
④ 영화 상영 시간의 변경을 알리려고
⑤ 영화표의 환불 절차를 안내하려고

04

대화를 듣고, 두 사람이 하는 말의 주제로 가장 적절한 것을 고르시오.

① 몸과 마음을 건강하게 유지하는 방법
② 현대인들이 운동을 하지 않는 이유
③ 건강 관련 정보를 얻는 요령
④ 건강한 식습관의 중요성
⑤ 운동의 장단기적 효과

05

대화를 듣고, 두 사람의 관계를 가장 잘 나타낸 것을 고르시오.

① photographer — film actress
② art collector — film director
③ reporter — interviewee
④ advertiser — editor
⑤ model — professor

06

대화를 듣고, 그림에서 대화의 내용과 일치하지 <u>않는</u> 것을 고르시오.

07

대화를 듣고, 이번 주 토요일에 남자가 할 일로 가장 적절한 것을 고르시오.

① 축제에 가기
② 시험 공부하기
③ 영화 보러 가기
④ 할머니 방문하기
⑤ 집 수리하는 것 돕기

08

대화를 듣고, 여자가 스터디 모임에 참석할 수 <u>없는</u> 이유를 고르시오.

① 화학 수업을 들어야 해서
② 수업 자료를 더 공부해야 해서
③ 아버지 생신 선물을 사야 해서
④ 부모님과 함께 외출하기로 해서
⑤ 다른 스터디 모임에 끼기로 해서

09

대화를 듣고, 남자가 지불할 금액을 고르시오.
① $20 ② $26 ③ $30 ④ $36 ⑤ $40

10

대화를 듣고, 공연 관람 에티켓에 관해 두 사람이 언급하지 <u>않은</u> 것을 고르시오.
① 휴대폰 무음으로 하기 ② 공연 중에 떠들지 않기
③ 앞 좌석 발로 차지 않기 ④ 공연 시간 지키기
⑤ 음료수 쏟지 않기

11

Maple 고등학교 에세이 대회에 관한 다음 내용을 듣고, 일치하지 <u>않는</u> 것을 고르시오.
① 에세이의 주제는 환경 보호에 대한 것이다.
② 제출은 학교에 직접 와서 해야 한다.
③ 4월 20일까지 제출해야 한다.
④ 2등과 3등의 상금 차이는 100달러이다.
⑤ 1등 수상작은 도시 신문에 실리게 될 것이다.

12

다음 표를 보면서 대화를 듣고, 두 사람이 딸을 위해 선택한 피아노 교습을 고르시오.

Piano Lessons for Kids

	Session	Time	Days
①	Mar.15 ~ Apr.5	5:00 ~ 6:30 p.m.	Mon. & Fri.
②	Mar.15 ~ Apr.5	6:30 ~ 8:00 p.m.	Tue. & Thur.
③	Mar.30 ~ Apr.15	5:00 ~ 6:30 p.m.	Tue. & Thur.
④	Mar.30 ~ Apr.15	5:00 ~ 6:30 p.m.	Mon. & Fri.
⑤	Mar.30 ~ Apr.15	6:30 ~ 8:00 p.m.	Mon. & Wed.

13

대화를 듣고, 여자의 마지막 말에 대한 남자의 응답으로 가장 적절한 것을 고르시오.

Man: _______________

① You'd better look for another parking space upstairs.
② Is there any way I could use your bicycle for a moment?
③ You should always wear a helmet when you ride a bike.
④ Would you return this book when you go to the law building?
⑤ First, go and see whether the place you left it in is a designated area.

14

대화를 듣고, 남자의 마지막 말에 대한 여자의 응답으로 가장 적절한 것을 고르시오.

Woman: _______________

① A balanced diet can help you get in shape.
② No way! It's not easy to do this program from home.
③ Of course you will. You can start with an easy routine.
④ That's fine. They don't have any classes for beginners.
⑤ No problem. You've gotten a lot stronger and healthier.

15

다음 상황 설명을 듣고, Bella가 Nathaniel에게 할 말로 가장 적절한 것을 고르시오.

Bella: Nathaniel, _______________

① would you help me with my fundraiser?
② you should really start saving your money.
③ I'm sometimes let down by my closest friends.
④ why don't you want to support our good cause?
⑤ it's great that you made such a large contribution.

[16~17] 다음을 듣고, 물음에 답하시오.

16

남자가 하는 말의 주제로 가장 적절한 것은?
① Safety concerns when glamping
② Ways to relax in the great outdoors
③ A new camping trend called 'glamping'
④ How to avoid discomfort while camping
⑤ Positive effects of glamping on the environment

17

새로운 캠핑이 제공하는 것으로 언급되지 <u>않은</u> 것은?
① 텐트 ② 전기 ③ 샤워시설
④ 난방기기 ⑤ 화장실

20 DICTATION

01

M: Hey, Ava. What are you going to focus on today at basketball practice?

W: I need to __________ __________ __________ __________ __________.

M: You should work on shooting. I think it's more important.

W: (Thanks for the suggestion.)

02

W: Good morning, Max. So, __________ __________ __________ __________ __________ for the school's marching band.

M: That's great! __________ __________ __________ __________ __________ __________ __________ __________ __________?

W: I'll probably play a brass instrument, but I'm not sure which one.

M: (Play the instrument you're best at.)

03

M: Good evening, ladies and gentlemen. Thank you for coming to the Fourth Annual International Film Festival here at historic Wilma Theater. I know many of you are excited about __________ __________ __________ __________ __________ __________,

Moonset Monarchy, by acclaimed director Mark Young. However, we're currently facing some __________ __________ __________ __________ __________ __________. The film was due to start momentarily, but as of now, we are postponing it for one hour. We __________ __________ __________ __________ __________ and are prepared to refund any tickets you have bought for this particular film. Thank you for your understanding.

04

W: Hey, Gilbert. What are you up to?

M: Hi, Mary. I just started listening to a new audio book about health.

W: Health? Is it about diets?

M: No, it's more about how to __________ __________ __________ __________ __________ __________.

W: That sounds really interesting.

M: We can do really simple things every day that will have significant effects in the long run. People want things right away, so they ignore __________ __________-__________ __________ of the stuff they do and eat.

W: So, what's the first thing you would recommend doing to get on the right path toward a healthy mind and body?

M: The first thing we need to do is inventory our lives. Find out what we've got, and then figure out how much of it we need and __________ __________ __________ __________ __________.

W: And, this inventory should include not just material possessions but food, people, work, hobbies and pretty much everything we deal with on a daily basis, right?

M: Yes, precisely.

05

[Knock on the door]

M: Please come in.

W: Hello, Mr. Anderson. I was told you wanted to see me.

M: Yes, Stacy. I was __________ __________. Please have a seat and take a look at this layout.

W: Oh, I really like it!

M: Great. Now I need your help choosing a couple of shots we can use for the brochure.

W: These two are really nice. I think they best capture what the film is about.

M: I took shots that I thought best __________ __________ __________, since the article focuses on your acting.

W: I'm really excited to be working with you. Your pictures make me look great.

M: I'm happy you like my work. We should take a few more shots before __________ __________ __________ __________ __________.

W: That sounds good. Can we do something with an action theme?

M: Sure. Come to the studio at three.

W: I __________ __________ __________ at four, so can we meet an hour earlier?

M: Of course.

06

W: Welcome to our school, Mr. Brown. Let me show you around.

M: Thanks. It's a pleasure to be working here. What's this room?

W: This is our teacher's lounge. It's where you can go between classes to relax and talk to the other teachers.

M: Wow, it seems quite nice. Is that a snack machine in the back?

W: It sure is. We also have two computers __________ __________ __________ __________ that you can use to access the Internet.

M: That's great. What's that on the table?

W: We sometimes have casual meetings in here, so we have two sofas and a phone on the table used to hold conference calls if we need to.

M: That's cool. What's __________ __________ __________ __________ next to the snack machine?

W: That's a poster for our upcoming Earth Day Fair. It __________ __________ __________ __________.

M: So the bulletin board announces upcoming events?

W: That's right. Sometimes we post other important information on there, so you should __________ __________ __________.

M: I see. What's the next stop on our tour?

W: We're going to the gym next.

07

W: How did you do on your test, Donald?

M: I'm not sure. I'll have my results by Wednesday of next week.

W: You studied hard, so I'm sure you'll __________ __________ __________ __________.

M: Thanks, Mom. By the way, can I go to the World Jazz Festival with my friends this Saturday?

W: Oh, no. Don't you remember what your father told you?

M: What's that?

W: Your father and I are __________ __________ __________ __________ __________. We really need your help.

M: Hmm. . . I guess I can't go. I'll go to the movies with them this Sunday instead.

W: Okay, but not on Sunday morning. We should __________ __________ __________ then. She's sick in bed.

M: Is it something serious?

W: No. She thinks it's just the flu.

M: __________ __________ __________! Don't worry, Mom. I'll meet my friends after visiting Grandma.

W: Thank you, Donald.

08

M: Hey, Claire. Are you all right? __________ __________ __________ __________ __________.

W: I have a big chemistry test tomorrow, but I just don't understand the material. I think I might fail.

M: Cheer up. Ryan, Jason, Taylor, and I started a study group. You can join us.

W: I'd love to, but I don't want to be a bother. __________ __________ __________ __________.

M: Don't worry. I'm sure everyone would love to have you around.

W: I really appreciate it. I need all of the help I can get.

M: We're getting together tonight at 6. Can you make it?

W: Hmm. . . I really don't think I can. I'm supposed to __________ __________ __________ __________ tonight. It's my father's birthday.

M: I see. Well, if you ever want to join us in the future, __________ __________ __________. Okay?

W: Thanks. I really appreciate it.

09

W: Hello. How may I help you?

M: Hi. How much is an Americano?

W: One is $5. But we're __________ __________ __________ this week. Americanos are buy one, get one free, so it's actually two for $5.

M: That's great. So I can get __________ __________
__________ __________ __________ __________.
I'll have four Americanos, then.

W: Is there anything else I can get you today?

M: Yeah, actually it's my coworker's birthday today, so
I'm thinking of __________ __________ __________
__________. How much for the devil's food cake?

W: That one is $20. __________ __________ __________
__________ __________ you can use?

M: I don't.

W: Well. I can give you one for 10% off your next
purchase.

M: Thanks. Is it okay if I use my credit card?

10

W: Sweetheart, I don't think these are the right seats.

M: Of course they are. These are the seat numbers
printed on our tickets.

W: Okay. I guess you're right. The play is about to
start. Did you __________ __________ __________
__________ __________ __________?

M: Of course.

W: It's good that you're so considerate. Remember the
last time we came to the theater? The couple behind
us would not be quiet. __________ __________
__________ __________ __________, too.

M: Yeah, they had no manners. The usher had to come
by three times to ask them to be silent.

W: Yeah, it was really annoying. It made it difficult
to enjoy the performance. It didn't help that you
__________ __________ __________ all over the
floor and the people in front of us got their shoes
wet and sticky.

M: __________ __________ __________. Anyway, the
play is starting now.

W: Great. I hope it goes better than last time.

11

M: Good morning, students and faculty! I would like
to announce the 20th Annual Maple High Essay
Contest. __________ __________ __________
__________ __________ more and more these days,
so this year we want to hear your ideas about how we
can protect the environment. There is a 1,000-word

limit on these essays, and __________ __________
__________ __________ via the school's homepage.
For those of you planning on participating,
__________ __________ __________ __________
__________ __________ April 20th. The top three
essays will be announced at the end of the month,
and prizes will be awarded. The first-place essay
will receive $500. The second- and third-place
essays will receive $200 and $100 respectively.
__________ __________ __________ __________
__________, the first-place essay will also be
published in the city newspaper. We encourage all
of you to participate. More entries mean more ideas,
and more ideas mean more help for the environment!

12

M: What are you doing, darling?

W: I'm looking at a leaflet on piano lessons for the kids.
I think Susan needs to learn how to play the piano.

M: I agree with you. But does she have time to take
any classes? __________ __________ __________
__________.

W: Don't worry about that. Her violin class is going to
finish on March 29th, so she's free after that.

M: I see. Then how about the one that starts at 6:30 p.m.?

W: I think it would be better for her __________
__________ __________ __________ __________
__________.

M: True. Well, there are a couple of classes that start at
5 p.m. Which one is better?

W: It doesn't matter as long as it's not on Thursday.
She has to __________ __________ __________
__________ __________ __________.

M: Okay, so there is only one class that she can take.
When is the deadline for registration?

W: The leaflet says it is March 10th, so we should hurry
before it fills up.

M: Oh, let's register right now.

13

M: You look upset, Nora. What's the matter?

W: I __________ __________ __________ __________
__________ this afternoon. It's very precious to me
because my father bought it for me when I got into
college.

M: What? The black one you always ride?

W: Yes.

M: What happened to it?

W: I parked it next to the law building.

M: Did you leave it __________ __________ __________ __________ __________ __________?

W: A designated bicycle parking area? What do you mean?

M: Oh, you didn't hear about the new regulation? On campus, you're only allowed to park bikes in designated areas.

W: So __________ __________ __________ __________ __________ because I parked it in the wrong place?

M: Could be.

W: How can I __________ __________ __________?

M: (First, go and see whether the place you left it in is a designated area.)

14

W: Hi, Louis! I never expected to see you here. What's up?

M: Hey, Francis. You were talking about your X-Cross exercise routine and got me curious.

W: I see. Are you looking to start?

M: I think so. You were telling me __________ __________ __________ __________ and how you're happier. I think I need that kind of change in my life.

W: Well, X-Cross does __________ __________ __________ __________ __________. It's also great for your mind.

M: Cool. I've been thinking I should get in shape. I've really let myself go these past few years.

W: Well, I think this program is perfect for you. Why don't you __________ __________ __________ __________ __________?

M: I think I will. I'll __________ __________ today.

W: Nice! I'll help you get started.

M: Thanks. But, like I said, I'm not in very good shape. Do you think I'll do all right in the class?

W: (Of course you will. You can start with an easy routine.)

15

W: Last month, a massive earthquake hit Japan. Many people died, and others __________ __________ __________ __________ __________. Bella decided to hold a fundraiser to __________ __________ and collect other things that could help those affected by the disaster. Almost everyone in her life __________ __________ __________ to donate clothing, canned goods, and money. However, one of her closest friends, Nathaniel, __________ __________ __________ __________ about helping the people who needed help. Later, Bella found out from a friend that Nathaniel actually donated all of his savings to a charity set up to __________ __________ __________ __________. This makes her feel good. What would Bella most likely say to Nathaniel when she sees him?

Bella: Nathaniel, (it's great that you made such a large contribution.)

16-17

M: Good afternoon, everyone. I'd like to talk to you today about recreational camping. In the early days of camping, many people used it as a way to be __________ __________ __________ __________ __________. Others disliked camping because __________ __________ __________ __________ leaky tents, damp sleeping bags, and terrible food. These inconveniences brought about the birth of the camping car and the recreational vehicle. There's a new camping trend gaining popularity these days. It's called 'glamping'. The word is a combination of the words *glamour* and *camping*. When you go glamping, you don't have to __________ __________ __________ or set up a sleeping bag. You don't even have to build a fire. Glamping is a way to take in nature from a hut, a prebuilt tent, or a treehouse. You don't have to give up your daily luxuries to go glamping. This pastime is gaining popularity because it allows you to be in the countryside __________ __________ __________ __________ __________. Glamping provides electricity, showers, and even a toilet. It's also easy to cook meals on __________ __________ __________ __________ __________ __________ when you go glamping.

실수 없는 수능 듣기 만점 공략!

Listening

수능 듣기 실전 모의고사 20회

정답 및 해설

목차

01회 실전 모의고사 ⋯⋯⋯⋯⋯⋯⋯⋯⋯ 02

02회 실전 모의고사 ⋯⋯⋯⋯⋯⋯⋯⋯⋯ 07

03회 실전 모의고사 ⋯⋯⋯⋯⋯⋯⋯⋯⋯ 12

04회 실전 모의고사 ⋯⋯⋯⋯⋯⋯⋯⋯⋯ 17

05회 실전 모의고사 ⋯⋯⋯⋯⋯⋯⋯⋯⋯ 22

06회 실전 모의고사 ⋯⋯⋯⋯⋯⋯⋯⋯⋯ 27

07회 실전 모의고사 ⋯⋯⋯⋯⋯⋯⋯⋯⋯ 32

08회 실전 모의고사 ⋯⋯⋯⋯⋯⋯⋯⋯⋯ 37

09회 실전 모의고사 ⋯⋯⋯⋯⋯⋯⋯⋯⋯ 42

10회 실전 모의고사 ⋯⋯⋯⋯⋯⋯⋯⋯⋯ 47

11회 실전 모의고사 ⋯⋯⋯⋯⋯⋯⋯⋯⋯ 52

12회 실전 모의고사 ⋯⋯⋯⋯⋯⋯⋯⋯⋯ 57

13회 실전 모의고사 ⋯⋯⋯⋯⋯⋯⋯⋯⋯ 62

14회 실전 모의고사 ⋯⋯⋯⋯⋯⋯⋯⋯⋯ 67

15회 실전 모의고사 ⋯⋯⋯⋯⋯⋯⋯⋯⋯ 72

16회 실전 모의고사 ⋯⋯⋯⋯⋯⋯⋯⋯⋯ 77

17회 실전 모의고사 ⋯⋯⋯⋯⋯⋯⋯⋯⋯ 82

18회 실전 모의고사 ⋯⋯⋯⋯⋯⋯⋯⋯⋯ 87

19회 실전 모의고사 ⋯⋯⋯⋯⋯⋯⋯⋯⋯ 92

20회 실전 모의고사 ⋯⋯⋯⋯⋯⋯⋯⋯⋯ 97

01 수능영어듣기 실전모의고사

01 ①	02 ②	03 ⑤	04 ①	05 ②	06 ④
07 ③	08 ④	09 ③	10 ⑤	11 ⑤	12 ①
13 ③	14 ④	15 ③	16 ②	17 ④	

01 짧은 대화의 응답

소재 새로 이사한 아파트

듣기 대본 해석
남: 새 아파트로 물건들 다 옮겼니, Wanda?
여: 응. 1층이라서 어렵지 않았어.
남: 멋진데. 너네 아파트에 옥외 테라스는 있니?
여: ① 응. 그래서 내가 이곳을 선택한 거야.

어휘
patio *n.* 옥외 테라스

정답 ①

문제풀이
1층이라는 여자의 말에 남자는 옥외 테라스가 있는지 물었으므로 ① '응. 그래서 내가 이곳을 선택한 거야.'가 가장 적절하다.

오답 보기 해석
② 아니. 내 가구를 옮기는 게 많이 어려웠어.
③ 난 주택이 좋은데 아파트는 너무 시끄럽거든.
④ 맞아. 난 항상 꼭대기 층에서 살고 싶었어.
⑤ 물론. 너 지난주 내 파티에 왔어야 하는데.

총 어휘 수 42

02 짧은 대화의 응답

소재 손가락 깁스

듣기 대본 해석
여: 오, 손가락에 깁스했네요. 다쳤어요?
남: 네. 훈련 중에 슬라이딩 태클을 당했는데 손으로 짚고 넘어졌어요.
여: 의사에게 가 보는 게 좋을 거예요. Dr. Kebb을 방문해 봤어요?
남: ② 갔다 왔어요. 괜찮을 거라고 했어요.

어휘
cast *n.* 깁스 〈문제〉injury *n.* 상처 referee *n.* 심판

정답 ②

문제풀이
여자는 손가락을 다친 남자에게 의사에게 가봐야겠다고 말했으므로 이에 대한 남자의 가장 적절한 응답은 ② '갔다 왔어요. 괜찮을 거라고 했어요.'이다.

오답 보기 해석
① 상처가 아주 심해 보여요.
③ 같이 연습하러 가는 건 어때요?
④ 아뇨. 저는 경기에 참가 안 할 것 같아요.
⑤ 심판이 그에게 레드 카드를 줬어야 했어요.

총 어휘 수 44

03 담화 주제

소재 꽃밭 가꾸기

듣기 대본 해석
여: 보통 당신의 자녀와 주말을 어떻게 보내십니까? 그들과 꽃밭을 만드는 것을 생각해 본 적이 있나요? 정원을 가꾸는 것은 자녀를 밖에 데리고 나가서 생활 기술을 가르치고 동시에 당신의 뜰을 밝아지게 만드는 멋진 방법입니다. 꽃밭은 아름답고, 다른 꽃들을 고르고 그것들이 자라는 것을 지켜보는 일은 아주 재미 있습니다. 만약에 당신의 자녀가 밖에서 충분한 시간을 보내지 않는 것이 염려되거나 책임감을 배우지 못하는 것이 걱정된다면 꽃밭은 그 두 가지 문제 모두에 도움을 줄 것입니다. 당신이 식물을 보살피는 동안 아이들은 무언가를 돌보는 것과 시작한 것을 끝내는 것이 왜 중요한지를 알 수 있습니다. 이는 아이들이 자연스럽게 개인적이고 사회적인 책임감을 발달시키도록 해줍니다. 이번 봄에 가족 시간을 위해 새로운 것을 시도해보세요. 꽃밭을 만들고 아이들이 꽃피우는 것을 지켜보세요!

어휘
brighten *v.* 밝히다, ~에 생기를 주다 be concerned about ~을 염려하다, ~에 관심을 가지다 responsibility *n.* 책임감 blossom *v.* 꽃을 피우다

정답 ⑤

문제풀이
아이들과 꽃밭을 가꾸면 아이들에게 어떤 점이 좋은지를 말해주고 있으므로 정답은 ⑤ '아이들과 꽃밭을 가꿀 때의 이로움'이다.

총 어휘 수 139

04 의견

소재 혼자 있는 시간

듣기 대본 해석
여: Jeff, 최근에 직장에서 당신을 못 봤네요. 어디에 있었나요?
남: 몇 주 휴가를 내고 인도로 배낭여행을 갔었어요.
여: 혼자 갔었나요?
남: 네. 저는 혼자 여행하는 것을 정말 즐겨해요.
여: 하지만 외롭게 느껴지지 않았나요?
남: 별로요. 저는 혼자 있는 것이 정신 건강에 좋다고 생각해요. 자기 반성을 할 수 있게 하고, 다른 사람들과 여행하는 것보다 스트레스를 덜 받아요.
여: 그럼 당신은 혼자 있는 시간을 갖는 것이 중요하다고 생각하나요?
남: 전적으로요.
여: 글쎄요, 개인적으로 저는 혼자 있을 때 정말 불안하고 염려가 돼요. 제 생각에 저는 좀 더 사회적 존재인가 봐요.
남: 저도 그랬었어요. 하지만 저는 혼자 있는 시간을 즐기는 것을 배웠고, 그게 제가 사회 생활 하는 데 정말 도움이 됐어요. 그것은 제 자신과 다른 사람들에게 좀 더 편안해지도록 도와주었어요.
여: 아하, 저는 당신이 뭘 의미하는지 알 것 같아요.

어휘
self-reflection *n.* 자기 반성 absolutely *ad.* 전적으로, 그럼(물론이지) uneasy *a.* 불안한 anxious *a.* 불안해하는, 염려하는 creature *n.* (생명이 있는) 존재 comfortable *a.* 편안한

정답 ①

문제풀이
남자는 혼자 있는 시간이 자기 반성에 좋고 정신 건강에도 좋다고 말하면서 그것이 사회 생활에도 도움이 됐다고 했다. 따라서 남자의 의견으로 ① '사람은 혼자만의 시간을 가질 필요가 있다.'이다.

총 어휘 수 135

05 대화자의 관계 파악

소재 구직자와의 인터뷰

듣기 대본 해석

여: 좋은 아침입니다.

남: Jackson씨군요. 앉으세요.

여: 감사합니다.

남: 당신의 자격증들을 살펴봤고 그리고 당신이 대학을 수석으로 졸업했다는 사실이 매우 인상 깊더군요.

여: 음. 저는 건축학을 전공했습니다. 저는 어릴 적 블록들을 가지고 놀기 시작한 후부터 그것에 관심을 갖고 있습니다. 그래서 저에겐 매우 자연스러운 일이지요.

남: 훌륭하군요. 또한 여기 보면 당신이 Carter & Young에서 인턴을 한 것으로 보이네요.

여: 네. 작년 여름방학 동안 그 사무실에서 일했습니다.

남: 좋습니다. 그럼. 저희 채용에 대해 어떻게 아셨죠?

여: 교수님께서 소개해 주셨습니다.

남: 알겠습니다. 만약 우리가 당신을 고용하기로 결정한다면. 어떤 종류의 건축에 관심을 갖고 계십니까?

여: 저는 상업 개발에 매우 관심이 많습니다.

남: 당신은 저희 회사에 잘 어울리는 것 같습니다.

여: 그렇게 말씀해 주시다니 감사합니다.

어휘

credential *n.* 자격증 **valedictorian** *n.* 졸업생 대표, 수석 졸업생
architecture *n.* 건축학 **hire** *v.* 고용하다 **commercial** *a.* 상업의

정답 ②

문제풀이

남자는 여자의 이력에 대한 질문을 하면서 채용에 대해 어떻게 알았는지 묻고 있고, 여자는 그에 알맞은 답을 하고 있으므로 면접하는 상황임을 알 수 있다. 따라서 정답은 ② '면접관 — 구직자'이다.

총 어휘 수 142

06 그림의 세부 내용 파악

소재 선거 포스터 제작

듣기 대본 해석

여: 안녕. Patrick!

남: 안녕. Teresa. 뭐하고 있니?

여: 나는 우리 선거 운동 포스터를 거의 끝냈어.

남: 대단해! 배경에 사용할 좋은 학교 사진 찾았어?

여: 응. 그리고 전경으로는 가리키고 있는 우리 사진을 사용했어.

남: 좋아 보인다. 우리 옆에 네가 그린 현수막도 마음에 들어.

여: 좋은 선거 운동 구호가 떠오르지 않았어. 미안해.

남: 괜찮아. 그런데 오른쪽에 있는 후보 번호가 좋아 보이지는 않는 듯해.

여: 네가 말하고 나서 보니. 그게 왼쪽에 있는 게 아마도 더 좋아 보이겠어. 하단에 우리 학교 이름과 우리가 출마한 직위는 어때?

남: 괜찮은 거 같아. 잘했어. Teresa.

여: 고마워. 기억해. 우리는 내일 아침 8시 30분까지 선거 캠페인을 시작해야 한다는 걸.

남: 알았어. 내가 늦어도 7시 30분까지는 거기 가 있을게. 고마워.

어휘

campaign *n.* 선거 운동, 캠페인 **slogan** *n.* 구호 **candidate** *n.* 후보 **election** *n.* 선거

정답 ④

문제풀이

남자가 후보 번호가 오른쪽에 있는 것이 좋아 보이지는 않는다고 한 것으로 보아 후보 번호는 오른쪽에 있어야 하나. 그림에서는 왼쪽에 있으므로 그림에서 대화 내용과 일치하지 않는 것은 ④번이다.

총 어휘 수 149

07 할 일

소재 남편의 양복 찾아다 주기

듣기 대본 해석

[휴대폰이 울린다.]

여: 여보. 집에 오는 중이에요?

남: 네. 그런데 도로가 매우 붐비네요. 무엇이 교통 체증을 유발하고 있는지 궁금하네요.

여: 사고 같은 게 난 거예요?

남: 어떻게 된 건지 잘 모르겠어요. 배고프면 나 없이 저녁 먹어요.

여: 좋아요. 언제 도착할 것 같아요?

남: 정말 모르겠어요. 부탁 좀 들어줄 수 있어요?

여: 물론이죠. 무슨 일인데요?

남: 세탁소에 들러서 내 회색 정장을 찾아줄래요? 내일 중요한 발표 때 그걸 입고 싶어서요.

여: 물론이죠. 지금 거기 가서 가져올게요.

남: 정말 고마워요. 여보. 내가 미리 돈은 냈으니까 그냥 가져오면 돼요. 곧 집에 도착할 수 있으면 좋겠네요.

여: 좋아요. 여보. 여기 오면 봐요.

어휘

on one's way ~ ~에 가는 중인 **presentation** *n.* 발표
in advance 미리

정답 ③

문제풀이

남편이 아내에게 양복점에서 자신의 회색 정장을 찾아달라고 부탁했으므로 정답은 ③ '회색 정장을 찾아오기'이다.

오답 보기 해석

① 저녁 만들기
② 집에 더 일찍 오기
④ 그에게 교통 상황 알려주기
⑤ 그의 발표 준비 도와주기

총 어휘 수 135

08 이유

소재 야구 경기 전 상대편 선수의 영상 보기

듣기 대본 해석

여: Tommy. 내일 상대팀 선발투수의 영상 본 적 있니?

남: 아직. 근데 진짜 놀랍다고 들었어.

여: 응. 맞아. 인터넷에서 모두 그에 대해서 난리야. 하이라이트 볼래?

남: 음... 보면 안 될 것 같아.

여: 왜? 왜 그렇게 잘하는지 보고 싶지 않아?

남: 그랑 경기할 때까지 기다리는 게 좋을 것 같아.

여: 근데 동영상 몇 개 보면 경기를 더 준비할 수 있지 않을까?

남: 훈련이 준비하는 더 좋은 방법인 것 같아.

여: 다른 선수들도 그 얘기 많이 했어. 동영상 보는 게 경기 준비에 도움이 안 된대.

남: 맞는 말이야. 동영상을 보는 건 시간 낭비야. 거실보다 체육관에서 시간을 보내는 게 더 좋을 것 같아.

starting pitcher (야구) 선발투수 **highlight** *n.* 하이라이트, 가장 흥미로운 부분 **prepare** *v.* 준비하다 **gym** *n.* 체육관

정답 ④

문제풀이

여자는 남자에게 야구 경기 전 상대팀 선수의 활약을 보여주는 동영상을 보라고 하지만 남자는 동영상을 보는 것보다 실제 연습하는 편이 더 나은 경기 준비라고 말하였으므로 정답은 ④ '연습하는 것이 낫다고 생각해서'이다.

총 어휘 수 128

09 숫자

소재 피자 주문

듣기 대본 해석

남: Brother's 피자에 전화 주셔서 감사합니다. 주문을 받을까요?
여: 네, 트리플 치즈 피자 라지로 주세요. 얼마가 될까요?
남: 스페셜토핑을 얹은 라지 사이즈는 보통 25달러지만 오늘은 고객 감사의 날이라 모든 라지 피자를 레귤러 사이즈 피자의 가격으로 사실 수 있습니다.
여: 아, 좋네요. 그러면 치킨윙 주문도 추가할게요.
남: 네. 이제 다 된 건가요?
여: 네, 그게 전부예요.
남: 좋아요. 피자는 20달러이고 치킨윙은 10달러, 전부 30달러가 되겠어요.
여: 이번 주문에서 쿠폰을 사용할 수 있나요?
남: 물론이죠. 쿠폰을 웹사이트에서 받으셨나요?
여: 네, 10퍼센트 할인이 되네요.
남: 배달원이 도착하면 그에게 건네주세요.

어휘

customer *n.* 고객

정답 ③

문제풀이

원래 라지 사이즈의 피자가 25달러인데 오늘이 고객 감사의 날이라서 레귤러 가격인 20달러이고, 10달러짜리 치킨윙을 추가했으므로 합이 30달러이다. 그리고 남자가 10퍼센트 할인 쿠폰을 사용할 수 있다고 말했으므로 여자는 27달러를 내게 된다. 따라서 정답은 ③ '$27'이다.

총 어휘 수 129

10 언급 유무

소재 흥미롭게 생긴 건물

듣기 대본 해석

남: 안녕. 컴퓨터로 무엇을 보고 있니?
여: 런던으로 여름 휴가 갔을 때 찍은 몇몇의 사진들이야. 한번 볼래?
남: 물론이지. [잠시 후] 이 건물 흥미롭네. 피클처럼 생겼네.
여: 맞아. 작은 피클인 오이 피클과 비슷해 보여서 런던 사람들은 그것을 "The Gherkin"이라고 불러.
남: 그것의 진짜 이름은 뭐니?
여: 30 Saint Mary Axe야. 그건 이 건물의 주소야.
남: 그 건물 안에는 뭐가 있니?
여: 음, 그것이 런던의 금융가에 위치하고 있어서, 많은 다른 금융 회사와 몇몇의 식당도 수용하고 있어.
남: 높이는 얼마인데?
여: 대략 180m 정도 된다고 생각해. 41층이나 돼.
남: 안에 들어 갔었니?
여: 응. 내부 사진을 찍었어. 사진 볼래?

어휘

gherkin *n.* 오이 피클 **address** *n.* 주소 **financial district** 금융가 **house** *v.* 수용하다 **along with** ～도 함께

정답 ⑤

문제풀이

건물의 겉모습, 주소, 용도, 층수에 관한 언급은 있지만 건축 년도에 관한 언급은 없으므로 정답은 ⑤ '건축 년도'이다.

총 어휘 수 118

11 내용 일치 · 불일치

소재 중고 물건 판매점

듣기 대본 해석

남: 여러분의 집은 필요 없는 물건들로 채워져 있나요? 먼지가 쌓여 있는 오래된 TV, 냉장고, 컴퓨터를 가지고 계신가요? 그럼, Big Bear Resale Services는 여러분께 딱 맞는 곳입니다. 저희는 20년 동안 고객들이 원하지 않는 물건들을 파는 사업을 해 왔습니다. 저희는 여러분의 오래된, 중고 물품으로부터 최상의 돈을 받을 수 있도록 최고의 골동품 가게, 폐품 처리장, 개인적인 구매자들과 일하고 있습니다. 여러분이 해야 할 일은 전화기를 들어서 저희에게 전화하는 것이 전부입니다. 저희는 여러분이 계신 곳에 가서 오래된 물건들을 살펴보고, 사진을 찍고, 관심이 있는 구매자를 찾기 위해 웹사이트에 사진을 올립니다. 그리고 나서 저희는 여러분의 물건들을 무료로 픽업하고 배달도 합니다. 오늘 Big Bear Resale Services에 전화주세요!

어휘

cluttered *a.* 어수선한, 필요 없는 **antique** *n.* 골동품 **scrapyard** *n.* 폐품 처리장 **assure** *v.* 장담하다, 확언하다 **appraise** *v.* 살피다, 뜯어보다 **buyer** *n.* 구매자

정답 ⑤

문제풀이

Big Bear Resale Services는 집에 있는 오래된 물건들을 팔아주는 곳으로 마지막 부분에서 물건을 픽업하고 배달하는 것도 무료로 해준다고 말했으므로 일치하지 않는 것은 ⑤ '픽업과 배달 서비스는 유료이다.'이다.

총 어휘 수 126

12 도표

소재 동아리 선택

듣기 대본 해석

여: Aaron, 안녕. 방과후 영어 동아리에 들어갈 생각이야.
남: 백 선생님께서도 나보고 계속 하나 들어가라 그러셔.
여: 그럼 같이 하나 들어가자. 전학 온 지 얼마 안 돼서 네가 거의 내 유일한 친구야.
남: 좋은 생각이야. 선생님께서 이 시간표 주셨어. 이 동아리는 어때? 난 항상 연기를 한번 해보고 싶었어.
여: 나도 그 동아리 진짜 들고 싶은데 월요일에는 학교 끝나고 피아노 연습 가야 돼. 토론 동아리는 어때? 토론하는 게 항상 흥미로웠어.
남: 난 독서를 많이 할 수 있는 동아리가 좋을 것 같아. 말하기랑 토론하기에는 별로 관심 없어.
여: 음, 이제 남은 동아리가 두 개로 좁혀졌네. 어떤 것을 고를까?
남: 이 동아리가 회원이 더 많은가 보네. 가입하자.
여: 응. 그래야 내가 친구를 사귈 기회가 더 많으니까.
남: 그러니까. 내가 우리 둘을 가입해 놓을게.

어휘

afterschool *a.* 방과후   **debate** *n.* 토론 *v.* 토론하다   **option** *n.*
선택, 옵션   **sign up** 가입하다

정답 ①

문제풀이

연기 동아리인 ③번은 여자가 시간이 안 된다고 했고 남자는 토론과 말하기보
다는 독서를 하고 싶다고 했으므로 남는 것은 ①번과 ④번이다. 이 둘 중에 회
원이 더 많은 곳으로 하자고 했으므로 정답은 ①번이다.

총 어휘 수 154

13 긴 대화의 응답

소재 회의 준비

듣기 대본 해석

여: 뭔가 지금 급하신가 봐요?
남: Craig 봤어요?
여: Craig요? 아침 일찍 나한테 전화해서 아프다고 했는데, 그래서 그는 안
　　왔어요.
남: 정말이에요? 그는 이번 달에 세 번이나 아프다고 전화했었어요.
여: 그는 몇 주 동안 꽤 아픈 것 같았어요. 무슨 문제가 있나요?
남: 그와 저는 오늘 사업 동업자들과 만나기로 되어 있었고, 그가 그 회의를
　　소집한 사람이거든요.
여: 오, 정말이에요?
남: 그는 가끔 굉장히 무책임하네요. 어쨌든, 그가 회의를 위해 준비했던
　　유인물을 본 적이 있나요?
여: 어떻게 생겼어요?
남: 지난 분기 동안 회사의 재정과 판매 순위에 관한 많은 정보와 데이터가
　　들어 있어요.
여: 제가 찾아보기 시작해보고, 찾으면 갖다 드릴게요.
남: ③ 고마워요. 제가 신세를 지네요.

어휘

in a hurry 서두르는   **call in sick** 아파서 결근한다고 전화하다
call a meeting 회의를 소집하다   **irresponsible** *a.* 무책임한
handout *n.* 유인물   **regarding** *prep.* ~에 관한   **finance** *n.* 재정

정답 ③

문제풀이

남자는 회의를 준비해야 하는데 Craig의 결근으로 여자가 회의 준비에 필요한
유인물을 찾아서 갖다 준다고 말했으므로 그에 대한 응답으로 가장 적절한 것은
③ '고마워요. 제가 신세를 지네요.'이다.

오답 보기 해석

① 회의를 취소해야 해요.
② 당신 병원에 가봐야 할 것 같아요.
④ 저는 이미 정보를 모두 복사했어요.
⑤ 네, 좋아요. Craig한테 도움 좀 받아요.

총 어휘 수 141

14 긴 대화의 응답

소재 서로 다른 게임 선호도

듣기 대본 해석

남: 안녕, Carol. 너 휴대폰으로 새로운 Candy Stomp 게임을 하고 있구나.
여: 응. 내 친구 James가 한번 해보라고 추천해 줬어.
남: 나도 그거 정말 해보고 싶었는데, 네가 끝나면 내가 그것을 해봐도 괜찮을까?

여: 문제없어. 몇 분 후에 너에게 줄게.
남: 너무 좋아. 너 Battle of the Clans 해본 적 있어? 그거 꽤 재미있어.
여: 그거 한 번 해봤는데, 나는 지루하게 느꼈는데.
남: 정말? 그거 매우 인기 있는데.
여: 음, 내 취향에는 너무 복잡했어. 나는 단순한 게임을 좋아해.
남: 그거 그렇게 복잡하지는 않은 것 같은데. 심지어 내 어린 사촌도 하던걸.
여: 나는 거기에 집중할 수 없었어. 나는 다른 사람들 같지 않나 봐.
남: 음, 모든 사람이 같은 의견을 갖는 것은 아니니까. 그렇지?
여: ④ 네 말이 맞아. 모든 사람들이 다른 선호도를 갖지.

어휘

recommend *v.* 추천하다   **popular** *a.* 인기 있는   **complicated**
a. 복잡한   **opinion** *n.* 의견   〈문제〉**broken** *a.* 고장 난, 깨진
relax *v.* 긴장을 풀다, 진정하다   **preference** *n.* 선호도

정답 ④

문제풀이

남자가 말한 게임은 많은 사람들이 좋아하는 게임인데 여자는 좋아하지 않는다고
말하고 있는 상황이다. 마지막에 남자가 모든 사람이 같은 의견을 갖는 것은
아니라고 말하며 되물었으므로 여자의 적절한 대답은 ④ '네 말이 맞아. 모든
사람들이 다른 선호도를 갖지.'이다.

오답 보기 해석

① 미안한데, 넌 할 수 없어. 내 폰이 고장 났어.
② 물론이야. 컴퓨터 게임을 하는 것은 내가 긴장을 풀도록 도와줘.
③ 문제 없어. 그게 바로 우정이지.
⑤ 너는 다른 게임을 찾아야 할 것 같아.

총 어휘 수 135

15 상황에 적절한 말

소재 기차표 구매하기

듣기 대본 해석

여: 뉴욕시티에서 친구를 만난 후 Taylor는 고향인 Minneapolis로 돌아가는
　　기차를 타러 Grand Central 역으로 가고 있습니다. 역으로 가는 길이
　　생각보다 차가 너무 막히고 택시는 천천히 가고 있습니다. Taylor는 기차
　　시간에 늦을까 봐 걱정됩니다. 역에 도착하자 출발 시간까지 이십 분 남아
　　있는 것을 봅니다. 표를 사는 줄은 굉장히 깁니다. 그는 역무원을 발견하고
　　표를 살 수 있는 다른 곳이 있는지 물어보고 싶어합니다. 이러한 상황에서
　　Taylor가 역무원에게 할 말로 가장 적절한 것은 무엇일까요?
Taylor: ③ 표를 살 수 있는 다른 곳이 있나요?

어휘

congested *a.* 차가 막히는, 혼잡한   **departure** *n.* 출발, 떠남

정답 ③

문제풀이

Taylor는 기차역에 시간적인 여유 없이 도착했는데 표를 사기 위해 기다려야
하는 줄이 매우 긴 것을 발견하고, 역무원에게 다른 곳에서 표를 살 수 있는지
묻고자 한다. 이 상황에 Taylor가 할말로 가장 적절한 것은 ③ '표를 살 수 있는
다른 곳이 있나요?'이다.

오답 보기 해석

① 여기 뉴욕에서 친구와 즐거운 시간을 보냈어요.
② 기차 플랫폼으로 갈 수 있는 방법을 가르쳐 주시겠어요?
④ 이곳은 제가 본 기차역 중에서 가장 좋은 기차역이네요.
⑤ Minneapolis로 가는 표 한 장 주세요.

총 어휘 수 130

소재 시에서 운영하는 조합 소개

듣기 대본 해석

여: 안녕하세요, 여러분. 저희 시에서 제공하는 사회적 행사에 대해 여러분 모두 아실 것이라 확신합니다만, 조합에 대해서는 아시나요? 저희 시의 조합은 우리 지역 공동체에 매우 중요합니다. 매일 열리기 때문에 회원들은 기금 마련, 자원봉사 프로젝트와 같은 지역사회 행사에 참여할 뿐 아니라, 신선한 농산물과 요리방법들을 교환할 수 있습니다. 조합은 공동체 내 회원들로 하여금 서로 돕는 데 참여하도록 하지요. 아마 여러분께서는 어떻게 조합에 가입하고, 참여하는지 궁금해하실 수 있겠네요. 회원들은 서로 소통하고, 예정된 행사들을 홍보하는 데 Twitter와 KakaoTalk과 같은 여러 소셜 미디어 수단들을 활용한답니다. 또한 우리는 Facebook 페이지를 갖고 있고, 때때로 기금마련을 위해 온라인 캠페인을 운영합니다. 이전에 저희가 했던 프로젝트들이 어떤 종류가 있는지 보려면 YouTube에 가보셔도 되고요. 여러분이 조합에 가입함으로써 동료 지역사회 일원들과 함께 하길 촉구하는 바입니다. 시간 내주셔서 감사합니다.

어휘

co-op *n.* 조합   **produce** *n.* 농산물   **upcoming** *a.* 다가오는, 곧 있을

정답 16 ② 17 ④

문제풀이

16 여자는 조합 활동 내용에 대해 상세히 이야기하면서 조합에 참여하기를 유도하고 있으므로 정답은 ② '조합을 통한 지역사회 (행사) 참여'이다.

17 여자는 조합원들이 소통하고, 행사를 홍보하는 소셜 미디어로 Twitter, KakaoTalk, Facebook을 언급하였고, 이전 프로젝트를 보기 위해 YouTube 페이지를 볼 것을 권하였다. 언급되지 않은 것은 ④ 'Instagram'이다.

오답 보기 해석

16

① 소셜 네트워킹의 다른 유형들
③ 소셜 네트워킹을 이용한 조직적 방법
④ 곧 있을 지역사회 행사에 참여하는 것
⑤ 지역사회 프로그램에 참여하는 것의 이점

총 어휘 수 158

DICTATION ANSWERS

01 Did you get everything moved into

02 fell on my hand

03 brighten up your yard / you're concerned about / caring for the plants / watch your children blossom

04 go backpacking / feel lonely / It allows time for self-reflection / I'm more of a social creature / enjoy time alone

05 looking over your credentials / it comes quite naturally to me / we decide to hire you / you would be a great fit for our company

06 come up with any good / would look better on the left / by seven thirty at the latest

07 on your way home / what's causing the bad traffic / do me a favor / I paid for it in advance

08 the opposing team's starting pitcher / is going crazy about him / we play against him / watching videos doesn't help them prepare for games

09 May I take your order / regular-sized one / In that case / Is it possible to use a coupon

10 It looks like a pickle / That's its address / it houses many different financial companies / It's forty-one stories high

11 cluttered with a bunch of junk / selling your unwanted items / for your old, used stuff / find an interested buyer / deliver them for free

12 has been pushing me to join one / I'd rather join a club / we have it narrowed down to two options

13 Are you in a hurry for some reason / who called the meeting / He can be so irresponsible / regarding the company's finances / I'll start looking for them

14 I try it out / Do you mind if I play / too complicated for my taste / not everyone can have the same opinion

15 The traffic on the way to the station / be late for his train / before the train's departure / if there is another place

16-17 participate in community events / to help one another / members use several social media outlets / I urge you to become one with

02 수능영어듣기 실전모의고사

01 ④	02 ①	03 ②	04 ②	05 ①	06 ⑤
07 ⑤	08 ③	09 ③	10 ⑤	11 ④	12 ④
13 ③	14 ②	15 ③	16 ⑤	17 ②	

01 짧은 대화의 응답

소재 컨디션이 좋지 않은 이유

듣기 대본 해석
남: 안녕, Lilly. 너 안 좋아 보여. 아주 피곤해 보이네.
여: 괜찮아. 하루 종일 두통이 있고 콧물이 날 뿐이야.
남: 심한 것 같아. 병원에 갔었니?
여: ④ 응. 오늘 아침에 의사를 만났어.

어휘
headache *n.* 두통　　**runny nose** 콧물　　**awful** *a.* 끔직한, 엄청

정답 ④

문제풀이
병원에 다녀왔냐고 묻는 남자의 질문에 적절한 대답은 ④ '응. 오늘 아침에 의사를 만났어.'이다.

오답 보기 해석
① 나는 간호사가 되기 위해 공부하고 있어.
② 아니. 나 아직 집에 안 갔어.
③ 너는 병원에 가야 해.
⑤ 좋을 것 같아. 내가 곧 낫기를 원해.

총 어휘 수 42

02 짧은 대화의 응답

소재 TV 프로그램

듣기 대본 해석
여: 너 내가 제일 좋아하는 텔레비전 프로그램 보고 있다고 들었어.
남: 그거 네가 좋아하는 거였어? 난 두 번째 회까지만 봤어. 지금까진 재미 없던데.
여: 맞아. 시작이 좀 지루하긴 한데 나중에 아주 재미있어져.
남: ① 그럼 계속 볼게.

어휘
boring *a.* 지루한, 재미없는

정답 ①

문제풀이
여자는 자신이 좋아하는 TV프로그램을 남자도 본다는 것을 알고, 시작은 지루하지만 나중에는 재미있어진다고 하였으므로, 남자가 이에 대해 할 말로 가장 적절한 것은 ① '그럼 계속 볼게.'이다.

오답 보기 해석
② 계속 봐봐.
③ 난 저 프로그램 한 번도 본 적 없어.
④ 너 다 보고 나한테 빌려줬으면 좋겠어.
⑤ 토요일 밤에 TV에서 하는 걸 볼 수 있어.

총 어휘 수 46

03 담화 목적

소재 캠핑장 이용 규칙

듣기 대본 해석
남: 안녕하세요, Walker Mountain State Park 캠핑장에 오신 것을 환영합니다. 저는 공원 관리원 Frank Reynolds이고 여기 주립 공원에서 지켜주셔야 할 규칙에 대해서 논하려고 합니다. 비누와 다른 세제용품에 있는 오염물질 때문에 지정된 곳에서만 샤워하고 설거지해주시기 바랍니다. 그리고 각 모닥불에 신경 쓰시고 자정 전에 꺼주시기 바랍니다. 불꽃놀이는 공원 부지 내에서 금지입니다. 아시다시피 방치된 모닥불과 불꽃은 야생동물들과 동료들을 위험에 빠트리는 산불을 일으킬 수 있습니다. 누군가가 이러한 규칙을 위반하는 것을 목격했을 경우 주저 없이 공원 경비원에게 알려주시기 바랍니다. 들어주셔서 감사하며 Walker Mountain State Park에서 즐거운 시간 보내시기 바랍니다.

어휘
discuss *v.* 상의하다, 논의하다　　**pollutant** *n.* 오염물질
designated *a.* 지정된　　**tend** *v.* ~에 신경 쓰다, 주의하다
extinguish *v.* 끄다, 없애다　　**prohibited** *a.* 금지된　　**premises** *n.* 부지, 지역, 구내　　**untended** *a.* 방치된, 돌봄을 받지 않은　　**hesitate** *v.* 망설이다, 주저하다　　**violate** *v.* 위반하다, 어기다

정답 ②

문제풀이
남자는 주립공원 관리원으로서 공원 내 캠핑장 이용 규칙에 대해서 설명하고 있으므로 정답은 ② '캠핑장 이용 수칙을 안내하려고'이다.

총 어휘 수 128

04 대화 주제

소재 명상의 이점

듣기 대본 해석
여: 안녕, Chase. 너 뭐 듣고 있어?
남: 안녕, Hailey. 명상에 관한 팟캐스트를 듣고 있어.
여: 명상. 어? 나는 그거 시도해 본 적 없는데.
남: 팟캐스트에서 많은 걸 배우고 있어. 사람들은 여러 가지 방법으로 명상으로 부터 좋은 점을 얻을 수 있다는 걸 아니? 예를 들면, 명상은 에너지를 북돋아 줘.
여: 흥미롭네. 그래서 만약에 내가 오후에 지쳤을 때 명상을 하면 도움이 되겠네.
남: 그럴 수 있지. 그들은 명상이 네가 밤에 잘 때 어떻게 도움을 주고 스트레스를 완화해 주는지에 대해서도 얘기하고 있어.
여: 정말? 그게 명상을 하는 사람들이 항상 그렇게 좋은 컨디션인 이유임에 틀림없어.
남: 맞아. 그들은 또 명상은 너의 건강을 증진시켜주고 정신을 선명하게 할 수 있다고도 말했어.
여: 그래서 명상이 정신적으로도 육체적으로도 좋은 거지?
남: 응, 너의 전체적인 건강에 좋아.
여: 나도 명상을 시작해야 한다고 생각해.
남: 나도 시작하려고 생각 중이야.

어휘
meditation *n.* 명상, 묵상　　**benefit** *v.* 득을 보다, 유용하다 *n.* 이득
boost *v.* 북돋우다　　**meditate** *v.* 명상하다　　**relieve** *v.* 없애다, 완화하다　　**sharpen** *v.* 분명하게 하다, 선명해지다　　**beneficial** *a.* 유익한, 이로운　　**mentally** *ad.* 정신적으로　　**physically** *ad.* 육체적으로

정답 ②

남자가 팟캐스트를 통해 들은 명상에 관한 좋은 점을 여자에게 말해주고 있으므로 정답은 ② '명상의 긍정적 효과'이다.

총 어휘 수 139

05 대화자의 관계 파악

소재 연극 연기 지도

듣기 대본 해석
남: Cindy, 대사를 외우는 건 어떻게 되어 가고 있나요?
여: 매우 잘 되고 있어요, Reynolds씨.
남: 당신이 빨리 할 수 있길 바라요. 우리는 시간이 많지 않아요.
여: 음, 외울 건 많은데 저는 겨우 오늘 아침에 대본을 받았어요.
남: 나도 알아요. 그렇지만 우리는 한 시간 더 공간을 대여했을 뿐이고, 우린 연기 억양 연습을 해야 해요.
여: 그래요, 지금 시작해요, 준비된 것 같아요.
남: 좋아요. 무대 왼쪽으로 와서 거기서부터 첫 대사를 해 봐요.
여: 네. *[잠시 후]* "아들을 낳을 때, 나는 두 번째 남편을 묻었어요." 어땠나요?
남: 좋아요. 이제, 같은 대사를 무대 오른쪽에서 해봅시다.
여: 알았어요. *[잠시 후]* "아들을 낳을 때, 나는 두 번째 남편을 묻었어요." 이게 나은가요?
남: 사실 그래요. 더 자연스러운 것 같아요.
여: 좋아요. 저는 개막공연이 너무 기대 되네요!
남: 그렇게 들으니 나도 기뻐요. 당신이 멋지게 해낼 거라고 믿어요.

어휘
line *n.* 대사   **script** *n.* 대본   **deliver** *v.* (강연, 연기, 대사 등을) 하다

정답 ①

문제풀이
Line, script, stage, opening 등의 단어에서 연극배우와 연출자와의 대화임을 유추할 수 있으므로 정답은 ① '감독 — 여배우'이다.

오답 보기 해석
② 미술 감독 – 심사위원
③ 상사 – 사무실 직원
④ 고객 – 미용사
⑤ 개인 트레이너 – 모델

총 어휘 수 151

06 그림의 세부 내용 파악

소재 얼음으로 만든 놀이터

듣기 대본 해석
남: 여기 정말 놀라워. 그렇지 않아?
여: 응, 좋은 시간을 보내고 있지만 꽤 춥네, 그렇지 않아?
남: 음, 한겨울이잖아. 저 뒤편에 고드름들 좀 봐. 뒤쪽에 특이한 얼음 조각품이 있어.
여: 동물을 타고 있는 원숭이를 말하는 거니?
남: 응. 원숭이가 타고 있는 게 어떤 동물이라고 생각해?
여: 돼지 같아. 그건 그렇고, 나는 전체 성을 얼음으로 지었다는 것을 믿을 수 없어.
남: 그래. 정말 멋있어 보여. 성 안을 확인해 보고 싶어?
여: 음, 나 지금 이 시소를 타는 게 너무 재미있어.
남: 나는 아냐. 네가 나보다 훨씬 커서 나는 계속 위에만 있잖아.
여: 맞아. 네가 말하고 보니, 항상 아래에 있는 것도 그렇게 재미있지 않아.
남: 그래. 그럼 우리 성으로 가볼래?

어휘
icicle *n.* 고드름   **peculiar** *a.* 특이한, 이상한   **sculpture** *n.* 조각품
now that ~이므로, ~이기 때문에

정답 ⑤

문제풀이
여자가 자신이 아래에만 있다고 했는데 위에 올라가 있으므로 정답은 ⑤번이다.

총 어휘 수 151

07 할 일

소재 손님 접대

듣기 대본 해석
여: 여보, 이번 금요일에 침실 재배치 도와줄 수 있어요?
남: 아무래도 못할 것 같아요. 다음 주 금요일에 할 수 있을까요?
여: 무슨 일이 생겼어요?
남: 네, 중요한 고객이 LA에서 오셔서 이번 주말에는 그녀를 접대해야 해요.
여: 주말 내내 바쁠까요?
남: 정확히 모르겠어요. 금요일 아침에 그녀가 도착하면 내가 공항에 데리러 가야 해요.
여: 그녀와 하루 종일 같이 보내야 해요?
남: 그녀가 도시를 관광하고 싶어 해서 내가 구경시켜 줘야 해요.
여: 그럼, 그녀가 중요한 고객이라면 저녁 식사에 초대하는 게 어때요?
남: 좋은 생각이에요. 프랑스 요리를 좀 해줄 수 있어요?
여: 알겠어요. 그러면 목요일에 식료품 장을 봐야겠어요.

어휘
rearrange *v.* 재배치하다   **entertain** *v.* 접대하다
be supposed to V ~하기로 되어 있다

정답 ⑤

문제풀이
여자의 '그럼, 그녀가 중요한 고객이라면 저녁 식사에 초대하는 게 어때요?'에서 고객을 저녁식사에 초대했음을 알 수 있으므로 여자가 남자를 위해 할 일로 적절한 것은 ⑤ '고객에게 식사 대접하기'이다.

총 어휘 수 123

08 이유

소재 새 유니폼 구매 요청

듣기 대본 해석
남: 안녕하세요, Temmel 선생님.
여: 안녕, John. 들어오렴. 무엇을 도와줄까?
남: 농구팀에 대해 드릴 말씀이 있어요.
여: 뭔데?
남: 음, 지난 시즌에 저희가 새로운 팀 유니폼을 샀던 것 아시죠.
여: 기억해. 모든 선수들에게 인기가 있었잖니.
남: 맞아요. 하지만 문제는 저희 라이벌 팀이 그들의 유니폼에 같은 색깔을 사용하고 있다는 거예요.
여: Mound High School 말이니?
남: 네. 제가 일전에 그 학교 학생들이 입고 있는 것을 봤어요.
여: 알았어. 그래서 너는 우리가 새로운 유니폼을 다시 사야 한다고 제안하는 거니?
남: 네. 그러면 다른 경기에선 다른 유니폼을 사용할 수 있어요.
여: 그래. 교장 선생님과 이야기해 보고 어떻게 생각하시는지 볼게.
남: 정말 감사해요, Temmel 선생님. 결정하시는 대로 저한테 알려주세요.

어휘

rival *n.* 맞수, 경쟁자   **principal** *n.* 교장

정답 ③

문제풀이

남자는 작년에 농구부의 새 유니폼을 구매했지만, 라이벌 팀에서 같은 색의 유니폼을 입은 걸 보고 새로운 유니폼을 다시 사야 한다고 제안하고 있다. 따라서 정답은 ③ '새 유니폼 구매를 요청하려고'이다.

총 어휘 수 129

09 숫자

소재 스쿠터 대여하기

듣기 대본 해석

여: 안녕하세요. 무엇을 도와드릴까요?
남: 안녕하세요. 오늘 오토바이 몇 대 빌리려고 해요.
여: 알겠습니다. 일단 50cc 스쿠터랑 125cc 오토바이가 있어요.
남: 그렇군요. 가격 차이는요?
여: 오토바이는 하루당 30달러예요. 스쿠터는 보통 25달러인데, 비수기 행사 중이라 추가로 10퍼센트 할인해 드려요.
남: 좋은데요! 그렇게 멀리까지 몰지는 않을 것 같으니까 스쿠터 두 대로 할게요.
여: 알겠습니다. 헬멧도 필요하신가요?
남: 그럼요. 탈 때 안전한 게 좋아요. 얼마예요?
여: 헬멧은 하루당 5달러인데, 행사에 포함은 안 돼요.
남: 그렇군요. 그럼 스쿠터 두 대랑 헬멧 두 개로 할게요.
여: 알겠습니다. 준비해 드릴게요.

어휘

rent *v.* 빌리다 *n.* 임대료   **promotion** *n.* 홍보, 판촉 행사

정답 ③

문제풀이

처음에 남자가 오늘 하루 빌린다고 했고, 스쿠터 두 대라 하루에 50달러인데 10퍼센트 할인을 해준다고 했으므로 45달러이고, 헬멧 두 개 대여료는 10달러이므로 정답은 ③ '$55'이다.

총 어휘 수 133

10 언급 유무

소재 지역사회 자원봉사

듣기 대본 해석

여: 안녕하세요, 여러분. 제 이름은 Terry Loggins이고요. 저는 오늘 지역사회에서 자원봉사 하는 것에 대해 여러분이 가지고 있을 만한 질문을 듣고자 여기 왔어요.
남: 안녕하세요, Terry. 저는 제 아이들을 얼마 동안 자원봉사에 참가시키고 싶었어요.
여: 마음 속에 생각해 둔 자원봉사는 어떤 종류인가요?
남: 음, 그들은 아직 중학생이니 너무 많이 할 수는 없어요.
여: 오, 그래도 가능한 자리가 있어요. 그들은 무료급식소나 노인복지시설에서 도와줄 수 있겠네요. 아니면 그들은 싱글맘이나 나이든 분들이 잔디 깎기나 쓰레기 치우기 같은 일상의 일을 하는 것을 도와줄 수 있어요.
남: 정말 좋은 추천이네요. 제가 어떻게 시작하면 되죠?
여: 시청에 들르세요. 그들은 모든 가능한 자원봉사 자리에 대한 목록을 가지고 있을 거예요.
남: 충분히 쉬워 보이네요.
여: 그것은 쉽고, 당신이 도와주는 사람들에게 큰 의미가 있을 거예요!

어휘

community *n.* 지역사회   **volunteer work** 자원봉사
soup kitchen 무료급식소   **retirement home** 노인복지시설
senior citizen 고령자, 노인   **mow** *v.* (잔디를) 깎다
recommendation *n.* 추천   **city hall** 시청

정답 ⑤

문제풀이

대화에서 자원봉사 할 사람, 장소, 활동 내용, 시작 방법에 관해서는 언급되어 있지만 봉사하게 될 시간에 관해서는 언급되지 않았으므로 정답은 ⑤ '자원봉사 하게 될 시간'이다.

총 어휘 수 144

11 내용 일치 · 불일치

소재 과학 박람회 소개

듣기 대본 해석

여: 우리는 과학 박람회의 첫 번째 라운드가 끝났고 학생들이 제출한 아이디어를 기초로 예선전을 통해 선발된 25명의 학생들이 있습니다. 마지막 라운드에 자격이 있는 모든 학생들은 오늘날의 세계에 관련이 있고 유용한 아이디어를 제출했습니다. 마지막 라운드는 5월 22일인 오늘부터 2주 동안 학생 센터 이벤트 홀에서 열릴 것입니다. 이번에는 학생들이 그들의 아이디어로 작동하는 모델을 만들 것입니다. 학생들은 아이디어가 작동할 수 있는지 뿐만 아니라 얼마나 많은 그리고 어떤 종류의 재료가 그것들을 만드는 데 사용되었는지에 따라 평가될 것입니다. 최우수 우승자는 특허권을 갖고 아이디어의 실제 원형을 제작하기 위해 5,000달러를 받게 될 것입니다.

어휘

preliminary *n.* 예선전   **submit** *v.* 제출하다   **qualify for** ~의 자격을 얻다   **relevant** *a.* 관련 있는, 적절한   **take place** 개최되다
patent *n.* 특허권

정답 ④

문제풀이

담화에서 학생들의 아이디어가 작동되는지 뿐만 아니라 사용한 재료의 수와 종류에 따라 평가된다고 했으므로 정답은 ④ '사용한 재료의 수와 종류는 평가에 반영되지 않는다.'이다.

총 어휘 수 127

12 도표

소재 에어컨 선택

듣기 대본 해석

남: 안녕하세요. 무엇을 도와드릴까요?
여: 안녕하세요. 새 아파트에 설치할 에어컨을 찾고 있어요.
남: 알겠습니다. 이 제품은 어때요? 창문에 다는 형식인데 전력 소요량이 낮아서 전기세를 꽤 아낄 수 있어요.
여: 아, 창문에 다는 건 별로 구입하고 싶지 않아요.
남: 알겠습니다. 음, 이 모델이 요즘 잘 팔려요. 리모컨도 함께 온답니다.
여: 리모컨 별로 필요 없을 것 같아요. 더 강력한 에어컨이면 좋겠어요.
남: 좋습니다. 풍향 조절 되는 모델을 원하세요?
여: 그럼요.
남: 그럼 이제 선택지가 두 모델로 줄어들었네요. 가격대는 어느 정도로 생각하고 계세요?
여: 가능하다면 250달러보다 적게 쓰고 싶네요.
남: 그럼 이 모델이 고객님께 딱 맞겠네요.
여: 좋네요. 이걸로 할게요.

어휘
power rating 전력 소요량, 전기요금률   **oscillate** *v.* 계속 오가다, 왔다 갔다 하다, 진동하다

정답 ④

문제풀이
여자가 창문에 달고 싶지 않다고 했으므로 ②번은 제외되고, 리모컨도 필요 없다고 했으므로 남는 것은 ④, ⑤번이다. ④번과 ⑤번은 파워는 같고 둘 다 풍향 조절이 되는데, 그 중에 가격이 250달러보다 싼 것을 원했으므로 정답은 ④번이다.

총 어휘 수 125

13   긴 대화의 응답

소재 교내 장기자랑 대회에서 탈락한 친구 위로하기

듣기 대본 해석
남: Laura. 너 상태가 안 좋아 보이는데. 괜찮니?
여: 괜찮아. 큰 문제는 아니야.
남: 말해봐. 나한텐 어떤 것도 말할 수 있잖아. 뭐가 문제야?
여: 음, 넌 내가 지난주 학교 장기자랑을 위해 얼마나 애썼는지 알지?
남: 응. 기억나. 저글링 공연에 몇 시간이나 들였잖아.
여: 맞아. 그래서 오늘 게시판을 확인해봤는데 장기자랑에서 탈락했어.
남: 정말? 어떻게 그럴 수가 있어? 잘하잖아.
여: 난 내 공연이 정말 완벽하다고 생각했어. 실수도 전혀 하지 않았고.
남: 네가 좌절한 거 이해해. 내가 연극부에 들어가려고 했을 때 나한테도 똑같은 일이 있었어.
여: 너무 속상해. 내 자신감이 완전히 무너졌어.
남: ③ 기운 내! 내년에 또 기회가 있을 거야.

어휘
bulletin board 게시판   **make it** 성공하다   **flawless** *a.* 완벽한, 나무랄 데 없는, 결점이 없는   **frustration** *n.* 좌절   **heartbreaking** *a.* 속상한, 가슴 아픈   **shot** *a.* 완전히 망가진   〈문제〉 **apologize** *v.* 사과하다

정답 ③

문제풀이
남자는 여자가 장기자랑에서 탈락했다는 소식을 듣고 위로하고 있다. 무척 속이 상하고 자신감이 무너졌다는 여자의 마지막 말에 남자의 응답으로 가장 적절한 것은 ③ '기운 내! 내년에 또 기회가 있을 거야.'이다.

오답 보기 해석
① 걱정 마. 나 혼자 할 수 있어.
② 쇼에 참여하게 된 걸 축하해.
④ 알겠어. 끝나면 전화할게.
⑤ 괜찮아. 나한테 사과할 필요 없어.

총 어휘 수 123

14   긴 대화의 응답

소재 오랜만에 만난 고교동창과의 대화

듣기 대본 해석
남: 안녕. 우리 전에 만난 것 같은데. 네 이름이 Jamie 아니었나?
여: 응. 맞아. 너 우리 고등학교 출신인 Ricky 맞지? 오랜만이네.
남: 응. 너를 마지막으로 본 게 졸업식인 것 같은데. 거의 8년이 되어가네!
여: 왜! 그렇게 오래 됐다니 믿어지지 않네. 요즘 어때?

남: 지난 몇 년간 LA에서 살고 있어. 배우로 내 이름을 알리려고 노력 중이야.
여: 정말? 주요 배역을 맡은 적이 있어?
남: 단지 속 쓰림 약 광고에서 뱀파이어 역을 한 것 밖에 없어.
여: 오, 나 그 광고 알아! 내가 가장 좋아하는 것들 중 하나야. 정말 재미있던데.
남: 고마워. 하지만 난 정말 할리우드 영화를 하고 싶어. 다음 주에 오디션이 몇 개 있어.
여: ② 네가 꿈을 쫓는 건 훌륭해.

어휘
commercial *n.* 광고   **heartburn** *n.* (소화불량에 의한) 속 쓰림   **feature** *n.* (영화 등의) 인기 있는 프로그램, 주요 작품

정답 ②

문제풀이
남자와 여자는 고등학교 졸업 이후 약 8년 만에 만나 근황을 얘기하고 있다. 남자는 배우가 되는 꿈을 이루기 위해 다음 주에 오디션을 볼 예정이라고 말하였으므로 이에 대한 여자의 응답으로 가장 적절한 것은 ② '네가 꿈을 쫓는 건 훌륭해.'이다.

오답 보기 해석
① 진정해. 너 자신한테 그렇게 엄격하지 않는 게 좋아.
③ 너 영화 오디션 보는 게 좋겠다.
④ 우리 영화 같이 보는 게 좋겠다.
⑤ 새로운 직업을 고려하는 게 좋을 거야.

총 어휘 수 138

15   상황에 적절한 말

소재 과학 수업의 팀 과제

듣기 대본 해석
남: Lucy와 Jayden은 지역 고등학교 학생들입니다. 이번 학기에 그들은 과학 수업을 같이 듣고 있습니다. 그 수업의 학생들에게 팀 과제가 주어졌습니다. Lucy와 Jayden은 팀으로 작업하면서 책임량을 반으로 나눴습니다. 문제는 Lucy는 미술 동아리에 가입했고 연습에 자주 참석해야 한다는 것입니다. 따라서 그녀는 제 시간에 그녀의 과제를 끝내지 못합니다. 처음에 Jayden은 Lucy의 상황을 이해합니다. 그러나 그는 그녀가 자신의 책임을 자꾸 미루자 화가 나기 시작합니다. Jayden은 Lucy에게 이에 대해 말하고 싶습니다. 이런 상황에서 그는 그녀에게 무슨 말을 해야 할까요?
Jayden: Lucy, ③ 네가 이 과제에 대한 너의 책임을 다하길 바라.

어휘
assign *v.* (특별한 임무를) 하라고 하다(맡기다)   **split** *v.* 나누다, 쪼개다   **responsibility** *n.* 책임   **put off** 미루다, 연기하다

정답 ③

문제풀이
팀 과제를 같이 하는데 친구가 자신이 맡은 부분을 하지 않아서 친구에게 화가 난 상황이다. 이럴 때는 친구에게 자기가 맡은 책임을 다하라고 말해주는 것이 가장 적절하므로 정답은 ③ '네가 이 과제에 대한 너의 책임을 다하길 바라.'이다.

오답 보기 해석
① 만약 네가 내 도움이 필요하면 꼭 말해줘.
② 나는 네가 미술 동아리에서 정말 잘 하길 바라.
④ 너는 학교와 집 생활의 균형을 맞추도록 노력해야 해.
⑤ 일이 너무 많다면 잠시 휴식을 취하는 게 어때?

총 어휘 수 116

16 담화 주제 / 17 세부 내용 파악

소재 교양과목 공부의 이점

듣기 대본 해석

여: 전국의 종합대학과 단과대학은 교양과목 프로그램에 대한 관심의 감소를 겪고 있습니다. 우리 나라의 영향력 있는 몇몇 인물들은 교양과목이 쓸모없다고 믿습니다. 그들은 더 좋은 직업으로 이끌 수 있기 때문에 다른 과목들을 공부하라고 학생들을 격려합니다. 교양과목이 유용한지 아닌지 잠깐 생각을 해보도록 합시다. 교양과목 강의는 다른 과목들이 줄 수 없는 아주 가치 있는 능력들을 줌으로써 미래의 직업을 위해 학생들을 준비시킵니다. 철학, 역사, 그리고 어학을 공부하는 것은 현실 세계에서의 생존에 필수적이고 수학 같은 과목들에서는 얻을 수 없는 학생들의 비판적 사고 능력을 길러 줍니다. 이러한 문제 해결 능력들은 다재 다능한 사람을 양성하는 데 도움을 줍니다. 교양과목에 대한 당신의 의견을 다시 한번 생각해 보시길 권고합니다. 여러 가지 방법으로 당신을 더 나은 사람으로 만들어줄 과목들을 신청하는 것을 고려하시기 바랍니다.

어휘

liberal arts 교양과목, 인문학　　**influential** *a.* 영향력 있는　　**subject** *n.* 과목, 주제　　**invaluable** *a.* 매우 유용한, 귀중한　　**critical thinking** 비판적 사고　　**essential** *a.* 필수적인　　**well-rounded** *a.* 다재 다능한　　**sign up** ~을 등록하다, 신청하다

정답 16 ⑤　17 ②

문제풀이

16 교양과목을 공부해서 얻을 수 있는 이점들을 이야기하고 있으므로 여자가 하는 말의 주제는 ⑤ '교양과목을 공부하는 것의 이점'이다.

17 여자는 철학, 역사, 어학, 수학은 언급했지만 교육학에 대한 언급은 하지 않으므로 정답은 ② '교육학'이다.

오답 보기 해석

16

① 교양과목과 전문적인 교육의 통합

② 교양과목 전공자들을 위한 취업 기회

③ 교양과목에 대한 관심 감소의 원인

④ 교양과목이 인류에 끼치는 영향

17

① 철학　　　③ 역사　　　④ 언어　　　⑤ 수학

총 어휘 수 144

01 had a headache and a runny nose / Have you been to a doctor's office

02 It's boring so far / it starts a bit slow

03 wash your dishes in designated areas / prohibited within park premises / endanger our wildlife as well as your fellow campers / Do not hesitate to contact

04 podcast about meditation / in a variety of ways / sharpen your mind / it's beneficial both mentally and physically

05 there's a lot to memorize / rented for another hour / deliver your opening line / let's try the same line / Did that work better

06 it is the middle of winter / built that entire castle out of ice / I'm always stuck on the top / Now that you mention it

07 rearrange the bedroom / I have to entertain her / I'm supposed to pick her up / spend the whole day / if she's an important client

08 popular with all of the players / the problem is our rival team / see what he thinks

09 rent a couple of motorbikes / What's the price difference / running an off-season promotion / in the promotion

10 involved in volunteering / take care of daily matters / How do I get started / a listing of all available volunteer positions

11 based on the ideas they submitted / both relevant and useful / The final round will take place / how much and what kind of material

12 it'll save you quite a bit on electricity / They come with a remote control / What's your price range / I'd like to spend less than

13 It's really no big deal / my performance was flawless / The same thing happened to me / My confidence is shot

14 make a name for myself / Have you got any big parts / one of my favorites

15 have split the responsibilities in half / finish her work on time / begins to get upset

16-17 a decrease in interest in liberal arts programs / Liberal arts courses prepare students for / gives students critical thinking skills / well-rounded person

03 수능영어듣기 실전모의고사

01 ④	02 ①	03 ④	04 ⑤	05 ③	06 ④
07 ①	08 ⑤	09 ③	10 ②	11 ②	12 ③
13 ④	14 ④	15 ①	16 ⑤	17 ④	

01 짧은 대화의 응답

소재 시험 이후의 계획

듣기 대본 해석

여: 기말고사가 끝나서 너무 행복해.
남: 나도 그래. 이번 주말에 나랑 소풍갈래?
여: 좋기는 한데, 나는 벌써 친척집에 방문할 계획이 있어.
남: ④ 아, 괜찮아. 우리는 다음에 갈 수 있잖아.

어휘

relative *n.* 친척

정답 ④

문제풀이

시험이 끝나고 주말에 소풍을 가자는 남자의 제안에 여자는 친척집 방문 계획이 있다고 말한다. 이에 대해 남자는 괜찮다며 다음에 갈 수 있다고 말하는 것이 자연스러우므로 정답은 ④ '아, 괜찮아. 우리는 다음에 갈 수 있잖아.'가 된다.

오답 보기 해석

① 글쎄, 날씨를 한번 보자.
② 그래 나도, 정말 신나.
③ 저녁에 너희 집에 들를게.
⑤ 우리는 시험 준비를 위해 공부를 좀 더 해야 해.

총 어휘 수 45

02 짧은 대화의 응답

소재 과제 완성하기

듣기 대본 해석

남: Clara, 물리 과제 완성하기에 너무 어렵다고 생각하지 않니?
여: 그것은 꽤 어려웠어. 하지만 난 어젯밤에 끝낼 수 있었어.
남: 농담이겠지! 분명히 너의 부모님께서 도와주셨을 거야, 그렇지?
여: ① 아니야. 내가 스스로 했어.

어휘

physics *n.* 물리학   assignment *n.* 과제   complete *v.* 완성하다
a. 완성된, 완료된   〈문제〉 on one's own 혼자서, 단독으로
chemistry *n.* 화학   a couple of 둘의, 몇 개의

정답 ①

문제풀이

과제를 부모님이 도와주셨을 거라고 말하는 남자의 말에 대한 대답으로 적절한 여자의 말은 ① '아니야. 내가 스스로 했어.'이다.

오답 보기 해석

② 아마도 다음주 월요일까지일거야.
③ 물론. 내가 해줄게.
④ 난 화학을 물리보다 좋아해.
⑤ 응. 그들은 며칠 뒤에 떠나.

총 어휘 수 43

03 요지

소재 학생들의 스포츠 활동

듣기 대본 해석

남: 여러분은 고등학교에서 체육 프로그램에 참여하는 것이 학생들의 성적에 부정적인 영향을 줄 것이라고 생각할 것입니다. 하지만, 최근의 연구에서, 일반적으로 운동을 하는 학생들이 하지 않는 학생들보다 학교에서 더 잘 생활한다고 보여줍니다. 운동은 학습, 기억, 집중에 긍정적인 영향을 주고, 그것은 교실에서 적극적인 학생들에게 이점을 줄 수 있습니다. 운동을 하는 학생들은 팀워크나 목표 설정과 같이 인생에서 가치 있는 다른 기술들에 대해서도 배우기 때문에 운동에 참여하는 효과는 때때로 학습적인 공부를 능가합니다. 경기에 이기고 다른 목표를 달성하기 위해서 코치, 트레이너, 팀원들과 노력하는 것은 학생들이 성공하는 데에 중요한 기술들을 가르쳐서 그들이 인생을 사는 동안 계속 그들에게 도움이 될 수 있습니다.

어휘

athletic *a.* 체육의, 경기의   have an impact on ~에 영향을 주다
advantage *n.* 이점   go beyond ~을 넘어서다, 능가하다

정답 ④

문제풀이

스포츠 활동이 학생들의 학업 성적과 인생을 사는 데 도움이 되는 이로움을 준다는 내용이므로 정답은 ④ '학생들의 스포츠 활동은 학업 이상의 것을 줄 수 있다.'이다.

총 어휘 수 118

04 의견

소재 정크푸드가 건강에 주는 영향

듣기 대본 해석

여: Tom, 여기서 대체 무슨 일이 일어난 거니?
남: 무슨 말씀이세요, 엄마?
여: 여기가 너무 지저분하잖니. 이 쓰레기들 좀 보렴!
남: 네, 맞아요, 죄송해요, 엄마. 제가 바로 치울게요.
여: 그리고 무엇이 지저분하게 했는지 보렴. 패스트푸드 봉지, 정크푸드 박스, 음료수 캔, 사탕 껍질들이 사방에 있구나. 네가 전부 먹은 건 아니지, 그렇지?
남: 제가 먹었어요. 너무 배가 고팠어요.
여: 하지만 이런 것들은 너한테 너무 안 좋아. 그것 중 어떤 것도 전혀 건강에 좋지 않아.
남: 네, 엄마는 저한테 정크푸드를 먹도록 절대 허락하지 않으시니까 엄마가 집에 안 계실 때 가끔 그것들을 많이 먹는 거예요.
여: 내가 너의 건강을 걱정하기 때문에 네가 그런 것들을 먹지 않았으면 하는 거야.
남: 저도 이해해요. 그리고 더 이상 정크푸드를 먹지 않도록 노력할게요.
여: 건강이 가장 중요하다는 것을 명심하렴.

어휘

messy *a.* 지저분한, 엉망인   once in a while 가끔, 때때로

정답 ⑤

문제풀이

엄마가 집을 비운 사이 많은 정크푸드를 먹은 아들에게 그것이 건강에 좋지 않다고 말하고 있는 상황이다. 따라서 ⑤ '건강을 위해 정크푸드를 삼가야 한다.'가 정답이다.

총 어휘 수 145

05 대화자의 관계 파악

소재 상사와 일상대화

듣기 대본 해석

남: 이런 날씨 어때요?

여: 끔찍해요, 그렇죠? 일기예보에 의하면 일주일 내내 비가 올 거라고 하네요.

남: 오늘도 여전히 야외에서 일해야 하나요?

여: 아니요. 당신은 사무실에서 할 일들이 있어요.

남: 잘 됐네요. 만약 야외에서 일하다 아플까 봐 걱정했거든요.

여: Frank. 당신에게 뭔가 줄곧 하려고 했던 말이 있어요.

남: 네. 무엇인가요?

여: 요즘 당신은 평소답지 않아요. 괜찮아요?

남: 솔직히 제 아들이 학교에서 많은 어려움을 겪고 있고 집에서는 쌀쌀맞거든요. 난 정말 그가 걱정돼요.

여: 이해해요. 저도 아이가 둘이 있거든요. 그런데 알다시피. 애들은 애들이죠. 아이들이 자연스럽게 성장하도록 놔두셔야 해요.

남: 조언 감사합니다 Stark씨. 제가 오늘 해야 할 일은 무엇이죠?

여: 이 서류들을 구분해주면 좋겠어요.

어휘

forecast *n.* 예보, 예측　**standoffish** *a.* 쌀쌀맞은

정답 ③

문제풀이

남자는 대화의 시작 부분에서 일을 어디서 해야 하는지 묻고 여자에게 아들에 대한 조언을 받았으며 마지막 부분에서 자신이 해야 할 일을 묻는 것으로 보아 두 사람의 관계는 ③ '상사 — 부하직원'임을 유추할 수 있다.

총 어휘 수 143

06 그림의 세부 내용 파악

소재 쇼를 위한 밴드의 전단지

듣기 대본 해석

남: Sandra, 무얼 하고 있니?

여: 내 새로운 밴드의 전단지야. 우리는 다음 주에 쇼가 있거든.

남: 오, 멋져 보인다. 그럼 너희 밴드 이름이 Bastion이구나.

여: 응. 우리 이름은 왼쪽 상단에 넣었어. 그리고 그것 옆에 해골도 그려 넣었지.

남: 그렇구나. 너희는 로큰롤 밴드 같아. 왼쪽에 그린 기타는 정말 멋진걸.

여: 응. 그건 내 기타인 Bender P-159야.

남: 네가 그림 오른쪽에 있는 것 같은데 네 기타는 어디 있니?

여: 내가 기타를 들고 있는 사진을 찾을 수가 없었어. 그래서 그것을 들고 있지 않은 사진을 선택했어.

남: 인상적이야. 날짜와 장소를 아래에 넣었구나?

여: 맞아. 우리는 27일 저녁 9시에 Denton Shelter House에서 연주할 거야.

남: 오, 멋지구나. 나도 가능하면 가고 싶네.

어휘

flyer *n.* 전단　**skull** *n.* 두개골, 해골　**venue** *n.* 장소

정답 ④

문제풀이

여자가 기타를 들고 있는 사진을 찾을 수가 없어서 기타를 들고 있지 않은 사진을 택했다고 했는데 그림에서는 기타를 어깨에 매고 있으므로 정답은 ④번이다.

총 어휘 수 148

07 부탁한 일

소재 생일파티 준비

듣기 대본 해석

여: 안녕, Oliver! 딱 맞춰 왔네!

남: 정말? 무슨 일이야?

여: 이번 주말 Elena의 생일파티를 위한 계획을 검토하려고.

남: 오. 좋아. 깜짝 파티를 할 거지?

여: 아니, 나는 우리가 Joe's Crab Shack에 가까운 친구 여러 명을 모이게 할 생각인데.

남: 좋아. 그녀가 한동안 거기 가고 싶어 했던 거 알아.

여: 나는 우리 친한 친구들 모두를 초대할까 생각 중이야.

남: 좋은 생각이야. 내가 도울 일은 없어?

여: 파티 상점에 가서 풍선이랑 "생일 축하" 표지를 사올래?

남: 물론. 바로 거기로 갈게.

여: 좋았어. 대단한 파티가 될 거야.

남: 그래, 정말 기대된다!

어휘

in time 시간 맞춰(늦지 않게)　**go over** 점검하다, 검토하다

a bunch of 다수의　〈문제〉**reserve** *v.* 예약하다　**directions** *n.* 길 안내

정답 ①

문제풀이

Elena를 위해 생일파티를 계획하고 있다는 여자의 말에 남자가 자신이 도울 수 있는 일을 물었고, 여자는 파티 상점에 가서 풍선과 "생일 축하" 표지를 사달라고 부탁했으므로 여자가 남자에게 부탁한 일은 ① '파티 장식품 사기'이다.

오답 보기 해석

② 북클럽 시작하는 것 도와주기

③ 충분한 테이블 예약하기

④ 친한 친구들에게 전화하기

⑤ 그녀에게 파티 가는 길 알려주기

총 어휘 수 118

08 이유

소재 친구의 제안 거절하기

듣기 대본 해석

여: 안녕 Julian. 무슨 일이야?

남: 별거 아냐. 학교 신문에 나온 이 음악 평론을 읽고 있어.

여: 멋지다. 무슨 앨범이야?

남: Kenny North의 새 앨범 Graduate School이야. 들어본 적 있니?

여: 물론이지. 요즘 여러 사람들이 얘기하던데.

남: 응. 살까 생각 중이야. 학교 끝나고 가서 나하고 같이 들어볼래?

여: 그러고 싶은데 안 되겠네. 오늘은 학교 끝나고 집에 바로 가야 하거든.

남: 정말? 왜?

여: 남동생이 대학교에서 와.

남: 그럼 버스 터미널로 태우러 가야 하겠구나?

여: 아빠가 가실 거야. 난 엄마 집 청소 하시는 거 도와드려야 해.

남: 알겠어. 오빠랑 즐거운 시간 보내.

어휘

review *n.* (책, 영화 등에 대한) 평론, 비평　**pick ~ up** ~을 차로 데리러 가다

정답 ⑤

문제풀이
새 음반을 들으러 같이 가자는 남자의 제안에 여자는 남동생이 집에 와서 집안
청소를 도와야 한다며 거절하고 있으므로 정답은 ⑤ '엄마가 청소하는 것을
도와야 해서'이다.

총 어휘 수 135

09 숫자

소재 스테이크와 감자 구입하기

듣기 대본 해석
여: Jenna의 정육점에 오신 것을 환영합니다. 무엇을 도와드릴까요?
남: 스테이크 고기를 좀 찾고 있어요.
여: 스테이크요? 어떤 스테이크요?
남: 글쎄요, 내일 장인, 장모님을 모시고 바비큐 파티를 할건데 그들에게 잘
　　보일 수 있는 걸로 주세요.
여: 음, 고급 티본스테이크 세일을 하고 있어요. 스테이크당 20달러예요.
남: 좋을 것 같아요. 네 개 주세요.
여: 알겠습니다. 그건 구운 감자랑 정말 잘 어울려요. 한 봉지 드릴까요?
남: 네. 얼마예요?
여: 보통 봉지당 9달러인데 단골손님이신 것 같으니 7달러에 드릴게요.
남: 좋아요. 감자 한 봉지 가져갈게요.
여: 알겠습니다. 그럼 고급 티본스테이크 네 개랑 감자 한 봉지입니다. 더
　　필요한 것 있으세요?
남: 없는 것 같아요. 여기 신용카드요.

어휘
butcher shop *n.* 정육점　　**barbecue** *n.* 바비큐　　**in-law** *n.* 인척
a. 인척 관계의(특히 시부모, 장인과 장모)　　**premium** *a.* 고급의, 아주 높은

정답 ③

문제풀이
남자는 장인, 장모님에게 대접할 20달러짜리 스테이크 4개와 본래 9달러인데
7달러로 깎아준 감자 한 봉지를 샀으므로 정답은 ③ '$87'이다.

총 어휘 수 135

10 언급 유무

소재 음악 캠프

듣기 대본 해석
[전화벨이 울린다.]
여: 여보세요?
남: 안녕 Stacy. 저 Dominic이에요. Russell 있나요? 제 아들이 오늘 그 애와
　　진짜 놀고 싶어해요.
여: 오, Russell은 여기에 없어요. 오늘 그는 음악 캠프에 있어요.
남: 음악 캠프요?
여: 네, 지역 오케스트라에서 여름마다 개최해요. 학생들은 전문적인 음악가들과
　　연습하게 돼요.
남: 멋지네요. 캠프는 어디서 해요?
여: 도서관 바로 건너편에 있는 강당에서요.
남: 그렇군요. 아직 자리가 남아 있나요?
여: 네, 제가 어제 막 Russell을 등록시켰는데, 아직 몇 자리 남았어요.
　　학생들을 태워 주는 셔틀버스도 있어요.
남: 멋지네요. 나이 제한이 있나요?
여: 10세 이상의 아이들을 위한 거예요. 오케스트라 웹 사이트에서 모든 정보를
　　찾을 수 있어요.
남: 좋아요! 확인해 볼게요. 제 아들이 가입하는 것을 좋아할 거예요.

어휘
awesome *a.* 굉장한, 멋진　　**auditorium** *n.* 강당, 객석
available *a.* 이용 가능한　　**sign ~ up** ~을 등록시키다
restriction *n.* 제한

정답 ②

문제풀이
음악 캠프의 시기와 위치, 셔틀버스 운행, 나이 제한에 관한 언급은 있지만 캠프
기간에 대한 언급은 없으므로 정답은 ② '캠프 기간'이다.

총 어휘 수 135

11 내용 일치 · 불일치

소재 최첨단 쌍방향 책상

듣기 대본 해석
남: 2009년 이후로 영국 전역에서 8살에서 10살 사이의 학생들이 매우 신선한
　　실험에 참가했습니다. 최첨단 쌍방향 책상으로 연필과 종이, 그리고 계산기를
　　대체하는 것이 학생들의 수학 실력을 향상시킬 수 있는지 알아보는 것이었
　　습니다! 영국의 Dunham University와 SinergyCom이 이 프로젝트를
　　고안했습니다. DeskTouch라고 불리는 이 최첨단 책상은 기술을 통해
　　학습을 향상시키도록 의도된 여러 연구 프로젝트 중에 하나입니다. 이 책상은
　　스마트폰이나 iPad같은 기기처럼 터치에 반응하는 소프트웨어에 최적화
　　되어있습니다. 모든 책상은 선생님이 수학문제를 학생들에게 만들어 보내고
　　이후에 그것들을 확인할 수 있는 중앙 책상과 통신합니다.

어휘
involve *v.* 참가시키다　　**enhance** *v.* 향상시키다　　**respond** *v.*
반응하다　　**afterwards** *ad.* 이후에

정답 ②

문제풀이
이 실험은 쌍방향 책상이 학생들의 수학 실력을 향상시킬 수 있는지 보기 위한
것이라고 했으므로 내용과 일치하지 않는 것은 ② '쌍방향 책상은 학생들의
공감능력 향상을 보기 위한 실험이다.'이다.

총 어휘 수 107

12 도표

소재 게스트 하우스 선택

듣기 대본 해석
여: 여보, Billy 학교 한 달도 안 남은 것 알지?
남: 응. 여름 방학 무척 기대하고 있더라. 올해는 좀 특별한 걸 할 생각이야.
여: 어떤 것을 생각하고 있는데?
남: 글쎄, 내가 Smoky 산맥에 항상 가고 싶다고 말한 거 알지?
여: 응. 신혼여행으로 거기 갈 뻔 했잖아.
남: 맞아. 그래서 인터넷을 보는데 그 산에 있는 오두막 목록을 찾았어. 어떤지
　　말해줘.
여: 음, 하룻밤에 60달러 넘게 쓰는 건 아니라고 생각해.
남: 응. 난 산에 머무르고 싶어. 거기 있는 도시는 관광객이 많을 거 같아.
여: 맞아. 그럼 두 개 남았네.
남: 흠... 온수욕조 있는 것으로 하자. 편안할 것 같아.
여: 그래. 어서 예약해.

어휘
honeymoon *n.* 신혼여행　　**chalet** *n.* 샬레, 오두막　　**touristy** *a.*
관광객이 많이 몰리는

정답 ③

문제풀이

하루에 60달러 넘게 쓰고 싶지는 않다고 했고, 산에 머무르고 싶다고 했으므로 남는 선택은 ②번과 ③번이다. 두 개중 온수욕조가 있는 것으로 하자고 했으므로 정답은 ③번이다.

총 어휘 수 142

13 긴 대화의 응답

소재 두꺼운 침낭 빌려주기

듣기 대본 해석

여: Eddie. 바빠 보이네. 다른 시간에 다시 올까?
남: 방금 마무리 중이었어. 네팔 여행을 위해 짐 싸는 것을 거의 끝냈어.
여: 좋네. 내가 추천한 것은 다 샀니?
남: 그래. 추천해줘서 고마워. 나는 새로운 부츠와 텐트를 샀어.
여: 멋지구나. 이런! 이게 너의 침낭이야? 너무 얇은 것 같은데. 밖에서 추위에 떨 거야.
남: 네 말이 맞지만 침낭이 너무 비싸. 새로운 것을 살 여유가 되지 않아.
여: 음... 내가 도움을 줄 수도 있겠다.
남: 정말? 내가 빌릴 침낭이라도 있니?
여: 음. 아버지께서 전혀 안 쓰시는 것이 있는데. 아버지께서 빌려주실지 내가 알아볼게.
남: ④ 그러면 좋겠다. 난 정말 돈을 아껴야 하거든.

어휘

sleeping bag 침낭 freeze v. 추위 죽을 지경이다. 얼다 afford v. (~을 사거나 할 금전적 · 시간적) 여유가 되다

정답 ④

문제풀이

침낭이 너무 비싸서 좀 더 두꺼운 침낭을 사지 못한 남자에게 여자는 아버지의 안 쓰는 침낭을 빌려줄 수 있도록 아버지께 여쭤본다고 하였으므로 이에 대한 남자의 응답으로 가장 적절한 것은 ④ '그러면 좋겠다. 난 정말 돈을 아껴야 하거든.'이다.

오답 보기 해석

① 괜찮아. 내가 새 침낭을 샀어.
② 추천해줘서 정말로 고마워.
③ 내가 그의 등산 부츠를 빌릴 수 있을까?
⑤ 굉장해. 그가 진짜로 즐거웠던 것 같더라.

총 어휘 수 128

14 긴 대화의 응답

소재 여자가 레드 와인을 반기지 않는 이유

듣기 대본 해석

여: 와줘서 고마워. 새로 이사한 아파트야.
남: 늦어서 미안해. 와인 사오느라.
여: 와인? 레드 와인은 아니지?
남: 맞는데. 레드 와인 싫어해?
여: 좋아해. 근데 거실에 최근에 이 하얀색 카펫 깔았단 말이야. 네가 여기에 흘리는 건 싫어.
남: 걱정 마. 각별히 조심할게.
여: 너 못 믿겠어. 우리 같이 스파게티 먹고 네 흰색 셔츠에 다 묻혔던 거 기억나?
남: 그건 딱 한 번 실수한 거였어. 너무 불합리해.

여: 네가 안 마시면 좀 더 마음이 편할 것 같아. 이 아파트 정말 깨끗하게 유지하고 싶어.
남: 정 그렇다면. 부엌으로 가지고 갈게.
여: ④ 알겠어. 거실에서만 마시지 마.

어휘

install v. 설치하다 spill v. 흘리다. 엎지르다 unreasonable a. 불합리한 spotless a. 티끌 하나 없는

정답 ④

문제풀이

여자는 남자가 사온 레드 와인이 자신이 최근 거실에 깐 하얀색 카펫을 더럽힐까 걱정하고 있다. 그러자 남자는 정 그렇다면 부엌으로 가지고 가겠다고 했는데, 이에 대해 가장 적절한 여자의 응답은 ④ '알겠어. 거실에서만 마시지 마.'이다.

오답 보기 해석

① 맞아. 저녁에 레드 와인 마시는 거 좋아해.
② 오늘은 네가 나한테 요리해 줄 차례인 것 같은데.
③ 미안한데 지금 마실 시간이 없어.
⑤ 걱정하지 마. 카펫에 와인 안 흘릴게.

총 어휘 수 134

15 상황에 적절한 말

소재 산으로 캠핑 가는 아들에게 재킷 챙겨주기

듣기 대본 해석

여: Mike는 고등학생인데 이번 주말에 그는 친구들과 함께 시간을 보낼 예정입니다. 그들은 산으로 캠핑을 가기로 결정했습니다. 하지만 Mike의 엄마인 Linda는 아들이 걱정됩니다. 그녀는 늦여름까지 캠핑을 해왔기 때문에 산이 꽤 추울 거라고 생각합니다. 그녀는 Mike에게 겨울 재킷을 가져가도록 충고하지만 그는 거절합니다. 그는 여름에 겨울 재킷을 입는 것이 우스꽝스럽다고 생각하고 엄마의 충고를 듣고 싶어 하지 않습니다. Linda는 그가 겨울 재킷이 필요한지 확실하지는 않지만 그녀는 만약을 위해 Mike가 겨울 재킷을 가져가도록 설득하려고 합니다. 이런 상황에서 Linda가 Mike에게 뭐라고 말할 것 같은가요?
Linda: ① 네가 생각하는 것보다 거기 위에는 더 추울지도 모른단다.

어휘

urge v. 충고하다 ridiculous a. 우스꽝스러운 just in case 만약을 위해서

정답 ①

문제풀이

산으로 캠핑을 가는 아들에게 엄마는 겨울 재킷을 가져가라고 하고, 아들은 여름에 겨울 재킷을 입는 것이 우스꽝스럽다고 생각하는 상황이다. 그럼에도 불구하고 만약의 경우를 대비해 재킷을 가져가라고 아들을 설득하고자 하는 상황에서 어머니인 Linda가 Mike에게 할 말은 ① '네가 생각하는 것보다 거기 위에는 더 추울지도 모른단다.'가 가장 적절하다.

오답 보기 해석

② 안전하게 지내고 허락된 곳에서만 캠핑을 하렴.
③ 떠나기 전 재킷을 빨고 가렴. 정말 더럽단다.
④ 네 옷들을 빨래하는 것을 끝내기 전까진 집을 떠날 수 없어.
⑤ 등산은 재미있지만 위험할 수 있어. 조심하렴.

총 어휘 수 124

16 담화 목적 / 17 세부 내용 파악

소재 예술 프로젝트에 대한 기금 마련

듣기 대본 해석

남: 크라우드 펀딩은 전 세계의 사람들이 그들의 예술적인 노력을 위한 자금을 모으는 멋진 방식이 되었습니다. 많은 창의적인 사람들이 실행시키고 싶은 아이디어들을 가지고 있지만 창작에 필요한 돈이 없습니다. 그것이 우리의 프로그램인 Donation Station이 관여하는 부분입니다. Donation Station은 예술가들과 창의적인 사람들을 그 프로젝트를 믿는 투자자들과 연결시켜 드립니다. 시작을 하기 위해서, Donation Station 웹사이트에서 프로필을 작성해 주시고, 당신의 프로젝트를 기술하시기만 하면 됩니다. 만약에 투자자가 그것을 좋아한다면, 그들은 당신에게 그 아이디어들이 생명력을 얻는 데 필요한 돈을 보내 줄 수 있습니다. 영화를 위한 좋은 아이디어가 있는데 그것을 제작할 돈이 부족합니까? Donation Station이 도움을 줄 수 있습니다. 아마도 당신은 새로운 패션 디자인이나 유용한 발명품을 가지고 있을 수도 있고, 아마도 책을 출판하는 데 도움이 필요할지도 모릅니다. Donation Station은 창의성이 우리 사회에서 필수적이고 전 세계가 발전하도록 도와준다는 것을 압니다. 그러한 이유로 우리는 당신의 꿈을 현실화하는 데에 도움을 주려는 것입니다. 당신의 아이디어가 순조롭게 시작되도록 지금 당장 저희 웹사이트에 가입하세요.

어휘

accumulate *v.* ～을 축적하다, 모으다　　**endeavor** *n.* 노력
bring ~ to life ～에 활기(생기)를 불어넣다　　**get ~ off the ground**
～을 순조롭게 출발(시작)하다

정답 16 ⑤　17 ④

문제풀이

16 남자는 예술적 아이디어들이 현실화될 수 있도록 자금을 지원하는 웹사이트 Donation Station을 소개하고, 신청 방법 및 예술 분야의 예들을 말하고 있으므로 정답은 ⑤ '창작자들이 프로젝트에 관한 자금지원을 받도록 도움을 주기 위하여'이다.

17 남자는 영화, 새로운 패션 디자인, 유용한 발명품, 출판에 대해서는 언급하였으나 만화는 언급하지 않았으므로 정답은 ④ '만화'이다.

오답 보기 해석

16
① 비슷한 생각을 가진 사람들을 모으기 위하여
② 예술가들의 도움에 감사하기 위하여
③ 예술작품 사는 법을 조언하기 위하여
④ 예술산업의 혁신을 장려하기 위하여

총 어휘 수 181

04 수능영어듣기 실전모의고사

01 ②	02 ②	03 ③	04 ③	05 ③	06 ③
07 ②	08 ⑤	09 ⑤	10 ⑤	11 ④	12 ①
13 ②	14 ①	15 ①	16 ①	17 ⑤	

01 짧은 대화의 응답

소재 음악적 능력

듣기 대본 해석
여: Daniel, 정말 훌륭한 기타리스트가 되어가고 있네요.
남: 그렇게 말해줘서 너무 감사해요. 악기를 연주해 본 적 있어요?
여: 나는 음악을 좋아하지만 음악적 능력은 전혀 없어요.
남: ② 괜찮아요. 연습만 하면 돼요.

어휘
appreciate v. 고마워하다   **instrument n.** 악기(= musical instrument), 기구, 도구   〈문제〉**tune v.** (악기를) 조율하다

정답 ②

문제풀이
음악적 능력이 없다는 여자의 말에 대한 남자의 응답으로는 연습하면 된다고 대답하는 것이 적절하므로 정답은 ② '괜찮아요. 연습만 하면 돼요.'이다.

오답 보기 해석
① 당신의 레슨이 저한테 정말 도움 됐어요.
③ 내가 정오쯤에 당신 집에 들를게요.
④ 나는 당신과 내 음악 모음을 공유할 수 있어서 기뻐요.
⑤ 잠깐만요! 당신은 연주하기 전에 기타를 조율해야겠어요.

총 어휘 수 37

02 짧은 대화의 응답

소재 저녁식사 정하기

듣기 대본 해석
남: 배고파져요. 오늘 무엇을 먹고 싶어요?
여: 모르겠어요. 또 외식하고 싶어요?
남: 우리는 외식으로 너무 많은 비용을 썼어요. 오늘 저녁은 집에서 먹는 게 어때요?
여: ② 좋아요. 내가 당신을 위해 요리를 해주면 어떨까요?

어휘
〈문제〉**bill n.** 계산서, 청구서   **care for** ～을 돌보다, 좋아하다

정답 ②

문제풀이
너무 자주 외식을 해서 오늘밤은 집에서 저녁 먹고 싶다는 남자의 말에 대한 여자의 응답으로 가장 적절한 것은 ② '좋아요. 내가 당신을 위해 요리를 해주면 어떨까요?'이다.

오답 보기 해석
① 네, 제 생각에는 팁이 계산서에 포함되지 않은 것 같아요.
③ 그 음식점의 파스타를 그다지 좋아하지 않았어요.
④ 물론이죠. 그러면 식료품점에 갈 필요가 없군요.
⑤ 맞아요. 길을 따라 가면 나오는 멕시코 음식점에 대해 들었어요.

총 어휘 수 43

03 담화 목적

소재 온라인상으로 팬들의 의견 받기

듣기 대본 해석
여: 안녕하세요 팬 여러분. 저는 팬 여러분들 중 몇 분께서 새로운 경기장과 시설에 관한 제안이 있다는 것을 들었습니다. 저희는 몇 개월 전에 경기장에 둔 상자 안에 팬 여러분들께서 넣어주신 제안들을 자세히 살펴보았습니다. 그러나, 우리는 이러한 과정을 여러분들께서 제안을 온라인 상에서 제출할 수 있도록 함으로써 더 쉽게 하기로 결정했습니다. 이는 팬 여러분들께서 언제, 어디서든지 할 수 있도록 할 것입니다. 이것은 꽤 간단합니다. 그냥 공식 웹사이트에 가서서, "제안" 링크를 클릭하시고, 제공되는 상자 틀 안에 여러분의 제안을 입력하시고 "제출"을 클릭하세요. 이러한 새로운 시스템은 또한 여러분의 제안에 적시에 더 쉽게 응답하도록 해줍니다. 시간 내주셔서 감사합니다.

어휘
facility n. 시설   **sort through** ～을 자세히 살피다   **submit n.** (서류, 제안서 등을) 제출하다   **in a timely manner** 적시에, 시기 적절하게

정답 ③

문제풀이
이제까지는 팬들이 의견을 상자에 넣는 방식이었지만 이 과정을 더 쉽게 하기 위해서 온라인 상에서 하게 되었음을 알려주고 있다. 따라서 여자가 하는 말의 목적은 ③ '팬들의 의견 제안 방식의 변경을 공지하려고'이다.

총 어휘 수 110

04 대화 주제

소재 한국 돌잔치와 관련된 특별한 전통

듣기 대본 해석
여: Jimmy. 당신을 위한 파티 초대장이에요.
남: 와, 당신 아들의 첫 번째 생일이네요. 정말 기쁜 일이네요!
여: 네. 파티에 와 줄 수 있으세요?
남: 부산에서요? 물론이죠 아기의 첫 번째 생일과 관련해 특별한 전통이 있다고 들었어요.
여: 네, 맞아요. 아기가 첫 번째 생일 파티에서 여러 가지 상징적인 물건들 중에 하나의 품목을 고르죠.
남: 그래서 아기가 선택하는 물건이 자신의 미래를 예측하나요?
여: 맞아요. 예를 들어, 제 아들이 연필을 고르면, 우리는 그것이 그가 학문 관련 직업으로 성공할 것이라고 믿어요.
남: 그렇군요. 아기가 무엇을 또 고를 수 있나요?
여: 음. 만약 아기가 돈을 선택하면 부자가 될 것이고, 실타래를 고르면 오래 살 것을 의미해요.
남: 일리 있네요. 당신 아기의 생일파티가 정말 기대되네요!

어휘
relating to ～과 관련된   **symbolic a.** 상징적인
academic career 학문 관련 직업 경력   **wealthy a.** 부유한
a spool of thread 실타래

정답 ③

문제풀이
아기의 돌잔치에서 아기가 물건을 선택하고 어떤 물건을 선택하는가에 따라 의미가 달라지는 한국의 독특한 전통을 말하고 있으므로 정답은 ③ '한국 돌잔치의 특별한 전통'이다.

총 어휘 수 133

05 대화자의 관계 파악

소재 교수님한테 학생 추천 받기

듣기 대본 해석

[전화벨이 울린다.]

여: 안녕하세요?

남: Aria, 안녕하세요. 저 Walter입니다.

여: 안녕하세요, Walter. 잘 지내시나요?

남: 네, 감사합니다. 지난번에 지금 저희와 일하고 있는 두 명의 인턴을 추천해 주셔서 정말 감사드린다는 말씀을 드리고 싶었어요. 우리는 그들이 열심히 일하고 헌신하는 것에 대해 정말로 높게 평가합니다.

여: 잘 됐군요! 제 학생들을 고용한 게 매우 도움이 되고 있다는 소식을 들으니 기뻐요.

남: 그들은 정말 잘 적응하고 있어요. 혹시 다른 학생들을 또 추천해주실 수 있는지 여쭤보려고 전화드렸습니다.

여: 물론이죠. 어떤 부서에서 필요하신가요?

남: 품질관리 일에 두 명이 필요합니다.

여: 알겠어요. 그 자리에 딱 맞는 학생들을 알고 있어요. 다음 주에 수업이 끝나고 그들에게 공지할게요.

남: 좋습니다. 그들에게 제 연락처를 주시고 제 번호로 바로 연락해 주길 바란다고 전해주십시오.

여: 그럴게요, Walter.

남: 감사합니다.

어휘

recommend *v.* 추천하다   **value** *v.* 평가하다. 존중하다. 소중히 하다
dedication *n.* 헌신. 전념

정답 ③

문제풀이

남자가 지난 번에 추천해준 두 명 학생이 일을 잘하고 있다면서 다른 학생들을 더 추천해줄 것을 부탁했고, 여자는 자신의 학생들이 잘하고 있다고 들으니 기쁘다며 다음 주 수업 후에 공지하겠다고 했으므로 둘 사이의 관계는 ③ '교수 — 회사 직원'으로 유추할 수 있다.

총 어휘 수 127

06 그림의 세부 내용 파악

소재 렌트할 자동차 선택

듣기 대본 해석

여: Isaac's Rent-a-Car에 오신 걸 환영합니다. 오늘 무엇을 도와드릴까요?

남: 안녕하세요. 오늘 오후에 차량을 가지고 가는 것을 예약했는데요. 제 이름은 Robert Clay입니다.

여: 잠시만요. 네, 바로 여기에 예약이 있네요, Clay씨. 저희 매장을 둘러보시고 어떤 차가 마음에 드시는지 말씀해 주세요.

남: 문이 네 개인 세단은 원하지 않아요. 혼자서 여행할 거예요.

여: 알겠습니다. 그럼 컨버터블은 어떠세요? 스포티해서 혼자 여행하는 분들에게 재미있습니다.

남: 오늘 날씨가 스모그가 많아요. 오염물질을 많이 들이마시고 싶지 않아요.

여: 네. 그럼 이 두 개로 좁혀지네요.

남: 음. 회색은 원치 않아요. 회색은 약간 우울한 색상이에요.

여: 음. 그럼 이게 가장 잘 맞을 것 같네요.

남: 좋네요. 그걸로 할게요. 여기 신용카드 있습니다.

어휘

smoggy *a.* 스모그가 많은   **inhale** *v.* 숨을 들이마시다   **pollution**
n. 오염. 공해

정답 ③

문제풀이

문이 네 개인 세단과 지붕을 열 수 있는 컨버터블은 원치 않는다고 했으므로 ③, ⑤번이 남게 되고, 대화의 마지막 부분에서 회색은 원하지 않는다고 했으므로 정답은 ③번이다.

총 어휘 수 145

07 할 일

소재 외국어로 된 호텔 예약 사이트 내용 해석 부탁하기

듣기 대본 해석

여: 야. 뭐해?

남: 이번 휴가 때 묵을 호텔을 인터넷에서 찾아보고 있어.

여: 재미있겠다. 어디로 가는데?

남: 도쿄. 가 본 적 있어?

여: 도쿄? 가 본 적 있지. Tokyo Palace 호텔에서 묵었어. 정말 좋았어.

남: 거기 방들 찾아봤는데 나한테는 너무 비싸더라.

여: 그렇구나. 그럼 호텔 예약하려면 이 사이트를 들어가 봐. tokyodeals.com이야.

남: 좋아. 지금 확인해 봐야지. *[잠시 후]* 아. 여기 있긴 한데 나한테는 좀 쓸모 가 없는 것 같아.

여: 왜?

남: 사이트가 일본어로 돼 있어. 나는 일본어 하나도 못 읽거든. 너는?

여: 물론이지. 대학에서 일본어를 공부했어. 내가 도와줄까?

남: 그럼 좋지! 도와줘서 고마워.

어휘

head *v.* ∼로 가다. 향하다   **useless** *a.* 쓸모 없는

정답 ②

문제풀이

남자는 여자가 알려준 호텔 예약 사이트에 들어갔으나 일본어로 되어 있어 읽지 못하자 여자에게 일본어를 읽을 수 있는지 물었고 여자는 자신이 도와주겠다고 했다. 따라서 여자가 남자를 위해 할 일은 ② '웹 사이트 읽어주기'이다.

총 어휘 수 125

08 이유

소재 사고로 인한 교통 체증

듣기 대본 해석

[전화벨이 울린다.]

여: 여보세요?

남: 엄마. 저 Tom이에요.

여: 어디 갔었니, Tom? 한 시간 전에 집에 오기로 되어 있었잖아. 7시야.

남: 아까 제 휴대폰 배터리가 나갔어요. 심지어 엄마한테 전화하려고 지금 다른 사람의 휴대폰을 빌려야 했어요.

여: 그래. 네가 지금 집이 아니고 나한테 전화하고 있으니, 이것은 네가 금방 집에 오지 않는다는 의미구나. 무슨 일이니?

남: 공원 앞에서 큰 사고가 있었던 거 못 들으셨어요?

여: 아니. 넌 괜찮아?

남: 네. 전 괜찮아요. 사고가 났을 때 저는 공원의 반대편에 있었어요.

여: 그럼 너는 왜 아직 집에 오지 않은 거니?

남: 경찰과 소방서에서 공원 주변 길을 막았어요. 교통상황이 정말 안 좋고, 지하철은 남은 시간 동안 운행하지 않을 거예요.

여: 끔찍한 소식이구나. 저녁 먹었니?

남: 조금 전에 과일과 샐러드를 약간 먹었어요. 전 괜찮아요.

여: 그래. 그럼 조심하고 이따 보자.

남: 네. 엄마. 이따 봬요.

어휘

be supposed to V ~하기로 되어 있다   **operate** *v.* 운행하다
awful *a.* 끔찍한

정답 ⑤

문제풀이

남자는 공원 앞에서 난 큰 사고 때문에 경찰과 소방서에서 길을 막았고, 지하철도 운행하지 않았기 때문에 늦는다고 했으므로 정답은 ⑤ '길이 통제되고 주변 교통수단을 이용할 수 없어서'이다.

총 어휘 수 160

09 숫자

소재 예술 센터 표 구매하기

듣기 대본 해석

남: 안녕하세요. Franklin 대학교 예술 센터에 오신 것을 환영합니다. 무엇을 도와드릴까요?
여: 안녕하세요. 성인 두 명이랑 어린이 두 명 표 좀 살게요.
남: 알겠습니다. *[키보드 치는 소리]* 44달러입니다.
여: 이 표를 사면 Harmony Blues 공연도 관람할 수 있나요?
남: 죄송하지만 관람할 수 없어요. 공연 표는 1인당 추가로 4달러가 들어요.
여: 그렇군요. 그럼 공연을 포함하면 표 값은 얼마인가요?
남: 성인은 18달러이고 어린이는 12달러입니다.
여: 네. 그럼 그 표로 성인 두 명이랑 어린이 두 명 표 주세요. 아! 까먹을 뻔 했는데 10퍼센트 할인 쿠폰이 있어요. 여기요.
남: *[잠시 후]* 죄송하지만 이 할인은 공연이 포함된 표에는 적용되지가 않아요.
여: 오, 그럼. 알겠습니다. 여기 카드요.
남: 감사합니다.

어휘

admission *n.* 입장   **performance** *n.* 공연   **discount** *n.* 할인

정답 ⑤

문제풀이

공연을 포함한 표는 성인 두 장에 36달러, 어린이 두 장에 24달러이므로 성납은 ⑤ '$60'이다.

총 어휘 수 126

10 언급 유무

소재 다큐멘터리 소개하기

듣기 대본 해석

여: Pablo, An Unfortunate Fact라는 다큐멘터리 본 적 있니?
남: 아니. 뭐에 대한 건데?
여: 기후 변화에 관한 거야. 다음 세대에게 닥칠 위험들을 다뤄.
남: 흠… 들어본 적 있는 것 같아. 난 과학 다큐멘터리 아주 좋아해. 어땠어?
여: 정말 많은 걸 깨닫게 해주는 프로그램이었어. 우리 지구의 미래에 대해서 신지하게 생각을 하게 되디리
남: 긴 다큐멘터리였어?
여: 거의 두 시간 정도 했어. 좀 지루할 때가 있지만 과학 다큐멘터리 좋아하면 재미있게 볼 수 있을 거야.
남: 정말 보고 싶은데 이번 주말에 시간이 없을 것 같아. 다음 주말에 아직도 상영 중일까?
여: 잘 모르겠어. 사이트에 들어가서 확인해 봐.
남: 아, 좋은 생각이야. 보고 나서 너랑 더 얘기해 보고 싶어.

어휘

climate *n.* 기후   **generation** *n.* 세대   **eye-opener** *n.* 눈을 뜨게 해주는(새로운 것을 깨닫게 해주는) 일 또는 경험

정답 ⑤

문제풀이

여자는 자신이 본 과학 다큐멘터리를 대화 소재로 꺼내면서 그것의 제목, 주제, 영화 길이, 관람 소감에 대해 이야기하고 있지만, 어디에서 상영 중인지는 언급하지 않았으므로 정답은 ⑤ '상영관 위치'이다.

총 어휘 수 140

11 내용 일치 · 불일치

소재 컴퓨터 게임 대회

듣기 대본 해석

남: 안녕하세요, 게이머 여러분! 저는 Nimbus이고요, 다음 주말에 PC Playground에서 2개의 대회를 개최할 겁니다. 이 대회들은 실시간 전략 게임 게이머들을 위한 것입니다. 이 대회들에서 두 가지 다른 게임을 할 건데요, Suncraft와 League of Heroes를 할 것입니다. Suncraft 대회에서는 Suncraft 프로게이머들과 함께 게임을 하게 될 것입니다. League of Heroes 대회에서는 참가자들이 무작위로 팀을 구성하게 될 것이고 컴퓨터 인공지능을 상대로 게임을 하는 스피드전이 이뤄질 것입니다. 이 대회들에서는 아마추어만 받아들입니다. 프로게이머는 참가가 불가능 합니다. 신청을 하기 위해서는 저희 웹 사이트 www.PCPlayg.co를 방문해서 1월 7일 전에 신청서를 제출해 주시기 바랍니다. 모두에게 행운이 있기를 바라며 굉장한 이벤트를 기대해 주십시오.

어휘

host *v.* 주최하다   **strategy** *n.* 전략   **side-by-side** *ad.* 나란히
random *a.* 무작위의   **compete** *v.* 경쟁하다   **accept** *v.* 받아들이다, 수락하다   **amateur** *n.* 아마추어   **outstanding** *a.* 뛰어난

정답 ④

문제풀이

남자는 League of Heroes 대회에서는 프로게이머는 참가가 불가능하고 이마추어만 가능하다고 하였으므로 일치하지 않는 내용은 ④ '이 대회에 아마추어는 참가가 불가능하다.'이다.

총 어휘 수 118

12 도표

소재 기부 내용 선택

듣기 대본 해석

여: 여보, 올해 기부를 할 자선 단체를 찾은 것 같아.
남: 잘 됐네! 또 어린이 자선 단체야?
여: 이번엔 아냐. 모든 연령대의 사람들을 도와줘. Make a Difference라는 자선 단체인데 해외의 어려움에 처한 사람들이나 여기 우리 나라 사람들을 도와줄지를 고를 수 있어.
남: 근데 작년에 시억 자신 단체에 기부를 히지 않았어? 올해는 해외에 있는 사람들을 도와 주는 게 좋을 것 같아.
여: 나도 그렇게 생각해. 요즘 뉴스를 많이 보는데 그 끔찍한 쓰나미 피해자들을 돕는 데 기부하는 게 좋을 것 같아.
남: 너무 끔찍해 보였어. 그렇지? 우리가 도울 수 있는 건 해야지.
여: 맞아. 그럼 얼마 정도 기부해야 한다고 생각해?
남: 300달러 이상을 기부할 수는 없을 것 같아.
여: 그럼 남은 게 이거 밖에 없네.
남: 좋아! 우리의 돈으로 남을 도울 수 있다는 건 정말 기분 좋은 일이야.

어휘

charity *n.* 자선 단체　　donate *v.* 기부하다　　overseas *a. ad.* 해외의
tsunami *n.* 쓰나미　　afford *v.* 여유(형편)가 되다　　〈문제〉disaster *n.*
재해　　relief *n.* 경감, 완화

정답 ①

문제풀이
남자와 여자가 기부할 프로그램을 고르고 있다. 해외에 있는 사람들을 돕자고
했으므로 ①~③중에 골라야 하고 쓰나미 피해자를 돕고 싶다고 했으므로
①, ③번이 남게 되는데 300달러 이상은 기부를 못한다고 했으므로 정답은
①번이다.

총 어휘 수 149

13　긴 대화의 응답

소재 여행에서 있었던 불행한 일들

듣기 대본 해석
남: Samantha. 뉴욕은 잘 갔다 왔어?
여: 정말 최악이었어.
남: 정말? 그거 안됐네. 뭐가 문제였는데?
여: 거의 모든 게 다 문제였어. 뉴욕에 도착할 때 항공사가 내 짐을 분실했다고
　　했어. 찾는 데 3일이나 걸렸어.
남: 최악이다. 근데 네가 어떤 기분인지 알아. 내가 로마에 갔을 때도 같은 일이
　　일어났거든.
여: 오, 그건 시작에 불과해. 내가 카페에서 커피를 마시고 있을 때 누가 내 서류
　　가방을 훔쳐 갔어.
남: 진짜? 정말 운이 없다.
여: 운이 없다고? 정말 화가 났어! 경찰도 어떻게 도와줄 수 없더라고. 그런데
　　내 불운은 거기가 끝이 아니야.
남: 진심이야?
여: 응. 시애틀로 돌아가는 비행기가 2시간 지연됐어. 그리고 내가 다시 짐을
　　찾으러 갔을 때 또 분실했다는 거야.
남: ② 안 좋은 일(불운)이 생겼다니 정말 안됐다.

어휘

baggage *n.* (여행용) 짐　　infuriate *v.* 격분시키다, 격노하게 하다
delay *v.* 미루다, 연기하다　　claim *v.* (자기 권리나 재산이라고 여겨)
요구하다

정답 ②

문제풀이
여자는 뉴욕 여행에서 짐을 잃어버리고, 도둑을 맞는 등 여러 안 좋은 일에 대해
남자에게 이야기 했으므로 이에 대한 남자의 응답으로 가장 적절한 것은
② '안 좋은 일(불운)이 생겼다니 정말 안됐다.'이다.

오답 보기 해석
① 뉴욕은 이때쯤 굉장히 아름다워.
③ 경찰들이 그걸 찾을 수 있어서 다행이야.
④ 한 시간 일찍 공항에 도착하는 게 좋아.
⑤ 난 다음에 여행갈 때 더 조심해야겠어.

총 어휘 수 149

14　긴 대화의 응답

소재 밀렵 당하는 코끼리를 돕는 방법
듣기 대본 해석
남: 안녕 Brittney. 너 보고 있는 것이 뭐니?
여: 아, 나는 온라인에서 코끼리를 지켜줄 방법을 검색하고 있어.

남: 너 코끼리를 돕는 것을 원하는구나, 그렇지?
여: 맞아. 코끼리들은 친절한 마음씨를 가진 감정적인 생명체야. 그들은 심지어
　　죽은 코끼리를 애도하기도 해.
남: 그거 흥미롭네. 나는 그것을 몰랐었어.
여: 그건 사실이야. 그런데 상아 때문에 코끼리를 사냥하는 밀렵꾼이 많잖아.
남: 아직도? 나는 사람들이 수십 년 전에 상아를 사용하는 것을 그만두었다고
　　생각했었어. 매년 얼마나 많은 코끼리들이 단지 그들의 상아 때문에
　　죽었을까?
여: 매년 40,000마리라고 몇몇 전문가들이 그러더라.
남: 끔찍하네. 사람들은 코끼리의 상아가 무엇에 필요하지?
여: 상아는 수집용 입상이나, 당구공, 그리고 전통 약을 만드는 데 사용될 수 있어.
남: 너무 슬프구나. 도움을 위해서 우리가 무엇을 할 수 있을까?
여: ① 음, 이 웹사이트에 돈을 기부하려고 생각하고 있어.

어휘

save *v.* 안전하게 하다, 지키다　　being *n.* 존재, 생명체　　mourn *v.*
애도하다, 슬퍼하다　　poacher *n.* 밀렵꾼　　ivory *n.* 상아　　tusk *n.*
엄니(상아)　　collectible *a.* 수집할 수 있는, 모을 수 있는　　figurine *n.*
작은 입상　　billiard ball 당구공　　traditional *a.* 전통의
medicine *n.* 약, 의학

정답 ①

문제풀이
밀렵 당하는 불쌍한 코끼리들을 위해 할 수 있는 일이 없는지 묻는 남자에게
여자가 해줄 응답은 ① '음, 이 웹사이트에 돈을 기부하려고 생각하고 있어.'가
적절하다.

오답 보기 해석
② 맞아. 많은 나라에서 코끼리를 죽이는 것은 불법이야.
③ 동물원에 있는 코끼리를 확인해 보는 것이 어때?
④ 문제 없어. 너는 이 다큐멘터리를 빌릴 수 있어.
⑤ 사람들은 상아를 얻기 위해 코끼리를 사냥해서는 안돼.

총 어휘 수 129

15　상황에 적절한 말

소재 아들의 운동과 다이어트에 대한 집착

듣기 대본 해석
남: Jane의 중학생인 아들 Tim은 운동과 몸매를 좋게 만드는 것에 매우
　　관심이 많습니다. Jane은 건강을 의식하는 것이 좋다는 것은 알지만, Tim이
　　너무 많이 한다고 생각합니다. 그녀는 그가 하루에 몇 시간씩 헬스장에 가고
　　살을 빼려고 식사를 거른다는 것을 알게 됩니다. 이는 그가 너무 말라 보여서
　　그녀가 걱정하게 합니다. 그는 건강지 않아 보입니다. 하지만 Tim은 살을
　　더 뺄 필요가 있다고 생각합니다. Jane은 그가 점점 집착하게 되어서,
　　그것이 심각한 건강 문제를 일으킬까 봐 걱정합니다. 그녀는 그가 운동하는
　　것과 다이어트를 하는 것에 대해 생각하는 방식을 바꾸게끔 하고 싶습니다.
　　이 상황에서 Jane이 Tim에게 이 할 가장 적절한 말은 무엇일까요?
Jane: Tim. ① 너의 운동과 다이어트 습관은 건강에 좋지 않아.

어휘

be concerned about ~에 관심을 갖다, ~을 염려하다
stay in shape 몸매를 좋게 유지하다　　lose weight 살을 빼다, 체중을
감량하다　　concern *v.* ~을 걱정하게 만들다　　skinny *a.* 마른
obsessed *a.* 사로잡힌, 집착하는　　lead to ~에 이르다

정답 ①

문제풀이
Jane은 아들의 운동과 다이어트 습관이 큰 문제를 일으킬 수 있다고 걱정하고
있으므로 정답은 ① '너의 운동과 다이어트 습관은 건강에 좋지 않아.'가 가장
적절하다.

② 너의 다이어트와 운동 요법은 효과가 좋구나.
③ 너는 여전히 건강이 안 좋아 보여(몸매가 엉망이야).
④ 너는 더 운동할 필요가 있어.
⑤ 너는 공부를 더 열심히 해야 해.

총 어휘 수 132

16 담화 목적 / 17 세부 내용 파악

소재 산악 자전거타기 시 주의점

듣기 대본 해석

남: 안녕하세요 여러분. 오늘 우리는 산악 자전거타기에 대해서 얘기해 보겠습니다. 아시다시피, 산악 자전거타기는 아주 좋은 운동 방법입니다. 그것은 또한 자연과 교감할 수 있는 훌륭한 방법입니다. 하지만 그것이 재미있고 건강에 도움이 될 수 있는 반면 위험하기도 합니다. 여러분의 다음 여행 전에 이런 것들을 꼭 명심하세요. 우선, 적절한 보호장비를 착용하세요. 항상 헬멧을 착용하세요. 산악 자전거를 탈 때 머리를 보호하는 것은 매우 중요합니다. 고려해야 할 또 다른 중요한 것은 물입니다. 산악 자전거타기는 신체적으로 매우 힘들기 때문에 충분한 물을 가져가는 것은 대단히 중요합니다. 산에 가기 전에 날씨도 확인해 봐야 합니다. 빗속에서 오도 가도 못하게 되기를 원치는 않을 것입니다. 그리고 마지막으로 지도와 나침반을 가져가세요. 그렇게 하면 만약 길을 잃었을 때 돌아 내려가는 길을 찾을 수 있습니다. 이러한 팁들을 다음 번에 산악 자전거를 탈 때 꼭 명심하세요.

어휘

take ~ into consideration ~을 고려하다 **proper** *a.* 적절한
protective *a.* 보호용의 **gear** *n.* 복장, 장비 **crucial** *a.* 중대한
exhausting *a.* 매우 힘든 **critical** *a.* 대단히 중요한, 비판적인
compass *n.* 나침반 〈문제〉**persuade** *v.* 설득하다 **take up**
계속하다 **potential** *a.* 잠재적인

정답 16 ① 17 ⑤

문제풀이

16 남자는 산악 자전거를 탈 때 고려해야 할 몇 가지를 말해주고 있으므로 남자가 하는 말의 목적은 ① '산악 자전거에 관한 충고를 제공하기 위해'이다.

17 남자는 헬멧, 물, 지도와 나침반을 챙기라고 했고 날씨도 확인하라고 했지만 여벌 옷에 대한 언급은 하지 않았으므로 정답은 ⑤ '여벌 옷'이다.

16

② 산악 자전거를 타도록 다른 사람들을 설득하기 위해
③ 산악 자전거의 건강상 이점을 확인하기 위해
④ 산악 자전거가 왜 인기 있는지에 관한 이유를 설명하기 위해
⑤ 산악 자전거를 타는 동안의 잠재적 위험에 대해 경고하기 위해

총 어휘 수 157

DICTATION ANSWERS

01 skilled guitar player / I appreciate you saying that

02 go out for dinner / spending too much money

03 We've been sorting through the suggestions / allowing you to submit suggestions online / click on the "Suggestions" link / makes it easier to respond

04 special tradition relating to / different symbolic objects / successful academic career

05 value their hard work and dedication / They're such a great fit / two openings in quality control / give them my contact information

06 Take a look at our lot / Well, I don't really want a four-door sedan / inhale too much of the pollution / a depressing color

07 Where are you heading / this website for booking a hotel / it'll be kind of useless

08 You were supposed to be home / My phone's battery died / there was a major accident / won't be operating for the rest of the day

09 include admission to / including the performance / the discount doesn't apply to

10 future generations face / a real eye-opener / It drags at points / it will still be in theaters

11 I'm hosting two contests / in a speed challenge / No professionals are allowed to enter / look forward to an outstanding event

12 people in need overseas / donate money to a local charity / We should do our part to help

13 could have gone any worse / The same thing happened to me / my bad luck continued beyond that / have to be joking / was delayed for two hours

14 They're very emotional beings / They even mourn their dead / stopped using ivory decades ago

15 working out and staying in shape / skipping meals to lose weight / change the way he thinks about working out and dieting

16-17 get in touch with nature / take these things into consideration / wear proper protective gear / bringing plenty of water is critical

05 수능영어듣기 실전모의고사

01 ③	02 ⑤	03 ②	04 ⑤	05 ③	06 ①
07 ⑤	08 ⑤	09 ④	10 ②	11 ②	12 ③
13 ④	14 ②	15 ④	16 ③	17 ②	

01 짧은 대화의 응답

소재 물건 구매

듣기 대본 해석
여: 엽서 어디서 샀어요? 비싼가요?
남: 선물가게에서 샀어요. 전체 세트당 10달러예요.
여: 정말이요? 저는 어제 동네에서 같은 엽서를 15달러에 샀어요.
남: ③ 당신이 정말 바가지를 쓴 것 같군요.

어휘
〈문제〉 **overcharge v.** 바가지를 씌우다　**misunderstanding n.** 오해
purchase n. 구매 **v.** 구매하다

정답 ③

문제풀이
같은 엽서 세트를 5달러나 더 주고 산 여자에게 남자가 할 말은 ③ '당신이 정말 바가지를 쓴 것 같군요.'가 적절하다.

오답 보기 해석
① 괜찮아요. 저는 신용카드로 지불할게요.
② 음, 그렇다면 내 돈을 되돌려 받아야겠어요.
④ 사과할게요. 오해가 있었어요.
⑤ 다음 구매 시에 5퍼센트 할인을 해 드릴게요.

총 어휘 수 42

02 짧은 대화의 응답

소재 겹친 행사

듣기 대본 해석
남: 다음 월요일에 제 딸이 초등학교에 입학해요. 하지만 저는 동시에 구직 인터뷰가 있어요.
여: 둘 다 할 수는 없잖아요.
남: 알아요. 어떤 게 더 중요하다고 생각하세요?
여: ⑤ 제 생각엔 직업을 구하는 거요.

어휘
elementary school 초등학교　〈문제〉 **get a job** 직업을 구하다

정답 ⑤

문제풀이
남자가 딸의 초등학교 입학과 구직 인터뷰 중에 더 중요한 일이 어떤 것이라고 생각하는지 물었으므로 어떤 것이 더 중요하다는 대답이 와야 한다. 따라서 ⑤ '제 생각엔 직업을 구하는 거요.'가 적절하다.

오답 보기 해석
① 오늘 밤 그를 인터뷰 하는 것이 기대돼요.
② 철저하게 준비되는 것이 중요한 것 같아요.
③ 꽃을 좀 가져와야 해요.
④ 그녀는 내년에 졸업할 거예요.

총 어휘 수 40

03 담화 주제

소재 온라인상 개인정보 도용을 막기 위한 요령

듣기 대본 해석
남: 최근 기술의 발전으로 사람들은 점점 더 많은 시간을 인터넷을 하면서 보내고 있습니다. 많은 분들이 알다시피 이는 여러분의 개인정보를 훔치려고 하는 인터넷상 약탈자들을 증가시키고 있습니다. 저는 오늘 신원 도용을 막을 수 있는 방법들을 여러분께 설명해 드리려고 합니다. 우선 여러분의 온라인 계정의 비밀번호를 수시로 바꾸는 것은 매우 중요합니다. 더 나아가 계정마다 비밀번호를 다르게 해놓는 것이 좋습니다. 이 비밀번호들은 숫자, 글자, 그리고 별표나 구두점 같은 특수문자를 포함하는 것이 좋습니다. 그리고 피싱 사이트들도 경계해야 합니다. 의심스러운 사이트에 개인정보를 입력할 때는 항상 조심하십시오. 마지막으로 공용 컴퓨터를 사용할 때 완전히 로그아웃을 하고 작업이 끝나면 브라우저를 닫으십시오.

어휘
predator n. 포식자, 약탈자　**identity theft** 신원 도용
asterisk n. 별표　**punctuation n.** 구두점　**suspicious a.** 의심스러운

정답 ②

문제풀이
남자는 개인정보 도용을 막을 수 있는 방법으로 비밀번호 변경, 비밀번호를 만드는 요령, 주의해야 할 사이트, 공용 컴퓨터 사용시 로그아웃 등을 말하고 있으므로 주제로 가장 적절한 것은 ② '온라인상 개인정보 도용 방지 요령'이다.

총 어휘 수 127

04 의견

소재 방해물을 치움으로써 학습 효율을 높이는 방법

듣기 대본 해석
남: Tiffany, 너 요즘 성적도 오르고 있고 수업 참여도 활발하게 하고 있어.
여: 알아차린 게 신기한데 그래, 맞아.
남: 어떻게 하는 거야? 학기 초에는 굉장히 힘들어하고 있었잖아.
여: 나는 집에서 수업 전에 교과서를 읽고, 방해되는 것들로부터 거리를 두려고 노력해 왔어.
남: 내가 어떻게 하면 네가 한 것처럼 집중과 흥미를 향상시킬 수 있을까?
여: 사실 꽤 간단해. 방해될 만한 것들을 다 치우는 거야.
남: 그럼 텔레비전도 끄고 인터넷을 하지도 말라는 거야?
여: 뭐, 적당하면 괜찮아. 근데 공부할 시간을 만들고 그 시간에는 공부만 해야 해.
남: 그건 그렇네. 난 어떨 땐 텔레비전 켜둔 채로 공부하는데 사실 방해 되더라고.
여: 널 방해하는 것들을 처리하면 분명 성적이 더 오를 거야.

어휘
distraction n. 방해물　**in moderation** 알맞게, 적당히
improve v. 개선되다, 향상시키다

정답 ⑤

문제풀이
남자가 여자에게 어떻게 성적을 올리고 공부에 집중하게 되었는지를 묻자, 방해될 만한 것들을 치움으로써 공부에만 집중한다고 대답하였으므로 여자의 의견으로 가장 적절한 것은 ⑤ '방해요소를 제거하여 학습 집중력을 높여야 한다.'이다.

총 어휘 수 155

05 대화자의 관계 파악

소재 영화배우의 스케줄 체크

듣기 대본 해석
여: 좋은 아침이에요, Boris. 오늘은 좀 어때요?
남: 많이 좋아졌어요, 감사해요. 리조트에서 굉장히 즐거운 시간을 보내고 있어요. 저번에 묵었던 곳보다 훨씬 편하네요.
여: 맘에 드셔서 다행이네요. 발코니에서의 경치가 장관이죠?
남: 아름다워요. 정말 떠나기 싫어요.
여: 음, 그럼 아침은 뭐 드실래요? 원하신다면 룸 서비스로 스테이크와 계란을 가져오라고 할 수 있어요.
남: 좋은 생각이에요. 오늘은 어떤 스케줄이 있어요? 잡지 촬영이 오늘인가요 내일인가요?
여: 내일이에요. 오늘은 지역 방송사에서 텔레비전 인터뷰가 있어요.
남: 그렇군요. 고마워요, Diane. 항상 챙겨줘서 고마워하고 있어요. 그나저나 영화촬영은 언제 시작해요?
여: 다음 주 월요일이에요. 세트장 매니저가 밤낮으로 준비하고 있어요.
남: 좋네요. 다시 한 번 고마워요.

어휘
balcony *n.* 발코니   **spectacular** *a.* 장관을 이루는, 극적인
magazine *n.* 잡지   **local** *a.* 지역의, 현지의   **station** *n.* 방송국, 역, 정류장   **around the clock** 24시간 내내, 밤낮으로

정답 ③

문제풀이
여자가 남자의 아침식사와 영화촬영 스케줄 등을 챙겨주는 것으로 보아 여자는 매니저, 남자는 영화배우임을 알 수 있으므로 정답은 ③ '영화배우 ― 매니저'이다.

총 어휘 수 138

06 그림의 세부 내용 파악

소재 새로 만든 홈페이지 디자인

듣기 대본 해석
여: 안녕하세요, Jayden 시금 컴퓨터로 뭘 하고 계세요?
남: 우리 홈페이지에 쓸 새로운 디자인을 만들고 있어요. 한번 봐요.
여: 훨씬 더 나아진 것 같네요. 새로운 색깔 조합이랑 레이아웃이 굉장히 마음에 드네요.
남: 고마워요. 사이트를 사용자에게 더 편리하게 만들고 싶었어요.
여: 나는 위쪽에 축구선수 사진도 좋아요. 그 아래에 저건 선수들 프로필로 연결되는 링크인가요?
남: 네, 맞아요. 팬들이 선수들에 대해 더 알 수 있게 하는 게 좋을 것 같더라고요.
여: 저 사진은 뭔가요?
남: 그것은 이달의 선수 사진이에요. 그는 모자를 거꾸로 쓰고 있어요.
여: 사진 밑에 있는 동영상은요?
남: 올해 여태까지의 하이라이트 몇 개를 보여주는 동영상이에요.
여: 팬들을 위한 게시판은요?
남: 페이지의 아래쪽에 하나 있어요.

어휘
color scheme 색채 배합   **biography** *n.* 전기, 프로필

정답 ①

문제풀이
위쪽에 축구선수 사진이 있다고 했는데 축구공 그림이 있으므로 일치하지 않는 것은 ①번이다.

총 어휘 수 138

07 할 일

소재 설거지 부탁

듣기 대본 해석
[전화벨이 울린다.]
여: 여보세요?
남: 안녕, 여보. 집에 오는 중이에요?
여: 아직이요. 방금 일을 마쳤어요. 5분 안에 퇴근할 거예요. 벌써 저녁 먹었어요?
남: 네, Richard랑 나는 햄버거를 먹었어요. 아, 오늘 당신한테 우편으로 큰 상자가 왔어요. 안에 뭐가 들었죠?
여: 그거 아마 Richard의 새 코트일 거예요. 며칠 전에 내가 인터넷에서 세일 중인 것을 발견했어요.
남: 아, 알았어요.
여: 그런데 나 오늘 엄청 긴 하루를 보냈어요. 내가 집에 갔을 때 설거지를 하기엔 너무 피곤할 것 같아요. 그것들 좀 해줄래요?
남: 물론이죠. 내가 Richard랑 할게요.
여: 좋아요. 내가 집에 가는 길에 식료품점에 잠깐 들려서 디저트를 사갈게요.
남: 좋아요.
여: 당신이 특별히 원하는 게 있나요?
남: 초콜릿이랑 아이스크림이면 괜찮아요. 집에 오면 봐요.

어휘
swing by 잠깐 들르다   **grocery store** 식품점, 슈퍼마켓
on the(one's) way (~으로) 가는 중에

정답 ⑤

문제풀이
여자는 오늘 긴 하루를 보냈다며 집에 가서 설거지를 못하겠다고 했고, 남자는 Richard와 함께 자신이 하겠다고 했으므로 남자가 여자를 위해 할 일은 ⑤ '설거지 해 주기'이다.

총 어휘 수 144

08 이유

소재 공항에 마중 나가지 못하는 이유

듣기 대본 해석
[휴대폰이 울린다.]
남: 여보세요?
여: 여보, 발표 어땠어?
남: 정말 잘 됐어. 나의 고객이 매우 인상 깊어했던 것 같아.
여: 잘 됐네. 오늘 집으로 올 거야?
남: 응. 오늘 오후 항공편을 예약했어.
여: 멋져. 아이들이 당신을 보면 굉장히 좋아할 거야. 너무 오랫동안 떠나 있었어.
남: 맞아. 집에 가서 가족과 함께 있게 되어 정말 신이 나. 공항에 나를 데리러 올 수 있어?
여: 아마도, 비행기가 몇 시에 도착해?
남: 4시 45분에 도착해.
여: 오, 음. 거기에 좀 늦게 도착할 수밖에 없을 것 같은데. 5시에 Alice를 피아노 레슨에 데려가야 해.
남: 문제없어. 택시타면 돼.
여: 미안해, 여보. 아, 당신이 돌아오는 길에 기념품 좀 사 올 수 있어?
남: 그럼. 오늘 밤에 봐.

어휘
make it home 집에 가다   **book** *v.* 예약하다   **flight** *n.* 항공편, 비행
land *v.* 착륙하다   **souvenir** *n.* 기념품, 선물

정답 ⑤

여자는 5시에 딸을 피아노 레슨에 데려가야 해서 비행기 도착시간에 공항에 도착할 수 있을 것 같지 않다고 말했으므로 여자가 공항에 마중 나갈 수 없는 이유는 ⑤ '딸을 피아노 레슨에 데려가야 해서'이다.

총 어휘 수 134

09 숫자

소재 연극 표 구입

듣기 대본 해석

여: 안녕하세요. 무엇을 도와드릴까요?

남: 안녕하세요. 저와 제 아내의 연극 표를 사고 싶습니다.

여: 음. 근데 지금 거의 매진입니다. 발코니에 위치한 C구역과 F구역에만 자리가 남았네요.

남: 그것들 중 하나라도 괜찮습니다. 얼마입니까?

여: C구역은 20달러이고 F구역은 15달러입니다.

남: 왜 C구역의 표가 더 비싸죠?

여: C구역이 시야가 더 좋습니다.

남: 그럼 C구역 표 두 장으로 할게요. 할인도 되나요?

여: 65세가 넘으신 고령자에게는 10퍼센트 할인을 해 드리고 있어요.

남: 저는 67살이고 제 아내는 지난 달에 65세가 됐습니다. 여기 신용카드랑 신분증이요.

여: 알겠습니다. 여기 표 받으세요. 오른쪽에 있는 문으로 입장하시면 됩니다. 즐거운 관람 되세요.

남: 감사합니다.

어휘

sold out (표가) 매진된

정답 ④

문제풀이

C구역 두 장이므로 40달러인데. 65세 이상 고령자 할인을 10퍼센트 받는다고 했으므로 남자가 지불해야 할 금액은 ④ '$36'이다.

총 어휘 수 150

10 언급 유무

소재 과외 수업

듣기 대본 해석

여: Felix, 과외 하면서 추가로 돈을 좀 벌려고 한다고 들었어.

남: 맞아. 누구 과외 선생님 찾는 사람 없어?

여: 음. 우리 여동생이 수학 때문에 좀 헤매고 있어서 도움이 필요할 것 같아.

남: 어떤 수학에서 도움이 필요한 건데?

여: 지금 고급 대수학 듣고 있어.

남: 오, 문제없어. 얼마나 자주 만날 수 있어?

여: 일주일에 두 번. 아마 화요일과 목요일이 가장 좋을 거야.

남: 응. 과외 시간은 얼마나 길어야 할까?

여: 일주일에 두 번이면, 한 시간이면 충분할 것 같아.

남: 그래. 어머님께서 얼마 정도 지불하실 생각이셔?

여: 한 수업 당 40달러면 괜찮을 것 같다고 하셨는데 상의해 볼 수 있을 거야.

남: 아니야. 그 정도면 괜찮아. 어머님께 내 휴대폰 번호 드리고 전화하시라고 하는 건 어때? 그럼 다른 더 자세한 얘기를 나눌 수 있잖아.

여: 그래. 알겠어.

어휘

tutoring *n.* 과외   **struggle** *v.* 허우적거리다, 버둥거리다

algebra *n.* 대수학   **negotiate** *v.* 협상하다

정답 ②

문제풀이

수업 과목(고급 대수학), 수업 횟수(일주일에 두 번), 수업 요일(화요일, 목요일), 수업료(40달러)는 언급했지만 수업 장소에 대해서는 언급하지 않았으므로 정답은 ② '수업 장소'이다.

총 어휘 수 156

11 내용 일치 · 불일치

소재 스노클링 투어

듣기 대본 해석

여: 돌고래, 물고기, 그리고 다른 바다 생물들과 수영하는 게 어떤 느낌일지 상상해 보신 적 있습니까? Johnny Bahama's 바다 투어에 참여해서 세계 최고의 스노클링 투어를 즐겨보세요. 오, 스노클링을 해본 적이 없으신가요? 문제 없습니다. 하는 내내 모든 과정을 여러분과 함께할 가이드들이 있습니다. 매일 아침 9시, 오후 1시, 오후 4시에 투어를 합니다. 스노클링은 체력적으로 힘든 활동이기 때문에 15세 이상인 분만 가능합니다. 그리고 모든 분들은 항상 구명조끼를 착용해 주시기 바랍니다. 호텔 로비나 아침 7시와 저녁 6시 사이에 110-555-7570으로 전화해서 예약하실 수 있습니다. 경청해 주셔서 감사드리고 이 아름다운 섬에서 좋은 시간 되시길 바랍니다.

어휘

marine *a.* 바다의, 해양의   **snorkeling** *n.* 스노클링   **demanding** *a.* 부담이 큰, 힘든

정답 ②

문제풀이

매일 아침 9시, 오후 1시, 오후 4시에 투어가 있다고 하였으므로, 하루에 총 세 번 투어가 있다. 따라서 일치하지 않는 것은 ② '하루에 네 번 투어가 있다.'이다.

총 어휘 수 133

12 도표

소재 딸의 도서관 여름 프로그램 선택

듣기 대본 해석

남: 여보, 도서관에서 어린이들을 위한 여름 프로그램을 개설한대요. 그 중 하나에 Leslie를 참가시킬 생각이에요.

여: 좋은 생각이네요. 그 프로그램에 대한 정보 있어요?

남: 물론이죠. 여기 받은 전단지에요.

여: [잠시 후] Leslie가 월요일에는 수영 수업 가야 돼서 그날 프로그램은 아무 것도 못 들어요.

남: 맞아요. 매일 오후 3시까지 하는 여름 캠프도 있죠?

여: 그래요. 그러니까 3시 30분 이후에 시작하는 프로그램을 찾아야 해요.

남: 알겠어요. 근데 그 애는 별로 화가로서의 소질은 없는 것 같으니까 다른 프로그램을 찾아보죠.

여: 네. 이제 이 두 개로 좁혀졌네요.

남: 그렇군요. 50달러는 좀 비싼 것 같지 않아요?

여: 나도 그렇게 생각해요. 그럼 이 프로그램에 등록해야겠어요.

남: 내일 도서관 가서 등록할게요.

어휘

enroll *v.* 등록하다   **flyer** *n.* 전단지   **sign ~ up** ~을 등록시키다

정답 ③

문제풀이

월요일은 안 된다고 했고, 매일 오후 세시까지는 여름 캠프가 있어서 3시 30분 이후인 프로그램 중에서 선택해야 한다. 그럼 말고 다른 프로그램을 찾자고 했으므로 ③번과 ④번이 남는다. 그 중에 50달러는 비싼 것 같으므로 다른 것을 선택하자고 했으므로 정답은 ③번이다.

총 어휘 수 142

13　긴 대화의 응답

소재 아들의 학교생활

듣기 대본 해석

남: Swanson씨, 안녕하세요. Edward의 아빠인 Daniel Hoult입니다.
여: 오, Hoult씨. 만나서 반가워요. 들어오세요.
남: 고마워요. 제 아들이 학교에서 어떻게 지내나요?
여: 음. Edward는 부지런한 학생이에요.
남: 정말입니까?
여: 네. 그는 항상 웃고 수업에 활발하게 참여하려고 노력해요.
남: 그런데 학교에서 약간 난폭하지는 않나요?
여: 아닙니다. 가끔 그의 친구들과 너무 흥분하긴 하지만 다른 학생들에게 피해를 주진 않아요.
남: 집에서는 다소 쉽게 짜증내거든요.
여: 음. 학생들은 종종 학교에서보다 집에서 매우 다르기도 해요.
남: 다른 학생들도 마찬가지라는 말씀이시죠?
여: 그렇습니다. Hoult씨. Edward는 여기에서 잘 하고 있어요. 그는 매사에 성실하게 최선을 다해요.
남: ④ 학교 생활을 정말 잘하고 있다니 안심이군요.

어휘

aggressive *a.* 난폭한, 공격적인　　**get irritated** 짜증나다
genuinely *ad.* 진정으로, 성실하게

정답　④

문제풀이

Edward의 아버지와 선생님의 대화 내용이다. 아들의 학교 생활을 걱정하는 아버지에게 여자는 Edward가 성실하게 최선을 다하는 학생이라고 말한다. 이에 적절한 대답은 ④ '학교 생활을 정말 잘하고 있다니 안심이군요.'이다.

오답 보기 해석

① 그가 어떤 학교 클럽에도 가입하지 않았으면 좋겠어요.
② 어떻게 학생들을 더 잘 가르칠 수 있는지 알고 싶네요.
③ 이제부터 학교에 제때 가라고 얘기할게요.
⑤ 수업에서 활동적으로 임하라고 충고해야 할 것 같아요.

총 어휘 수 126

14　긴 대화의 응답

소재 멀리 계신 아빠 방문

듣기 대본 해석

남: Jenny, 주말 동안 갔던 하이킹 여행 어땠어? 가족들과 함께 간 거야, 맞지?
여: 사실, 이번엔 아빠랑만 갔는데, 평생의 경험(일생일대의 경험)이었어!
남: 너랑 너희 아빠랑만?
여: 응. 우린 많은 이야기를 했지. 나는 다 컸고 내 인생에 책임을 져야 한다고 느꼈어.
남: 네가 그럴 거라고 생각해. 나도 우리 아빠가 많이 그리워. 아빠께서는 일 년 동안 멀리 가 계셔.
여: 두바이에 계시지, 맞지? 네가 겨울 방학 동안 아빠께 방문하는 게 어때?
남: 아빠도 나한테 오라고 하셨지만, 내가 시간이 없어. 겨울 대학진학 준비 프로그램에 참가해야 해.

여: 오, 대학진학 준비 프로그램이 아주 힘들다고 들었어.
남: 맞아. 숙제랑 읽기가 많아. 내가 아빠를 방문할 수 없어서 기분이 안 좋아.
여: ② 안됐지만 아빠가 상황을 이해하실 거라 믿어.

어휘

responsible for ～에 책임이 있는　　**demanding** *a.* 부담이 큰, 힘든
〈문제〉**that's a shame** 안됐군요, 유감이다

정답　②

문제풀이

두바이에 계신 아빠가 보고 싶지만 겨울에 대학진학 준비 프로그램 참가로 방문을 못해서 기분이 좋지 않다고 말하는 남자에게 여자가 해줄 수 있는 말은 ② '안됐지만 아빠가 상황을 이해하실 거라 믿어.'가 가장 적절하다.

오답 보기 해석

① 지금은 많이 바쁘지 않아서 너랑 같이 그를 보러 갈 수 있어.
③ 네가 정말 열심히 해왔으니까 시험에 통과할 거라고 확신해.
④ 그렇긴 하지만 그는 너랑 캠핑 가기에는 너무 바쁘신 게 틀림없어.
⑤ 과제들은 선생님들께 이메일로 제출해야 해.

총 어휘 수 142

15　상황에 적절한 말

소재 문제가 생긴 차

듣기 대본 해석

여: 출근하는 길에 Carl의 차에 문제가 생깁니다. 그는 서비스 센터에 가서 공회전할 때 차가 가끔 시동이 꺼진다고 얘기합니다. 정비공은 자동차를 보고 점화 플러그를 교체해야 한다는 것을 알아냅니다. Carl에겐 다행히도 이는 꽤나 간단하고 저렴한 해결책이어서 그는 정비공에게 플러그를 교체할 것을 요구합니다. Carl은 시간이 많지 않아서 정비공에게 언제쯤 자동차 수리가 끝나는지 물어보고 싶어합니다. 이러한 상황에서 Carl이 정비공에게 뭐라고 말할까요?
Carl: ④ 점화 플러그를 교체하는 데 얼마나 걸릴까요?

어휘

stall *v.* (갑자기) 시동이 꺼지다　　**idle** *v.* (엔진이) 공회전하다, 빈둥거리다
a. 게으른, 가동되지 않는　　**spark plug** 점화 플러그　　**mechanic** *n.*
정비공　　〈문제〉**get a second opinion** 다른 사람의 의견을 얻다

정답　④

문제풀이

담화의 마지막 부분에서 Carl이 좀 바빠서 점화 플러그를 교체하는 데 얼마나 걸리는지 물어보고자 한다고 했으므로 정답은 ④ '점화 플러그를 교체하는 데 얼마나 걸릴까요?'이다.

오답 보기 해석

① 다른 정비공에게도 물어봐야 할 것 같아요.
② 차 수리하는 데 얼마 정도 들까요?
③ 차에 점화 플러그가 없는 것 같아요.
⑤ 좋네요! 심각한 문제일까 봐 걱정했어요.

총 어휘 수 111

16　담화 주제　/　17　세부 내용 파악

소재 치매 예방법

듣기 대본 해석

남: 치매는 오늘 날 세계에 점점 더 흔해지고 있습니다. 이는 사람의 언어능력, 이해능력, 기억력 그리고 사고 처리에 부정적으로 영향을 미치는 끔찍한 병입니다. 이 병은 보통 연세가 많으신 분들이 가장 영향을 많이 받지만,

치매는 40세만큼이나 젊은 성인들까지 걸리는 것으로 알려져 있습니다.
많은 연구를 통해서 의사들은 이제 이 병이 예방될 수 있다고 자신 있게
말합니다. 독일에서 쓰이는 예방법 중 하나는 은행잎 추출물을 사용한
치료법입니다. 이 유명한 약초는 순환계를 향상시킬 뿐만 아니라 뇌 기능을
상승시키기 위해서도 중국과 다른 나라들에서 수천 년 간 쓰여져 왔습니다.
임상 연구는 이 약초가 기억력을 회복하고 뇌로 가는 혈류량을 증가시키는
능력이 있음을 보여주었습니다. 사실 약초가 굉장히 강해서 복용 20분
내에 효과가 감지될 수 있습니다. 몇 개월 간 지속적으로 복용을 하면 치매
환자들은 큰 호전을 경험할 수 있을 것입니다.

어휘

Alzheimer's disease 치매 **prevalent** *a.* 일반적인, 흔한
comprehension *n.* 이해력 **preventative** *a.* 예방을 위한
measure *n.* 조치 **ginkgo biloba** 은행잎 추출물
circulatory system 순환계 **detect** *v.* 감지하다, 발견하다
dramatic *a.* 극적인, 인상적인

정답 16 ③ 17 ②

문제풀이

16 남자는 오늘날 치매가 점점 흔해지고 젊은 사람들에게까지 나타나고 있다
고 말하면서 치매 치료에 도움을 주는 ginkgo biloba(은행잎 추출물)를
소개하고 있다. 따라서 남자가 하는 말의 주제는 ③ '치매 환자를 도와준다고
입증된 보조제를 제안하기 위해'이다.

17 독일에서 쓰이는 방법이지만 수천 년 전부터 중국과 다른 나라들에서도 쓰여
왔다고 했으므로 내용과 일치하지 않는 것은 ② '독일 외 다른 나라에선
쓰지 않는다.'이다

오답 보기 해석

16
① 사람들에게 새로운 약초 보조제에 대해 알리기 위해
② 기억력과 뇌활동 개선에 대한 조언을 주기 위해
④ 사람들에게 약초 복용의 위험성을 상기시키기 위해
⑤ 사람들이 치매 경고 증상을 인식하도록 돕기 위해

총 어휘 수 145

DICTATION ANSWERS

01 at the gift shop

02 enter elementary school

03 how you can prevent identity theft / passwords for
each of your accounts / also be cautious of phishing
websites / into suspicious websites

04 starting to excel in class / separate myself from
distractions / okay in moderation

05 the balcony is spectacular / what's on the schedule /
when do we start filming / is working around the clock

06 color scheme and the new layout / wearing his cap
backward / a message board for the fans

07 Are you on your way home / I found it on sale / too
tired to wash the dishes / swing by the grocery store

08 booked a flight / You've been gone so long / take Alice
to her piano lesson / catch a taxi / pick up a couple of
souvenirs

09 we're nearly sold out / The view is better / Senior
citizens over the age of

10 earn some extra money / struggling in math / She's
taking advanced algebra / willing to pay

11 the world's finest snorkeling tours / guides who will be
with you every step / wear a life jacket

12 we should enroll Leslie in / can't attend any programs /
don't think she's much of / sign her up

13 is a diligent student / never gives others a hard time /
genuinely tries his best at

14 the experience of a lifetime / responsible for my life /
Why don't you visit him / pre-college program is very
demanding

15 pulls into a service station / is in a bit of a hurry /
when his car will be fixed

16-17 becoming more and more prevalent / One
preventative measure used / increase blood flow /
After several months of steady use

06 수능영어듣기 실전모의고사

01 ①	02 ④	03 ③	04 ⑤	05 ②	06 ⑤
07 ①	08 ②	09 ③	10 ③	11 ⑤	12 ⑤
13 ①	14 ④	15 ②	16 ①	17 ③	

01 짧은 대화의 응답

소재 야외 바비큐

듣기 대본 해석
남: 안녕, Amanda. 뭘 굽고 있어?
여: 내일 저녁 디저트를 위한 파이를 구울 거야.
남: 대단하네. 내일 야외 바비큐 저녁 식사야. 맞지?
여: ① 응, 여름 저녁을 보내는 데에 최고일 거야.

어휘
dessert *n.* 디저트   **outdoor** *a.* 야외의

정답 ①

문제풀이
남자가 내일 야외 바비큐 식사가 맞는지 확인 차 묻는 데 대해 맞다고 대답하는 답변이 가장 자연스럽다. 따라서 ① '응, 여름 저녁을 보내는 데에 최고일 거야.'가 정답이다.

오답 보기 해석
② 너의 그 유명한 치킨 샐러드를 만들 거니?
③ 모든 사람들을 파티에 초대하는 게 어때?
④ 스낵 좀 가져와. 그건 큰 일이 아니니까.
⑤ 파이 굽는 데 도움이 필요하니?

총 어휘 수 36

02 짧은 대화의 응답

소재 동전 바꾸기

듣기 대본 해석
여: 드디어 주말이다. 오락실에 가서 게임이나 하자.
남: 그거 좋겠다. 그런데 나 동전이 떨어졌어. 너 20달러 잔돈으로 가지고 있니?
여: 그럴 거야. 어떻게 줄까?
남: ④ 10달러 지폐 하나랑 5달러 지폐 하나, 그리고 나머지는 동전으로 줘.

어휘
change *n.* 동전, 잔돈   〈문제〉**a penny for your thoughts**
[속담] 무엇을 멍하니 생각하고 있니

정답 ④

문제풀이
남자는 여자에게 잔돈이 있는지 물었고, 여자는 어떻게 바꿔줄지를 물었으므로 남자의 대답으로 적절한 것은 ④ '10달러 지폐 하나랑 5달러 지폐 하나, 그리고 나머지는 동전으로 줘.'이다.

오답 보기 해석
① 뭘 그리 멍하게 생각해.
② 난 동전만 있는 거 같아.
③ 오락실은 두 블록만 가면 돼.
⑤ 내가 어디서 잔돈으로 바꾸는 기계를 찾을 수 있는지 아니?

총 어휘 수 46

03 담화 목적

소재 교내 토네이도 대비 훈련 안내

듣기 대본 해석
[차임벨이 울린다.]
여: 안녕하세요 학생 여러분. 교감 선생인 Lee입니다. 토네이도가 많이 일어나는 철이 오고 있어서 오늘 점심을 먹은 후에 토네이도 대비 훈련을 실시할 예정입니다. 비상벨이 울릴 때 선생님의 지시에 따르도록 합시다. 서두르지 않으면서 질서 있게 방을 나가주시기 바랍니다. 선생님들께서 여러분을 지하실로 안내할 것이고 거기서 여러분은 토네이도가 일어날 경우 어떻게 자신을 보호해야 하는지 배우게 될 것입니다. 지역 소방관들도 참여하여 절차를 도와줄 것입니다. 대비 훈련은 마치는 데 30분 정도밖에 걸리지 않을 것입니다. 이 대비 훈련은 여러분의 안전을 위한 것이니 부디 집중해 주시기를 바랍니다. 협조해 주셔서 감사합니다.

어휘
drill *n.* 훈련   **instruction** *n.* 지도, 지시   **orderly** *a.* 질서 있는
usher *v.* 안내하다   **in the event of** 만약 ~하면, ~할 경우
in attendance 참석한   **procedure** *n.* 절차, 방법

정답 ③

문제풀이
토네이도가 자주 발생하는 철을 맞아 교내에서 실시되는 토네이도 대비 훈련에 대해 실시 시간, 절차, 소요 시간 등을 말하고 있는 것으로 보아 여자가 하는 말의 목적은 ③ '교내 토네이도 대비 훈련에 대해 안내하려고'이다.

총 어휘 수 112

04 의견

소재 카페 매출 신장 방안

듣기 대본 해석
여: Justin, 우리 앉아서 카페에 대해 얘기 좀 해요.
남: 네. 무슨 일 있어요?
여: 아시다시피, 우리는 이익을 내지 못하고 있어요.
남: 네, 저도 알아요. 길 건너편에 Blackbeans가 문을 연 후로 우린 계속 힘들었어요.
여: 음, 우리가 가격을 내려야 한다고 생각해요.
남: 정말이요? 저는 그래야 하나고 생각하지 않아요.
여: 그렇지만 우리 고객들을 카페로 다시 오게 하는 유일한 방법일 것 같아요.
남: 저는 우리는 제공하지만 Blackbeans에서는 제공하지 않는 메뉴에 집중해야 한다고 생각해요.
여: 그거 정말 좋은 생각이에요!
남: 우리가 더 좋은 다양한 메뉴를 제공한다고 사람들에게 알려야 해요. 그것에 관해 광고해야 될까요?
여: 물론이죠. 내일 초안을 바로 구상해볼게요.
남: Blackbeans에서는 제공하지 않고 우리가 제공하는 모든 메뉴들의 사진과 우리 로고면 완벽한 광고를 만들 수 있을 거예요.
여: 좋은 제안이에요.

어휘
suffer *v.* 악화되다, 시달리다, 고통 받다   **offer** *v.* 제공하다, 제안하다
remind *v.* 상기시키다, 다시 한번 알려주다   **variety** *n.* 여러 가지, 다양성

정답 ⑤

문제풀이
Blackbeans가 문을 연 후로 이익이 나지 않기 때문에 남자는 Blackbeans에서는 팔지 않는 메뉴에 집중하자고 말하고 있다. 따라서 답은 ⑤ 'Blackbeans에서 제공하지 않는 메뉴를 제공해야 한다.'이다.

총 어휘 수 136

05 대화자의 관계 파악

소재 조각가와의 인터뷰

듣기 대본 해석

남: 안녕하세요, Sampson씨!

여: 안녕하세요, Steve. 오늘 와주셔서 감사합니다.

남: 시작하겠습니다. 이번에 당신은 사람의 표정에 초점을 맞추고 있네요.

여: 네, 맞아요. 제가 사람의 표정에 혼신을 다하기로 정했던 것은 처음이에요.

남: 즐거웠나요?

여: 정말 즐거웠어요. 실제로, 이제 저는 추상적인 예술보다는 인간의 몸에 대한 작업에 집중해볼까 생각하고 있어요.

남: 재미있을 것 같네요. 저는 이 조각품의 이 모델 표정이 좋아요. 그녀는 당신이 아는 사람인가요?

여: 네, 그녀는 우리 이웃에 커피숍을 가지고 있어요. 저는 그녀에게 저를 위한 자세를 부탁했고 그녀는 기꺼이 도와줬어요.

남: 그렇군요. 부탁 하나 해도 될까요?

여: 물론이죠. 뭔데요?

남: 저희 기사에 사진을 싣고 싶습니다. 당신이 가장 좋아하는 작품 옆에 서 주시겠어요?

여: 물론이죠.

어휘

appreciate *v.* 고맙게 여기다 **expression** *n.* 표정 **devote** *v.* (시간 · 노력 · 돈을) 쏟다, 바치다, 기울이다 **abstract** *a.* 추상적인 **sculpture** *n.* 조각 **neighborhood** *n.* 이웃

정답 ②

문제풀이

대화에서 조각품이 나오고 어떤 것을 소재로 한 작업인지 이야기하고 있으므로 여자는 조각가이고, 대화의 마지막에 남자가 기사에 싣고 싶다고 하는 것으로 보아 남자는 여자를 취재하러 온 기자임을 알 수 있다. 따라서 정답은 ② '기자 — 조각가'이다.

총 어휘 수 140

06 그림의 세부 내용 파악

소재 어린이집 인테리어

듣기 대본 해석

남: 어린이집을 열 준비가 거의 된 것 같은데요, Pam.

여: 우리는 지난 몇 주 동안 많은 노력을 들였어요. 놀이방을 보세요.

남: 좋아 보여요. 구석이 있는 로켓은 굉장해요!

여: 네, 아이들이 거기서 놀기 재미있을 거예요. 뒤 벽에 별도 좀 그렸어요.

남: 그리고 오른쪽에 달도 보여요.

여: 맞아요. 좌석 배치는 어떤 것 같아요?

남: 잘된 것 같아요. 원통형 의자가 제법 우주 공간 같아요.

여: 나도 그렇게 생각했어요. 우리는 그것들의 크기를 다르게 하려고 노력했어요.

남: 하지만 탁자가 좀 부적절한 거 같네요.

여: 나도 그렇게 생각해요. 이 방에 사각 탁자는 어울리지 않아요.

남: 아이들은 상관없을 거예요.

어휘

arrangement *n.* 배열, 배치 **cylinder** *n.* 원통, 원기둥 **out of place** 어울리지 않는, 제 자리에 있지 않는 **square** *a.* 정사각형 모양의

정답 ⑤

문제풀이

대화의 마지막 부분에서 남자와 여자는 사각 탁자는 어울리지 않는다고 했는데 그림에서는 원형 탁자이므로 정답은 ⑤번이다.

총 어휘 수 132

07 할 일

소재 여자의 도움 제안

듣기 대본 해석

여: 안녕하세요 Smith 선생님. 뭐하세요?

남: 안녕, Serena. 책을 찾고 있어.

여: 무엇 때문에요?

남: 내 영어수업을 듣는 학생들이 재미있어 할 만한 책들을 찾고 있어. 학생들이 여름 동안 읽을 한 권을 선택했으면 하거든.

여: 아 여름 독서 목록을 만드시는 거군요. 지금까지 어떤 책들을 선택하셨어요?

남: 몇 개 밖에 안돼. 훨씬 더 많이 필요하지. 학생들이 흥미 있어 하는 책을 찾는 게 쉽지가 않네.

여: 제가 도와드릴 수 있을 것 같아요. 전 시간이 남을 때 책을 많이 읽거든요.

남: 정말이니?

여: 네. 제가 가장 좋아하는 것들을 목록으로 만들어서 이메일로 보내드릴 수 있어요.

남: 정말 친절하구나. 도와줘서 고마워.

여: 뭘요. 즐거운 여름방학 보내세요.

어휘

look up 찾아보다 **reading list** (추천) 도서 목록

정답 ①

문제풀이

남자가 학생들이 여름에 즐겁게 읽을 만한 책 찾기가 쉽지 않다고 하자, 여자는 남자에게 자신이 좋아하는 책 목록의 일부를 보내주겠다고 하였으므로 정답은 ① '도서 목록 만들어 보내 주기'이다.

총 어휘 수 132

08 이유

소재 집에 들어오는 시간

듣기 대본 해석

[휴대폰이 울린다.]

여: 여보세요, 아빠. 무슨 일이세요?

남: 안녕, Elsa. 집에 곧 오니?

여: 아직 학교에 있어요. 언제 끝날지 잘 모르겠어요.

남: 집에 오는 길에 피자 두서너 판 사올 수 있는지 궁금하구나. 남동생이 배가 고프단다.

여: 음, 아직 할 일이 남아있어요. 과학 전시회가 내일 있는 것 아시잖아요.

남: 맞다. 이제 기억이 나는구나. 저녁은 학교 근처에서 먹을 거니?

여: 네, 근처 작은 식당에서 간단히 먹을 거예요.

남: 알았다. 그럼 집에는 언제 올 것 같니?

여: 8시는 되어야 하지 않을까 싶어요. 저를 태우러 오실 수 있으세요?

남: 그러지 못할 것 같구나. 오늘 늦게까지 일해야 한단다. 남동생에게 전화해서 오늘 저녁은 스스로 챙겨먹으라고 얘기해주겠니?

여: 물론이죠. 제가 그에게 전화할게요.

어휘

be starving 배가 고파 죽을 지경이다 **grab a bite** 간단히 먹다

정답 ②

문제풀이

대화의 마지막 부분에서 여자가 자신을 데리러 올 수 있는지 물었는데, 남자는 늦게까지 일해야 해서 안 된다고 했으므로 정답은 ② '늦게까지 일해야 해서'이다.

총 어휘 수 144

09 숫자

소재 치킨 주문

듣기 대본 해석

[전화벨이 울린다.]

남: Together Chicken에 전화해 주셔서 감사합니다. 무엇을 도와드릴까요?

여: 안녕하세요. 내일 필요한 주문을 하려고요. 동아리 모임 때문에 치킨 20마리가 필요합니다.

남: 알겠습니다. 어떤 치킨으로 드릴까요?

여: 음. 갈릭 치킨과 훈제 치킨으로 할게요.

남: 네. 몇 마리씩 드릴까요?

여: 열 마리씩 살게요. 얼마예요?

남: 갈릭 치킨은 한 마리당 10달러이고 훈제 치킨은 15달러입니다.

여: 음. 제가 생각했던 것보다 좀 비싸네요.

남: 아! 깜박할 뻔 했네요. 치킨 열 마리 이상 주문할 시 10퍼센트 할인을 해 드리고 있어요.

여: 오, 좋네요! 오후 열두 시에 Jason Bourne Academy로 배달해 주세요.

남: 알겠습니다. 그때 배달해 드리겠습니다.

어휘

meeting *n.* 모임, 회의   **pricey** *a.* 비싼

정답 ③

문제풀이

여자는 10달러짜리 갈릭 치킨 열 마리와 15달러짜리 훈제 치킨 열 마리를 주문하였으므로 총액이 100달러+150달러=250달러인데, 열 마리 이상 구매하여 10퍼센트 할인을 받게 되었다. 그러므로 정답은 ③ '$225'이다.

총 어휘 수 137

10 언급 유무

소재 겨울철 호주 여행

듣기 대본 해석

남: 안녕 Maggie. 이번 겨울 방학에 뭐 할 거야? 계획 있어?

여: 음, 알아보고 있는 중인데 호주에 있는 Cairns로 여행 갈까 생각 중이야.

남: 음... 매우 좋은 생각은 아닌 것 같아.

여: 왜 안 되는데?

남: 음, 우선, 성수기이기 때문에 관광객들로 붐빌 거야.

여: 정말?

남: 확실해. 성수기에는 또한 거기가 더 많이 비싸.

여: 몰랐어.

남: 호주가 남반구에 있기 때문에 그때 거기는 정말 덥기도 해. 거긴 여름 일 거야.

여: 오, 나는 꽤 온화할 거라고 생각했는데. 나는 더위를 정말 싫어해. 그때 호주를 방문하는 것에 대해 좋은 점이 있을까?

남: 글쎄, 낮이 좀 더 길어서, 해변에서 좀 더 시간을 가질 수 있을 거야.

여: 그건 좋은 것 같네. 그런데 아마도 난 이번 겨울에 갈 다른 곳을 찾아야 할 것 같아.

어휘

look into ~을 조사하다, 주의 깊게 살피다   **first off** 우선
peak season 성수기   **be packed with** 붐비다, 북적거리다
hemisphere *n.* 반구

정답 ③

문제풀이

두 사람의 대화에서 겨울철 호주 여행시 관광객의 수, 물가, 날씨, 낮의 길이에 관한 언급은 있었지만 교통수단에 관한 언급은 없었으므로 정답은 ③ '교통수단'이다.

총 어휘 수 148

11 내용 일치 · 불일치

소재 잠을 많이 자는 나무늘보

듣기 대본 해석

남: 오늘, 저는 나무늘보에 대해 이야기하겠습니다. 나무늘보는 세계에서 가장 잠이 많은 동물 중 하나입니다! 나무늘보는 하루에 18시간을 잡니다. 왜 이 동물이 그렇게 잠을 많이 잘까요? 과학자들은 이것이 나무늘보가 스스로를 보호하는 방법이라고 생각합니다. 나무늘보는 나무 높은 곳에서 쉬고 잠을 자지만 먹는 먹이는 땅 아래에 있습니다. 나무늘보는 매우 천천히 움직이는 동물이기 때문에 땅에서 음식을 찾는 동안 포식자들에게 매우 취약합니다. 시간이 흐르면서 이 졸린 동물은 아주 적은 먹이로 사는 법을 배워서 사냥하는 데 적은 시간만 필요합니다. 그러나 이는 왜 나무늘보가 그렇게 잠을 많이 자는지 설명할 수 없습니다. 아마도 잠자는 것이 에너지를 아끼는 데 도움을 줄지도 모르죠. 아니 나무늘보가 정말 게으른 것일지도 모르고요!

어휘

sloth *n.* 나무늘보   **protect** *v.* 보호하다, 지키다   **vulnerable** *a.* 취약한   **predator** *n.* 포식자, 포식동물   **conserve** *v.* 아끼다, 보존하다

정답 ⑤

문제풀이

나무늘보는 아주 적은 먹이를 먹고 산다고 했으므로 일치하지 않는 것은 일치하지 않는 것은 ⑤번이다.

총 어휘 수 138

12 도표

소재 중고차 선택

듣기 대본 해석

남: 안녕하세요. 무엇을 도와드릴까요?

여: 안녕하세요. 아들을 위한 중고차를 찾고 있어요.

남: 찾고 계신 특정한 모델이 있나요?

여: 음, 그가 빠른 걸 좋아해서 스포츠카를 여러 대 둘러봤어요.

남: 그렇군요. 재고에 몇 대 있는 것 같아요. *[마우스 클릭 소리]* 우리가 갖고 있는 중고 스포츠카 목록이에요.

여: 흠... 5년 이상 된 차는 별로인 것 같아요.

남: 음. 근데 이 차의 전 주인은 이 다섯 개 승에서 운전을 가장 덜 했어요.

여: 저도 알지만, 50,000마일보다 적게 몰았던 좀 더 새 차를 찾고 있어요.

남: 알겠습니다. 가격은 얼마 정도 예상하세요?

여: $15,000 넘게 쓰고 싶진 않아요.

남: 그럼 이 두 가지로 좁혀졌네요.

여: 좋네요. 뭔가 잘못됐을 때 돈을 더 쓰고 싶지 않으니까 보증기간이 더 긴 걸로 할게요.

남: 알겠습니다. 가서 한번 살펴 보죠.

어휘

particular *a.* 특정한   **previous** *a.* 이전의   **warranty** *n.* 보증기간

정답 ⑤

문제풀이

여자는 5년 이하이고 50,000마일보다 적게 탔으며 15,000달러를 넘지 않는 것을 원하고 있으므로 ②번과 ⑤번이 남게 된다. 그 중에 보증기간이 긴 것으로 한다고 했으므로 정답은 ⑤번이다.

총 어휘 수 165

13 긴 대화의 응답

소재 출처 언급의 중요성

듣기 대본 해석

여: 뭐 하고 있어?

남: 경제학 리포트 마무리하려고. 너는 다 했어?

여: 응. 나는 어제 제출했어.

남: 너는 항상 빨리 끝내는구나. 나도 오늘 밤까지 리포트를 끝낼 수 있었으면 좋겠다.

여: 걱정 마. 너는 잘 할 거야. 시간 많잖아. *[잠시 후]* 저 그래프 정말 좋다. 멋져 보여!

남: 고마워. 나도 좋아. 내가 조사하면서 찾은 웹사이트에서 복사한 거야.

여: 정말? 네 자료출처에 사이트 목록을 작성했어?

남: 아니, 안 했는데. 해야 돼?

여: 당연하지! 네가 다른 사람의 자료를 사용할 때 출처를 항상 언급해야 해.

남: 나는 그게 인터넷에도 적용되는지 몰랐어. 알려줘서 고마워.

여: ① 언제든 괜찮아. 출처 언급을 기억하지 않으면 곤란하게 될 수도 있어.

어휘

source *n.* 원천, 자료, 출처　　**cite** *v.* 인용하다　　**apply to** ~에 적용되다
〈문제〉 **hand in** 제출하다

정답 ①

문제풀이

남자가 그래프를 인터넷 사이트에서 베꼈다고 하자 여자는 출처를 밝혔는지 물었고 남자에게 다른 사람의 자료를 사용할 때는 반드시 출처를 언급해야 함을 알려주었다. 남자가 거기에 대한 고마움을 표시했을 때 적절한 여자의 대답은 ① '언제든 괜찮아. 출처 언급을 기억하지 않으면 곤란하게 될 수도 있어.'이다.

오답 보기 해석

② 맞아. 난 우선 그 그래프를 사용하지 말았어야 했어.

③ 걱정 마. 이 그래프는 네가 필요할 모든 정보를 주고 있어

④ 그 그래프는 사실 사무실에 있는 다른 사람한테 있던 거야.

⑤ 천만에. 내일 우린 함께 우리의 보고서를 제출할 수 있어.

총 어휘 수 128

14 긴 대화의 응답

소재 태블릿 컴퓨터 장시간 사용

듣기 대본 해석

여: Rudy, 저게 너의 새 태블릿 컴퓨터니? 정말 좋아 보인다.

남: 고마워. 지난 주말에 샀어.

여: 어디서 샀니?

남: William's Electronics 마트에서 샀어.

여: 내가 사용해봐도 될까?

남: 물론이지. 해봐.

여: 정말 끝내준다. 이거 분명 최신 모델일 거야. 어떻게 시작메뉴로 가지?

남: 기기 밑에 있는 둥근 버튼을 누르기만 하면 돼.

여: *[잠시 후]* 오, 좋아. 너 많은 멋진 앱들을 다운받느라 바빴던 것 같네.

남: 맞아. 사실 산 뒤로 다운받느라 많은 시간을 보냈어.

여: 너 매일 사용하니?

남: 그럼. 매일 대략 4시간 정도 사용하지.

여: 정말? 4시간? 너무 오래 사용하는 것 아니야?

남: ④ 맞아, 그래. 사용 시간을 줄여야 할 것 같아.

어휘

neat *a.* 훌륭한　　**bottom** *n.* 아래쪽　　**device** *n.* 장치, 기구
〈문제〉 **cut down on** ~을 줄이다　　**budget** *n.* 예산, 비용

정답 ④

문제풀이

여자는 새로 산 남자의 태블릿 컴퓨터에 대해 여러 가지 질문을 하고 남자가 하루에 4시간 사용한다는 말에 너무 오래 사용 하는 게 아닌지 묻고 있으므로 그에 적절한 정답은 ④ '맞아, 그래. 사용 시간을 줄여야 할 것 같아.'이다.

오답 보기 해석

① 어떤 태블릿 컴퓨터를 추천할래?

② 맞아. 너는 정말 새 태블릿 컴퓨터가 필요해.

③ 어떤 앱을 요즘 가장 많이 사용하니?

⑤ 그 태블릿 컴퓨터는 사실 내 예산으론 너무 비쌌어.

총 어휘 수 142

15 상황에 적절한 말

소재 새로운 팀에서 친구 만들기

듣기 대본 해석

남: Dave는 최근 새로운 야구팀으로 이적했습니다. 그는 항상 팀원들과 잘 지내지 못했어요. 첫 훈련 후에 팀 매니저인 Roy가 탈의실에서 파티를 할 것을 제안합니다. Roy는 이 파티가 Dave가 선수들과 친해질 수 있는 좋은 기회라고 생각합니다. Dave는 처음에 망설이지만 조금 생각하다가 파티에 가기로 합니다. Dave는 그 파티에서 몇몇 팀원들과 끈끈한 친구 관계를 만들었습니다. Dave는 Roy에게 자기가 파티를 즐겼고 새로운 팀에 잘 적응했다는 것을 알려주고 싶어합니다. 이러한 상황에서 Dave는 Roy에게 뭐라고 말할까요?

Dave: ② 새로운 친구를 만드는 것을 도와줘서 고마워요.

어휘

transfer *v.* 이적하다, 이동하다　　**opportunity** *n.* 기회　　**hesitant** *a.* 주저하는　　**deliberation** *n.* 숙고, 숙의　　**comfortable** *a.* 편한, 쾌적한

정답 ②

문제풀이

새로 이적한 팀에서 팀원들과 잘 지내지 못하는 Dave에게 매니저인 Roy는 탈의실 파티를 제안하고, Dave는 파티에서 몇몇의 팀원들과 우정을 쌓게 되어 고맙다는 인사를 하려는 상황이므로 ② '새로운 친구를 만드는 것을 도와줘서 고마워요.'가 정답이다.

오답 보기 해석

① 친구 사귀는 데에 조언 좀 해줄 수 있을까요?

③ 오늘 파티에 참석하지 못할 것 같아요.

④ 내일 훈련 때 만나요, Roy.

⑤ 저는 전의 팀에서 정말 친한 친구들이 많았어요.

총 어휘 수 120

16 담화 주제 / 17 세부 내용 파악

소재 보다 현명한 소비자가 되는 방법

듣기 대본 해석

남: 청취자 여러분 안녕하세요. 오늘 저는 여러분들에게 더 현명한 쇼핑객이 되는 법과 여러분의 돈을 현명하게 사용하는 법을 말하고 싶습니다. 예리한 소비자가 되기 위해서 여러분이 이용할 수 있는 몇 가지 요령이 여기 있습니다. 첫째, 여러분들이 필요로 하는 것과 원하는 것 사이에 차이를 고려하세요. 필요한 것들의 리스트를 만들고 가장 중요한 것들을 쇼핑 리스트에서 더 높은 위치에 (더 우선 순위에) 두는 것을 확실히 하세요. 둘째, 구매를 하기 전에 약간의 제품 조사를 하세요. 전자 제품, 자동차, 가전제품 같은 다양한 범위의 제품에 대한 후기들과 평판들을 제공하는 몇몇 웹사이트가 온라인

상에 있습니다. 셋째, 여러분들이 사는 것의 가격을 의식하고 여러분들이 적절하게 청구 되었는지 확신하기 위해 영수증을 확인하도록 하세요. 마지막으로, 쿠폰과 할인판매를 찾도록 하세요. 여러분들은 싼 거래를 인터넷에서 찾을 수 있습니다. 여러분들의 돈을 절약하는 쿠폰을 제공하는 스마트폰 앱도 있습니다. 다음에 여러분들이 쇼핑하러 가실 때 이러한 조언들을 명심하세요. 들어 주셔서 감사합니다.

어휘
keen *a.* 예리한, 날카로운　　**necessities** *n.* 필수품　　**review** *n.* 후기, 비평, 평론　　**appliance** *n.* 기기　　**be conscious of** ~을 자각하다, 알고 있다　　**receipt** *n.* 영수증　　**charge** *v.* 청구하다　　**keep ~ in mind** ~을 명심하다

정답 16 ①　17 ③

문제풀이
16 남자는 더 현명한 쇼핑객이 되어 돈을 현명하게 사용하는 방법을 알려주고 있으므로 정답은 ① '보다 현명한 소비자가 되는 방법'이다.

17 남자는 쇼핑 리스트, 웹 사이트, 영수증, 스마트폰 앱에 대한 언급은 했지만 중고 거래에 관한 언급은 하지 않았으므로 정답은 ③ '중고 거래'이다.

오답 보기 해석
16
② 구매 후기를 찾을 수 있는 곳
③ 효과적인 쇼핑 리스트를 쓰는 방법
④ 더 의식 있는 쇼핑객이 되어야 하는 이유
⑤ 쇼핑할 때 쿠폰을 사용하는 것에 대한 이점

총 어휘 수 170

DICTATION ANSWERS

01 bake a pie for

02 I'm out of coins / How do you want it

03 follow your teacher's instructions / in an orderly fashion / how to protect yourself in the event of a tornado / be in attendance

04 We're not making a profit / We've been suffering ever / lower our prices / focus on what we offer / we offer a better variety

05 focusing on human expression / I asked her to pose for me / Would you mind standing

06 put a lot of work into it / the seating arrangement / seems a bit out of place / just doesn't fit

07 students are interested in reading / in my free time / some of my favorites

08 Your brother is starving / grab a quick bite / he's going to have to feed himself

09 place an order / that's a bit pricier

10 I've been looking into it / it'll be packed with tourists / the days are a bit longer

11 vulnerable to predators / conserve its energy

12 Are you interested in a particular model / we have a few of those in stock / this one drove the least / with the longer warranty

13 finish my report by tonight / list the site in your sources / cite sources

14 Do you mind if I give it a try / on the bottom of the device / you've been busy downloading

15 getting along with his teammates / hesitant to go at first / feels comfortable with his new team

16-17 between things you need and things you want / Make a list of necessities / research before making a purchase / make sure you were charged appropriately

01 ③	02 ④	03 ①	04 ⑤	05 ③	06 ⑤
07 ③	08 ②	09 ②	10 ②	11 ⑤	12 ⑤
13 ⑤	14 ③	15 ⑤	16 ②	17 ③	

01 짧은 대화의 응답

소재 트레이너 채용

듣기 대본 해석
남: 훈련 시설에서 일하기 시작했다는 말 사실이야?
여: 응. 이번 달 초에 시작했어.
남: 나 체육관에서 시간 보내는 거 좋아하는데. 다른 사람을 더 채용할 거래?
여: ③ 응. 트레이너 더 필요하대.

어휘
facility *n.* 시설, 기관　　**hire** *v.* 고용하다

정답 ③

문제풀이
남자가 다른 사람을 채용할지를 물었으므로 적절한 대답은 ③ '응. 트레이너 더 필요하대.'이다.

오답 보기 해석
① 아니. 난 그 훈련 시설 안 좋아해.
② 고마워. 이 일이 진짜 필요했어.
④ 미안하지만 난 일자리가 필요 없어.
⑤ 알았어. 도와줄게.

총 어휘 수 38

02 짧은 대화의 응답

소재 우유에 대한 알레르기

듣기 대본 해석
여: 제 아들이 걱정돼요. 아침 식사 후에 갑자기 얼굴이 붉어졌어요.
남: 그렇군요. 어디 한 번 봅시다. [잠시 후] 그에게 무엇을 먹였나요?
여: 음. 그는 오늘 아침에 빵과 우유를 먹었어요.
남: ④ 당신의 아들은 우유 알레르기가 있을지도 몰라요.

어휘
turn red 얼굴이 붉게 변하다　　**feed** *v.* ~에게 먹을 것을 주다
〈문제〉 **allergy** *n.* 알레르기

정답 ④

문제풀이
두 사람의 대화를 통해 두 사람은 의사와 아들을 데려온 엄마임을 알 수 있다. 엄마가 아이에게 빵과 우유를 먹였다고 했을 때 나올 수 있는 응답은 ④ '당신의 아들은 우유 알레르기가 있을지도 몰라요.'이다.

오답 보기 해석
① 그는 거의 2살이에요.
② 그의 가장 좋아하는 음식은 닭고기예요.
③ 아이들은 건강에 좋은 음식을 먹어야 해요.
⑤ 저의 아들을 돌봐주셔서 감사합니다.

총 어휘 수 42

03 담화 목적

소재 헌혈증 기증

듣기 대본 해석
여: 좋은 아침입니다. 여러분. 저는 교감인 Rebecca Smith입니다. 여러분 대부분이 학급 친구인 Helena Simson을 알고 있을 것이라 생각합니다. 그녀의 어머니가 위험성이 큰 수술을 앞두고 병원에 계십니다. 저는 방금 Helena의 담임 선생님으로부터 그녀의 어머니가 곧 수술하기로 되어 있다는 소식을 들었습니다. 저는 수술을 위해서 많은 양의 B형 혈액이 필요하다는 통지를 받았습니다. 이런 때에. 서로를 돕는 것은 우리에게 달려있다고 굳게 믿습니다. 그러니 만약 여러분 중 누구라도 Helena의 어머니에게 혈액을 기증하고 싶은 학생은 헌혈증을 제 사무실로 가져오기 바랍니다. 여러분의 피는 누군가의 목숨을 살릴 수도 있습니다. Helena와 그녀의 어머니를 대신해서 여러분의 따뜻한 도움에 감사드립니다.

어휘
vice principal 교감　　**high-risk** *a.* 위험성이 큰　　**surgery** *n.* 수술
on behalf of ~을 대신해서, ~을 대표하여

정답 ①

문제풀이
학급의 친구인 Helena의 어머니가 큰 수술을 앞두고 있는데 B형 혈액이 필요하니 헌혈증을 기증해 달라는 내용이므로 정답은 ①번이다.

총 어휘 수 123

04 의견

소재 새 휴대폰 구입

듣기 대본 해석
여: 아빠, 질문 하나 해도 되요?
남: 물론이지. 뭔데?
여: 제 휴대폰을 업그레이드하고 싶어요.
남: 네가 가지고 있는 휴대폰에 문제가 있니?
여: 그건 아닌데, 2년 동안 사용해서 새 것을 가지고 싶어서요.
남: Lizzy, 휴대폰에 문제가 없는데 왜 바꾸고 싶어하는 거지?
여: 그게 너무 오래 됐고 스마트폰도 아니잖아요.
남: 휴대폰의 가장 중요한 기능은 전화를 하는 것이라는 것을 알고 있잖아. 나는 사업가지만 스마트폰을 가지고 있지 않단다.
여: 제발요, 아빠. 요즘 휴대폰은 전화하는 것 이상이라는 것을 아시잖아요.
남: 내가 내 말을 잘 이해시키지 못했나 보다. 너는 단지 최신 유행이란 이유로 어떤 것을 필요하다고 느껴서는 안 되는 거야.
여: 네, 아빠. 제가 더 생각해 볼게요.

어휘
replace *v.* 바꾸다, 교체하다　　**trend** *n.* 유행, 경향, 추세

정답 ⑤

문제풀이
휴대폰에 문제가 없는데 스마트폰으로 바꾸고 싶어하는 딸에게 아빠는 단지 최신 유행이라는 이유로 뭔가가 필요하다고 느껴서는 안 된다고 말해주고 있으므로 남자의 의견으로 가장 적절한 것은 ⑤ '맹목적으로 최신 유행을 쫓으려고 하지 마라.'이다.

총 어휘 수 138

05 장소 파악

소재 스케이트장에서의 대화

듣기 대본 해석
여: 내가 생각했던 것보다 더 재미있다.
남: 그렇지? 내가 어렸을 적에 매년 겨울에 스케이트 타러 갔었어.
여: 그런데 잠시 쉬면 안 될까? 너무 피곤해.
남: 알았어. 그럼 좀 앉아있자. 뭐 마실 것 좀 갖다 줄까?
여: 응. 소다음료가 좋을 것 같아. 근데 그 스케이트 신고 사러 가기 힘들지 않을까?
남: 아니. 카운터로 갈 필요 없어. 전화를 걸면 주문한 것을 갖다 줄 거야.
여: 잘됐다. 나 진짜 뭔가 마시고 싶거든.
남: 나도. 이렇게 땀이 많이 날 줄 몰랐어. 우리가 얼음 위에 있는 내내 추울 줄 알았어.
여: 그건 네가 안 쉬어서 그런 거잖아. 우리가 링크를 몇 번이나 돌았는지 알고 있니?
남: 미안해. 너무 재미있어서 쉬는 것을 까먹어서 그래.

어휘
order *n.* 주문   **sweat** *v.* 땀 흘리다   **lap** *n.* (경주 트랙의) 한 바퀴
rink *n.* 스케이트 링크

정답 ③

문제풀이
여자가 남자에게 스케이트를 신고 음료를 사러 가기 힘들지 않겠느냐고 물어봤고, 링크를 몇 바퀴나 돌았는지 물었으므로 장소는 ③ '아이스링크'이다.

총 어휘 수 156

06 그림의 세부 내용 파악

소재 연극 무대 디자인

듣기 대본 해석
남: Hannah, 이것이 네가 지난 학기에 공연했던 연극의 사진이지?
여: 맞아. 우리 그 공연에서 진짜 열심히 했었지.
남: 호랑이는 정말 진짜처럼 보여. 마치 토끼가 그의 친구 사슴을 붙잡고 있는 호랑이에게 놔달라고 빌고 있는 것 같은데?
어: 맞아. 호랑이의 토끼에 관한 이솝 우화야.
남: 세트가 정말 멋있어 보여.
여: 고마워. 연극부가 모두 모여서 그것을 전부 디자인했어. 배경에 바위들 보여? 내가 그것들을 칠했어.
남: 와! 잘했네. 오른편에 있는 저 나무도 진짜처럼 보여. 그것이 아프리카에 있는 것 같은 느낌을 주네.
여: 그래. 그게 우리가 원했던 거야.
남: 네가 의상도 디자인했어?
여: 아니. 의상은 Fat Panda's 의상샵에서 대여했어.
남: 그렇구나. 음. 이 연극에서 네가 정말 많이 애쓴 것 같아.

어휘
semester *n.* 학기   **performance** *n.* 공연   **beg** *v.* 애원하다
costume *n.* 의상

정답 ⑤

문제풀이
무대의 오른편에 나무가 있다고 했는데 꽃들이 있으므로 그림과 일치하지 않는 것은 ⑤번이다.

총 어휘 수 139

07 한 일

소재 보고서 철자 오류 수정

듣기 대본 해석
남: Sophie, 네가 냉전에 관한 보고서를 썼다고 들었어.
여: 응. 네가 너무 바빠서 날 도와줄 수 없었지.
남: 미안해. 그런데 내 보고서를 끝내서 오늘 시간이 생겼어.
여: 음. 이미 다 썼어!
남: 알아. 네가 데스크톱에 파일을 저장했길래 네가 학교에 있는 동안 내가 읽어봤어.
여: 오. 마음에 드니?
남: 응. 마음에 들어. 냉전의 환경적 문제에 관한 네 생각이 매우 흥미롭더라.
여: 고마워. 그 부분을 찾는 데 많은 시간을 들였거든.
남: 하지만 철자 오류가 조금 있어서 내가 수정했어.
여: 고마워.
남: 원한다면, 철자 검사 프로그램 사용법을 알려줄게.
여: 좋은 생각이야.

어휘
Cold War 냉전   **save** *v.* 저장하다   **correct** *v.* 정정하다, 바로잡다

정답 ③

문제풀이
남자는 여자를 위해 데스크톱에 저장되어 있던 보고서를 읽고 철자 오류를 수정해 주었으므로 남자가 여자를 위해 한 일은 ③ '보고서 철자 오류 수정해 주기'이다. 반면, ⑤ '철자 검사 프로그램 사용법 알려주기'는 한 일이 아니라 할 일이다.

총 어휘 수 125

08 이유

소재 제때 도착하지 않은 상품의 주문 취소하기

듣기 대본 해석
[전화벨이 울린다.]
남: 안녕하세요. Genie's 온라인 매장입니다.
여: 안녕하세요. 제가 지난주에 주문한 책 몇 권 때문에 연락 드렸습니다.
남: 네. 뭐가 문제입니까? 책에 손상이 있나요?
여: 아니요. 도요일까지 도착했어야 하는데 벌써 월요일이지만 아직 여기로 안 왔어요.
남: 그렇군요. 주문을 확인하겠습니다. 주문 번호 7자리를 불러주시겠어요?
여: 지금 주문 번호가 없어요. 제 이름은 Ella Hanley인데, 도움이 될까요?
남: 네. 확인하는 동안 조금만 기다려 주세요.
여: 알겠습니다.
남: *[키보드 치는 소리]* 죄송하지만 배송이 지연된 것 같습니다. 목요일까지는 도착할 겁니다.
여: 목요일이요? 그건 납득할 수 없네요. 수요일 수업 때 그 책들이 필요합니다.
남: 정말 죄송합니다.
여: 제 주문 취소해 주시겠어요? 동네 서점에서 살게요.

어휘
in regards to ~에 관해서   **damage** *v.* 훼손하다, 피해를 입히다
digit *n.* ~자리 숫자   **delay** *v.* 미루다, 연기하다   **unacceptable** *a.* 받아들일 수 없는   **cancel** *v.* 취소하다

정답 ②

문제풀이
여자는 지난주에 주문한 책이 도착하지 않자 전화를 걸어 확인한 결과 책이 필요한 수요일이 지나 목요일에 도착한다는 것을 알게 되었다. 따라서 여자가 주문을 취소하려는 이유는 ② '상품이 제때 도착하지 않아서'이다.

총 어휘 수 137

소재 진로 박람회 티켓 구입

듣기 대본 해석

[전화벨이 울린다.]

여: Henderson 고용 및 교육 사무실입니다. 도와드릴까요?

남: 안녕하세요. 제가 이번 달 말에 있는 진로 박람회에 관한 전단을 보았어요. 남은 표가 있는지 궁금해서요.

여: 네. 아직 표가 있습니다.

남: 좋네요. 저는 5장이 필요해요. 얼마인가요?

여: 미리 구매하신다면, 10달러입니다. 현장에서는 20달러입니다.

남: 알았어요. 단체 할인이 있나요?

여: 까먹을 뻔했네요. 저희는 단체 할인을 제공합니다. 5명에서 10명까지의 단체는 10퍼센트 할인을 받고 10장 이상의 표를 사시면 20퍼센트를 할인을 받으실 수 있습니다.

남: 너무 좋아요. 저는 10퍼센트 할인을 받을 수 있네요. 그럼 지금 살게요.

여: 문제 없어요. 신용카드나 직불카드가 지금 있으시면, 지금 당신의 정보를 좀 물을게요.

어휘

flyer *n.* 전단　　**in advance** 미리　　**at the door** 현장에서
debit card 직불카드　　**handy** *a.* 유용한, 편리한, 사용하기 편한 곳에 있는

정답 ②

문제풀이

미리 구매하면 인당 10달러라고 했고 5장이 필요하다고 했으므로 50달러이다. 5명에서 10명까지는 10퍼센트 할인을 받는다고 했으므로 정답은 ② '$45'이다.

총 어휘 수 137

소재 보아뱀이 새끼를 낳는 방식

듣기 대본 해석

여: 안녕 Theo. 주말 잘 보냈어?

남: 응. 특별한 건 안 했어. 내가 관심 있게 여긴 파충류에 관한 짧은 다큐멘터리를 보긴 했어.

여: 정말? 파충류 어떤 점에 관한 건데?

남: 응. 너 파충류가 알을 낳는다는 건 알고 있었니?

여: 물론. 그런 건 상식이라고 생각했는데.

남: 그렇지. 하지만 뱀 중에서 몇몇 종은, 예를 들면 보아뱀 같은 건 살아있는 상태의 새끼를 낳아.

여: 말도 안 돼. 어떻게 그렇게 하지?

남: 뱃속에서 알을 품고 일단 부화하면 낳는 거지.

여: 믿을 수 없네. 보아뱀이 새끼를 몇 마리 낳아?

남: 6마리에서 39마리까지 새끼를 낳을 수 있어.

여: 믿을 수 없다. 전혀 몰랐어.

남: 사실이야. 보아 새끼들은 또한 태어난 지 10일 이내에 허물을 벗어.

여: 와, 동물들은 정말 놀랍다. 그렇지?

어휘

reptile *n.* 파충류　　**common knowledge** 상식　　**boa constrictor**
보아뱀　　**incubate** *v.* (알을) 품다, 부화하다　　**hatch** *v.* 부화하다
shed *v.* (옷을) 벗다, 없애다

정답 ②

문제풀이

보아뱀이 새끼 낳는 방법, 부화하는 장소, 낳는 새끼의 수, 새끼들의 허물 벗기에 대한 언급은 있지만 먹이에 대한 언급은 없으므로 정답은 ② '새끼의 먹이'이다.

총 어휘 수 127

소재 에펠탑 소개

듣기 대본 해석

여: 오늘은 에펠탑에 대해 말하겠습니다. 에펠탑은 세계에서 가장 잘 알려진 기념물 중 하나이지만, 원래 감시탑으로 지어졌다는 것을 아십니까? 그 탑의 건설은 1887년에 시작되었고 2년 후에 완성되었습니다. 에펠탑이 건설되는 동안, 그것은 세계에서 사람이 만든 가장 높은 구조물로 추정되는 워싱턴 기념비를 능가했습니다. 탑에는 관광객들이 이용할 수 있는 세 개의 층이 있고, 그것은 입장료를 받는 세계에서 가장 방문자가 많은 기념물입니다. 방문객들은 일층과 이층까지 계단이나 엘리베이터로 올라갈 수 있습니다. 첫 번째 층에서 두 번째 층으로 오르는 것처럼, 지상에서 첫 번째 층까지 300개가 넘는 계단이 있습니다. 마지막 층은 엘리베이터로만 대중들에게 입장 가능합니다.

어휘

recognized *a.* 알려진　　**construction** *n.* 건설, 공사　　**surpass** *v.*
능가하다, 뛰어넘다　　**monument** *n.* 기념물　　**assume** *v.* 추정하다
access *v.* 이용하다, 접근하다　　**ascend** *v.* 올라가다　　**accessible**
a. 입장(이용) 가능한

정답 ⑤

문제풀이

에펠탑은 세 개의 층을 관광객이 이용할 수 있고 첫째 층과 둘째 층은 걷거나 엘리베이터를 이용할 수 있지만, 가장 위층은 엘리베이터로만 이용할 수 있다고 했으므로 정답은 ⑤ '가장 위층까지 관광객들이 걸어서 이용할 수 있다.'이다.

총 어휘 수 138

소재 주말 휴가 예약

듣기 대본 해석

여: ABC여행사에 오신 것을 환영합니다. 오늘은 무엇을 도와드릴까요?

남: 안녕하세요. 저는 제 사업 파트너들과 저의 주말 휴가를 예약하고 싶어요.

여: 제가 도와드릴게요. 언제 여행을 가실 계획이에요?

남: 이번 달 마지막 주말에 가려고 해요.

여: 알겠어요. 해외로 여행하고 싶으세요, 미국 내에 머무르고 싶으세요?

남: 저는 이국적인 곳으로 가고 싶은데요. 미국 외 어딘가는 어떨까요?

여: 당신 패키지에 호텔을 포함시키고 싶으신가요?

남: 네. 그럼요. 가능하다면 일체의 경비가 포함되도록 하고 싶어요.

여: 물론이죠. 여기 좀 보세요. 1인당 단 850달러로 당신 조건을 만족시키는 목적지가 있어요.

남: 저희 비용 범위에서 좀 벗어나는군요. 저는 1인당 750달러 이상을 쓰지 않으려고 해요.

여: 그럼 하나의 선택만 남네요.

남: 저는 늘 거기 가길 원했어요. 4자리 예약해주세요.

어휘

getaway *n.* 휴가　　**exotic** *a.* 외국의, 이국적인　　**all-inclusive** *a.*
일체의 경비가 포함된　　**destination** *n.* 목적지　　**range** *n.* 범위

정답 ⑤

문제풀이

남자는 해외로 가길 원하므로 ③~⑤번이 남고, 호텔 등 일체의 경비가 포함된 여행을 원하므로 ④번과 ⑤번이 남는다. 둘 중 남자가 생각한 가격대에 맞는 것은 ⑤번이다.

총 어휘 수 148

13 긴 대화의 응답

소재 크게 음악을 틀어둔 버스 안

듣기 대본 해석
여: 안녕, Stan!
남: 안녕, Candace. 나는 네가 버스 타고 집에 가는 줄 몰랐어.
여: 음, 보통 운전해서 가는데, 이번 주에 나의 자동차가 정비소에 있어. 아무튼, 너도 집에 가는 길이야?
남: 오 아니 이건 우리 집에 가는 버스가 아니야. 나는 사실 쇼핑몰에 가고 있어.
여: 미안. 넘어지겠다고?
남: 아니. 나는 쇼핑몰에 가고 있다고 말했어. 아이를 위해 사고 싶은 새로운 장난감이 있거든.
여: 그렇구나. 그 쇼핑몰은 우리 집과 정말 가까워. 그래서 나는 거기를 매우 잘 알아.
남: Candace, 미안한데 잘 안 들려. 이 버스의 음악이 너무 시끄러워.
여: 그래. 나는 그들이 음악을 시끄럽게 켜 놓을 때가 너무 싫어. 내가 버스를 탈 때, 나는 단지 휴식을 취하고 하루에 대해 생각하기를 원해.
남: 왜 헤비메탈 음악을 틀어야 하지? 이건 최악이야.
여: ⑤ 동의해. 내가 가서 운전기사님에게 소리를 조금 낮추어 달라고 요청할게.

어휘
 incredibly *ad.* 굉장히, 엄청나게   〈문제〉 **reflect** *v.* 깊이 생각하다. 반영하다   **in public** 사람들이 있는 데서

정답 ⑤

문제풀이
남자는 버스 내 음악이 너무 커서 여자의 말을 들을 수 없다고 했고, 최악이라고 얘기했으므로 이에 대한 여자의 응답으로 가장 적절한 것은 ⑤ '동의해. 내가 가서 운전기사님에게 소리를 조금 낮추어 달라고 요청할게.'이다.

오답 보기 해석
① 버스를 타는 것은 하루를 되돌아보는 데 아주 좋지.
② 나도 그렇게 생각해. 그는 더 안전한 것을 가지고 놀아야 해.
③ 맞아. 사람들이 있는 데서 크게 말하는 것은 예의가 아니야.
④ 좋네. 나 버스에서 음악 듣는 거 정말 좋아해.

총 어휘 수 159

14 긴 대화의 응답

소재 할로윈 파티 계획하기

듣기 대본 해석
여: 안녕 Andrew. 얘기 좀 하고 싶은데.
남: 물론, Grace. 무슨 일이야?
여: 할로윈 파티에 대한 거야. 준비는 다 한 거야?
남: 아직. 같이 계획하는 게 좋을 것 같아. 그렇게 생각하지 않니?
여: 응, 그게 좋을 것 같아. 나한테 몇몇 게임과 이벤트에 대한 생각이 있어.
남: 좋아. 작년에 부모님들이 사탕을 가져왔고 우리는 아이들과 의상 경연을 했지.
여: 그건 좀 평범한 것 같지 않아? 좀 더 특별한 걸 하는 게 어때? 예를 들면 유령의 집을 만드는 것처럼.
남: 네 말은 도서관을 이용해서 유령의 집을 만들고 싶다는 거야?
여: 정확해. "유령이 나오는 도서관 관광"이라고 부르면 되잖아. 아이들이 좋아할 것 같지 않아?
남: ③ 그거 좋은 생각이야. 아이들이 신나 할 거야.

어휘
 arrangement *n.* 준비   **costume** *n.* 의상   **haunted** *a.* 유령이 나오는

정답 ③

문제풀이
두 사람은 할로윈 파티에 대해 계획하고 있는데 여자가 도서관을 유령의 집으로 만드는 것을 제안하고 있다. 이에 대한 남자의 응답으로 가장 적절한 것은 ③ '그거 좋은 생각이야. 아이들이 신나 할 거야.'이다.

오답 보기 해석
① 난 아이들이 그렇게 재미있어 하는 걸 본 적이 없어.
② 난 유령의 집 디자인을 꽤 잘해.
④ 문제 없어. 부모님들께 우리 계획을 알려드릴게.
⑤ 그거 좋은 계획이네. 아이들은 의상 경연을 좋아하잖아.

총 어휘 수 137

15 상황에 적절한 말

소재 숙제 제출 기한 연장

듣기 대본 해석
남: Aiden은 그의 고등학교 농구 팀의 주장인데, 그 때문에 방과 후에도 바쁩니다. 그는 또한 체스 동아리, 영화 동아리, 학생회 같은 학교에서의 다른 방과 후 활동에도 참여를 합니다. 그는 이런 활동들로 바쁘지 않은 얼마 안 되는 시간을 숙제와 시험공부에 사용합니다. Aiden은 Lincoln 선생님 수업의 중요한 과제를 위해 책을 읽어야 하는데, 내일 마감 전까지 끝내지 못할 것입니다. 그는 선생님께 과제 기간을 더 연장해 주실 수 있는지 물어보려고 합니다. 이러한 상황에서, Lincoln 선생님께 Aiden이 할 말로 가장 적절한 것은 무엇일까요?
Aiden: ⑤ 숙제의 제출기한을 연장해주실 수 있으세요?

어휘
 take part in 참여하다   **extracurricular** *a.* 과외의   **assignment** *n.* 과제, 임무   **deadline** *n.* 기한, 마감시한   **extension** *n.* 연장, 확대   〈문제〉 **priority** *n.* 우선사항   **due date** 만기일   **postpone** *v.* 연기하다, 미루다

정답 ⑤

문제풀이
Aiden이 농구 팀 주장일과 여러 방과 후 활동으로 너무 바빠서 숙제를 마감 전까지 끝낼 수 없으므로 기한을 연장해 줄 수 있는지 물어야 하므로 ⑤ '숙제의 제출기한을 연장해주실 수 있으세요?'가 적절하다.

오답 보기 해석
① 우선사항을 다시 생각해 주셔야 합니다.
② 이 과제의 제출기한이 언제죠?
③ 회의를 더 뒤의 날짜로 다시 잡으실 수 있나요?
④ 이 책들을 이틀 더 가지고 있어도 될까요?

총 어휘 수 119

16 담화 목적 / 17 세부 내용 파악

소재 방콕의 주말 시장

듣기 대본 해석
여: 안녕하세요 학우 여러분. 저는 오늘 여러분께 태국의 수도인 방콕에 있는 아주 특별한 시장에 대해서 얘기드리고자 합니다. Chatuchak 시장은 세계에서 가장 큰 주말 시장입니다. 이 시장에는 27에이커에 걸쳐 있는 8,000개가 넘는 가판대가 있습니다. 400,000명이 넘는 사람들이 주말마다 이 시장을 방문합니다. 방문자들은 현지 태국 음식을 즐길 수 있고, 기념품을 사거나 빈티지 운동화도 사고, 새끼 다람쥐나 원숭이 같은 특이한 애완동물도 살 수 있습니다. 태국에서 유명하다는 저렴하면서도 고품질의 비단으로

만들어진 것 또한 살 수 있습니다. 그 비단은 태국 전통 의상에 쓰입니다. 비단 스카프, 담요, 그리고 넥타이도 살 수 있습니다. 시장의 어디에서 사느냐에 따라 비단 스카프를 4달러에서 40달러를 주고 살 수 있습니다. 그러나 비단만이 Chatuchak 시장에 있는 특별한 기념품이 아닙니다. 지갑도 살 수 있고, 무에타이 복싱 바지, 보석, 그리고 도자기도 살 수 있습니다. 이제 제가 지난 봄에 Chatuchak 시장을 방문했을 때 찍은 사진들을 보여드리겠습니다.

어휘

market *n.* 시장 **stall** *n.* 가판대 **souvenir** *n.* 기념품 **exotic** *a.* 이국적인 **specialty** *n.* 특징 **purse** *n.* 지갑 **ceramic** *n.* 도자기 〈문제〉 **popularity** *n.* 인기

정답 16 ② 17 ③

문제풀이

16 여자는 방콕에 있는 주말 시장 Chatuchak 시장의 규모, 방문자 수, 즐길 거리, 쇼핑거리, 기념품 등을 말하고 있으므로 정답은 ② '방콕에 있는 Chatuchak 시장을 소개하려고'이다.

17 여자는 비단 제품의 우수한 품질, 용도, 제품 종류, 가격대에 대해 언급하였지만 가장 많이 사는 기념품이라고는 언급하지 않았으므로 정답은 ③ '가장 많이 사는 기념품이다.'이다

오답 보기 해석

16

① 태국 비단 옷을 추천하기 위해서
③ 태국의 여러 가지 기념품을 소개하기 위해서
④ 태국 문화에서 시장의 중요성을 설명하려고
⑤ Chatuchak 시장의 규모와 인기를 설명하려고

총 어휘 수 174

08 수능영어듣기 실전모의고사

01 ①	02 ③	03 ⑤	04 ⑤	05 ④	06 ②
07 ④	08 ④	09 ②	10 ④	11 ②	12 ③
13 ⑤	14 ⑤	15 ③	16 ②	17 ①	

01 짧은 대화의 응답

소재 예약 확인

듣기 대본 해석

[전화벨이 울린다.]

남: Bird's Car Rental에 전화해 주셔서 감사합니다. 무엇을 도와드릴까요?
여: 네. 제가 온라인으로 한 예약을 확인하려고 전화드렸습니다.
남: 물론이죠. 예약 번호를 가지고 있나요?
여: ① 죄송하지만, 적어 두는 것을 잊었어요.

어휘

confirm *v.* ~을 확인하다   reservation *n.* 예약

정답 ①

문제풀이

여자는 예약을 확인하고 싶어서 전화를 걸었고 남자가 예약 번호를 알고 있는지 물었으므로 여자의 적절한 응답은 ① '죄송하지만, 적어 두는 것을 잊었어요.'이다.

오답 보기 해석

② 도와드릴 누군가를 바로 보낼게요.
③ 다음에 빌릴 때 10%를 할인 받을 수 있어요.
④ 당신이 스포츠카를 예약했다고 여기에 나와 있네요.
⑤ 제 예약을 미니밴으로 바꾸고 싶어요.

총 어휘 수 38

02 짧은 대화의 응답

소재 업무 숙 식사

듣기 대본 해석

여: 이런! 시간 좀 봐요. 우리 먹으러 곧 가야 해요.
남: 잠시만요. 저는 일의 마지막 부분을 끝내고 싶어요.
여: 점심 먹고 할 수 있잖아요. 신선한 공기를 마시러 밖으로 나가요.
남: ③ 가세요. 저는 정말 오후 5시 전에 이것을 마쳐야만 해요.

어휘

〈문제〉 look forward to ~을 고대하다   complete *v.* 완료하다, 끝마치다

정답 ③

문제풀이

남자는 업무를 조금 더 해야 하는 상황이고 여자는 먹으러 나가자고 하고 있으므로 그 말에 대한 응답으로 ③ '가세요. 저는 징밀 오후 5시 진에 이것을 마쳐야만 해요.'가 가장 적절하다.

오답 보기 해석

① 우리가 결정하기 전에 메뉴를 확인하는 게 어때요?
② 저는 이번 주말의 만남이 기대되지 않아요.
④ 저는 우리가 지난 번에 먹었던 모든 게 너무 좋았다고 생각했어요.
⑤ 좋은 저녁 식사 장소를 추천해 줄 수 있어요?

총 어휘 수 48

03 담화 주제

소재 피클과 건강

듣기 대본 해석

남: 여러분은 햄버거를 좋아하십니까? 햄버거와 같이 나오는 피클도 좋아하십니까? 여러분은 피클이 실제로 건강에 꽤 좋다는 것을 아십니까? 맞습니다. 피클은 맛도 좋을 뿐 아니라 지방과 칼로리도 낮습니다. 피클은 또한 상처 입은 후에 혈액을 진해지게 만들어서 몸의 회복을 돕는 비타민 K가 다량으로 함유되어 있습니다. 피클의 반만 먹어도 여러분이 하루에 필요한 비타민K의 17퍼센트가 공급됩니다. 그러나 피클의 나트륨 함량이 높기 때문에, 과도하게 먹으면 고혈압을 야기할 수도 있습니다. 피클 한 개를 다 먹으면 하루 나트륨 권장량의 절반 이상을 섭취하게 됩니다. 피클은 매일 즐기되 너무 많이 먹지 않도록 명심하십시오.

어휘

fat *n.* 지방   recover *v.* 회복되다   injury *n.* 부상   thicken *v.* (농도가) 진해지다   requirement *n.* 요구량   in excess 과도하게   high blood pressure 고혈압   sodium *n.* (화학) 나트륨   fulfill *v.* (의미, 약속 등을) 다하다, 수행하다   recommendation *n.* 권고(량), 추천

정답 ⑤

문제풀이

남자는 피클이 가지고 있는 영양분과 그것이 건강에 미치는 영향에 대해 설명하고 있으므로 정답은 ⑤ '피클의 섭취와 건강과의 관계'이다.

총 어휘 수 124

04 의견

소재 고장 난 컴퓨터 수리

듣기 대본 해석

여: 여보, 내 컴퓨터 이상해. 화면이 자꾸 깜박거려.
남: 흠... 그럼 이번 주말에 새 컴퓨터 사러 쇼핑 가자.
여: 새 것을 살 필요는 없을 것 같아. 이것도 꽤 새 거야.
남: 요즘에는 기술이 너무 빨리 발전해서 사람들은 거의 2년마다 컴퓨터를 바꿔.
여: 맞아. 근데 너무 낭비하는 것 같아. 화면만 바꾸면 되지 않을까?
남: 니도 그렇게 생각해. 근데 새 컴퓨터는 무척 얇고 빨라.
여: 당신 말이 맞는데, 근데 화면 외에는 이상한 게 없어. 아직 2년은 더 쓸 수 있을 것 같아.
남: 그래. 당신이 원한다면.
여: 우리 이걸 고치도록 해보자. 내가 그걸 수리점으로 가지고 갈게.

어휘

flicker *v.* 깜빡거리다   replace *v.* 교체하다   sleek *a.* 매끈한, (모양이) 날렵한

정답 ⑤

문제풀이

남자는 컴퓨터 화면이 깜빡거린다는 여자의 말에 컴퓨터를 새로 사자고 하지만 여자는 화면(모니터) 말고는 문제가 없다면서 버리지 말자고 한다. 이것으로 보아 여자의 의견은 ⑤ '컴퓨터의 일부만 교체하고 가급적 버리지 말아야 한다.'이다.

총 어휘 수 129

05 대화자의 관계 파악

소재 저널리스트가 되고 싶은 학생

듣기 대본 해석
남: 안녕하세요, Towns 선생님.
여: 안녕, Hugh. 우리가 지난주에 나눈 이야기에 대해 더 생각해 보았니?
남: 네. 결정을 내렸어요. 저널리스트가 되고 싶어요.
여: 저널리스트라고? 왜 그렇게 생각하니?
남: Voice News에서 많은 뉴스 클립들을 보아왔어요. 기자들의 일이 정말 흥미롭고 열정적인 것 같아요.
여: 그렇구나. 저널리스트가 되기 위해 어떤 종류의 기술들이 필요할 것 같니?
남: 자연스럽게 호기심도 많아야 하고 질문을 하거나 조사하는 것도 잘해야 할 것 같아요.
여: 그래. 내 생각에는 지역대학에 성공적인 저널리스트가 되기 위해 필요한 여러 기술들을 가르쳐주는 좋은 코스가 있을 것 같구나.
남: 정말이요?
여: 그래. 여러 좋은 점들을 들어왔어. 또한 네가 학교 신문부에 가입하는 게 좋을 것 같다. 너는 그곳에서 여러 과정에 대해 많이 배울 수 있을 거야.
남: 좋은 생각이네요. Towns 선생님, 조언해주셔서 감사합니다.
여: 언제든지 오렴, Hugh.

어휘
intense *a.* 열정적인, 강렬한, 극심한 **investigate** *v.* 조사하다

정답 ④

문제풀이
남자는 저널리스트가 되고 싶다면서 저널리스트가 되기 위한 조언을 구하고 있고, 여자는 도움이 될 만한 것들을 알려주고 있으므로 두 사람의 관계는 ④ '학생 — 진로 상담교사'임을 추측할 수 있다.

총 어휘 수 149

06 그림의 세부 내용 파악

소재 포토존

듣기 대본 해석
남: 이 줄은 다 뭐니, Dee?
여: 사람들이 같이 온 친구랑 사진을 찍기 위해 기다리고 있는 거야. 줄 서자.
남: 좋아. 하지만 이 포토존이 좀 촌스러운 것 같지 않니?
여: 응. 좀 유치하지? 우리 소파에 앉아야 하나? 난 서 있는 게 낫겠다.
남: 응. 그리고 원 모양 쿠션은 너무 누덕누덕하다. 오래 돼 보여.
여: 소파 옆에 큰 꽃 좀 봐.
남: 저거 해바라기인가? 우리 무도회 주제와는 정말 안 어울려.
여: 벽에는 별들도 있어. 같은 사진에 밤과 낮이 있는 것 같아. 뭘 생각한 거지?
남: 벽에 있는 포스터는 맘에 든다. 여기 고등학교에서 우리의 시간을 기념하고 있어.
여: 네 말이 맞는 것 같아.
남: 좋아, 우리 순서다. 웃어!

어휘
companion *n.* 동행, 친구, 짝 **cheesy** *a.* 질 낮은, 값싼, 촌스러운
ragged *a.* 누더기의, 다 찢어진 **prom** *n.* 무도회
commemorate *v.* 기념하다

정답 ②

문제풀이
남자가 소파에 원 모양의 쿠션이 있다고 했는데 그림에서는 하트 모양의 쿠션이 있으므로 정답은 ②번이다.

총 어휘 수 132

07 할 일

소재 커피 사다 주기

듣기 대본 해석
남: 안녕, Rachel! 점심 먹으러 갈 거야?
여: 그러고 싶지만 오늘은 너무 바빠. 너는 어때?
남: 응. 쉬는 시간이 있어서 뭐 좀 먹으러 가려고. 너 먹을 만한 음식을 좀 사올까?
여: 물어봐줘서 고맙지만 이 보고서를 작성하는 게 날 불안하게 해. 식욕이 전혀 없어.
남: 정말? 그거 참 안됐구나. 그럼 커피는 어때? 스타빈스 커피 좋아하니?
여: 응, 물론. 거기 바닐라 라떼 좋아해.
남: 좋아. 바닐라 라떼 하나로 하지. 30분 내로 돌아올게. 오, 어떤 사이즈가 좋을까?
여: 와, 넌 정말 친절해. Tall 사이즈가 좋겠어. 너무 고마워!
남: 괜찮아. 곧 돌아올게.

어휘
have a break 휴식을 취하다 **nervous** *a.* 초조해(불안해) 하는
appetite *n.* 식욕

정답 ④

문제풀이
남자가 너무 바빠 먹을 시간도 없고, 불안해서 식욕이 없다는 여자를 위해 커피를 사다 주겠다고 하였으므로 정답은 ④ '커피 사다 주기'이다.

총 어휘 수 134

08 이유

소재 친구에게 빌린 DVD

듣기 대본 해석
남: 안녕, Carrie. 무슨 일이니?
여: DeWitt 선생님 수업 때 발표할 내용을 검토하고 있어. 꽤나 스트레스 받네.
남: 이해해. 근데, 너 지난번 내가 빌려줬던 페루에 관한 DVD 갖고 왔니?
여: 어머나, 완전히 잊고 있었네. 정말 미안해 Conner. 내일 갖고 올게.
남: 뭐라고? 또 잊었다고? 내가 오늘 오후 내 발표를 위해 필요하다고 말했었잖아.
여: 미안해. 깜빡 잊었어. 오늘 아침에 내 남동생 수학 숙제를 도와주느라고 갖고 오는 걸 잊었어.
남: 네 설명이 문제를 해결해 주지는 못해, Carrie.
여: 정말 미안해. 점심시간에 집에 가서 갖다 줄게.
남: 알겠어. 점심시간 끝날 무렵 여기에서 기다릴게.
여: 응. 다시 한번 미안해. 이따 봐.

어휘
presentation *n.* 발표 **slip one's mind** (깜빡) 잊어 버리다

정답 ④

문제풀이
대화의 중간 부분에서 여자는 아침에 동생의 수학 숙제를 도와주느라 DVD 가져오는 것을 깜빡 잊었다고 했으므로 정답은 ④ '동생의 숙제를 도와주느라 잊어서'이다.

총 어휘 수 132

09 숫자

소재 아기 신발 교환

듣기 대본 해석

여: 실례합니다. 이 아기용 신발을 다른 것으로 교환하고 싶습니다.

남: 왜 교환하시려고요?

여: 실은, 친구가 이것을 이 매장에서 제 딸을 위해 사준 것인데, 한 달 전에 또 다른 사람으로부터 똑같은 신발을 받았습니다.

남: 오, 알겠습니다. 여기 다양한 종류의 신발이 있습니다. 마음에 드는 것이 보입니까?

여: 좀 보죠... 오, 이게 제 딸에게 잘 어울릴 것 같네요. 신발 옆의 리본이 아주 귀엽네요. 이건 얼마죠?

남: 60달러입니다.

여: 그러면, 교환 후에 제가 얼마를 더 지불해야 하죠?

남: 손님이 다시 가져오신 신발은 45달러였으므로 나머지만 지불하시면 됩니다.

여: 알겠습니다. 여기 제 신용카드입니다. 오, 우리 딸 머리띠도 하나 필요합니다. 하나 고르도록 도와주실래요?

남: 예, 물론이지요. 이것이 여기서 가장 잘 나가는 것들 중 하나입니다. 2달러 밖에 안 합니다.

여: 좋아요. 그것도 살게요.

어휘

exchange *v.* 교환하다　　**look good on** ~에게 어울리다

정답 ②

문제풀이

새로 사려고 하는 신발이 교환을 위해 가져간 신발보다 15달러가 비싸고, 2달러 짜리 머리띠를 산다고 했으므로 여자가 지불할 금액은 ② '$17'이다.

총 어휘 수 155

10 언급 유무

소재 최신 훈련 시설

듣기 대본 해석

여: 저희 시설에 오신 것을 환영합니다. Fecc 박사님.

남: 안녕하세요, Johnson 씨. 당신을 드디어 만나게 되어서 좋습니다. 이 훈련 시설은 믿을 수가 없군요.

여: 저희 팀의 시설이 매우 자랑스러워요. 일 얘기를 시작하기 전에 둘러보시겠어요?

남: 둘러보고 싶군요. 고마워요. 그런데, 지난 시즌 리그에서 EPL이 이 시설을 최고로 뽑았다고 들었어요.

여: 사실이에요. 세계적으로 유명한 트레이너인 Pete Parker가 설계했어요.

남: 네, 그에 대해 들은 적 있어요. 완성하는 데 오래 걸렸나요?

여: 2년 정도밖에 안 걸렸어요. 저희는 지난 봄에 여기서 훈련을 시작할 수 있었어요.

남: 여기에 어떤 종류의 편의시설이 있죠?

여: 음, 어디부터 시작할까요? 올림픽 사이즈의 수영장, 테니스 코트, 사우나, 한증실, 여러 가지가 계속 있답니다.

남: 놀라워요. 오... 여기에 레스토랑도 있군요. 이 장소는 정말로 믿을 수 없군요.

어휘

facility *n.* 시설, 기관　　**renowned** *a.* 유명한　　**amenities** *n.* 편의시설　　**steam room** 한증실　　**incredible** *a.* 믿을 수 없는

정답 ④

문제풀이

설계자(Pete Parker)와 건축 기간(about two years), 완공 시기(last spring), 포함된 내부 시설(an Olympic-sized swimming pool, a tennis court, a sauna, a steam room)은 언급되었지만 ④ '건축 비용'에 대한 언급은 없다.

총 어휘 수 149

11 내용 일치 · 불일치

소재 EcoBag 홍보

듣기 대본 해석

남: 오늘 아침, 저는 환경을 위한 위대한 새 발명품에 대해 말하겠습니다. 그것은 EcoBag이라 불립니다. 여러분께서 추측하시듯이, 그것은 환경 친화적인 가방입니다. 교수의 딸인 Amanda Stevens은 전 세계 학교에 사회적 인식을 불러일으키고자 이 위대한 가방을 만들었습니다. EcoBag은 전체가 재활용된 플라스틱으로 만들어졌습니다. 심지어 지퍼조차 이런 방식으로 만들어졌습니다. 가방의 끈과 손잡이는 재활용된 천과 플라스틱을 혼합하여 만들어져서 튼튼할 뿐만 아니라 편안하고 가볍습니다. 여러분이나 여러분의 자녀가 그것에 맞지 않게 자랐을 때, 그것은 재활용될 수 있습니다. 더 나아가 만약에 여러분이 온라인으로 그것을 구매하면, 회사는 어려움에 처한 학생에게 가방을 하나 기부할 것입니다. 보시다시피, EcoBag은 환경과 어려운 사람들을 도움으로써 여러분의 역할을 할 수 있는 훌륭한 방법입니다.

어휘

invention *n.* 발명　　**awareness** *n.* 의식　　**entirely** *ad.* 완전히, 전부　　**blend** *n.* 혼합 *v.* 섞다, 혼합하다　　**lightweight** *a.* 가벼운　　**outgrow** *v.* ~보다 더 커지다. (옷 등에 비해 사람이) 자라서 맞지 않게 되다　　**purchase** *v.* 구매하다　　**the needy** 어려운 사람들

정답 ②

문제풀이

가방의 모든 부분을 재활용 플라스틱으로 만들었다고 강조하면서 지퍼까지도 그러한 방식으로 만들었다고 했으므로 내용과 일치하지 않는 것은 ② '지퍼를 제외한 가방 전체가 재활용된 플라스틱으로 만들어졌다.'이다.

총 어휘 수 135

12 도표

소재 동물들을 돕는 기부 프로그램 선택

듣기 대본 해석

남: 여보, 뭐 보고 있어?

여: Guardian's 자선단체에 대한 안내 책자야. 동물들을 돕기 위한 기부를 받는대.

남: 그래. 좋은 프로그램이네. 기부할 생각인 거야?

여: 글쎄, 당신은 어떻게 생각해? 동물 도와주는 거 좋아하지?

남: 당연하지. 작년에 지역 동물 보호소에 일회적으로 기부했었던 것 기억나? 올해는 다른 것을 해보자.

여: 그래. 최근에 나는 야생 동물 보호구역과 어떻게 이 보호구역들이 학대 당하고 다친 동물들을 자연 서식지로 돌려보내는지에 관한 기사를 읽었어.

남: 흥미롭네. 동물 보호구역에 매월 기부를 하는 게 좋을 것 같아.

여: 좋은 생각이야. 달마다 기부를 하는 게 더 비용이 알맞고 뜻깊어. 얼마를 기부할까?

남: 10달러 이상인 건 무리야.

여: 알겠어. 그럼 이 선택이 제일 좋겠다.

어휘

brochure *n.* 책자   **charity** *n.* 자선단체   **abused** *a.* 학대당한
injured *a.* 다친, 부상을 입은   **habitat** *n.* 서식지   **sanctuary** *n.*
보호구역

정답 ③

문제풀이

올해는 야생 동물 보호구역에 기부를 하자고 했으므로 ③~⑤중에 고르면
되고, 매월 하자고 했으므로 ③번과 ④번이 남게 된다. 한 달에 10달러 이상은
무리라고 했으므로 정답은 ③번이다.

총 어휘 수 146

13 긴 대화의 응답

소재 팬이 직접 마스코트를 정하는 이벤트

듣기 대본 해석

여: 야, 좋은 소식 있어! 우리 팀 사이트에서 재미있는 이벤트를 하고 있어.
남: 진짜? 뭔데?
여: 사람들이 "여러분의 마스코트를 선택하세요"라고 부르는 이벤트인데 다음
　　경기에서 할 거래.
남: 잘 이해가 안 가. 무슨 마스코트를 쓸지 팬들이 정할 수 있게 해준다는 거야?
여: 그렇지. 팬들이 팀의 마스코트가 뭐가 될지 고를 수 있다는 거야.
남: 그리고 그 마스코트는 팬들이 투표해서 고르는 그 어떤 것도 된단 말이야?
여: 응. 팬들이 투표해서 고르는 그 어떤 것이든 말이야.
남: 특별하네. 이벤트에 누구든 참여할 수 있는 거야?
여: 아니. 다음 경기를 보러 오는 팬들만 참여할 수 있대.
남: 재미있네. 나도 다음 마스코트 정하는 것에 참여하고 싶어.
여: 그럼 토요일에 하는 경기 표를 구해야 될 거야.
남: ⑤ 알았어. 지금 하나 살 거야.

어휘

mascot *n.* 마스코트   **vote** *n.* 투표 *v.* 투표하다   **participate** *v.*
참여하다   **attend** *v.* 참석하다

정답 ⑤

문제풀이

여자는 남자가 마스코트 정하는 이벤트에 참여하려면 토요일에 있을 다음
경기를 봐야 한다고 하였다. 이에 대한 남자의 응답으로 가장 적절한 것은
⑤ '알았어. 지금 하나 살 거야.'이다.

오답 보기 해석

① 미안하지만 팬들만 투표할 수 있어.
② 이것들이 우리가 고를 수 있는 마스코트들이야.
③ 아니. 넌 이벤트에 참가할 수 없어.
④ 이벤트에 참여하려면 빨리 신청해야 돼.

총 어휘 수 132

14 긴 대화의 응답

소재 토론팀에서의 활동

듣기 대본 해석

남: 우리 견학 계획 바뀐 것 들었어?
여: 아니. 아무것도 못 들었는데.
남: 응. 금요일에 비가 와서 놀이공원에 가지 못하거든. 대신 과학 박물관에
　　갈 거야.
여: 아쉽네. 하지만 넌 좋겠다. 너 지난주에 가족하고 놀이공원에 간 거 맞지?

남: 응. 그리고 나는 과학 박물관이 열었을 때부터 정말 가고 싶었거든. 우리
　　과학동아리 구성원들에게 좋은 경험이 될 거야.
여: 음. 사실 난 이번 주 금요일에 견학을 못 가.
남: 정말? 왜 못 가는데?
여: 토론팀에서 해야 할 일이 있거든.
남: 정말? 금요일에 토론이 있는 줄은 몰랐어.
여: 그건 아닌데 다음 주 토론을 준비해야 하거든.
남: 알겠어. 넌 정말 팀에 헌신적이구나.
여: ⑤ 팀의 구성원이 되려면 열심히 해야 돼.

어휘

be supposed to V ~하기로 되어 있다   **amusement park** 놀이공원
obligation *n.* 의무, 해야 할 일   **dedicated** *a.* 전념하는, 헌신적인

정답 ⑤

문제풀이

토론 준비로 견학을 못 가는 여자에게 남자가 팀에 헌신적이라고 말했으므로
이에 대한 여자의 응답으로 가장 적절한 것은 ⑤ '팀의 구성원이 되려면 열심히
해야 돼.'이다.

오답 보기 해석

① 과학 박물관에서 기념품 사다 줄게.
② 이 견학을 정말 기다려 왔어.
③ 나는 과학 박물관이 열었을 때 방문했어.
④ 토론팀은 금요일에 겨뤄야 해.

총 어휘 수 160

15 상황에 적절한 말

소재 날씨에 대한 걱정으로 밖에서 뛰는 것 미루기

듣기 대본 해석

여: Bill이 그의 친구 Martin으로부터 전화를 받았을 때 그는 집에서 TV를
　　보고 있습니다. 그 두 친구는 보통 때 꽤 활동적이지만 날씨가 좋지 않아서
　　몇 주 동안 같이 놀지 못했습니다. 오늘 저녁 Martin은 뛰러 나가자고
　　제안합니다. Bill은 정말 뛰러 나가고 싶고 밖에서 운동하고 싶지만 그는
　　여전히 날씨에 대해 걱정하고 있습니다. 지난 여름, 그는 도시에서 꽤 멀리
　　자전거를 타러 나갔고 강한 뇌우를 만났습니다. 그 나쁜 기억 때문에, 그는
　　Martin의 제안을 거절하기로 결정합니다. 이런 상황에서 Bill이 Martin에
　　게 할 말로 가장 적절한 것은 무엇일까요?
Bill: Martin. ③ 비가 오지 않을 것이 확실할 때 뛰러 가자.

어휘

catch *v.* (폭풍우 등이) 엄습하다, 급습하다   **thunderstorm** *n.* 뇌우
decline *v.* 거절하다

정답 ③

문제풀이

Bill은 작년 여름에 멀리 나가서 자전거를 타다가 강한 뇌우를 만났던 나쁜 기억
때문에 밖에서 뛰어 놀자는 Martin의 제안을 거절하기로 한다. 따라서 Bill이
Martin에게 할 말은 ③ '비가 오지 않을 것이 확실할 때 뛰러 가자.'이다.

오답 보기 해석

① 네가 길을 안내하면 내가 너를 따라갈게.
② 비가 올지 안 올지 나는 언제든 알 수 있어.
④ 운동 장비를 사용한 후 항상 잘 말려야 돼.
⑤ 안 좋은 날씨에 자전거를 탈 때는 항상 주의해.

총 어휘 수 123

소재 목적에 맞게 고친 제품

듣기 대본 해석

남: 모든 사람들은 다른 목적에 맞게 고친 제품을 사용하는 것이 환경에 좋다고 알고 있지만 새로운 것을 사는 것만큼이나 품질이 좋을까요? 당신이 Greenbacks로부터 구매할 때, 그 대답은 항상 "네."입니다. 우리는 버려진 물건들을 수집하고 그것들을 흥미롭고 품질이 높은 새로운 물건으로 다른 용도에 맞게 만듭니다. 또한 가격도 매우 합리적입니다. 우리의 상품 목록에는 100달러가 넘는 것이 없습니다. 우리는 버려진 상업 나무로 만든 가구, 낡은 옷으로 만든 전등 갓, 오래된 사다리로 만든 책장을 팝니다. 만약에 봄에 새로운 화분이 필요하다면, 다른 곳 말고 Greenbacks를 찾으세요. 우리는 상자, 부츠, 항아리 같은 많은 것들을 당신의 정원에 멋지고 새로운 모습을 선사하기 위해서 재정비했습니다. 우리의 물품 모두가 독특해서 구매를 하시면 멋진 화제거리가 될 것입니다. 목적에 맞게 바꾸기 운동의 다른 많은 것들에 참여하기 위해서는 우리의 홈페이지 www.greenbacksrepurpose.com을 확인해 주세요. Greenbacks와 함께 현명하고 세련된 삶을 시작하세요.

어휘

repurpose *v.* 다른 목적에 맞게 만들다(바꾸다)   **discarded** *a.* 버려진 **reasonable** *a.* 합리적인, 비싸지 않은   **inventory** *n.* 재고품, 상품 목록 **lamp shade** 전등 따위의 갓   **planter** *n.* (분재용) 장식 용기, 화분 **crate** *n.* 상자   **conversation piece** 화제거리

정답 16 ②   **17** ①

문제풀이

16 폐품을 이용해서 목적에 맞게 고친 제품을 파는 회사를 홍보하는 내용이므로 정답은 ② '재활용 제품을 판매하는 회사를 홍보하려고'이다.

17 가구, 전등갓, 책장, 화분에 대한 언급은 있었지만 액자에 대한 언급은 하지 않았으므로 정답은 ① '액자'이다.

오답 보기 해석

17

② 가구　　　③ 전등갓　　　④ 책장　　　⑤ 화분

총 어휘 수 150

01 confirm a reservation

02 Let's get outside

03 helps your body recover after injury / if eaten in excess / cause high blood pressure

04 The screen keeps flickering / every two years / new computers are so sleek and fast / there's nothing wrong with this one / take it to

05 made a decision / interesting and intense / be good at asking questions / join the school newspaper

06 is a little cheesy / the circle-shaped pillow is so ragged / commemorates our time here

07 going to go out for lunch / pick something up for you / I don't really have an appetite / that is so nice of you

08 going over my presentation / slipped my mind / doesn't solve my problem

09 look good on her / pay the rest / Would you help me choose one / This is one of our best sellers

10 designed by world-renowned trainer / What kinds of amenities are in / and the list goes on and on

11 made entirely out of recycled plastic / When you or your child outgrows it / purchase one online

12 made a one-time donation / abused and injured animals / monthly donation to a sanctuary

13 it's taking place / Fans will be allowed to choose / whatever mascot the fans vote on / that attend the next game

14 go to the amusement park / This will be a great experience for / I have an obligation / dedicated to your team

15 receives a call / suggests they go for a run / head out for a run / he was caught in a strong thunderstorm / decline Martin's offer

16-17 using repurposed products / repurpose them into new items / look no further than / Start living smart and stylish

01 ③	02 ③	03 ①	04 ④	05 ⑤	06 ⑤
07 ③	08 ④	09 ⑤	10 ②	11 ③	12 ③
13 ⑤	14 ①	15 ⑤	16 ③	17 ④	

01 짧은 대화의 응답

소재 스마트 워치 반품

듣기 대본 해석

남: 안녕하세요. 이 스마트 워치 반품하고 싶어요.

여: 알겠습니다. 언제 구매하셨죠?

남: 영수증 확인해 볼게요. *[잠시 후]* 한 달이 좀 넘은 것 같네요.

여: ③ 죄송합니다만 30일 이후로는 반품을 받지 않습니다.

어휘

purchase *v.* 구입하다　**receipt** *n.* 영수증　〈문제〉**final** *a.* 변경할 수 없는, 최종적인　**refund** *n.* 환불

정답 ③

문제풀이

반품을 원하는 남자가 영수증 확인 후 한 달이 넘은 것 같다고 말하고 있으므로 그에 적절한 응답은 ③ '죄송합니다만 30일 이후로는 반품을 받지 않습니다.'이다.

오답 보기 해석

① 죄송하지만, 저희 매장에 있는 모든 제품은 반품이 안됩니다.

② 다음 주에 액정을 고칠 수 있을 겁니다.

④ 환불을 원하시면 영수증이 필요할 겁니다.

⑤ 이 제품에 문제가 많았어요.

총 어휘 수 42

02 짧은 대화의 응답

소재 비행기 도착 예정 시간

듣기 대본 해석

여: 실례합니다. 시애틀에는 언제 착륙하죠?

남: 저녁 7시쯤에 시애틀에 도착할 예정입니다.

여: 알겠습니다. 그럼 예정보다 약간 늦어지는 거군요.

남: ③ 네. 불편을 드려서 정말 죄송합니다.

어휘

behind schedule 예정보다 늦게　〈문제〉**inconvenience** *n.* 불편

정답 ③

문제풀이

여자가 시애틀에 언제 도착하는지 묻고 남자는 예상 시간을 답해주는 것으로 보아 승객과 승무원의 대화임을 알 수 있다. 예정보다 늦어지는 거냐고 확인하는 여자의 말에 적절한 남자의 응답은 ③ '네. 불편을 드려서 정말 죄송합니다.'이다.

오답 보기 해석

① 문제없습니다. 저희는 금방 떠날 겁니다.

② 좋습니다. 정말 즐거운 비행이었습니다.

④ 맞습니다. 우린 공항에 정시에 도착할 겁니다.

⑤ 불편하게 해 드려서 죄송합니다. 금방 물을 가져다 드리겠습니다.

총 어휘 수 36

03 담화 목적

소재 체육관 보수공사로 인한 이용 통제

듣기 대본 해석

[벨이 울린다.]

여: 안녕하세요, 여러분. 주목해 주시겠습니까? 저는 교장인 Jones입니다. 날씨로부터 받은 피해로, 학교의 체육관이 앞으로 3주간 공사 때문에 문을 닫을 것입니다. 학생들은 체육관이 공사 중인 기간에 체육관을 이용할 수 없습니다. 이번 폐쇄로 인한 문제에 대해 사과드립니다만 이는 학생들의 안전을 위한 것입니다. 저는 보수된 체육관이 2월 22일 다시 문을 열었을 때 더 안전하고 훨씬 멋있을 거라고 여러분께 장담합니다. 체육관에서 실시하기로 계획되었던 모든 활동들은 길 아래 커뮤니티 센터로 옮겨갈 것입니다. 변경된 일정은 웹사이트에서 확인할 수 있습니다. 상황을 이해해 줘서 고맙습니다.

어휘

principal *n.* 교장　*a.* 주요한　**damage** *n.* 피해, 훼손　**under construction** 공사 중　**apologize** *v.* 사과하다　**assure** *v.* 장담하다　**renovated** *a.* 개조된　**revised** *a.* 변경된

정답 ①

문제풀이

여자는 학생들에게 체육관 보수공사가 있어서 당분간 폐쇄된다는 것을 알리며 앞으로 3주간 체육관을 이용할 수 없다고 하였으므로, 정답은 ① '보수공사로 인한 이용 통제를 공지하려고'이다.

총 어휘 수 118

04 대화 주제

소재 음악 들으며 조깅하는 것의 위험성

듣기 대본 해석

여: 여보, 나 시내를 달릴 거예요.

남: 알겠어요. 근데 헤드폰을 가지고 가네요. 달리는 동안에 음악을 들을 거예요?

여: 물론이죠. 막 새로운 Maroon 5 앨범을 구했거든요. 이 앨범을 들어보길 기대하고 있어요.

남: 달리는 동안에 음악을 듣지 않는 게 좋겠어요.

여: 왜 안 돼요? 뛰는 것은 지루해요. 음악을 들으면 좀 더 견딜 만해요.

남: 헤드폰을 쓰면 지나가는 차량의 소리를 못 들을 거예요. 그건 매우 위험해요.

여: 흠… 그런 생각을 전혀 못했어요.

남: 네. 밖에 있을 때 주위 환경에 대해서 주의하는 것이 중요해요. 난 당신이 다치기를 원치 않아요.

여: 알았어요. 집에 왔을 때 이 앨범을 들어야겠어요.

남: 여보, 난 그저 당신이 조심하기를 바라요.

어휘

look forward to ~을 학수고대하다　**bearable** *a.* 견딜 수 있는　**be aware of** ~을 알아 차리다, ~을 알다

정답 ④

문제풀이

여자가 시내를 달리러 나가는데 헤드폰을 가지고 나가자 남자는 달릴 때 음악을 들으면 자동차 소리를 못 듣기 때문에 위험하다고 말해주고 있으므로 두 사람이 하는 말의 주제는 ④ '헤드폰 끼고 음악 들으며 뛰는 것의 위험성'이다.

총 어휘 수 130

05 대화자의 관계 파악

소재 뉴스 보도 방식

듣기 대본 해석
여: 안녕하세요, Sam. 손에 들고 있는 게 뭐예요?
남: 안녕, Erica. 사실 이건 우리가 최근에 받은 항의 편지들이에요.
여: 정말이요?
남: 네. 확실히 몇몇의 시청자들은 우리의 뉴스 내용을 좋아하지 않아요.
여: Sam, 당신은 지역 뉴스를 좀 더 가볍게 만들고 싶어하던 사람이잖아요.
남: 나도 알고 있지만, 우리가 시청자들을 실망시킨다면 그것은 소용이 없는 것 같아요.
여: 그럼 저는 더 진지한 뉴스를 보도하기 시작해야 하나요?
남: 그럴 것 같아요. 우리 회의를 소집해서 이 문제를 토론해보면 어떨까요?
여: 좋은 생각이에요. 저는 어떻게 해야 하죠?
남: 모든 스텝들에게 연락해서 점심 식사 후 회의실에서 모두 만나게 해줄래요?
여: 네, 알았어요. 그렇지만 저는 우리가 뉴스를 진행하고 있었던 방식이 정말 좋았다고 말하고 싶네요.
남: 네, 저도 그래요. 회의 때 모두 이야기해 봅시다.

어휘
audience *n.* 시청자, 청중   **light-hearted** *a.* 편안한 마음으로, 마음이 가벼운   **disappoint** *v.* 실망시키다   **serious** *a.* 진지한
boardroom *n.* 회의실

정답 ⑤

문제풀이
여자가 진지한 뉴스를 보도해야 하는지 물은 점이나 진행하고 있었던 방식이 좋았다고 말하는 것에서 여자는 뉴스 진행자임을 알 수 있고, 남자는 뉴스 보도를 위해 지시하고 회의를 소집하는 것으로 보아 프로듀서임을 알 수 있다. 그러므로 정답은 ⑤ '뉴스 진행자 — 프로듀서'이다.

총 어휘 수 138

06 그림의 세부 내용 파악

소재 누군가가 침입했던 방

듣기 대본 해석
여: 오, 이런! 너 아파트에 무슨 일이 있었니, Alvin?
남: 왜! 누가 침입해서 집을 망가뜨려 놓은 것 같네.
여: 응. 여기 있던 사람이 너의 거울을 깨뜨렸네.
남: 내 테이블도 부서졌어. 끔찍하다.
여: 테이블 옆에 방망이가 있네. 아마도 그걸 사용해서 다 부쉈나 봐.
남: 그런 것 같아. 이런 적이 없었는데. 왜 누군가가 나한테 이런 일을 했을까?
여: 적어도 나무는 손상되지 않았는데.
남: 가져간 것은 없는 것 같아. 일단 없어진 건 없는 것 같은데. 책은 바닥에 내가 놓은 그대로 있어.
여: 그들이 어떻게 들어왔는지 궁금해.
남: 아마도 열려있는 창문으로 기어들어 왔을 거야.
여: 그랬을 수도 있겠다. 문을 사용한 것처럼 보이지는 않아.

어휘
destroy *v.* 파괴하다, 부수다   **crawl** *v.* (엎드려) 기다

정답 ⑤

문제풀이
대화의 마지막 부분에서 남자가 침입자는 열려 있는 창문으로 들어왔을 거라고 했는데 창문이 닫혀 있으므로 그림과 일치하지 않는 것은 ⑤번이다.

총 어휘 수 122

07 부탁한 일

소재 동아리 지도교사 섭외

듣기 대본 해석
여: 안녕, Daryl. 내가 뭐 도와줄까?
남: 네, Peterson 선생님. 선생님께 여쭤보고 싶은 게 있어요.
여: 그럼, 알다시피 어떤 것이든 물어봐도 좋아.
남: 몇몇 친구들과 저는 영화 만드는 데 정말 관심이 많고 우리가 영화 동아리를 시작한다면 어떨지 알고 싶어요.
여: 음, 내 생각에는 일단 너희들이 Stevenson 선생님과 이야기를 해야 할 것 같구나. 그는 동아리 활동을 담당하는 선생님이니까.
남: 네, 제가 Stevenson 선생님께 말씀드렸어요. Stevenson 선생님은 저희를 지도해 주실 선생님이 필요하다고 말씀하셨어요.
여: 그래, 그래서 너희가 생각하고 있는 사람은 누구니?
남: 저희는 선생님께서 비디오 제작에 계셨던 걸로 알고 있어요.
여: 오, 그걸 알고 있었니? 그래서 너희는 내가 너희 동아리를 지도해 주기를 원하는 거니?
남: 그러면 정말 좋을 것 같아요. 해주실 수 있으세요?
여: 물론 할 수 있지. 사실 아주 재미있을 것 같구나.
남: 정말 감사합니다, Peterson 선생님!

어휘
in charge of ~을 맡고 있는, 담당해서   **supervise** *v.* 지도하다, 감독하다

정답 ③

문제풀이
학생인 남자는 새로운 영화 동아리를 만들려 하는데 교사인 여자에게 그 동아리의 지도를 부탁하고 있다. 그러므로 남자의 부탁으로 가장 적절한 것은 ③ '새 동아리를 지도하는 것'이다.

오답 보기 해석
① Stevenson 선생님께 말하는 것
② 그녀의 강의에 등록하는 것
④ 그의 새로운 영화에 참여하는 것
⑤ 그에게 카메라 사용법을 보여주는 것

총 어휘 수 135

08 이유

소재 스페인어 시간에 있을 연설에 대한 걱정

듣기 대본 해석
남: 엄마, 커피 남은 게 있나요?
여: 있는 것 같은데. 왜 그러니?
남: 한 잔 마시고 싶어서요.
여: 커피를 마시기에는 너무 늦은 것 같은데. 커피에는 카페인이 많이 들어 있어서 마시면 잠잘 시간이 지나서도 잠이 오지 않을 거야.
남: 에너지가 좀 필요한 것 같아서요.
여: 왜 늦게까지 깨어있어야 하니?
남: 내일 스페인어 수업시간에 연설을 해야 해서 연습하고 싶어서요.
여: 지난주 내내 네 방에서 그것을 연습하는 것을 들었는데.
남: 네, 사실 지난 주부터 계속 연습했어요.
여: 그럼 이제 준비가 됐어야지.
남: 음, 제가 실수를 해서 모두가 절 비웃을까 봐 두려워요.
여: 그렇구나. 내 생각에는 네가 걱정할 필요가 없을 것 같구나. 만약 실수를 해서 모두가 웃는다면 그냥 같이 웃어 버리렴.
남: 네, 조언 감사해요 엄마.
여: 언제든. 자 이제 잘 준비를 하렴.

어휘
give a speech 연설하다　**make a mistake** 실수하다

정답 ④

문제풀이
여자가 왜 늦게까지 깨어있어야 하는지 물었을 때 남자는 스페인어 수업시간에 해야 할 연설을 연습하고 싶다고 했으므로 정답은 ④ '내일 할 연설을 연습하고 싶어서'이다.

총 어휘 수 149

09 숫자

소재 과학 센터 표 구매

듣기 대본 해석
남: Chester 과학 센터에 오신 것을 환영합니다. 어떻게 도와드릴까요?
여: 안녕하세요. 어른 두 명, 아이 한 명의 티켓이 필요해요.
남: 네. 어른은 30달러, 아이는 20달러예요.
여: 좋아요. 이 표로 박물관에 있는 모든 것을 이용할 수 있나요?
남: 음. 표는 직접 해보는 과학 쇼와 수족관을 포함해서 모든 쇼와 주요 명소를 포함하고 있어요.
여: 멋지네요. 천체 투영관은요? 그것도 표 가격에 포함되어 있나요?
남: 아니요. 하지만 천체 투영관과 레이저쇼뿐만 아니라 모든 쇼와 주요 명소를 포함하고 있는 Science Center Plus 표를 구매할 수 있어요.
여: 알았어요. 그 표는 얼마인가요?
남: 한 사람당 5달러를 추가하면 됩니다.
여: 좋아요. 그걸로 3장 주세요.
남: 네. 어른 두 명, 아이 한 명 맞죠?
여: 맞아요. 여기 제 카드요.

어휘
main attraction 주요 명소, 주요 명물　**hands-on** *a.* 직접 해보는
aquarium *n.* 수족관　**planetarium** *n.* 천체 투영관

정답 ⑤

문제풀이
어른 한 명당 30달러인데 두 명이므로 60달러, 아이는 한 명 당 20달러인데. Science Center Plus 표는 한 사람당 5달러로 세 명이면 15달러이다. 따라서 전체 지불할 금액은 95달러(=60달러+20달러+15달러)이므로 정답은 ⑤ '$95'이다.

총 어휘 수 132

10 언급 유무

소재 연례 마라톤에 대한 대화

듣기 대본 해석
남: Cathleen. 이번 달 27일에 연례 마라톤 열리는 거 알고 있었니?
여: 응 알고 있어.
남: 너도 참가할 거야?
여: 그러고 싶지만. 26마일을 달리는 게 나한테는 너무 어려울 것 같아.
남: 응. 꽤나 멀지. 하지만 다 달릴 필요는 없어. 필요하면 걸어도 돼.
여: 정말? 나쁘지 않은데.
남: 올해는 뛰는 사람이 많아. 웹사이트에 따르면, 거의 2,000명이 등록을 했어.
여: 왜! 정말 많다.
남: 너도 알다시피 좋은 목적을 위해서잖아. 참가비는 40달러인데, 수익금은 강변공원을 미화하는 데 사용될 거야.
여: 알았어.

남: 완주를 하면 티셔츠와 네 이름이 새겨진 상패도 받을 수 있어. 우리 같이 할 수 있어. 내가 끝내도록 도와줄게.
여: 좋아. 잠깐 생각할 시간을 줘. 다음 주가 되기 전에 참가할지 말지 알려줄게.

어휘
register *v.* 등록하다　**beautify** *v.* 아름답게 하다　**plaque** *n.* 명판

정답 ②

문제풀이
두 사람은 완주 거리, 현재 등록 인원, 수익금 사용처, 완주 기념품에 관한 언급은 했지만 ② '당일 복장'에 관한 언급은 하지 않았다.

총 어휘 수 173

11 내용 일치 · 불일치

소재 Miller Brody의 일생

듣기 대본 해석
여: 여러분, 좋은 아침이에요. 오늘 저는 여러분께 미국의 심리학자인 Miller Brody에 대해 이야기 하고 싶어요. 그는 1920년 Tennessee에서 태어났고, 열심히 일하는 사업가와 가정 주부 사이의 외아들이었어요. 그는 1945년 Minnesota 대학에서 심리학 박사가 되었고 다음 해에 Montana 대학에서 강의를 시작했어요. 그는 종종 동료 교수들과 충돌이 있었지만, 그가 잘 생겼고 재미있어서 학생들은 그를 많이 좋아했어요. 그의 경력 동안 그는 사회 계층과 지위가 사람들에게 끼치는 심리적 영향에 대해 많은 책을 펴냈습니다. 그는 결혼 후 유럽으로 갔고, 거기서 그는 미국에서 사회적 계층 체계의 기원을 발견하길 바라며 다른 나라에서 온 학자들을 만났습니다. Miller Brody는 2002년에 자연적 원인으로 사망했습니다.

어휘
psychologist *n.* 심리학자　**conflict** *n.* 충돌　**career** *n.* 사회생활, 경력　**publish** *v.* 출판하다　**pass away** 사망하다

정답 ③

문제풀이
그는 자주 그의 동료 교수들과 갈등을 겪었다고 했으므로 내용과 일치하지 않는 것은 ③ '동료 교수들과 충돌 없이 잘 지냈다.'이다.

총 어휘 수 140

12 도표

소재 Madison 관광 선택

듣기 대본 해석
여: 여보, 로비에서 이 팜플렛 찾았어. Madison 관광지에 대한 정보가 있더라.
남: 좋네. 내일 할 것을 찾아보자.
여: 그래. 일단 카누를 타고 싶은데 다섯 시간은 너무 길지 않아?
남: 맞아. 그리고 그건 너무 비싸. 좀 더 저렴한 걸 찾아보자.
여: 응. 우린 나비 정원을 보러 갈 수도 있어. 이맘때쯤 예쁘다고 들었어.
남: 갈 수도 있는데 호텔에서 가는 셔틀버스를 제공해 주지 않아.
여: 그렇네. 거기까지 가는 게 힘들겠다.
남: 맞아. 그럼 이제 선택지가 두 개 남았네. 어떤 게 더 재미 있을 것 같아?
여: 걸으면서 관광하기에는 내일 날씨가 너무 더울 것 같아.
남: 동감이야. 그럼 이걸로 하자.

어휘
pamphlet *n.* 팜플렛　**tourist attraction** 관광지　**canoeing** *n.* 카누 타기　**shuttle** *n.* 셔틀버스

정답 ③

문제풀이

카누는 시간도 길고 비싸서 제외되고, 남자가 70달러보다는 덜 비싼 활동을 찾자고 하였으므로 River Zipline도 제외된다. 나비 정원은 셔틀을 제공해 주지 않아서 제외된다. 따라서 남은 선택지는 ③번과 ④번인데 걷는 것은 너무 덥다고 했으므로 두 사람이 선택한 관광지는 ③ '와인 시음'이 된다.

총 어휘 수 137

13 긴 대화의 응답

소재 극장에서 생긴 일

듣기 대본 해석
여: 안녕, Tom! 어젯밤 그 연극 재미있었어?
남: 음, 연극 자체는 정말 좋았는데 나는 극장에서 그렇게 즐기지는 못했어.
여: 오, 나는 네가 그 연극을 보고 엄청 좋아할 거라고 생각했는데. 무슨 일이 있었는데?
남: 주연을 담당하는 배우를 좋아해서 정말 그 연극을 보고 싶었거든. 그런데 두어 사람과 말다툼을 했어.
여: 극장에서? 왜 말다툼 한 건데?
남: 그들이 내 자리에 앉아있었고 내가 지적한 후에도, 그 자리가 그들 것이라고 우기더라고.
여: 사람들이 그럴 때 정말 화가 나!
남: 그게 다가 아니야. 안내원이 그 상황을 해결하려고 왔고, 우리 표를 자세히 보더라고. 자세히 보니 직원이 나한테 잘못된 표를 인쇄해 준 것 같았어. 그래서 나는 훨씬 뒷자리에 앉아야 했어.
여: 너 정말 화가 났겠다. 결국 어떻게 했어?
남: ⑤ 연극을 본 후에, 극장에 항의했어.

어휘
argument *n.* 논쟁, 말다툼　　**insist** *v.* 주장하다, 우기다　　**annoy** *v.* 짜증나게 하다　　**usher** *n.* 안내원　　**handle** *v.* 다루다, 해결하다
a close(r) look 자세히 살핌

정답 ⑤

문제풀이
남자는 어제 연극을 보러 갔다가 잘못된 표를 받아서 뒤에서 연극을 봐야 했던 일을 여자에게 말해주었고 마지막에 여자는 그래서 어떻게 했는지를 물었다. 남자는 극장 측의 잘못으로 화가 났으므로 적절한 응답은 ⑤ '연극을 본 후에, 극장에 항의했어.'이다.

오답 보기 해석
① 그 안내원에게 그들을 조용히 시켜달라고 말했어.
② 그 주연을 담당하는 배우를 만났어.
③ 안내원에게 내가 화장실에 가도 되냐고 물었어.
④ 나는 그 훌륭한 공연을 절대 잊지 못할 거야.

총 어휘 수 166

14 긴 대화의 응답

소재 동물 실험 반대 캠페인

듣기 대본 해석
여: 이봐, Cameron. 너 피켓 표지에 뭐라고 한 거야? "동물 실험 반대?"
남: 오, 안녕, Ellie. 그래, 동물 실험 제품에 반대하는 캠페인이야.
여: 내가 아는 많은 사람들도 그것에 반대하고 있는데 나는 왜 그런지 잘 모르겠어.
남: 자, 사람들은 인간이 쓰기 위해 개발된 제품을 시험하기 위해 동물을 이용해선 안 돼. 이 사진들에 실험실에서 동물들에게 행해지는 모든 종류의 잔인한 행동들이 나와 있어.

여: 와, 정말 충격적이야. 난 사람들이 동물들을 그렇게 다루는지 몰랐어.
남: 사람들은 단지 제품 하나의 효과를 연구하기 위해 하루에 수백 마리의 동물들을 죽여!
여: 네가 이 캠페인에 그렇게 열정적인 게 대단하다고 생각해. 내가 기부를 할 수 있어?
남: 그거 좋겠다, Ellie. 우리 웹사이트에 가면 네가 필요한 정보가 있어.
여: ① 좋아. 나도 도울 수 있게 되어서 기뻐.

어휘
picket *n.* 피켓　　**campaign** *n.* 캠페인, 사회 운동　　**lab** *n.* 실험실
passionate *a.* 열정적인　　**donation** *n.* 기부, 기부금
〈문제〉 **appreciate** *v.* 고맙게 여기다, 환영하다

정답 ①

문제풀이
동물 실험 반대 캠페인을 하는 친구를 만나서 기부가 가능한지 물었고 친구는 웹사이트에 들어가면 정보가 나와있다고 알려준다. 이에 대한 여자의 대답은 ① '좋아. 나도 도울 수 있게 되어서 기뻐.'가 가장 적절하다.

오답 보기 해석
② 우리는 너의 기부를 환영해. 너무 고마워.
③ 그 사진들을 안 보는 게 낫겠어. 너무 슬퍼.
④ 충고 고마워. 다시는 그렇게 하지 않도록 명심할게.
⑤ 여기에 이름 쓰고 사인만 하면 돼. 그게 우리가 필요한 전부야.

총 어휘 수 137

15 상황에 적절한 말

소재 고아원에서 자원봉사하자고 친구 설득하기

듣기 대본 해석
남: Kenny는 친구 Katie에게 같이 새 영화를 보러 가자고 합니다. Katie는 오늘 오후에 고아원에서 봉사를 해야 하기 때문에 거절을 합니다. Kenny는 Katie에게 왜 자원봉사를 하냐고 물어보자 Katie는 다른 사람들, 특히 어린이들을 도와주는 것은 무척 보람 있는 일이라고 답합니다. Kenny가 남을 도와주는 것을 좋아하기 때문에 자원봉사하는 것을 생각해 본 적이 있습니다. 그러나 어린이들과 잘 놀아주지 못하는 것 같아 고아원에서 봉사할 수는 없을 것 같다고 생각합니다. Katie는 Kenny가 자기와 함께 고아원에서 봉사활동을 했으면 좋겠고 그가 할 수 있도록 격려하고 싶어 합니다. 이러한 상황에서 Katie가 Kenny에게 할 말로 가장 적절한 것은 무엇일까요?
Katie: ⑤ 봉사는 매우 재미있고 아이들이 너를 좋아할 거라고 확신해.

어휘
decline *v.* 거절하다, 감소하다　　**orphanage** *n.* 고아원　　**volunteer** *v.* 자원봉사하다　　**rewarding** *a.* 보람 있는　　**encourage** *v.* 격려하다, 고무하다

정답 ⑤

문제풀이
Katie가 고아원에 봉사활동을 하러 간다는 것을 알게 된 Kenny는 이에 동참하고 싶어 하지만 자신이 아이들과 잘 놀지 못한다고 생각하여 주저하고 있다. Katie는 Kenny가 함께 자원봉사하기를 바라고 그를 격려하고자 하므로, 그녀가 할 말로 가장 적절한 것은 ⑤ '봉사는 매우 재미있고 아이들이 너를 좋아할 거라고 확신해.'이다.

오답 보기 해석
① 우리가 고를 수 있는 다른 영화들이 있어.
② 너는 자원봉사에 대한 보상은 받지 않을 거야.
③ 우리는 이미 자원봉사하는 사람들을 충분히 보유하고 있어.
④ 나는 고아원에서 일함으로써 돕고 싶어.

총 어휘 수 119

소재 세계 최대의 호텔

듣기 대본 해석

남: Las Vegas에 있는 Venetian Hotel은 특별한 경험이 될 수 있습니다. 1999년에 문을 연 이래로 Venetian Hotel은 세계에서 가장 큰 호텔입니다. 7,000개 이상의 방을 갖추고 있으며, 호텔은 5개의 별개의 구역으로 나눠져 있습니다. 세계 곳곳의 다양한 음식을 제공하는 식당가는 A지역에 있는데, 그곳에는 피아노를 연주해주는 바도 있습니다. B지역에는 카지노가 있는데, 거기서 고객들이 매일 밤 크게 이깁니다. C지역에는 쇼핑몰이 있는데, 코치, 프라다, 루이비통과 같은 디자이너 브랜드가 다 모여있는 곳입니다. D지역은 Venetian 호텔의 오락구역이며, 그곳에서는 전세계의 유명 연극이 매일 밤낮으로 공연됩니다. 여러분은 서커스, 마술쇼를 보실 수 있고 Barbara Streisand 노래 혹은 많은 다른 Vegas풍의 쇼를 보실 수 있습니다. 마지막으로 E지역에는 로비와 무도회장이 있습니다. 이 지역에서는 보통 회의와 세미나가 개최됩니다. 만약 Las Vegas에 가시게 되면 꼭 세계에서 가장 큰 호텔인 Venetian Hotel을 방문하세요.

어휘

distinct *a.* 별개의, 뚜렷한   **variety of** 다양한   **patron** *n.* 고객, 후원자

정답 16 ③   **17** ④

문제풀이

16 남자는 라스베가스에 있는 세계 최대 호텔의 5개 구역을 설명해주고 있다. 따라서 남자가 하는 말의 목적은 ③ '세계 최대의 호텔을 소개하려고'이다.

17 오락구역인 D구역에서 매일 밤낮으로 공연을 한다고 했으므로 정답은 ④ 'Area D'이다.

총 어휘 수 181

DICTATION ANSWERS

01 return this smartwatch

02 behind schedule

03 Due to damage from the weather / while it is under construction / the renovated gym / revised schedule

04 go for a run / makes it more bearable / be aware of your surroundings / when I get home

05 complaint letters we've received recently / Why don't we call a meeting / Get in touch with

06 destroyed the place / My table is broken / crawled in through

07 interested in making movies / in charge of club activities / you used to be / sounds like a lot of fun

08 keep you up past your bedtime / stay up late / give a speech / you should be ready by now

09 include everything in the museum / Is it included / an additional five dollars per person

10 holding the annual marathon / too difficult for me to run / registration fee / Give me a while

11 a doctorate in psychology / in conflict with his fellow professors / social class and status / passed away

12 go canoeing / offer a shuttle / leaves us with two options / too hot tomorrow for a walking tour

13 played the main role / got into an argument / so annoying / I had to sit farther back

14 a campaign against testing products on animals / hundreds of animals / so passionate about this campaign

15 declines his offer / work at the orphanage / encourage him to volunteer

16-17 divided into five distinct areas / famous acts from around the world / be sure to visit the largest hotel

10 수능영어듣기 실전모의고사

01 ①	02 ②	03 ⑤	04 ①	05 ②	06 ⑤
07 ③	08 ①	09 ④	10 ③	11 ⑤	12 ②
13 ②	14 ⑤	15 ④	16 ⑤	17 ③	

01 짧은 대화의 응답

소재 에어컨 고장

듣기 대본 해석
남: 와, 여기 정말 덥네. 에어컨 켜자, Amy.
여: 제대로 작동이 안 돼. 고칠 때까지 사용할 수 없어.
남: 자, 그럼 최대한 빨리 고쳐야지.
여: ① 좋아, 내가 지금 서비스 센터에 연락할게.

어휘
properly *ad.* 제대로 **fix** *v.* ~을 고치다

정답 ①

문제풀이
남자가 고장 난 에어컨을 빨리 고쳐야겠다고 말했으므로 여자의 응답은 서비스 센터에 연락한다는 ① '좋아, 내가 지금 서비스 센터에 연락할게.'가 가장 적절하다.

오답 보기 해석
② 내가 확실히 그것을 관리할게.
③ 우리는 같은 모델 제품을 사야 된다고 생각해.
④ 가능하다면 우리는 에너지를 절약하려고 해야 해.
⑤ 그가 가능한 빨리 와야 한다는 것을 반드시 알도록 해.

총 어휘 수 42

02 짧은 대화의 응답

소재 세차 가격

듣기 대본 해석
여: 오늘 날씨가 좋아.
남: 응. 세차를 해야겠어.
여: 세차하는 데에 얼마나 드니?
남: 보통 20달러 정도 들어.
여: 정말? 너무 비싸지 않아?
남: ② 별로 그렇지 않아. 그들이 일을 정말 잘해.

어휘
expensive *a.* 값비싼

정답 ②

문제풀이
세차 가격이 너무 비싸지 않냐는 말에 ② '별로 그렇지 않아. 그들이 일을 정말 잘해.'가 적절하다.

오답 보기 해석
① 사실, 세차를 할 필요가 있을지 모르겠어.
③ 나도 그렇게 생각해. 그들은 돈이 없어.
④ 내 차를 세차하지는 않아.
⑤ 그것은 내 차가 아니야.

총 어휘 수 40

03 담화 목적

소재 애완동물을 가진 아파트 주민들에 대한 협조 요청

듣기 대본 해석
남: 최근 몇 주간 동네 애완견들이 밤 늦게 짖는 것에 대한 항의가 많이 들어왔습니다. 이 애완견들은 특히 아침 일찍 출근해야 하는 주민들에게 골칫거리가 되었습니다. 상황은 어젯밤 주민 한 명이 경찰에 신고해 문제를 해결하기 위해 우리 동네로 경찰이 출동하는 지경까지 이르렀습니다. 이러한 소란에 더해져 애완동물 주인들이 애완동물들의 배설물을 치우지 않고 있다는 항의까지 들어왔습니다. 우리 Greenville 아파트는 주민들에게 동네의 청결과 조용함을 유지하기 위해 필요한 조치를 취하기를 권고합니다. 협조해주셔서 감사합니다.

어휘
nuisance *n.* 골칫거리, 성가신 일 **resident** *n.* 주민, 거주자
disturbance *n.* 소란, 방해

정답 ⑤

문제풀이
애완견이 밤늦게 짖거나 동물 주인이 배설물을 치우지 않아 아파트 주민들에게 피해를 끼치고 있다고 말하면서 적절한 조치를 취할 것을 요청하고 있으므로 정답은 ⑤ '애완동물이 이웃에 피해를 끼치지 않도록 요청하려고'이다.

총 어휘 수 107

04 의견

소재 산에서 쓰레기 다시 가져오기

듣기 대본 해석
여: Daniel, 여기 경치 좋다. 산 공기가 정말 맑고 경치가 굉장한데.
남: 맞아. 정말 멋지다. 그런데 우리 내려가는 게 좋을 것 같아.
여: 떠나기 싫지만 어두워지고 있어. 곧 가야 돼.
남: 우선, 이 쓰레기 어디에 버려야 되는 거지?
여: 쓰레기를 버릴 장소가 없어 보여. 우리가 그냥 가져가자.
남: 좋아. 그런데 여기 쓰레기통이 있으면 훨씬 더 편할 텐데.
여: 맞아. 그런데 그렇게 하면 쓰레기통을 비울 직원이 있어야 할 거야.
남: 글쎄. 사람들은 쓰레기통이 없으면 아무데나 쓰레기를 버리지.
여: 맞아. 그런데 쓰레기통이 있으면 금방 쓰레기가 가득 차고 넘쳐서 쓰레기가 쓰레기통 주변에 많이 쌓일 거야.
남: 네 말이 맞을 수도 있겠다.
여: 우리가 쓰레기를 다시 가져가는 것이 그리 힘든 일은 아니라고 생각해.
남: 그래, 힘든 일이 아니지.

어휘
amazing *a.* 놀라운, 굉장한 **fill up** 가득 차다 **build up** ~이 쌓이다
a big deal 큰일, 힘든 일

정답 ①

문제풀이
남자는 산 위에 쓰레기통이 있으면 더 편리할 것이라고 말했지만, 여자는 쓰레기통이 있으면 쓰레기통을 비울 사람이 필요하고 쓰레기통 주변에 쓰레기가 쌓이게 된다면서 쓰레기를 되가져가는 것은 그리 힘든 일이 아니라고 말했다. 따라서 정답은 ① '산에서 자신의 쓰레기를 다시 가지고 와야 한다.'이다.

총 어휘 수 155

05 대화자의 관계 파악

소재 연기 실수에 대한 사과

듣기 대본 해석

여: 실례합니다. Wise 선생님. 시간 있으신가요?
남: 물론이야, Shelly. 들어오렴. 뭘 도와줄까?
여: 지난밤 저의 연기에 대해 사과 드리고 싶어요. 제가 선생님과 다른 사람들을 실망 시켜드렸어요.
남: 그래. 네가 평소처럼 그 공연에 몰입하진 않았지. 너무 많은 실수를 했어.
여: 알아요. 좀 더 집중했었어야 했어요. 제가 최근 너무 좌절을 해서 제 연기에 영향을 끼쳤어요.
남: 무엇에 좌절했는데?
여: 음, 제가 수학시간에 너무 뒤떨어져 있어요. 그것에 스트레스를 받고 있어요.
남: 알았다. 학업에 집중할 수 있도록 공연 몇 개는 너 대신 다른 사람이 하게 할까?
여: 아니요, 괜찮아요. 저희 선생님께 말씀드렸어요. 그녀는 제가 지난 시험을 재시험 볼 수 있도록 동의했어요.
남: 좋아. 그러면, 지난밤에 대한 것은 잊으렴. 내일 공연에 집중하자.
여: 알겠습니다. 고맙습니다. Wise 선생님.

어휘

performance *n.* 공연, 연기   **let ~ down** ~을 실망시키다
stress out 스트레스를 받다

정답 ②

문제풀이

여자는 지난 공연에서 자신의 연기 실수에 대해 사과하고 있고, 남자는 문제점을 말해주면서 이제는 잊으라고 말하며 내일 공연에 집중하자고 하는 것으로 보아 두 사람의 관계는 ② '감독 ― 배우'임을 유추할 수 있다.

총 어휘 수 150

06 그림의 세부 내용 파악

소재 시내 봄 축제

듣기 대본 해석

여: 나 봄 축제 보려고 시내에 나오는 게 정말 좋아, Carl. 진짜 재미있어!
남: 나도. 할 게 정말 많아.
여: 당연하지. 우선 뭐 좀 먹자.
남: 그래. 근데 ATM에서 현금 뽑아야 돼.
여: 시식 판매대가 은행 앞에 있으니까 딱 좋네.
남: 좋다! 먹은 다음에는 뭐 할래?
여: 음, 난 놀이기구 타는 게 좋아, 특히 저 큰 관람차.
남: 난 너랑 같이 못 탈 것 같아. 고소공포증이 있거든.
여: 아쉽네. 그럼, 저쪽에 있는 사람들처럼 나무 아래서 날 기다리면 되겠네. 그리고 밴드 음악을 들어도 되고.
남: 안타깝게도 지금은 연주하는 밴드가 없어.
여: 기다리는 동안 분명 뭔가 할 게 있을 거야.
남: 그래. 어쨌든, 이제 뭐 먹으러 가자!

어휘

food booth 시식 판매대

정답 ⑤

문제풀이

대화의 끝부분에서 지금은 연주하는 밴드가 없다고 했는데 그림에서는 밴드가 무대에서 공연을 하고 있으므로 정답은 ⑤번이다.

총 어휘 수 137

07 부탁한 일

소재 교통 검색 어플리케이션

듣기 대본 해석

여: 안녕하세요, Brown 선생님. 여기서 만나다니 반갑습니다. 버스 기다리세요?
남: 응. 어디 가는 거니, Laura?
여: 집에 가요. 저도 버스를 탈 거예요. 어떤 버스 기다리세요?
남: 52번. 거의 10분째 기다리고 있어. 아, 너 스마트폰 있니?
여: 네, 왜 물으세요?
남: 거기에 대중교통 검색 어플리케이션이 있다고 들었어. 내 버스가 언제 올지 알려줄 수 있니?
여: 물론이죠. 사실, 그 앱을 오늘 아침에 제 휴대폰에 설치했어요. 잠시만요. *[잠시 후]* 보세요. 여기, 52번 버스는 약 5분 뒤에 도착한대요.
남: 오, 그거 잘됐네. 고마워, Laura.
여: 천만에요. 오, 제 버스가 오네요. 내일 뵐게요, Brown 선생님.

어휘

public transportation 대중교통   **install** *v.* 설치하다

정답 ③

문제풀이

남자는 버스를 오래 기다려서 여자에게 대중교통 검색 어플리케이션을 이용해서 버스가 언제 오는지 봐달라고 부탁하고 있으므로 정답은 ③ '언제 그의 버스가 도착하는지 확인하기'이다.

오답 보기 해석

① 그를 어딘가로 데려다 주기
② 버스 요금 빌려주기
④ 버스 정류장 위치 알려주기
⑤ 어플리케이션 찾는 법 보여주기

총 어휘 수 123

08 이유

소재 조깅을 하지 않는 이유

듣기 대본 해석

여: 실례합니다. 우리 서로 아는 사이 아닌가요?
남: Cynthia! 저예요, Mason!
여: 오, 이런. 제가 너무 당황스럽네요. 잘 지내죠?
남: 나는 잘 지내요. 당신이 이사간 후로 우리가 이야기를 나누지 못한 것 같아요.
여: 맞는 것 같아요. 아직도 음악 연주를 해요? 당신은 드럼을 좋아했었잖아요.
남: 그래요, 여전히 연주하기를 좋아해요.
여: 조깅은 어때요? 당신이랑 조깅을 많이 했던 걸로 기억하는데.
남: 사실 오랫동안 조깅을 하지 않았어요.
여: 정말이요? 왜 안 했어요?
남: 제가 일 년 전쯤 음주 운전자한테 치였었어요. 저는 달릴 수가 없어요.
여: 끔찍하네요. 그 소식을 들으니 유감이에요. 그렇게 한 사람을 잡았길 바라요.
남: 네, 잡았어요. 사실 그는 멈춰서 경찰을 불러줬었어요. 어쨌든, 저는 가야 해요.
여: 네, 저도요. 연락하기로 해요!
남: 물론이죠.

어휘

embarrassed *a.* 쑥스러운, 당황스러운   **move away** 이사하다

정답 ①

문제풀이

남자는 일 년 전쯤에 교통사고를 당해서 그 뒤로 달릴 수가 없기 때문에 조깅을 하지 않는다고 말하고 있으므로 정답은 ① '교통사고 부상 때문에'이다.

총 어휘 수 139

09 숫자

소재 채소 구입

듣기 대본 해석

남: 안녕하세요, Smith씨.

여: 안녕하세요, Baron씨. 오늘은 모든 야채가 정말로 신선해 보이네요.

남: 네, 특히 양파와 당근을 추천해 드리고 싶습니다. 그것들은 막 도착했거든요.

여: 정말로 신선해 보이는군요. 얼마죠?

남: 양파는 한 개에 2달러이고 당근은 킬로그램 단위로 팔립니다. 당근 1킬로그램은 6달러입니다.

여: 그러면 당근 1킬로그램과 양파 2개 주세요.

남: 알겠습니다. 다른 것도 사실 건가요?

여: 네, 수프를 좀 만들기 위해 호박이랑 감자를 약간 사야 해요.

남: 호박 하나에 5달러이고 감자 1킬로그램은 4달러입니다.

여: 호박 2개와 감자 1킬로그램이면 충분합니다. 배달이 되나요?

남: 그럼요, 물론이지요. 사람을 시켜 약 2시간 내로 가져다 드리도록 하겠습니다.

여: 좋습니다. 여기 제 신용카드 받으세요.

어휘

fresh *a.* 신선한　　**carrot** *n.* 당근　　**by the kilogram** 킬로그램 단위로　　**deliver** *v.* 배달하다

정답 ④

문제풀이

여자는 당근 1킬로그램(6달러), 양파 2개(4달러), 호박 2개(10달러)와 감자 1킬로그램(4달러)을 사기로 했으므로 지불해야 할 총 금액은 ④ '$24'이다.

총 어휘 수 128

10 언급 유무

소재 잘못 배송된 책

듣기 대본 해석

[전화벨이 울린다.]

남: Shine On Top 서점입니다. 무엇을 도와드릴까요?

여: 제가 온라인에서 2권의 책을 주문했고 오늘 아침에 받았는데요, 한 권의 책에 실수가 있네요.

남: 알겠습니다. 이름 좀 알려주시겠어요?

여: 네, 제 이름은 Rebecca Jackson입니다.

남: 구매내역을 확인해볼게요. *[키보드 치는 소리]* 수필 모음집 한 권과 과학 교과서 한 권을 주문하셨네요, 맞나요?

여: 네, 문제는 제가 받은 수필집이 제가 주문한 것이 아니라는 겁니다.

남: 아, 죄송합니다. 받은 책 제목이 뭐죠?

여: A Big Dream이에요. 제가 주문한 건 John Thomas의 Just a Dream이고요.

남: 실수에 대해 사과드립니다. 지금 바로 제대로 된 책을 보내겠습니다.

여: 제가 지금 가지고 있는 책은 어떻게 해야 하죠?

남: 우편으로 돌려 보내 주시겠어요? 우편요금은 저희가 낼게요.

여: 알겠습니다. 내일 보낼게요.

어휘

apologize *v.* 사과하다　　**postage** *n.* 우편요금

정답 ③

문제풀이

여자가 책을 주문했는데 한 권이 잘못 배송되어 서점에 전화한 상황이다. 여자가 주문했던 책의 권 수, 여자가 주문했던 책의 종류, 잘못 배송된 책의 처리 방법, 운송료 지급에 관한 언급은 있었지만, 잘못 배송된 책의 작가에 대한 언급은 없었으므로 정답은 ③ '잘못 배송된 책의 작가'이다.

총 어휘 수 145

11 내용 일치 · 불일치

소재 가족 초대 행사

듣기 대본 해석

여: 여러분 안녕하세요. 저는 이곳 Maple's Academy의 아트 디렉터 Lilly Stevens입니다. 오늘 우리 학교의 특별한 학교공개 행사에 대해서 안내하고자 합니다. 이 이벤트는 학생 여러분이 가족들을 학교로 모셔와서 이번 학기 동안 여러분이 만든 작품들을 감상할 수 있게 합니다. 그리고 부모님뿐만 아니라 할아버지, 할머니, 형제자매, 그리고 다른 친척들도 모시고 와도 됩니다. 그리고 조각, 홀치기 염색과 같이 여러분이 여러분의 친척들과 함께 참여할 수 있는 여러 가지 행사들이 열릴 것입니다. 학교 공개 행사는 활동 센터에서 3월 26일, 수요일 오후 5시부터 9시까지 진행될 예정입니다. 공간에 100명만 들어갈 수 있기 때문에 인터넷으로 신청을 해주시기 바랍니다. 더 많은 정보를 보려면 우리 사이트를 방문 해 주세요.

어휘

announce *v.* 발표하다, 알리다　　**open house** (학교 · 기숙사 등의) 공개일　　**artwork** *n.* 미술품　　**sibling** *n.* 형제자매　　**relative** *n.* 친척 *a.* 연관 있는　　**sculpt** *v.* 조각하다　　**tie-dye** *v.* 홀치기 염색을 하다　　**accommodate** *v.* 공간을 제공하다, 수용하다

정답 ⑤

문제풀이

100명만 수용할 수 있기 때문에 온라인상에서 등록해야 한다고 말했으므로 일치하지 않는 것은 ⑤ '선착순으로 입장한다.'이다.

총 어휘 수 126

12 도표

소재 배 타기와 스노클링 관광 스케줄 선택

듣기 대본 해석

여: 여보, 뭐 보고 있어?

남: 배 타기랑 스노클링 관광 스케줄이야. 집에 가기 전에 스노클링 좀 하면 좋을 것 같아.

여: 좋은 생각이야. 그 관광 가자, 애들한테 좋은 경험이 될 거야. 일곱 시간 프로그램은 어때?

남: 일곱 시간은 애들이랑 배에 타있기에는 너무 길어. 지겨워하거나 그대로 있기 힘들어하지 않을까?

여: 그럴 것 같아. 그럼 좀 더 짧은 것으로 하자.

남: 응. 점심을 제공해 주는 프로그램이 좋을까?

여: 별로 필요하진 않을 것 같은데. 여행 올 때 음식 많이 샀잖아. 내가 샌드위치 몇 개 만들게.

남: 알겠어. 우리가 따로 사고 싶지 않으면, 당연히 물안경 필요할 거야. 오리발은 어떡하지? 필요할까?

여: 당연하지. 스노클링은 오리발이 있으면 훨씬 재미있어.

남: 그래. 그럼 우릴 위한 안성맞춤의 관광 프로그램을 찾은 것 같아.

어휘

snorkeling *n.* 스노클링　　**necessary** *a.* 필요한　　**goggles** *n.* 고글, 물안경　　**fin** *n.* 오리발

정답 ②

문제풀이

7시간은 너무 길다고 했고, 점심은 제공해 주지 않는 것으로 하자고 했으므로 ①, ③, ⑤번은 제외된다. ②, ④번 중에 물안경과 오리발은 필요하다고 했으므로 두 사람이 선택한 것은 ②번이다.

총 어휘 수 163

13 긴 대화의 응답

소재 아이스하키 경기 후 마중 약속

듣기 대본 해석

여: 너 오늘 Devils와 Rangers의 아이스하키 경기 볼 계획이니?
남: 물론이죠! 나는 이 경기가 정말 신이 나요.
여: 표는 샀어?
남: 물론이죠.
여: 경기가 몇 시에 끝나지?
남: 보통 저녁 9시 30분에서 10시 사이에 끝나요.
여: 아, 그래? 경기가 그렇게 늦게 끝나는 줄 몰랐네. 내가 차로 너를 데리러 갈게.
남: 그거 좋겠네요, 엄마. 우리 어디서 만나야 되죠?
여: 내가 경기장에 도착하면 너한테 전화할게.
남: 네, 좋아요. 반드시 휴대폰을 가지고 있도록 할게요.
여: 너 휴대폰 벨소리 들을 수 있겠니? 경기장은 매우 시끄럽잖니.
남: 전화가 오면 느낄 수 있도록 휴대폰을 진동 모드로 해 놓고 제 앞 주머니에 넣어둘게요.
여: ② 그래, 좋아. 그러면 내 전화를 놓치지 않겠구나.

어휘

stadium *n.* 경기장　　**on vibrate** 진동으로

정답 ②

문제풀이

엄마는 아이스하키 경기가 끝날 때쯤 아들을 데리러 갈 예정인데, 엄마가 아들한테 전화했을 때 경기장이 시끄러워서 벨소리를 들을 수 있냐고 묻자 아들은 휴대폰을 진동으로 바꾸고 앞주머니에 넣겠다고 한다. 이에 대한 가장 적절한 엄마의 응답은 ② '그래, 좋아. 그러면 내 전화를 놓치지 않겠구나.'이다.

오답 보기 해석

① 통화할 때 항상 예의 바르게 행동해야 해.
③ 네가 집에 올 때 지하철을 타는 것이 좋겠어.
④ 휴대폰으로 통화할 때 꼭 부드럽게 말하도록 하렴.
⑤ 휴대폰을 꺼두어야 해.

총 어휘 수 138

14 긴 대화의 응답

소재 자녀의 취업에 관한 걱정

듣기 대본 해석

여: 여보, 친구들과 어땠어요?
남: 아주 좋았어요. 맛있는 점심을 먹고 공원에 갔어요.
여: 아주 즐거웠던 것 같네요.
남: 정말 그랬어요. 우리 모두 정말 좋은 시간 보냈고, 계속 좋은 시간을 보내고 싶어서 내가 친구들을 커피 마시러 초대했어요.
여: 훌륭한 생각이에요.
남: 오, Lauren이 내게 그녀의 딸이 Phoenix에 일자리를 얻었다고 하더군요.
여: 잘됐네요. 그녀가 부러워요? Alyssa가 일자리를 구하는 것에 대해 정말 걱정했었잖아요.
남: 아마 조금이요. 그렇지만 우리 Alyssa도 곧 일자리를 찾을 거라고 생각해요.
여: 당신 전보다 덜 걱정하는 것 같네요.
남: 글쎄요, 내가 그것에 대해 할 수 있는 것이 없다고 깨달았어요.
여: 맞아요, 걱정해보았자 바뀌는 건 아무것도 없어요.
남: ⑤ 네, 걱정은 상황을 더 좋지 않게 만들 뿐이라는 걸 이제 알아요.

어휘

land a job 일자리를 얻다　　**envious** *a.* 부러워하는　　**concerned** *a.* 걱정하는　　**realization** *n.* 깨달음

정답 ⑤

문제풀이

여자는 걱정이 아무것도 해결해주지 않는다고 말하고 있고 남자도 이에 동조하는 맥락이므로 남자의 응답으로 가장 적절한 것은 ⑤ '네, 걱정은 상황을 더 좋지 않게 만들 뿐이라는 걸 이제 알아요.'이다.

오답 보기 해석

① 맞아요. 그녀가 괜찮은 직장을 찾을 방법은 없어요.
② 그래요. 난 늘 그녀의 딸이 좋은 직장을 갖기를 원했었죠.
③ 놀라워라! 난 파티에 그들을 초대하지 않았는데.
④ 걱정할 필요 없어요. Alyssa가 당신이 걱정한다는 것을 알았어요.

총 어휘 수 149

15 상황에 적절한 말

소재 어린아이의 믿음

듣기 대본 해석

여: Rachel과 그의 아버지는 십 분 동안 쇼핑몰 주차장을 차로 돌고 있습니다. 토요일이고 주차장은 거의 찼습니다. Rachel의 아버지는 눈에 띄게 답답해하고 있습니다. 그 때, Rachel은 인형을 꺼내고 인형한테 그들이 주차 공간 찾는 것을 도와달라고 말합니다. Rachel의 아버지는 그녀에게 무엇을 하고 있는지 물었습니다. 그녀는 그녀가 가장 좋아하는 만화에 나오는 인물 중 하나가 항상 말하기를 만약에 도움이 필요하면 친구한테 부탁해야 한다고 했다는 것을 이야기해줍니다. 그녀의 아버지는 이것은 만화에서 말하고 있는 도움의 종류가 아니라고 설명하려 하지만, Rachel은 주장합니다. 갑자기 그들은 그들 앞에 주차 공간이 나는 것을 봅니다. Rachel은 그녀의 아버지에게 무엇이라고 말할 것 같은가요?
Rachel: ④ 봐요, 나는 그녀가 우리를 도와줄 줄 알았어요!

어휘

visibly *ad.* 눈에 띄게, 분명히　　**frustrated** *a.* 불만스러워 하는, 답답해 하는　　**insist** *v.* 주장하다　　〈문제〉 **calm down** 진정하다

정답 ④

문제풀이

주차 공간이 없는 상황에서 Rachel은 만화에서 도움이 필요하면 친구한테 부탁해야 한다고 했다면서 가방에서 인형을 꺼내서 주차 공간 찾는 것을 도와달라고 말한다. 아버지는 그것은 도움이 안 되는 일이라고 설명해 주려 했지만 그 때 그들 앞에 주차 공간이 나타난다. 이 상황에서 Rachel이 할 수 있는 말은 ④ '봐요, 나는 그녀가 우리를 도와줄 줄 알았어요!'가 가장 적절하다.

오답 보기 해석

① 이 모든 것에 대해 죄송해요, 아빠.
② 진정해요, 아빠. 괜찮을 거예요.
③ 정말이요? 그녀에게 부탁하면 안 되나요?
⑤ 우리는 버스를 탔어야 했어요.

총 어휘 수 129

16 담화 목적 / 17 세부 내용 파악

소재 감시 카메라 남용의 문제점

듣기 대본 해석

남: 안녕하세요, 여러분. 저는 오늘 밤 폐쇄회로 또는 감시 카메라에 관해 간단히 이야기하는 시간을 가졌으면 합니다. 우리 나라에는, 어느 순간이든 3백만 대 이상의 감시 카메라가 작동하고 있습니다. 어떤 사람들은 이 카메라들이 범죄자들이 카메라 주변을 조심하기 때문에 범죄가 일어나는 것을 막아준다고 믿습니다. 그러나, 우리 대부분은 감시 카메라가 사생활을 침해할

수 있다고 느낍니다. 이러한 카메라들이 우리의 학교, 사무실, 상점, 그리고 우리 차에 이르기까지 모든 곳에 있습니다. 이 카메라들이 잠재적 범죄자들을 녹화할 수도 있는 반면에, 아무 죄가 없는 행인들도 녹화합니다. 사람들이 그들의 이웃이나 다른 사람들을 감시하기 위해 감시 카메라를 설치한다는 이야기도 있습니다. 이런 행동은 확실히 법에 어긋나지만, 거의 처벌받지 않습니다. 경찰들 또한 우리가 감시 카메라의 수를 줄이고 순찰 경찰관들의 수를 늘려야 한다는 것에 동의하는 것 같습니다. 우리는 사생활에 대한 우리의 권리를 보호하기 위해서 우리 도시에서 감시 카메라의 수를 줄이도록 같이 힘써야 합니다.

어휘

closed-circuit *n.* 폐쇄회로　**prevent A from -ing** A가 ～하는 것을 막다　**crime** *n.* 범죄　**commit** *v.* (일, 죄 등을) 저지르다　**criminal** *n.* 범죄자 *a.* 범죄의　**invade privacy** 사생활을 침해하다　**potential** *a.* 잠재적인, 가능성이 있는　**innocent** *a.* 아무 죄가 없는, 순진한　**passerby** *n.* 오가는 사람, 행인　**install** *v.* 설치하다　**punish** *v.* 처벌하다, 벌주다　〈문제〉**demonstrate** *v.* 입증하다, 보여주다

정답　16 ⑤　17 ③

문제풀이

16 남자는 감시 카메라가 사생활 침해의 소지가 있으니 그 수를 줄여야 한다고 말하고 있으므로 담화의 목적은 ⑤ '감시 카메라의 수를 줄일 것을 제안하기 위해서'이다.

17 남자가 감시 카메라가 설치된 곳으로 학교, 사무실, 상점, 자동차는 언급했지만 엘리베이터는 언급하지 않았다. 따라서 정답은 ③ '엘리베이터'이다.

오답 보기 해석

16

① 감시 카메라의 설치 방법을 알려주기 위해서
② 사람들이 감시 카메라를 구매하도록 설득하기 위해서
③ 감시 카메라가 어떻게 범죄를 막는지 설명하기 위해서
④ 감시 카메라의 효과를 입증하기 위해서

총 어휘 수 160

DICTATION ANSWERS

01 get it fixed

02 pay about twenty dollars

03 a nuisance to members of our community / gotten to the point where / On top of this disturbance / take the necessary action

04 we'd better start hiking back down / throw away all of this garbage / empty them / build up around it

05 do you have a minute / let you and the others down / having an effect on my performance / focus on your studies

06 The food booths are in front of / I'm afraid of heights / wait for me under the tree

07 taking a bus / public transportation application / will be arriving in / here comes my bus

08 I'm so embarrassed / remember jogging with you / I was hit by a drunk driver / keep in touch

09 look really fresh / How much are they / Anything else / have them delivered

10 ordered two books online / not the one I ordered / apologize for the error / pay for the postage

11 show off the artwork / grandparents, siblings, and other relatives / is scheduled to take place / register online

12 schedule of the boat and snorkeling tours / take a tour / they'll get bored or restless / more fun with fins

13 planning to watch the ice hockey game / pick you up / I'll give you a call / keep it on vibrate

14 had a great lunch / I invited them over for coffee / Are you feeling envious / came to the realization

15 is becoming visibly frustrated / asks her to make / All of a sudden

16-17 operating at any given moment / invade privacy / spy on their neighbors / reduce the number of surveillance cameras / protect our right to privacy

11

수능영어듣기
실전모의고사

본문 p.68

01 ⑤	02 ⑤	03 ④	04 ③	05 ①	06 ②
07 ①	08 ①	09 ②	10 ③	11 ③	12 ④
13 ④	14 ③	15 ⑤	16 ③	17 ②	

01 짧은 대화의 응답

소재 새 TV 구입

듣기 대본 해석
남: 자기, 이 새 TV 샀어?
여: 응. 우리가 선명한 화질의 더 좋은 것이 필요하다고 말했던 것 기억 안 나?
남: 기억 나. 그런데 왜 내게 알려주지도 않고 샀어?
여: ⑤ 난 당신이 새로운 TV 사는 걸 괜찮다고 말한 줄 알았어.

어휘
clear *a.* 선명한, 확실한 〈문제〉 **hang** *v.* 걸다 **regularly** *ad.*
정기적으로

정답 ⑤

문제풀이
왜 말해주지 않고 새 TV를 샀는지 묻는 남자의 말에 가장 적절한 대답은 ⑤ '난
당신이 새로운 TV 사는 걸 괜찮다고 말한 줄 알았어.'이다.

오답 보기 해석
① 아니, 이건 우리 집에는 너무 커.
② 그걸 사기 전에 네 조언이 필요했어.
③ 물론이지. 내가 그 TV를 벽에 걸게.
④ 당신은 거실을 주기적으로 청소해야 해.

총 어휘 수 46

02 짧은 대화의 응답

소재 친구의 생일파티

듣기 대본 해석
여: Robert, Helena의 17번째 생일이 얼마 남지 않았어.
남: 아. 깜박할 뻔 했어. 3월 23일이었지. 그녀를 위해 깜짝 파티를 해주는
   게 어때?
여: 좋은 생각이야. 그렇다면 그녀가 가장 좋아하는 음식인 사과파이를 내가
   준비할게.
남: ⑤ 좋아. 나는 음료를 가져올게.

어휘
just around the corner 임박하여 〈문제〉 **be proud of**
~을 자랑으로 여기다 **beverage** *n.* 음료

정답 ⑤

문제풀이
Helena의 생일 파티 준비에 관한 내용이다. 사과파이를 준비하겠다는 여자의
말에 적절한 응답은 ⑤ '좋아. 나는 음료를 가져올게.'이다.

오답 보기 해석
① 그녀는 틀림없이 네가 입상한 것이 자랑스러울 거야.
② 맞아, 그 빵집에서 맛있는 사과파이를 팔아.
③ 너의 생일에 특별한 케이크를 만들어줄게.
④ 나는 알코올 음료는 좋아하지 않아.

총 어휘 수 39

03 담화 목적

소재 연극 동아리 가입

듣기 대본 해석
여: 안녕하세요, 저는 언론학을 전공하는 3학년생인 Grace Stamos입니다.
   여러분이 신입생으로 입학한 지 3개월이 되었군요. 대학 생활을 즐기고
   계신가요? 모든 것이 여러분이 생각한 대로 되고 있습니까? 만약 여러분이
   더 많은 것을 하기를 찾으신다면, 연극 동아리에 가입하는 것을 생각해
   보십시오. 연극 동아리는 50년간 대학에서 큰 부분을 차지해 왔고 입학하는
   많은 신입생들이 참여했습니다. 여러분이 동아리에 들어오면 새 친구를
   사귀기가 쉽고, 여러분이 공연할 때 도시에 있는 모든 멋진 클럽과 극장에
   가게 될 것입니다. 여러분이 동아리를 매우 즐기게 될 것이라고 저는 확신
   합니다. 만약 여러분이 새로운 사람을 만나고 싶고 이곳에서 여러분의 시간을
   최대한으로 활용하고 싶다면 오늘 연극 동아리에 가입하세요!

어휘
involve *v.* 참여시키다, 관련시키다 **performance** *n.* 공연, 성과
positive *a.* 확신 있는, 적극적인

정답 ④

문제풀이
여자는 대학 생활에서 더 많은 것을 원한다면 연극 동아리에 가입할 것을
권유하면서, 동아리를 가입했을 때의 활동과 이점을 이야기하고 있으므로 정답은
④ '연극 동아리 가입을 권유하려고'이다.

총 어휘 수 132

04 대화 주제

소재 탄산수의 이점

듣기 대본 해석
남: 왜! 너무 덥다. 마실 것 좀 가져왔니, Katie?
여: 물론이지.
남: 고마워. [잠시 후] 잠깐만, 왜 소다를 가져왔어?
여: 그거 탄산수야.
남: 탄산수라고? 왜 일반 물이 아니지? 이건 맛이 좀 이상한데.
여: 음. 탄산수는 일반 물에서 얻을 수 없는 이점을 가지고 있어. 다이어트와
   소화불량에 정말 좋아.
남: 그렇구나. 왜 그렇지?
여: 그것은 식욕을 억제해. 그래서 다이어트에 좋지. 내가 탄산수를 마신 이후로,
   거의 4킬로그램이 빠졌어.
남: 믿을 수 없어.
여: 그것은 또한 이 지역 수돗물보다 훨씬 건강해. 여기 수돗물이 몇 달 동안
   적절하게 여과되지 않고 있었다는 걸 뉴스에서 봤어.
남: 알았어. 나도 탄산수 마시기를 시작해야겠네.

어휘
indigestion *n.* 소화불량 **suppress** *v.* 참다, 억누르다
appetite *n.* 식욕 **tap water** 수돗물 **filtered** *a.* 여과된

정답 ③

문제풀이
여자가 탄산수를 가져와서 남자는 왜 탄산수를 마시는지 묻고 여자는 탄산수의
좋은 점을 말해주고 있으므로 두 사람 대화의 주제는 ③ '탄산수가 건강에 좋은
이유'이다.

총 어휘 수 121

05 대화자의 관계 파악

소재 집 계약

듣기 대본 해석

[휴대폰이 울린다.]

남: 안녕하세요, Tanner 부인. 저는 Joseph Lancaster입니다.

여: Lancaster씨, 연락이 와서 기쁘네요. 집은 결정하셨어요?

남: 네. 저와 제 아내는 Main Street의 집으로 결정했어요.

여: 아, 세 개의 화장실과 두 개의 침실이 있는 집이요. 정말 훌륭한 집이지요. 나와 있는 것 중에 최고예요.

남: 네. 우리는 마당에 탁 트인 공간이 너무 좋아요.

여: 아이들을 키우기에 완벽해요. 뛰어 놀 공간이 많을 거예요.

남: 네, 맞아요. 마당에 작은 정원을 만들어도 괜찮은지도 궁금해요.

여: 정원을 만들면 좋을 거라고 확신해요. 제가 집주인과 몇 년 동안 일해 왔어요.

남: 좋아요. 그럼 제가 언제 계약서를 볼 수 있어요?

여: 오늘 오후에 사무실에 들르실 수 있어요? 집주인도 여기로 올 거예요.

남: 물론이죠. 4시경에 갈게요.

어휘

property *n.* 부동산, 재산   **plenty of** 많은   **contract** *n.* 계약서

정답 ①

문제풀이

남자는 집을 구하고 있고, 여자는 집이 좋다고 말해주고 집주인이라는 말을 하는 것으로 보아 부동산 중개업자임을 알 수 있다. 따라서 정답은 ① '고객 — 부동산 중개업자'이다.

총 어휘 수 155

06 그림의 세부 내용 파악

소재 아빠가 만들어 주신 어린 시절의 놀이터

듣기 대본 해석

남: 여보 봐요, 내가 다락에서 이 오래된 사진을 발견했어요.

여: 어머나. 아주 오랫동안 이 사진을 못 봤는데, 저랑 제 남동생 Tim이 어렸을 때 아버지가 우리를 위해 만들어 주신 놀이터에요.

남: 그럼 이 작은 소녀는 당신이네요. 당신은 그네를 타고 있네요.

여: 맞아요. 저 귀엽지 않았나요?

남: 당신 손을 잡아주고 있는 사람이 당신 아버지고요. 그는 아주 젊어 보이네요!

여: 음, 맞아요. 우리 모두 그래요!

남: 모래에서 놀고 있는 아이가 Tim, 맞죠?

여: 네, 그는 항상 더러워지는 걸 좋아했어요.

남: 저 미끄럼틀은 너무 재미있어 보이네요.

여: 정말 재미있었어요. 모든 이웃 아이들이 와서 타고 싶어 했죠.

남: 그럼 이 사진은 언제 찍은 거죠?

여: 언제 같아요?

남: 모든 것들이 매우 푸르른 것을 보니 아마 여름일 것 같은데요.

여: 네, 그래요. 우리가 학교에 갈 필요가 없기 때문에 여름은 항상 최고였죠.

남: 정말 멋진 정글짐이에요. 당신은 너무 좋은 여름을 보낸 것 같아요.

여: 정말 그래요. 아버지 덕분에요.

어휘

attic *n.* 다락(방)   **awesome** *a.* 아주 좋은, 멋진

정답 ②

문제풀이

아버지가 여자의 손을 잡고 있다고 했는데 그림에서 아버지는 여자의 그네를 밀어주고 있으므로 ②번이 그림과 일치하지 않는다.

총 어휘 수 175

07 할 일

소재 새로운 드러머 찾기

듣기 대본 해석

여: 오, 시내에 있는 재즈 카페에서 연주할 재즈밴드 오디션 공고를 보고 있구나. 관심 있니?

남: 난 없어. 내 여동생이 참가하는 것에 관심 있어해. 재즈밴드에서 기타를 치거든.

여: 그녀의 밴드가 이 오디션에 참여한대?

남: 그러고 싶대. 문제는 지난주에 드러머가 팔이 부러졌어.

여: 오, 이런! 그럼 그는 아직 드럼을 칠 수 없겠네.

남: 응. 그래서 밴드 리더가 새로운 드러머를 가능한 빨리 찾으려고 노력 중이야.

여: 흠… 내가 그를 만나볼 수 있을까?

남: 왜? 너 드럼 칠 줄 아니?

여: 응, 조금 칠 수 있어. 그리고 오랫동안 밴드에 참여하고 싶기도 했고.

남: 잘됐다! 내 여동생에게 그의 휴대폰 번호를 물어봐서 너에게 곧 알려줄게.

여: 고마워. 내가 그들과 함께 연주할 만큼 잘 하면 좋겠다.

어휘

notice *n.* 공고문, 안내문, 공지사항 *v.* 알아채다   **participate** *v.* 참가하다

정답 ①

문제풀이

남자는 여자에게 밴드 리더의 휴대폰 번호를 여동생에게 물어보고 알려주겠다고 했으므로 정답은 ① '밴드 리더의 전화번호 알려주기'이다.

총 어휘 수 140

08 이유

소재 작아져서 입을 수 없게 된 청바지

듣기 대본 해석

남: Stacy, 네 청바지가 바닥에 있어. 좀 치워주겠니?

여: 잠깐 그냥 거기에 두면 안 될까요, Brian? 오늘 중에 자선단체에 갖다 줄 거예요.

남: 정말? 그런데 새 것 같은데.

여: 네, 기본적으로는 새 거예요. 몇 번밖에 안 입었어요.

남: 왜 주려고 하는데? 상발 실이 좋아 보이는데.

여: 알아요. 그리고 그 청바지 좋아해요. 그런데 입을 수 없어요.

남: 무슨 말이야? 왜 안 돼?

여: 저에게 너무 작아요.

남: 좋아. 그런데, 꽉 낀 청바지는 유행인데. 요즘 애들이 정말 꽉 끼는 청바지 입고 다니는 것 줄곧 봤거든.

여: 네, 그런데 게다가 너무 짧기까지 해요.

남: 아하.

여: 그 청바지 지난 여름에 샀는데 그 이후로 키가 거의 2인치 자랐어요.

남: 음, 곧 너에게 새 청바지를 사줘야겠구나.

어휘

charity *n.* 자선단체   **in style** 유행인

정답 ①

문제풀이

여자가 그 청바지를 좋아하지만 사이즈가 작아지고 길이도 짧아져서 못 입겠다고 말했으므로 정답은 ① '키가 커지면서 바지가 맞지 않게 되어서'이다.

총 어휘 수 139

09 숫자

소재 헤드폰 구입하기

듣기 대본 해석
남: 안녕하세요. 새로운 헤드폰을 사려고 해요.
여: 네. 생각해 보신 특별한 브랜드나 스타일이 있으세요?
남: 글쎄요. 통근할 때 착용할 거라서 편한 것이었으면 좋겠어요.
여: 알겠어요. 제 생각엔 이것을 매우 좋아하실 것 같네요.
남: 어떤 특징들이 있나요?
여: 요즘에 광장히 인기가 좋아요. 편안함을 위해서 조절 가능한 밴드가 있고요, 최적화된 소리를 위해 신기술을 사용했어요.
남: 좋아 보이네요. 얼마인가요?
여: 50달러에 팔리고 있지만 이번 주에 10퍼센트 할인이 돼요.
남: 좋네요! 그리고 웹사이트에서 10달러를 할인해주는 쿠폰을 찾았어요. 이 제품에 쿠폰을 사용할 수 있나요?
여: 물론이죠. 할인된 가격에 추가 10달러를 깎아 드릴게요.
남: 알겠어요. 현금으로 계산할게요.
여: 네. 문제없어요.

어휘
optimal *a.* 최적의　　**retail** *v.* (특정 가격에) 팔리다

정답 ②

문제풀이
원래는 50달러지만 10퍼센트 할인을 받을 수 있고, 거기에 10달러 추가 할인을 받을 수 있는 쿠폰을 사용할 수 있다. 그러므로 남자가 지불할 금액은 ② '$35'이다.

총 어휘 수 131

10 언급 유무

소재 컴퓨터 게임 토너먼트

듣기 대본 해석
여: 자기야. 내일 Albert를 컴퓨터 게임 대회에 데려가는 건 어때?
남: 좋은 생각이야! PC Playground Arena에서 개최된다고 포스터에서 봤어.
여: 거기 맞아! 매달 마지막 토요일에 대회를 개최한대.
남: 근데 Albert가 그 대회에 관심을 가질까? 일인칭 슈팅 게임을 즐기기에는 너무 어린 것 같아.
여: 난 그렇게 생각하지 않아. 분명히 좋아할 거야. 가자는 건 사실 걔 생각이었어.
남: 알겠어. 뭘 싸가야 할까?
여: 점심 싸가고 간식이랑 음료수, 그리고 우리가 응원할 수 있게 Ryan이랑 Jason 티셔츠를 가져가는 게 좋을 것 같아.
남: 오후 행사인 것치고는 꽤 많이 챙겨야 되네. 일찍 출발해야 할까?
여: 너무 일찍 출발하는 건 별로일 것 같아. 열두 시에 시작하니까 열한 시쯤 출발하자.
남: 그래, 열한 시까지 다 준비해 놓을게.

어휘
tournament *n.* 토너먼트　　**take place** 개최되다
first-person shooter 1인칭 슈팅 게임

정답 ③

문제풀이
두 사람은 장소(PC Playground Arena), 요일(토요일), 준비물(간식, 음료수, 티셔츠), 시작 시간(12시)은 언급하였으나 대상 연령에 대해서는 언급하지 않았으므로 정답은 ③ '대상 연령'이다.

총 어휘 수 146

11 내용 일치 · 불일치

소재 겨울 캠프 자원봉사자 모집

듣기 대본 해석
여: 주목해 주세요, 여러분. New Poets Society는 시와 예술에 관심 있는 새로운 학생들의 지원을 받고 있습니다. 겨울 방학 동안 시 캠프가 있을 예정인데 우리는 본 캠프에 자원봉사로 가능한 한 많은 학생들이 참여해 주었으면 합니다. 자원봉사 캠프 상담자들은 어린 학생들을 지켜봐 주시고 적절한 행동과 안전의 모델이 되어주실 책임이 있습니다. 겨울 캠프는 12월 23일에 그리고 1월 7일에 시작하며, 모든 수업은 Minneapolis에 있는 Walker Art Center에서 개최될 것입니다. 지원서는 8월 31일까지 제출되어야 합니다. 캠프 상담자들은 일주일에 3일, 최소 8시간 동안 일해야 합니다. 만약 겨울 캠프에 추가적인 정보를 원하시면 웹사이트 www.winterpoets.com을 방문해 주십시오.

어휘
volunteer *n.* 자원봉사자　　**participate** *v.* 참가(참여)하다
appropriate *a.* 적절한　　**submit** *v.* 제출하다　　**additional** *a.* 추가의

정답 ③

문제풀이
캠프의 모든 수업은 Walker Art Center에서 진행된다고 말하였으므로 내용과 일치하지 않는 것은 ③ '수업마다 다른 장소에서 캠프를 진행한다.'이다.

총 어휘 수 127

12 도표

소재 CCTV 고르기

듣기 대본 해석
여: 저기, Samuel, 당신 집에 CCTV 시스템 사지 않았어요?
남: 샀어요. 왜요?
여: 아, 남편이랑 제가 하나 사려고 다니고 있는데, 제가 그것들에 대해 정말 많이 몰라서요. 저 좀 도와줄 수 있어요?
남: 물론이죠. 그 책자 좀 볼게요. *[잠시 후]* 네. 당신은 먼저 비디오 해상도를 고려하고 싶을 거예요.
여: 음, 어떤 것을 추천해 주시겠어요?
남: 제 생각엔 해상도가 높을수록 더 좋아요.
여: 좋아요. 높은 해상도로 할게요.
남: 어두운 데서 볼 수 있는 적외선이 필요할 거라고 생각해요?
여: 적외선이 달린 것은 훨씬 비싸네요. 그게 필요할 거라고 생각하지 않아요.
남: 좋아요. 다음으로 고려할 것은 저장 용량이에요.
여: 어, 제가 너무 많은 용량이 필요할 거라고 생각하진 않아요. 당신은 어떻게 생각해요?
남: 제 것도 많은 공간을 사용하지 않고 있어요. 32기가면 충분할 거라고 생각해요.
여: 좋아요. 이 제품이 저한테 좋을 것 같아요.

어휘
resolution *n.* 해상도, 해결　　**recommend** *v.* 추천하다　　**go with** ~로 하다　　**infrared** *a.* 적외선의　　**storage capacity** 저장 용량

정답 ④

문제풀이
해상도가 높고, 적외선이 포함되지 않은 것, 용량은 32기가라고 했으므로 정답은 ④번임을 알 수 있다.

총 어휘 수 149

13 긴 대화의 응답

소재 집에서 공룡영화를 보는 부녀의 대화

듣기 대본 해석

남: Debra, 영화 어떻게 생각해?
여: 좋았어요, 아빠! 다시 한 번 봐요.
남: 네가 좋아할 줄 알았다. 하지만 간식을 먹고 다른 것 보자.
여: 다른 건 보고 싶지 않아요. Before Time 다시 봐요!
남: 방금 봤잖니. 이제 다른 것을 넣자. 진심이야. Teddy Rex 어때? 좋은 영화라고 들었는데.
여: 알겠어요. 하지만 Before Time만큼 좋아야 할 거예요!
남: 훨씬 더 재미있을 거야. 네가 마음 바뀌기 전에 빨리 트는 게 좋겠다.
여: 안 바꿀 거예요. 이제 Teddy Rex 틀어줘요, 아빠.
남: 좀 놀랍구나 Debra. 우리가 Before Time을 보기 시작하기 직전에 공룡들이 무섭다고 말했잖아.
여: ④ 그러게요, 하지만 그것들이 그렇게 흥미로운지 몰랐어요.

어휘

snack *n.* 간식　　dinosaur *n.* 공룡

정답 ④

문제풀이

남자는 여자가 영화 'Before Time'을 보기 전에는 공룡들이 무섭다고 하고서는 본 후에는 그것을 한 번 더 보자고 한 것에 놀라고 있다. 이에 대한 여자의 응답으로 가장 적절한 것은 ④ '그러게요, 하지만 그것들이 그렇게 흥미로운지 몰랐어요.'이다.

오답 보기 해석

① 놀랍지 않아요. 당신이 그 영화 좋아할 줄 알았어요.
② 난 왜 사람들이 공룡영화를 좋아하는지 모르겠어요.
③ 우리 쉬면서 간식을 좀 먹는 게 좋을 것 같아요.
⑤ 공룡영화를 한 편 더 보면 당신은 겁에 질릴 거예요.

총 어휘 수 127

14 긴 대화의 응답

소재 전공 선택

듣기 대본 해석

남: Lynn, 너 대학 전공 벌써 정했어?
여: 정했어. 난 최근에 온라인 저널리즘으로 결정했어. 너는 어때?
남: 나는 아직 결정 못 했어.
여: 나는 네가 회계학을 전공할 거라고 생각했는데. 너는 숫자와 돈 관리에 재주가 있잖아.
남: 맞아. 하지만 내가 숫자를 가지고 하는 일을 하고 싶은지 잘 모르겠어. 나는 예술이랑 예술 역사에도 관심이 있거든.
여: 그래서 무엇을 전공할지 확신하지 못하고 있구나?
남: 그래, 내가 무엇을 해야 할지 모르겠어.
여: 음, 너 상담 센터에 있는 Marshall 선생님을 찾아가 봤어?
남: 내가 왜 그녀를 찾아가야 해? 나는 어떤 행동적 문제가 없는데.
여: Marshall 선생님은 네가 무엇을 제일 잘하는지 볼 수 있는 적성검사를 해주실 수 있어. 내 생각엔 그것이 네가 결정하는 데 도움을 줄 것 같아.
남: ③ 정말? 당장 도움을 받으러 가야겠어.

어휘

major in ~을 전공하다　　figure *v.* (~이라고) 생각하다, 중요하다
accounting *n.* 회계　　knack *n.* 재주, 요령　　counseling *n.* 상담
behavioral *a.* 행동의, 행동에 관한　　aptitude *n.* 적성
make a decision 결정하다

정답 ③

문제풀이

자신의 전공을 정하지 못하고 있는 남자에게 여자는 학교 상담 센터의 Marshall 선생님을 찾아가면 적성검사를 해주신다고 말하며 그것이 도움이 될 거라고 했다. 거기에 대한 남자의 적절한 대답은 ③ '정말? 당장 도움을 받으러 가야겠어.'이다.

오답 보기 해석

① 나는 네가 너의 꿈을 좇아야 한다고 생각해.
② 난 회계학을 전공해야 할 것 같아.
④ 너는 전공을 곧 선택해야 해.
⑤ 예술에는 많은 직업들이 없어.

총 어휘 수 133

15 상황에 적절한 말

소재 인터넷으로 구매한 야구 카드

듣기 대본 해석

남: Morty는 물건들을 모으는 것을 좋아합니다. 야구 카드는 그가 모으기 가장 좋아하는 물건입니다. 몇 주전, Morty는 인터넷에서 개봉하지 않은 야구 카드 20팩을 20달러에 판다는 항목별 광고를 봤습니다. 그는 구매하기로 하고 즉시 카드 판매자에게 돈을 보냈습니다. 일주일 동안 기다리고 매일 우편함을 확인하지만 카드는 오지 않았습니다. 그는 일주일을 더 기다리기로 결심했지만 카드는 여전히 오지 않았습니다. 그는 더 이상 기다리지 못하고 오늘 카드 판매자에게 전화하기로 합니다. 신호가 세 번 가자 판매자는 전화를 받습니다. 이러한 상황에서 Morty가 카드 판매자에게 뭐라고 말할까요?
Morty: ⑤ 아직 카드를 못 받았습니다. 혹시 보내셨나요?

어휘

collect *v.* 수집하다　　classified ad (신문의) 안내광고, 항목별 광고란
transfer *v.* 보내다, 이체하다　　dealer *n.* 판매자, 밀매인　　impatient
a. 짜증난, 어서 ~하고 싶어 하는

정답 ⑤

문제풀이

인터넷으로 야구 카드를 구매했는데 이주일이 지나도 오지 않자 판매자에게 전화를 건 상황이다. 따라서 Morty가 할 말은 ⑤ '아직 카드를 못 받았습니다. 혹시 보내셨나요?'가 적절하다

오답 보기 해석

① 환불금을 저한테 벌써 보내셨나요?
② 카드 한 세트 더 구매할 수 있을까요?
③ 당신의 야구 카드 모음집은 얼마나 큰가요?
④ 당신이 다른 카드 판매자들을 알고 있나 궁금합니다.

총 어휘 수 124

16 담화 주제 / 17 세부 내용 파악

소재 여러 일들을 하기 위해 이용되는 동물들

듣기 대본 해석

남: 안녕하세요 여러분. 우리의 마지막 수업에서 동물들이 어떻게 오락을 위해서 학대되고 이용되는지 서커스에서의 코끼리와 곰을 예로 들어가며 이야기했습니다. 오늘 수업에서는 사람들이 교통수단 외의 여러 일들을 하기 위해 어떻게 동물들을 이용하는지에 대해서 이야기를 해 보겠습니다. 여러분은 쇼핑몰이나 거리를 걸을 때 첫 번째 동물을 보셨을 겁니다. 이것은 맹도견이며 맹인들이 일상생활을 하는 것을 도와줍니다. 맹도견은 보통 골든리트리버이며 주인이 길을 걷고 장애물을 피하는 것을 도와줍니다.

이런 개들은 동반자가 되어 주기도 하며 일반적으로 돌보는 일을 잘 하는 동물입니다. 다음으로 이야기할 동물은 송로돼지입니다. 북아메리카와 유럽 사람들은 돼지를 이용해서 송로라고 불리는 맛있고 비싼 버섯을 찾아냅니다. 돼지들은 땅 밑에 있는 음식을 찾는 것에 대한 본능적인 친화성이 있어서 이 임무에 완벽합니다.

어휘

mistreat *v.* 학대하다   **avoid** *v.* 피하다. 막다   **obstacle** *n.* 장애물
companionship *n.* 우정   **affinity** *n.* 친밀감. (~에 대한) 기호

정답 16 ③ 17 ②

문제풀이

16 남자는 이번 수업에서 사람들이 여러 일들을 하기 위해 어떻게 동물을 이용하는지에 대해 이야기하자면서 맹도견과 송로돼지의 예를 들었으므로 정답은 ③ '동물들이 사람을 돕는 방법'이다.

17 남자는 학대 받는 동물로 코끼리와 곰을 언급했고, 사람을 도와주는 동물의 예로 맹도견과 송로돼지를 언급했지만 사슴에 관한 언급은 없으므로 정답은 ② '사슴'이다.

오답 보기 해석

16

① 학대 받는 동물들을 구조하는 방법
② 멸종위기에 처한 동물들을 구하기 위한 노력
④ 오락에서 동물들의 역할
⑤ 도움을 위해 동물들을 사용하는 것의 부정적 영향들

17

① 코끼리
③ 곰
④ 개
⑤ 돼지

총 어휘 수 170

DICTATION ANSWERS

01 without letting me know

02 just around the corner

03 as you thought it would be / joining the Drama Club / get involved / once you join the club / get the most out of your time

04 tastes a bit strange / good for dieting and indigestion / it hasn't been properly filtered / drinking sparkling water

05 one of the best on the market / plenty of room to play / take a look at the contract

06 playing on the swing / must be your father / loved to come over and play / What a great jungle gym

07 participate in the audition / as soon as possible / join a band / let you know

08 giving them to charity / What do you mean / tight jeans were in style / I have grown

09 during my commute / an adjustable band / use it on this item / pay for it in cash

10 computer game tournament / it's taking place / He seems a bit young to enjoy / What should we pack for the event / I'll have everything ready by

11 participate in these camps / all classes will be held / Applications should be submitted

12 consider the video resolution / the higher the resolution, the better / need infrared to see in the dark

13 What did you think of / get a snack / as good as / before you change your mind

14 I figured you'd major in / have a knack for / have you gone to / what you're best at

15 came across a classified ad / wait another week / He grew impatient

16-17 perform tasks other than transportation / helps blind people / avoid obstacles / search for delicious and expensive fungi / buried up to three feet underground

01 ⑤	02 ⑤	03 ⑤	04 ③	05 ④	06 ③
07 ④	08 ①	09 ④	10 ⑤	11 ④	12 ①
13 ②	14 ①	15 ⑤	16 ①	17 ①	

01 짧은 대화의 응답

소재 면접 일정

듣기 대본 해석

여: 안녕하세요. 제가 지원서를 다 작성했는데요. 제가 해야 할 다른 것이 있나요?
남: 아니요, 됐어요. 가셔도 됩니다.
여: 알겠어요. 면접 일정을 잡기 위해 언제 저에게 전화하실 거예요?
남: ⑤ 우리는 지금 당장은 바빠서 다음 주에 당신에게 연락할 거예요.

어휘

fill out 작성하다　　**application** *n.* 지원(서)

정답 ⑤

문제풀이

면접 일정을 위해서 언제 전화를 줄 건지를 물었으므로 적절한 응답은 ⑤ '우리는 지금 당장은 바빠서 다음 주에 당신에게 전화할 거예요.'이다.

오답 보기 해석

① 당신은 건강 검진을 받아야 해요.
② 당신은 우선 지원서를 작성해야 해요.
③ 당연하죠. 면접관이 이제 당신을 만날 거예요.
④ 우리는 당신을 위해 어제 약속을 잡았어요.

총 어휘 수 44

02 짧은 대화의 응답

소재 전시회 티켓

듣기 대본 해석

님: Rosa, 널 위해 특별한 것을 준비했어. 뭔지 궁금하지?
여: 오, 그래 제발. 어서 말해줘.
남: 내가 Van Gogh 전시회 티켓 두 장을 예매했어!
여: ⑤ 믿을 수 없어! 내가 그의 작품을 좋아하는 것을 어떻게 알았어?

어휘

exhibition *n.* 전시회

정답 ⑤

문제풀이

Rosa를 위해 Van Gogh의 전시회 티켓 두 장을 예매했다는 남자의 말에 적절한 응답은 ⑤ '믿을 수 없어! 내가 그의 작품을 좋아하는 것을 어떻게 알았어?'이다.

오답 보기 해석

① 네 말이 맞아. 너무 비싸.
② 선물이 뭔지 알고 싶어.
③ 네 말이 맞아. 반 고흐는 최고의 예술가야.
④ 티켓이 고작 10달러라고? 정말 싸다.

총 어휘 수 43

03 담화 목적

소재 스포츠 음료 홍보

듣기 대본 해석

여: 안녕하세요, 선수 여러분. 여러분이 모두 알다시피 경기 중에 에너지 수준을 높게 유지하는 것은 쉽지 않습니다. 스포츠를 하는 것은 자연적으로 에너지를 소진시킵니다(체력을 저하시킵니다). 경쟁에서의 우위를 유지하는 것을 도와줄 방법이 있습니다. Rad CraCra를 마시세요. Rad CraCra는 당신이 경기를 계속하게 해줍니다. 비타민과 미네랄의 특수한 배합은 높은 수준의 에너지를 유지하도록 도와줍니다. 저렴하기도 합니다. Rad CraCra 한 캔이 약 1달러 정도 하는데 이것만으로도 경기 내내 활기차게 뛸 수 있습니다. 고품질 제품이지만 다른 스포츠 음료의 반값입니다. 더 비싼 다른 제품들보다 효과도 오랫동안 지속됩니다. 그러므로 더 많은 힘이 필요할 때는 Rad CraCra를 찾아주세요.

어휘

drain *v.* 빠지다, (체력이) 쇠진하다　　**competitive edge** 경쟁 우위, 경쟁력

정답 ⑤

문제풀이

여자는 스포츠 음료 Rad CraCra가 운동 경기 중 체력 저하를 막고, 몸에 좋은 성분을 포함하고 있으며 가격도 저렴하다고 말하면서 그것을 홍보하고 있으므로 정답은 ⑤ '스포츠 음료를 홍보하려고'이다.

총 어휘 수 121

04 대화 주제

소재 시험으로 인한 긴장감 해소법

듣기 대본 해석

여: Joe, 무슨 일 있니? 표정이 안 좋아.
남: 엄마, 영어 시험 때문에 긴장돼요.
여: 진정해! 일주일 내내 공부했으니까 분명 잘 할 거야.
남: 그냥 너무 걱정돼요. 어떤 것에도 집중을 못하겠어요.
여: 요가를 좀 해보거나 친구와 이야기를 나눠봤니?
남: 선화로 Molly랑 이야기했는데, 별로 도움이 되지 않았어요. 엄마는 스트레스 받을 때 어떻게 진정해요?
여: 신정해야 할 때 엄마는 보통 조깅을 해.
남: 도움이 될까요? 조깅을 하면 피곤해질 것 같아요.
여: 운동은 뇌에 엔돌핀을 분비시켜서 머리를 맑게 해줘. 분명 네 기분도 나아지게 할 거야.
남: 그래요? 그럼 호수 전체를 한 바퀴 돌고 와야겠어요. 도와주셔서 감사해요, 엄마.

어휘

concentrate *v.* 집중하다　　**release** *v.* 분비하다, 방출하다　　**entire** *a.* 전체의

정답 ③

문제풀이

시험 때문에 긴장된다는 아들에게 엄마는 요가를 하거나 친구와의 수다를 제안하기도 하고, 조깅을 해서 기분을 전환할 것을 권하고 있으므로 이 대화의 주제는 ③ '시험으로 인한 긴장을 완화하는 방법'이다.

총 어휘 수 133

05 대화자의 관계 파악

소재 헌혈하기

듣기 대본 해석

여: 안녕하세요. 헌혈하러 오셨나요?
남: 네. 그런데 좀 긴장되네요. 헌혈은 처음이거든요.
여: 잘 오셨어요. 처음에 하셔야 하는 것은 이 양식을 작성하시는 겁니다.
남: 네. [잠시 후] 끝났어요. 다음에는 뭘 하죠?
여: 이제 혈액형을 확인하기 위해서 손가락을 찔러야 해요.
남: 네. 그런데 전 바늘이 좀 무서워요.
여: 약간만 아플 거예요. [잠시 후] 좋습니다. 현재 복용하고 있는 약이 있나요?
남: 음. 며칠 전에 알레르기 약을 좀 먹었어요. 괜찮을까요?
여: 문제가 될 것 같지는 않네요. 여기 앉으셔서 소매를 걷어 주세요.
남: 모임에 좀 늦을 것 같은데요. 오래 걸리진 않겠죠?
여: 헌혈하는 데 보통 20분 정도 걸립니다. 헌혈해 주셔서 정말 감사합니다.

어휘

donate v. 헌혈하다. 기부하다   **prick v.** 찌르다   **blood type** 혈액형
be afraid of ~을 두려워하다   **medication n.** 약   **donation n.**
기부. 기증

정답 ④

문제풀이

남자는 헌혈하러 처음 온 사람이고, 여자는 안내를 하며 헌혈을 도와주는
상황이므로 두 사람의 관계는 ④ '간호사 — 헌혈자'로 생각할 수 있다.

총 어휘 수 140

06 그림의 세부 내용 파악

소재 어릴 때 눈사람과 놀던 사진

듣기 대본 해석

남: 여보, 내 어린 시절 사진 좀 봐요.
여: 당신 그 때 정말 귀여웠네요. 야구 유니폼 입은 당신 좀 봐요.
남: 네. 전 야구를 정말 좋아했거든요. 겨울에도 유니폼을 입었는걸요. 저게 내
　　처음 글러브에요.
여: 정말이요? 왼손에는 눈 뭉치를 들고 있네요. 어렸을 때는 왼손잡이였어요?
남: 네. 어릴 땐 양손잡이였어요. 어떤 손을 써야 할지 모르겠더라고요.
여: 당신이 만든 눈사람 맘에 드는데요. 당신의 모자를 준 것 같은데요.
남: 맞아요. 내 Ravens 야구모자를 쓰고 있어요. 난 Lions 모자를 쓰고 있어요.
여: 그럼 당신은 투수고 눈사람은 타자네요? 눈사람이 당신의 배트를 가지고
　　있어요.
남: 네. 어릴 때 친구가 별로 없어서 겨울에는 스스로 만들곤 했어요.
여: 정말 사랑스럽네요, 여보.

어휘

childhood n. 어린 시절   **ambidextrous a.** 양손잡이의
adorable a. 사랑스러운, 귀여운

정답 ③

문제풀이

여자가 남자의 왼손에 눈 뭉치를 들고 있다고 말했는데 그림에서는 야구공을
들고 있으므로 정답은 ③번이다.

총 어휘 수 138

07 할 일

소재 인쇄물 출력

듣기 대본 해석

여: Bill. 수정 테이프 가지고 있나요?
남: 네. 수정 테이프가 왜 필요해요?
여: 오늘 제휴사 회의를 위한 인쇄물에 잘못된 게 있어요. 그걸 고쳐야 해요.
남: 제 생각에는 당신이 컴퓨터에서 잘못된 부분을 고치고 다시 프린트해야 할
　　것 같아요. 제휴사 회의는 중요해요.
여: 알아요. 하지만 우리 프린트가 작동하지 않고 회의는 30분 내에 있어요.
남: 네. 알아요. 당신은 인력관리부서로 내려가서 거기 프린터를 사용해야 할
　　거예요.
여: 그렇지만 저는 컬러 복사가 필요해요. 거기 프린터는 흑백만 돼요.
남: 그렇지 않으면 당신은 우리 것을 수리해줄 누군가가 올 때까지 기다려야
　　할 거예요.
여: 저는 그렇게 오래 기다릴 수 없어요. 길에 있는 인터넷 카페에 컬러 프린터가
　　있을 것 같아요?
남: 저도 잘 모르지만 제가 거기 전화번호를 찾아볼 테니 당신이 전화를 걸어
　　볼 수 있어요.
여: 그거 좋네요, Bill. 도와줘서 고마워요.
남: 천만에요.

어휘

human resources department 인력관리부   **repair v.** 수리하다
look up 찾아보다

정답 ④

문제풀이

남자가 인터넷 카페에 컬러 프린터가 있을지는 모르지만 카페 전화번호를
찾아줄 테니 전화해보라고 했으므로 여자가 할 일은 ④ '인터넷 카페에 전화
하기'이다.

총 어휘 수 145

08 이유

소재 바쁜 대학 생활

듣기 대본 해석

남: 안녕, Sammie. 새 학교는 좀 어때?
여: 괜찮아. 시간표에 적응해 가고 있어.
남: 잘됐네. 아, Jeff 기억나? 주말에 같이 해변에 가기로 했어.
여: 좋네. 바르셀로나에서 학기 끝내고 돌아왔나 보네.
남: 맞아. 해변가로 가서 밀린 얘기도 하고 집으로 돌아온 거 축하해 줄 거야.
　　같이 가자.
여: 나도 그러고 싶은데 못 갈 것 같아. 과제가 엄청 많아.
남: 학교가 널 주말에도 바쁘게 하는 거야?
여: 가끔은. 이번 주말은 특히 더 바빠. 월요일까지 중요한 화학 리포트를
　　제출해야 되고 화요일에는 영어 시험이 있어.
남: 대학교 생활은 아주 힘든가 보다.
여: 맞아. 일주일 내내 너무 힘들었어.

어휘

beach n. 해변   **chemistry n.** 화학   **stressful a.** 스트레스가 많은,
힘든

정답 ①

문제풀이

남자는 오랜만에 집으로 돌아온 Jeff를 맞아주기 위해 주말에 해변에 같이
가자고 여자에게 제안하였으나 여자는 주말에 해야 할 과제가 많아서 갈 수
없다고 하였으므로 정답은 ① '과제를 해야 해서'이다.

총 어휘 수 129

09 숫자

소재 고속도로 개통으로 단축될 시간과 고속도로 이용 요금

듣기 대본 해석
여: 여보, 내일 Grove Beach에 가는 것이 어때요?
남: 여기에서 너무 멀지 않나요? 구불구불한 길로 산을 넘어가는 데 약 40분이 걸리잖아요.
여: 더 이상 그 길로 갈 필요가 없어요. 지난달에 개통된 새 고속도로로 가면 돼요.
남: 정말이요? 그러니까 우리가 그 구불구불하고 위험한 산길로 운전해 갈 필요가 없다는 말인가요?
여: 맞아요. 그 고속도로를 이용해서 거기에 도달하는 데 15분 정도밖에 걸리지 않아요.
남: 와, 굉장한데요.
여: 하지만 공짜가 아니에요. 사용료를 내야 해요.
남: 얼만데요?
여: 음, 정부의 원래 계획은 5달러를 부과하는 거였어요. 하지만 시민단체들이 정부에게 요금을 내려달라고 요청했어요.
남: 그래서 요금이 내렸나요?
여: 그래요. 정부는 결국 원래 계획했던 것 보다 2달러 적게 부과하게 되었어요.
남: 오, 그렇군요.

어휘
curvy *a.* 굽은   **fantastic** *a.* 멋진   **free** *a.* 무료의   **original** *a.* 원래의   **civil organization** 시민단체   **request** *v.* 요청하다
lower *v.* 낮추다

정답 ④

문제풀이
구불구불한 산길을 넘는 데 약 40분이 걸렸지만 고속도로를 이용하면 15분 정도밖에 걸리지 않으므로 약 25분이 단축될 것이고, 고속도로 요금은 원래 5달러였지만 시민단체의 요청으로 정부가 2달러 적게 청구하기로 하여 3달러가 되었으므로 정답은 ④ '약 25분 — $3'이다.

총 어휘 수 129

10 언급 유무

소재 캠핑 계획

듣기 대본 해석
남: 여보, 다음 주 토요일에 우리랑 캠핑 갈래요?
여: 모르겠어요. 거기에서 재미있을지 모르겠어요.
남: 재미있을 거예요. 호수가 정말 아름다워요. 내가 불 피우는 법과 텐트 치는 법을 알려줄게요.
여: 알았어요, 갈게요. 그런데 내가 지루해지지 않게 계속 참여시켜 줘야 해요.
남: 물론이죠, 여보. 우리가 가려는 곳은 아주 잘 알려져 있어요. 당신이 인터넷으로 찾아 볼 수도 있어요.
여: 거기까지 여기서 얼마나 걸려요?
남: 차로 3시간 30분 정도 걸리는데 가는 길의 경치가 너무 아름다워요.
여: 정말 기대가 되네요. 그런데 거기서 우리 뭘 먹을까요?
남: 물고기를 잡아 먹고 물론 핫도그나 햄버거 같은 다른 음식들도 먹을 거예요.
여: 알았어요. 짐 싸는 데 도울 일이 있나요?
남: 없어요! 내가 다 할 수 있어요. 당신은 그냥 친구가 되어주기만 하면 돼요.

어휘
build a fire 불을 피우다   **scenery** *n.* 경치   **pack** *v.* 짐을 싸다
company *n.* 친구

정답 ⑤

문제풀이
캠핑 가는 요일, 남자가 여자에게 알려줄 일, 캠핑 가는 데 걸리는 시간, 캠핑에서 먹을 음식은 언급되었지만 짐 싸야 할 항목에 대한 언급은 없으므로 정답은 ⑤ '짐을 싸야 할 항목'이다.

총 어휘 수 166

11 내용 일치 · 불일치

소재 Georgetown's Musical Mondays 행사

듣기 대본 해석
남: 여러분 안녕하세요. 여러분들도 아시다시피, 날씨가 따뜻해지고 있는데요, 이는 강가에서 Georgetown's Musical Mondays가 시작할 때라는 것을 의미합니다. 첫 번째 행사는 다음 주 월요일인 4월 22일 여섯 시에 개최될 예정입니다. 유명한 블루스 밴드인 Back Section Action이 Riverside Park에서 공연하러 올 예정이고요. 그 밴드의 리드보컬이 공연 후에 팬들과 만날 것입니다. 그 밴드는 6시에 무대에 오를 것이며 대략 8시에 끝날 예정입니다. 우리의 모든 행사와 마찬가지로, 이 공연도 모든 연령대를 위한 공연이므로 여러분의 친구와 가족 모두를 데리고 오세요. 모든 참석자는 5달러의 요금을 지불해야 하며, 수익금 전액은 Georgetown 예술문화협회에 전달될 예정입니다. 시간 내주셔서 감사합니다.

어휘
kick off 시작하다   **take place** 일어나다. 개최되다   **entire** *a.* 전체의
proceeds *n.* 수익금

정답 ④

문제풀이
이 공연은 모든 연령대를 위한 공연이라고 언급했으므로 내용과 일치하지 않는 것은 ④ '초등학생 이상의 어린이부터 입장할 수 있다.'이다.

총 어휘 수 127

12 도표

소재 자전거 강좌 선택

듣기 대본 해석
남: 여보, 우리가 Adam한테 보조바퀴 없이 자전거 타는 법을 가르치기 시작해야 할 것 같아요.
여: 좋은 생각이긴 한데 여기 주변에서 하는 건 안전하지 않다고 생각해요. 거리가 항상 너무 북적이잖아요.
남: 그게, Freedom Park에서 하는 자전거 수업에 관한 이 전단지를 봤어요. 이 강사들은 아이들이 처음 자전거 타는 것을 가르치는 걸 전문으로 하고 있어요.
여: 정말 좋네요.
남: 나도 그렇게 생각해요. 우리가 남자선생님을 고용해야 할까요, 아니면 여자선생님을 고용해야 할까요?
여: 제 생각엔 여자선생님을 선택해야 할 것 같아요. 그 애는 학교에 여자선생님들을 좋아하는 것 같아 보여요.
남: 좋아요. 이 수업은 듣지 못하겠네요. 월요일에는 야구 연습이 있어요.
여: 남은 두 수업 중에서 좀 더 경험이 많은 분으로 해야 될 것 같아요.
남: 나도 동의해요. 우리에게 맞는 강사를 찾은 것 같네요.

어휘
flyer *n.* (광고 · 안내용) 전단   **instructor** *n.* 강사

정답 ①

문제풀이

아들에게 알맞은 자전거 강좌를 찾고 있는 두 사람은 여자선생님을 원하고, 월요일은 야구 연습 때문에 안 된다고 했으며 경력이 더 많은 선생님을 원하고 있다. 따라서 모든 조건을 만족시키는 강좌는 ①번이다.

총 어휘 수 141

13 긴 대화의 응답

소재 교내 장기자랑 참가 결정

듣기 대본 해석

여: 그래서 Larry, 너 올해 장기자랑에 나갈 거야?
남: 확실하지 않아요.
여: 왜 확실하지 않아? 너 저글링 정말 잘하고 무척 열심히 연습해 왔잖아.
남: 내가 실수하고 모든 사람들이 나보고 웃을까 걱정이 되거든요.
여: 넌 자신감을 갖고 너 자신을 믿을 필요가 있어, Larry. 많은 사람들이 사람들 앞에서 공연할 때 무대 공포증을 갖는단다.
남: 도와주시려 해서 감사해요, 엄마.
여: 그래, 한번 해볼 거지?
남: 음... 아직 모르겠어요.
여: 시도해봐! 자신감을 보여줘! 두려워하는 것은 너답지 않아!
남: 작년에 무대에서의 큰 실수 후에, 저한테 자신감이 있는지 확신을 못하겠어요.
여: 안심해. 누구도 완벽하지 않고 모든 사람은 실수를 한단다.
남: 그럼, 엄마는 제가 올해 더 잘할 거라고 생각하세요?
여: ② 물론이지. 너는 열심히 연습해 왔잖니.

어휘

take part in ~에 참가하다   **talent show** 장기자랑
make a mistake 실수하다   **stage fright** 무대 공포증
give ~ a shot ~을 시도해 보다   **confidence** *n.* 자신감
disaster *n.* 완전한 실패, 재해   **relax** *v.* 휴식을 취하다, 안심하다

정답 ②

문제풀이

장기자랑에 나가기를 망설이는 아들에게 엄마가 용기를 주고 있는 상황이다. 작년에 했던 실수 이후로 자신감을 잃은 아들이 이번에 나가면 잘할 수 있을지 물을 때 엄마가 할 수 있는 응답은 ② '물론이지. 너는 열심히 연습해 왔잖니.'가 적절하다.

오답 보기 해석

① 너는 전에 무대 공포증이 있었던 적이 없었어.
③ 네가 없었더라면 난 그걸 할 수 없었을 거야.
④ 아니. 나는 너무 긴장돼서 공연을 할 수 없어.
⑤ 그래. 내가 한번 시도해 봐야겠어.

총 어휘 수 139

14 긴 대화의 응답

소재 독일에 살다 온 이유

듣기 대본 해석

여: Nicholas, 제가 일전에 시내에서 당신을 본 것 같아요. 당신은 아주 매력적인 여성분과 이야기하고 있었어요.
남: 아, 기억나요. Clarice Heisenberg와 이야기하고 있었어요. 그녀는 저희 가족사업을 위해 일하고 있어요. 그녀가 저희의 모든 해외 계좌들을 관리하고 있죠.
여: 제가 들으려는 의도는 아니었는데 당신이 다른 언어로 이야기하는 것을 알아챌 수 밖에 없었어요.
남: 네, Clarice는 독일에서 왔어요. 그녀가 영어로 말할 수 있긴 하지만 그녀는 독일어로 말하는 게 더 쉽고, 저는 연습하는 것을 좋아해요.

여: 나는 당신이 독일어를 하는지 몰랐어요.
남: 네, 저는 사실 독일에서 태어나서 어릴 때 십 년 동안 살았어요.
여: 정말요? 몰랐어요. 왜 독일에서 살았죠?
남: 저희 아버지의 사업이 거기에 근거지를 두고 있었어요.
여: 흥미롭네요. 언젠가 독일로 돌아갈 거예요?
남: ① 네. 저는 아이들이 조금 더 크면 돌아갈 거예요.

어휘

attractive *a.* 매력적인   **handle** *v.* 다루다, 관리하다   **overseas** *a.* 해외의 *ad.* 해외에서   **account** *n.* 계좌

정답 ①

문제풀이

남자는 어릴 때 독일에서 10년을 살았다고 말했고, 여자는 다시 돌아갈 것인지를 물었으므로 그에 적절한 남자의 대답은 ① '네, 저는 아이들이 조금 더 크면 돌아갈 거예요.'이다.

오답 보기 해석

② 사실은, 내가 어릴 때 미국을 떠나지 않았으면 좋았을 거예요.
③ 그래요. 해외에서 의사소통 하는 것은 힘들 거예요.
④ 맞아요. 열심히 하는 것은 모든 것을 가능하게 만들죠.
⑤ 나는 정말 외국에서 공부하고 싶었지만 여유가 없었어요.

총 어휘 수 143

15 상황에 적절한 말

소재 기부자들에게 감사 표하는 방법

듣기 대본 해석

남: 엄청난 토네이도가 최근에 근처 동네를 강타하자 Greg과 Henry는 피해를 입은 사람들에게 도움을 주기 위해 자선 행사를 열었습니다. 배려심 깊은 사람들이 돈과 통조림 식품과 생수 같은 기본적인 생필품을 기부해주어서 행사는 성공적이었습니다. Greg과 Henry는 기부에 감사해 하는 피해자들에게 이러한 물건들을 보내주었습니다. Greg과 Henry는 기부를 한 사람들에게 감사한 마음을 표현하기로 했습니다. Henry는 이메일을 보내는 것으로 충분할 것이라고 생각합니다. Greg은 이메일이 편리하다는 것에는 동의하지만 손글씨 편지가 더 사적이고 진심 어리기 때문에 손글씨 편지를 보내야 한다고 생각합니다. 이러한 상황에서 Greg은 Henry에게 뭐라고 말할까요?
Greg: ⑤ 감사한 마음을 보여주는 데에는 손글씨 감사 편지가 가장 좋은 방법이라고 생각해.

어휘

charity *n.* 자선   **necessities** *n.* 필수품   **suffice** *v.* 충분하다
convenient *a.* 편리한   **personal** *a.* 사적인, 개인적인   **sincere** *a.* 진심 어린

정답 ⑤

문제풀이

Greg과 Henry는 함께 자선 행사를 했고, 기부해준 사람들에게 고마움을 표하고자 한다. Greg은 이메일로도 충분하다고 생각하는 Henry에게 감사한 마음을 보여주는 데는 손으로 쓴 편지가 좋다고 말하려 하므로 ⑤ '감사한 마음을 보여주는 데에는 손글씨 감사 편지가 가장 좋은 방법이라고 생각해.'가 정답이다.

오답 보기 해석

① 이메일은 감사하는 마음을 보여주는 좋은 방법이야.
② 그들이 무엇을 기부했는지는 상관 없어. 마음이 중요한 거지.
③ 감사한 마음을 표현하기 위해 선물 바구니를 만드는 게 좋을 것 같아.
④ 감사 편지를 쓰는 데에 그렇게 많은 시간을 투자하면 안 된다고 생각해.

총 어휘 수 128

16 담화 주제 / 17 세부 내용 파악

소재 여름에 시원하게 지내는 법

듣기 대본 해석

남: 이번 여름은 좀 더웠습니다. 그렇지 않았나요? 사실, 전 지구가 지구 온난화로 점점 더 뜨거워지고 있습니다. 만약에 여러분께서 더위를 이기고 시원함을 유지하고 싶으시다면, 적절한 옷을 입으십시오. 밝은 색은 빛과 함께 열도 반사하지만 어두운 색은 그것을 흡수합니다. 그래서 더 밝은 색의 옷을 입는 것이 여러분을 더 시원하게 해줍니다. 또한 여러분은 열을 발생시키는 전자제품들을 사용하지 않을 때 꺼 두어야 합니다. 예를 들어, 전화기를 충전하고 있지 않을 때는 전화기 충전기의 선을 꽂아둘 필요가 없습니다. 또, 시원함을 유지하기 위해서 시계가 있는 것들의 플러그를 뽑는 것이 현명합니다. 전자레인지와 커피메이커가 열을 발생시키고 전기를 낭비하는 시계가 딸린 전자제품의 좋은 예들입니다. 컴퓨터 또한 많은 열을 발생시킵니다. 그래서 여러분이 컴퓨터를 쓰지 않을 때는 컴퓨터를 꺼야 합니다. 마지막으로, 가능한 아래층으로 내려오세요. 지하가 집의 다른 곳보다 항상 더 시원합니다. 보통 다른 층들보다 약 5~10도 더 시원합니다.

어휘

reflect *v.* 비추다, 반사하다 **absorb** *v.* 흡수하다 **generate** *v.* 발생시키다 **charger** *n.* 충전기 **unplug** *v.* 플러그를 뽑다

정답 16 ① 17 ①

문제풀이

16 남자는 지구 온난화로 점점 더워지는 지구에서 시원함을 유지할 수 있는 몇 가지 방법을 소개하고 있다. 따라서 남자가 하는 말의 주제는 ① '더운 날씨에 시원하게 지내는 것에 대한 조언'이 된다.

17 남자는 처음에 전화기 충전기를 언급했고 다음에 전자레인지와 커피메이커, 그리고 컴퓨터를 언급했으므로 언급되지 않은 것은 ① '냉장고'이다.

오답 보기 해석

16

② 비상 상황에 해야 하는 일

③ 환경을 위해 에너지를 절약하는 방법

④ 디지털 전자제품의 에너지 소비량

⑤ 전기 콘센트 과부하의 위험성

총 어휘 수 162

13 수능영어듣기 실전모의고사

01 ⑤	02 ①	03 ③	04 ②	05 ⑤	06 ⑤
07 ④	08 ⑤	09 ④	10 ⑤	11 ④	12 ②
13 ①	14 ①	15 ④	16 ③	17 ①	

01 짧은 대화의 응답

소재 저녁 식사

듣기 대본 해석

여: 영화 시작하기 전에 시간이 좀 있네. 저녁 먹자.
남: 좋아. 배고파 죽겠어. 뭐 먹고 싶어?
여: 일식이 먹고 싶어. 넌 어때?
남: ⑤ 좋은 생각이야. 근처에 괜찮은 식당을 알고 있어.

어휘

starve v. 굶주리다　　in the mood for ∼할 기분이 나서

정답 ⑤

문제풀이

여자가 일식이 먹고 싶다고 말하며 남자의 의견을 물었을 때 가장 적절한 대답은 ⑤ '좋은 생각이야. 근처에 괜찮은 식당을 알고 있어.'이다.

오답 보기 해석

① 나도. 중국 음식 엄청 좋아해.
② 좋은 생각이야. 팝콘 먹자.
③ 난 액션보다 로맨스 영화가 좋아.
④ 글쎄. 영화 끝나고 저녁을 먹고 싶어.

총 어휘 수 38

02 짧은 대화의 응답

소재 신입사원의 사무실 위치 찾기

듣기 대본 해석

남: 그게, 저 여기서 막 일하기 시작해서 제 사무실이 어딘지 모르겠어요.
여: 마케팅 부장님인 Sarah씨에게 물어보세요.
남: 그분이 어디 있는지 아세요? 전 그녀를 한 번도 못 만나봤거든요.
여: ① 그녀는 그녀의 사무실에 있을 겁니다. 제가 둘을 소개시켜 줄게요.

어휘

marketing manager 마케팅 책임자　　〈문제〉fit n. 어울림. 조화

정답 ①

문제풀이

남자는 자신의 사무실 위치를 알기 위해 마케팅 부장을 만나야 하는데 그녀를 만난 적조차 없으므로 이에 대한 여자의 응답으로 가장 적절한 것은 ① '그녀는 그녀의 사무실에 있을 겁니다. 제가 둘을 소개시켜 줄게요.'이다.

오답 보기 해석

② 만약 그러한 경우라면. 당신은 새로운 사무실을 찾아야 해요.
③ 제 사무실은 이 건물의 6층에 있어요.
④ 여긴 당신의 사무실이 아니에요. 당신의 사무실은 저기예요.
⑤ 새로운 팀 멤버가 아주 적합한 사람 같네요.

총 어휘 수 45

03 담화 목적

소재 채식주의자가 되는 이유

듣기 대본 해석

여: 지난 시간에 우리는 많은 종교, 특히 불교와 힌두교에서 고기를 먹지 않는 것이 일반적이라고 배웠습니다. 오늘 수업에서 저는 고기를 먹지 않고 채식주의자가 되는 여러 다른 이유들을 알아보고 싶습니다. 많은 사람들은 채식주의가 건강에 좋다고 믿기 때문에 채식주의를 선택합니다. 그들은 고기를 적게 먹고 섬유질을 많이 먹는 것이 심장병, 암. 당뇨병에 걸릴 위험을 낮출 것이라고 믿습니다. 채식주의자는 윤리적인 신념 또한 가지고 있습니다. 그들은 소나 닭 같은 특정 동물들을 크게 만들기 위해 다른 화학약품을 먹이는 것을 좋아하지 않습니다. 어떤 이유로든 동물을 죽이는 데에 반대하는 사람들도 있습니다. 채식주의자가 되고 싶은 어떤 다른 이유들이 있을까요? 우리와 함께 생각을 공유해 주세요.

어휘

Buddhism n. 불교　　Hinduism n. 힌두교　　vegetarian n. 채식주의자　　vegetarianism n. 채식주의　　fiber n. 섬유질　　diabetes n. 당뇨병　　ethical a. 윤리적인. 도덕상의　　chemical n. 화학약품

정답 ③

문제풀이

사람들이 왜 채식주의자가 되는지를 알아보는 강의이다. 건강상의 이유. 윤리적인 신념 등으로 채식주의자가 된다고 말하고 있으므로 여자가 하는 말의 목적은 ③ '채식주의자가 되는 이유를 설명하려고'이다.

총 어휘 수 128

04 의견

소재 TV 자막을 이용한 영어 실력 향상

듣기 대본 해석

여: 저게 블루레이 재생기인가요? 조금 특이하게 생겼네요.
남: 청각 장애가 있는 사람들을 위한 자막이 제공돼요.
여: 정말이요? 아주 흥미로운 생각이네요. 그런 기술이 있는지 몰랐어요.
남: 모든 TV 프로그램에서 지원되는 것은 아니지만 대부분 지원이 되고 인터넷으로 더 주문할 수도 있어요.
여: 청각 장애가 없으신데 왜 이 기계를 갖고 계신가요?
남: 일년 동안 우리와 지내게 될 교환 학생이 있는데 이 재생기가 그녀의 영어 실력 향상에 도움이 될 것이라고 생각했어요.
여: 아주 사려 깊으시네요. 그런데 그녀가 TV 보는 것을 좋아하는지 어떻게 아세요?
남: 이메일로 물어봤어요. 미국 드라마 보는 것을 좋아하지만 대화 속도가 가끔은 너무 빨라서 알아듣기 어렵다네요.
여: 그렇다면 이 기기가 아주 도움이 되겠네요.
남: 그러면 좋겠어요. 기기가 싸지는 않았거든요.

어휘

subtitle n. 자막　　hearing disability 청각 장애　　exchange student 교환 학생　　thoughtful a. 사려 깊은

정답 ②

문제풀이

남자의 집에서 지낼 교환 학생이 말하길 그녀는 미국 드라마 보는 것을 좋아하지만 빠른 대화 속도로 인해 어려움을 겪는다고 한다. 그런 교환 학생의 영어 실력 향상에 TV 자막이 도움이 될 것이라고 말한 것으로 보아 남자의 의견으로 적절한 것은 ② 'TV 자막을 활용하면 효과적으로 외국어를 학습할 수 있다.'이다.

총 어휘 수 143

05 장소 파악

소재 밴드 배틀 대회

듣기 대본 해석
여: 와. 이곳은 정말 붐비는 구나. 엄청 시끄럽네!
남: 응. 오늘이 대회 마지막 날이야. 최종 4개 밴드팀이 곧 공연할 거야.
여: 그렇구나. 난 이곳이 이렇게 붐비고 시끄러울 줄 몰랐어.
남: Clara. 이건 로큰롤 대회야. 당연히 시끄럽지.
여: 생각은 했었지. 하지만 이 정도일 줄은 몰랐어. 이건 정말 대단해.
남: 그래. 믿어지지 않을 정도지. 그렇지? 매년 열리는 밴드들의 배틀 대회가 지난 몇 년간 많은 인기를 누리고 있어.
여: 확실히 그랬어. 내 생각엔 모든 밴드들이 이 공연을 위해 최고의 노래들을 아껴두고 있었던 같아. 그렇지?
남: 응. 우리 형이 말하길 그의 밴드는 최종 결승을 위해 가장 시끄럽고 강력한 노래를 할 거라고 했어.
여: 정말 말 되네.
남: 난 그의 공연이 정말 기대가 돼.
여: 나도 그래.

어휘
competition *n.* 경쟁. 대회　　**performance** *n.* 공연. 연주회

정답 ⑤

문제풀이
밴드 대회가 시작되기 전 남자와 여자가 나누고 있는 대화이므로 두 사람이 대화하고 있는 장소는 ⑤ '밴드 대회장'임을 알 수 있다.

총 어휘 수 134

06 그림의 세부 내용 파악

소재 고양이와 찍은 사진

듣기 대본 해석
남: 안녕. Maro. 뭐 보고 있어?
여: 내 고양이 Dubu랑 내 사진이야. 한번 봐.
남: *[잠시 후]* 이 사진에서 너 정말 어려 보인다. 언제 찍은 거야?
여: 분명 내가 Dubu를 받은 지후였을 거야. 나 안경을 썼었잖아.
남: 너 안경 쓴 거 본 적 없는데. Dubu의 색깔이 맘에 든다. 멋있게 완전한 회색이야.
여: 응. 이 셔츠 어떻게 생각해?
남: 내 생각에는 좀 저렴해 보이는 것 같은데. 난 물방울 무늬는 정말 별로거든. 목줄에 달려있는 건 하트 펜던트야?
여: 응. 귀여운 것 같아서 사줬지. 그는 또한 가장 좋아하는 장난감을 가지고 놀고 있어.
남: 공이네. 맞지?
여: 응. 나는 그에게 새로운 장난감을 항상 사주는데 여전히 저 공을 엄청 좋아해.
남: 멋지다. 좋은 고양이 같아.

어휘
solid *a.* 다른 색이 섞이지 않은(완전한)　　**cheesy** *a.* 싸구려의
polka dot 물방울무늬

정답 ⑤

문제풀이
대화의 마지막 부분에서 고양이가 가지고 있는 장난감은 공이라고 했는데 그림에서는 물고기를 가지고 있으므로 정답은 ⑤번이다.

총 어휘 수 138

07 부탁한 일

소재 집 안 대청소 후 외식

듣기 대본 해석
여: 이제야 집 청소를 마쳤어요.
남: 네. 쉽지 않았어요. 그렇게 힘들지 몰랐어요.
여: 오늘 날씨가 너무 더운 것도 도움이 되지 않았어요.
남: 그래도 결국. 우리가 해냈어요. 모든 게 훨씬 좋아 보이네요.
여: 맞아요. 오. 시간을 봐요. 우리가 저녁을 놓칠 뻔 했어요. 뭘 만들어야 할까요?
남: 아무것도 만들고 싶지 않아요. 나가서 저녁을 먹으러 갑시다. 우린 그럴 자격이 있어요.
여: 좋은 생각이에요. 우리가 이제 막 청소했는데 부엌을 어지럽히고 싶지 않아요.
남: 그래요. 나도 쉬고 싶고 남은 시간을 즐기고 싶어요.
여: 나가기 전에 개들한테 먹이 좀 줄래요? 저는 저녁 먹기 위해서 빨리 씻고 싶어요.
남: 물론이죠.
여: 고마워요. 여보.

어휘
miss *v.* 놓치다　　**make a mess** 어지럽히다　　**relax** *v.* 휴식을 취하다

정답 ④

문제풀이
청소를 마치고 저녁 식사를 하러 나가기로 했는데 여자는 나가기 전에 개들한테 먹이를 줄 것을 남자에게 부탁하고 있다. 따라서 정답은 ④ '저녁 전에 개들한테 먹이주기'이다.

오답 보기 해석
① 옷장 청소하기
② 저녁을 위한 음식 준비하기
③ 식당에 미리 전화하기
⑤ 집에 있는 모든 불 끄기

총 어휘 수 131

08 이유

소재 같이 오토바이 탈 시간 정하기

듣기 대본 해석
여: 안녕. Marcus. 너 오토바이 수리 끝났니?
남: 응. 오늘 아침에 직장에 타고 왔어. 마치 새 것 같았어. 오늘 일 끝나고 같이 타러 갈까?
여: 안 될 것 같은데. 내일 오후에 가자.
남: 토요일 오후? 오늘 밤은 왜 안 돼?
여: 음. 우리가 어떻게 다음 주에 그 중요한 출장을 가게 된 건지 너도 알잖아? 난 오늘 퇴근 전에 모든 준비를 마쳐야 해.
남: 오. 그런데 난 내일은 타러 못 갈 것 같은데.
여: 왜? 주말에 무슨 계획 있니?
남: 응. 내일 아침에 여동생을 만나기로 했어.
여: 뭐 할 건데?
남: 그녀는 새 아파트로 이사를 해서 내 도움이 필요해.
여: 힘들겠구나. 어쨌든. 여동생과 즐거운 시간이 되길 바라. 곧 같이 오토바이 탈 시간을 맞춰보자.
남: 좋아.

어휘
brand new 완전 새 것인　　**exhausting** *a.* 힘든. 기진맥진하게 만드는

정답 ⑤

문제풀이

대화의 마지막 부분에서 여자가 내일 무슨 계획이 있는지 묻자 남자는 여동생의 이사를 도와줘야 한다고 했으므로 정답은 ⑤ '여동생 이사를 도와줘야 해서'이다.

총 어휘 수 144

09 숫자

소재 공항에 마중 가기

듣기 대본 해석

남: Marcia가 떠난 지 벌써 일 년이 되었다니 믿을 수가 없어요.

여: 알아요. 어서 그녀와 이야기를 나누고 싶어요.

남: 그녀가 탄 한국에서 오는 비행기는 언제 도착하죠?

여: 오후 6시요.

남: 좋아요. 그럼 5시쯤 여기서 출발하면 시간에 맞게 거기에 도착할 거예요.

여: 네, 근데 요즘 도로 공사 때문에 차가 많이 막혀요. 더 일찍 출발해야 될 거예요.

남: 좋아요. 30분 일찍은 어때요?

여: 좋은 생각이에요. 제가 지금 식료품점에 가서 오늘 저녁거리를 사올게요.

남: 출발할 수 있게 시간 맞춰 올 거죠?

여: 물론이죠. 그때 봐요.

남: 아주 좋아요. 절대 늦지 마요. 오늘은 정말 중요한 날이에요!

여: 알아요. 늦지 않을게요.

어휘

flight *n.* 항공기, 항공편   **road work** 도로 공사

정답 ④

문제풀이

원래는 5시쯤에 출발하려고 했지만 도로 공사 때문에 차가 막히므로 30분 더 일찍 출발하기로 했다. 그러므로 답은 ④ '4시 30분'이다.

총 어휘 수 130

10 언급 유무

소재 중고 판매점

듣기 대본 해석

여: Jason, 다음 달 대회를 위한 컴퓨터 게임 샀어?

남: 응. Big Panda's 중고 판매점에서 샀어. 새 것 같은데 15달러밖에 안 줬어.

여: 정말? 새 것 가격의 반이네. 그 가게는 얼마나 멀어?

남: 이 길 따라 쭉 내려가면 그 옛날 고등학교 근처에 있어.

여: 그럼 꽤 가깝네.

남: 응. 중고 책, 게임, 그리고 영화로 가득 차 있는 이층짜리 빌딩에 있어.

여: 우왜 꽤 크구나. 나도 거기 가서 게임을 좀 봐야겠어. 언제 문 닫아?

남: 밤 열 시에 닫는 것 같아. 근데 확실하게 전화해서 물어 보는 게 나을 거야.

여: 좋은 생각이야.

남: 아! 그리고 학생증 보여주면 10퍼센트 할인해 줘.

여: 좋다! 도와줘서 고마워.

어휘

resale *n.* 재판매, 중고 판매

정답 ⑤

문제풀이

남자가 여자에게 중고 판매점에 대해 말해주고 있는 상황이다. 매장의 위치, 규모, 문 닫는 시간, 할인 혜택은 언급되었지만 택배 서비스에 대한 언급은 하지 않았으므로 정답은 ⑤ '택배 서비스'이다.

총 어휘 수 147

11 내용 일치 · 불일치

소재 멜론 나무

듣기 대본 해석

여: 오늘 아침 저는 멜론 나무에 대해 말하려 합니다. 그것은 남아메리카의 남쪽 지역이 원산지이고, 그것의 오렌지색 꽃은 봄에 2주 동안 매일 밤 자정에 볼 수 있습니다. 멜론 나무는 그 지역에 사는 야생 꿀벌에 의해 수분됩니다. 수분될 때, 꽃들은 밤에 빛나는 것처럼 보입니다. 멜론 나무가 만드는 열매는 이 특정한 지역에서만 발견되는 특별한 종의 멜론입니다. 그 맛은 수박이나 칸탈루프와 비슷하며 매우 달콤하고 즙이 많습니다. 그러나 그 열매는 먹지는 못하는데 그 멜론 나무를 수분하는 벌들이 독성이 있고 식물에 그들 독의 강한 자취를 남기기 때문입니다. 과일은 먹을 수 없지만 씨는 햇볕으로 인한 심한 화상을 치료하기 위해 사용되는 효과 좋은 연고로 가공될 수 있습니다.

어휘

pollinate *v.* 수분하다   **inhabit** *v.* 살다, 거주하다   **glow** *v.* 빛나다
poisonous *a.* 독성이 있는   **trace** *n.* 자취, 흔적   **process** *v.* 가공
(처리)하다   **ointment** *n.* 연고   **severe** *a.* 극심한, 심각한

정답 ④

문제풀이

멜론 나무의 열매는 달고 즙이 많지만 수분하는 벌들이 독성이 있고 식물에 그들 독의 강한 자취를 남기기 때문에 먹을 수 없다고 했으므로 내용과 일치하지 않는 것은 ④ '열매는 달고 즙이 많아 사람이 먹을 수 있다.'이다.

총 어휘 수 131

12 도표

소재 태블릿 선택

듣기 대본 해석

남: 여보, 새로운 태블릿을 살 때가 된 것 같아. 지금 우리가 갖고 있는 건 너무 오래됐고 느려.

여: 나도 그렇게 생각했어. 원하는 걸 찾았어?

남: 응. 우리가 살 수 있는 것들의 목록을 만들어봤어. 한번 봐봐.

여: *[잠시 후]* 이거 괜찮은 것 같아. 제일 싸기도 하고.

남: 응. 그게 싸. 그런데 별로 크지가 않아. 사실 우리가 지금 갖고 있는 것보다 작아.

여: 정말? 그럼 이게 화면이 제일 크네. 그리고 아주 인기 있는 브랜드 것이기도 하고.

남: 그걸 살까도 생각 했었어. 근데 태블릿에 250달러 이상을 쓰는 건 합리적인 것 같지 않아. 좀 더 저렴한 걸 찾아보자.

여: 그래. 그럼 이 두 개 중에서 골라야 된다는 거네. 이게 더 비싼데 보증 기간이 더 길어.

남: 그래. 보증 기간이 더 긴 게 중요한 것 같아. 고장 나면 비교적 쉽게 교체할 수 있잖아.

여: 좋아. 그럼 이걸로 하자.

어휘

tablet *n.* 태블릿   **justify** *v.* 정당화하다, 합리화하다   **warranty** *n.*
보증 기간, 품질 보증서

정답 ②

문제풀이

가장 저렴한 ①번은 너무 작다고 했고, 250달러 이상 쓰는 것은 합리적이지 않다고 했으므로 ②번과 ③번이 남는다. 그 중에 비싸지만 보증 기간이 긴 것으로 하자고 했으므로 정답은 ②번이다.

총 어휘 수 160

13 긴 대화의 응답

소재 생체공학적 다리

듣기 대본 해석

남: 안녕 Lana. 너 휠체어 어디 있어?
여: 오늘은 가져오지 않았어.
남: 그럼 이제 목발을 사용하는구나?
여: 아니. 난 목발도 필요 없어.
남: 그렇구나. 그럼 어떻게 돌아다니려고 해? 도움 없이 걷는 게 힘들잖아.
여: 이제는 휠체어나 목발 없이도 걸을 수 있어. 다시 사용할 필요가 없어.
남: 뭐? 말도 안돼! 평생 걸을 수 없었잖아!
여: 나 C-Braces를 맞췄어.
남: C-Braces가 뭐야?
여: 그건 내 다리에 붙여서 내가 다른 도움 없이 걸을 수 있는, 특별하고 컴퓨터로 조절되는 버팀대야. 새로운 기술이지.
남: 그럼 기본적으로 이제 네가 걸을 수 있다는 얘기야?
여: 맞아. 이제 내 생체공학적 다리로 돌아다닐 수 있어.
남: ① 대단하다. 기술이 참 놀랍지 않니?

어휘

crutch *n.* 목발   **brace** *n.* 버팀대   **bionic** *a.* 생체 공학적인

정답 ①

문제풀이

도움 없이는 걸을 수 없었던 여자가 갑자기 혼자 걷게 되자 남자는 이유를 물었고 여자는 C-Braces라는 생체공학적 다리를 맞췄다고 말해주고 있다. 남자의 마지막 반응은 ① '대단하다. 기술이 참 놀랍지 않니?'가 적절하다.

오답 보기 해석

② 너는 지금 당장 C-Braces를 맞춰야 해.
③ 충고 고마워. 새로운 목발을 살게.
④ 맞아. 난 곧 걸을 수 있게 될 거야.
⑤ 너와 같은 상태를 가진 사람들은 다시 걸을 수 있다고 들었어.

총 어휘 수 120

14 긴 대화의 응답

소재 아늘의 컴퓨터 게임 시간 제한

듣기 대본 해석

여: 뭐하고 있어요, George?
남: 컴퓨터에 새로운 게임을 다운로드 받고 있어요.
여: 왜 다른 새로운 게임을 다운로드 받는 거예요?
남: 음. Teddy가 이런 교육용 게임을 좋아하고 무료라서 안 받을 이유가 없는 것 같아요.
여: 그에게 이미 게임이 충분히 있다고 생각하지 않아요?
남: 그렇게 생각하지 않아요. 그는 아주 빠르게 배우는 나이예요.
여: 알았어요. 그렇지만 만약에 당신이 너무 많은 게임을 다운로드 받으면. 그는 게임에 중독되고 밖에 나가서 놀고 싶어 하지 않을 수도 있어요.
남: 그것에 대해선 걱정하지 않아요. 우리는 그 애를 체조랑 야구에도 등록시켰잖아요.
여: 좋은 생각이지만 그런 활동들은 고작 일주일에 두 번인걸요. 게임은 매일 할 수 있잖아요.
남: 네, 당신의 요점을 알았어요. 아이가 컴퓨터에 쓰는 시간을 제한해야겠어요.
여: ① 당신이 균형 있는 해결책을 찾을 수 있을 거라고 생각해요.

어휘

addicted *a.* 중독된   **enroll** *v.* 등록하다   **gymnastics** *n.* 체조
see (one's) point ~의 요점을 알다

정답 ①

문제풀이

아들이 컴퓨터하는 시간을 제한해야겠다고 말하는 남자에게 여자가 해 줄 수 있는 말은 ① '당신이 균형 있는 해결책을 찾을 수 있을 거라고 생각해요.'가 적절하다.

오답 보기 해석

② 이 새 게임을 다운로드 하는 데에 도움이 필요해요.
③ 요즘은 아이들이 운동하는 게 너무 비싸요.
④ 그가 경기하는 야구팀의 이름을 나한테 말해줄 수 있어요?
⑤ 당신이 그 게임을 하기 위해서는 더 새로운 하드웨어가 필요한 것 같아요.

총 어휘 수 138

15 상황에 적절한 말

소재 집에 두고 온 보고서

듣기 대본 해석

여: Michael은 오늘 회사에 제출해야 할 중요한 보고서가 있습니다. 그는 독감에 걸려서 지난번의 보고서를 며칠 정도 늦게 제출했습니다. 그의 상사는 지연된 것에 대해 기분이 좋지 않았기 때문에 그는 이번 것은 제 시간에 제출하도록 의욕이 있는 상태입니다. 그가 회사에 도착했을 때. 그는 문서를 찾으려고 서류 가방을 열었고 거기에 그것들이 없다는 것을 알게 되었습니다. 그는 처음에 당황하고 어떻게 반응해야 할지 모릅니다. 그는 집에 있는 그의 아내에게 전화를 걸고 그녀는 그가 문서들을 주방 탁자 위에 놓고 갔다고 그에게 말합니다. 그는 보고서를 잃어버리지 않아 기뻐하지만 재빨리 제출해야만 합니다. 이 상황에서. Michael은 그의 아내에게 뭐라고 말하겠습니까?
Michael: ④ 내 사무실로 문서들을 갖다 줄래요?

어휘

turn in 제출하다   **flu** *n.* 독감   **delay** *n.* 지연, 지체   **briefcase** *n.* 서류 가방

정답 ④

문제풀이

Michael은 반드시 마감 전에 제출하려 했던 중요한 보고서를 집에 두고 왔음을 아내에게 전화해서 확인했는데, 그는 당장 그 보고서가 필요한 상황이다. 이런 상황에서 Michael이 이내에게 할 말로 가장 적절한 것은 ④ '내 사무실로 문서들을 갖다 줄래요?'이다.

오답 보기 해석

① 나는 지난주에 보고서를 제출했어요.
② 내가 도울 일이 있으면 알려주세요.
③ 문서들이 주방 탁자 위에 있어요.
⑤ 보고서 쓰는 것을 좀 도와줄래요?

총 어휘 수 131

16 담화 목적 / 17 세부 내용 파악

소재 코 호흡의 중요성

듣기 대본 해석

여: 안녕하세요, 여러분. 저는 오늘 적절한 호흡법이 여러분의 전반적인 건강에 얼마나 좋은 영향을 주는지 이야기하고 싶습니다. 먼저, 여러분은 코를 통해 숨을 쉬어야 합니다. 입으로 하는 호흡이 더 일반적이지만 코를 사용하면 사실 훨씬 더 자연스럽고 그래서 더 건강해집니다. 코는 우리가 숨을 쉴 때 공기 중에서 발견될 수 있는 모든 불순물에 대해 여과기로 작용합니다. 입으로 호흡하는 것은 공기를 전혀 정화시키지 못해서 먼지와 때가 걸러질

수 없습니다. 이는 여러분이 감기나 다른 공기로 전염되는 병을 더 쉽게 걸리게 만듭니다. 입으로 숨을 쉬면 찬 공기가 폐로 들어오도록 해서 호흡기에 염증이 생기게 합니다. 그러나 코를 통해 숨을 쉬면 여러분의 몸에 활력을 불어넣고 더 많은 에너지를 줍니다. 공기를 여과하고 따뜻하게 유지함으로써 코의 통로는 폐에 들어오기 적합한 공기만 들어오게 합니다. 이는 공기에 의존하는 모든 섬세한 기관들이 가장 잘 작동할 것이라는 것을 의미합니다.

어휘

breathing *n.* 호흡　**benefit** *n.* 이점, 혜택　*v.* 혜택을 주다　**overall** *a.* 전반적인　**impurity** *n.* 불순물　**airborne** *a.* 공기로 운반되는　**lung** *n.* 폐　**respiratory** *a.* 호흡의, 호흡성의　**organ** *n.* 장기(기관)　**inflamed** *a.* 염증이 생긴　**vitalize** *v.* 활력을 불어넣다　**nasal** *a.* 코의　**passage** *n.* 통로　**fit** *a.* 적합한　**delicate** *a.* 섬세한　〈문제〉 **delicacy** *n.* 섬세함, 여림

정답　16 ③　17 ①

문제풀이

16 여자는 입으로 하는 호흡과 코로 하는 호흡을 비교하면서 코로 하는 호흡의 중요성을 설명하고 있으므로 정답은 ③ '코로 하는 호흡의 중요성을 강조하려고'이다.

17 Mouth breathing의 단점으로 폐에 불순물 유입, 질병 감염에 대한 취약성, 폐에 찬 공기 유입, 호흡기 염증 유발 등이 언급되었으나 불면증 유발은 언급되어 있지 않으므로 정답은 ① '불면증 유발'이다.

오답 보기 해석

16
① 입으로 호흡하는 것을 효과적으로 피할 수 있는 방법을 설명하려고
② 호흡기관의 섬세함을 강조하려고
④ 여과된 공기를 마시는 것의 이점을 설명하려고
⑤ 호흡의 여러 가지 방법을 기술하려고

총 어휘 수　168

14 수능영어듣기 실전모의고사

01 ⑤	02 ⑤	03 ④	04 ④	05 ③	06 ⑤
07 ②	08 ④	09 ③	10 ③	11 ②	12 ⑤
13 ③	14 ②	15 ①	16 ⑤	17 ②	

01 짧은 대화의 응답

소재 테니스 경기 보러 가기

듣기 대본 해석
남: Mia. 테니스 경기 갈 준비 됐어?
여: 거의. 수학 숙제 마지막 문제 몇 개만 풀면 돼.
남: 얼마 정도 더 걸릴 것 같아?
여: ⑤ 15분 넘게 걸리진 않을 거야.

어휘
match *n.* 경기, 시합 〈문제〉 **turn in** ~을 제출하다

정답 ⑤

문제풀이
테니스 경기에 가기 전 수학 문제를 풀고 있는 여자에게 남자는 얼마나 더 걸릴 것인지 묻고 있으므로 정답은 ⑤ '15분 넘게 걸리진 않을 거야.'이다.

오답 보기 해석
① 경기 갈 준비 다 됐어.
② 대신 영화 보러 가자.
③ 우리 내일 아침에 출발해야 해.
④ 너 숙제 제출하는 것 까먹었어.

총 어휘 수 43

02 짧은 대화의 응답

소재 감기 기운

듣기 대본 해석
여: 얘, Kevin, 여기 좀 춥네. 창문을 좀 닫자.
남: 오늘 몸이 그다지 좋지 않네.
여: 무슨 일이야? 오늘 아침에 활기차게 보였는데.
남: ⑤ 내 생각엔 반 친구한테서 감기가 옮은 것 같아.

어휘
〈문제〉 **rewarding** *a.* 보람 있는 **catch a cold** 감기에 걸리다

정답 ⑤

문제풀이
오늘 아침에는 활기차 보였는데 왜 몸이 안 좋은 거냐고 묻는 여자의 말에 대한 남자의 응답으로 가장 적절한 것은 ⑤ '내 생각엔 반 친구한테서 감기가 옮은 것 같아.'이다.

오답 보기 해석
① 창문을 닫아줘서 고마워.
② 오늘 날씨가 훌륭해.
③ 맞아. 난 자주 운동을 해왔거든.
④ 다른 사람들을 돕는 것은 정말 보람 있는 일이야.

총 어휘 수 39

03 담화 목적

소재 공원 내 스포츠 광장 건립 반대

듣기 대본 해석
남: 여러분, 안녕하세요. 저는 Scott McGee이고, 저는 오늘 밤 Central Park에 스포츠 광장을 건립하려는 도시의 계획에 대해 말씀드리려 합니다. Central Park는 모두에게 휴식과 재미를 주는 공간이라는 것에 여러분 모두 동의하신다고 확신합니다. 우리는 그곳으로 봄, 여름에 소풍을 가고 일년 내내 운동과 건강관리를 위해 그곳을 이용합니다. 하지만, 우리가 만약 도시의 스포츠 광장 건립을 허락한다면 우리는 더 이상 그런 것들을 할 공간이 없을 것입니다. 스포츠 경기나 다른 이벤트를 보러 광장으로 가는 사람들 때문에 심한 교통 체증만 보게 될 것입니다. 이는 우리의 삶의 질을 낮출 거라고 저는 확신합니다! 저는 여기 여러분 모두가 저의 의견에 동감하시리라 생각합니다.

어휘
construct *v.* 건설하다 **relaxation** *n.* 휴식 **wellness** *n.* 건강, 건강관리 **opinion** *n.* 의견, 견해

정답 ④

문제풀이
남자는 시민들의 휴식과 운동의 공간인 Central Park에 스포츠 광장이 건립되면 어떻게 될지 설명하면서 도시의 스포츠 광장 건립 계획을 반대하고 있으므로 정답은 ④ '공원 내 스포츠 광장 건립 계획에 반대하려고'이다.

총 어휘 수 125

04 대화 주제

소재 바나나 껍질의 다양한 용도

듣기 대본 해석
여: Cody, 그거 버리지마.
남: 왜? 그냥 바나나 껍질이잖아.
여: 바나나 껍질은 쓸모가 아주 많아.
남: 응, 화단에 주려고 네가 껍질로 퇴비 만드는 걸 봤어. 그런 걸 말하는 거야?
여: 음, 응. 그렇긴 한데 그것 외에도 바나나 껍질은 여러 가지로 쓰여. 예를 들어 멀레기 분 곳이나 가려운 발진에 그걸 바르면 좋다는 거 알고 있었어?
남: 신기하다. 그래서 혹시 벌레한테 물릴 때에 대비해서 오래된 바나나 껍실을 모으겠다는 거야?
여: 그건 아냐. 사실 그 껍질로 내 가죽 신발 광내려고 했어.
남: 내 신발 광낼 때도 하나 써봐야지. 또 어디에 쓰여?
여: 창문 밖에다 놓으면 새들과 나비들이 모여들 거야.
남: 좋네. 왜 나보고 버리지 말라고 했는지 이제 알겠어.

어휘
peel *n.* 껍질 *v.* 껍질을 벗기다 **compost** *n.* 퇴비 **relieve** *v.* 없애다, 덜어주다 **rash** *n.* 발진 **polish** *v.* 광을 내다 **attract** *v.* 끌어들이다

정답 ④

문제풀이
여자는 바나나 껍질을 버리려는 남자에게 벌레 물림과 발진 완화, 신발 광 내기 등 다양한 쓸모를 이야기하고 있으므로 정답은 ④ '바나나 껍질의 다양한 용도'이다.

총 어휘 수 141

05 대화자의 관계 파악

소재 영화감독의 학교방문

듣기 대본 해석

[전화벨이 울린다.]
여: 여보세요?
남: 여보세요, 저는 Ryan James입니다. 저는 막 당신의 이메일을 받았고, 당신의 초대를 받아들이고 싶습니다.
여: 정말이에요? 잘 됐네요. 바쁜 스케줄 와중에도 우리 학교를 방문하기 위하여 시간을 내어 주셔서 정말 감사드립니다.
남: 괜찮습니다. 저는 사실 이 졸업식에서 연설하기를 무척 기대하고 있습니다.
여: 당신의 영화가 여기 Henderson County 고등학교의 많은 학생들에게 영감이 되었어요.
남: 오, 당신으로부터 그런 말을 듣다니 굉장히 기분이 좋네요.
여: 저희 학생들 몇 명이 당신과 직접 이야기하고 싶어해요. 졸업식 전에 팬미팅을 해주실 수 있나요?
남: 되고 말고요. 저는 저의 팬들을 존경하고 그들, 특히 어린 팬들의 얘기를 듣는 것을 좋아해요.
여: 학생들이 당신을 직접 만나게 돼서 무척 신나할 거예요.

어휘

appreciate *v.* 감사하다　　**look forward to** ~을 기대하다
inspiration *n.* 영감, 영감을 주는 것　　**ecstatic** *a.* 황홀해하는, 열광하는
in person 직접, 몸소　　**meet-and-greet** *n.* 팬미팅

정답 ③

문제풀이

남자가 여자가 있는 학교에 와서 졸업식 때 연설을 해주기로 했고 여자는 그의 영화에 학생들이 영감을 받았다고 했으므로 두 사람의 관계는 ③ '영화감독 ― 교사'로 유추할 수 있다.

총 어휘 수 132

06 그림의 세부 내용 파악

소재 기숙사 방

듣기 대본 해석

남: 네가 기숙사 방 꾸민 것 맘에 들어, Clara.
여: 고마워. 책상하고 침대 옮기느라 꽤 힘들었어.
남: 침대 위에 있는 건 봉제 인형이지?
여: 응. 내가 어릴 때부터 가지고 있었어. 이름은 Geoffrey인데 기린이야.
남: 멋지다. 오, 좋은 지도인데. 핀을 꽂아둔 곳은 모두 네가 가 본 곳이니?
여: 맞아. 난 그 옆에다 내 스케줄을 쓰기 위해 화이트보드를 놓았어. 너도 알지만 내가 건망증이 심하잖아.
남: 저 전등도 맘에 든다. 방을 잘 밝혀 주는구나.
여: 저건 할머니에게 받은 또 다른 선물이야.
남: 책상 위에 노트북 컴퓨터 좋은 거구나. 집에서 가져 온 거야?
여: 응. 아빠가 떠나는 선물로 나에게 주셨어.
남: 네 방은 내 방보다 훨씬 아늑해 보인다. 맘에 들어.
여: 오? 이제는 네 방이 궁금한걸.

어휘

dorm *n.* 기숙사　　**forgetful** *a.* 잘 잊어 먹는, 건망증이 있는
light up 밝히다

정답 ⑤

문제풀이

책상 위에 노트북 컴퓨터가 있다고 했는데 책이 있으므로 정답은 ⑤번이다.

총 어휘 수 146

07 부탁한 일

소재 새집 만들기

듣기 대본 해석

여: 저는 이 길이 항상 좋았어요, 아빠.
남: 그렇다니 아빠도 기쁘구나. 아빠도 아주 좋아한단다.
여: 저는 예쁜 새들을 볼 수 있는 게 좋아요.
남: 그래. 새들이 여기 많이 나와 있구나.
여: 아빠, 새들은 어디서 자나요?
남: 새들은 나무에서 살지. 새들은 나뭇가지 저 위에 새집을 짓는데 둥지라고 부른단다.
여: 새들은 서로 둥지를 공유하나요?
남: 나도 그건 확실히 모르겠구나, 얘야. 그렇지만 집이 없는 새들도 있을 거야.
여: 정말이요? 그건 슬프네요. 우리가 새들을 위해 집을 만들어 줄 수 있어요?
남: 집이 없는 새들 때문에 네가 슬프다면, 물론 할 수 있지.
여: 정말 그래요, 아빠. 모든 새들이 멋진 집을 가지고 있었으면 해요.
남: 그래. 그럼 다음 주 주말에, 새집을 만들어서 정원에 걸자꾸나.
여: 좋아요! 고마워요, 아빠.

어휘

trail *n.* 오솔길　　**homeless** *a.* 집이 없는

정답 ②

문제풀이

아빠가 집이 없는 새들도 있을 거라고 하자 딸은 집이 없는 새들 때문에 슬프다며 새들을 위해 집을 만들어 주자고 한다. 따라서 딸이 아빠한테 부탁한 일은 ② '새집 만들어 주기'이다.

총 어휘 수 133

08 이유

소재 콘서트에 못 가게 된 이유

듣기 대본 해석

여: Jim, 오늘 왜 그렇게 우울해 보이니?
남: 내가 Eric Benet 콘서트 기다려 왔다는 것 알지? 내가 제일 좋아하는 가수잖아.
여: 물론이지. 너 아주 신나 있었잖아. 무슨 문제 있어?
남: 내가 콘서트에 갈 수 없게 되었거든.
여: 왜? 그거 취소됐어?
남: 아니. 회의 때문에 상하이에 가야만 해.
여: 사장님이 그 회의에 참석하기로 했던 거 아니었어?
남: 응. 그랬지. 그렇지만 사장님이 지난 주 일요일에 테니스를 치다가 팔이 부러지는 바람에 갈 수 없게 됐어.
여: 안타깝구나. 그럼 그 티켓은 어떻게 할 거니?
남: 이미 내 남동생한테 줬어.
여: 작년에 결혼한 그 남동생 말하는 거지?
남: 맞아. 티켓 받고 좋아하더라.
여: 그에게는 잘된 일이네. 언젠가 Eric Benet을 볼 기회가 있을 거야, Jim.

어휘

turn out ~인 것으로 드러나다　　**cancel** *v.* 취소하다
be supposed to V ~하기로 되어 있다　　**attend** *v.* 참석하다

정답 ④

문제풀이

남자는 원래 회의에 참석하기로 했던 상사의 팔이 부러져서 상사를 대신해서 상하이에서 열리는 회의에 참석해야 하기 때문에 콘서트에 가지 못하게 되었다고 말했으므로 정답은 ④ '상사 대신 출장을 가야 해서'이다.

총 어휘 수 129

09 숫자

소재 등산 용품 구매하기

듣기 대본 해석

남: 안녕하세요. 무엇을 도와드릴까요?

여: 등산화를 찾고 있어요. 저 가죽 등산화 좀 봐도 될까요?

남: 사실 그것들은 남성용 등산화예요.

여: 알아요. 십대인 제 아들 것을 사려고요. 얼마예요?

남: 원래 100달러였지만 이번에 20퍼센트 할인을 하게 됐어요. 저번 시즌에 굉장히 유행했죠. 그가 좋아할 거라고 확신해요.

여: 저도 그렇게 생각해요. 9 사이즈로 한 켤레 주세요. 아! 그리고 우리 둘이 쓸 등산 스틱도 필요해요.

남: 네. 분홍색, 보라색, 초록색, 그리고 파란색이 있습니다.

여: 보라색 하나랑 파란색 하나 살게요. 얼마예요?

남: 한 개당 20달러입니다.

여: 등산 스틱에도 20퍼센트 할인이 적용되나요?

남: 죄송하지만 할인은 등산화에만 적용됩니다.

여: 알겠어요. 여기 카드요.

어휘

apiece *ad.* 각각, 하나에   **apply to** ~에 적용되다

정답 ③

문제풀이

20퍼센트 할인 중인 100달러짜리 등산화 한 켤레와 정가로 판매 중인 20달러짜리 등산 스틱 2개이므로 80달러+40달러=120달러가 되어 정답은 ③ '$120'이다.

총 어휘 수 146

10 언급 유무

소재 여드름 관리

듣기 대본 해석

남: 오, 안돼! 내 얼굴에 뾰루지가 너무 많아요.

여: 작은 여드름이 났구나. 사춘기를 지날 때는 그게 조금 나는 것이 정상이란다. 네가 십대를 벗어날 때가 되면 그건 거의 완전히 없어질 거야.

남: 네, 그걸 전부 이해하긴 해요. 하지만 이런 여드름들을 보는게 정말 싫어요.

여: 그게 좋지 않다는 거 나도 알아.

남: 제가 그것에 대해 무엇을 할 수 있나요?

여: 피부를 깨끗하게 유지하고 여드름을 자극하지 말도록 해봐.

남: 네, 그렇게 할 수 있어요.

여: 네가 여드름을 봤을 때, 그것을 짜고 싶은 욕구를 참아야 해.

남: 정말이요? 그렇지만 저는 여드름을 즉시 없애고 싶어요.

여: 그래. 대부분의 사람들이 그렇지만. 그것들을 터트리는 건 더 악화시킬 뿐이야.

남: 어떤 음식이 여드름을 유발시킬까요?

여: 만약에 네가 여드름이 잘 난다면, 너는 기름기 있는 음식들은 피해야 한단다.

어휘

pimple *n.* 여드름, 뾰루지   **acne** *n.* 여드름   **puberty** *n.* 사춘기
irritate *v.* (피부 등을) 자극하다   **resist** *v.* 견디다, 저항하다
squeeze *v.* 찌다   **prone** *a.* ~하기 쉬운   **greasy** *a.* 기름진

정답 ③

문제풀이

여자는 여드름이 나기 시작한 사춘기 남자에게 깨끗한 피부를 유지할 것, 여드름을 자극하지 말 것, 여드름을 짜지 말 것, 기름진 음식을 피할 것을 조언으로 언급하였으나 ③ '여드름에 연고 바르기'는 언급하지 않았다.

총 어휘 수 140

11 내용 일치 · 불일치

소재 메이플 시럽

듣기 대본 해석

여: 오늘 저는 여러분께 우리가 메이플 시럽이라고 부르는 아주 달콤한 간식에 대해서 얘기해 드릴 겁니다. 유럽 식민지화되기 전에 북미의 원주민들은 메이플(단풍) 나무에 구멍을 뚫어 흘러 나오는 액체를 모아 그 시럽을 모았습니다. 그들은 메이플 시럽이 많은 요리에 쓰일 수 있는 자연 감미료임을 발견했습니다. 오늘날 캐나다의 퀘벡 주가 세계 최대의 메이플 시럽 생산지입니다. 그곳은 전체 메이플 시럽의 3/4을 생산합니다. 사탕 수수나 옥수수 시럽과 같은 다른 감미료들에 비해 메이플 시럽은 중요한 비타민과 영양분의 좋은 공급원입니다. 많은 의사들은 매일 메이플 시럽을 적당량 섭취하는 것이 심장병 예방에 도움이 되고 면역 체계를 강화시킬 수 있다고 생각합니다.

어휘

sweet treat 사탕, 과자 등의 단 음식   **colonization** *n.* 식민지화
native *a.* 토박이의   **tap** *v.* 가볍게 두드리다, (나무에 자국을 내고) 수액을 받다   **sap** *n.* 수액   **seep** *v.* 스미다   **sweetener** *n.* 감미료
province *n.* 주, 지방   **superior** *a.* 우수한   **source** *n.* 원천, 근원
consume *v.* 소모하다, 섭취하다   **moderate** *a.* 보통의, 적당한
immune system 면역 체계

정답 ②

문제풀이

원주민들은 메이플 시럽이 여러 요리에 쓰일 수 있는 자연 감미료임을 발견했다고 했으므로 일치하지 않는 것은 ② '주로 상처 치료에 널리 사용되었다.'이다.

총 어휘 수 130

12 도표

소재 전자레인지 선택

듣기 대본 해석

여: 안녕하세요. 뭐 찾는 것 있으세요?

남: 네. 새 전자레인지 사려고요. 추천하는 것 있으세요?

여: 네, 이거 한번 보세요.

남: 가격이 $100도 안 되는 걸로 봐서는 별로일 것 같네요.

여: 그럴지도 모르겠네요. 이건 어때요? 서번 수에 새로 들어온 모델이에요. 굉장히 인기 있는 것 같아요.

남: 겉모습은 괜찮은데 싼 제품의 전력량과 같아요. 좀 더 센 모델을 찾고 있어요.

여: 알겠습니다. 이것도 굉장히 잘 나가고, 거의 신상품이에요. 이것도 지난 주에 들어왔어요.

남: 이 모델의 장단점은 뭐예요?

여: 그건 회전을 하는데요, 근데 좀 작아요. 내부 크기가 0.9 세제곱 피트밖에 안돼요.

남: 우리는 좀 큰 요리들도 데워먹어서 더 큰 게 아마도 더 좋을 것 같네요.

여: 알겠습니다. 이건요?

남: 좋네요. 회전도 하고 내부 크기도 더 커 보여요. 오, 판넬 스티커에 1.2 세제곱 피트라고 써있네요. 이걸로 할게요.

여: 네. 카트에 싣는 것을 도와드릴게요. 앞쪽 계산대로 가져가세요.

어휘

microwave *n.* 전자레인지   **recommend** *v.* 추천하다   **visually**
ad. 시각적으로   **appealing** *a.* 매력적인   **pros and cons** 장단점
rotate *v.* 회전하다   **interior** *n.* 내부

정답 ⑤

문제풀이

100달러가 안 되는 것은 별로일 것 같다고 했고, 전력이 센 것을 찾았으므로 ③~⑤번이 남는데 이 중 회전을 하고 내부가 1.2 세제곱 피트인 것은 ⑤번이다.

총 어휘 수 193

13　긴 대화의 응답

소재　언어의 정확성과 유창성

듣기 대본 해석

여: Issac, 우리 프랑스어 선생님 어때?

남: 내 생각엔 괜찮은데 너는 별로 좋아하지 않는 것처럼 보여.

여: 어학 실습은 많이 하지만 기초 문법은 충분하지 않은 것 같아.

남: 그게 맘에 들지 않아?

여: 나는 문법이 새로운 언어를 배우는 데 가장 중요한 부분이라고 생각하기 때문에 그게 좋지가 않아.

남: 너의 생각을 뒷받침할 만한 최근 연구가 있어?

여: 그렇진 않아.

남: 그럼, 너는 왜 그렇게 생각해?

여: 나는 만약에 문법적으로 옳은 문장을 사용해서 말하지 않는다면, 웃기게 들릴 거라고 생각해.

남: 나는 언어 교육의 많은 최근 이론들에 근거할 때 그렇게 생각하지 않아.

여: 정말? 그 이론들에서 뭐라고 주장하는데?

남: ③ 그들은 정확성보다 유창성이 더 중요하다고 말해.

어휘

on the basis of ~에 근거하여　〈문제〉**theory n.** 이론　**fluency n.** 유창성　**accuracy n.** 정확도　**emphasize v.** 강조하다

정답　③

문제풀이

남자가 문법을 중시하는 여자의 의견에 대해 최근 언어 교육 이론을 근거로 그렇지 않다고 반박하자 여자는 이론의 내용을 묻고 있으므로 응답으로 가장 적절한 것은 ③ '그들은 정확성보다 유창성이 더 중요하다고 말해.'이다.

오답 보기 해석

① 프랑스어가 영어보다 더 어려워.

② 우리는 이론에 의존해야 할 것 같아.

④ 그 이론들은 올바른 문법의 사용을 강조해.

⑤ 그들은 이론과 실제가 다르다고 지적해.

총 어휘 수　115

14　긴 대화의 응답

소재　친구를 위한 생일파티에 대한 상의

듣기 대본 해석

남: 안녕, Stacy, 이번 주말에 뭐해?

여: 아직 확실하지 않아. 왜 물어 보는 거야?

남: Bruno를 위해서 깜짝 생일 파티를 열려고 해. 그는 30살이 되잖아. 네가 온다면 그가 좋아할 거라 생각해.

여: 좋은 생각이야. 나는 그가 파티를 할지 궁금했었어. 난 가면 좋지.

남: 좋아. 음, 나는 모든 사람들이 5시에 나의 집에 왔으면 해.

여: 나에게 딱 좋네. 내가 파티 도와 줄까? 내가 간식거리 같은 것을 사갈 수 있어.

남: 내 생각에는 간식은 많을 것 같아. 너는 몸만 와.

여: 정말 내가 도울 수 있는 게 없을까? Bruno는 좋은 친구잖아. 그가 우리한테 얼마나 의미 있는지 그에게 보여주고 싶어.

남: 음, 그러면, 네가 파티를 위해 할 일이 있지.

여: 그게 뭔데?

남: Susie가 직장에서 우리 모두의 사진을 가지고 콜라주를 만들 거야. 그녀가 사진 고르는 걸 네가 도와주면 좋을 거라고 생각해.

여: ② 물론이지. 내가 그것을 할 수 있어. 도움이 될 수 있어서 기뻐.

어휘

surprise birthday party 깜짝 생일 파티　**bring yourself** 몸만 (빈 손으로) 와　**contribute v.** 기여하다　**collage n.** 콜라주

정답　②

문제풀이

여자가 생일 파티를 위해 무언가를 돕고 싶다고 하자 남자가 사진을 찾아주면 좋을 것 같다고 했으므로 가장 적절한 여자의 응답은 ② '물론이지. 내가 그것을 할 수 있어. 도움이 될 수 있어서 기뻐.'이다.

오답 보기 해석

① 내가 반드시 그녀를 파티에 초대할게.

③ 좋아. 점심 후에 사진을 몇 장 찍을게.

④ 내가 콜라주를 만들었는데 진짜 멋져 보여.

⑤ 좋았어. 내가 꼭 간식을 좀 가져올게.

총 어휘 수　174

15　상황에 적절한 말

소재　퇴직 후 혼자 여행하기

듣기 대본 해석

남: Neil은 성공한 변호사이고 몇 년 동안 퇴직을 고대하고 있는 중이었습니다. 그가 마침내 퇴직했을 때, 그는 낚시, 카페에서 커피를 마시거나 운동으로 시간을 보냈습니다. 그는 그의 새로운 일상에 꽤 지루해져 갔고 그가 좀 더 흥미 있는 무언가를 해야만 한다고 결심했습니다. 그는 몇 달 동안 동남아시아를 쭉 여행하기를 원합니다. Neil이 그의 계획을 아내와 의논할 때, 그녀는 그렇게 오랜 여행을 감당하지 못할 것이라며 그와 함께 가는 것을 거절했습니다. Neil은 그의 아내에게 그가 다시는 여행할 기회를 갖지 못할 것이기 때문에 그가 혼자 갈 수 있도록 아내를 설득하고 싶어 합니다. 이 상황에서, Neil은 그의 아내에게 뭐라고 말할까요?

Neil: ① 나는 항상 이런 긴 여행을 하는 것을 원해왔어요.

어휘

look forward to ~을 고대하다　**retirement n.** 퇴직　**handle v.** 다루다, 감당하다　**convince v.** 납득시키다

정답　①

문제풀이

퇴직 후의 일상에 지루함을 느낀 Neil은 동남아시아 여행을 하려고 한다. 하지만 아내가 동참을 거절하자 혼자라도 가겠노라고 아내를 설득하려는 상황이므로 Neil이 아내에게 할 말로 가장 적절한 것은 ① '나는 항상 이런 긴 여행을 하는 것을 원해왔어요.'이다.

오답 보기 해석

② 이제 내가 퇴직했으니, 나는 내가 원하는 언제든 낚시를 갈 수 있어요.

③ 나는 정말로 우리가 뭔가 흥미롭게 할 것을 찾길 바래요.

④ 나는 우리가 함께 배낭여행을 가야 한다고 생각해요.

⑤ 당신 말이 맞는 것 같아요. 그렇게 오랫동안 여행하는 것은 나한테 너무 어려워요.

총 어휘 수　123

16　담화 목적　/　17　세부 내용 파악

소재　아침에 먹기 좋은 과일 추천

듣기 대본 해석

남: 여러분은 얼마나 자주 아침을 드십니까? 너무 바빠서 하루의 가장 중요한 식사를 위해 시간을 낼 수 없는 자신을 발견하십니까? 다음 번에 급할 때는, 문을 나서는 길에 과일을 집으세요. 과일은 당신이 몹시 필요로 하는 아침 활력을 당신에게 줄 수 있는 훌륭한 방법입니다. 당신이 단 한 종류의 과일만 선택해야 한다면 사과를 고르십시오. 사과는 가장 건강한 과일입니다. 당신은 "하루에 사과 하나를 먹으면 의사가 필요 없다"는 옛 속담을 들은

기억이 있을 겁니다. 사과는 비타민C로 가득 차 있고 섬유질이라 우리가 체중을 관리하는 것을 도와줄 수 있습니다. 사과는 또한 뼈를 튼튼하게 하고 콜레스테롤을 낮추는 데도 좋습니다. 사과는 심장병과, 폐암, 유방암, 대장암 그리고 간암을 예방합니다. 사과는 영양적으로 이점을 가지고 있어서 당신을 건강한 삶으로 이끌어 줄 수 있습니다. 과일은 먹기 쉽고 아주 짧은 준비 시간을 필요로 합니다. 그러니 다음 번에 당신이 충분한 아침을 먹기에 너무 바쁘면, 사과를 집으세요.

어휘

in a hurry 바쁜, 서둘러 **grab** *v.* 붙잡다 **boost** *n.* 힘, 증가 **proverb** *n.* 속담 **packed with** ~로 가득 찬 **fibrous** *a.* 섬유질의 **weight** *n.* 체중 **strengthen** *v.* 강화하다, 더 튼튼하게 하다 **prevent** *v.* 예방하다, 막다 **lung** *n.* 폐, 허파 **breast** *n.* 가슴, 유방 **colon** *n.* 결장 **liver** *n.* 간 **cancer** *n.* 암 **preparation** *n.* 준비

정답 16 ⑤ 17 ②

문제풀이

16 남자는 바빠서 아침을 먹을 수 없다면 과일을 먹으라고 권한 후, 특히 사과의 좋은 점을 언급하며 추천하고 있다. 그러므로 남자가 하는 말의 목적은 ⑤ '건강에 도움이 되도록 아침에 과일 먹는 것을 제안하려고'이다.

17 남자는 사과의 건강상 이점으로 비타민C의 공급원이고, 체중 관리에 좋으며, 뼈를 튼튼하게 하고, 여러 가지 암을 예방한다고 언급했지만 소화를 촉진시키킨다고는 언급하지 않았으므로 정답은 ② '소화를 촉진시킨다.'이다.

오답 보기 해석

16
① 과일을 신선하게 유지하는 비결을 제공하려고
② 아침 식사를 거르는 것의 위험에 대해 경고하려고
③ 하루 중 사과를 먹기에 가장 좋은 시간대를 추천하려고
④ 아침 식사를 즐길 새롭고 신나는 방법을 제안하려고

총 어휘 수 157

DICTATION ANSWERS

01 the last couple of questions / How much longer

02 not feeling so well / You were so full of energy

03 a place for relaxation and fun / use it for exercise and wellness / What we will have is a lot of car traffic / this will decrease our quality of life

04 many uses for banana peels / relieve bug bites / keep old banana peels around / didn't want me to throw it out

05 accept your invitation / I actually look forward to speaking / Your movies have been an inspiration / have a meet-and-greet before the ceremony / meet you in person

06 a stuffed animal / all of the places you've been / It really lights up / as a going away gift / looks a lot more homey

07 where do birds sleep / share their nests with each other / feel sad about the homeless birds / put them in our yard

08 looking so down / It turns out that / Was it canceled / your boss supposed to attend / You'll have another chance to

09 take a look at / they just went on sale / apply to the hiking poles

10 when you're going through puberty / try not to irritate it / the urge to squeeze it / you're prone to acne

11 Before European colonization / three-quarters of the world's supply / a superior source / consuming a moderate amount of maple syrup / strengthen the immune system

12 I doubt that one's any good / its pros and cons

13 there's too much language practice / learning a new language / grammatically correct sentences / I don't think so

14 what are you up to / throwing a surprise birthday party / need me to help with the party / contribute in some way

15 looking forward to retirement / He became quite bored with his new routine / she can't handle traveling / Neil wants to convince his wife

16-17 grab some fruit on the way out / An apple a day keeps the doctor away / are fibrous, so they can help you / strengthening your bones / grab an apple

15 수능영어듣기 실전모의고사

01 ③	02 ⑤	03 ④	04 ②	05 ⑤	06 ③
07 ②	08 ①	09 ③	10 ②	11 ④	12 ④
13 ①	14 ⑤	15 ④	16 ⑤	17 ③	

01 짧은 대화의 응답

소재 선물 내용 알아 맞추기

듣기 대본 해석
여: 이 상자 안에 네게 줄 선물이 있어. 절대 맞힐 수 없을걸!
남: 맞혀 볼게. 음... 옷 같은 거 맞지?
여: 맞아! 도대체 어떻게 알았어?
남: ③ 내가 어떤 사이즈의 옷을 입는지 어제 네가 물었잖아.

어휘
how on earth 도대체 어떻게 〈문제〉**eventually** *ad.* 결국

정답 ③

문제풀이
여자가 남자에게 선물을 주면서 절대 맞히지 못할 거라고 했는데, 남자가 맞혔고 여자는 어떻게 알았는지 묻고 있다. 이에 대한 응답으로는 ③ '내가 어떤 사이즈의 옷을 입는지 어제 네가 물어봤잖아.'가 가장 적절하다.

오답 보기 해석
① 그 가게가 결국 문을 닫을 줄 알았어.
② 그 옷들은 품질이 좋다는 걸 알았어.
④ 내가 그 상자를 탁자 위에 올려두지 말았어야 했어.
⑤ 너 그 날짜를 기억하려고 네 휴대폰에 입력해뒀잖아.

총 어휘 수 45

02 짧은 대화의 응답

소재 과학 보고서 도와주기

듣기 대본 해석
남: Helen, 학교 끝나고 내 과학 보고서 좀 도와줄 수 있니?
여: 물론이지. 도서관에서 만나는 게 어때?
남: 좋아. 계산기를 가져가야 할까?
여: ⑤ 내 생각엔 계산기를 쓰진 않을 것 같아. 그냥 교과서만 가져와.

어휘
calculator *n.* 계산기

정답 ⑤

문제풀이
계산기를 가져가야 하는지에 대한 대답이 와야 하므로 적절한 대답은 ⑤ '내 생각엔 계산기를 쓰진 않을 것 같아. 그냥 교과서만 가져와.'이다.

오답 보기 해석
① 고마워. 하지만 나 새 계산기를 샀어.
② 점심을 가져오지 않아도 돼. 무료야.
③ 올 때 내 과학 보고서 가지고 와줘.
④ 다른 데에서 만나자. 도서관이 지금 문을 닫았어.

총 어휘 수 41

03 담화 목적

소재 지하철 공사를 위한 기금 마련

듣기 대본 해석
남: 안녕하세요, 여러분. 지하철은 우리 시민들에게 가장 안전하고 시간 면에서 효율적인 교통수단입니다. 그런 이유에서 더 많은 사람들이 이용하고 도시 주변에 있는 더 많은 목적지로 데려다 주는 지하철 시스템이 필요합니다. 우리는 교통부와 접촉을 하였지만, 현재 그들은 우리 시민들의 대부분을 수용할 지하철 시스템을 만들기에 기금이 충분하지 않다고 생각합니다. 하지만 우리 사회에 최선의 것을 하는 것이 우리의 의무이기 때문에 우리는 앞으로 세 달 동안 기금을 마련할 방법에 대해 토론할 것입니다. 이는 다른 사회적 프로그램과 서비스를 포함할 수도 있습니다. 제 생각을 듣기 위해 시간을 내주신 여기 모든분들께 감사드립니다.

어휘
efficient *a.* 효율적인 **transportation** *n.* 교통수단, 수송 **citizen** *n.* 시민 **destination** *n.* 목적지, 도착지 **contact** *v.* 연락하다 **accommodate** *v.* 공간을 제공하다, 수용하다 **raise money** 돈을 마련하다

정답 ④

문제풀이
남자는 지하철이 가장 안전하고 시간을 효율적으로 사용할 수 있는 교통수단이므로 도시에 필요하지만 교통부에서 기금이 부족하여 더 만들 수 없다고 했기 때문에 앞으로 세 달 동안 기금 마련을 위한 토론을 하겠다고 알려주고 있다. 따라서 정답은 ④ '지하철 공사 기금 마련을 위한 토론을 알리려고'이다.

총 어휘 수 111

04 대화 주제

소재 국립 공원의 애완동물 입장 제한

듣기 대본 해석
남: 나 이번 주말에 Yosemite 국립 공원에 드라이브하러 갈 생각이야.
여: 정말? 멋진 여행이 될 것 같아.
남: 공원 내에 애완동물을 데려가는 데 대해 어떤 규정이 있는지 알고 있니?
여: 실제로 국립 공원은 애완동물에 대해 꽤 엄격한 규정이 있어.
남: 그래? 하지만 애완동물은 가장 좋은 여행의 동반자인 걸. 왜 그렇게 규정이 엄격하지?
여: 음. 애완동물은 국립 공원에 서식하는 더 작은 동물들을 해칠 수 있어.
남: 아, 네가 옳다고 생각되네. 나도 그런 것을 원하진 않아.
여: 너도 알다시피, 그 공원 규정은 너의 애완동물을 보호하기 위한 것이기도 해.
남: 어떻게 그렇지?
여: 사람들의 애완동물이 야생동물한테 공격받거나 때로는 죽임을 당하는 경우가 많이 있어 왔어.
남: 오, 이런! 그러면, 이번 여행에 내 애완동물은 반드시 집에 두고 가야 되겠다. 정보 고마워.

어휘
policy *n.* 정책, 방침 **companion** *n.* 동반자 **inhabit** *v.* 살다, 서식하다

정답 ②

문제풀이
남자는 주말에 국립 공원에 드라이브를 갈 예정이고, 여자가 애완동물 입장에 관한 엄격한 규정이 있다는 것과 그 이유를 설명해 주고 있다. 그러므로 ② '국립 공원에서 애완동물에 대한 규정이 엄격한 이유'가 두 사람이 하는 말의 주제로 가장 적절하다.

총 어휘 수 129

남자가 장애물을 들이받아서 창문이 깨졌다고 했는데 그림에서는 헤드라이트가 깨졌으므로 정답은 ③번이다.

총 어휘 수 141

05 대화자의 관계 파악

소재 요리 경연 대회

듣기 대본 해석

여: 오늘 저녁 당신의 요리를 잘 먹었습니다. 굉장히 독특한 맛들을 낼 수 있으시군요.

남: 감사합니다. 여러 가지 조합으로 실험을 많이 해왔어요.

여: 이렇게 닭고기를 튀기는 것은 어디서 배웠나요? 이 기술을 쓰는 사람은 한 번도 본 적이 없어요.

남: 그게, 우리 할머니께서 저를 키우셨는데 저는 그녀가 주방에 있는 것을 보곤 했어요. 제가 아는 모든 것을 할머니에게서 배웠어요.

여: 훌륭한 선생님 같군요. 주요리를 만드는 데에는 어떤 영감이 있었나요?

남: 멕시코 남부에서 현지 맛을 2년 동안 공부했어요. 이 예술(요리)에 대한 제 관점을 완전히 바꾸었지요.

여: 자신의 일에 완전히 전념하시는 것 같군요. 여기 와 주셔서 감사합니다.

남: 기회를 주셔서 감사합니다.

여: 대회 다음 라운드에서도 저희와 함께 해주시기를 바랍니다.

남: 정말이요? 기회를 주셔서 감사합니다.

어휘

unique *a.* 독특한, 특별한　　combination *n.* 조합　　inspiration *n.* 영감　　perspective *n.* 관점, 시각　　dedicated *a.* 전념하는, 헌신하는

정답 ⑤

문제풀이

여자는 남자의 요리가 맛있었다며 남자의 요리에 대한 여러 가지 질문을 하고 있고 남자에게 다음 라운드에 가게 됐다고 말하고 있는 것으로 보아 두 사람의 관계는 ⑤ '심사위원 — 대회참가자'이다.

총 어휘 수 133

06 그림의 세부 내용 파악

소재 장애물을 들이받은 자동차 사고

듣기 대본 해석

여: 안녕, Spencer. 오늘 아침 회의에 왜 그렇게 늦었어?

남: 나에게 힘든 하루였어. 정말 많은 문제가 있었거든.

여: 정말? 무슨 일이었는데?

남: 음, 회의에 늦지 않으려고 집에서 정말 일찍 나갔는데 가는 길에 도로공사를 하고 있더라고.

여: 그렇구나. 그래서 도로를 막은 거야?

남: 맞아. 나는 그다지 주의를 기울이지 않았고 장애물을 들이받아서 내 차의 창문이 깨졌어.

여: 끔찍하다.

남: 그게 다가 아니야. 내 GPS가 우회경로를 찾아내지 못해서 일반 지도를 사용해야 했어.

여: 그런 지도는 난 몇 년 동안 보지 않았지.

남: 난 길을 잃어버려서 스마트폰을 가진 여자분에게 도와달라고 부탁해야 했어.

여: 처음 보는 사람의 친절함에 의지할 수 있다니 좋구나.

남: 네 말이 맞는 것 같아. 더 나쁜 상황이 되었을 수도 있었는데.

어휘

construction *n.* 공사, 건설　　detour *n.* 우회길　　count on 의지하다, 기대다

정답 ③

07 할 일

소재 어머니의 크리스마스 방문

듣기 대본 해석

남: 여보, 나 왔어요. 무슨 일 있어요?

여: 방금 엄마한테 전화 받았어요. 엄마가 휴가를 보내기 위해 우리 집에 오신대요!

남: 그거 좋은데요!

여: 네, 나도 좋아요. 그런데 크리스마스는 겨우 이틀 뒤인데 난 엄마의 방문에 대해 계획을 하지 않았어요!

남: 여보, 괜찮아요. 걱정하지 말아요.

여: 집도 준비를 해야 하고 엄마께 드릴 선물도 사지 못했어요.

남: 내가 도와줄게요. 내가 집에서 일할까요, 아님 선물 사러 갈까요?

여: 음, 내가 당신보다 엄마의 취향을 좀 더 잘 아니까 내가 선물을 사야 된다고 생각해요.

남: 네, 그렇네요. 그러면 내가 집안을 조금 치울게요. 어머님은 언제 도착하실까요?

여: 엄마의 비행기는 오후 7시에 도착하니까 내가 내일 일 끝나고 공항에 모시러 갈게요.

남: 네, 좋은 생각이네요.

어휘

taste *n.* 기호, 취향　　make sense 말이 되다, 이치에 맞다, 의미가 통하다　　pick up ∼을 (차에) 태우러 가다

정답 ②

문제풀이

어머니의 선물을 사는 일과 집안 일 중 여자는 자신이 어머니의 취향을 더 잘 알기 때문에 선물을 사겠다고 했고 남자는 집을 치우겠다고 했으므로 정답은 ② '집안 청소 하기'이다.

총 어휘 수 144

08 이유

소재 프레젠테이션 준비

듣기 대본 해석

여: 안녕하세요, Shepherd씨.

남: 안녕하세요, Paula. 오늘 저녁에 있을 회의 준비가 모두 되었나요?

여: 밤새 내내 준비해서 드디어 이제 프레젠테이션 준비가 끝났습니다.

남: 잘됐네요. 세탁소에서 제 정장을 찾았나요?

여: 네, 사무실 옷장에 있습니다.

남: 열심히 이 일을 해준 것에 대해 정말 고마워요. 이제 제 프레젠테이션을 좀 봐야겠군요.

여: 이메일로 보내드렸는데요. 수신함을 확인해보세요. 오, 그런데 회의가 1시로 일정이 변경되었습니다.

남: 뭐라고요? 그건 너무 이른데요. 회의 전에 먹을 시간이 없겠군요.

여: 걱정 마세요. 점심을 이미 주문했습니다. 사무실에서 드실 수 있어요.

남: 오, 잘됐군요. 고마워요.

closet *n.* 옷장, 벽장   reschedule *v.* 일정을 변경하다

정답 ①

문제풀이
여자가 회의 시간이 1시로 변경되었다고 말하자 남자가 너무 이르다며 회의 전에 점심 먹을 시간이 없겠다고 했고 여자는 미리 점심을 주문했으니 사무실에서 먹을 수 있다고 했으므로 정답은 ① '회의 시작 시간이 변경되어서'이다.

총 어휘 수 129

09 숫자

소재 숙박 요금 계산

듣기 대본 해석
남: 안녕하세요. 체크아웃 준비 되셨나요?
여: 네. 몇 분 늦어서 죄송해요.
남: 괜찮습니다.
여: 잘됐군요. 저번에 묵었던 곳은 5분 늦게 나왔다고 15달러를 연체료로 청구했거든요.
남: 걱정 마세요. 몇 분 늦으신다고 저희한테 피해가 가진 않아요. 카드로 내시겠어요?
여: 아니요. 여기 현금 있어요.
남: 알겠습니다. 금액이 세금 포함해서 120달러네요.
여: 네? 어제 왔을 때는 110달러라고 그러셨잖아요.
남: 그건 숙박료입니다. 하지만 여기 어젯밤에 영화를 주문하셨던 것으로 나타나는데요.
여: 그렇군요. 주문한 영화가 그렇게 비쌀 줄은 몰랐네요. 여기 150달러요.
남: 네. *[잠시 후]* 여기 거스름돈이요.

어휘
check out (호텔에서 비용을 지불하고) 나가다, 확인하다
inconvenience *n.* 불편, 피해   **change** *n.* 거스름돈, 변화 *v.* 바꾸다

정답 ③

문제풀이
여자가 낼 숙박료는 120달러인데 150달러를 냈다고 했으므로 거스름돈의 액수는 ③ '$30'이다.

총 어휘 수 147

10 언급 유무

소재 조건에 맞는 아파트

듣기 대본 해석
여: 여보, 아파트 안내 광고를 좀 봐요. 올해가 가기 전에 어느 아파트를 임대할지 결정해야 해요.
남: 맞아요. Demarest랑 Willington 중 어느 지역이 더 좋아요?
여: 사실 나는 Demarest가 더 좋지만 그 아파트들은 보통 훨씬 더 비싸요.
남: 그럼 Willington 지역을 봐요. 이 곳도 제법 살기 좋은 곳이에요.
여: 좋아요. 우리가 지불할 수 있는 최대 임대 비용은 한 달에 2,000달러 인 것 같아요.
남: 맞는 말이에요. 집의 크기는요? 우리가 적어도 세 개의 침실이 필요하다고 생각하지 않아요?
여: 그래요. 우리 아이들이 각자 자기 방을 쓰고 싶어하니까요.
남: 좋아요. 그들은 또한 7층 이상의 아파트에서 살고 싶어해요.
여: 동의해요. 아파트가 높을수록 경치가 더 좋아요.
남: 글쎄. 우리의 요구조건을 모두 만족시킬 아파트를 찾는 게 쉽지는 않을 거예요.

어휘
classified ad (항목별) 광고   rent *v.* 임대하다 *n.* 임대료
requirement *n.* 필요조건, 요구

정답 ③

문제풀이
위치는 Demarest와 Willington 중 하나로, 가격은 2,000달러 이하로, 침실의 개수는 3개로, 선호하는 층은 7층 이상으로 언급되었으나 편의시설에 관한 내용은 없으므로 정답은 ③ '편의시설'이다.

총 어휘 수 154

11 내용 일치 · 불일치

소재 Berry Delicious Day에 관한 안내

듣기 대본 해석
남: 안녕하세요 학생 여러분. 저는 Dustin Swift이고, Blue Mystic Berry Farm을 대표하여 말씀드리겠습니다. 저는 Berry Delicious Day에 대해서 소개해 드리고자 합니다. 딸기, 블루베리와 함께, 우리는 여러분이 직접 블랙베리, 라즈베리, 보이즌베리를 수확해볼 수 있는 Berry Delicious Day를 이번 토요일에 개최합니다. 행사는 오전 10시에 시작해서 오후 2시까지 계속됩니다. 무료이기 때문에 부모님께 말씀을 드려 온 가족을 모시고 오세요. 여러분이 따게 될 베리는 노숙자 쉼터를 돕기 위해 판매될 파이를 만드는 데 사용될 것입니다. 반드시 옷을 알맞게 입으시길 바랍니다. 소매가 긴 셔츠와 바지를 입으셔서 베리 덤불에 찔리지 않도록 하세요. 몇몇 베리들은 애완동물에게 해롭기 때문에 애완동물을 집에 두고 오시기를 요청합니다. 토요일에 여기 Blue Mystic Berry Farm에서 여러분들을 뵙기를 바랍니다.

어휘
announce *v.* 알리다, 발표하다   **harvest** *v.* 수확하다
free of charge 무료로   **benefit** *v.* ~에게 유익하다, 이롭다
appropriately *ad.* 알맞게   **bush** *n.* 덤불   **harmful** *a.* 해로운

정답 ④

문제풀이
베리 덤불에 찔리지 않도록 긴 셔츠와 바지를 입으라고 당부했으므로 내용과 일치하지 않는 것은 ④ '참가자는 활동을 위해 반바지를 입는 것이 좋다.'이다.

총 어휘 수 151

12 도표

소재 캠핑카 선택

듣기 대본 해석
남: 내가 이번 여름 우리 캠핑 여행을 위해서 레저용 자동차 대여를 찾아 봤어. 예약을 빨리 해야 될 것 같아.
여: 맞아. 그래야지. 너무 늦을 때까지 기다리면 안 되니까.
남: 음. 내가 다섯 가지 다른 옵션이 있는 회사를 찾았어.
여: 어디 보자. *[잠시 후]* 온 가족이 가는 거니까 최소한 네 명이 잘 수 있는 차가 필요해.
남: 맞아. 근데 좀 더 큰 걸 대여하는 게 좋을 것 같아. 적어도 다섯 명이 잘 수 있는 게 더 나을 것 같아.
여: 알겠어. 근데 물 연결 필요해?
남: 있으면 좋지. 그러면 샤워를 할 수 있으니까.
여: 알겠어. 스토브랑 냉장고는? 요리의 대부분은 야외에서 하잖아.
남: 이 옵션은 포함시키자. 음식 저장해 두려고 아이스박스 챙기는 건 정말 귀찮은 일이야.
여: 알겠어. 그럼 이제 선택지가 이 두 개로 좁혀졌네.

남: 굳이 돈을 더 낼 필요는 없는 것 같아. 더 싼 걸로 하자.
여: 좋아. 어서 예약해.

어휘
RV *n.* 레저용 자동차　　**reservation** *n.* 예약　　**hookup** *n.* 연결
hassle *n.* 번거로운 일, 귀찮은 일　　**cooler** *n.* 아이스박스

정답 ④

문제풀이
먼저 적어도 다섯 명이 잘 수 있는 차로 하자고 했으므로 ②~⑤번 중에 고르게
되고 물 연결과 스토브, 냉장고도 포함시키면 ④번과 ⑤번이 남게 되는데 이
중에 싼 걸로 하자고 했으므로 정답은 ④번이다.

총 어휘 수 179

13　긴 대화의 응답

소재 티켓 챙기기

듣기 대본 해석
여: 여보, 우리 늦겠어요. 아직 준비 안 됐어요?
남: 서두르려고 하는데 휴대폰을 잃어버린 것 같아요.
여: 아까 소파에서 본 것 같은데요.
남: 아, 여기 있다. 좋아. 가기 전에 살펴야 할 게 있어요?
여: 오, 우리가 없는 동안 누가 물고기 먹이를 주죠?
남: 진정해요. Garcia 부인이 돌봐준댔어요.
여: 좋아요. 티켓을 꼭 가져가야 해요. 출력은 했죠?
남: 아니요. 하지만 휴대폰에 저장해 놨어요.
여: 휴대폰에 저장했다고요? 이젠 프린트로 출력할 필요가 없는 거예요?
남: 없어요. 바로 여기 전자 티켓이 있어요. 가판대에서 보여주기만 하면 돼요.
여: 전자 티켓이라. 꽤 편리해 보이는데 그래도 혹시 모르니까 출력하는 게
　　좋을 것 같아요.
남: ① 좋은 생각이에요. 내가 지금 그걸 할게요.

어휘
kiosk *n.* 매점, 가판대　　**convenient** *a.* 편리한　　**in case** (~할)
경우에 대비해서

정답 ①

문제풀이
만약에 사태에 대비해서 출력을 해두는 게 나을 것 같다고 말하는 여자의
말에 대한 남자의 대답으로 적절한 것은 ① '좋은 생각이에요. 내가 지금 그걸
할게요.'이다.

오답 보기 해석
② 내가 Garcia 부인에게 집 열쇠를 줬어요.
③ 우리는 충분한 물고기 먹이가 있어야 해요.
④ 알았어요. 그가 그것들을 우리한테 가져올 수 있는지 알아볼게요.
⑤ 알겠어요. 나는 이미 휴대폰을 켰어요.

총 어휘 수 151

14　긴 대화의 응답

소재 놓고 온 물건 가져다 줄 것 요청하기

듣기 대본 해석
[휴대폰이 울린다.]
남: 여보세요?
여: Charlie, 나 Riley야.
남: 안녕 Riley. 무슨 일이야?

여: 음, 지금 회의 때문에 EPL 본부로 가는 중이야.
남: 우리 새 경기장에 대해서 발표할 준비 돼 있어?
여: 응, 근데...
남: 근데 뭐? 무슨 문제 있어?
여: 그게, 발표 자료들을 다 사무실 책상에 두고 온 것 같아. 네가 어떻게 나에게
　　갖다 줄 수 있는 방법은 없을까?
남: 나도 도와주고 싶은데 내가 가져갈 수 있는 방법이 없어. 지금 사무실이
　　아니거든.
여: 근데 벌써 12시고 회의는 1시간 뒤에 시작해. 거기 다시 가서 자료들을
　　가져오면 시간 안에 도착할 수가 없어.
남: 정말 어떻게 할 수 없는 문제네. Kyle에게 전화해 봐. 아마 사무실에 있을
　　거야.
여: ⑤ 알았어. 그에게 전화해서 자료를 가져다 줄 수 있는지 물어볼게.

어휘
dilemma *n.* 진퇴양난, 궁지

정답 ⑤

문제풀이
여자는 발표에 필요한 자료들을 모두 사무실에 놓고 와서 난처한 상황이며
남자도 현재 사무실에 있지 않아 가져다 줄 수 없어 다른 사람에게 전화해볼
것을 제안했다. 이에 대해 가장 적절한 여자의 응답은 ⑤ '알았어. 그에게
전화해서 자료를 가져다 줄 수 있는지 물어볼게.'이다.

오답 보기 해석
① 그 경기장은 한 시까지 문을 열지 않아.
② 그래. 자료들을 최대한 빨리 가져다 줄게.
③ 내가 발표를 취소할 수 있을 거라고 생각하니?
④ 나쁘진 않네. 언제까지 발표가 준비돼야 하니?

총 어휘 수 149

15　상황에 적절한 말

소재 게임 결승전에서 우승하지 못한 친구 위로하기

듣기 대본 해석
남: Ryan과 Jason은 Counter Strike: GO라는 유명한 일인칭 슈팅 게임의
　　결승전에서 방금 패배했습니다. Ryan은 시합 초반부에 큰 실수를 몇 번
　　했으며, 이러한 실수들로 인해 그들은 경기에서 패배합니다. Jason은
　　경기 후에 Ryan이 밖에서 혼자 길에 앉아 있는 것을 발견합니다. 그는
　　Ryan이 속상하고 자신한테 실망한 듯 보이는 모습을 알게 됩니다. Jason은
　　속상하지 않고 오히려 결승전까지 간 것이 자랑스럽습니다. 그는 Ryan에게
　　그는 최선을 다했고 그의 노력 덕분에 결승전까지 올 수 있었음을 알고
　　있으며, Ryan에게 힘을 내라고 말하고 싶어합니다. 이러한 상황에서
　　Jason이 Ryan에게 할 말로 가장 적절한 것은 무엇일까요?
Jason: ④ 네가 없었더라면 우리는 결승까지 가지 못했을 거야.

어휘
upset *a.* 속상한　　**disappointed** *a.* 실망한, 낙담한　　〈문제〉 **cancel**
v. 취소하다

정답 ④

문제풀이
게임 결승전에서 실수를 해서 낙담해 있는 친구에게 위로를 해주고 싶은
상황이다. 또 Jason은 Ryan덕분에 결승전까지 갈 수 있었다는 것을 말해주고
싶다고 했으므로 Jason이 할 말로 적절한 것은 ④ '네가 없었더라면 우리는
결승까지 가지 못했을 거야.'이다.

오답 보기 해석

① 나한테 친절하게 대해줘서 정말 고마워.

② 빨리 가서 경기에 최선을 다하자.

③ 챔피언전 이긴 걸 축하해.

⑤ 그들이 챔피언전을 취소해서 좋지 않아?

총 어휘 수 131

16 담화 주제 / 17 세부 내용 파악

소재 환경오염의 원인과 해결책

듣기 대본 해석

남: 요즘 인간은 오염의 영향으로부터 고통을 받기 시작하고 있습니다. 오염의 원인이 되는 많은 요인들이 있습니다. 그것들 중에 몇몇은 자연적이지만, 그것들의 대부분은 인간이 만들었고 예방이 가능합니다. 분명한 것부터 시작하면, 사람들은 종종 쓰레기로 거리와 수로를 오염시킵니다. 우리의 환경을 보호하고 아름답게 하는 데 도움을 주기 위해 스스로 뒤처리를 하는 것은 우리의 의무입니다. 재활용은 환경을 돕기 위한 좋은 방법인데 그것은 쓰레기 매립지로 가는 소비자의 폐기물의 양을 줄여주기 때문입니다. 개인 자동차는 또한 공기 오염에 상당히 기여합니다. 그러므로, 자전거 타기 또는 대중교통수단 이용이 우리 환경에 큰 도움을 줄 수 있습니다. 발전소 또한 공기를 오염시킬 수 있습니다. 만약 우리가 가정에서 에너지 사용을 줄인다면, 발전소로부터의 배기가스를 줄일 수 있습니다. 우리는 반드시 에너지 효율이 좋은 전구를 사용하고 에너지 효율이 좋은 가전제품에 투자를 해야 합니다. 이것은 공기 오염을 줄일 뿐만 아니라 우리로 하여금 돈을 절약하게 해 줄 것입니다.

어휘

man-made *a.* 인공의　**preventable** *a.* 예방 가능한
pick up after ~의 뒤처리를 하다　**landfill** *n.* 쓰레기 매립지
plant *n.* 공장　**emission** *n.* 배출가스　**efficient** *a.* 효율적인
appliance *n.* 가전제품

정답 16 ⑤　17 ③

문제풀이

16 남자는 사람들의 어떤 행동이 환경을 오염시키는지 그리고 그를 막기 위한 해결책을 제시하고 있으므로 남자가 하는 말의 주제는 ⑤ '환경 오염에 대한 원인과 해결책'이다.

17 남자는 환경오염을 줄이기 위한 방법으로 쓰레기 줍기, 재활용과 대중교통 수단의 이용, 에너지 아껴 쓰기를 제시했으므로 언급하지 않은 것은 ③ '태양 에너지 사용하기'이다.

오답 보기 해석

16

① 사람들이 오염에 기여하는 방법

② 공기 질 향상을 위해 해야 할 것들

③ 오염이 환경에 끼치는 영향

④ 에너지 절약 습관을 갖는 것의 이점

17

① 쓰레기 줍기

② 재활용 하기

④ 대중교통수단 사용하기

⑤ 에너지 아껴 쓰기

총 어휘 수 156

01 How on earth

02 How about we meet

03 the safest and most time-efficient method / accommodates most of our citizens / spending the next three months discussing

04 have rather strict rules / the best travel companions / to protect your pet / leave my pet at home

05 fry the chicken like that / the inspirations for the main dish / dedicated to your work / the next round of the competition

06 road construction on the way / paying attention / find a detour / count on the kindness of strangers

07 Christmas is only two days away / bought her a gift / that makes sense / pick her up at the airport

08 pick up my suit from the dry cleaners / hard work you put in here / has actually been rescheduled / ordered lunch

09 charged us a fifteen-dollar late fee / charge it to your card / includes sales tax / you ordered a movie

10 before the end of the year / a good area to live in / The higher the apartment is / meets all of our requirements

11 It's free of charge / dress appropriately / avoid getting pricked by / leave your pets at home

12 offers five different options / take showers / narrows it down

13 Aren't you ready yet / feed the fish / You printed them out / That sounds quite convenient

14 I'm on my way to / Is there any way you can / make it in time / quite a dilemma

15 it was due to these mistakes / disappointed in himself / did his best / thanks to his hard work

16-17 suffer from the effects of pollution / cuts down on the amount of consumer waste / using public transportation / invest in energy-efficient appliances

01 ④	02 ②	03 ②	04 ⑤	05 ⑤	06 ②
07 ⑤	08 ⑤	09 ①	10 ③	11 ②	12 ③
13 ②	14 ③	15 ⑤	16 ④	17 ⑤	

01 짧은 대화의 응답

소재 영화표 구입

듣기 대본 해석

남: Wrong Number 영화표 두 장 살 수 있나요?
여: 물론이죠. 몇 시 영화로 하시겠어요?
남: 저녁 7시요. 어른 2명 앞 쪽이요.
여: ④ 그 쇼는 발코니 자리밖에 남아있지 않네요.

어휘

〈문제〉 **available** *a.* 이용할 수 있는

정답 ④

문제풀이

남자는 극장에서 원하는 좌석을 말하고 있으므로 그에 대한 여자의 응답으로
④ '그 쇼는 발코니 자리밖에 남아있지 않네요.'가 적절하다.

오답 보기 해석

① 예, 이쪽으로 저를 따라오세요.
② 죄송합니다. 줄 서서 기다리셔야 합니다.
③ Wrong Number는 더 이상 상영되지 않습니다.
⑤ 안 됩니다. 당신은 매니저와 이야기해야 해요.

총 어휘 수 36

02 짧은 대화의 응답

소재 머그잔 사용

듣기 대본 해석

여: 오, 너 커피 머그산을 쓰고 있구나.
남: 응. 일회용 컵을 쓰는 것은 환경에 절대로 좋지 않아.
여: 전적으로 동의해. 나도 내 머그잔을 하나 사서 너와 함께 동참해야겠다.
남: ② 나에게 남는 머그잔들이 있어. 너한테 하나 줄 수 있어.

어휘

disposable *a.* 일회용의   〈문제〉 **prefer A to B** A를 B보다 선호하다
from now on 이제부터

정답 ②

문제풀이

머그잔을 사서 머그잔 사용하기에 동참하겠다는 여자의 말에 적절한 남자의
응답은 ② '나에게 남는 머그잔들이 있어. 너한테 하나 줄 수 있어.'이다.

오답 보기 해석

① 오늘 아침에 환경에 대한 뉴스를 들었어.
③ 종이컵을 쓰는 것은 참 편리해.
④ 틀렸어. 난 차를 커피보다 더 좋아해.
⑤ 이제부터 커피를 마시지 않겠어.

총 어휘 수 48

03 담화 목적

소재 교내 식당 시설 개선

듣기 대본 해석

여: 안녕하세요, 학생 여러분. 오늘 점심 식사 하실 계획이시죠? 아마 여러분이
"네."라고 말할 거라고 생각합니다. 그러면 여러분은 학교 식당에 대해
어떻게 생각하시나요? 시설이 좋다고 생각하시나요? 이마 아닐 겁니다. 최근
많은 학생들이 식당에 대해 꽤 불평을 하고 있습니다. 그들 중 몇몇은 학교
웹사이트에 글을 올리기도 했습니다. 저도 그 중 한 명입니다. 불행하게도,
학교는 저희의 얘기를 듣고 있는 것 같지 않습니다. 교내 식당은 우리 학교에
좋지 않은 평판만 주고 있습니다. 우리가 시설을 개선하지 않는다면 그런
평판은 계속 악화될 것입니다. 우리 모두 더 나은 학교 생활을 보장받기
위해 빨리 식당을 보수해야 합니다.

어휘

facility *n.* 시설, 설비   **complaint** *n.* 불평   **reputation** *n.* 평판,
명성   **renovate** *v.* 보수하다, 개조하다

정답 ②

문제풀이

여자는 교내 식당 시설에 대해 많은 학생들이 불만을 제기하고 있으며, 학교의
평판이 나빠지고 있으니 빨리 보수되어야 한다고 말하고 있다. 따라서 정답은
② '교내 식당의 시설 개선을 요청하려고'이다.

총 어휘 수 118

04 대화 주제

소재 휴대폰과 건강

듣기 대본 해석

남: 와, 내 휴대폰이 정말 뜨거워졌어.
여: 너무 오랫동안 사용하면 안 돼.
남: 휴대폰이 건강에 좋지 않다는 것에 대해 어떻게 생각해?
여: 음. 지나친 장시간 휴대폰 사용이 뇌종양을 일으킬 수 있다고 보여준 많은
    연구를 알고 있어.
남: 나도 전에 라디오에서 들었어.
여: 진자파는 우리 몸에 위험해. 그리고 이 사실이 많은 연구에서 밝혀져 왔지.
남: 나도 알아. 하지만 일 때문에 나는 상당히 자주 휴대폰을 사용해야 하거든.
여: 그럼, 네가 소심해서 사용할 수 있는 방법들이 있어. 예를 들어, 네가 이어폰을
    사용하면 휴대폰 자체와 직접적인 접촉을 피하잖아.
남: 맞아. 나도 이어폰을 좀 더 자주 착용하기 시작해야겠어.
여: 다른 안전 예방책도 있어. 인터넷에서 찾아볼 수 있을 거야.

어휘

harmful *a.* 해로운   **excessive** *a.* 지나친, 과도한   **tumor** *n.* 종양
avoid *v.* 피하다, 막다

정답 ⑤

문제풀이

뇌종양 유발 및 전자파에 대한 노출 등 과도한 휴대폰 사용이 건강에 미치는
부정적인 영향에 대해 대화를 나누고 있으므로 정답은 ⑤ '휴대폰 사용이 건강에
미치는 영향'이다.

총 어휘 수 140

05 심정 파악

소재 코치 교체 후 연패

듣기 대본 해석

남: 안녕, Monica. 경기 어땠어?
여: 글쎄. 내가 너한테 이건 말할 수 있어. 당분간은 다른 경기를 보지 않을 거라고.
남: 왜? 나는 네가 미식축구를 정말 좋아한다고 생각했어. 너네 팀이 작년에 정말 잘하지 않았어?
여: 응. 그들은 수퍼볼에서 우승했지. 그런데 그 후에 코치가 은퇴했어. 새 코치가 왔고 팀이 전에 없이 형편없이 경기하고 있어!
남: 너는 이번 새 코치의 팬이 아닌 것처럼 들리네.
여: 그 코치 때문에 팀이 경기를 못하는 것 같아.
남: 그가 그렇게 별로야?
여: 글쎄. 그 팀의 기록을 봐. 올해 우리는 원정경기에서 한 번도 못 이겼어.
남: 진정해. 나는 그들이 이번 시즌에 경기가 차츰 좋아질 거라고 확신해.
여: 나는 그러길 바라지만 정말 그럴 것 같지가 않아. 지난주에도 그들보다 훨씬 약한 팀에 졌거든.
남: 오늘 경기는 어땠는데?
여: 그들은 리그에서 최고의 팀과 경기했고 물론 졌지.

어휘

retire *v.* 은퇴하다   **away game** 원정 경기   **league** *n.* (스포츠 경기의) 리그

정답 ⑤

문제풀이

여자가 좋아하는 미식축구팀이 코치가 교체된 후 계속 지고 있어서 여자는 그것이 새 코치 때문이라고 말하는 것으로 보아 여자의 심정은 ⑤ '스트레스를 받는'이 가장 적절하다.

오답 보기 해석

① 당황스러운
② 죄책감을 느끼는
③ 행복한
④ 느긋한

총 어휘 수 149

06 그림의 세부 내용 파악

소재 새 사무실 안내

듣기 대본 해석

여: 여기가 당신의 사무실이에요. Smith씨.
남: 와! 제가 상상했던 것보다 훨씬 좋아요. 창 밖을 봐요. 산의 경치가 얼마나 아름다운지!
여: 사랑스러워요, 그렇죠? 그것이 우리가 그 방향을 마주보게 의자를 놓은 이유예요.
남: 멋지네요. 그리고 저 책상 위에 있는 것이 저의 새 노트북 같군요.
여: 물론이죠. 지난주에 그걸 샀어요. 당신이 필요한 모든 것이 이미 노트북에 다 들어 있을 거예요.
남: 그런데 저 시계는 제가 어떻게 좀 해야 할 것 같아요.
여: 무슨 뜻이죠?
남: 얼마나 큰지 보세요. 너무 주의를 산만하게 하네요.
여: 당신이 원한다면 시계를 없애셔도 돼요.
남: 제가 커피를 좋아하는 것을 어떻게 알았어요?
여: 당신이 커피를 즐겨 마시게 보였어요, Smith씨. 농담이에요. 저희 모든 사무실마다 전기 커피포트가 있어요. 어쨌든. 저희 빌딩에 오신 것을 환영해요.
남: 정말 감사합니다.

어휘

distracting *a.* 주의집중을 방해하는 · **get rid of** ~을 없애다

정답 ②

문제풀이

대화의 앞부분에서 창 밖 경치가 좋아서 의자를 그 방향으로 마주보게 놓았다고 했는데 그림에서는 반대 방향으로 놓여 있으므로 정답은 ②번이다.

총 어휘 수 141

07 부탁한 일

소재 아빠의 은퇴 파티 준비

듣기 대본 해석

남: Linda. 아빠 은퇴 기념파티 할 장소 정했니?
여: 두세 군데 생각해뒀어. 첫 번째는 새로 생긴 멕시칸 그릴이고 다른 한 곳은 그리스 식당이야.
남: 음. 너도 알다시피 아빠가 그리스 음식을 좋아하시니까 그리스 식당으로 가는 게 어떨까?
여: 그게 좋겠다.
남: 아빠 선물도 벌써 샀니?
여: 아니, 안 샀어. 너는?
남: 나도 안 샀어. 내 생각에 우리가 선물을 같이 사야 할 것 같아. 아마 아빠가 좋아하시는 비타민을 사드릴 수 있을 거야.
여: 그거 훌륭한 선물이겠다.
남: 좋았어. 내가 내일 일하면서 살게. 카드는 네가 살 수 있어?
여: 물론이지. 좋은 데 알아.
남: 완벽하네. 그럼 내일 보자.
여: 그래. 그때 봐.

어휘

retirement *n.* 퇴직, 은퇴

정답 ⑤

문제풀이

남자와 여자가 같이 아빠의 은퇴 기념파티를 준비하면서 식당을 정하고 선물을 준비하는 대화이다. 남자가 선물을 사겠다고 했고 여자에게 카드를 살 수 있는지 물었으므로 정답은 ⑤ '카드 사기'이다.

오답 보기 해석

① 예약하기
② 비타민 사기
③ 선물 추천하기
④ 저녁 준비하기

총 어휘 수 124

08 이유

소재 아빠에게 화가 난 엄마

듣기 대본 해석

여: 거실 청소해 주어서 고마워, Thomas.
남: 괜찮아요, 엄마.
여: 근데, 나의 USB 드라이브 봤니?
남: 못 본 것 같은데요. 왜요?
여: 음, 내 생각에는 탁자 위에 놓아둔 것 같은데 오늘은 찾을 수 없는 것 같아서.
남: 아, 맞아요. 아빠가 가지고 가시는 걸 봤어요.
여: 응? 아빠가 사무실에 가지고 가셨다고?

남: 네. 아빠가 함께 일하시는 분의 컴퓨터에서 파일을 꺼내는 데 그것이 필요하다고 말씀하셨어요.
여: 정말? 설마 그럴 리가. 그가 내 USB 드라이브를 먼저 물어보지 않고 가지고 갔다고?
남: 아빠가 엄마에게 물어보지 않으셨다는 거죠?
여: 절대로 안 물었지. 아빠는 거기에 우리 가족 사진 몇 장이 있다는 것을 알아. 그건 나에게 매우 중요해.
남: 아마 아빠가 묻는 것을 잊으셨나 봐요.
여: 때때로 나는 너의 아빠가 이해가 안 돼. 행동하기 전에 생각을 안 하셔.
남: 진정하세요, 엄마. 모두 잘 될 거라고 확신해요.

어휘
coworker *n.* 동료

정답 ⑤

문제풀이
엄마는 아빠가 자신의 허락을 받지 않고 가족 사진이 들어 있는 중요한 USB를 회사에 가져가서 화가 나 있다. 따라서 정답은 ⑤ '자신의 USB 드라이브를 허락 없이 가져가서'이다.

총 어휘 수 140

09 숫자

소재 옷 구매하기

듣기 대본 해석
여: 안녕하세요. 아들한테 줄 새 스웨터를 사려고 하는데요.
남: 도와드리겠습니다. 나이가 어떻게 되죠?
여: 15살이요. 보통 성인 중간사이즈로 입어요.
남: 좋습니다. 자, 고를 수 있는 몇 가지 소재가 있는데요, 면하고 울 중에서 어떤 게 좋으세요?
여: 가격 차이가 어떻게 되죠?
남: 면 스웨터는 55달러이고 울은 20달러 더 비싸요. 면으로 된 것이 요즘 정말 인기가 많아요.
여: 좋네요. 그럼 면으로 된 걸로 할게요. 청바지도 사고 싶은데요.
남: 네. 이 스키니 진이 스웨터하고 잘 어울려요. 정상가는 50달러지만 10퍼센트 세일하고 있습니다.
어: 스웨터도 할인이 적용되나요?
남: 죄송하지만 할인은 청바지에만 적용됩니다.
어: 괜찮습니다. 이쨌든 둘 다 주세요. 여기 카드 있습니다.
남: 감사합니다.

어휘
apply to ～에 적용되다

정답 ①

문제풀이
여자는 아들 옷으로 55달러짜리 면 스웨터와 10퍼센트 세일 중인 50달러짜리 스키니 진을 선택했다. 그러므로 55달러와 45달러를 합쳐 총 ① '$100'를 지불해야 한다.

총 어휘 수 143

10 언급 유무

소재 소설에 관한 대화

듣기 대본 해석
남: Amy, 벌써 다른 책을 읽고 있니?
여: 응. 지난번 책은 다 읽었고 오늘 아침 이 책을 읽기 시작했어. The Prized Prince라는 책이야.

남: 들어본 것 같은데. 최근 베스트셀러 목록에 있던 것 아니니?
여: 맞아. 200만 부가 넘게 팔렸지.
남: 정말 많이 팔렸구나! 그 책은 무엇 때문에 그렇게 인기가 많을까?
여: 무엇보다도 Steve Queen에 의해 쓰여졌잖아. 너도 알다시피 그는 정말 유명해.
남: Steve Queen? 그러면 그 책은 틀림없이 공포소설이겠구나.
여: 아니. 실은 이번에는 로맨스 소설이야.
남: 아. 난 로맨스 소설을 좋아하지는 않아. 그건 지루하거든.
여: 이것은 보통 로맨스 소설과는 약간 달라. 난 그것을 영화로 만들 계획이라고 온라인에서 읽었어.
남: 멋지네. 그런 경우면 한번 시도해 보고 싶은걸.
여: 그래. 내가 다 읽으면 너에게 빌려줄게.

어휘
horror novel 공포소설　　in that case 그런 경우에는, 그렇다면
give it a shot ～을 시도하다

정답 ③

문제풀이
두 사람은 책의 판매 부수, 저자, 장르, 영화 제작 계획에 대해서는 언급했지만, 출판사에 대해서는 언급하지 않았으므로 정답은 ③ '출판사'이다.

총 어휘 수 146

11 내용 일치 · 불일치

소재 Science Fair 소개

듣기 대본 해석
여: 좋은 아침입니다, 여러분. 저는 올해의 Science Fair에 대해 말하려 합니다. 올해 모든 사람들은 팀이 되어 일할 것이고 여러분은 처음부터 끝까지 여러분의 프로젝트를 촬영할 것입니다. 팀은 서너 명의 학급친구들로 구성될 것입니다. 모든 팀은 올해의 과학 카탈로그에서 서로 다른 주제를 고를 것입니다. 올해의 주제는 수중 호흡, 경주용 차 디자인, 쓰레기 압축하는 과정, 로봇 가정부의 움직임을 포함하고 있습니다. 물론 프로젝트는 작동이 되는 모델을 만들 필요는 없고 개념의 입증만 있으면 됩니다. 모든 팀원의 이름과 여러분이 정한 주제를 지원서와 함께 5월 5일 오후 5시까지 제출해 주십시오. 질문이 있으면 과학 선생님께 이메일을 보내세요. 여러분 모두의 작업을 보는 것이 기대가 됩니다.

어휘
include *v.* 포함하다　　proof *n.* 입증, 증거　　concept *n.* 개념
application *n.* 지원서

정답 ②

문제풀이
주제는 올해의 과학 카탈로그에서 팀 별로 서로 다른 주제를 골라야 하므로 ② '주제는 제한 없이 자유롭게 선택하면 된다.'가 일치하지 않는다.

총 어휘 수 131

12 도표

소재 자동차 바퀴(휠) 구입

듣기 대본 해석
여: 무엇을 도와 드릴까요?
남: 제 차에 쓸 새로운 바퀴(휠)를 찾고 있어요. 제가 그것을 구입했을 때 딸려 나온 공장 것들은 맘에 들지 않아요.
여: 알겠습니다. 22 또는 24인치 휠이 손님의 차에 맞을 것 같네요.
남: 제가 좀 낮게 타는 것을 좋아해서 22인치 휠이 저한테 더 맞을 것 같군요.

여: 알겠습니다. 색상이 섞인 것이 좋으세요, 단색의 검은 가장자리가 좋으세요?
남: 색이 섞인 것은 나한테 너무 화려하고요, 검은색 휠이 좋아요. 더 스포티해요.
여: 네. 이 모델 좋아하실 것 같네요.
남: 멋지네요! 가격이 얼마예요?
여: 이번 주에 세일해서 1,200달러예요. 40퍼센트 할인가예요.
남: 나한테 여전히 너무 비싸네요. 1,000달러 미만으로 쓰려고 하거든요.
여: 좋아요. 그러면 이것이 손님이 찾고 있는 제품인 것 같네요.
남: 더 저렴한데 마찬가지로 좋아보이는군요. 그걸로 할게요.

어휘
rim *n.* 가장자리, 테

정답 ③

문제풀이
남자가 22인치 휠이 본인한테 더 알맞다고 했으므로 ①, ③, ⑤번 중에 선택해야
하는데 색은 검정이 좋다고 했으므로 ③, ⑤번이 남는다. 그런데 1,000달러
미만으로 하고 싶다고 했으므로 정답은 ③번이다.

총 어휘 수 150

13　긴 대화의 응답

소재　좋아하는 일과 잘하는 일 사이에서의 고민

듣기 대본 해석
남: Chloe, 뭐해?
여: 그냥 몇 주 전에 했던 군대 적성 검사 결과 보고 있었어.
남: 오, 나도 봐도 돼?
여: 그럼.
남: [잠시 후] 우와! 결과가 대단한데. 공간 추론 능력이랑 문제 해결 능력이
　　뛰어나다고 써있어. 건축가나 전략가가 되는 게 가장 좋을 거야.
여: 응, 근데 결과가 맘에 드는지는 모르겠어.
남: 진짜? 왜?
여: 음, 우리 부모님께서는 내가 군대에 들어가길 바라시지만 난 항상 작가가
　　되고 싶었어. 지금은 그렇게 잘 쓰는 작가는 아닌 것 같지만 연습하고
　　있었어.
남: 그렇구나. 네가 좋아하는 일이랑 네가 잘하는 일 사이에서 결정을 하는 건
　　항상 어려운 일이야.
여: 맞아. 네가 나라면 어떻게 하겠니?
남: ② 네가 열정을 갖고 있는 일을 하는 게 좋을 것 같아.

어휘
aptitude *n.* 적성　　**spatial reasoning** 공간 추론　　**strategist** *n.*
전략가

정답 ②

문제풀이
좋아하는 일과 잘하는 일 사이에서 고민하고 있는 여자에게 남자가 해줄 수 있는
적절한 조언은 ② '네가 열정을 갖고 있는 일을 하는 게 좋을 것 같아.'이다.

오답 보기 해석
① 내가 너라면 군대 적성 검사를 받아 볼 것 같아.
③ 아직 내가 하고 싶은 일을 결정하지 못했어.
④ 요즘 성공적인 건축가가 되는 것은 정말 어려운 일이야.
⑤ 넌 가능한 많은 군사 전략 책들을 모으는 편이 낫겠어.

총 어휘 수 142

14　긴 대화의 응답

소재　남편을 위한 스마트폰

듣기 대본 해석
남: 안녕하세요 Lewis 부인. 컴퓨터로 뭐하고 계세요?
여: 오, 안녕하세요. Chris. 저는 제 남편을 위한 새로운 스마트폰을 찾고 있어요.
남: 그렇군요. 그의 생일이 다가온다거나 하는 건가요?
여: 맞아요. 그는 다음 달에 47살이 돼요.
남: 그가 새로운 스마트폰을 가지게 되어 정말 기뻐하겠네요.
여: 그는 아직 몰라요. 그렇지만 그는 현재 그의 전화기가 정말 느리다고 항상
　　불평해요.
남: 전화기가 얼마나 오래 되었죠?
여: 약 4년 됐어요.
남: 네. 스마트폰이 요즘 매우 빨리 구식이 돼요.
여: 맞아요. 그는 현재의 전화기를 가지고 인터넷 검색을 하는 데 많은 어려움이
　　있고, 보다 최신 앱을 실행할 수 없어요.
남: 당신은 아마도 그에게 최신 모델 중에 하나를 사줘야겠네요. 그래야지
　　오래갈 거예요.
여: ③ 당신 말이 맞지만, 저는 어느 모델이 가장 좋은지 모르겠어요.

어휘
complain *v.* 불평하다　　**outdated** *a.* 구식의　　**browse** *v.* 인터넷을
돌아다니다

정답 ③

문제풀이
여자가 남자에게 남편의 전화기에 대한 얘기를 했고, 남자는 최신 모델 중 하나를
사줘야겠다고 했으므로 그에 적절한 응답은 ③ '당신 말이 맞지만, 저는 어느
모델이 가장 좋은지 모르겠어요.'이다.

오답 보기 해석
① 네. 구식 전화기로는 새로운 앱을 실행할 수 없어요.
② 그의 전화기는 잘 작동하지만 별로 세련되지는 않아요.
④ 맞아요. 저는 제가 어렸을 때 스마트폰을 결코 가지지 못했어요.
⑤ 네. 하지만 그는 평소에 그의 전화기가 얼마나 느린지 불평해요.

총 어휘 수 131

15　상황에 적절한 말

소재　건강한 음식의 선택

듣기 대본 해석
여: Nancy는 체중감량 클리닉에서 일하는 직원입니다. 그녀는 개인 트레이너는
　　아니지만 클리닉에서 5년 넘게 일해서 영양에 대해 그리고 어떻게 건강을
　　유지하는지에 대해 잘 압니다. 어느 오후에 그녀는 아파트 건물의 복도에서
　　친구인 Maya와 마주칩니다. 그녀는 식료품 가방을 나르고 있었습니다.
　　그녀가 Nancy를 봤을 때 그녀는 Nancy에게 자기가 산 음식에 대해
　　묻기 위해 멈춰 섰습니다. 그녀는 자기가 건강한 음식을 사려고 노력하지만
　　그녀 자신과, 남편, 아들을 위해 사야 하고 그녀의 선택에 대해 모두가
　　만족하기를 바랍니다. 이런 상황에서 Nancy는 Maya에게 뭐하고 말할
　　것 같은가요?
Nancy: ⑤ 너의 영양 목표에 맞는 음식들 몇 가지를 그들이 고르게 해 봐.

어휘
well-versed in ~에 정통한　　**nutrition** *n.* 영양　　〈문제〉**pregnant**
a. 임신한

정답 ⑤

문제풀이
Nancy의 친구 Maya는 건강한 음식을 사고 싶지만 자신과, 남편, 아들의
기호도 고려해야 한다며 조언을 구하고 있다. 이에 맞는 응답은 ⑤ '너의 영양
목표에 맞는 음식들 몇 가지를 그들이 고르게 해 봐.'이다.

① 넌 체중감량 클리닉에 등록해야 해.
② 나는 체중감량과 영양에 대해 많이 알아.
③ 과식은 심각한 건강 문제를 일으키지.
④ 네가 임신 중이라면 자연히 더 많이 먹게 될 거야.

총 어휘 수 131

16 담화 목적 / 17 세부 내용 파악

소재 먼지를 줄이는 청소 방법

듣기 대본 해석

여: 여러분 안녕하세요. 제 이름은 Mary Anne Philips이고 저는 Big City 위생국의 수간호사입니다. 오늘 저는 알레르기 유발 항원, 특히 먼지에 대해서 얘기를 해보고 싶습니다. 먼지는 우리의 건강에 많은 악영향을 주기 때문에 우리는 집을 최대한 청결하게 유지하기 위해 노력해야 해야 합니다. 집에 있는 먼지의 양을 대폭 줄일 수 있는 몇 가지의 청소 방법이 있습니다. 먼저, 진공청소기를 얼마나 자주 쓰시나요? 최소한 일주일에 두 번은 사용해야 할 것 같습니다. 둘째, 베개와 소파 쿠션을 일주일에 한 번씩 밖에서 터는 것도 먼저를 제거합니다. 종종 바닥을 걸레로 닦는 것은 불편하겠지만 청소기를 쓰면서 놓쳤을 먼지와 흙을 치우기 위해서는 필수적으로 해야 하는 겁니다. 마지막으로 침구류를 자주 세탁하는 것이 좋은데 이는 본인이나 같이 사는 사람이 알레르기가 있을 때는 특히 더 중요합니다. 이런 도움이 되는 조언들을 명심한다면 깨끗하고 건강한 집을 유지할 수 있을 것입니다. 시간 내 주셔서 감사합니다.

어휘

briefly *ad.* 간략히 　**allergen** *n.* 알레르겐(알레르기를 일으키는 항원)
strive *v.* 분투하다, 노력하다 　**drastically** *ad.* 대폭, 과감하게
vacuum cleaner 진공청소기 　**beat** *v.* 두드리다 　**mop** *v.* 닦다

정답 16 ④ **17** ⑤

문제풀이

16 여자는 먼지를 줄일 수 있는 청소 방법들을 제시하고 있으므로 여자가 하는 말의 목적은 ④ '먼지를 줄이는 청소 요령을 알려주려고'이다.

17 여자는 진공청소기 사용하기, 베개와 쿠션 털기, 바닥 닦기, 침구 세탁하기에 대해서는 언급하였으나, 환기에 대한 언급은 하지 않았으므로 정답은 ⑤ '환기시키기'이다.

총 어휘 수 180

DICTATION ANSWERS

01 in the front section

02 a disposable cup / I couldn't agree more

03 planning on having lunch / a few complaints about the cafeteria / bad reputation / renovate the cafeteria

04 cell phones being harmful to your health / excessive or long-term cell phone use / dangerous to our health / you avoid direct contact with the phone itself

05 you're not a fan of / the team's record / I seriously doubt it

06 much nicer than I imagined / facing that direction / I might have to do something / free to get rid of it

07 have you decided where to eat / That works for me / get him some of the vitamins / Can you buy a card

08 by the way / left it on the coffee table / he didn't ask / He doesn't think before he does things

09 rather go with cotton or wool / costs twenty dollars more / are a great match with / applies to the jeans

10 Wasn't it on the best-seller list / a horror novel / I'm not a very big fan of / give it a shot

11 from start to finish / choose a different topic / submit your applications / email your science teacher

12 you'll be needing / will better suit me / They're sportier / spend less than one thousand dollars

13 Do you mind if I / spatial reasoning and problem solving / join the military / if you were me

14 turns forty-seven / his current phone is really slow / smartphones get outdated pretty quickly / browsing the Internet

15 has been working for over five years / runs into a friend of hers / stops to ask her a question / wants everyone to be happy with her choices

16-17 negative health effects / as clean as possible / at least twice a week / Keep these helpful tips in mind

17 수능영어듣기 실전모의고사

본문 p.104

01 ④	02 ③	03 ④	04 ②	05 ⑤	06 ①
07 ②	08 ⑤	09 ④	10 ③	11 ④	12 ③
13 ③	14 ①	15 ⑤	16 ②	17 ④	

01 짧은 대화의 응답

소재 물건 가격 흥정

듣기 대본 해석
여: 이 바지 정말 맘에 들어요. 얼마죠?
남: 100달러입니다. 디자이너 바지인데 최신 유행이에요.
여: 이런. 가격이 저한테 좀 비싸네요. 할인해 주실 수 있나요?
남: ④ 음. 오늘 10퍼센트 할인을 해드릴 수 있어요.

어휘
trendy *a.* 최신 유행의 〈문제〉 **sold out** 다 팔리고 없는 **tailor** *v.* 맞추다

정답 ④

문제풀이
남자는 바지가 좀 비싸다며 할인해 줄 수 있냐는 여자의 말에 맞는 대답을 해야 한다. 따라서 ④ '음. 오늘 10퍼센트 할인을 해드릴 수 있어요.'가 정답이다.

오답 보기 해석
① 죄송하지만 품절됐어요.
② 여기서 그것을 맞추실 수 있어요.
③ 저는 보통 디자이너 바지를 팔지 않아요.
⑤ 음, 전 다른 물건들을 보고 싶군요.

총 어휘 수 43

02 짧은 대화의 응답

소재 회사에 지각하지 않게 가기

듣기 대본 해석
남: 일어나, Annie! 열 시가 넘었어! 분명 회사에 지각할거야!
여: 진정해! 자동차로 이십 분밖에 안 걸려.
남: 잊었어? 네 자동차는 수리점에 있잖아.
여: ③ 그럼 택시를 잡아야겠네.

어휘
relax *v.* 진정하다, 휴식을 취하다 **repair shop** 수리점 〈문제〉 **flat tire** 바람이 빠진 타이어

정답 ③

문제풀이
여자의 차가 수리점에 있고, 차로 가야 늦지 않으므로 여자가 할 적절한 말은 ③ '그럼 택시를 잡아야겠네.'이다.

오답 보기 해석
① 괜찮아. 오늘은 내 차를 몰고 갈게.
② 혹시 이 주변에 수리점 있어?
④ 이런! 너 타이어 펑크 난 것 같아.
⑤ 난 식료품점에 먼저 들러야 돼.

총 어휘 수 41

03 담화 목적

소재 걷기의 중요성

듣기 대본 해석
여: 여러분은 건강을 어떻게 유지하십니까? 규칙적으로 운동을 하십니까? 걸으십니까? 여러분은 걷기가 건강에 주는 이점을 알고 계십니까? 간단히 말해서, 여러분이 더 많이 걸으면 여러분의 삶은 더 나아질 것입니다. 심장병으로 고생했던 Roger Williams라는 제 친구 이야기를 해 드릴게요. 그는 몇몇 의사들로부터 그의 병이 결코 완전히 치료되지 못할 것이라고 들었습니다. 의사들의 진단에도 불구하고 그는 더 이상 심장병을 조금도 앓고 있지 않습니다. 그를 도왔던 것은 걷기였습니다. 그는 걷기를 일상의 중요한 부분으로 만들었습니다. 많은 사람들이 걷기가 그들의 삶을 더 낫게 변화 시킨다는 것을 보여줄 것입니다. 걷기는 특정한 유형의 사람들에게만 이로운 것이 아니라 모든 사람들에게 필수적입니다.

어휘
regularly *ad.* 규칙적으로 **aware of** ~을 인지하다, 알다 **suffer from** ~로 고통 받다 **cure** *v.* 치료하다, 고치다 **diagnosis** *n.* 진단, 진찰 **testify** *v.* 증언하다, 증명하다 **necessary** *a.* 필수의, 필연적인

정답 ④

문제풀이
걷기를 통해 자신의 병을 이겨낸 친구 이야기를 예로 들면서 걷기는 모든 사람들에게 필요하다고 말하며 걷기의 중요성을 강조하고 있으므로 정답은 ④ '걷기 운동의 중요성을 알려주려고'이다.

총 어휘 수 122

04 의견

소재 경고 표지판 세우기

듣기 대본 해석
여: 안녕하세요, Anderson씨.
남: 오늘 아침 저를 만나 주셔서 감사합니다. 제가 이 길을 당신께 보여드리고 싶었어요.
여: 네, 왜 그런지 알겠어요. 아주 위험해 보여요.
남: 정말 위험해요. 운전자에게 급커브에 대한 주의를 요하는 경고 표지판이나 전등이 충분하지 않아요.
여: 집에서 길이 보이나요?
남: 네, 보여요. 저는 차 사고를 많이 목격했어요.
여: 당신 생각에는 사람들이 너무 속력을 내서 사고가 일어난다고 생각하세요?
남: 정말이지 사람들이 너무 속도를 낸다고 생각해요. 저는 더 많은 경고 표지판이 사고 건수를 크게 줄여줄 거라고 믿어요.
여: 시에 항의를 한 적 있으신가요?
남: 제가 몇 번이나 했지만 아무도 신경 쓰지 않는 것 같은 게 저한테 전화나 이메일로 답변을 준 적이 한 번도 없어요.
여: 알았어요. 제가 사무실에 도착하자마자 담당하는 사람들과 연락을 해 볼게요.
남: 정말이요? 잘됐어요. 우리는 더 많은 경고 표지판이 필요하다고 꼭 말해 주세요.

어휘
warning sign 경고 표지판 **significantly** *ad.* 상당히, 크게 **reduce** *v.* 줄이다, 축소하다 **file a complaint** 항의를 제기하다 **get in touch with** ~와 연락하다 **in charge** 담당하고 있는

정답 ②

남자는 급커브 지역에 경고 표지판이나 전등이 없어서 사람들이 속력을 내고 그래서 사고가 많이 난다면서 급커브 지역에 경고 표지판이나 전등을 설치해야 한다고 말하고 있다. 따라서 정답은 ② '급커브 지역에 경고 표지판이나 전등을 설치해야 한다.'이다.

총 어휘 수 163

05 대화자의 관계 파악

소재 건물 세부정보 확인

듣기 대본 해석

[전화벨이 울린다.]

여: 여보세요. Brittney Smith입니다.

남: 안녕하세요. Smith씨. 저는 Dominic Antonoff입니다. 당신이 어제 저한테 건물 몇 개를 보여주셨는데 제가 몇 가지 질문을 해도 괜찮을지 모르겠네요.

여: 안녕하세요. Antonoff씨. 어떤 건물에 관심이 있으시죠?

남: Water Street에 있는 거요. 그 건물에 대형냉장고 있나요?

여: 제가 확인할 동안 잠깐 시간을 주세요. *[잠시 후]* 네. 있어요.

남: 좋아요. 그런데 중앙 난방과 냉방 시스템도 가지고 있나요?

여: 있어요. 문제 있나요?

남: 흠... 문제가 될 것 같아요. 6번가에 있는 건물은 어때요? 여전히 가능해요?

여: 네. 그것도 아직 가능합니다.

남: 제가 만약 가게 앞에 딸린 공간을 개조한다면 문제가 될까요?

여: 제 생각엔 괜찮을 것 같아요.

남: 좋습니다. 그리고 건물주에게 제가 식당 공간에 걸어놓는 등을 설치해도 되는지 물어봐 주셨나요?

여: 네. 제가 여쭤봤어요. 그분이 괜찮을 거라고 하셨어요.

어휘

wonder *v.* ~일지 모르겠다, 궁금하다   **walk-in freezer** 대형냉장고
available *a.* 이용할 수 있는

정답 ⑤

문제풀이

남자는 여자에게 건물의 시설과 개조 가능 여부에 관해 질문하고 있고 여자는 이에 답해주고 있으므로 두 사람의 관계는 ⑤ '부동산 중개인 – 고객'이다.

총 어휘 수 145

06 그림의 세부 내용 파악

소재 리조트에 놀러 갔던 가족 사진

듣기 대본 해석

여: 안녕 Jay. 휴가 어땠어?

남: 좋았어. 우리 가족은 머물렀던 리조트를 정말 좋아했어. 여기 사진이 있어.

여: *[잠시 후]* 멋지다. 벽에 있는 건 섬 지도니?

남: 맞아. 우리는 하와이의 Big Island에서 머물렀어.

여: 가족들 모두 경치를 정말 즐기고 있는 것 같네.

남: 맞아. 아내하고 나는 리조트에서 단지 휴식하는 건 즐겼어. 그리고 저건 니가 가장 좋아하는 선글라스야.

여: 멋지네. 공을 가지고 노는 건 네 아이들이야?

남: 응. 내 아들 딸이야. 애들이 거기 날씨를 정말 좋아하더라.

여: 아내는 어떤 음료를 마시고 있어? 좋아 보이는데.

남: 저건 Blue Hawaiian이야. 하와이에서는 대중적인 음료야.

여: 그럼, 누가 이 사진을 찍었어?

남: 내 남동생이 찍었어. 난 내 스마트폰으로 찍고 싶었는데 그날 잃어버렸어.

여: 바닥에 있는 저거 아냐?

남: 응. 나 참 멍청하지.

어휘

vacation *n.* 휴가   **take a picture** 사진을 찍다

정답 ①

문제풀이

벽에 걸려 있는 것은 섬 지도라고 했는데, 그림에서는 화산이 그려져 있으므로 그림과 일치하지 않는 것은 ①번이다.

총 어휘 수 152

07 할 일

소재 Rain Valley Park 방문

듣기 대본 해석

여: 여보, 저기 Rain Valley Park 표지판이 보여요.

남: 저 사람들 좀 봐요! 여기가 틀림없어요.

여: 맞아요. 오, 주차장은 저기 있네요!

남: 아주 좋아요. 거기 주차하고 계곡까지 걸어갈 수 있어요. 거기까지 가는 데 오래 걸릴 거라고 생각해요?

여: 내가 생각하기엔 20분 정도 걸릴 거예요. 우리가 거기 도착하면 강가에 앉아있을 수 있을 거예요.

남: 와! 정말 차가 많군요.

여: 우리가 주차 공간을 찾을 수 있을까요?

남: 내가 찾을 거예요. 걱정 마세요. 당신은 차에서 내려서 입장권을 사세요. 저쪽에 줄이 있는 것 같은데.

여: 좋은 생각이에요. 내가 출력해 온 지도 가지고 있어요?

남: 네. 제가 가지고 있어요. 내가 반드시 가지고 갈게요.

여: 아주 좋아요. 공원 입구에서 만나요.

어휘

sign *n.* 표지판, 신호   **parking lot** 주차장   **parking space**
주차 공간   **entry permit** 입장권   **entrance** *n.* 입구

정답 ②

문제풀이

남자가 여자에게 차에서 내려서 입장권을 사라고 말했고 여자는 알았다고 대답했으므로 답은 ② '입장권 사기'이다.

총 어휘 수 149

08 이유

소재 친구 숙제 도와주기

듣기 대본 해석

[전화벨이 울린다.]

남: 여보세요?

여: 이봐, Mel. 나 Katie야.

남: 아, Katie. 요즘 어때?

여: 별 일 없어. 그런데 너, Levine 선생님께서 오늘 내주신 수학 문제 모두 다 했어?

남: 네가 전화하기 직전에 막 다했어.

여: 난 정말 수학을 이해 못 하겠어. 네가 그것들을 도와줄 어떤 방법이 있을까?

남: 물론, 문제 없어.

여: 좋아. 너 내일 학교에 일찍 올 생각이야? 그럼 우리가 만나서 네가 나에게 문제 푸는 것을 도와줄 수 있을 거야.

남: 음… 내가 내일 학교에 일찍 갈 수 있을 것 같지가 않아. 걸어서 남동생을
　　학교에 바래다 줘야 하거든.
여: 엄마가 동생을 왜 안 데려다 주셔?
남: 음. 엄마는 내일 아침에 바쁘실 거야. 지금 내가 널 도와줄 수 있어. 우리
　　Cup 카페에서 만나는 거 어때?
여: 좋은 생각이야. 너무 고마워.

어휘
assign **v.** 부과하다, 맡기다

정답 ⑤

문제풀이
남자는 내일 아침에 엄마가 바쁘셔서 동생을 학교까지 걸어서 바래다 줘야 하기
때문에 학교에 일찍 갈 수 없을 것 같다고 했으므로 정답은 ⑤ '걸어서 남동생을
학교에 바래다 줘야 하기 때문에'이다.

총 어휘 수 127

09　숫자

소재　전시회 티켓 구입

듣기 대본 해석
남: 서울 아트 센터에 오신 걸 환영합니다. 무엇을 도와 드릴까요?
여: 우리 가족의 오늘 전시회의 티켓을 사야 하거든요.
남: 네. 몇 장 필요하세요?
여: 음. 남편, 딸, 제 것이 필요한데요. 딸이 고등학생이에요. 그러니까 성인
　　두 명에 학생 한 명이 되겠네요.
남: 좋습니다. 성인표는 각각 60달러이고, 학생은 40달러입니다. 따님은
　　학생증 가지고 있나요?
여: 네. 여기 있어요.
남: 좋습니다. 그럼 성인 둘, 학생 한 명 맞죠?
여: 맞습니다. 아! 제가 딸이 학교에서 받은 쿠폰이 있는 걸 깜빡 했네요. 아직
　　사용할 수 있나요?
남: 아직 유효한지 확인해 볼게요.
여: 그럴 거예요. 지난주에 받았거든요.
남: [잠시 후]맞습니다. 따님의 표는 반값에 사실 수 있어요.
여: 좋아요. 여기 카드 있어요.

어휘
exhibition **n.** 전시회　　valid **a.** 유효한　　half price 반값

정답 ④

문제풀이
성인 티켓은 60달러인데 2명이므로 120달러. 학생은 40달러이고 1명인데
할인쿠폰이 있어서 반값에 가능하다고 했으므로 20달러가 된다. 따라서 여자가
지불해야 할 금액은 ④ '$140'이다.

총 어휘 수 142

10　언급 유무

소재　학업 상담

듣기 대본 해석
남: 잠깐 이야기 할 수 있을까요, Whitman 선생님?
여: 그럼, 물론이지. 무엇을 도와줄까?
남: 전 공부를 아주 열심히 하는데 성적은 계속 좋지 않아요.
여: 문제점을 좀 찾아보자. 하루에 얼마나 오래 공부하니?
남: 저는 주중에 집에서 거의 자정까지 공부하니까 약 4시간 정도 되는 것
　　같아요. 하지만 제 동생들이 자주 집중을 못하게 해요.

여: 네가 밤에 늦게까지 공부할 때 방해받기 쉽겠구나. 도서관에서 공부하지
　　그러니?
남: 맞아요. 제 생각에도 저의 공부 습관을 바꿔야 할 것 같아요.
여: 그래. 너는 또 네가 사용하고 있는 교재들이 최고인지 확인해야 해.
남: 아. 알겠어요.
여: 너는 네가 왜 대학에 가고 싶어 하는지 알고 있니?
남: 그것에 대해서는 별로 생각해보지 않은 것 같아요.
여: 네가 무엇을 하고 싶은지에 대한 명확한 생각이 있다면, 네가 공부에서 더
　　많은 것을 얻을 거라고 믿어.
남: 네, 조언 감사합니다. Whitman 선생님.

어휘
distract **v.** 집중이 안 되게 하다　　sibling **n.** 형제, 자매　　make sure
확인하다, 확실히 하다

정답 ③

문제풀이
공부는 열심히 하고 있는데 성적이 좋지 않다는 남학생이 선생님께 조언을
구하고 있다. 하루에 공부하는 시간, 공부하는 장소, 사용하는 교재, 대학 진학을
원하는 이유는 언급했지만 수업을 듣는 태도에 대해서는 언급하지 않았으므로
정답은 ③ '수업을 듣는 태도'이다.

총 어휘 수 162

11　내용 일치 · 불일치

소재　파충류 박람회

듣기 대본 해석
남: 안녕하세요 학생 여러분. 코브라와 직접 맞닥뜨리고 싶습니까? 악어를
　　만져보고 먹이를 주고 싶습니까? 그렇다면 이번 주말 Mega Village
　　축제 마당에서 열리는 Reptile World 박람회에 오세요. 이번 박람회는
　　도마뱀과 이구아나부터 비단뱀과 악어까지 여러분이 가장 좋아하는
　　파충류를 모두 포함하고 있습니다. 이 박람회는 Mega Village 야생동물
　　협회에서 개최하는 것으로 관람객들이 독특한 야생동물들과 가까이 직접
　　다가가는 것을 허용합니다. 굉장히 많은 정보를 얻을 수 있고 교육적입니다.
　　무료 입장이지만 미리 표를 예약해 주시기 바랍니다. 더 많은 정보는
　　Mega Village 야생동물협회 홈페이지에서 확인해 주시기 바랍니다.
　　들어 주셔서 감사합니다.

어휘
crocodile **n.** 악어　　reptile **n.** 파충류　　exhibit **n.** 박람회
unique **a.** 독특한　　admission **n.** 입장　　reserve **v.** 예약하다

정답 ③

문제풀이
관람객들에게 독특한 야생동물들에게 가까이 직접 다가가는 것을 허용한다고
했으므로 내용과 일치하지 않는 것은 ③ '동물들에게 가까이 다가가서는 안
된다.'이다.

총 어휘 수 112

12　도표

소재　가족 여행용 렌터카 대여

듣기 대본 해석
여: 무엇을 도와드릴까요?
남: 가족 여행을 위한 차를 대여하고 싶어요. 한 대 추천해 주시겠습니까?
여: 네, 저희에게 이코노미, 패밀리, 럭셔리 차종이 있어요. 가족이 몇 분이신가요?
남: 저를 포함해서 네 명입니다.

여: 제 생각에는 패밀리 사이즈나 럭셔리 사이즈가 적당할 것 같군요.

남: 그것들과 이코노미 사이즈의 차이는 무엇인가요?

여: 대여 가격과 주행 마일 수의 차이 외에, 이코노미 차는 충분한 공간이 없어서 네 분이서 타시면 조금 불편하실 거예요.

남: 그렇군요. 그리고 저희는 짐을 위한 공간이 필요해서 대여할 차가 좀 넓어야 해요.

여: 그러면, 럭셔리 사이즈를 대여하시는 건 어떠세요? 일곱 명에게도 공간이 충분해서 가족들이 아주 편안하실 거예요.

남: 하지만 대여비가 저한테는 너무 비싸네요. 오, 여기 럭셔리 차와 같은 수용 인원수를 가진 패밀리 차가 있네요.

여: 죄송합니다. 손님. 이 모델은 지금 이용이 가능하지 않습니다. 모두 대여되었어요.

남: 그러면 다른 선택이 없네요. 저걸로 대여할게요.

어휘

include *v.* 포함하다 **suitable** *a.* 적당한 **besides** *prep.* ~외에
gas mileage 주행 마일 수, 연비 **spacious** *a.* 널찍한 **capacity**
n. 용량, 수용력 **available** *a.* 이용 가능한

정답 ③

문제풀이

가족 4명과 짐을 위한 충분한 공간이 필요하므로, 좁은 이코노미는 제외된다. 직원이 럭셔리를 추천했지만, 남자가 너무 비싸다고 하였으므로 럭셔리도 제외된다. 럭셔리와 같은 수용 인원수를 가진 패밀리 타입이 있으나 이용 가능한 차가 없다. 그러므로 4명과 짐을 수용할 수 있으면서 럭셔리만큼 비싸지 않고, 현재 이용 가능한 차가 있는 차종은 ③번이다.

총 어휘 수 177

13 긴 대화의 응답

소재 사업에 대한 조언

듣기 대본 해석

여: 안녕, Rodrick.

남: 오, 안녕, Karen. 오랜만이야.

여: 그래 오랜만이야. 알다시피 내가 네 회사를 떠난 지 1년쯤 됐네. 거기에서 일했던 것이 그리워.

남: 우리도 너를 그리워해. 너 약간 달라 보여. 살이 좀 빠셨니?

여: 그래. 나는 보다 건강하게 먹고 이 강도 높은 규칙적인 운동을 하고 있어.

남: 멋진데. 너무 무리하게 하지는 마. 내 친구가 운동하다가 부상을 입었어.

여: 걱정하지 마. 나는 꽤 조심하고 있어.

남: 그렇구나. 너의 새로운 사업은 어때?

여: 음, 그거 정말 스트레스 받아. 할 일은 정말 많고 일 할 시간은 충분하지 않아.

남: 이해가 되네. 나도 처음 내 사업을 시작했을 때 힘든 시간을 보냈어.

여: 사업을 시작하는 것은 항상 어려운 것 같아. 나에게 조언 좀 해 줄래?

남: ③ 열심히 일은 하되 삶에서 중요한 것을 잊지 마.

어휘

lose weight 살을 빼다 **overdo** *v.* 무리하다, 지나치게 하다
incredibly *ad.* 믿을 수 없을 정도로, 엄청나게

정답 ③

문제풀이

여자가 사업에 관해 조언을 해달라고 했으므로 적절한 응답은 ③ '열심히 일은 하되 삶에서 중요한 것을 잊지 마.'이다.

오답 보기 해석
① 너의 새로운 사업에서 모든 것이 잘 되리라 확신해.

② 나의 이전 직원이 성공하는 것을 보면 항상 기분이 좋아.

④ 너를 만나서 반가웠어. 언젠가 너의 사무실에 들를게.

⑤ 너는 세 시간 이상 강도 높게 운동해서는 안 돼.

총 어휘 수 143

14 긴 대화의 응답

소재 야구 경기 응원

듣기 대본 해석

여: 너 지난밤에 야구 경기 봤니?

남: 봤어. 정말 훌륭한 경기였어! 나는 Los Angeles가 Detroit를 이겨서 너무 기뻤어.

여: 나는 사실 Detroit 팬이지만, Los Angeles 팀이 정말 잘 싸웠어.

남: LA의 투수가 대단했어. 정말 인상 깊었지.

여: 응, 그랬어. 그런데 경기가 끝날 무렵에 그가 팔을 다친 것 같던데.

남: 나도 봤어. 나는 구원투수를 보기 기대했는데 아무도 나오지 않았어.

여: 정말 긴 게임이었어. 선수들이 정말 지쳤을 거야.

남: 그래. 13회를 했잖아. 정말 긴 게임이지!

여: 맞아.

남: Detroit는 언제 다시 경기해?

여: 목요일 밤에.

남: 나는 너희 집에 가서 너랑 같이 그들을 응원할 거야.

여: ① 좋아. 그들이 이겼으면 좋겠어!

어휘

pitcher *n.* (야구에서) 투수 **impress** *v.* 깊은 인상을 주다
relief pitcher 구원투수

정답 ①

문제풀이

여자가 응원하는 Detroit팀의 다음 경기는 목요일 밤이고 남자는 여자와 같이 응원하고 싶다고 말했으므로 그에 대한 여자의 대답은 ① '좋아. 그들이 이겼으면 좋겠어!'가 적절하다.

오답 보기 해석

② 나도 너와 함께 너의 팀을 응원할게.

③ 물론이지! 7시쯤 갈게.

④ 대단한 걸. 그들 또한 응원하러 올 지도 몰라.

⑤ 사실은 이번 주말에 정말 바빠.

총 어휘 수 130

15 상황에 적절한 말

소재 전화기를 사용하며 걷다가 다른 사람과 부딪힌 상황

듣기 대본 해석

남: Candace는 바쁜 직장 여성입니다. 어느 날, 그녀는 중요한 업무 회의가 있어서 그녀의 전화기로 이메일을 작성하면서 버스 정류장으로 걸어가는 중입니다. 이름이 Larry인 한 중년의 남성이 아침 조깅을 위해 나옵니다. 그는 허우적대다가 Candace쪽으로 휘청거렸고, 그녀는 젖은 땅에 중요한 문서를 떨어뜨립니다. Larry는 그것들을 집어서 말리려고 애썼지만 엉망이 되었습니다. 그는 매우 미안해하고 그의 어설픔에 미안함을 느낍니다. Candace는 그녀도 사고 당시에 다른 데 정신이 팔려 있었기 때문에 그녀의 잘못도 있다고 생각합니다. 이 상황에서, Candace는 Larry에게 뭐라고 말하겠습니까?

Candace: ⑤ 저도 책임이 있어요. 전화기를 사용하지 말았어야 했어요.

어휘

business meeting 업무 회의　　**struggle** *v.* 몸부림치다, 허우적거리다, 버둥거리다, 고투하다　　**stumble** *v.* 발이 걸리다, 발을 헛디디다, 휘청거리다　　**apologetic** *a.* 미안해하는　　**clumsiness** *n.* 어색함, 서투름

정답 ⑤

문제풀이

Candace가 휴대폰으로 이메일을 작성하면서 걸어가다가 조깅하러 가던 Larry와 부딪혔고 그로 인해 Candace의 문서가 엉망이 된 상황에서 Larry가 사과했다. Candace는 본인에게도 책임이 있다고 생각하므로 그녀가 할 말로는 ⑤ '저도 책임이 있어요. 전화기를 사용하지 말았어야 했어요.'가 적절하다.

오답 보기 해석

① 당신에게 문제가 생기면, 꼭 저에게 알려주세요.
② 당신이 밖에서 달릴 때 좀 더 조심해야겠어요.
③ 이 문서들을 깨끗이 하기 위해 당신이 할 수 있는 것은 아무것도 없는 것 같아요.
④ 걱정 마세요. 몇 분 안에 또 다른 버스가 올 거예요.

총 어휘 수 120

16 담화 목적 / 17 세부 내용 파악

소재 해외 자원봉사 프로그램의 이점

듣기 대본 해석

남: 안녕하세요 학생 여러분. 오늘 여러분께 해외 자원봉사 여름 프로그램에 대해서 말씀 드리고자 합니다. 해외 자원봉사는 쉽지 않은 경험이 될 수 있습니다. 여러분들은 분명 어려움에 직면할 수 있고 적응하는 데 어려움을 겪을 것입니다. 하지만 그러한 경험은 놀랍도록 보람이 있으며 틀림없이 여러분이 세상을 바라보는 시각을 바꿔놓을 것입니다. 여러분들이 어려움에 처한 사람들을 도우면서 여러분의 우선순위가 무엇인지 알게 될 것입니다. 외국 땅에 사는 것이 당신을 바꿀 것이기 때문에 당신의 세계관이 넓어질 것입니다. 여러분은 새로운 풍습과 규범을 갖게 될 것입니다. 지금까지 꿈꿔보지도 못한 음식들을 먹어보게 되고 외국어로 의사소통을 하기 위해서 노력을 할 것입니다. 가장 중요한 것은, 도움이 필요한 사람들을 돕게 되는 것입니다. 여러분은 아프리카 사람들에게 어떻게 물을 정화하는지를 가르치고, 인도에서 아기들 밥을 먹이고, 미얀마에서 집을 짓고, 인도네시아에서 아픈 어린이들을 돌보고 있는 자신을 발견하게 될 것입니다. 해외 자원봉사는 정말 둘도 없는 기회이며, 여러분은 분명히 그로 인해 더 나은 사람이 될 것입니다.

어휘

adjust *v.* 적응하다　　**rewarding** *a.* 보람이 있는　　**perspective** *n.* 시각, 견지　　**expand** *v.* 확대되다　　**strain** *v.* 힘껏 노력하다, 안간힘을 쓰다

정답 16 ② 17 ④

문제풀이

16 남자는 해외 자원봉사를 했을 때 사람들이 얻을 수 있는 세계관의 확장과 다양한 경험 등 여러 가지 이점에 관해 이야기하였으므로 남자가 하는 말의 목적은 ② '해외 자원봉사의 이점을 알려주려고'이다.

17 남자는 물 정화방법 가르치기, 아기들 밥 먹이기, 집 짓기, 아픈 아이들 치료하기에 관한 언급은 했지만 영어 가르치기에 관한 언급은 하지 않았으므로 정답은 ④ '영어 가르치기'이다.

총 어휘 수 152

DICTATION ANSWERS

01 and they're really trendy / Can you give me a discount

02 be late for work / in the repair shop

03 health benefits of walking / suffered from heart disease / Despite their diagnosis / not beneficial for only certain types of people

04 to make the driver aware of all the really sharp turns / reduce the number of accidents / filed a complaint with the city / get in touch with the people in charge / we need more warning signs

05 Which building are you interested in / It might be an issue / it's still available / install hanging lights in the dining area

06 the resort we stayed at / a map of the islands on the wall / your kids playing with the ball / take a picture with my smartphone / How silly of me

07 This must be the right place / walk down to the valley / go buy our entry permits / It's with my things / at the entrance to the park

08 did you finish all of the math problems / Is there any way you could help me / walk my brother to school / she's going to be busy

09 How many do you need / got a coupon from her school / if it's still valid

10 How long do you study each day / I'm often distracted by / change my study habits

11 pet and feed a crocodile / include all of your favorite reptiles / allows visitors to get up close / We offer free admission

12 rent a car for my family trip / would be suitable for / the car we end up with should be a bit spacious / all rented out

13 been eating healthier / got injured while exercising / incredibly stressful / Do you have any tips

14 What a game / I was really impressed / towards the end of the game, though / cheer them on with you

15 He is struggling / they're ruined / feels sorry for his clumsiness

16-17 summer abroad volunteer programs / incredibly rewarding / help others in need / strain to communicate / feeding babies

01 ②	02 ④	03 ①	04 ②	05 ③	06 ③
07 ⑤	08 ①	09 ③	10 ④	11 ③	12 ③
13 ⑤	14 ④	15 ⑤	16 ④	17 ②	

01 짧은 대화의 응답

소재 새로 생긴 초밥집

듣기 대본 해석

남: 안녕 Pat, 너 초밥 Safari 식당에 가 봤니?
여: 가봤지. 나는 개업 첫 주말에 가봤어. 멋지던데.
남: 나는 내일 갈 예정이야. 여기서 가까워?
여: ② 응. 걸어서 5분 밖에 안 걸려.

어휘

opening *n.* 개막, 개통, 개업   **close** *a.* 가까운

정답 ②

문제풀이

새로 생긴 식당이 여기서 가까운지 물었으므로 그에 적절한 응답은 ② '응. 걸어서 5분밖에 안 걸려.'이다.

오답 보기 해석

① 물론. 나는 외국 음식을 먹는 것을 좋아해.
③ 아니. 난 요리를 잘 하지 못해.
④ 확실하지 않아. 나는 거기서 먹어 본 적이 없거든.
⑤ 그래. 내일은 문을 닫을 거야.

총 어휘 수 40

02 짧은 대화의 응답

소재 일기예보 확인하기

듣기 대본 해석

여: Wade, 너 흠뻑 젖었네. 무슨 일 있었어?
남: 밖에 비가 정말 많이 쏟아지고 있어. 내가 우산 가져가는 것을 생각하지 못했거든.
여: 그래, 안됐네. 매일 일기예보를 확인하지 않아?
남: ④ 평상시에는 그렇지만, 오늘 아침은 아주 바빴어.

어휘

soaked *a.* 흠뻑 젖은   **weather forecast** 일기예보

정답 ④

문제풀이

일기예보를 매일 확인하지 않느냐는 여자의 질문에 적절한 남자의 대답은 ④ '평상시에는 그렇지만, 오늘 아침은 아주 바빴어.'이다.

오답 보기 해석

① 고마워. 이런 날씨에 정말 하나 필요해.
② 응. 내일 날씨 확인해 봐.
③ 괜찮아. 내 우산 빌려도 돼.
⑤ 내일 날씨가 좋다니 기쁘네.

총 어휘 수 41

03 담화 목적

소재 야외 활동 시 뇌우 대처법

듣기 대본 해석

남: 대부분의 사람들은 날씨가 좋을 때 야외에서 노는 것을 즐깁니다. 그렇지만 날씨가 매우 빠르게 더 나쁜 상황으로 변할 수 있다는 것을 명심하는 것이 중요합니다. 여러분은 이런 일이 일어날 경우에 무엇을 해야 할지 알아야 합니다. 만약에 여러분이 뇌우를 만나면, 여러분은 빌딩 안이나 차 안에 대피처를 찾아야 합니다. 그런 것이 가능하지 않다면, 여러분 주변에서 가장 낮은 지역을 찾고 탁 트인 공간은 피해야 합니다. 만약 여러분이 탁 트인 공간에 있고 주변에 있는 모든 것보다 더 크다면, 여러분은 번개를 맞을 위험이 커집니다. 항상 나무와 전신주는 피하세요. 이런 조언을 따른다면 여러분은 다음에 나쁜 날씨가 덮쳤을 때 준비가 되어 있을 것입니다.

어휘

thunderstorm *n.* 뇌우   **shelter** *n.* 대피처   **avoid** *v.* 피하다
telephone pole 전신주

정답 ①

문제풀이

야외에서 갑자기 뇌우를 만나게 될 때 어떻게 행동하면 되는지를 알려주고 있다. 따라서 남자가 하는 말의 목적으로 적절한 것은 ① '야외 활동 시 뇌우에 대처하는 방법을 알려주려고'이다.

총 어휘 수 116

04 대화 주제

소재 나라마다 다른 개인 위생

듣기 대본 해석

남: 너 괜찮아? 걱정이 있어 보여.
여: 너 Dimitri 알지?
남: 물론이지. 그는 이탈리아 사람이잖아. 정말 친절한 친구야.
여: 응, 맞아. 나도 그를 좋아해. 그렇지만 그는 항상 입 냄새가 난다는 거 알고 있니?
남: 사실은 나도 알아. 그게 너를 화나게 해?
여: 그는 재미있고 같이 이야기를 나누면 재미있지만 입 냄새는 참을 수가 없어.
남: 편하게 생각해. 개인 위생의 기준은 나라마다 다르단다.
여: 그래? 다른 나라에 가본 적이 없어서 몰랐어.
남: 개인 위생에 대한 개념은 세계 여러 나라마다 다른 거야.
여: 이런 차이가 사회적 문제가 될 수도 있겠다. 그렇지?
남: 그래. 맞아. 나는 사람들이 모두 다르다는 것을 이해하려고 노력하는 것이 중요하다고 생각해.
여: 충고 고마워. 나는 Dimitri와 이제 더 잘 지낼 수 있을 것 같아.
남: 그렇게 말해주니 기쁘네.

어휘

bad breath 입 냄새   **unbearable** *a.* 참을 수 없는
personal hygiene 개인 위생   **get along** 사이 좋게 지내다

정답 ②

문제풀이

여자가 이탈리아에서 온 친구에게 입 냄새가 나서 참기 힘들다고 말하자 남자는 개인 위생에 대한 생각이 나라마다 다르므로 사람들이 서로 다름을 이해하도록 노력해야 한다고 말하고 있다. 따라서 두 사람의 대화 주제는 ② '나라마다 다른 개인 위생의 인식 차이'이다.

총 어휘 수 135

소재 관광 중 입은 상처

듣기 대본 해석
여: 저기, 죄송한데요. 혹시 반창고 하나 있나요?
남: 물론입니다. 제가 인솔하는 모든 투어에 항상 구급상자를 들고 다녀요. 무슨
    일이 있었나요?
여: 박물관 계단에서 넘어져서 무릎이 까졌어요.
남: 그럼 큰 게 필요하겠네요. 잠깐만요. *[잠시 후]* 여기 있어요.
여: 고마워요. 그리고 저와 제 남편 둘 다 여행을 굉장히 즐기고 있다고 말씀
    드리고 싶었어요.
남: 좋네요. 즐거운 시간을 보낼 수 있도록 최선을 다하고 있습니다.
여: 그럼 동굴 안에는 언제 들어가나요?
남: 1시쯤 거기 도착할 겁니다.
여: 별로 안 걸리네요. 그 동굴은 긴 역사를 갖고 있지 않나요?
남: 맞아요. 1800년대 중반에 Jesse James와 그의 노상강도 패거리의
    은신처로도 쓰였어요.
여: 흥미롭네요. 이곳에는 재미있는 역사 이야기들이 많네요. 그렇죠?
남: 맞아요. 굉장히 역사가 깊은 곳이에요. 자연의 아름다움도 많이 담고 있고요.

어휘
bandage *n.* 밴드, 붕대   **first-aid kit** 구급상자   **scrape** *v.* 긁다,
긁히다   **ensure** *v.* 보장하다   **hideout** *n.* 은신처   **bandit** *n.*
노상강도

정답 ③

문제풀이
남자는 자신이 인솔하는 투어에 항상 구급상자를 가지고 다닌다고 하였고,
사람들이 즐거운 시간을 보낼 수 있도록 최선을 다 하고 있다고 하였다. 여자는
자신과 남편이 여행을 즐기고 있다고 말하고, 다음 관광 일정에 대해 묻는 것으로
보아 두 사람의 관계는 ③ '관광객 ― 관광 가이드'임을 알 수 있다.

총 어휘 수 161

소재 재즈 밴드에 관한 대화

듣기 대본 해석
여: 와! 이 밴드 정말 좋다. Joey!
남: 응. 내가 가장 좋아하는 재즈 밴드 중 하나야. Jazz Hands라고 불려.
여: 재미있는 이름인데. 여자 바이올리니스트가 있는 게 좋은데. 진짜 멋져.
남: 다들 재능이 엄청나지. 뒤에 기타리스트는 시에서 최고의 기타리스트 중
    한 명이야.
여: 대단하다. 보컬이 노래하면서 기타를 치는 게 멋진데.
남: 응. 목소리가 정말 좋더라. 음역이 넓어.
여: 그런데 피아노 연주자는 어울리지 않는 것 같아. 나머지는 서 있는데 그만
    앉아 있잖아.
남: 음. 그는 피아노를 치고 있잖아. 피아노 치면서 서 있을 수는 없어. 페달을
    써야 하거든.
여: 오, 맞아. 어쨌든, 날 이 재즈 클럽에 데려와 줘서 정말 기뻐, Joey.
남: 네가 같이 와 줘서 내가 기쁘지.

어휘
awesome *a.* 멋진   **range** *n.* 범위(폭)   **out of place** 어울리지 않는,
부적절한

정답 ③

문제풀이
대화의 중간 부분에서 여자가 보컬이 노래하면서 기타를 치는 게 멋있다고
했는데 그림에서 보컬은 기타가 없으므로 정답은 ③번이다.

총 어휘 수 137

소재 교환학생 다녀온 친구

듣기 대본 해석
[휴대폰이 울린다.]
남: 여보세요?
여: 안녕, Ted. 나 Grace야. 어떻게 지냈어?
남: Grace! 돌아왔어?
여: 응. 교환학생 프로그램이 끝나서 어젯밤에 비행기를 타고 돌아왔어.
남: 그랬어? Stone 선생님이 네가 다음 주 월요일에 학교로 돌아온다고 말씀
    하셨어. 중국은 어땠어?
여: 멋졌어. 중국어로 사람들에게 말하는 데 훨씬 더 자신감이 생겼어.
남: 훌륭해! 우리 모두 네가 중국에서 보낸 시간에 대해 이야기하길 기대하고
    있어. 특히 선생님들이.
여: 나도 가능한 빨리 그들을 만나고 싶어. 하지만 수업의 처음 2주를 놓쳐서
    조금 걱정이 돼.
남: 그래… 다음 주에 퀴즈가 2개 있어.
여: 정말? 난 퀴즈 준비가 안 됐는데.
남: 선생님들께서 주신 자료물이 나한테 있어. 네가 원하면 가져다 줄게.
여: 그래 줄래? 정말 잘됐네!
남: 친구 좋다는 게 뭐니?

어휘
exchange *n.* 교환   **since** *conj.* ~ 때문에   **prepare for** ~를
준비하다

정답 ⑤

문제풀이
선생님에게서 받은 자료물을 갖다 주겠다는 남자의 말로 미루어 보아 정답은
⑤ '수업시간에 받은 자료 갖다 주기'이다.

총 어휘 수 137

소재 우천으로 취소된 테니스 경기

듣기 대본 해석
여: Davis. 어디 가니?
남: 엄마의 꽃가게에 가고 있어. 엄마가 우체국에 볼 일이 있어서 내가 가게를
    좀 봐야 하거든.
여: 정말 친절하구나. 오, 너 지난 일요일에 테니스 경기에 갔었지. 그렇지?
    경기 어땠어?
남: 그 경기는 사실은 일요일이 아니라 토요일이었어.
여: 아. 어쨌든, 너 멋진 시간을 보냈음이 틀림없겠구나. 너 테니스 좋아하잖아.
남: 나는 경기장에 갔었는데 경기가 취소되었어.
여: 진짜? 왜?
남: 폭풍우(뇌우) 때문이야. 경기가 시작되기도 전에 우천으로 취소됐어.
여: 아. 맞아! 토요일에 날씨가 진짜 별로였지. 정말 안됐네.
남: 그래. 나는 정말 그 게임을 보러 가는 데 들떠 있었어. 내가 해야 하는 숙제와
    공부 때문에 이번 시즌에 경기 볼 시간이 없었거든.
여: 그래. 네 심정 알겠어. 경기를 놓쳤다니 유감이야.

어휘
head *v.* 가다, 향하다   **run an errand** 심부름 하다   **rain out**
우천으로 경기가 취소되다

정답 ①

문제풀이

남자는 경기 전 시작된 폭풍우로 테니스 경기가 취소되었다고 했으므로 경기를
관람하지 못한 이유는 ① '폭우로 경기가 취소돼서'이다.

총 어휘 수 141

09 숫자

소재 골동품 구입

듣기 대본 해석

여: 왜 이 골동품들 진짜인가요?
남: 네. 몇 개는 저희 할머니가 저에게 주신 거예요.
여: 저기 있는 램프들은 비싼가요?
남: 황동 램프는 40달러이고 유리 램프는 60달러입니다.
여: 유리 램프가 정말 멋있긴 한데 제가 사기엔 비싼 것 같네요.
남: 정말 그게 맘에 드시면 황동 램프와 같은 가격으로 드릴게요.
여: 와, 정말이요? 좋아요. 그걸 살게요! 저 아름다운 접시들은 얼마예요?
남: 더 큰 접시들은 각각 10달러이고 작은 접시들은 각각 5달러예요.
여: 네, 제가 이 큰 접시 두 개 살게요.
남: 제가 손님께 권해드릴 만한 또 다른 품목이 있나요?
여: 저 의자가 아주 마음에 드네요.
남: 네, 아주 예쁜 의자이지 않나요? 사실 마지막 남은 겁니다. 다른 것들은
   70달러에 팔렸지만 손님께는 50달러에 드릴게요.
여: 네, 좋아요. 고마워요!

어휘

antique *n.* 골동품   brass *n.* 놋쇠, 황동   afford *v.* (~을 살 금전적·
시간적) 여유·형편이 되다   item *n.* 품목   interest somebody in
(~을 사거나 먹도록) 권하다

정답 ③

문제풀이

유리 램프를 황동 램프 가격인 40달러에, 큰 접시 두 개는 20달러에, 그리고
의자를 50달러에 판다고 했으므로 합계는 110달러이다. 따라서 여자가 지불할
금액은 ③ '$110'이다.

총 어휘 수 154

10 언급 유무

소재 새로 산 컴퓨터

듣기 대본 해석

남: 여보. 오늘 택배 도착했어.
여: 좋다. 이 새 컴퓨터 빨리 설치하고 싶었어.
남: 우리 예전 컴퓨터보다 많이 커 보인다.
여: 맞아. 그리고 훨씬 빠르기도 해. 21인치 모니터랑 레이저 프린터가 포함된
   세트로 샀어.
남: 꽤 복잡해 보인다. 내가 컴퓨터에 대해서 좀 더 유식했으면 좋겠어.
여: 굉장히 쉬워. 여보, 어떻게 쓰는지 가르쳐 줄게.
남: 좋네. 이 컴퓨터로 Cacao Chat 할 수 있어? 회사 동료들이 다 그 얘기
   하더라고.
여: 당연하지. 또 영상통화도 무료로 즐길 수 있어.
남: 좋다. 보증기간도 있어?
여: 응. 2년 동안 무슨 일이 있으면 와서 고쳐준대.
남: 그럼 잃어버리지 않게 보증서를 안전한 곳에 보관하자.
여: 좋은 생각이야.

어휘

savvy *n.* 지식 *a.* 지식이 많은   warranty *n.* 보증서, 보증기간

정답 ④

문제풀이

두 사람은 21인치 모니터, 레이저 프린터, 무료 영상통화, 2년의 보증기간에 대해
언급했지만 백신에 대한 언급은 없었으므로 정답은 ④ '무료 백신'이다.

총 어휘 수 149

11 내용 일치·불일치

소재 자선 콘서트 소개하기

듣기 대본 해석

남: 여러분 안녕하세요. 저는 GBC 뉴스의 Ronnie Maroon입니다. 우리의
   아름다운 도시에서 자선 음악회가 열린다는 사실을 알리게 되어 기쁩니다.
   그 음악회는 The Great Tusk Concert라는 음악회이고 세상에서 가장
   큰 동물 복지 단체인 Earth Wildlife Federation의 후원을 받고 있습니다.
   The Great Tusk Concert는 음악, 영화, TV 업계에서 유명한 인사들의
   공연을 선보일 것이며, 그들은 화려한 저녁을 위해 지역사회를 하나로 화합
   시키기를 기대하고 있습니다. 행사는 7월 15일 Metropolitan Opera
   House에서 개최될 예정입니다. 이 행사의 수익금은 세계 각지에서 학대와
   혹사를 당하고 있는 코끼리들의 복지에 쓰일 것입니다. 더 많은 정보와 표
   구매를 위해서는 www.thegreattuskconcert.com라는 행사 사이트를
   방문해 주십시오.

어휘

feature *v.* ~을 특징으로 하다   proceeds *n.* 수익금   abuse *n.*
학대, 남용   mistreatment *n.* 학대, 혹사

정답 ③

문제풀이

남자는 자선 음악회에 대해 소개하면서 행사 날짜는 7월 15일이라고 하였으므로
일치하지 않는 것은 ③ '행사 날짜는 6월 15일이다.'이다.

총 어휘 수 122

12 도표

소재 RV캠프장 선택

듣기 대본 해석

여: 여보, 뭐하고 있어요?
남: 다음 달에 있을 우리 RV(레크리에이션 차) 여행 옵션을 확인하고 있어요.
   우리가 가려는 호수 주변에 5개의 캠핑장이 있어요.
여: 멋지네요. 선택하는 거 도와줄까요?
남: 물론이죠. 그런데, 우리의 선택에서 어떤 것들을 고려해야 하죠?
여: 음. 물을 쓸 수 있는 게 꽤 중요할 것 같아요.
남: 맞아요. 우리 차량은 샤워기를 가지고 있으니까 사용하려면 물을 연결할
   수 있어야 하겠네요.
여: 그래요. 그러면 이 3개 중에서 하나를 골라야 해요.
남: 좋아요. 내 생각에는 애완동물은 금지라니까 이건 빼야겠어요.
여: 네, 난 정말 Baxter를 데리고 가고 싶어요. 정말 좋아 할거예요.
남: 그럼 이 2개로 좁혀지네요.
여: 당신 생각에 전기 없이 3일을 지낼 수 있을 것 같아요?
남: 가능하긴 한데, 필요할지도 모르니까 있는 게 나을 것 같아요.
여: 좋아요. 그럼 이 캠핑장으로 예약해야겠네요.

어휘

hookup *n.* (전기, 수도 등의 외부와의) 연결부　　**prohibit** *v.* 금지하다
electricity *n.* 전기

정답 ③

문제풀이

처음에 물을 사용할 수 있어야 한다고 했으므로 A, C, E중에 골라야 하고, 애완동물을 데려가고 싶으므로 E는 제외된다. A, C중에서 전기가 되는 것으로 선택하자고 했으므로 정답은 ③번이다.

총 어휘 수 169

13　긴 대화의 응답

소재　옛 친구와의 만남

듣기 대본 해석

남: 지난밤에 내게 무슨 일이 일어났는지 아니, Maria?
여: 무슨 일이 일어났어?
남: 너 Dan이 누군지 아니?
여: 물론이지. 우리 고등학교 동안 라크로스 경기 같이 했었는데, 그가 졸업반 때 텍사스로 이사 갔잖아.
남: 맞아. 근데 그가 어젯밤에 나한테 Face Friend 메시지를 보냈어.
여: 정말? 그는 어떻게 지내?
남: 내 생각에 그는 다시 여기에 일하러 이사올 생각인 것 같고 그가 여기서 어울리던 사람들과 연락하고 싶었던 것 같아.
여: 그를 만나면 너무 좋을 것 같아. 많이 변했는지 궁금하다.
남: 음, 곧 그를 볼 수 있을 거야. 그는 2주 후에 아파트를 구하기 위해 여기에 올 거래.
여: 왜! 좋은 소식이네!
남: 그래. 시내 어딘가에서 점심 먹을 거야. 너도 올래?
여: ⑤ 물론이야. 만날 일이 기대되네.

어휘

hang out 어울리다

정답 ⑤

문제풀이

남자는 예전에 살던 곳으로 다시 이사오기 전에 연락을 취한 Dan에 대해 여자에게 이야기해 주었고 여자도 고등학교 때 같이 경기 하던 친구라 어떻게 변했는지 궁금해하고 있다. 남자가 Dan과 점심 약속을 잡았다며 여자에게 합류 의향을 물었을 때 가장 적절한 여자의 대답은 ⑤ '물론이지. 만날 일이 기대되네.'이다.

오답 보기 해석

① 나는 그렇게 생각하지 않아. 그는 더 빨리 전화했어야 했어.
② 너한테 소식 듣는 건 항상 좋아. 몸 조심해.
③ 유감이지만 그 소식이 사실이기에는 너무나 좋아서 믿을 수 없구나.
④ 사실 나는 그 사람이 누군지 몰라.

총 어휘 수 135

14　긴 대화의 응답

소재　대학 선택

듣기 대본 해석

남: 안녕 Leah, 네가 원하는 대학에 들어갔니?
여: 응, Paul. 실은 두 군데 대학에서 입학 허가를 받았어.
남: 두 개 대학? 그럼, 어디로 갈지 벌써 정한 거야?
여: 두 학교 모두 좋은 학교야. 가장 큰 차이점은 Upstate 대학교는 주립대학이고, Lakeside는 사립이란 거지.

남: 두 학교 다 평판이 좋잖아.
여: 맞아. 그 둘 중에서 어떻게 한 군데를 골라야 할지 모르겠어.
남: 딜레마에 빠졌구나. 그렇지만 난 네가 어떻게 결정할 수 있을지 알고 있어.
여: 어떻게? 난 정말 조언이 필요해.
남: 동전을 던져봐. 동전이 공중에 있을 때, 넌 동전이 어느 쪽으로 떨어지길 바라는지 알게 될 거야.
여: 한번 해볼게. [잠시 후] 네 말이 맞았어. 그게 공중에 떠 있을 때, 난 Upstate 대학을 원했거든.
남: ④ 만약 그렇다면, 그곳이 네가 가야 하는 대학이야.

어휘

dilemma *n.* 딜레마　　**flip** *v.* 톡(툭) 던지다

정답 ④

문제풀이

여자가 두 개의 대학으로부터 입학 허가를 받고 고민하자 남자가 조언을 해주고 있다. 남자는 동전을 던져서 동전이 공중에 있을 때 마음속으로 떨어지기를 바라는 면을 알아 보라고 조언하고, 여자는 그렇게 해서 정말로 자신이 원하는 대학을 알게 되었다. 이에 대한 남자의 대답으로 적절한 것은 ④ '만약 그렇다면, 그곳이 네가 가야 하는 대학이야.'이다.

오답 보기 해석

① 나는 내가 너에게 도움을 요청한 것이 정말 기뻐.
② 나는 네가 그 대학에 들어갔으면 좋겠어.
③ 정말로 너희 부모님께 조언을 구해야 해.
⑤ 대학에서 너 자신에 대해 많이 배워.

총 어휘 수 136

15　상황에 적절한 말

소재　동물 보호소 동물들의 식단 관리

듣기 대본 해석

여: Valerie는 최근에 자신의 동물 보호소를 시작하였고 그녀의 일에 매우 열정적입니다. 그녀는 동물들이 잘 관리되고 있다는 것을 확실히 하기 위해 자신의 직원들을 훈련시킵니다. 그녀는 각 종들이 다른 식단 요구를 갖고 있기 때문에 직원들이 동물들 먹이는 것을 특별히 신경쓰길 원합니다. 어느 날, 그녀는 몇몇 동물들이 아프기 시작한 것을 알아차립니다. 그녀가 철창 안을 들여다 보는데 구조된 너구리가 새 모이를 먹고 있는 것을 봅니다. 그녀는 동물들이 계속 잘못된 종류의 음식을 먹고 죽을까 봐 걱정합니다. 그녀는 이 문제를 다루기 위한 회의에 직원들을 불러들입니다. 이 상황에서, Valerie가 그녀의 직원들에게 할 말로 적절한 것은 무엇입니까?
Valerie: ⑤ 우리는 반드시 동물들이 적합한 음식을 먹도록 해야 합니다.

어휘

animal shelter 동물 보호소　　**passionate** *a.* 열정적인
in good hands 안심할 수 있는, 잘 관리되는　　**species** *n.* 종
dietary *a.* 음식물의

정답 ⑤

문제풀이

동물 보호소에 있는 동물들이 잘못된 음식을 먹고 죽을까 봐 걱정이 된 Valerie가 직원회의를 소집한 상황에서 직원들에게 할 말로 가장 적절한 것은 ⑤ '우리는 반드시 동물들이 적합한 음식을 먹도록 해야 합니다.'이다.

오답 보기 해석

① 어떤 방문자도 동물 보호소 내에 들어오지 못하도록 해주세요.
② 기금을 받기 위해 고군분투 하는 중이라 문을 닫아야 할 것 같아요.
③ 방문자들이 동물들에게 사람이 먹는 음식을 주지 못하도록 해야 합니다.
④ 동물들을 위해 더 신선한 음식을 사야 할 것입니다.

총 어휘 수 128

16 담화 주제 / 17 세부 내용 파악

소재 햇볕으로 인한 화상을 다루는 방법

듣기 대본 해석

여: 여러분, 좋은 아침입니다. 오랫동안 사람들은 햇빛이 우리의 피부에 줄 수 있는 손상에 대해 알고 있었지만 "애프터 썬 케어"와 같은 특정 제품들이 이 손상을 무효로 만들 수 있다고 믿게 했습니다. 사실 애프터 썬 제품이라고 불리는 이런 제품들은 제품 속에 든 기름이 우리 피부 속에 열을 가두어 두기 때문에 사실 우리 몸이 가지고 있는 치유 과정을 방해할 수 있습니다. 그러면 우리가 우리 자신을 보호하기 위해 무엇을 할 수 있을까요? 우리가 일광 화상을 어떻게 다루어야 할까요? 단지 피부를 시원하게 두는 것이 방법입니다. 여러분은 시원한 물에 몸을 담그거나 식초를 사용할 수 있습니다. 수건을 식초에 담그고 그것을 일광 화상을 입은 자리에 두면 식초가 당신 피부의 열을 빼낼 겁니다. 놀랍지만 약간 냄새가 나죠. 여러분이 그 냄새를 맡길 원하지 않으시면, 알로에 베라 막이나 얇게 썬 오이도 같은 역할을 합니다.

어휘

damage *n.* 손상, 피해　　**undo** *v.* 무효로 만들다, 원상태로 돌리다　　**hinder** *v.* 저해하다, 막다　　**trap** *v.* 가두다　　**vinegar** *n.* 식초　　**soak** *v.* 담그다　　〈문제〉**alternative** *n.* 대안

정답 16 ④　17 ②

문제풀이

16 여자는 일광 화상을 입은 다음 제품을 바르는 것은 도움이 되지 않는다고 말하면서 다른 적당한 방법으로 시원한 물에 몸 담그기, 식초에 담근 수건 대고 있기 등을 알려주고 있다. 따라서 여자가 하는 말의 주제는 ④ '애프터 썬 제품의 대안'이다.

17 여자는 일광 화상을 입었을 때 찬물에 몸을 담그거나 식초, 알로에, 오이를 이용하라고 말했지만 우유에 대해서는 언급하지 않았으므로 정답은 ② '우유'이다.

오답 보기 해석

16
① 피부에 바르는 천연 재료의 효과
② 자외선 차단제를 항상 사용해야 하는 이유
③ 규칙적인 일광욕의 장점
⑤ 가장 좋은 애프터 썬 케어 제품

총 어휘 수 149

01 its opening weekend / I'm going to check it out

02 you're soaked / check the weather forecast

03 enjoys having fun outdoors / the weather can change for the worse / find yourself caught in a thunderstorm / getting struck by lightning

04 it's fun to talk with him / Personal hygiene is looked at differently / I appreciate the advice

05 carry a first-aid kit / having a great time on the trip / I'm doing my best

06 They're all super talented / That's awesome / He's got great range

07 student exchange program is finished / I'm not prepared for the quizzes / What are friends for

08 where are you headed / run some errands / It was rained out

09 the one made of glass / I don't think I can afford it / I can interest you in

10 I've been looking forward to / more computer-savvy / get a warranty on / let's be sure to keep the warranty papers

11 a benefit concert will be held / some of the biggest names in / experiencing abuse and mistreatment

12 What are you up to / water hookup / since it prohibits pets / That narrows it down to

13 during our senior year / used to hang out with / you might see him soon / we're going to set up a lunch

14 I got accepted to two universities / That's quite a dilemma / Flip a coin

15 her animals are in good hands / different dietary needs / calls her staff in for a meeting

16-17 we can undo this damage / hinder your body's own healing process / traps heat inside the skin / soak a towel in vinegar / pull the heat out of your skin

19 수능영어듣기 / 실전모의고사

01 ②	02 ⑤	03 ③	04 ②	05 ②	06 ③
07 ③	08 ⑤	09 ⑤	10 ⑤	11 ②	12 ④
13 ③	14 ①	15 ③	16 ③	17 ④	

01 짧은 대화의 응답

소재 식사 주문

듣기 대본 해석

여: 저는 주문할 준비가 된 것 같은데, 주문 받아주실래요?
남: 물론이죠. 오늘 아침에 뭐가 좋으세요?
여: 베이컨과 계란 그리고 사이드 메뉴로 구운 감자를 주세요. 언제 될까요?
남: ② 그것은 15분 안에 준비될 것입니다.

어휘

〈문제〉 **waffle** *n.* 와플(밀가루 · 달걀 · 우유 등을 섞어 구운 것) **popular** *a.* 인기 있는

정답 ②

문제풀이

음식이 언제 준비되는지 물었으므로 남자의 응답으로 가장 적절한 것은 ② '그것은 15분 안에 준비될 것입니다.'이다.

오답 보기 해석

① 카페는 약 1시간 거리예요.
③ 애플 파이를 곁들인 와플은 인기 있는 메뉴입니다.
④ 사람들은 감자가 건강에 좋지 않다고 말해요.
⑤ 마트에서 며칠 전에 좀 사왔어요.

총 어휘 수 42

02 짧은 대화의 응답

소재 티켓 구하기

듣기 대본 해석

남: 이번 토요일에 올림픽 경기장에서 하는 Dragon Heart 콘서트를 정말 보고 싶어!
여: 응, 나도. 아직 티켓을 구할 수 있을까?
남: 잘 모르겠어. 하지만, 내 친구 Kevin이 티켓 판매소에서 일하고 있어.
여: ⑤ 네가 꼭 그에게 전화해서 물어봐야겠는데.

어휘

stadium *n.* 강당   〈문제〉 **definitely** *ad.* 분명히

정답 ⑤

문제풀이

남자의 친구 Kevin이 티켓 판매소에서 일하고 있다고 했으므로, 여자의 응답은 ⑤ '네가 꼭 그에게 전화해서 물어봐야겠는데.'가 알맞다.

오답 보기 해석

① 와, 나도 Dragon Heart 좋아해!
② 나는 이번 토요일에 정말로 바빠.
③ 유감스럽게도 매진됐다고 그가 말했어.
④ 나 그 콘서트 표를 두 장 가지고 있어.

총 어휘 수 43

03 담화 목적

소재 법률 분야 인턴십 모집 안내

듣기 대본 해석

여: 여러분 안녕하세요! 오늘 저는 여러분이 놓치고 싶어하지 않을 기회에 대해서 말씀 드리고자 합니다. 여러분 중에 로스쿨에 진학하고 싶으신 분이 계시다면, 제가 여러분과 공유하려는 인턴십은 직접 실무에 참여하는 경험을 얻을 수 있는 좋은 기회입니다. 그러나, 몇 가지 알아둘 점들이 있습니다. 이 인턴십 지원은 우리 학교에 현재 등록된 대학생과 대학원생에게 해당됩니다. 그러나, 이 기회를 얻을 수 있는 학부생들은 오로지 현재 졸업반 학생들임을 명심하십시오. 법대생들과 그 분야를 접해본 지원자가 선호될 것입니다. 마지막으로, 지원자들은 28세 이하여야 합니다. 법 분야에서 어렵지만 보람 있는 일을 시작하고 싶다면 오늘 지원하십시오.

어휘

hands-on *a.* 직접 해 보는. 직접 실무에 참여하는   **undergraduate** *a.* 학부의 *n.* 학부생   **be eligible for** ~에 자격이 있다   **senior** *a.* 졸업할 학년의   **candidate** *n.* 지원자. 후보자   **exposure** *n.* 노출. 접함   **preference** *n.* 선호   **career** *n.* 경력. 직업

정답 ③

문제풀이

법률 관련 분야에서 실무적인 경험을 쌓을 수 있는 인턴십에 지원할 수 있는 자격 조건으로 '등록된 학생인지 여부. 졸업반인 학부생. 지원가능 연령 등'을 말하고 있으므로 답은 ③ '인턴십에 지원할 수 있는 자격을 알리려고'이다.

총 어휘 수 131

04 대화 주제

소재 맨발로 뛰기의 장점

듣기 대본 해석

여: Cody. 뭐해?
남: 맨발로 뛰는 것의 장점에 대해 읽고 있어.
여: 요즘 사람들이 그거 많이 해보고 있다고 들었어.
남: 맞아. 어떤 연구자들은 맨발로 뛰는 게 건강에 굉장히 좋다고 생각해.
여: 어떤 이점이 있는데?
남: 일단 균형감각을 발달시켜 줄 수 있어.
여: 정말? 어떻게?
남: 신발을 신은 채로 뛰면 발이 (좁은) 신발 안에 밀어 넣어져 있어. 신발이 없으면 발가락을 펼 수 있어서 균형을 더 잘 잡을 수 있지.
여: 그렇구나. 다른 건 안 도와줘?
남: 다리 근육에도 좋아. 보통 운동화는 뒤꿈치에 굽이 있어서 아킬레스건이랑 종아리 근육이 많이 쓰이질 않아.
여: 왜 많은 사람들이 맨발로 뛰기 시작했는지 알겠어. 한번 해봐야겠다.
남: 나도 한번 해보려고.

어휘

benefit *n.* 이점   **balance** *n.* 균형   **cramped** *a.* 비좁게 있는   **tendon** *n.* 건. 힘줄   **calf** *n.* 종아리

정답 ②

문제풀이

두 사람은 맨발로 뛰었을 때의 균형감 향상과 다리 근육 단련 효과에 대해 이야기하고 있으므로 두 사람이 하는 말의 주제로 가장 적절한 것은 ② '맨발로 뛰기의 장점'이다.

총 어휘 수 139

소재　자동차 수리 맡기기

듣기 대본 해석

남: 안녕하세요. 무엇을 도와드릴까요?

여: 그게, 최근에 사고가 났었어요. 그 이후로 계기판에 계속 빨간 불이 깜박거려요.

남: 한번 확인해 볼게요. 다른 문제는 없으신가요?

여: 있어요. 시속 70킬로미터 이상으로 달릴 때 차에서 딸깍거리는 소리가 나요.

남: 흠… 타이어의 문제 같네요.

여: 제 보험이 필요한 수리에 대한 모든 비용을 다 대줄 거예요. 그렇죠?

남: 유감스럽지만 저희는 그것에 관해서는 잘 모르겠습니다. 직접 보험사에 전화를 해보셔야 할 것 같습니다.

여: 점심 시간 후에 한 번 전화해 볼게요. 수리하는 데에 얼마나 걸릴까요?

남: 글쎄요. 차에 정확히 어떤 문제가 있느냐에 따라 다릅니다. 한번 점검한 다음에 알려드릴 수 있을 것 같습니다.

여: 이 주변에서 볼 일이 좀 있어요. 제가 나중에 와도 될까요?

남: 괜찮습니다. 전화번호를 남겨 주세요. 뭐가 문제인지 더 잘 알아내면 연락 드릴게요.

여: 알겠습니다.

어휘

dashboard *n.* 계기판　　**errand** *n.* 일, 심부름

정답　②

문제풀이

여자는 차에 문제가 있어 자동차 수리공인 남자에게 수리를 맡기고 있으므로 두 사람의 관계는 ② '자동차 수리공 — 고객'이다.

총 어휘 수　176

06　그림의 세부 내용 파악

소재　캠핑장 정리

듣기 대본 해석

여: 안녕, Peter. 늦어서 미안해. 나 너무 바빴어.

남: 괜찮아. 내가 캠핑장을 거의 다 설치했어. 내가 지금까지 해놓은 것 어때?

여: 아주 살했어. 텐트를 강가에 친 것이 마음에 들어.

남: 응, 우리 그러면 수영도 낚시도 쉽게 할 수 있어. 강가에서 저녁을 즐기는 것도 멋질 거야.

여: 아, 그래서 테이블과 의자를 텐트와 강 사이에 놓았구나. 그런데 아이스박스는 어디에 뒀어? 그것은 그늘에 둬야 해.

남: 오, 깜빡했어. 지금 텐트 안에 있어. 내가 그걸 가지고 가서 나무 아래 둘게.

여: 그러면 그게 모닥불 옆에 놓일 거야. 게다가 나무 너무 가까이에 불을 피우는 것은 위험할 수도 있어.

남: 맞는 말이네. 그건 나중에 옮기도록 하고 강 근처에 새로 불을 만들자. 그건 그렇고, 나무 사이에 해먹을 걸었어. 어떻게 생각해?

여: 완벽해. 잘 했어!

어휘

campsite *n.* 캠핑장, 야영지　　**set up** ~을 설치[설비]하다　　**shade** *n.* 그늘　　**make sense** 말이 되다, 이치에 닿다　　**hang (-hung-hung)** *v.* 걸다

정답　③

문제풀이

아이스박스는 텐트 안에 있다고 했는데 밖에 나와 있으므로 정답은 ③번이다.

총 어휘 수　168

07　부탁한 일

소재　친구에게 잠시 가방 맡기기

듣기 대본 해석

여: Jeff, 늦어서 진짜 미안해.

남: 진심으로 걱정했잖아. 네가 못 오는 줄 알았어. 전화도 해봤는데 네가 전화를 안 받더라고.

여: 그게, 택시를 타서 반쯤 왔을 때 휴대폰을 집에 놔두고 왔다는 걸 알아차려서 다시 가야 했어. 게다가 오는 도중에 차도 좀 막혔어.

남: 맞아. 금요일 저녁에는 항상 그런 식으로 막혀.

여: 몰랐어. 아, 버스 정류장 주변에 혹시 편의점 있어?

남: 저 쪽에 하나 있어. 왜?

여: 휴대폰 가지러 집에 다시 갔을 때 충전기를 깜박하고 안 가져왔어. 하나 사야 돼. 내 가방 좀 봐줄래?

남: 알겠어. 여기서 기다릴게.

여: 고마워. 몇 분 안 걸릴 거야.

어휘

traffic jam 교통 체증　　**convenience store** 편의점　　**charger** *n.* 충전기　　〈문제〉**keep an eye** 주시하다

정답　③

문제풀이

여자는 집에서 휴대폰 충전기를 놓고 와서 편의점에서 하나 사려고 하는데 그 동안 잠시 남자에게 자신의 가방을 봐(맡아) 달라고 부탁하고 있으므로 정답은 ③ '가방 맡아주기'이다.

오답 보기 해석

① 휴대폰 가지러 가기

② 휴대폰 충전하기

④ 휴대폰 충전기 사주기

⑤ 버스 정류장에 데려다 주기

총 어휘 수　136

08　이유

소재　집에서 공부하려는 이유

듣기 대본 해석

남: 안녕, Kate. 내일 볼 시험 준비됐니?

여: 아닌 것 같아. 하루 종일 공부하고 있을 것 같아. 넌 어때?

남: 난 새로운 학생 센터에 있는 카페에서 계속 공부했어.

여: 아, 거기 어때?

남: 꽤 멋져. 거기에는 새로 연 레스토랑 몇 군데랑 탁구 테이블이 있는 레크레이션 룸 그리고 농구 코트가 있어.

여: 대단한 걸. 시험 끝나고 탁구 치러 가야겠다.

남: 거기에 생긴 새로운 피자가게도 정말 좋아.

여: 좋네. 그럼 거기서 점심 먹고 카페에서 같이 공부하는 건 어때?

남: 나도 점심 먹고 싶어. 하지만 거기서 공부하는 건 별로 좋은 생각이 아니야.

여: 정말? 왜 그런데?

남: 카페 테라스가 아직 공사 중이라 꽤 시끄러워.

여: 알았어. 그러면 나도 집에 가서 공부해야겠어

어휘

recreation room 레크리에이션 룸, 오락실　　**awesome** *a.* 굉장한, 엄청난　　**under construction** 공사 중인

정답　⑤

문제풀이

새로 생긴 학생 센터에 있는 카페에서 같이 공부하는 게 어떠냐는 여자의 말에 남자는 카페 테라스가 아직 공사 중이라 시끄러워서 거기서 공부하는 것은 좋은 생각이 아니라고 했다. 따라서 남자가 집에서 공부하려는 이유는 ⑤ '카페 외부 공사로 인한 소음이 시끄러워서'이다.

총 어휘 수 134

09 숫자

소재 토네이도 지역을 돕기 위한 기부

듣기 대본 해석

남: DeLaney 선생님. 안녕하세요. 바쁘신가요? 말씀드릴 게 좀 있어서요.

여: 아, Taylor. 들어오렴. 무엇이 필요하니?

남: 지난주에 Kentucky주에 닥친 토네이도에 관해서 들으셨을 거예요.

여: 들었지. 끔찍했어. 많은 집들이 완전히 파괴되었잖니.

남: 음. 많은 학생들이 피해자들에게 돈을 기부하기 위해 모였어요. 모든 학생들이 3달러를 냈어요.

여: 정말 잘한 일이구나. 도움이 될 거라고 확신해.

남: 저도 그러길 바라요. 모두들 도울 수 있어서 기뻐했어요.

여: 25명의 학생 모두가 기부했다고? 꽤 많은 돈일 텐데.

남: 네. 여기 저희가 모금한 돈이에요. 혹시 선생님께서 저희를 대신해서 돈을 보내 주실 수 있나 궁금해서요.

여: 물론이지. 나도 20달러를 기부할게.

남: 감사해요 DeLaney 선생님. 이 돈이 정말 도움이 되기를 바라요.

여: 확실히 도움이 될 거야. Taylor.

어휘

destroy *v.* 파괴하다   **donate** *v.* 기부하다   **pitch in** ~을 기부하다
on one's behalf ~을 대신(대표)하여

정답 ⑤

문제풀이

25명 학생 모두가 3달러를 기부했으므로 75달러이고, DeLaney 선생님이 20달러를 기부했으므로 여자가 토네이도 지역에 전달할 총 기부금은 ⑤ '$95'이다.

총 어휘 수 132

10 언급 유무

소재 브로콜리의 건강상 이점

듣기 대본 해석

남: 오늘 기분이 너무 좋아. 막 시작한 새로운 식단이 엄청나거든. 너는 어때? 어떻게 하고 있어?

여: 너만큼 좋지는 않아. 나도 네 식단을 시도해야겠어. 어떤 종류의 음식을 먹고 있어?

남: 나는 더 많은 야채를 먹고 있어. 너에게도 이걸 추천하고 싶어. 브로콜리가 너한테 좋아.

여: 정말? 브로콜리에 어떤 건강상 이점들이 있어?

남: 어, 우선. 브로콜리는 녹는 섬유질이 가득 차 있고, 그것이 콜레스테롤을 낮추는 데 좋아.

여: 알겠어. 또 다른 건?

남: 브로콜리는 비타민 C와 K가 가득한데. 그 비타민들은 뼈 건강을 증진시켜줘. 브로콜리는 또한 암을 예방하고 건강을 유지시켜주는 산화방지제의 훌륭한 원천이지.

여: 대단해. 나는 약간의 살도 좀 빼고 싶은데. 브로콜리가 그것을 도와줄 수 있을까?

남: 물론 그럴 거야. 브로콜리가 섬유질로 가득하다고 말했던 것 기억해? 이건 많은 칼로리를 먹지 않고도 네가 배부르게 느끼게끔 만들어주는 것을 의미해.

여: 왜. 브로콜리는 정말 슈퍼푸드구나!

어휘

recommend *v.* 추천하다   **benefit** *n.* 이점   **soluble** *a.* 녹는
fiber *n.* 섬유질   **antioxidant** *n.* 산화방지제

정답 ⑤

문제풀이

브로콜리는 섬유질을 많이 함유해 콜레스테롤을 낮추고, 비타민 C와 K가 많아서 뼈 건강을 증진시키며 산화방지제가 있어 암을 예방하고 포만감을 주어서 체중 감소에도 도움을 줄 수 있다고 언급하였다. 그러나 식욕증진에 대한 것은 언급되지 않았으므로 정답은 ⑤번이다.

총 어휘 수 162

11 내용 일치 · 불일치

소재 큰까마귀에 대한 설명

듣기 대본 해석

남: 북쪽 지방의 까마귀로 널리 알려진 큰까마귀는 북반구에서 주로 발견되는 크고 까만 새입니다. 이것은 까마귀 종류 중 가장 흔합니다. 사실. 진화론적 관점에서 이 종은 매우 성공적으로 발전해왔습니다. 큰까마귀는 수천 년 동안 인간과 공존해 왔고 어떤 지역에서는 너무 많아서 성가시게 여겨지기도 했습니다. 까마귀 생존 성공의 중요한 부분은 그것의 식습관에서 옵니다. 이 새들은 썩은 살. 곤충. 곡물 낟알들. 베리. 과일. 작은 동물과 음식물 쓰레기를 먹으면서 영양의 원천을 찾는 데 능하고 기회를 잘 잡습니다. 까마귀는 대단한 포식동물로 여겨져 왔고 전미 미식 축구 연맹의 Baltimore Ravens를 포함해서 다른 많은 스포츠팀의 마스코트로 사용되어 왔습니다.

어휘

widely *ad.* 널리   **Northern Hemisphere** 북반구   **numerous**
a. 많은   **pest** *n.* 성가신 것. 해충   **crucial** *a.* 중요한   **versatile** *a.*
다재 다능한   **opportunistic** *a.* 기회주의적인   **nutrition** *n.* 영양
grain *n.* 곡물. 낟알   **predator** *n.* 포식자. 포식동물

정답 ②

문제풀이

큰까마귀는 수천 년 동안 인간과 공존해 왔다고 했으므로 내용과 일치하지 않는 것은 ② '인간과 공존한 지는 오래되지 않았다.'이다.

총 어휘 수 128

12 도표

소재 스포츠 센터 여름 프로그램 선택

듣기 대본 해석

여: Garrett. 스포츠 센터에서 이번 여름 프로그램 시간표 받았어. 그건 나를 이렇게 생각하게 만들었어. 이번 여름에 운동 좀 하자고. 하루 종일 안에서 아무것도 안 하는 건 너무 아쉬울 거야.

남: 맞아. 어떤 수업 보고 있어?

여: 수영 수업은 어때? 수영을 더 잘하고 싶어.

남: 사실 나 물 공포증이 있어.

여: 그럼 에어로빅은 어때? 재미있을 것 같아.

남: 괜찮을 것 같은데 수요일 밤에 독서 모임 있잖아.

여: 맞아. 그럼 이제 선택지가 두 개밖에 없네.

남: 수업이 저렴해서 좋네. 우리 부모님은 30달러보다 비싼 수업료는 내실
여유가 없으셔.
여: 그럼 너는 어느 게 좋아?
남: 일단 화요일이랑 목요일 수업은 우리가 들을 수 없네. 고학년 애들을 위한
거야.
여: 맞아. 그럼 이 수업 신청하자.
남: 좋은 생각이야.

어휘
afford *v.* 여유(형편)이 되다　**sign up** 등록하다　〈문제〉**racquetball**
n. 라켓볼

정답 ④

문제풀이
두 사람이 같이 수강할 프로그램을 고르고 있다. 남자가 수영은 싫다고 했고,
에어로빅은 독서 모임이 있는 수요일 밤이라 안 된다고 했으므로 ④번과 ⑤번이
남는다. 그런데 화요일과 목요일 수업은 연령이 더 높은 아이들을 위한 거라
듣지 못한다고 했으므로 두 사람이 수강할 강좌는 ④번이다.

총 어휘 수 148

13　긴 대화의 응답

소재 발을 다친 강아지

듣기 대본 해석
남: 여기 앉으세요. 당신의 강아지에게 무슨 문제가 있나요?
여: 글쎄요, 제대로 걷지를 못해요.
남: 발을 한번 보도록 할게요. *[잠시 후]* 아, 문제가 있네요. 왼쪽 발이 좀 부어
올랐네요. 왜 그런지 아세요?
여: 잘 모르겠는데요.
남: 다행히 그렇게 심각한 건 아니에요. 부기는 대략 일주일 내외로 가라 앉을
겁니다.
여: 일주일 내로요? 사실, 그는 다음 주에 Handsome Dog Contest에
참가해야 해요.
남: Dog-Lovers Club이 주최하는 대회 말씀이신가요?
여: 맞아요. 대회에 나가도 괜찮을까요? 참가하지 못 할까 봐 걱정되네요.
남: 걱정 마세요. 오, 그러면 9일 남았네요. 그때까지는 완전히 괜찮아질 겁니다.
여: 다행이네요. 정말 거정 많이 했거든요.
남: ③ 아니에요, 그는 괜찮을 거예요. 대회에서 행운을 빌게요.

어휘
swollen *a.* 부어 오른, 부은　**take part in** ~에 참가하다　**host** *v.*
주최하다　**participate** *v.* 참가하다

정답 ③

문제풀이
강아지가 발이 부어서 대회에 참여하지 못 할까 봐 걱정을 많이 했다는 여자의
말에 남자는 걱정 말라며 그때까지는 완전히 나을 것이라고 했으므로 적절한
마지막 응답은 ③ '아니에요, 그는 괜찮을 거예요. 대회에서 행운을 빌게요.'이다.

오답 보기 해석
① 당신의 개는 매우 심각한 부상을 입었어요.
② 어디서 애완동물을 잃어버린 것 같아요?
④ 왜 애완동물을 서브기로 결심했는지 말해 줄 수 있어요?
⑤ 유감스럽게도 당신의 애완동물은 대회에 참가할 수 없을 거예요.

총 어휘 수 142

14　긴 대화의 응답

소재 경기 침체 극복하기

듣기 대본 해석
여: 안녕하세요, Goodman씨. 요즘 가게는 어떠세요?
남: 사실 요즘에 매출이 그리 좋지 않아요.
여: 유감이네요. 요즘 경기가 나쁘잖아요.
남: 네, 조만간 조치를 취해야겠어요.
여: 어떻게 경기를 바꾸려 하세요?
남: 제가 경기를 바꿀 수는 없지만 제가 사업하는 방식을 바꿀 수는 있죠.
여: 말하자면 물건 가격을 낮추는 것 같은 건가요?
남: 음. 일간지에 쿠폰을 발행할까 생각 중이에요. 사람들에게 같은 돈으로 더
많은 혜택을 주고 싶어요.
여: 아주 인정이 많으시네요. 그런데 그렇게 하면 손해가 아닐까요?
남: 처음에는 그러겠죠. 그러나 힘든 시기에 제가 사람들을 돕는다고 사람들이
여길 것이고 그것이 단골 고객층을 만드는 데 도움이 될 거예요.
여: ① 당신이 그럴 여유가 있는 한 아주 좋은 생각이에요.

어휘
lately *ad.* 최근에　**economy** *n.* 경기　**lower** *v.* ~을 낮추다
accommodate *v.* ~을 수용하다　**in a time of need** 어려울(힘들) 때
loyal customer base 단골 고객층　〈문제〉**loan** *n.* 대출, 대부

정답 ①

문제풀이
남자는 경기는 좋지 않지만 일간지에 쿠폰을 발행함으로써 고객들에게 더
많은 혜택을 주어 초반 손해를 감수하고서라도 단골층을 확보하겠다고 하므로
이에 대한 응답으로 가장 적절한 것은 ① '당신이 그럴 여유가 있는 한 아주 좋은
생각이에요.'이다.

오답 보기 해석
② 당신이 단골 고객층을 갖고 있어서 좋네요.
③ 제가 대출을 조금 받을 수 있을까요?
④ 그 판촉은 조금 도움이 됐다고 확신해요.
⑤ 광고는 대개 꽤 효과적이에요.

총 어휘 수 146

15　상황에 적절한 말

소재 그랜드캐니언 방문

듣기 대본 해석
여: Casey는 뉴욕시에 살지만, 그녀는 Arizona주의 Tucson에 사는 그녀의
친구 Danny의 집을 방문하기로 결심합니다. Casey는 긴 여행을 했고
Danny는 그녀를 보고 반가워합니다. 그는 그녀에게 그의 도시를 관광 시켜
줍니다. 모든 명소를 다 본 후, Casey는 Danny에게 그녀가 항상 그랜드
캐니언을 보길 원했다고 말합니다. 그들은 다음 날 그랜드캐니언으로
출발하고 그 관광지를 보기 위한 훌륭한 장소를 찾습니다. 그들은 그곳에
조금 있다가, Danny가 더 완벽한 경관을 보기 위해 헬리콥터를 타서
협곡을 돌 것을 제안합니다. 하지만 Casey는 높은 곳을 매우 두려워하고
헬리콥터를 타지 않기를 원합니다. 이 상황에서 Casey는 Danny에게
뭐라고 말할까요?
Casey: ③ 그거 재미있을 것 같아. 하지만 난 헬리콥터를 타지 않을래.

어휘
journey *n.* 여행　**be delighted** 반가워하다, 좋아하다　**sight** *n.*
명소, 관광지　**canyon** *n.* 협곡　**set out** 출발하다
〈문제〉**check out** 나가다, 체크아웃 하다

정답 ③

문제풀이

Danny는 그랜드캐니언에서 더 좋은 경관을 보기 위해 Casey에게 헬리콥터를 타자고 제안하지만, Casey는 높은 곳에 대한 공포가 있어 헬리콥터를 타지 않길 원하는 상황이므로 Casey가 Danny에게 할 말로 가장 적절한 것은 ③ '그거 재미있을 것 같아. 하지만 난 헬리콥터를 타지 않을래.'이다.

오답 보기 해석

① 우리 뉴욕 헬리콥터 투어를 하자.
② 괜찮아. 나는 우리가 다음 헬리콥터를 탈 수 있을 것이라고 확신해.
④ 좋아. 나는 항상 위에서 그 협곡을 보길 원했어.
⑤ 그랜드캐니언 박물관에 가서 더 많은 정보를 얻자.

총 어휘 수 136

16 담화 주제 / 17 세부 내용 파악

소재 자신을 좀 더 정돈되게 하는 방법들

듣기 대본 해석

남: 당신은 자주 당신의 지저분한 책상 위에서 무언가를 미친 듯이 찾고 있는 자신을 발견하나요? 당신이 단지 너무 정리를 못해서 모임 또는 약속을 놓친 적이 있나요? 자, 저는 오늘 당신이 좀 더 독립적이고 정돈되도록 하는 방법에 약간의 조언을 드리기 위해 여기에 왔습니다. 첫째, 책상을 정돈하세요. 물건을 모아 두는 사람이 되지 마세요. 당신이 필요로 하지 않거나 중요하지 않은 것은 버리세요. 둘째, 당신의 업무를 기억하기 위해 달력, 일정 계획표 또는 스마트폰을 사용하세요. 달력과 일정 계획표는 약간 구식이지만 그것들은 당신을 정돈되게 해 줄 수 있습니다. 기술은 당신의 친구이고 당신의 일정을 체계화하는 데 도움을 줄 수 있는 많은 앱들이 있습니다. 셋째, 당신이 끝낼 필요가 있는 것들의 목록을 만드세요. 할 일 목록은 당신의 하루를 체계화할 좋은 방법이고 도움을 줄 수 있는 많은 멋진 스마트폰 앱들도 있습니다. 마지막으로 당신의 모든 계획을 완수하세요. 미루는 것을 멈추고 일정을 지키세요. 해야 할 일 목록에 그 항목을 위한 시간 범위를 정하세요. 시간을 절약하기 위해 항목들을 합치세요. 당신이 이러한 조언들을 따른다면, 저는 당신이 더 체계적이고 생산적인 삶을 영위하리라 확신합니다.

어휘

frantically *ad.* 미친 듯이　　**hoarder** *n.* 축적가　　**keep track of** ~을 계속 파악하다　　**follow through** ~을 완수하다　　**procrastinate** *v.* 미루다, 질질 끌다　　**stick to** ~을 계속하다, 고수하다　　**combine** *v.* 결합하다

정답 16 ③ 17 ④

문제풀이

16 남자는 체계적인 생활을 위해 책상을 정리정돈 하거나 시간 계획을 짜는 방법에 대해 조언하고 있으므로 남자가 하는 말의 주제는 ③ '보다 체계적인 생활을 하기 위한 조언들'이다.

17 달력, 일정 계획표, 스마트폰, 할 일 목록은 언급되었지만 시계에 대한 언급은 없으므로 정답은 ④ '시계'이다.

오답 보기 해석

16
① 할 일 목록의 필요성
② 자신의 책상을 정돈하는 방법
④ 달력과 일정 계획표를 사용하는 이유
⑤ 스마트폰 앱을 사용하는 것의 이점

총 어휘 수 175

DICTATION ANSWERS

01 Can you take my order / When will that be ready

02 Can we still get tickets / works at the ticket counter

03 to get hands-on experience / keep in mind that / are eligible for this opportunity / start a challenging, yet rewarding career

04 the benefits of running barefoot / improve your balance / your foot is cramped up inside / trying it out myself

05 check them out / starts making a clicking noise / what exactly is wrong with your car / errands I need to run

06 in the shade / I'll go get it / That makes sense

07 you were going to make it / got halfway here / a traffic jam / I forgot to grab my charger

08 are you ready for the exam / I'll be studying all day / is still under construction

09 were completely destroyed / donate money to the victims / on our behalf

10 broccoli is full of soluble fiber / promote great bone health / without actually eating many calories

11 found mostly in the Northern Hemisphere / has coexisted with humans / finding sources of nutrition / great predator

12 sit inside all day doing nothing / My parents can't afford anything / sign up for this one

13 His left foot is a bit swollen / he's supposed to take part in / participate in the contest

14 the way I do business / lowering your prices / in a time of need / build a loyal customer base

15 After seeing all the sights / great spot to view the landmark / to get a more complete view / is very afraid of heights

16-17 how you can become more independent and organized / keep track of your tasks / make lists of things you need to do / follow through on all your plans / Set time frames

01 ①	02 ②	03 ④	04 ①	05 ①	06 ②
07 ⑤	08 ④	09 ③	10 ④	11 ①	12 ④
13 ⑤	14 ③	15 ⑤	16 ③	17 ④	

01 짧은 대화의 응답

소재 농구 수업에서 집중 연습할 기술

듣기 대본 해석

남: Ava. 농구 연습에서 오늘은 뭐에 집중할 거야?
여: 패스와 슛 중에서 골라야 돼.
남: 슛 연습을 하는 게 좋을 것 같아. 그게 더 중요하다고 생각해.
여: ① 제안해줘서 고마워.

어휘

〈문제〉 **suggestion** *n.* 제안

정답 ①

문제풀이

여자가 슛과 패스 중 어떤 것에 더 집중해서 연습할지 정해야 된다고 하자 남자는 슛이 더 중요한 것 같다고 추천했으므로 그에 대한 여자의 대답은 ① '제안해줘서 고마워.'가 적절하다.

오답 보기 해석

② 응. 나는 슈팅을 잘해.
③ 괜찮아. 나 농구 별로 안 좋아해.
④ 넌 오늘 농구 연습에 가야 해.
⑤ 난 네가 농구에 관심 있는 줄 알았어.

총 어휘 수 35

02 짧은 대화의 응답

소재 악단에서 연주할 악기

듣기 대본 해석

여: 안녕, Max. 나 학교 악단에 시험 쳐 보기로 결심했어.
남: 좋은 생각이야! 어떤 악기를 연주할 건데?
여: 아마 금관악기를 연주할 건데 어떤 것을 할지는 확실치 않아.
남: ② 네가 가장 잘하는 악기를 연주해.

어휘

marching band 악단　**brass instrument** 금관악기
〈문제〉 **tryout** *n.* 오디션　**relieve** *v.* 없애주다, 덜어주다

정답 ②

문제풀이

여자가 악단 시험을 본다고 했는데 금관악기 중 어떤 악기로 할지 모르겠다고 말했으므로 적절한 응답은 ② '네가 가장 잘하는 악기를 연주해.'이다.

오답 보기 해석

① 내가 더 나은 연주자가 되도록 도와줘.
③ 너 오디션에서 드럼을 쳐서는 안 돼.
④ 악단 대회는 이번 주말이야.
⑤ 악기 연주는 스트레스를 해소하는 데 좋아.

총 어휘 수 41

03 담화 목적

소재 국제 영화제

듣기 대본 해석

남: 안녕하세요, 신사 숙녀 여러분. 이곳 역사적인 Wilma Theater에서 열리는 제 4회 국제 영화 축제에 와 주셔서 감사합니다. 찬사를 받고 있는 감독 Mark Young이 만든, 다음 상영작 Moonset Monarchy를 많은 분들께서 기대하고 계시리라 생각합니다. 하지만 저희는 현재 영사기에 기술적인 장애가 있는 상황입니다. 영화가 곧 시작하기로 되어 있었으나, 현재로서는 한 시간 동안 미루고자 합니다. 지연된 것에 대해 진심으로 사과 드리며, 이 특정 영화를 위해 구매하신 티켓은 환불을 해 드릴 준비가 되어있습니다. 양해해 주셔서 감사합니다.

어휘

acclaimed *a.* 칭찬(호평)을 받고 있는　**technical** *a.* 기술적인
film projector 영사기　**momentarily** *ad.* 곧, 금방, 잠깐 (동안)
as of now 현재로서는　**sincerely** *ad.* 진심으로

정답 ④

문제풀이

남자는 영사기에 문제가 생겨서 영화 상영 시간이 늦춰졌음을 알려주고 있으므로 정답은 ④ '영화 상영 시간의 변경을 알리려고'이다.

총 어휘 수 96

04 대화 주제

소재 몸과 마음을 건강하게 유지하는 방법

듣기 대본 해석

여: 안녕, Gilbert. 뭐하고 있어?
남: 안녕, Mary. 나 방금 건강과 관련 있는 새로운 오디오북을 듣기 시작했어.
여: 건강이라고? 식습관에 관한 거야?
남: 아니. 그건 어떻게 너의 몸과 마음을 건강하게 유지하느냐에 관한 거야.
여: 흥미롭게 들리네.
남: 우리는 장기적으로 중요한 영향을 끼치는 정말 단순한 일들을 매일 할 수 있어. 사람들은 효과를 바로 원해서 우리가 하는 것과 먹는 것들의 장기적인 효과를 무시하는 거야.
여: 그래서 건강한 마음과 건강한 몸을 향하는 바른 길로 가기 위해 네가 추천하려는 첫 번째 것은 뭐야?
남: 우리가 해야 할 첫 번째 일은 우리 생활에서의 목록을 만드는 거야. 우리가 가지고 있는 것을 파악한 다음에 그 중에서 우리가 얼마나 필요하고 나머지는 얼마나 없애야 하는지를 알아내야 해.
여: 그럼, 그 목록은 단지 물질적인 소유물이 아니라 음식, 사람, 일, 취미, 그리고 매일매일 우리가 다루는 꽤 많은 모든 것들을 포함해야 하는구나, 그렇지?
남: 그래, 정확해.

어휘

significant *a.* 중요한　**in the long run** 결국에는, 장기적으로는
ignore *v.* 무시하다　**long-term effect** 장기적 효과　**stuff** *n.* 물건, 물질　**recommend** *v.* 추천하다　**path** *n.* 길, 방향　**inventory** *v.* ~의 목록을 만들다 *n.* 목록, 재고　**figure out** 이해하다, 알아내다
deal with 다루다, 처리하다　**on a daily basis** 매일매일

정답 ①

문제풀이

남자는 여자에게 방금 읽기 시작한 오디오북의 내용을 얘기해주고 있다. 단순한 일들이 장기적으로 중요한 결과를 만들어낸다고 말하면서 건강한 마음과 몸을 유지할 수 있는 방법을 소개하고 있다. 따라서 두 사람 대화의 주제는 ① '몸과 마음을 건강하게 유지하는 방법'이다.

총 어휘 수 157

05 대화자의 관계 파악

소재 책자 사진 선택

듣기 대본 해석

[문을 두드리는 소리]

남: 들어오세요.

여: 안녕하세요, Anderson씨. 저를 만나고 싶어 하셨다고 들었어요.

남: 네, Stacy. 당신을 기다리고 있었어요. 앉아서 이 배치를 좀 살펴봐 주세요.

여: 오, 정말 좋은데요!

남: 잘됐네요. 이제 책자에 쓸 사진 두어 장을 고르는 데 당신의 도움이 필요해요.

여: 이 두 장이 정말 훌륭하네요. 이 사진들이 영화가 무엇에 관한 것인지를 가장 잘 포착해내는 것 같아요.

남: 기사가 당신의 연기에 초점을 맞추기 때문에 제 생각에 당신의 캐릭터를 가장 잘 표현하는 사진들을 찍었어요.

여: 당신과 일하는 것이 정말 신나요. 당신 사진들은 저를 멋지게 보이도록 만들어요.

남: 제 작품을 좋아해 주신다니 기뻐요. 감독에게 넘기기 전에 몇 장 더 찍어야 해요.

여: 좋은 생각이에요. 액션을 주제로 찍을까요?

남: 네. 스튜디오로 세 시까지 오세요.

여: 제가 네 시에 약속이 있으니 한 시간 더 일찍 만나도 될까요?

남: 물론이죠.

어휘

layout *n.* 배치, 설계   **shot** *n.* 촬영, 사진   **represent** *v.* 표현하다, 나타내다   **hand over** 넘겨주다   **appointment** *n.* 약속

정답 ①

문제풀이

남자가 기사에 쓸 여자의 사진을 찍었고 여자는 영화와 캐릭터를 이야기하는 것으로 보아 ① '사진작가 — 여배우'의 관계임을 알 수 있다.

오답 보기 해석

② 예술품 수집가 — 영화 감독

③ 기자 — 인터뷰 대상자

④ 광고인 — 편집자

⑤ 모델 — 교수

총 어휘 수 152

06 그림의 세부 내용 파악

소재 교사 휴게실 안내

듣기 대본 해석

여: 저희 학교에 오신 걸 환영합니다. Brown씨. 학교 안내를 해 드릴게요.

남: 감사합니다. 여기서 일하게 돼서 영광이에요. 이 방은 뭐죠?

여: 여기는 교사 휴게실이에요. 쉬는 시간에 휴식을 취하고 다른 선생님들과 이야기를 나누는 장소예요.

남: 우와, 꽤 좋아 보이네요. 저기 뒤에 있는 건 스낵 자판기인가요?

여: 맞아요. 왼쪽 벽에 인터넷에 접속할 수 있는 컴퓨터도 두 대 있어요.

남: 좋네요. 이 탁자에 있는 건 뭐죠?

여: 여기서 가끔 편하게 회의를 해서 의자 두 개와 필요할 때 전화 회담에 사용되는 전화기가 탁자 위에 있어요.

남: 좋네요. 자판기 옆의 게시판에는 뭐가 붙어 있는 거예요?

여: 조만간 있을 지구의 날 행사 포스터예요. 4월에 열려요.

남: 그럼 게시판은 다가오는 행사들을 홍보하는 건가요?

여: 맞아요. 가끔 다른 중요한 정보도 붙여 놓으니까 주기적으로 확인하는 게 좋아요.

남: 그렇군요. 다음은 어디로 가는 거죠?

여: 다음엔 체육관으로 갈 거예요.

어휘

lounge *n.* 휴게실   **relax** *v.* 쉬다, 휴식을 취하다   **snack machine** 스낵 자판기   **casual** *a.* 태평스러운, 편한   **bulletin board** 게시판   **announce** *v.* 발표하다, 알리다   **periodically** *ad.* 정기적으로, 주기적으로

정답 ②

문제풀이

여자가 인터넷에 접속할 수 있는 컴퓨터가 두 대 있다고 했는데 그림에는 한 대만 있으므로 정답은 ②번이다.

총 어휘 수 173

07 할 일

소재 주말 계획

듣기 대본 해석

여: 시험 어땠니, Donald?

남: 잘 모르겠어요. 다음 주 수요일까지는 결과가 나올 거예요.

여: 너는 공부를 열심히 했으니까, 좋은 점수 받을 거야.

남: 고마워요, 엄마. 그런데 이번 주 토요일에 친구들이랑 World Jazz Festival에 가도 될까요?

여: 오, 안돼. 아버지께서 하신 말씀 잊었니?

남: 무슨 말이요?

여: 우리는 집을 개조할 계획이야. 너의 도움이 정말 필요하단다.

남: 흠... 가면 안되겠네요. 그럼 대신에 일요일에 친구들이랑 영화 보러 가야겠어요.

여: 그래. 하지만 일요일 아침은 안돼. 그때는 할머니를 찾아 뵈어야 하거든. 편찮으시대.

남: 심각하신가요?

여: 아니야. 그저 독감이라고 말씀하시더구나.

남: 다행이네요! 걱정 마세요, 엄마. 할머니를 뵙고 나서 친구들을 만날게요.

여: 고맙다, Donald.

어휘

remodel *v.* 개조하다   **serious** *a.* 심각한   **relief** *n.* 안도, 안심

정답 ⑤

문제풀이

남자는 토요일에 World Jazz Festival에 가려고 했으나 집 수리를 돕기 위해 가지 않기로 했으므로 정답은 ⑤ '집 수리하는 것 돕기'이다. 할머니 방문하기는 일요일 아침이다.

총 어휘 수 138

08 이유

소재 스터디 그룹 모임

듣기 대본 해석

남: Claire. 괜찮니? 너 우울해 보여.

여: 내일 중요한 화학 시험이 있는데, 나는 자료를 이해 못하겠어. 내일 시험에 떨어질 것 같아.

남: 힘내. Ryan, Jason, Taylor와 나는 그룹 스터디를 시작했어. 너도 같이 하자.

여: 나도 하고 싶은데, 나는 성가시게 하고 싶진 않아. 나는 정말 뒤쳐져 있어.

남: 걱정 마. 나는 모든 사람들이 네가 있는 것을 좋아한다고 확신해.

여: 진짜로 고마워. 나는 내가 얻을 수 있는 모든 도움이 필요해.

남: 우리는 오늘 밤 6시에 모일 거야. 너도 올 수 있지?

여: 흠... 나 진짜 못 갈 것 같은데. 오늘 밤 부모님이랑 밖에 나가기로 되어 있어. 아버지 생신이거든.

"

남: 알았어. 그럼 네가 나중에 우리와 함께 하기를 원한다면 나에게 알려줘.
　　알았지?
여: 고마워. 정말 고마워.

어휘
down in the dumps 우울한　　**material** *n.* 자료　　**bother** *n.*
성가신 사람　　**appreciate** *v.* 감사하다　　**be supposed to V**
~하기로 되어 있다

정답 ④

문제풀이
6시 스터디 모임에 나올 수 있냐는 남자의 질문에 여자는 아버지 생신이라
부모님과 함께 나가야 해서 못 간다고 했다. 따라서 정답은 ④ '부모님과 함께
외출하기로 해서'이다.

총 어휘 수 137

09　숫자

소재 커피와 케이크 사기

듣기 대본 해석
여: 안녕하세요. 어떻게 도와드릴까요?
남: 안녕하세요. 아메리카노 한 잔에 얼마예요?
여: 5달러입니다. 그런데 이번 주는 판촉행사 진행 중이에요. 아메리카노를 한 잔
　　사시면 한 잔 공짜로 드려요. 그러니까 5달러에 두 잔을 드실 수 있어요.
남: 잘됐네요. 그럼 제가 네 잔을 두 잔 가격으로 살 수 있다는 말이죠. 그럼
　　아메리카노 네 잔 주세요.
여: 또 다른 필요한 것이 있나요?
남: 네. 실은 오늘이 제 동료의 생일이라서 그에게 케이크를 사 주려고요. 초콜릿
　　케이크는 얼마인가요?
여: 20달러예요. 사용할 수 있는 쿠폰이 있나요?
남: 없어요.
여: 음. 다음 번 구매 시 10퍼센트 할인쿠폰을 드릴 수 있어요.
남: 감사해요. 신용카드 사용해도 되나요?

어휘
run a promotion 판촉행사를 진행하다　　**buy one, get one free**
한 개를 사면 한 개를 무료로 더 받다　　**devil's food cake** 초콜릿 케이크
purchase *n.* 구매

정답 ③

문제풀이
한 잔에 5달러인 아메리카노가 한 잔 사면 한 잔이 공짜이므로 네 잔의 가격이
10달러이고, 20달러짜리 케이크를 산다고 했으므로 남자가 지불할 금액은
③ '$30'이다.

총 어휘 수 119

10　언급 유무

소재 공연 에티켓

듣기 대본 해석
여: 여보, 우리가 제대로 된 좌석에 앉은 것 같지가 않아요.
남: 아니에요. 이 좌석 번호가 우리 티켓에 인쇄돼 있는 번호예요.
여: 그래요. 당신이 맞는 것 같아요. 연극이 곧 시작할 것 같아요. 휴대폰
　　무음으로 했어요?
남: 물론이죠.

여: 당신은 배려심이 있어서 다행이에요. 지난번 영화관에 갔을 때 기억나요?
　　우리 뒷좌석에 있던 커플이 많이 떠들었잖아요. 그들은 우리 자리를 계속
　　발로 차기도 했어요.
남: 네. 정말 매너가 없었죠. 안내 담당자가 세 번이나 와서 조용히 해달라고
　　요청했었지요.
여: 네. 정말 짜증났었어요. 공연을 제대로 즐기기가 어려웠었어요. 당신이
　　온 바닥에 음료를 다 쏟아서 우리 앞줄에 있던 사람들 신발이 다 젖었고
　　끈적해진 것도 그 상황에 도움이 안됐죠.
남: 다시 상기시키지 말아요. 어쨌든, 이제 곧 공연이 시작할 것 같아요.
여: 좋아요. 지난번보다는 더 나은 경험이 되길 바라요.

어휘
considerate *a.* 배려하는, 사려 깊은　　**usher** *n.* 좌석 안내원
annoying *a.* 짜증스러운　　**spill** *v.* 쏟다, 흘리다

정답 ④

문제풀이
공연을 보러 온 두 사람은 휴대폰 무음으로 하기, 공연 중에 떠들지 않기, 앞
좌석 발로 차지 않기, 음료수 쏟지 않기를 언급했지만 공연 시간을 지키는 것에
대한 언급은 하지 않았으므로 정답은 ④ '공연 시간 지키기'이다.

총 어휘 수 147

11　내용 일치 · 불일치

소재 학교 에세이 대회 공지

듣기 대본 해석
남: 안녕하세요, 학생과 교수단 여러분! 저는 해마다 열리는 제 20회 Maple
　　고등학교 에세이 대회를 발표하려고 합니다. 환경 문제가 요즘 점점 더 주요
　　뉴스가 되고 있어서 올해 저희는 우리가 환경을 보호할 수 있는 방법에
　　대한 여러분의 생각을 듣고 싶습니다. 에세이들은 1,000단어를 넘으면
　　안 되고, 학교 홈페이지를 통해 제출되어야만 합니다. 참가를 계획하시는
　　분들께서는 4월 20일까지 참가해 주세요. 제일 잘한 세 편을 이달 말에
　　발표하고 시상을 하겠습니다. 1등은 500달러를 받게 됩니다. 2등과
　　3등은 각각 200달러와 100달러를 받게 될 것입니다. 상금과 함께 1등
　　수상작은 도시 신문에 실리게 될 것입니다. 여러분 모두가 참여하시길
　　바랍니다. 더 많은 참가는 더 많은 아이디어를 의미하고, 더 많은 아이디어는
　　환경을 위한 더 많은 노력을 의미합니다!

어휘
faculty *n.* 교수단, 교수들　　**announce** *v.* 발표하다, 알리다
protect *v.* 보호하다　　**submit** *v.* 제출하다　　**via** *prep.* 통하여
award *v.* (상을) 주다, 수여하다　　**respectively** *ad.* 각각　　**publish**
v. 출판(발행)하다

정답 ②

문제풀이
제출은 학교 홈페이지를 통해서 하라고 했으므로 내용과 일치하지 않는 것은
② '제출은 학교에 직접 와서 해야 한다.'이다.

총 어휘 수 147

12　도표

소재 피아노 레슨 선택

듣기 대본 해석
남: 여보, 뭐 하는 중이죠?
여: 아이를 위한 피아노 레슨 전단지를 보고 있어요. Susan은 피아노 치는
　　법을 배울 필요가 있다고 생각해요.

남: 맞는 말이에요. 그렇지만 Susan이 수업을 들을 수 있는 시간이 있어요? 그녀의 일정이 꽉 차 있잖아요.

여: 그건 걱정 마세요. 바이올린 수업이 3월 29일에 끝나니까 그 이후론 시간이 비어요.

남: 알았어요. 그렇다면 오후 6시 30분에 시작하는 수업 어때요?

여: 내 생각엔 그녀가 집에 너무 늦게 오지 않는 게 좋을 것 같아요.

남: 맞아요. 음, 오후 5시에 시작하는 수업이 몇 개 있어요. 어느 것이 좋을까요?

여: 목요일만 아니면 상관없어요. 매주 목요일엔 치과에 가야 하니까.

남: 좋아요. 그렇다면 그녀가 참여할 수 있는 수업이 딱 하나 있네요. 등록 마감일이 언제죠?

여: 전단지에 3월 10일이라고 적혀있어요. 수업이 다 차기 전에 서둘러야겠어요.

남: 오, 지금 당장 등록해요.

어휘

leaflet *n.* 광고용 전단지　　**deadline** *n.* 기한, 마감시간　　**register** *v.* 등록하다

정답 ④

문제풀이

Susan이 3월 30일부터 시간이 된다고 했으므로 ①번과 ②번은 제외된다. 또한 6시 30분에 시작하는 수업은 너무 늦다고 했으므로 ⑤번은 제외된다. 그리고 매주 목요일은 치과에 가야 한다고 했으므로 화요일, 목요일 수업인 ③번도 제외되므로 정답은 ④번이다.

총 어휘 수　162

13　긴 대화의 응답

소재　자전거 주차

듣기 대본 해석

남: 기분이 안 좋아 보여, Nora. 무슨 일이니?

여: 낮에 학교에서 내 자전거를 잃어버렸어. 나에게 아주 소중한 건데 대학교에 들어올 때 아버지께서 사 주셨거든.

남: 뭐? 네가 항상 타던 그 검은색 자전거?

여: 맞아.

남: 어떻게 된 거야?

여: 법학관 옆에 주차했어.

남: 너 자전거를 지정된 자전거 주차 구역에 둔 거니?

여: 지정된 자전거 주차 구역? 무슨 말이니?

남: 아, 너 새로운 규정에 대해 듣지 못했니? 캠퍼스 안에서 지정된 구역에만 자전거 주차가 허용돼.

여: 그러면 내가 잘못된 장소에 주차해서 견인된 거야?

남: 그럴 수도 있지.

여: 다시 찾으려면 어떻게해야 하지?

남: ⑤ <u>먼저, 가서 네가 주차한 곳이 지정된 구역인지 확인해봐.</u>

어휘

designated *a.* 지정된　　**regulation** *n.* 규정

정답 ⑤

문제풀이

여자가 자전거를 잃어버렸다고 하자 남자는 지정된 구역을 제외하고는 자전거를 주차할 수 없다는 새로운 규정에 대해 말해주었고, 여자는 어떻게 자전거를 찾아야 되는지 물었다. 그러므로 주차했던 곳이 지정된 곳인지 알아보라고 말하는 ⑤ '먼저, 가서 네가 주차한 곳이 지정된 구역인지 확인해봐.'가 가장 적절하다.

오답 보기 해석

① 위층의 다른 주차 구역을 찾아보는 게 좋을 거야.
② 네 자전거 잠시만 써도 될까?
③ 자전거 탈 때 항상 헬멧을 써야 해.
④ 법학관에 가면 이 책 반납해줄래?

총 어휘 수　127

14　긴 대화의 응답

소재　X-Cross 운동 시작하기

듣기 대본 해석

여: 안녕, Louis! 너를 여기서 볼 것이라고 기대 못했는데. 무슨 일이야?

남: 안녕, Francis. 네가 너의 규칙적인 X-Cross 운동에 대해 얘기해서, 궁금해졌거든.

여: 그렇구나. 시작해보려고?

남: 그럴까 해. 네가 나에게 얼마나 기분이 좋은지 그리고 얼마나 더 행복한지 말했잖아. 나의 삶에 그런 종류의 변화가 필요하다고 생각해.

여: 음, X-Cross가 너를 훨씬 건강하게 해 줘. 또한 너의 정신에도 좋아.

남: 맞아. 좋은 몸 상태를 유지해야 한다고 생각해왔어. 나는 정말로 지난 몇 년 동안 내 마음대로 했거든.

여: 음, 이 프로그램이 너에게 딱 맞는 것 같아. 한번 해 보는 것이 어때?

남: 그래야겠어. 오늘 등록할 거야.

여: 먼저, 네가 시작하는 것을 도와 줄게.

남: 고마워. 하지만, 내가 말한 것처럼 나는 몸 상태가 좋지 않아. 수업에서 내가 잘 할거라 생각하니?

여: ③ <u>물론이지. 너는 쉬운 운동으로 시작할 수 있어.</u>

어휘

exercise routine (규칙적인) 운동　　**get in shape** 좋은 몸 상태(몸매)를 유지하다　　**let oneself go** 자제력을 잃다　　**give it a shot** 시도해 보다　　**sign up** 등록하다

정답 ③

문제풀이

남자가 새로운 운동을 시작하려는데 자신 없어하고 있고, 여자는 도와준다고 말하고 있으므로 남자가 자신이 잘 할 수 있을지 물었을 때 적절한 여자의 응답은 ③ '물론이지. 너는 쉬운 운동으로 시작할 수 있어.'이다.

오답 보기 해석

① 균형 잡힌 식단이 네가 좋은 몸 상태를 유지하도록 도울 수 있어.
② 절대 아냐! 집에서 이 프로그램을 하는 것은 쉽지 않아.
④ 괜찮아. 초보자들을 위한 수업은 없어.
⑤ 문제 없어. 너는 훨씬 더 강해졌고, 건강해졌어.

총 어휘 수　152

15　상황에 적절한 말

소재　지진 피해자들을 위한 기부

듣기 대본 해석

여: 지난달, 거대한 지진이 일본을 강타했습니다. 사람들이 많이 죽었으며 집과 재산을 잃었습니다. Bella는 재난으로 영향을 받은 사람들을 도울 수 있는 돈과 다른 것들을 모으기 위해 모금행사를 열기로 결정했습니다. 그녀가 아는 거의 모든 사람들이 옷과 통조림 제품 그리고 돈을 기부하기 위해 그 행사에 참석했습니다. 그러나, 그의 가장 가까운 친구인 Nathaniel은 도움이 필요한 사람들을 돕는 것에 대해 관심이 없는 것 같았습니다. 나중에 Bella는 Nathaniel이 사실 지진의 피해자들을 돕기 위해 세워진 자선 단체에 그가 모은 돈을 전부 기부했다는 것을 친구로부터 들었습니다. 이는 그녀를 기분 좋게 만듭니다. Bella가 Nathaniel을 보면, 그녀는 그에게 뭐라고 말할까요?

Bella: Nathaniel, ⑤ <u>네가 그렇게 큰 기부를 했다니 대단해.</u>

어휘

massive *a.* 거대한, 심각한　　**property** *n.* 재산
hold a fundraiser 모금행사를 열다　　**disaster** *n.* 재난, 재해
donate *v.* 기부하다　　**canned goods** 통조림 제품　　**charity** *n.* 자선단체　　**victim** *n.* 피해자, 희생자　　〈문제〉 **let down** 실망시키다
cause *n.* 대의명분, 취지　　**contribution** *n.* 기부금, 성금

정답 ⑤

문제풀이

Bella는 친구인 Nathaniel이 기부에 관심이 없는 줄 알았다가 그가 모은 돈을
다 기부한 것을 알고 기쁨을 표현하려 하므로 정답은 ⑤ '네가 그렇게 큰 기부를
했다니 대단해.'이다.

오답 보기 해석

① 자선기금 마련을 도와주겠니?
② 너는 정말 돈을 모으기 시작해야 돼.
③ 나는 가끔 나의 가장 친한 친구한테 실망을 해.
④ 왜 우리의 좋은 취지를 지지하지 않으려는 거니?

총 어휘 수 124

16 담화 주제 / 17 세부 내용 파악

소재 글램핑의 좋은 점

듣기 대본 해석

남: 여러분 안녕하세요. 오늘 저는 여러분에게 레크리에이션 캠핑에 대해서
이야기하려고 왔습니다. 처음에는 많은 사람들이 캠핑을 자연과 최대한
가까워지는 방법으로 사용했지요. 다른 사람들은 캠핑을 물이 새는 텐트,
축축한 침낭, 그리고 맛없는 음식이 연상되기 때문에 싫어합니다. 이러한
불편은 캠핑카와 레저용 자동차들의 출현을 낳았습니다. 요즘 새로운 캠핑
유행이 인기를 얻고 있습니다. 이름은 '글램핑'입니다. 이 단어는 '글래머'와
'캠핑'을 섞은 단어예요. 글램핑을 가면 텐트를 치거나 침낭을 풀 필요가
전혀 없습니다. 불을 피울 필요도 없습니다. 글램핑은 오두막이나 미리 세워진
텐트 또는 나무 위 오두막 안에서 자연을 느끼는 방법입니다. 글램핑을 가기
위해서 일상의 호화로움을 버릴 필요가 없는 것입니다. 이 취미는 캠핑의
불편함 없이 시골을 즐길 수 있게 해주기 때문에 인기를 끌고 있습니다.
글램핑은 전기, 샤워시설, 그리고 화장실까지 제공해 줍니다. 또, 글램핑을
할 때 제공되는 조리 기구들로 쉽게 요리를 할 수도 있습니다.

어휘

recreational *a.* 레크리에이션의, 오락의   **associate** *v.* 연상하다,
연관 짓다   **leaky** *a.* 새는, 구멍이 난   **damp** *a.* 축축한
inconvenience *n.* 불편   **glamour** *n.* 화려함   **assemble** *v.*
조립하다   **luxury** *n.* 호화로움, 사치   **equipment** *n.* 장비

정답 16 ③ 17 ④

문제풀이

16 기존 캠핑의 불편한 점을 보완한 새로운 형태의 캠핑인 글램핑을 소개하고
   있으므로 남자가 하는 말의 주제는 ③ '글램핑이라는 새로운 캠핑 추세'가
   된다.

17 글램핑은 미리 쳐진 텐트나 오두막에서 한다고 했고, 전기, 샤워시설, 화장실이
   제공된다고 했으므로 언급되지 않은 것은 ④ '난방기기'이다.

오답 보기 해석

16
① 글램핑을 할 때의 안전의식
② 야외에서 휴식을 취하는 방법
④ 캠핑을 할 때 불편을 피하는 방법
⑤ 글램핑이 환경에 끼치는 긍정적 영향

총 어휘 수 186

01 choose between passing and shooting

02 I decided to try out / What instrument are you going
    to play

03 the next film to be screened / technical difficulties with
    our film projector / sincerely apologize for the delay

04 keep your body and mind healthy / the long-term
    effects / get rid of the rest

05 expecting you / represented your character / handing
    them over to the director / have an appointment

06 along the left wall / on the bulletin board / takes place
    in April / check it periodically

07 get a good grade / planning to remodel the house /
    visit your grandmother / That's a relief

08 You look down in the dumps / I'm really far behind /
    go out with my parents / let me know

09 running a promotion / four for the price of two / buying
    him a cake / Do you have any coupons

10 put your cell phone on silent / They kept kicking our
    seats / spilled your drink / Don't remind me

11 Environmental issues are making headlines / they
    must be submitted / please have your entries in by /
    Along with the prize money

12 Her schedule is full / not to come home so late / go to
    the dentist every Thursday

13 lost my bike on campus / in a designated bicycle parking
    area / my bike was picked up / get it back

14 how great you feel / make you a lot healthier / give it a
    shot / sign up

15 lost their homes and property / raise money / attended
    the event / did not seem to care / help the earthquake
    victims

16-17 as close as possible to nature / they associated it
       with / assemble a tent / without the discomfort of
       camping / cooking equipment that's provided for
       you

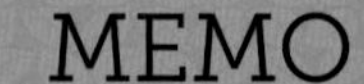

MEMO

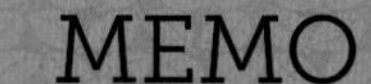